NUMERICAL PREDICTION AND DYNAMIC METEOROLOGY

NUMERICAL PREDICTION AND DYNAMIC METEOROLOGY

SECOND EDITION

George J. Haltiner, Ph.D.
Roger Terry Williams, Ph.D.

U.S. Naval Postgraduate School

JOHN WILEY & SONS
New York Chichester Brisbane Toronto

Library of Congress Cataloging in Publication Data:

Haltiner, George J
Numerical prediction and dynamic meteorology.

First ed. (1971) published under title: Numerical
weather prediction.
Bibliography: p.
Includes indexes.
1. Numerical weather forecasting. 2. Dynamic
meteorology. I. Williams, Roger Terry, 1936- joint
author. II. Title.

QC996.H35 1980 551.6′34 79-25544
ISBN 0-471-05971-4

Printed in the United States of America

10 9 8 7 6 5 4 3 2 1

PREFACE

This book is an enlarged edition of the first one. The first author heartily welcomed Professor R. T. Williams to share in the task of updating a text in a rapidly growing field because of his broad knowledge of atmospheric dynamics and numerical weather prediction. Although the dynamics of large-scale motions are included to provide a basis for NWP, the treatment may also stand on its own merits for use in courses in dynamic meteorology.

For the most part the text is self-contained in order to provide easy reference to basic concepts and for readability by scientists in other fields. However, because of the brevity of treatment of a number of topics, as necessitated by limited size of the text, a previous introductory course may be desirable, especially for undergraduates.

We thank our colleagues at the Postgraduate School, the Navy Fleet Numerical Weather Central, and the Navy Environmental Prediction Research Facility in Monterey for many helpful suggestions, particularly E. H. Barker, S. D. Burk, C.-P. Chang, K. L. Davidson, R. L. Elsberry, R. L. Haney, T. E. Rosmond, A. L. Schoenstadt and visiting Professors R. A. Anthes, Pennsylvania State University; H. E. Fleming, NESS; and N. O. Jensen, Denmark.

Our appreciation goes especially to Dr. K. Miyakoda, GFDL, NOAA, Princeton University for his critical and thorough review of the entire manuscript, which resulted in the addition of several topics, references and the elimination of many minor errors as well.

Our reference list includes not only specific articles referred to in the text but others that were helpful to us. Nevertheless, we were unable to list every author from whom we have indirectly benefited in the past; for this we apologize.

Our thanks go to the department clerical staff, especially to Ms. Marion Marks, who typed many pages of notes for classroom use from which this text evolved.

Finally, we dedicate this book to our wives, Mary Haltiner and Jan Williams, who, with love, patience, and forbearance, supported us in this effort.

George J. Haltiner
R. T. Williams

June 1979

CONTENTS

Abbreviations xiii

Partial List of Symbols xv

CHAPTER 1 THE GOVERNING EQUATIONS 1

1-1 Introduction 1
1-2 Equation of Motion 3
1-3 Continuity Equation 5
1-4 Equation of State 5
1-5 First Law of Thermodynamics 6
1-6 The Complete System of Equations 7
1-7 Coordinate Systems 8
1-8 Map Projections 10
1-8-1 Polar Stereographic Projection 11
1-8-2 Mercator Projection 13
1-8-3 Lambert Conformal Projection 13
1-8-4 Additional Remarks 14
1-9 Alternate Vertical Coordinates 14
1-9-1 Pressure Vertical Coordinate 17
1-9-2 Isentropic Vertical Coordinate Θ 19
1-10 Some Energy Relations 20
1-10-1 Kinetic Energy 20
1-10-2 Potential Energy 20
1-11 Available Potential Energy 23
1-12 Vorticity and Divergence Equations 26
1-12-1 Divergence Equations 27

CHAPTER 2 WAVE MOTION IN THE ATMOSPHERE: PART I 29

2-1 Introduction 29
2-2 Linearized Equations 29
2-3 Pure Sound Waves 31
2-4 Sound Waves and Internal Gravity Waves 33
2-5 Surface Gravity Waves 36
2-6 Inertial Gravity Waves and Rossby Waves 40
2-7 Response to Initial Conditions 45
2-8 Geostrophic Adjustment 47

CHAPTER 3 SCALE ANALYSIS **53**

3-1 Introduction 53
3-2 Shallow-Water Equations 54
3-3 Baroclinic Equations 59
3-4 Midlatitude Analysis 62
3-5 Tropics 67
3-6 Planetary Scale 67
3-7 Balance System 68

CHAPTER 4 ATMOSPHERIC WAVES: PART II **70**

4-1 Introduction 70
4-2 Rossby Waves 70
4-3 Conditions for Barotropic Instability 72
4-4 Some Unstable Profiles 75
4-5 Linear Shear 79
4-6 Barotropic Effects in the Atmosphere 81
4-7 Baroclinic Instability 81
4-8 Baroclinic Instability with Linear Shear 83
4-9 Two-Level Model 86
4-10 Wave Structure 91
4-11 Vertical Energy Propagation 96
4-12 Barotropic Equatorial Waves 99
4-13 Vertical Structure of Equatorial Waves 102

CHAPTER 5 NUMERICAL METHODS **108**

5-1 Introduction 108
5-2 Finite Difference Methods 108
5-3 The Advection Equation 110
5-4 Some Basic Concepts 120
5-5 Stability Analysis 122
5-5-1 The Matrix Method 123
5-5-2 Von Neumann Method 127
5-5-3 The Energy Method 129
5-6 Examples of the Von Neumann Method 129
5-6-1 Euler Scheme 130
5-6-2 Uncentered Differencing, Von Neumann Method 130
5-6-3 Trapezoidal Implicit Scheme 132
5-6-4 Euler Backward Scheme 134
5-6-5 Fourth-Order Space Differencing 135
5-6-6 Oscillation Equation 138
5-6-7 Two-Dimensional Advection Equation 139
5-6-8 External Gravity Waves, Leapfrog Scheme 140

5-6-9 Staggered Grid 141
5-7 Forward-Backward Scheme, Pressure Averaging, and Semi-Implicit Methods 142
5-7-1 Forward-Backward Scheme 143
5-7-2 Pressure Averaging 144
5-7-3 Time Averaging 145
5-7-4 Semi-Implicit Method 148
5-7-5 Lax Wendroff Scheme 149
5-8 A Summary of Some Difference Schemes 150
5-9 Parabolic Equations 153
5-10 Elliptic Equations 157
5-10-1 Relaxation Method 157
5-10-2 Direct Methods 159
5-10-3 Gaussian Elimination 164
5-10-4 Buneman Variant 165
5-10-5 Helmholtz Equation on a Sphere 167
5-10-6 Reduction of a Three-Dimensional Elliptic Equation to Two-Dimensional Equations 168
5-11 Nonlinear Instability and Aliasing 170
5-11-1 Discrete Mesh 173
5-11-2 Primitive Equations Considerations 176

CHAPTER 6 GALERKIN METHODS 181

6-1 Introduction 181
6-2 Example with Spectral and Finite Element Methods 182
6-3 Time Dependence 186
6-4 Barotropic Vorticity Equation with Fourier Basis Functions 187
6-5 Transform Method 193
6-6 Spectral Model of Shallow-Water Equations 197
6-7 Advection Equation with Finite Elements 201
6-8 Barotropic Vorticity Equation with Finite Elements 203

CHAPTER 7 NUMERICAL PREDICTION MODELS 208

7-1 Filtered Models 208
7-1-1 Quasi-Geostrophic Equivalent Barotropic Model 208
7-1-1-1 Energetics of the Barotropic Model 210
7-1-2 Quasi-Geostrophic Multilevel Baroclinic Model 211
7-1-3 Linear Balanced Model 213
7-1-4 Nonlinear Balanced Model 214
7-2 Primitive Equation Models 215
7-2-1 Constraints from Continuous Equations 217
7-2-2 Vertical Differencing 219

7-3 Staggered Grid Systems 226
7-4 Example of a Staggered Primitive Equation Model 230
7-4-1 Equations in Curvilinear Coordinates 230
7-4-2 Horizontal Differencing 231
7-4-3 Energy Conservation 235
7-5 Potential Enstrophy Conserving Scheme 237
7-5-1 Continuous Integral Constraints 238
7-5-2 Difference Equations 239
7-5-3 Constraints Enforced 242
7-6 Spherical Grids 243
7-7 Fine Mesh Modeling 248
7-7-1 One-Way Influence 249
7-7-2 Boundary Conditions 250
7-7-3 Two-Way Interaction 254
7-7-4 Initialization on a Bounded Region 255
7-8 Baroclinic Spectral Models 257
7-9 Isentropic Coordinate Models 262
7-10 Upper Boundary Conditions 264
7-11 Mountain Effects 265

CHAPTER 8 BOUNDARY LAYER REPRESENTATIONS 267

8-1 Introduction 267
8-2 Reynolds Equations 268
8-3 Bulk Formulas 269
8-4 Eddy Viscosity, *K*-Theory 272
8-5 Combined Prandtl and Ekman Layers 272
8-5-1 Prandtl Layer (Neutral Stratification) 273
8-5-2 Ekman Layer 274
8-6 Nonneutral Surface Layer 277
8-6-1 Matching Ekman Spiral 283
8-7 Similarity Solutions for the Entire PBL 285
8-7-1 Deardorff Mixed Layer Model 285
8-7-2 Surface Layer 286
8-7-3 Matching Solutions for the Surface and Mixed Layers 288
8-7-4 Surface Wind Direction 290
8-7-5 Modified Transfer Coefficients 291
8-8 A Prediction Equation for *h* 293
8-8-1 Further Comments on PBL Parameterization 294
8-9 High-Resolution Model 295
8-9-1 The Coefficient of Eddy Viscosity 295
8-9-2 Surface Temperature 298
8-9-3 Some Prediction Model Details 299
8-10 Mean Turbulent Field Closure Models (Second-Order Closure) 300

CHAPTER 9 INCLUSION OF MOISTURE 308

9-1 Moisture Conservation Equation 308
9-1-1 Modified Thermodynamic Equation 310
9-1-2 Equivalent Potential Temperature and Static Energy 310
9-2 Convective Adjustment 312
9-2-1 Case A. Dry Convection, $q < q_s$ 312
9-2-2 Case B. Moist Adjustment $q \geq q_s$ 313
9-3 Modeling Cloud Processes 315
9-3-1 Nonconvective Condensation 317
9-4 Cumulus Parameterization 319
9-4-1 Introduction 319
9-4-2 Kuo Method 321
9-5 Parameterizations Involving Cloud Models 323
9-6 Arakawa and Schubert Model 328
9-6-1 Large-Scale Budget Equations 331
9-6-2 Cloud Budget Equations 334

CHAPTER 10 RADIATION PARAMETERIZATION 340

10-1 Terrestrial Radiation 340
10-2 Absorbing Substances 343
10-3 Simplified Transmission Functions 343
10-4 Discretization, Long-Wave Radiation 345
10-4-1 Clear Sky 345
10-4-2 Cloudy Sky 348
10-5 Solar Radiation 349
10-5-1 Clear Sky 350
10-5-2 Cloudy Sky, One Cloud Layer 351
10-5-3 Two Contiguous Cloud Layers 352
10-5-4 Two Separated Cloud Layers 353
10-6 Miscellany 354

CHAPTER 11 OBJECTIVE ANALYSIS AND INITIALIZATION 356

11-1 Introduction 356
11-2 A Three-Dimensional Analysis 358
11-3 Statistical Methods, Multivariate Analysis 359
11-4 Initialization 365
11-4-1 Introduction 365
11-4-2 Damping Techniques 367
11-4-3 Static Initialization 368
11-4-4 Variational Method 369
11-4-5 Normal Mode Expansions 377

11-4-6 Variational Normal Mode Initialization 377
11-5 Dynamic Balancing 385
11-6 Four-Dimensional Data Assimilation 387
11-7 Newtonian Relaxation or "Nudging" 389
11-8 Smoothing and Filtering 392
11-8-1 Two-Dimensional Smoothers 397
11-8-2 Bandpass Filters 397
11-8-3 Boundary Effects 398

CHAPTER 12 OCEAN DYNAMICS AND MODELING 399

12-1 Introduction 399
12-2 Wind-Driven Barotropic Models 399
12-3 Nonlinear Effects 404
12-4 Barotropic Numerical Models 404
12-5 Simple Thermohaline Models 406
12-6 Baroclinic Numerical Models 409
12-7 Bottom Topography Effects 413
12-8 Synoptic Scale Eddies 414
12-9 Mixed Layer Models 415
12-10 Problems in Ocean Modeling 421

CHAPTER 13 WEATHER AND CLIMATE PREDICTION 423

13-1 Introduction 423
13-2 Current Forecasting Skill 423
13-2-1 Short Range 424
13-2-2 Medium and Longer Ranges 427
13-2-3 Additional Comments on Forecasting 428
13-3 Predictability of the Atmosphere 428
13-4 Statistical-Dynamical Prediction 433
13-4-1 Simple Empirical Corrections 433
13-4-2 Stochastic-Dynamical Prediction 434
13-5 Climate and Climate Prediction 435

Appendix Mathematical Relations 440

References 444

Index 471

ABBREVIATIONS

AGU:	American Geophysical Union
AMS:	American Meteorological Society
AWS:	Air Weather Service (U.S. Air Force)
BAMS:	*Bulletin of AMS*
CMS:	Canadian Meteorological Society
CAC:	Climate Analysis Center
ECMRWF:	European Center for Medium Range Weather Forecasting
FGGE:	First Garp Global Experiment (or GWE)
FNWC:	Fleet Numerical Weather Central (U.S. Navy)
GARP:	Global Atmospheric Research Project
GFDL:	Geophysical Fluid Dynamics Laboratory (NOAA)
GISS:	Goddard Institute for Space Studies
J. Appl. Met.:	*Journal of Applied Meteorology (AMS)*
J. Atmos. Sci.:	*Journal of Atmospheric Sciences (AMS)*
Mon. Wea. Rev.:	*Monthly Weather Review (AMS)*
NCAR:	National Center for Atmospheric Research
NEPRF:	Navy Environmental Prediction Research Facility
NESS:	National Environmental Satellite Service (NOAA)
NMC:	National Meteorological Center (NOAA)
NOAA:	National Oceanic and Atmospheric Administration
NPS:	Naval Postgraduate School, Monterey, CA
NWP:	Numerical Weather Prediction
NWS:	National Weather Service
PBL:	Planetary boundary layer
Quart. J. Roy. Met. Soc.:	*Quarterly Journal of Royal Meteorological Society*
WMO:	World Meteorological Organization

PARTIAL LIST OF SYMBOLS

a Radius of earth; constant
a_o Clear sky albedo
a_s Surface albedo
c Phase velocity
c_f Finite difference phase velocity
c_i, c_r Imaginary and real parts of c
c_p Specific heat at constant pressure
c_l Specific heat of liquid water
c_v Specific heat at constant volume
$dS = dx/dy$
e Vapor pressure
e_s Saturation vapor pressure
$f = 2\,\Omega \sin\varphi =$ Coriolis parameter
g Gravity
g_a Gravitation
h Horizontal; free surface height; moist static energy; mixed layer depth
i,j,k Unit vectors
$i = \sqrt{-1}$; index
j Index
k Vertical wave number; constant; index
k_v Absorption coefficient
l Liquid water content of air; index; mixing length
m Index; map factor
n Index; normal direction
p Pressure; vertical coordinate; wave number
p_s Terrain surface pressure
q Specific humidity, potential vorticity; wave number
q_s Saturated value of q
q_w Saturated value of q at water temperature
r Radial distance; relative humidity
$\mathbf{r}$ Radius vector
s Scalar distance, surface index; dry static energy.
t Time coordinate
u x-component of velocity
u_* Friction velocity
u^* Pressure-corrected water vapor mass
v y-component of velocity; volume
w z-component of velocity; precipitable water vapor
x,y,z Space coordinates
z,z_p Pressure height;
z_o Roughness length
A Available potential energy; wave amplitude; area
Ac Cloud absorbtivity
B_v Black-body radiation
C Fractional cloud cover; curve; cloud production; rate; condensation
C_D Drag coefficient

C_E	Energy exchange coefficient
C_u,C_Θ	Turbulent transfer coefficient
D	Horizontal divergence
$E =$	c_pT, enthalpy, total potential energy
E_v	Evaporation
$F =$	f^2L^2/gH Rotational Froude number; friction force; flux
G	Group velocity
H	Mean height of free surface or depth of the troposphere; total energy; scale height
H_L	Latent heat flux
H_S	Sensible heat flux
$I =$	c_vT, internal energy
I_v	Radiation intensity
J	Jacobian
K	Kinetic energy per unit mass; coefficient of eddy viscosity; diffusion coefficient
K_H	Horizontal curvature
L	Wavelength; latent heat; horizontal scale length; Monin-Obukhov length
L_r	Rossby radius of deformation
$\mathcal{L}$	Differential operator, wavelength
$dM =$	$\rho dx\, dy\, dz = -g^{-1}\, dx\, dy\, dp$
N	Index
P	Pressure; potential energy; precipitation
$P_{m,n}$	Legendre function
Q	Diabatic heating per unit mass per unit time
R	Gas constant for air; response function; regression coefficient
R_c	Cloud albedo
$R_i =$	Richardson Number
R_{ij}	Residual during relaxation process
R_v	Gas constant for water vapor
S	Surface; solar radiation
T	Temperature; time scale
T_a	Air temperature
T_c	Cloud temperature
T_g	Ground temperature
T_r	Truncation error
T_s	Sea temperature; saturated air temperature
U	Basic current in x-direction, velocity component in direction of map coordinate
V	Horizontal velocity; characteristic velocity; velocity component in direction of map coordinate; volume
$\mathbf{V}_a$	Absolute velocity
$\mathbf{V}_g$	Geostrophic wind
$\mathbf{V}_T$	Thermal wind
$\mathbf{V}_x$	Divergent wind component
$\mathbf{V}_\psi$	Rotational wind component
W	Characteristic vertical velocity; amplitude; weight factor
$Y_{m,n}$	Spherical harmonic
Z	$-\ln(p/p_o)$; vertical coordinate
α	Specific volume; angle; coefficient of thermal expansion
β	df/dy Rossby parameter
γ	c_p/c_v; lapse rate
γ_d	Dry adiabatic lapse rate
γ_m	Moist adiabatic rate
Γ	Static stability

δ	Differential; Kronecker delta; declination angle; variation; optical thickness
$\times$	Vector product
Δ	Finite difference
∇	Del operator
$\nabla_t, \nabla_x, \nabla_F$	Finite difference del operators
∂	Partial differentiation
ε	Arbitrary variable; error; rotational Froude number; dissipation rate
ζ	Vertical component of vorticity; vertical coordinate
ζ_g	Geostrophic vorticity
κ	R/c_p
η	Absolute vorticity; cloud parameter
θ	Potential temperature; colatitude; phase angle
θ_s	Wet-bulb potential temperature
θ_e	Equivalent potential temperature
λ	Inverse static stability parameter; longitude; Lagrange multiplier; eigenvalue; fractional entrainment
$\mu =$	$2\pi/\mathcal{L}$ = wave number; diffusion coefficient; micron
υ	Frequency; kinematic coefficient of eddy viscosity; eigenvector
π	3.14159. . .; normalized pressure
ρ	Density
ρ_v	Density of water vapor
σ	Static stability parameter; vertical coordinate; Stefan-Boltzmann constant; surface element; computational stability constant
$\dot{\sigma} =$	$d\sigma/dt$, vertical velocity in σ-system.
Σ	Summation
τ	Friction force; stress; transmission function
φ	Latitude; basis function
ϕ	Geopotential; colatitude
ϕ_s	Surface geopotential
χ	Velocity potential function for divergent component
ψ	Stream function for rotational velocity component
$\omega =$	dp/dt = vertical velocity in p-system; frequency
Ω	Angular velocity of earth

CHAPTER 1

The Governing Equations

1-1 INTRODUCTION

Weather forecasting is not a new science (or art); it has a long history because of the importance of weather in human activity. The weather affects our lives in a multitude of ways through agriculture, industry, transportation, communications, recreation, etc. As in other fields, certain events, inventions, and scientific innovations marked the important advances in weather prediction.

In a brief history of forecasting, Reed (1977) mentions that the invention of the barometer in 1643 by Torricelli is considered by many to be the beginning of meteorology as a science. The barometer soon became a useful tool because of the close relationship between atmospheric pressure and local weather. Surprisingly, however, the first synoptic map of surface pressure was not constructed until 1820 and then only with data nearly 50 years old. Although the map's potential for weather forecasting was quickly recognized, there remained an obstacle, the lack of a rapid means of communicating observational data to a central location for analysis. This problem was overcome by the invention of the telegraph in 1845, which was soon followed by the first current synoptic weather maps displayed at the World Fair in London during 1851. National services were established in many countries during the next several decades to provide weather forecasts and storm warnings.

During the period, 1850-1920, called the *empirical era,* weather organizations grew in size and broadened to provide forecasts for the general public, agriculture, flood warnings, transportation, etc. The surface pressure map was the primary tool for there was little upper air information and the approach was almost wholly empirical. Although rarely applied to forecasting, theoretical research was being pursued that laid a foundation for its eventual application. An important milestone was the recognition by V. Bjerknes in 1904 that forecasting is fundamentally an initial-value problem in mathematical physics and, moreover, that the basic system of equations to be solved was already known, at least in general form. But Bjerknes realized that this system of highly nonlinear partial differential equations did not possess closed solutions, except possibly in grossly simplified forms that had little direct use in forecasting. In addition the data were wholly inadequate to determine the initial conditions. During and immediately following World War I, L. F. Richardson sought to solve the system of equations numerically using desk calculators. The discouraging results of his pioneering effort, published in book form in 1922, gave pressure changes an order of magnitude greater than observed. Few people realized the fundamental importance of Richardson's work and no one seemed to care to repeat the months of calculations to determine the cause of the failure. The invention of the radiosonde resulted in the widespread use of upper air data during the 1930s and led to further empirical improvements in forecasting with increasing application to a rapidly growing aviation industry.

Theoretical research continued with important contributions by Rossby, Petterssen, J. Bjerknes, Charney, Eady, Eliassen, Fjørtoft, Obukhov, and others that led to some direct applications to practical problems and more importantly laid the foundation for a radical departure from pure empiricism. But, it was another invention, the electronic computer in the late 1940s, that stimulated a new breakthrough. Using the recently invented computer at Princeton University Charney, Fjørtoft, and von Neumann (1950) produced the first successful dynamical-numerical forecast at 500 mb with an equivalent-barotropic vorticity model, a far simpler model than Richardson's version. Their accuracy was nearly comparable to that achieved by highly skilled forecasters using subjective and empirical techniques. Thus dawned the age of dynamical forecasting by numerical methods, commonly referred to as *numerical weather prediction* (NWP), which soon became the primary basis for modern weather prediction.

In 1954 a numerical prediction group was set up in the Washington, D.C., area consisting of Air Force, Navy, and Weather Bureau personnel. Improved NWP models soon surpassed the skill of manual forecasts at 500 mb. In fact, even when given the numerical predictions, experienced forecasters were unable to score better on a regular basis at 500 mb, though not so with the sea-level pressure prognoses.

During the past three decades, there have been rapid advances in all phases of NWP, concomitant with a remarkable development in electronic computers. It would be remiss not to mention the unique contribution of meteorological satellites as an observational platform that has provided new insights about weather producing systems and has been very valuable for short-range forecasting, especially over and near sparse data areas. However, it has not yet nearly reached its potential in providing initial conditions for NWP.

This text describes the physical and mathematical basis of numerical weather prediction and *attempts* to present recent practices and trends in research.

As an initial-value problem, dynamical-numerical weather forecasting requires a closed set of appropriate physical laws expressed in mathematical form, suitable initial and boundary conditions, and an accurate numerical method of integrating the system of equations forward in time. Implied here is the collection and checking of surface- and upper-air meteorological observations, an objective determination of the meteorological variables to serve as initial conditions over a set of gridpoints covering the forecast region, preferably subjected to several dynamical constraints, the actual numerical prediction, the display and distribution of the forecasts, and, finally, verification of the results.

This text does not treat the subject matter exactly in the order listed above nor are all topics treated in detail, especially those related to taking observations and the transmission of data and forecasts. Chapter 1 presents the basic physical laws in various forms. Chapters 2, 3, and 4 deal with the meteorological dynamics that form the background for large-scale numerical weather prediction. Chapters 5, 6, and 7 are concerned with numerical methods and problems associated with integration. Chapter 8 is devoted to the planetary boundary layer, Chapter 9 with the treatment of moisture including clouds and precipitation, and Chapter 10, which is less general, describes a particular method of handling the complex solar and terrestrial radiative transfers. Although the determination of initial conditions is the first step in carrying out a numerical forecast, this subject is not discussed until Chapter 11. The reason for its late appearance is that the initialization procedure depends on the integration scheme and the physical processes being simulated which therefore should be discussed first. Chapter 12 provides a short introduction to some of the unique features of ocean modeling. Chapter 13 treats current forecasting skill, the limits on the predictability of the atmosphere, and very briefly the feasibility of forecasting seasonal and climatic trends.

1-2   EQUATION OF MOTION

Newton's second law of motion for a "fixed" or inertial reference frame may be expressed as $\vec{V} = u\vec{i} + v\vec{j} + w\vec{k}$

$$\frac{d_a \mathbf{V}_a}{dt} = \mathbf{M} \tag{1-1}$$

where $\mathbf{M}$ represents the vector sum of the forces per unit mass. The subscript a denotes the values of velocity and acceleration as observed in the inertial frame. However, since these quantities are observed on earth, which is moving through space, it is desirable to express the equation of motion in terms of variables measured relative to the earth. The principal motion that must be accounted for is the rotation of the earth, while other motions such as the orbital movement around the sun, etc., may be neglected. Assuming the earth to be rotating at angular velocity $\mathbf{\Omega}$, the absolute velocity $\mathbf{V}_a$ of a particle may be written as the sum of the velocity relative to the earth $\mathbf{V}$ and the velocity due to the rotation.

$$\mathbf{V}_a = \mathbf{V} + \mathbf{\Omega} \times \mathbf{r} \tag{1-2}$$

Here $\mathbf{r}$ represents the position vector of the particle as measured from the origin at the earth's center.

Now let **i**, **j**, and **k** be unit vectors along an orthogonal set of axes in the absolute frame of reference and **i′**, **j′**, and **k′** in the rotating frame. Then an arbitrary vector A may be expressed in the two frames as

$$\mathbf{A} = A_x\mathbf{i} + A_y\mathbf{j} + A_z\mathbf{k} = A'_x\mathbf{i}' + A'_y\mathbf{j}' + A'_z\mathbf{k}'$$

and its time derivative as

$$\frac{d\mathbf{A}}{dt} = \frac{dA_x}{dt}\mathbf{i} + \frac{dA_y}{dt}\mathbf{j} + \frac{dA_z}{dt}\mathbf{k}$$

$$= \frac{dA'_x}{dt}\mathbf{i}' + \frac{dA'_y}{dt}\mathbf{j}' + \frac{dA'_z}{dt}\mathbf{k}' + A'_x\frac{d\mathbf{i}'}{dt} + A'_y\frac{d\mathbf{j}'}{dt} + A'_z\frac{d\mathbf{k}'}{dt}$$

The derivatives of the unit vectors are given by $d\mathbf{i}'/dt = \mathbf{\Omega} \times \mathbf{i}'$, etc.; hence

$$\frac{d_a\mathbf{A}}{dt} = \frac{d\mathbf{A}}{dt} + \mathbf{\Omega} \times \mathbf{A} \tag{1-3}$$

where d_a/dt represents the rate of change with respect to the fixed system and d/dt with respect to the rotating system.

Thus it has been shown that the total derivative of an arbitrary vector as measured in the fixed system is expressible as the sum of the derivative in the rotating system and the term $\mathbf{\Omega} \times \mathbf{A}$.

From this theorem it follows that

$$\frac{d_a\mathbf{V}_a}{dt} = \frac{d\mathbf{V}_a}{dt} + \mathbf{\Omega} \times \mathbf{V}_a$$

Substituting further from (1-2) gives

$$\frac{d_a\mathbf{V}_a}{dt} = \frac{d(\mathbf{V} + \mathbf{\Omega} \times \mathbf{r})}{dt} + \mathbf{\Omega} \times (\mathbf{V} + \mathbf{\Omega} \times \mathbf{r})$$

or (1-4)

$$\frac{d_a\mathbf{V}_a}{dt} = \frac{d\mathbf{V}}{dt} + 2\mathbf{\Omega} \times \mathbf{V} + \mathbf{\Omega} \times (\mathbf{\Omega} \times \mathbf{r})$$

The principal forces (per unit mass) in atmospheric motions are the pressure force, gravitation $\mathbf{g}_a$, and the friction force **F**. Introducing these forces and the expression for the absolute acceleration (1-4) into (1-1) gives the equation of relative motion

$$\frac{d\mathbf{V}}{dt} = -\alpha\nabla p - 2\mathbf{\Omega} \times \mathbf{V} + \mathbf{g} + \mathbf{F} \tag{1-5}$$

where α is the specific volume and gravity **g** is the sum of gravitation and the centrifugal force $-\mathbf{\Omega} \times (\mathbf{\Omega} \times \mathbf{r})$. That is

$$\mathbf{g} = \mathbf{g}_a - \mathbf{\Omega} \times (\mathbf{\Omega} \times \mathbf{r})$$

The second term on the right of (1-5), $-2\mathbf{\Omega} \times \mathbf{V}$, is referred to as the *coriolis force*.

1-3 CONTINUITY EQUATION

The second fundamental law is the conservation of mass, which may be expressed in mathematical form as follows. Consider an infinitesimal volume $\delta x\, \delta y\, \delta z$ as shown in Figure 1-1. The mass inflow per unit time into the x-face is $\rho u\, \delta y\, \delta z$, where ρ is the density and u is the x component of velocity. The outflow from the opposite face is $[\rho u + (\partial \rho u/\partial x)\delta x]\delta y\, \delta z$. The difference between the inflow and the outflow per unit volume is $-\partial(\rho u)/\partial x$, which represents the x contribution to the local rate of change of mass per unit volume, namely, the rate of density change. Considering all three directions, the result is

$$\frac{\partial \rho}{\partial t} = -\nabla \cdot (\rho \mathbf{V}) = -\rho \nabla \cdot \mathbf{V} - \mathbf{V} \cdot \nabla \rho \tag{1-6}$$

Alternate forms are obtainable by combining local derivatives and using $\alpha = 1/\rho$,

$$-\frac{1}{\rho}\frac{d\rho}{dt} = \frac{1}{\alpha}\frac{d\alpha}{dt} = \nabla \cdot \mathbf{V} \tag{1-7}$$

1-4 EQUATION OF STATE

As confirmed by the early discoveries of Boyle and Charles, the three thermodynamic variables p, α, and T are not independent. For every substance there exists a relationship known as the equation of state of the form

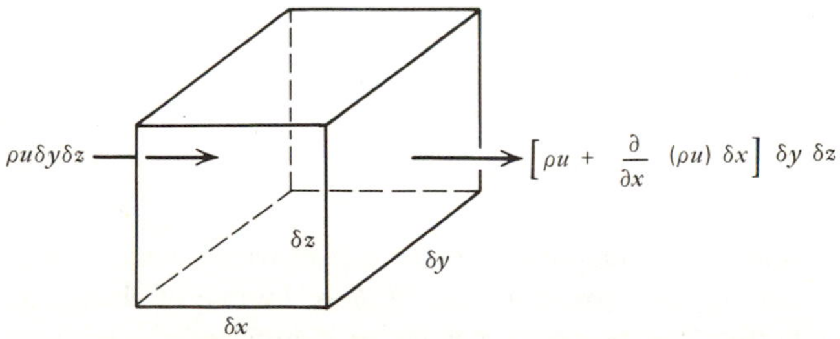

Figure 1-1. Mass conservation.

$$f(p, \alpha, T) = 0$$

For real substances this relationship is highly complex, and no simple analytical expression exists. However, there are analytic forms that are satisfactory over limited ranges of the variables. A general equation may be derived by assuming certain idealized conditions. For example, a *perfect* gas may be defined as one that obeys Boyle's and Charles' laws exactly, in which case it is readily shown that the equation of state takes the form

$$p\alpha = RT \tag{1-8}$$

Although no perfect gas exists, (1-8) may be used to approximate real gases for many processes and will suffice for our purposes here. Although the atmosphere is, in fact, a mixture of gases, (1-8) is nevertheless satisfactory, provided the gas constant R is a weighted average of the gas constants of the individual gases constituting the atmosphere.

1-5 FIRST LAW OF THERMODYNAMICS

The first law of thermodynamics expresses the principle of conservation of energy. The latter states that the change in energy of a system is equal to the net transfer of energy across the boundaries of the system. In complete generality, this principle embraces all types of energy: potential, kinetic, thermal, radiant, magnetic, electrical, chemical, etc.; however, for application to the meteorological thermodynamics considered here, the relationship may be considerably simplified. As will be shown later, Newton's law of motion implies a balance of certain forms of mechanical energy. As a consequence, the change in the sum of the organized kinetic energy of motion and the potential energy due to the field of gravity is equal to part of the work done by the pressure and frictional forces. Thus these particular terms may be omitted from the first law of thermodynamics. The remaining work done on (or by) the gas by the pressure and frictional forces is a consequence of the expansion and deformation of the gas.

If the chemical, magnetic, and electrical effects are omitted, the first law of thermodynamics may be written in the simple form

$$Q = \frac{dI}{dt} + W$$

where Q is the rate of heat energy addition, W is the rate at which work is done by the gas on its surroundings by expansion, and dI/dt is the rate of change of internal energy. For a perfect gas the rate of change of internal energy per unit mass is given by $c_v dT/dt$, where c_v is the specific heat at a constant volume, while the work done per unit mass per unit time during a reversible expansion of a nonviscous gas is $p\, d\alpha/dt$. Substituting these expressions into the thermodynamical equation gives

$$Q = c_v \frac{dT}{dt} + p \frac{d\alpha}{dt} \tag{1-9a}$$

Use of (1-8) gives the alternate form

$$Q = c_v \frac{dT}{dt} - \alpha \frac{dp}{dt} = c_p T \frac{d(\ell n \theta)}{dt} \tag{1-9b}$$

where

$$\theta = T(p_0/p)^{\kappa} \quad \kappa = \mathrm{R}/c_p \qquad p_0 = 1000 \text{ mb}$$

When there are changes of phase of the water substance, for example, from vapor to liquid, (1-9b) takes the form of

$$Q - L\frac{dq}{dt} - c_\ell \ell \frac{\mathrm{dT}}{\mathrm{dt}} = c_p \frac{dT}{dt} - \alpha \frac{dp}{dt} \tag{1-10}$$

where q is the specific humidity of the water-vapor constituent, ℓ is the liquid water mass per unit mass of air, L is the latent heat, c_ℓ is the specific heat of the liquid water and Q now represents other forms of heating than latent heat.

1-6 THE COMPLETE SYSTEM OF EQUATIONS

For dry air, (1-5), (1-7), (1-8), and (1-9) comprise a *complete system* of *six scalar equations* and *six unknowns, p, α, T, u, v,* and w. The friction force F and diabatic heating Q are assumed to be either known functions or expressible in terms of the other variables; hence, in principle, all future states can be determined by solution of this system.

When moisture is included, modifications are necessary in the equation of state and the first law of thermodynamics; in addition, an equation is needed to express the conservation of the water substance. For the present, only dry air will be considered; in Chapter 9 the effects of moisture will be discussed.

For large-scale motions of the air, the atmosphere may be assumed to be in hydrostatic equilibrium, that is, the vertical acceleration may be neglected along with the vertical component of the coriolis force. When the hydrostatic approximation is valid, (1-5) is equivalent to the pair of

$$\frac{d\mathbf{V}_H}{dt} = -\alpha \nabla p - \mathbf{f} \times \mathbf{V}_H + \mathbf{F}_H \tag{1-11}$$

$$0 = -\alpha \frac{\partial p}{\partial z} - g \tag{1-12}$$

Here $\mathbf{V}_H$ is the horizontal wind velocity, ∇ is the two-dimensional del operator, $\mathbf{F}_H$ is the horizontal component of the frictional force, $\mathbf{f} = f\mathbf{k}$, and $f = 2\Omega \sin\varphi$ is the *coriolis parameter* (which is the vertical component of the earth's vorticity).

1-7 COORDINATE SYSTEMS

The vector forms of the equations of motion are compact and facilitate the physical interpretation of the various terms; however, application to real problems and, in particular, numerical weather prediction, requires a depiction in terms of a coordinate system. Since the large-scale motions of the atmosphere are quasi-horizontal with respect to the earth's surface, spherical coordinates are quite useful. Toward this end, the generalized expressions for several vector operators [(A-17) to (A-24) at the end of the book] may be used to transform (1-5) to spherical coordinates.

Let $x_1 = \lambda$, $x_2 = \varphi$, and $x_3 = r = z + a$ where λ, φ, r, a, and z are the longitude, latitude, radial distance, mean radius of the earth, and the height above mean sea level. The curvilinear distance elements ds in the coordinate directions and the corresponding metric coefficients h_j are

$$ds_1 = r\cos\varphi\, d\lambda \qquad ds_2 = r d\varphi \qquad \text{and} \qquad ds_3 = dr$$
$$h_1 = r\cos\varphi \qquad h_2 = r \qquad \text{and} \qquad h_3 = 1$$

$$u = ds_1/dt = r\cos\varphi\, d\lambda/dt; \; v = ds_2/dt = r d\varphi/dt$$

$$w = ds_3/dt = dr/dt = dz/dt$$

$$\mathbf{V} = u\mathbf{i}' + v\mathbf{j}' + w\mathbf{k}' \tag{1-13}$$

The symbols u, v, and w represent the curvilinear velocity components toward the east, the north, and in the vertical; and $\mathbf{i}'$, $\mathbf{j}'$, and $\mathbf{k}'$ are unit orthogonal vectors in these directions. The vector equation of motion (1-5) may be expressed in spherical coordinates by utilizing the foregoing values of h_1, h_2, and h_3 and the operators (A-17) to (A-22), or using (A-23) directly. In the former procedure the total derivative $d\mathbf{V}/dt$ is calculated bearing in mind the $\mathbf{i}'$, $\mathbf{j}'$, and $\mathbf{k}'$ vary with latitude and longitude and must be differentiated, as well as u, v, and w, as indicated in (A-22). The procedure is straightforward and may be found in Haltiner and Martin (1957). Another approach is to use the expansion (see A-8).

$$d\mathbf{V}/dt = \partial\mathbf{V}/\partial t + \tfrac{1}{2}\nabla(\mathbf{V}\cdot\mathbf{V}) + (\nabla \times \mathbf{V}) \times \mathbf{V}$$

in (1-5) and then apply the generalized vector operators (A-17) and (A-21) to compute the products and the vector components. The following results are obtained for several of the less obvious terms:

$$\begin{aligned}
2\boldsymbol{\Omega}\times\mathbf{V} &= 2\Omega\,(\mathbf{j}\cos\varphi + \mathbf{k}\sin\varphi)\times(u\mathbf{i}+v\mathbf{j}+w\mathbf{k})\\
&= (2\Omega\cos\varphi\, w - fv)\,\mathbf{i} + fu\mathbf{j} - 2\Omega\cos\varphi\, u\mathbf{k}
\end{aligned}$$

$$\begin{aligned}
\boldsymbol{\nabla}\times\mathbf{V} &= \frac{1}{r}\left[\frac{\partial w}{\partial\varphi} - \frac{\partial}{\partial r}(rv)\right]\mathbf{i} + \frac{1}{r}\left[\frac{\partial}{\partial r}(ur) - \frac{1}{\cos\varphi}\frac{\partial w}{\partial\varphi}\right]\mathbf{j}\\
&\quad + \frac{1}{r\cos\varphi}\left[\frac{\partial v}{\partial\lambda} - \frac{\partial}{\partial\varphi}(u\cos\varphi)\right]\mathbf{k}
\end{aligned}$$

$$\begin{aligned}
(\boldsymbol{\nabla}\times\mathbf{V})\times\mathbf{V} + \tfrac{1}{2}(\mathbf{V}\cdot\mathbf{V}) &= [\mathbf{V}\cdot\boldsymbol{\nabla}u - (uv\tan\varphi - uw)/r]\mathbf{i}\\
&\quad + [\mathbf{V}\cdot\boldsymbol{\nabla}v - (u^2\tan\varphi + vw)/r]\mathbf{j}\\
&\quad + [\mathbf{V}\cdot\boldsymbol{\nabla}w - (u^2 + v^2)/r]\mathbf{k}
\end{aligned}$$

where, by (A-17),

$$\mathbf{V}\cdot\boldsymbol{\nabla}A = \frac{u}{r\cos\varphi}\frac{\partial A}{\partial\lambda} + \frac{v}{r}\frac{\partial A}{\partial\varphi} + w\frac{\partial A}{\partial z}$$

Expanding the remaining terms and separating into component equations leads to

$$\begin{aligned}
\frac{du}{dt} &= -\frac{1}{\rho}\frac{\partial p}{\partial x} + \left(2\Omega + \frac{u}{r\cos\varphi}\right)(v\sin\varphi - w\cos\varphi) + F_\lambda\\
\frac{dv}{dt} &= -\frac{1}{\rho}\frac{\partial p}{\partial y} - \left(2\Omega + \frac{u}{r\cos\varphi}\right)u\sin\varphi - \frac{vw}{r} + F_\varphi \qquad (1\text{-}14)\\
\frac{dw}{dt} &= -\frac{1}{\rho}\frac{\partial p}{\partial z} - g + \left(2\Omega + \frac{u}{r\cos\varphi}\right)u\cos\varphi + \frac{v^2}{r} + F_z
\end{aligned}$$

$$\begin{aligned}
\text{where } \frac{d(\;)}{dt} &= \frac{\partial(\;)}{\partial t} + \frac{\partial(\;)}{\partial\lambda}\frac{d\lambda}{dt} + \frac{\partial(\;)}{\partial\varphi}\frac{d\varphi}{dt} + \frac{\partial(\;)}{\partial z}\frac{dz}{dt}\\
&= \frac{\partial(\;)}{\partial t} + u\frac{\partial(\;)}{\partial x} + v\frac{\partial(\;)}{\partial y} + w\frac{\partial(\;)}{\partial z}
\end{aligned}$$

and x, y, and z are the curvilinear coordinates toward the east, north, and local vertical. As pointed out by Phillips (1966) the foregoing equations are not exact because the ellipticity of the earth is ignored; however the angular momentum principle is conserved, that is,

$$\frac{d}{dt}[r\cos\varphi\,(u + \Omega r\cos\varphi)] = r\cos\varphi\, F_\lambda \qquad (1\text{-}15)$$

where F_λ represents the forces toward the east.

Since the atmosphere is a relatively thin layer enveloping the earth, the radius r may be replaced with little error by the mean radius at sea level, a, and in the velocity components (1-13) as well. However, in order to maintain the *angular momentum* principle, as noted by Phillips (1966), the terms involving w on the right sides of (1-14) must be omitted. The result is an approximate form of (1-15) with r replaced by a. In addition, certain terms in the last equation are omitted for consistency with respect to equivalent vector invariant form (1-11). The resulting approximate equations are:

$$\frac{du}{dt} = -\frac{1}{\rho}\frac{\partial p}{\partial x} + \left(f + \frac{u \tan\varphi}{a}\right) v + F_\lambda \tag{1-16}$$

$$\frac{dv}{dt} = -\frac{1}{\rho}\frac{\partial p}{\partial y} - \left(f + \frac{u \tan\varphi}{a}\right) u + F_\varphi \tag{1-17}$$

$$\frac{dw}{dt} = -\frac{1}{\rho}\frac{\partial p}{\partial z} - g + F_z \tag{1-18}$$

Here the vertical component of the earth's vorticity, $f = 2\Omega \sin\varphi$, is called the coriolis parameter. The angular momentum principle corresponding to the last set of equations is just (1-15) with r replaced by a, which is a consistent approximation.

When the vertical scale of the disturbances is much smaller than the horizontal scale, the vertical acceleration dw/dt may be neglected; and (1-18) without friction reduces to the *hydrostatic equation*

$$0 = -\frac{1}{\rho}\frac{\partial p}{\partial z} - g \tag{1-20}$$

The thermodynamic equation 1-9b involves total derivatives that can be readily expanded in any coordinate system (A-21) so (1-9b) will suffice for the present.

1-8 MAP PROJECTIONS

For various purposes—analysis, prediction, and depiction of the meteorological variables—it is useful to map all or part of the surface of the earth on a plane. Such map projections should be as nearly like the spherical surface as possible, but it is obvious that some features will be lost. It is very important to preserve the angle between intersecting curves, for example the right angles between latitude circles and meridians. Maps possessing this valuable property are called *conformal*. If distances were preserved from sphere to projection, the map would be termed *isometric*. While this feature is not maintained among the maps used by meteorologists, the distortion of distance can be kept to a tolerable level.

Three commonly used maps are the *polar stereographic,* which is convenient for mapping a hemisphere or a bit more; the *Mercator cylindrical* projection which is especially good for an equatorial band, and the *Lambert conical* projection, all of which are shown in Figure 1-2. The polar stereographic and Mercator maps are special cases of the Lambert conical projection. When the spherical surface has been mapped onto a plane it may be desirable to set up a new system of coordinates on the plane and further transform the equations of motion into the map coordinates.

1-8-1 Polar Stereographic Projection

This projection has been widely used in numerical weather prediction. The mapping from sphere to plane is accomplished by the transformation

$$r = 2a \tan(\phi/2) \qquad \text{and} \qquad \theta = \lambda \tag{1-21}$$

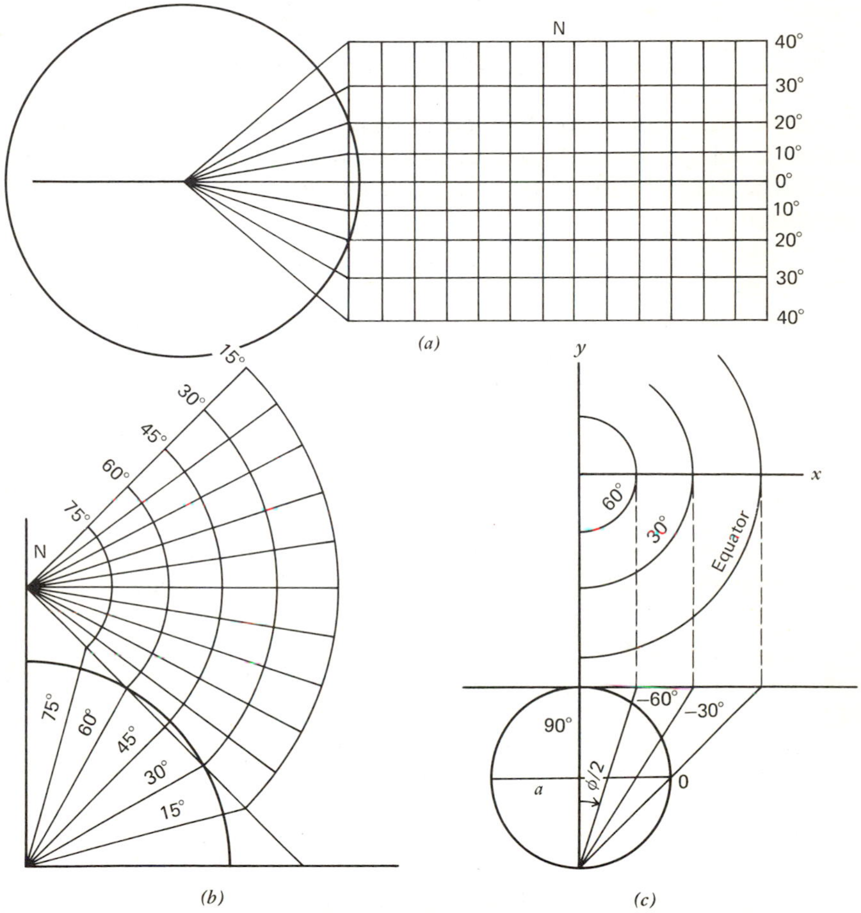

Figure 1-2. (*a*) Mercator cylindrical projection true at 20° latitude, (*b*) Lambert conical projection true at 30° and 60° latitude, (*c*) polar stereographic projection true at 90°.

The first formula follows immediately from Figure 1-2. The symbol a represents the mean earth radius and r is the radius of a latitude circle on the map with colatitude ϕ with $\phi = \pi/2 - \varphi$; (1-21) can be written as

$$r = a\, m(\varphi)\cos\varphi \qquad \theta = \lambda \qquad m(\varphi) = 2/(1 + \sin\varphi) \tag{1-22}$$

where $m(\varphi)$ is the image scale.

Cartesian coordinates may be introduced on the map with $x = r\cos\theta$, $y = r\sin\theta$, which can be written in terms of φ and λ

$$x = \frac{2a\cos\varphi\cos\lambda}{1 + \sin\varphi} \qquad y = \frac{2a\cos\varphi\sin\lambda}{1 + \sin\varphi} \qquad z = z \tag{1-23}$$

Differentiating these expressions leads to relationships between map distances and distance on the sphere (dx_s, dy_s), which may be put in a matrix form:

$$\begin{pmatrix} dx \\ dy \end{pmatrix} = \frac{2}{1 + \sin\varphi}\begin{pmatrix} -\sin\lambda & -\cos\lambda \\ \cos\lambda & -\sin\lambda \end{pmatrix}\begin{pmatrix} dx_s \\ dy_s \end{pmatrix} \tag{1-24}$$

As before, the coefficient $2/(1 + \sin\varphi)$ represents the magnification $m(\varphi)$ of distance from sphere to map and the matrix a rotation of the spherical coordinates. The metric coefficients h_x and h_y for the polar stereographic projection are, therefore

$$h_x = h_y = 1/m(\varphi) = (1 + \sin\varphi)/2 \tag{1-25}$$

It is also clear from (1-24) that the wind velocities in the direction of the map coordinates (U, V) are related to the velocities toward the east and north (u_s, v_s) on the earth by a relationship similar to (1-24), that is,

$$\begin{pmatrix} U \\ V \end{pmatrix} = \begin{pmatrix} -\sin\lambda & -\cos\lambda \\ \cos\lambda & -\sin\lambda \end{pmatrix}\begin{pmatrix} u_s \\ v_s \end{pmatrix} \tag{1-26}$$

where $U = h_x\dot{x}$ and $V = h_y\dot{y}$ (1-27)

To obtain the equations of motion in the map coordinate the foregoing relationship may be substituted into (1-16 to 1-19). The results are

$$\frac{dU}{dt} - V\left(f - \frac{xV - yU}{2a^2}\right) - \frac{W}{a}[(1 + \sin\varphi)\Omega y - U] = -m\alpha\frac{\partial p}{\partial x} \tag{1-28}$$

$$\frac{dV}{dt} = U\left(f - \frac{xV - yU}{2a^2}\right) + \frac{W}{a}[(1 + \sin\varphi)\Omega x + V] = -m\alpha\frac{\partial p}{\partial y} \tag{1-29}$$

$$\frac{dW}{dt} - \frac{1}{a}[U^2 + V^2 + \Omega(1 + \sin\varphi)(xV - yU)] = -\alpha\frac{\partial p}{\partial z} - g \tag{1-30}$$

where $f = 2\Omega\sin\varphi$, F is omitted, and, for example,

$$dU/dt = \partial U/\partial t + m\left(U\frac{\partial U}{\partial x} + V\frac{\partial U}{\partial y}\right) + W\frac{\partial U}{\partial z} \tag{1-31}$$

When the hydrostatic approximation is used in place of (1-30), the terms explicitly involving W on the left in the horizontal equations (1-28 to 1-29) must be omitted for they exactly cancel all the terms, except dW/dt, on the left side of (1-30) when a kinetic energy equation is formed,

$$d(U^2 + V^2 + W^2)/dt = \ldots .$$

Equations 1-28 to 1-31 then reduce to a form similar to (1-16) to (1-18)

$$\frac{dU}{dt} - V\left(f - \frac{xV - yU}{2a^2}\right) = -m\alpha\frac{\partial p}{\partial x} \tag{1-32}$$

$$\frac{dV}{dt} + U\left(f - \frac{xV - yU}{2a^2}\right) = -m\alpha\frac{\partial p}{\partial y} \tag{1-33}$$

$$0 = -\frac{1}{\rho}\frac{\partial p}{\partial z} - g \tag{1-34}$$

The equation of continuity needs little alteration, that is,

$$\frac{\partial\rho}{\partial t} + m^2\left[\frac{\partial(\rho U/m)}{\partial x} + \frac{\partial(\rho V/m)}{\partial y}\right] + \frac{\partial(\rho W)}{\partial z} = 0 \tag{1-35}$$

1-8-2 Mercator Projection

The Mercator projection is defined by the equation

$$x = (a\cos\varphi_0)\lambda \qquad y = a\cos\varphi_0\,\ell n[(1 + \sin\varphi)/\cos\varphi]$$

where φ_0 is the latitude at which the projection is "true." The map factor is $m(\varphi) = \cos\varphi_0/\cos\varphi = 1/h_x = 1/h_y$; and the horizontal equations of motion are

$$\frac{\partial U}{\partial t} + m\left(U\frac{\partial U}{\partial x} + V\frac{\partial U}{\partial y}\right) + w\frac{\partial U}{\partial z} - \left(f + \frac{U\tan\varphi}{a}\right)V = -\frac{m}{\rho}\frac{\partial p}{\partial x} \tag{1-36}$$

$$\frac{\partial V}{\partial t} + m\left(U\frac{\partial V}{\partial x} + V\frac{\partial V}{\partial y}\right) + w\frac{\partial V}{\partial z} + \left(f + \frac{U\tan\varphi}{a}\right)U = -\frac{m}{\rho}\frac{\partial p}{\partial y} \tag{1-37}$$

1-8-3 Lambert Conformal Projection

The Lambert conformal projection is defined by the equations:

$$r = r_0\left[\tan\left(\frac{\pi}{4} - \frac{\varphi}{2}\right)\right]^K \qquad \theta = K(\lambda - \lambda_0) \tag{1-38}$$

The two constants r_0 and K may be chosen to make the projection "true" at latitudes φ_1 and φ_2. When this is done (1-38) may be written as

$$r = (a/K)\,m(\varphi)\cos\varphi \qquad \theta = K(\lambda - \lambda_0) \tag{1-39}$$

where

$$m(\varphi) = \left(\frac{\cos\varphi}{\cos\varphi_1}\right)(K-1)\left(\frac{1+\sin\varphi_1}{1+\sin\varphi}\right)K$$

$$K = \ell n\left(\frac{\cos\varphi_1}{\cos\varphi_2}\right) \div \ell n\left\{\frac{\tan[(\pi/4)-(\varphi_1/2)]}{\tan[(\pi/4)-\varphi_2/2)]}\right\} \qquad (1\text{-}40)$$

The equations of motion are identical in form to (1-32) to (1-34).

1-8-4 Additional Remarks

Global integrations of the prediction equations have been made for climatological studies for about a decade and also some global forecasts have been made on a limited basis for both short and extended ranges. As computer power increases, multilevel global forecasts on a 100 to 200 km mesh will be made on a routine basis. Global models have the advantage that no lateral boundary conditions have to be imposed, whereas limited areas require a treatment of the lateral boundaries. The global forecasts will be supplemented by limited area fine mesh models to provide sufficient resolution for the shorter synoptic scales and mesoscale phenomena.

1-9 ALTERNATE VERTICAL COORDINATES

The height z (or radial distance r) is not the most convenient vertical coordinate for many purposes. Other vertical coordinates that have been used with advantage are: pressure, p; $\ell n p/p_0$; pressure normalized with surface pressure, $\sigma = p/p_s$; and potential temperature, θ.

Consider a generalized vertical coordinate ζ [Kasahara (1974)], which is assumed to be related to the height z by a single-valued monotonic function. In terms of the z coordinate, ζ is a function of x, y, z, and t, that is, $\zeta = \zeta(x,y,z,t)$. On the other hand, in terms of ζ as a vertical coordinate, z becomes a dependent variable, so that $z = z(x,y,\zeta,t)$. Any other scalar (or vector) dependent variable, say A, may be expressed in terms of either coordinate system as $A(x,y,z,t)$ or $A(x,y,\zeta,t)$. These functions become identical when either z or σ is replaced by its functional form in terms of the other, that is,

$$A(x,y,\zeta,t) \equiv A(x,y,z(x,y,\zeta,t),t)$$

Now if a partial derivative is taken with respect to s where s is x, y, or t, the result is

$$\left(\frac{\partial A}{\partial s}\right)_\zeta = \left(\frac{\partial A}{\partial s}\right)_z + \frac{\partial A}{\partial z}\left(\frac{\partial z}{\partial s}\right)_\zeta \qquad s = x,y,\text{ or } t \qquad (1\text{-}41)$$

where the subscript ζ or z denotes the particular vertical coordinate. Similarly, the vertical derivatives are related as follows:

$$\frac{\partial A}{\partial \zeta} = \frac{\partial A}{\partial z}\frac{\partial z}{\partial \zeta} \text{ or, alternatively, } \frac{\partial A}{\partial z} = \frac{\partial A}{\partial \zeta}\frac{\partial \zeta}{\partial z} \tag{1-42}$$

If (1-42) is substituted into (1-41), the result is

$$\left(\frac{\partial A}{\partial s}\right)_\zeta = \left(\frac{\partial A}{\partial s}\right)_z + \frac{\partial A}{\partial \zeta}\frac{\partial \zeta}{\partial z}\left(\frac{\partial z}{\partial s}\right)_\zeta \tag{1-43}$$

The last expression may be used successively with $s = x$ and y to form the gradient of A and similarly with the components of a vector $\mathbf{B}$ to give the two-dimensional divergence with the results,

$$\nabla_\zeta A = \nabla_z A + \frac{\partial A}{\partial \zeta}\frac{\partial \zeta}{\partial z}\nabla_\zeta z \tag{1-44}$$

$$\nabla_\zeta \cdot \mathbf{B} = \nabla_z \cdot \mathbf{B} + \frac{\partial \mathbf{B}}{\partial \zeta}\frac{\partial \zeta}{\partial z} \cdot \nabla_\zeta z \tag{1-45}$$

When $s = t$, the result is

$$\left(\frac{\partial A}{\partial t}\right)_\zeta = \left(\frac{\partial A}{\partial t}\right)_z + \frac{\partial A}{\partial \zeta}\frac{\partial \zeta}{\partial z}\left(\frac{\partial z}{\partial t}\right)_\zeta \tag{1-46}$$

The total derivative in ζ-coordinates is

$$\frac{dA}{dt} = \left(\frac{\partial A}{\partial t}\right)_\zeta + \mathbf{V} \cdot \nabla_\zeta A + \dot{\zeta}\frac{\partial A}{\partial \zeta} \tag{1-47}$$

where $\mathbf{V}$ is the horizontal velocity henceforth, $\dot{\zeta} = d\zeta/dt$ is the *vertical velocity* in the ζ system and A can be a scalar or a vector (assuming the metric terms are taken care of).

The foregoing expressions may be used to transform the equations of motion from the z-coordinate into the ζ-coordinate. By virture of (1-44) the horizontal pressure force transforms as follows

$$-\alpha\nabla_z p = -\alpha\nabla_\zeta p + \alpha\frac{\partial p}{\partial z}\nabla_\zeta z = -\alpha\nabla_\zeta p - \nabla_\zeta \phi \tag{1-48}$$

where $\phi = gz$ is the geopotential.
Thus the horizontal equation of frictionless motion in ζ coordinates becomes

$$\frac{d\mathbf{V}}{dt} = -\alpha\nabla_\zeta p - \nabla_\zeta \phi - f\mathbf{k} \times \mathbf{V} + \mathbf{F} \tag{1-49}$$

Using (1-42) the *hydrostatic equation*, $\alpha(\partial p/\partial z) + g = 0$, becomes

$$\alpha\frac{\partial p}{\partial \zeta}\frac{\partial \zeta}{\partial z} + g = 0 \quad \text{or} \quad \alpha\frac{\partial p}{\partial \zeta} + \frac{\partial \phi}{\partial \zeta} = 0 \tag{1-50}$$

Transforming the continuity equation;

$$d(\ell\text{n } \rho)/dt + \nabla_z \cdot \mathbf{V} + \partial w/\partial z = 0 \tag{1-51}$$

is straightforward but requires somewhat more manipulations. First note that application of (1-42) and (1-45) to the divergence terms gives

$$\nabla_z \cdot \mathbf{V} + \frac{\partial w}{\partial z} = \nabla_\zeta \cdot \mathbf{V} - \frac{\partial \zeta}{\partial z}\frac{\partial \mathbf{V}}{\partial \zeta} \cdot \nabla_\zeta z + \frac{\partial w}{\partial \zeta}\frac{\partial \zeta}{\partial z} \tag{1-52}$$

Moreover

$$w = dz/dt = (\partial z/\partial t)_\zeta + \mathbf{V} \cdot \nabla_\zeta z + \dot{\zeta}\partial z/\partial \zeta \tag{1-53}$$

Hence

$$\frac{\partial w}{\partial \zeta} = \frac{\partial}{\partial t}\left(\frac{\partial z}{\partial \zeta}\right) + \mathbf{V} \cdot \nabla_\zeta \frac{\partial z}{\partial \zeta} + \frac{\partial \mathbf{V}}{\partial \zeta} \cdot \nabla_\zeta z + \frac{\partial \dot{\zeta}}{\partial \zeta}\frac{\partial z}{\partial \zeta} + \dot{\zeta}\frac{\partial}{\partial \zeta}\left(\frac{\partial z}{\partial \zeta}\right) \tag{1-54}$$

Substituting the foregoing equation into (1-52) leads to

$$\nabla_z \cdot \mathbf{V} + \frac{\partial w}{\partial z} = \nabla_\zeta \cdot \mathbf{V} + \frac{\partial \zeta}{\partial z}\left(\frac{\partial}{\partial t} + \mathbf{V} \cdot \nabla_\zeta + \dot{\zeta}\frac{\partial}{\partial \zeta}\right)\frac{\partial z}{\partial \zeta} + \frac{\partial \dot{\zeta}}{\partial \zeta} \tag{1-55}$$

Furthermore, since $\partial \zeta/\partial z = (\partial z/\partial \zeta)^{-1}$, the middle term is just $d[\ell\text{n}(\partial z/\partial \zeta)]/dt$, which can now be combined with $d(\ell\text{n } \rho)/dt$ in (1-51) to give

$$d[\ell\text{n}(\rho\, \partial z/\partial \zeta)]/dt = d(\ell\text{n } \partial p/\partial \zeta)/dt$$

Thus the transformed continuity equation becomes

$$\frac{d}{dt}\left(\ell\text{n}\frac{\partial p}{\partial \zeta}\right) + \nabla_\zeta \cdot \mathbf{V} + \frac{\partial \dot{\zeta}}{\partial \zeta} = 0 \tag{1-56}$$

The thermodynamic equation is not changed in appearance since it can be expressed in terms of the total derivative of potential temperature, $\theta = T(p_0/p)^\kappa$, and T as follows;

$$c_p T(d\ \ell\text{n } \theta)/dt = Q \tag{1-57a}$$

or

$$c_p \frac{dT}{dt} - \alpha \frac{dp}{dt} = Q \tag{1-57b}$$

The next step will be to apply these general equations to some specific selections for ζ.

1-9-1 Pressure Vertical Coordinate

If $\zeta = p$, then $\nabla_\zeta p = \nabla_p p \equiv 0$ and $\partial p/\partial p = 1$ so the equation of motion (1-49) and the hydrostatic equation (1-50) become

$$\frac{d\mathbf{V}}{dt} = -\nabla_p\phi - f\mathbf{k}\times\mathbf{V} + \mathbf{F} \tag{1-58}$$

$$\frac{\partial\phi}{\partial p} = -\alpha \tag{1-59}$$

In the continuity equation (1-56), with $\zeta = p$ the first term, $\ell n(\partial p/\partial p)$, vanishes; hence

$$\nabla_p\cdot\mathbf{V} + \partial\omega/\partial p = 0 \tag{1-60}$$

where $\omega = dp/dt = \dot{p}$ is the vertical velocity in the p-system. Note that this equation is *linear*. This equation may be integrated from $p = 0$, where $\omega = 0$, to an arbitrary level p to yield an equation for ω, that is,

$$\omega = -\int_0^p \nabla_p\cdot\mathbf{V}\,dp \tag{1-61}$$

At the surface the kinematic boundary condition assumes no normal flux, hence

$$\omega_s = dp_s/dt = \partial p_s/\partial t + \mathbf{V}_s\cdot\nabla p_s \tag{1-62}$$

Thus if the integration is taken to $p_s(x,y,t)$ and equation for the surface pressure tendency is obtained, that is,

$$\frac{\partial p_s}{\partial t} + \mathbf{V}_s\nabla\cdot p_s = -\int_0^{ps} \nabla_p\cdot\mathbf{V}\,dp \tag{1-63}$$

Finally, dp/dt in the thermodynamic equation (1-57b) may be replaced by ω, but no other change is necessary.

Some obvious advantages of p-coordinate over z are that the continuity equation (1-60) is linear and also the pressure force in (1-58). The latter also simplifies the geostrophic and thermal wind relationships by the elimination of density, for example,

$$\frac{\partial\mathbf{V}_g}{\partial p} = -f^{-1}\mathbf{k}\times\nabla\frac{\partial\phi}{\partial p} \qquad \text{and} \qquad \Delta\mathbf{V}_g = -f^{-1}\mathbf{k}\times\nabla\,\Delta\phi$$

Normalized Pressure Coordinate $\sigma = p/p_s$ (Phillips, 1957). For this vertical coordinate bear in mind again that, $p_s = p_s(x,y,t)$, then

$$-\alpha\nabla_z p = -\alpha\nabla_\sigma p - \alpha(\partial p/\partial z)\nabla_\sigma z = -\alpha\nabla_\sigma(\sigma\, p_s) - \nabla_\sigma\phi$$

Since $\alpha \nabla_\sigma(\sigma p_s) = \alpha\sigma\nabla p_s$, the equation of motion (1-49) becomes

$$\frac{\partial \mathbf{V}}{\partial t} + \mathbf{V}\cdot\nabla_\sigma \mathbf{V} + \dot{\sigma}\frac{\partial \mathbf{V}}{\partial \sigma} = -\nabla_\sigma \phi - (RT/p_s)\nabla p_s - f\mathbf{k} \times \mathbf{V} + \mathbf{F} \quad (1\text{-}64)$$

In the hydrostatic equation (1-50), $\partial p/\partial\sigma = \partial(\sigma\, p_s)/\partial\sigma = p_s$, hence

$$\partial\phi/\partial\sigma + \alpha\, p_s = 0 \quad (1\text{-}65)$$

The first term in the continuity equation (1-56) becomes $d(\ell n\ \partial p/\partial\sigma)/dt$; and since $\partial p/\partial\sigma = p_s$, the continuity equation in σ-coordinates is

$$d(\ell n\ p_s)/dt + \nabla_\sigma\cdot\mathbf{V} + \partial\dot{\sigma}/\partial\sigma = 0 \quad (1\text{-}66)$$

An alternate form is obtained by expanding the first term $\dot{p}_s/p_s$, giving

$$\partial p_s/\partial t + \mathbf{V}\cdot\nabla p_s + \dot{\sigma}\,\partial p_s/\partial\sigma + p_s\,\nabla_\sigma\cdot\mathbf{V} + p_s\,\partial\dot{\sigma}/\partial\sigma = 0$$

Since p_s does not vary with σ, $\partial p_s/\partial\sigma = 0$; hence

$$\partial p_s/\partial t = -\nabla\cdot(p_s\mathbf{V}) - \partial(p_s\dot{\sigma})/\partial\sigma \quad (1\text{-}67)$$

The boundary conditions on the "vertical velocity," $\dot{\sigma} = d\sigma/dt$, are:

At the surface; $p = p_s$; hence $\sigma = 1$ and $\dot{\sigma} = 0$

Top of the atmosphere; $p = 0$; hence $\sigma = 0$ and $\dot{\sigma} = 0$ (1-68)

With these conditions (1-67) may be integrated over the entire atmosphere, or over part of it, as follows:

$$\frac{\partial p_s}{\partial t} = -\int_0^1 \nabla\cdot(p_s\mathbf{V})\, d\sigma \quad (1\text{-}69)$$

which is an equation for the surface pressure tendency. Integrating from $\sigma = 0$ to arbitrary level σ will give an equation for the vertical velocity $\dot{\sigma}$ at level σ;

$$\sigma\frac{\partial p_s}{\partial t} + \int_0^\sigma \nabla\cdot(p_s\mathbf{V})\, d\sigma = -p_s\dot{\sigma} \quad (1\text{-}70)$$

If the value of $\partial p_s/\partial t$ is obtained from (1-69), it can be used in (1-70) to calculate $\dot{\sigma}$, which, in turn, can be used in the momentum equation (1-64) to evaluate $\dot{\sigma}\partial\mathbf{V}/\partial\sigma$ and similarly in the thermodynamic equation. These steps are part of the procedure to determine the local time changes of $\mathbf{V}$, T, etc. in a numerical weather prediction model.

The reason $\dot{\sigma} = 0$ at the surface is that the flow must be along the surface (normal component zero) for which $\sigma \equiv 1$. It is this simplified lower boundary condition that provides the advantage of the σ-coordinate over the p-coordinate.

An immediate result is a concise form (1-69) for computing the surface pressure tendency.

1-9-2 Isentropic Vertical Coordinate θ

Isentropic surfaces (constant entropy), or equivalently, potential temperature surfaces gained popularity as a vertical coordinate in the 1930s and 1940s. Although little used for many years, the θ-coordinate has enjoyed a mild resurgence in the middle 1970s. An attractive feature of the θ coordinate is that for *dry adiabatic* motions each parcel conserves its potential temperature; hence $d\theta/dt = 0$; and the isentropic surfaces become material surfaces, which is not true for diabatic conditions. However, this coordinate system has other desirable features and is not confined to the study of adiabatic motions. For example, the θ coordinate gives better resolution in the vicinity of fronts.

Again transforming the horizontal pressure force with (1-44) gives

$$-\alpha \nabla_z p = -\alpha \nabla_\theta p - \alpha \frac{\partial p}{\partial z} \nabla_\theta z = -\alpha \nabla_\theta p + g \nabla_\theta z \tag{1-71}$$

Since $\theta = T(p_0/p)^\kappa$, $\nabla_\theta \ln T - (R/c_p)\nabla_\theta \ln p = \nabla_\theta \ln \theta = 0$; therefore $-\nabla_\theta p = -(p\, c_p/RT)\nabla_\theta T$. Hence the horizontal pressure (1-71) may be written

$$-\alpha \nabla_z p = -\nabla_\theta (c_p T) - \nabla_\theta \phi$$

Substituting this expression into the equation of horizontal motion gives

$$\frac{\partial \mathbf{V}}{\partial t} + \mathbf{V}\cdot\nabla_\theta \mathbf{V} + \dot{\theta}\frac{\partial \mathbf{V}}{\partial \theta} = -\nabla_\theta (c_p T + \phi) - f\mathbf{k} \times \mathbf{V} \tag{1-72}$$

The quantity, $c_p T + \phi = M$, is usually referred to as the *Montgomery streamfunction*. The hydrostatic equation may be derived by using the definition of potential temperature in terms of p and T, taking the logarithm and then differentiating:

$$\frac{1}{\theta} = \frac{1}{T}\frac{\partial T}{\partial \theta} - \frac{R}{p\, c_p}\frac{\partial p}{\partial \theta}$$

Next replace $\partial p/\partial \theta$ with $-\rho \partial \phi/\partial \theta$, giving

$$\frac{\partial}{\partial \theta}(c_p T + \phi) = \frac{c_p T}{\theta}. \tag{1-73}$$

The *continuity equation* (1-56) becomes

$$\frac{d}{dt}\left(\ln \frac{\partial p}{\partial \theta}\right) + \nabla_\theta \cdot \mathbf{V} + \frac{\partial \dot{\theta}}{\partial \theta} = 0 \tag{1-74}$$

which can also be expanded and integrated (with respect to θ) to give an equation for the surface pressure tendency $\partial p_s/\partial t$.

The thermodynamic equation (1-57a) needs no change. The boundary conditions on $\dot{\theta}$, analogous to (1-68), are:

$$\dot{\theta} = 0 \text{ at } \theta = \theta_{top}$$

$$\dot{\theta} = \partial\theta_s/\partial t + \mathbf{V}_s \cdot \nabla\theta_s, \text{ at } \theta = \theta_s \qquad (1\text{-}75)$$

1-10 SOME ENERGY RELATIONS

In dynamical analysis of atmospheric phenomena the study of the energetics of the various disturbances is of vital importance. The energy relations are also of importance in numerical weather prediction. Diagnosis of energy transformations and conservation properties of numerical models are valuable tools in designing differencing schemes, representation of physical processes and detecting sources of error.

1-10-1 Kinetic Energy

An equation involving the kinetic energy per unit mass is readily obtained by scalar multiplication of the equation of motion by **V**. For example, the pressure coordinate form (1-58) gives

$$dK/dt = \partial K/\partial t + \mathbf{V}\cdot\nabla K + \omega\partial K/\partial p = -\mathbf{V}\cdot\nabla_p\phi + \mathbf{V}\cdot\mathbf{F} \qquad (1\text{-}80)$$

where $K = V^2/2$ and $\mathbf{V}\cdot\mathbf{F}$ represents the frictional sink. This equation may be put in flux form by multiplying the equation of continuity by K and adding it to (1-80), giving

$$\partial K/\partial t + \nabla\cdot K\mathbf{V} + \partial(K\omega)/\partial p = -\nabla\cdot(\phi\mathbf{V}) + \phi\nabla\cdot\mathbf{V} + \mathbf{V}\cdot\mathbf{F} \qquad (1\text{-}81)$$

Also the continuity equation may be used to express the term $\phi\nabla\cdot\mathbf{V}$ as follows:

$$\phi\nabla\cdot\mathbf{V} = -\phi\partial\omega/\partial p = -\partial(\phi\omega)/\partial p + \omega\partial\phi/\partial p$$

Finally, $\partial\phi/\partial p = -\alpha = -RT/p$, hence (1-81) becomes

$$\frac{\partial K}{\partial t} + \nabla\cdot[(K+\phi)\mathbf{V}] + \frac{\partial[(K+\phi)\omega]}{\partial p} = -\frac{RT\omega}{p} + \mathbf{V}\cdot\mathbf{F} \qquad (1\text{-}82)$$

The second and third terms are flux divergence terms, while the fourth and fifth terms represent sources or sinks of kinetic energy.

1-10-2 Potential Energy

The potential energy due to gravity of a column of air per unit horizontal area extending from the surface to the top of the atmosphere is given by the integral

$$P = \int_0^\infty gz\rho dz = \int_0^{p_s} \phi \frac{dp}{g} = \frac{\phi p}{g}\bigg|_0^{p_s} - \frac{1}{g}\int p d\phi$$

where the vertical variation of g has been neglected and integration by parts has been used to obtain the last form, as well as the hydrostatic equation. The latter is used again to give

$$p = \phi_s p_s/g + \frac{1}{g}\int_0^{p_s} RT\,dp \tag{1-83}$$

The *internal energy* of the same column is

$$I = \int_0^\infty c_v T\,\rho dz = \int_0^{p_s} \frac{c_v T\,dp}{g} \tag{1-84}$$

Using the relation, $c_v + R = c_p$, gives the final expression for the combined internal energy and the potential energy due to gravity, which is referred to as *total potential energy,* that is,

$$P + I = g^{-1}\int_0^{p_s} E\,dp + g^{-1}\phi_s p_s \tag{1-85}$$

where $E = c_p T$ is the *enthalpy*.

This result shows that the total potential energy of a column of the atmosphere is proportional to the integral of the enthalpy plus a term proportional to surface height above sea level. Hence to obtain an equation for the total potential energy, the thermodynamic energy equation (1-57b) may be used as follows:

$$\frac{\partial E}{\partial t} + \mathbf{V}\cdot\nabla E + \omega\frac{\partial E}{\partial p} = \frac{RT}{p}\omega + Q \tag{1-86}$$

where dE/dt has been expanded into partial derivatives.

Next multiply the continuity equation (1-60) by E and add it to (1-86) to obtain a flux form, that is,

$$\frac{\partial E}{\partial t} + \nabla\cdot(E\mathbf{V}) + \frac{\partial(E\omega)}{\partial p} = \frac{RT\omega}{p} + Q \tag{1-87}$$

Comparing (1-82) and (1-87) shows that the term $RT\omega/p$ appears in both equations but with opposite signs. When potential energy is increasing locally by virtue of this term, kinetic energy is decreasing, and vice versa. In a closed region integration of this term represents the *transformation between kinetic and potential energies*. This *transformation function* will vanish when the two equations, (1-82) and (1-87), are summed to give an equation for the local change of $K + E$ as follows

$$\frac{\partial(K+E)}{\partial t} + \nabla\cdot[(K+E+\phi)\mathbf{V}] + \frac{\partial}{\partial p}[(K+E+\phi)\omega] = Q + \mathbf{V}\cdot\mathbf{F} \qquad (1\text{-}88)$$

Next, integrate this equation over the entire mass of the atmosphere, an infinitesimal element of which is $\rho\, dxdydz = -\, dxdydp/g$.

$$\begin{aligned}&\frac{1}{g}\iint\int_0^{p_s} \frac{\partial}{\partial t}(K+E)dpdxdy + \frac{1}{g}\iint\int_0^{p_s} \nabla\cdot[(K+E+\phi)\mathbf{V}]\, dpdxdy \\ &+ \frac{1}{g}\iint [(K+E+\phi)\omega]_s\, dxdy = \overline{Q} + \overline{\mathbf{V}\cdot\mathbf{F}}\end{aligned} \qquad (1\text{-}89)$$

The terms $\overline{Q}$ and $\overline{\mathbf{V}\cdot\mathbf{F}}$ represent, respectively, the total heat added or lost by the atmosphere to space and the underlying surface and the total frictional dissipation. Vertical integration has been applied to the third integral. Next the differential operators $\partial/\partial t$ and $\nabla\cdot$ are moved outside the integration with respect to p, taking into account the variable upper limit p_s by use of Leibniz rule for differentiation of an integral.

$$\begin{aligned}&\iint \frac{1}{g}\left\{\frac{\partial}{\partial t}\int_0^{p_s} (K+E)dp - \frac{\partial p_s}{\partial t}(K+E)_s + \nabla\cdot\int_0^{p_s} [(K+E+\phi)\mathbf{V}]dp\right. \\ &\left. - \nabla p_s\cdot[(K+E+\phi)\mathbf{V}]_s + [(K+E+\phi)\omega]_s\right\} dxdy = \overline{Q} + \overline{\mathbf{V}\cdot\mathbf{F}}\end{aligned} \qquad (1\text{-}90)$$

where the $(\overline{})$ represents the triple integral as above.

Now the $\partial/\partial t$ can come outside the integral sign, and the third term involving the horizontal flux divergence vanishes by virtue of the Gauss divergence theorem because no lateral boundaries exist over the spherical earth (excluding mountains intersecting p-surfaces), leaving

$$\begin{aligned}&\frac{\partial}{\partial t}(\overline{K} + \overline{E}) - \iint\left\{(K+E)_s\frac{\partial p_s}{\partial t} + \nabla p_s\cdot[(K+E+\phi)\mathbf{V}]_s\right. \\ &\left. - \frac{1}{g}[(K+E+\phi)_s\omega_s]\right\} dxdy = \overline{Q} + \overline{\mathbf{V}\cdot\mathbf{F}}\end{aligned} \qquad (1\text{-}91)$$

According to the surface boundary condition (1-62), $\partial p_s/\partial t + \mathbf{V}\cdot\nabla p_s = \omega_s$; hence the terms involving $(K+E)_s$ cancel. On the other hand, the term $\phi_s(\omega - \mathbf{V}\cdot\nabla\phi)_s$ may be replaced by $\phi_s\, \partial p_s/\partial t$. Thus the total energy equation (1-91) reduces to

$$\frac{\partial}{\partial t}[\overline{K} + \overline{E} + \frac{1}{g}\overline{\phi_s p_s}] = \overline{Q} + \overline{\mathbf{V}\cdot\mathbf{F}} \qquad (1\text{-}92)$$

where $\overline{\phi_s p_s}$ is only a two-dimensional integral.

The left side of (1-92) is the time rate of change (actually the total derivative d/dt) of the total kinetic plus potential energy as defined in (1-85), while the right side represents the total energy added to the system and the frictional dissipation of kinetic energy. Under adiabatic, frictionless conditions the right side of (1-92) vanishes and the total energy is conserved.

1-11 AVAILABLE POTENTIAL ENERGY

As is often the case in nature, the mere existence of some kind of potential energy does not assure its availability for conversion to other forms of energy. To clarify this situation with respect to atmosphere processes, Lorenz (1955) defined a quantity called *available potential energy* which is the *difference* between the total potential energy of the atmosphere at a given time and a hypothetical state obtained by adiabatically rearranging the temperature field to a stable stratification in which the p, T, and therefore θ, surfaces coincide. According to (1-82) the rate of conversion of potential to kinetic energy over a closed region is given by the integral, $-(R/g)\int\int\int(T\omega/p)dxdydp$, which is proportional to the vertically integrated covariance, $\overline{T\omega}$, of T and ω over isobaric surfaces (the covariance $\overline{T\omega} = \overline{T'\omega'} + \bar{T}\bar{\omega}$), and since $\bar{\omega} = 0$, as will be proven below, the covariance becomes $\overline{T\omega} = \overline{T'\omega'}$. At Lorenz' hypothetical state of the atmosphere the temperature is constant over the isobaric surfaces, hence $\overline{T\omega} = 0$. Next, apply the Gauss divergence theorem to the vertically integrated continuity equation (1-61) giving

$$\bar{\omega}\int\int dxdy = \int\int\omega\, dxdy = -\int\int_0\int^p \nabla_p\cdot\mathbf{V}\, dxdydp \qquad (1\text{-}93)$$

which is zero provided the surface is closed or V_n vanishes at the boundaries. Thus $\int\int \nabla_p\cdot\mathbf{V}\, dxdy = 0$ and $\bar{\omega} = 0$ over a closed isobaric surface. It follows that at the hypothetical adiabatically rearranged state of the atmosphere $\overline{T\omega} = \bar{T}\bar{\omega} = 0$, and *no further conversion of potential to kinetic energy can take place.*

It is now evident why the name *available potential energy* is appropriate for the difference between the potential energy of the atmosphere at some arbitrary state and the idealized hypothetical state, since having arrived at the latter adiabatically, and no further conversion to kinetic energy is possible, this difference is the only part of the total potential energy which would be available for conversion to kinetic energy.[1]

To obtain a mathematical expression for available potential energy A, for simplicity ignore orography, let $p_s = 1000$ mb and introduce potential temperature, $\theta = T(p_s/p)^\kappa$, into (1-85). Then

$$TPE = (c_p/g)\int_0^{po} Tdp + g^{-1}\phi_s p_s = g^{-1}c_p p_s^{-\kappa}\int_0^{po}\theta p^\kappa dp + \phi_s p_s/g$$

[1] The "reference state" is somewhat arbitrary since there is no guarantee that it can be attained by natural processes.

where $\kappa = R/c_p$. Next integrate by parts, giving

$$TPE = \frac{c_p p_s^{-\kappa}}{g(1+\kappa)}\left[(\theta p^{1+\kappa})_0^{p_s} + \int_{\theta S}^{\theta T} p^{1+\kappa}\, d\theta\right] + \phi_s p_s g$$

Disregarding the constant terms, the total potential energy of the atmosphere averaged over an area and denoted by a bar is

$$\overline{TPE} = \frac{c_p p_s^{-\kappa}}{g(1+\kappa)} \int \overline{p^{1+\kappa}}\, d\theta \tag{1-94}$$

where the vertical coordinate is now potential temperature. If the atmosphere is now rearranged to Lorenz' hypothetical state, where the pressure over the isentropic (θ) surface is equal to the average of the initial pressure distribution, say $\bar{p}$, then the available potential energy over the area will be the difference between (1-94) and the $\overline{TPE}$ of the hypothetical state, that is,

$$\bar{A} = \frac{c_p p_s^{-\kappa}}{g(1+\kappa)} \int (\overline{p^{1+\kappa}} - \bar{p}^{1+\kappa})\, d\theta \tag{1-95}$$

In order to put this in a more workable form, let $p = \bar{p} + p'$ and then expand $p^{1+\kappa}$ in a series as follows

$$p^{1+\kappa} = (\bar{p}+p')^{1+\kappa} = \bar{p}^{1+\kappa} + \frac{(1+\kappa)\,\bar{p}^{\kappa}p'}{1!} + \frac{\kappa(1+\kappa)\bar{p}^{\kappa-1}p'^2}{2!} + \ldots$$

Now take the area average, which will cause the middle term on the right to vanish, and substitute the result into (1-95), giving

$$\bar{A} \doteq \frac{1}{2}\kappa\, c_p g^{-1} p_s^{-\kappa} \int_{\theta S}^{\theta T} \bar{p}^{1+\kappa}\, \overline{(p'/p)^2}\, d\theta \tag{1-96}$$

Thus the available potential energy over an area is dependent on the variance of pressure over the isentropic surfaces which, in turn, is closely related to the variance of θ (or T) over pressure surfaces. If $\bar{\theta}$ and $\bar{T}$ represent averages over a $\bar{p}$ surface then

$$p \doteq \bar{p}[\theta(p)] \qquad \text{and} \qquad p' \doteq \bar{p}(\theta-\theta') - \bar{p}(\theta) = \theta'\, \partial\bar{p}/\partial\theta$$

Hence, $\overline{(p'/p)^2} = (1/\bar{p}^2)\, \overline{(\theta'\, \partial p/\partial\theta)^2} = (1/\bar{p}^2)\, \overline{\theta'^2}\, (\partial\bar{p}/\partial\theta)^2$ and (1-96) becomes

$$\bar{A} = \frac{1}{2}\kappa\, c_p g^{-1} p_s^{-\kappa} \int_{\theta S}^{\theta T} \frac{\bar{p}^{\kappa}}{\bar{p}}\, \overline{\theta'^2} \left(\frac{\partial\bar{p}}{\partial\theta}\right)^2 d\theta$$

$$= \frac{\kappa\, c_p}{2g\, p_s^{\kappa}} \int_{p_s}^{0} \bar{p}^{(\kappa-1)}\, \overline{\theta^2} \left(\frac{\theta'}{\bar{\theta}}\right)^2 \left(\frac{\partial\bar{\theta}}{\partial\bar{p}}\right)^{-1} dp \tag{1-97}$$

Substituting the following relations into (1-97) leads to the final form of $\bar{A}$;

$$(\partial\bar{p}/\partial\theta)\kappa\bar{\theta}/(\gamma_d p) = -1/(\gamma_d - \gamma) \qquad \gamma = -\partial T/\partial z,\ \gamma_d = g/c_p$$

$$\bar{\theta} = \bar{T}(p_s/p)^{\kappa} \qquad \text{and} \qquad \theta'/\theta \doteq T'/T$$

$$\bar{A} \doteq \frac{1}{2}\int_0^{p_s} \frac{\bar{T}}{\gamma_d - \bar{\gamma}} \overline{\left(\frac{T'}{\bar{T}}\right)^2}\, dp \tag{1-98}$$

For the typical values, $\gamma \doteq 2\gamma_d/3$, $\overline{T'^2} = (15°)^2$, and

$$\bar{A}/\overline{TPE} \sim {}^1/_{200} \tag{1-99}$$

hence less than 1 percent of the total potential energy is available for conversion to kinetic energy. The kinetic energy K and total potential energy TPE in a column of atmosphere per unit cross section are, respectively,

$$K = \frac{1}{2g}\int_0^{p_s} V^2\, dp \qquad TPE = \frac{c_v}{gR}\int_0^{p_s} c^2\, dp \tag{1-100}$$

where $c^2 = c_p RT/c_v$ is the square of the speed of sound.

Taking an average of $V/c \sim {}^1/_{20}$ leads to the rough estimate

$$\bar{K}/\overline{TPE} \sim {}^1/_{2000} \qquad \text{and} \qquad \bar{K}/\bar{A} \sim {}^1/_{10} \tag{1-101}$$

Thus, despite the fact that only a very small fraction of the total potential energy is available for conversion to kinetic energy, it is still roughly ten times the observed mean kinetic energy. If kinetic energy is not generated, it is not for lack of available potential energy as defined, but rather the mechanism to release it.

With respect to weather prediction a numerical scheme with an erroneous conversion of only 0.01 percent of the TPE could result in a 20 percent increase in kinetic energy which would be an unacceptable error.

Conservation laws similar to (1-87 to 1-92), but involving A instead of E, can be developed, but will be omitted here.

In any event, the nonlinear advection terms do not generate kinetic energy in the mean, hence a proper numerical treatment of the advection terms must avoid the false generation of kinetic energy, a subject that will be taken up in Chapter 5.

1-12 VORTICITY AND DIVERGENCE EQUATIONS

For the purposes of studying the dynamics of geophysical systems and also for numerical weather prediction, it is often advantageous to replace the vector equation of horizontal motion (or the two scalar component equations) by two other scalar equations known as the *vorticity* and *divergence* equations.

Vorticity Equation. The three-dimensional vector vorticity is simply the curl of the velocity, which is a generalization of the concept of angular velocity. In the case of solid rotation vorticity is simply twice the angular velocity. In the atmosphere the large-scale flow is quasi-horizontal with the vertical velocity several orders of magnitude smaller than the horizontal velocity. Because of this and the nature of the large-scale dynamics, the vertical component of vorticity turns out to be of principal importance. Consequently, only the horizontal wind vector and the vertical component of its vorticity, $\zeta = \mathbf{k}\cdot\nabla \times \mathbf{V}$, are usually needed. In spherical coordinates

$$\zeta = (1/a \cos \varphi)\, \partial v/\partial\lambda - a^{-1}\, \partial u/\partial\varphi + u \tan \varphi/a \qquad (1\text{-}102)$$

To derive an equation for the time rate of change of ζ, it is convenient to write (1-16 to 1-17) in vector form and use the relationship (A-9), $(\mathbf{V}\cdot\nabla)\mathbf{V} = \nabla(V^2/2) + \zeta\mathbf{k} \times \mathbf{V}$.

$$\underset{1}{\frac{d\mathbf{V}}{dt} = \frac{\partial \mathbf{V}}{\partial t}} + \underset{2}{\nabla(V^2/2)} + \underset{3}{\zeta\mathbf{k} \times \mathbf{V}} + \underset{4}{w\frac{\partial \mathbf{V}}{\partial z}} = \underset{5}{-\alpha\nabla p} - \underset{6}{f\mathbf{k} \times \mathbf{V}} + \mathbf{F} \qquad (1\text{-}103)$$

where $f = 2\Omega \sin \varphi$ is the coriolis parameter. For convenience, define $\eta = \zeta + f$ and combine the third and sixth terms to give $\eta\mathbf{k} \times \mathbf{V}$ and then operate on the entire equation with $\mathbf{k} \cdot \nabla \times$. The vector operations given in the appendix may be used to simplify the results. For example, the second term vanishes because the curl of the gradient is zero. Most products are straightforward except perhaps the following:

$$\mathbf{k}\cdot[\nabla \times (\eta\mathbf{k} \times \mathbf{V})] = \mathbf{k}\cdot[\eta\mathbf{k}\nabla\cdot\mathbf{V} - \mathbf{V}\nabla\cdot\eta\mathbf{k} - (\eta\mathbf{k}\cdot\nabla)\mathbf{V} + (\mathbf{V}\cdot\nabla)\eta\mathbf{k}]$$

The middle two terms on the right will vanish since $\mathbf{k}\cdot\mathbf{V} = \mathbf{k}\cdot\nabla = 0$.

The result is the *vorticity equation*

$$\underset{1}{\frac{\partial \zeta}{\partial t}} + \underset{3,6}{\mathbf{V}\cdot\nabla\eta} + \underset{4}{w\frac{\partial \zeta}{\partial z}} = \underset{3,6}{-\eta\nabla\cdot\mathbf{V}} + \underset{4}{\mathbf{k}\cdot\nabla w \times \frac{\partial \mathbf{V}}{\partial z}} + \underset{5}{\mathbf{k}\cdot\nabla p \times \nabla\alpha} + \mathbf{k}\cdot\nabla \times \mathbf{F} \qquad (1\text{-}104)$$

where the numbers indicate the source of each term from (1-103). To put the equation in the usual form note that $\partial f/\partial t = \partial f/\partial z = 0$; thus (1-104) becomes

$$\frac{\partial(\zeta+f)}{\partial t} + \mathbf{V}\cdot\nabla(\zeta+f) + w\frac{\partial(\zeta+f)}{\partial z}$$
$$= -(\zeta+f)\nabla\cdot\mathbf{V} + \mathbf{k}\cdot\nabla w \times \frac{\partial \mathbf{V}}{\partial z} + \mathbf{k}\cdot\nabla p \times \nabla\alpha + \mathbf{k}\cdot\nabla \times \mathbf{F} \quad (1\text{-}105)$$

where the left side is just $d(\zeta+f)/dt$. Most applications of the vorticity equation involve further approximations, which will be taken up later.

1-12-1 Divergence Equation

The three dimensional divergence is $\nabla_3\cdot\mathbf{V}_3$; however, the horizontal divergence, $D = \nabla\cdot\mathbf{V}$ is usually treated separately for reasons that will become apparent. In spherical coordinates, $\nabla\cdot\mathbf{V} = (1/a \cos\varphi)\partial u/\partial\lambda + a^{-1}\partial v/\partial\varphi - v \tan\varphi/a$.

An equation involving the local time derivative of D is obtainable by taking the horizontal divergence of the vector equation of horizontal motion. A preliminary result is

$$\frac{\partial D}{\partial t} + \nabla\cdot[(\mathbf{V}\cdot\nabla)\mathbf{V}] + \nabla\cdot(f\mathbf{k}\times\mathbf{V}) + \nabla w\cdot\frac{\partial \mathbf{V}}{\partial z} + w\frac{\partial D}{\partial z}$$
$$= -\nabla\cdot(\alpha\nabla p) + \nabla\cdot\mathbf{F} \quad (1\text{-}106)$$

However, for purposes of application, the equation must be expanded further and eventually simplifed by omitting terms of lesser magnitude. In particular, the horizontal advection term is somewhat more involved. The result with some approximations is

$$\frac{\partial D}{\partial t} + \mathbf{V}\cdot\nabla D + w\frac{\partial D}{\partial z} + \nabla w\cdot\frac{\partial \mathbf{V}}{\partial z} + D^2 - 2J(u,v) + (\mathbf{k}\times\mathbf{V})\cdot\nabla f$$
$$- f\zeta = -\nabla\cdot(\alpha\nabla p) + \nabla\cdot\mathbf{F} \quad (1\text{-}107)$$

where $J(u,v) = (\partial u/\partial x)(\partial v/\partial y) - (\partial u/\partial y)(\partial v/\partial x)$ is the Jacobian. With regard to the vorticity and divergence equations it would make little sense to replace the two scalar equations of horizontal motion with the higher order vorticity and divergence partial differential equations, unless there are some potential advantages. This formulation does provide a method of introducing simplifying approximations while retaining certain physical processes. More specifically the approximations may be for one of the following purposes: (1) to simplify a dynamical analysis, (2) to filter or remove certain types of motion, or (3) to simplify numerical prediction models, and possibly other reasons.

The first five terms of (1-107) are small and are generally neglected, also dropping the first three effects the removal of certain types of disturbances. Similarly, the terms involving the vertical velocity, the metric terms and $\zeta\nabla\cdot\mathbf{V}$ are frequently neglected in the vorticity equation (1-105). The omission of the various terms may be justified under suitable assumptions by a scale analysis, which will be presented in Chapter 3.

The vorticity and divergence equations as derived here involved height z as a vertical coordinate. In subsequent sections other coordinate systems will be considered, which give rise to some variations in the form of the equations. In particular, the commonly used vertical coordinate, p, affords some simplifications. For example, the horizontal pressure force has the form, $-\nabla\phi$, hence $\mathbf{k}\cdot\nabla \times \nabla\phi = 0$. Thus the first term on the right in the divergence equation (1-107) becomes $-\nabla^2\phi$ and there is no term corresponding to $\mathbf{k}\cdot\nabla p \times \nabla\alpha$ in 1-104.

CHAPTER 2

Wave Motion in the Atmosphere: Part I

2-1 INTRODUCTION

There are a variety of phenomena occurring in the atmosphere having the horizontal space and time scales as shown in Figure 2-1. Here the tropics and middle latitudes are presented separately and the horizontal scales are divided into five parts: planetary scale, synoptic scale, mesoscale, convective scale, and microscale. This chapter investigates the types of wave solutions that can be obtained from the linearized atmospheric prediction equations. Some of the solutions do not correspond to any of the phenomena in Figure 2-1; this information is needed for the construction of numerical prediction models.

2-2 LINEARIZED EQUATIONS

In order to understand the extremely complex motions of the atmosphere, it is desirable first to isolate and analyze some simple types of motion in this chapter. For this purpose consider motion only in the x–z plane. Assume uniformity in the lateral direction (y) and also neglect the rotation of the earth, friction, and diabatic heating. The Newtonian momentum equations, thermodynamic equation, and the continuity equation are then expressible in the form

$$
\begin{aligned}
\frac{du}{dt} + \alpha \frac{\partial p}{\partial x} &= 0 \\
\frac{dw}{dt} + \alpha \frac{\partial p}{\partial z} + g &= 0 \\
\alpha \frac{dp}{dt} + p\gamma \frac{d\alpha}{dt} &= 0 \\
\alpha \nabla \cdot \mathbf{V} - \frac{d\alpha}{dt} &= 0
\end{aligned}
\qquad (2\text{-}1)
$$

where

$$\gamma = \frac{c_p}{c_v}, \qquad \alpha = \frac{1}{\rho}$$

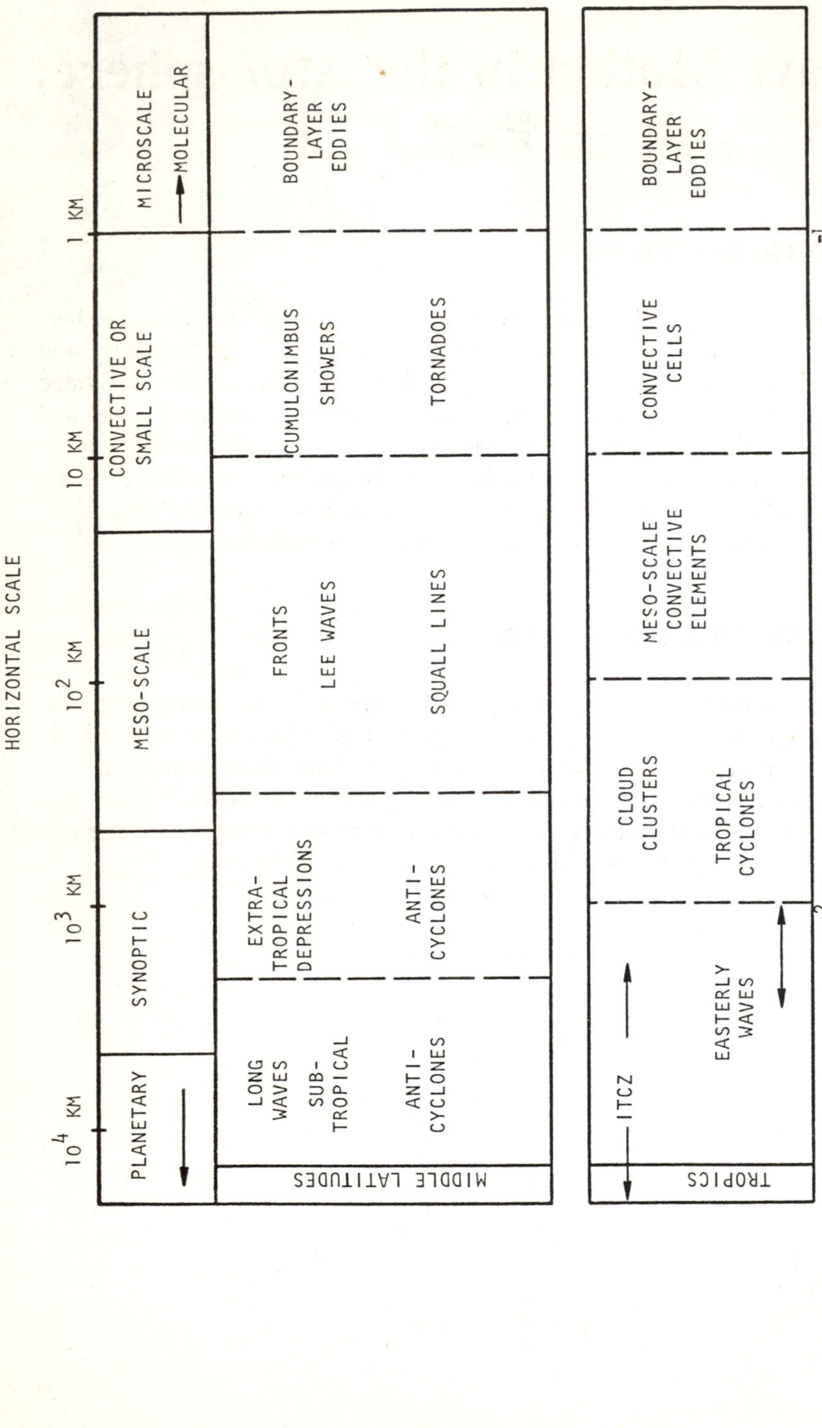

Figure 2-1 Some atmospheric phenomena as a function of scale.

Now these equations will be linearized by the so-called perturbation method. For simplicity assume a constant basic current U and basic state thermodynamic variables $\overline{p}(z)$ and $\overline{\alpha}(z)$ in hydrostatic balance: $\overline{\alpha}\partial\overline{p}/\partial z = -g$. Next, express the dependent variables as the sum of the basic or undisturbed value plus a perturbation (e.g., $u = U + u'$), and substitute these expressions into the system (2-1). After subtracting the equations for the basic flow only and neglecting the products of perturbation quantities, the resulting linear equations for the perturbation quantities are:

$$
\begin{aligned}
&\frac{\partial u'}{\partial t} + U\frac{\partial u'}{\partial x} + \overline{\alpha}\frac{\partial p'}{\partial x} = 0 \\
&\delta_1\left(\frac{\partial w'}{\partial t} + U\frac{\partial w'}{\partial x}\right) + \overline{\alpha}\frac{\partial p'}{\partial z} - \frac{g\alpha'}{\overline{\alpha}} = 0 \\
&\overline{\alpha}\left(\frac{\partial p'}{\partial t} + U\frac{\partial p'}{\partial x}\right) - gw' + \overline{p}\gamma\left(\frac{\partial \alpha'}{\partial t} + U\frac{\partial \alpha'}{\partial x} + w'\frac{\partial\overline{\alpha}}{\partial z}\right) = 0 \\
&\left(\frac{\partial u'}{\partial x} + \frac{\partial w'}{\partial z}\right)\overline{\alpha} - \delta_2\left(\frac{\partial \alpha'}{\partial t} + U\frac{\partial \alpha'}{\partial x}\right) - w'\frac{\partial\overline{\alpha}}{\partial z} = 0
\end{aligned}
\tag{2-2}
$$

The symbols δ_1 and δ_2 merely identify certain vertical acceleration and the compressibility terms during the subsequent analysis and will take on values of either unity or zero according to whether the terms are omitted or included.

2-3 PURE SOUND WAVES

Sound waves are compression waves that can be isolated by setting $g = 0$, $\delta_1 = \delta_2 = 1$, and by letting $\overline{p}$ and $\overline{\alpha}$ be constants. Now assume the perturbation quantities are harmonic in x, z, and t with constant coefficients as follows:

$$
\begin{aligned}
u' &= Se^{i(\mu x + kz - \nu t)} \qquad & w' &= We^{i(\mu x + kz - \nu t)} \\
p' &= Pe^{i(\mu x + kz - \nu t)} \qquad & \alpha' &= Ae^{i(\mu x + kz - \nu t)}
\end{aligned}
\tag{2-3}
$$

These are plane waves with μ and k as wave numbers in the x and z directions and with υ as the frequency. The actual physical quantities are obtained by taking the real parts of the solutions. Since the equations (2-2) are linear, any linear combination of solutions will also be a solution, hence only a single harmonic need be considered. Substituting the functions (2-3) into (2-2) leads to a system of homogeneous algebraic equations for the amplitudes S, W, P and A as follows:

$$
\begin{aligned}
&(\mu U - \upsilon)S + \bar{\alpha}\mu P = 0 \\
&(\mu U - \upsilon)W + \bar{\alpha}kP = 0 \\
&\bar{\alpha}(\mu U - \upsilon)P + \bar{p}\gamma(\mu U - \upsilon)A = 0 \\
&\mu\bar{\alpha}S + \bar{\alpha}kW - (\mu U - \upsilon)A = 0
\end{aligned}
\tag{2-4}
$$

The foregoing systems may be written in matrix form as

$$
\begin{bmatrix}
(\mu U - \upsilon) & 0 & \bar{\alpha}\mu & 0 \\
0 & (\mu U - \upsilon) & \bar{\alpha}k & 0 \\
0 & 0 & \bar{\alpha}(\mu U - \upsilon) & \bar{p}\gamma(\mu U - \upsilon) \\
\alpha\mu & \alpha k & 0 & -(\mu U - \upsilon)
\end{bmatrix}
\begin{bmatrix} S \\ W \\ P \\ A \end{bmatrix} = 0 \tag{2-5}
$$

Nonzero values for the amplitudes S, W, P and A, are possible only if the determinant of the set of homogeneous equations vanishes. When the determinant is expanded the following frequency equation is obtained

$$\bar{\alpha}(\mu U - \upsilon)^2[-(\mu U - \upsilon)^2 + \gamma\bar{p}\bar{\alpha}(k^2 + \mu^2)] = 0 \tag{2-6}$$

It is of fourth order and hence has four solutions:

$$\upsilon = \pm\ \mu U \tag{2-7a}$$

which correspond to simple advection, and

$$\upsilon = \mu U \pm (k^2 + \mu^2)^{1/2}\sqrt{\gamma R\bar{T}} \tag{2-7b}$$

where the mean equation of state has been used. Note that the presence of a mean wind merely adds U to the propagation in the x-direction.

The phase speed is the velocity of the phase lines ($\mu x + kz =$ constant) in the normal direction, and it is related to the frequency as follows:

$$c = \upsilon\mathcal{L}/2\pi \tag{2-8}$$

where $\mathcal{L}$ is the wavelength normal to the phase lines. The expression $\mathcal{L} = 2\pi(k^2 + \mu^2)^{-1/2}$ can be derived (with trigonometry) with the use of $\mathcal{L}_x = 2\pi\mu^{-1}$ and $\mathcal{L}_z = 2\pi k^{-1}$. With this relation for $\mathcal{L}$, (2-8) can be written

$$c = \upsilon(k^2 + \mu^2)^{-1/2} \tag{2-9}$$

Setting $U = 0$ and using (2-9) in (2-8) gives

$$c = \pm\sqrt{\gamma R\bar{T}} \tag{2-10}$$

which is the well-known formula for the speed of sound. Note that the speed is independent of the direction of propagation.

2-4 SOUND WAVES AND INTERNAL GRAVITY WAVES

Gravity waves arise from the differential effect of gravity on air parcels of different density at the same level. When gravitational effects are included it is necessary to consider the height dependence of $\bar{p}$ and $\bar{\alpha}$ as governed by the hydrostatic and state equations:

$$0 = -\bar{\alpha}\frac{\partial \bar{p}}{\partial z} - g$$

$$\bar{p}\bar{\alpha} = R\bar{T}$$

For an isothermal atmosphere the solutions to these equations give

$$\bar{p} = \bar{p}(0)\, e^{-z/H} \qquad \bar{\alpha} = \bar{\alpha}(0)\, e^{z/H} \tag{2-11}$$

where $H = R\bar{T}/g$ is called the scale height. Under these conditions simple wave solutions of the form:

$$u' = S\bar{\alpha}^{1/2}\, e^{i(\mu x + kz - \upsilon t)} \qquad w' = W\bar{\alpha}^{1/2}\, e^{i(\mu x + kz - \upsilon t)}$$

$$p' = P\bar{\alpha}^{-1/2}\, e^{i(\mu x + kz - \upsilon t)} \qquad \alpha' = A\bar{\alpha}^{\frac{3}{2}}\, e^{i(\mu x + kz - \upsilon t)} \tag{2-12}$$

lead to the matrix equation

$$\begin{bmatrix} -\upsilon & 0 & \mu & 0 \\ 0 & -\delta_1\upsilon & k + \dfrac{i}{2\bar{\alpha}}\dfrac{\partial\bar{\alpha}}{\partial z} & ig \\ 0 & \left(-g + \dfrac{\gamma R\bar{T}}{\bar{\alpha}}\dfrac{\partial\bar{\alpha}}{\partial z}\right)i & \upsilon & \gamma R\bar{T}\upsilon \\ \mu & k + \dfrac{i}{2\bar{\alpha}}\dfrac{\partial\bar{\alpha}}{\partial z} & 0 & \delta_2\upsilon \end{bmatrix} \begin{bmatrix} S \\ W \\ P \\ A \end{bmatrix} = 0 \tag{2-13}$$

with elements that are not functions of position or time. Here U is omitted since it merely adds to the propagation in the x-direction. Next introduce (2-11) into (2-13) and set the determinant equal to zero, which gives the following frequency equation:

$$\delta_1\delta_2\upsilon^4 - \{\gamma R\overline{T}(k^2 + \mu^2\delta_1) + \frac{g}{4H}[(2\delta_2 - 1)\gamma + 2(1-\delta_2)]$$

$$+ g(\gamma - 1)(\delta_2 - 1)ik\}\,\upsilon^2 + \mu^2 g^2(\gamma - 1) = 0$$

The g terms in the υ^2 coefficient may be dropped in comparison to $\gamma R\overline{T}k^2$ when the vertical wavelength $2\pi/k$ is smaller than $4\pi H$, which is almost always the case. Also, the last term can be rewritten with the potential temperature, which gives

$$\delta_1\delta_2\upsilon^4 - \gamma RT(k^2 + \mu^2\delta_1)\upsilon^2 + \mu^2\frac{\gamma R\overline{T}g}{\overline{\theta}}\frac{\partial\overline{\theta}}{\partial z} = 0 \tag{2-14}$$

The four roots of this equation correspond to a pair of sound waves and a pair of internal gravity waves. The gravity waves can be excluded by setting g to zero, which gives the same result as in Section 2-2. To isolate the gravity waves, take $\delta_2 = 0$ (incompressibility) and $\delta_1 = 1$, which gives

$$\upsilon^2 = \frac{\mu^2 \dfrac{g}{\overline{\theta}}\dfrac{\partial\overline{\theta}}{\partial z}}{k^2 + \mu^2} \tag{2-15}$$

Using (2-9), the phase speed becomes

$$c = \pm\frac{\mu}{\mu^2 + k^2}\left(\frac{g}{\overline{\theta}}\frac{\partial\overline{\theta}}{\partial z}\right)^{1/2} \tag{2-16}$$

This formula can also be derived without the isothermal condition. These gravitational oscillations are stable if the lapse rate is subadiabatic (i.e., if $\partial\overline{\theta}/\partial z > 0$), but an amplified disturbance occurs if the lapse rate is superadiabatic (i.e., if $\partial\overline{\theta}/\partial z < 0$).

If the depth of the disturbance is large compared to the horizontal scale, $\mu^2 >> k^2$, then, from (2-15)

$$\upsilon \doteq \pm\left(\frac{g}{\overline{\theta}}\frac{\partial\overline{\theta}}{\partial z}\right)^{1/2} \tag{2-17}$$

This is the Brunt-Vaisäla frequency for essentially vertical oscillations. On the other hand when the vertical scale is much smaller than the horizontal scale, the hydrostatic approximation is valid and δ_1 may be set to zero in (2-14). In this case,

$$\upsilon^2 = \frac{\mu^2}{k^2}\frac{g}{\overline{\theta}}\frac{\partial\overline{\theta}}{\partial z}$$

which follows from (2-15) when $k^2 >> \mu^2$. A horizontally propagating solution with vertical variation can be constructed by adding solutions with $+k$ and $-k$ as follows:

$$e^{i(\mu x + kz - \upsilon t)} + e^{i(\mu x - kz - \upsilon t)} = 2 \cos kz \, e^{i(\mu x - \upsilon t)}$$

This can be done as long as υ is independent of the sign of k. Here the propagation is horizontal so that

$$c = \frac{\upsilon}{\mu} = \pm \frac{1}{k} \left(\frac{g}{\overline{\theta}} \frac{\partial \overline{\theta}}{\partial z} \right)^{1/2} \tag{2-18}$$

where $k \gtrless 0$ gives the same pair of υ's.
The sound and gravity waves solutions to (2-14) can also be isolated by assuming that υ^2 is large for sound waves and small for gravity waves.

There are no meteorological phenomena in which sound waves play a significant dynamical role, and it is often desirable to eliminate them from the equations. It can be seen from (2-14) that the sound waves are excluded if the hydrostatic approximation ($\delta_1 = 0$) or the incompressibility condition ($\delta_2 = 0$) is used. Internal gravity waves are important for smaller scale atmospheric motion such as thermal convection and mountain lee wave phenomena. Under proper conditions internal gravity waves may propagate energy high into the atmosphere as indicated by the $\overline{\alpha}^{1/2}$ dependence of the velocity amplitudes in the solutions (2-12). They also play a role in the so-called geostrophic adjustment process, which will be discussed later.

Equation 2-2 has an additional set of wave solutions for the isothermal atmosphere that are not of the form (2-12). These waves have no vertical velocity and they propagate horizontally with the speed of sound. It can be shown by direct substitution that (2-2) is satisfied by the following solutions:

$$\begin{aligned} u' &= Se^{(\gamma - 1)z/\gamma H} \, e^{i\mu(x - ct)} \\ w' &= 0 \\ p' &= Pe^{-z/\gamma H} \, e^{i\mu(x - ct)} \\ \alpha' &= Ae^{(2\gamma - 1)z/\gamma H} \, e^{i\mu(x - ct)} \end{aligned} \tag{2-19}$$

where $c = \pm \sqrt{\gamma R \overline{T}}$. This solution is called the *Lamb wave*. Note that this wave automatically satisfies a $w = 0$ condition at a boundary. This solution is very similar to the external gravity wave, which will be discussed in a later section. The Lamb wave carries very little energy in the atmosphere, but it is important in numerical weather prediction because it places a severe restriction on the maximum time step that may be used during numerical integration of the hydrostatic equations.

2-5 SURFACE GRAVITY WAVES

In this section the troposphere will be replaced by a one-layer, homogeneous incompressible fluid. The mathematically and physically simpler solutions enhance the understanding of more complex atmospheric processes, as well as describing surface ocean waves.

Since the fluid is incompressible and homogeneous, $\alpha' \equiv 0$, and an upper surface will exist that will be permitted to be free, the linearized equations of motion (2-2) are (dropping primes) as follows:

$$\frac{\partial u}{\partial t} + U\frac{\partial u}{\partial x} + \frac{1}{\bar{\rho}}\frac{\partial p}{\partial x} = 0 \tag{2-20a}$$

$$\delta\left(\frac{\partial w}{\partial t} + U\frac{\partial w}{\partial x}\right) + \frac{1}{\bar{\rho}}\frac{\partial p}{\partial z} = 0 \tag{2-20b}$$

$$\frac{\partial u}{\partial x} + \frac{\partial w}{\partial z} = 0 \tag{2-20c}$$

The hydrostatic equation applies to the undisturbed flow

$$\frac{\partial \bar{p}}{\partial z} = -g\bar{\rho}$$

Integrating this equation from $z = 0$ to the top of the undisturbed fluid H gives

$$g\bar{\rho}H = p_0 \tag{2-21}$$

Next assume the perturbation quantities to be of the harmonic form

$$\begin{aligned} u &= \psi(z)e^{i\mu(x-ct)} \\ w &= \Phi(z)e^{i\mu(x-ct)} \\ \frac{p}{\bar{\rho}} &= P(z)e^{i\mu(x-ct)} \end{aligned} \tag{2-22}$$

Substituting (2-22) into (2-20) and simplifying leads to

$$\begin{aligned} (U - c)\psi(z) + P(z) &= 0 \\ i\mu\delta(U - c)\Phi(z) + P'(z) &= 0 \\ i\mu\psi(z) + \Phi'(z) &= 0 \end{aligned} \tag{2-23}$$

Eliminating $P(z)$ from the first two equations of (2-23) and then further elimination of $\psi(z)$ between the resulting equation and the last equation of (2-23) gives

$$\Phi''(z) - \mu^2\delta\Phi(z) = 0 \tag{2-24}$$

Consider two cases: $\delta = 1$, in which *vertical accelerations* are *permitted* and $\delta = 0$, where the *perturbations are hydrostatic*. The solutions are respectively,*

$$\Phi(z) = a_1 e^{\mu z} + a_2 e^{-\mu z} \qquad \delta = 1$$

$$\Phi(z) = a_1' z + a_2' \qquad \delta = 0$$

where the a's are arbitrary constants to be determined by the boundary conditions. At the lower boundary, which is assumed to be horizontal, the vertical velocity vanishes. Hence $a_1 = -a_2 \equiv a$ when vertical accelerations are present ($\delta = 1$) and

$$\Phi(z) = a(e^{\mu z} - e^{-\mu z}) \qquad \delta = 1 \tag{2-25}$$

Expanding the exponential terms as power series leads to the approximation

$$\Phi(z) = 2a\mu z + \cdots$$

In the hydrostatic case ($\delta = 0$), $a'_2 = 0$, and placing $a'_1 = a$ gives

$$\Phi(z) = az \tag{2-26}$$

The second boundary condition is that the total pressure of a surface particle (which must remain at the boundary) remains unchanged. Hence

$$d(\overline{p} + p)/dt = 0$$

at the free surface. This may be approximated by linearizing and applying this condition at $z = H$. Thus,

$$\frac{\partial p}{\partial t} + U\frac{\partial p}{\partial x} + w\frac{\partial \overline{p}}{\partial z} = 0 \qquad \text{at} \qquad z = H \tag{2-27}$$

Utilizing the solutions (2-25) and (2-26) and the system (2-23) gives the following results:

CASE 1. Nonhydrostatic ($\delta = 1$):

$$\begin{aligned} \psi(z) &= ia(e^{\mu z} + e^{-\mu z}) \\ P(z) &= -ia(U - c)(e^{\mu z} + e^{-\mu z}) \end{aligned} \tag{2-28}$$

Substituting (2-25) and (2-28) into (2-27) and simplifying yields the roots of the frequency equation

$$c = U \pm \left(\frac{gL}{2\pi}\tanh\frac{2\pi H}{\mathcal{L}}\right)^{1/2} \tag{2-29}$$

* Note that this exponential solution is of the form (2-3) and hence have could been obtained as a particular case of (2-5).

CASE 2. Hydrostatic ($\delta = 0$):

$$\psi(z) = \frac{a'i}{\mu}$$
$$P(z) = -\frac{ia'(U - c)}{\mu} \tag{2-30}$$

Substituting (2-26) and (2-30) into (2-27) and simplifying gives

$$c = U \pm \sqrt{gH} \tag{2-31}$$

Waves traveling with the phase velocity given by (2-31) are generally referred to as "shallow-water" or "long" waves. When the ratio $H/\mathcal{L}$ in (2-29) is relatively large (about 0.5 is sufficient), the phase velocity is approximately

$$c \doteq U \pm \sqrt{\frac{g\mathcal{L}}{2\pi}}$$

The waves are then called "deep-water" waves, and the fluid particle trajectories are nearly circular. On the other hand, for small values of $H/\mathcal{L}$ (≤ 0.04), (2-29) reduces to (2-31), and the particle trajectories are very elongated ellipses and thus nearly horizontal lines. If one assumes a homogeneous atmosphere, the hydrostatic equation gives $gH = p_0/\rho = RT$, and (2-31) may be written

$$c = U \pm \sqrt{RT} \tag{2-32}$$

Thus the speed of "long" gravity waves is nearly the speed of sound waves given by (2-10) and the Lamb wave.

The phase velocity for the so-called long gravity waves given by (2-31) was obtained when vertical accelerations were omitted, that is, when the perturbations are hydrostatic. This result could have been obtained in a somewhat more direct manner as follows. Assuming hydrostatic equilibrium, it follows immediately that for any point in the fluid, $g\bar{\rho}(h - z) = p$, where h is the height of the free surface. Placing $h = H + h'$ and $p = \bar{p} + p'$ leads to $g\bar{\rho}h' = p'$, and thus to (dropping primes)

$$g\frac{\partial h}{\partial x} = \frac{1}{\bar{\rho}}\frac{\partial p}{\partial x}$$

etc.

Thus the first equation in (2-20) may be written as

$$\frac{\partial u}{\partial t} + U\frac{\partial u}{\partial x} + g\frac{\partial h}{\partial x} = 0 \tag{2-33}$$

where u and h are now the perturbation quantities.

A second equation in u and h is obtainable by integrating the continuity equation (2-20c) in the vertical. However, this mass conservation equation may be easily derived directly in terms of h as follows (see Figure 2-2):

$$\frac{\partial(\bar{\rho}h)}{\partial t} = -\frac{\partial(\bar{\rho}uh)}{\partial x}$$

Linearizing and simplifying, yields

$$\frac{\partial h}{\partial t} + U\frac{\partial h}{\partial x} + H\frac{\partial u}{\partial x} = 0 \tag{2-34}$$

where h and u are now perturbation quantities. Since h and hence u are not functions of z, they may be taken to be of the form

$$u = u_0 e^{i\mu(x-ct)} \qquad h = h_0 e^{i\mu(x-ct)}$$

where u_0 and h_0 are constants. Substituting the expressions into (2-33) and (2-34) and setting the determinant of the homogeneous system to zero again gives the phase velocity for shallow-water waves,

$$c = U \pm \sqrt{gH}$$

which is identical to (2-31), as might have been expected.

The gravity waves just described are usually termed *external,* since their maximum amplitude is at the boundary of the fluid. There are also *internal* gravity waves that may develop on interfaces of density or when the density varies continuously as in Section 2-4. The propagation speeds of such *internal* gravity waves may be quite different from those mentioned earlier. For example, in the simple case of two semiinfinite layers separated by a zero-order discontinuity of both density and velocity, the wave speed is given by (see Haltiner and Martin, 1957).

$$c = \frac{\rho U + \rho' U'}{\rho + \rho'} \pm \left[\frac{gL(\rho - \rho')}{2\pi(\rho + \rho')} - \frac{\rho\rho'(U - U')^2}{(\rho + \rho')^2}\right]^{1/2}$$

where the primes deonte the parameters for the upper layer. To obtain this result the perturbations were assumed to vanish at $\pm\infty$. The phase velocity of the "deep-water" waves discussed earlier may be obtained as a special case of the foregoing formula by placing ρ' equal to zero. Other special cases include nonshearing waves, $U = U'$, and pure shearing waves ($\rho = \rho'$). Note that, if the quantity under the radical sign becomes negative, the phase velocity is

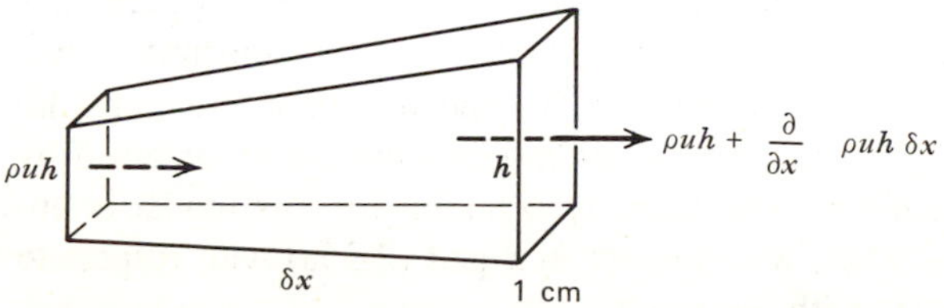

Figure 2-2 Illustrating mass continuity.

complex and unstable waves occur. These growing solutions are called Kelvin-Helmholtz waves.

2-6 INERTIAL GRAVITY WAVES AND ROSSBY WAVES

In this section the effects of the earth's rotation will be added to the hydrostatic one-layer equations that were developed in the last section. The deflection caused by the coriolis force will affect the lower frequency gravity waves. In addition Rossby waves will be found that depend on the spatial variation of the coriolis parameter. The equations of motion are expressible in the form

$$\frac{\partial u}{\partial t} + u\frac{\partial u}{\partial x} + v\frac{\partial u}{\partial y} - fv + g\frac{\partial h}{\partial x} = 0 \qquad (2\text{-}35a)$$

$$\frac{\partial v}{\partial t} + u\frac{\partial v}{\partial x} + v\frac{\partial v}{\partial y} + fu + g\frac{\partial h}{\partial y} = 0 \qquad (2\text{-}35b)$$

Because of the hydrostatic assumption and constant density, the horizontal pressure force is independent of height. By assuming that the velocity field is initially independent of height, it will remain so; thus the vertical advection terms have been omitted in (2-35). With the incompressibility assumption, the continuity equation is linear:

$$\frac{\partial u}{\partial x} + \frac{\partial v}{\partial y} + \frac{\partial w}{\partial z} = 0 \qquad (2\text{-}36)$$

Integrating (2-36) with respect to z gives

$$\left(\frac{\partial u}{\partial x} + \frac{\partial v}{\partial y}\right) h + w_h - w_0 = 0 \qquad (2\text{-}37)$$

In accordance with the kinematic boundary condition, w must vanish at the lower boundary (i.e., $w_0 = 0$). On the other hand, the vertical velocity $w = dz/dt$ at the upper boundary represents the rate at which the free surface is rising. Thus $w_h = dh/dt$, and (2-37) becomes

$$h\left(\frac{\partial u}{\partial x} + \frac{\partial v}{\partial y}\right) = -\frac{dh}{dt} = -\left(\frac{\partial h}{\partial t} + u\frac{\partial h}{\partial x} + v\frac{\partial h}{\partial y}\right) \qquad (2\text{-}38)$$

which is the same form as obtained in Section 2-3, but derived here in a somewhat different manner. Equations 2-35a, 2-35b, and 2-38 constitute a system of three equations in three unknowns, u, v, and h. These equations are called the shallow-water equations. An important equation can be obtained by combining these three equations. The vorticity equation for this model is obtained by differentiating (2-35b), with respect to x and (2-35a) with respect to y and forming the difference, with the result

$$\frac{\partial \zeta}{\partial t} + u\frac{\partial \zeta}{\partial x} + v\frac{\partial \zeta}{\partial y} + \beta v = -(\zeta + f)\left(\frac{\partial u}{\partial x} + \frac{\partial v}{\partial y}\right) = (\zeta + f)\frac{1}{h}\frac{dh}{dt} \tag{2-39a}$$

which can also be written as

$$\frac{d}{dt}\left(\frac{\zeta + f}{h}\right) = 0 \tag{2-39b}$$

where $\beta = \partial f/\partial y$.

This equation shows that the quantity $(\zeta + f)/h$, called the *potential vorticity*, is conserved. This is a special case of the general potential vorticity theorem that was derived by Ertel (1942). Equation 2-39b corresponds to conservation of absolute angular momentum, as may be seen by considering the effect of height changes on a moving column of fluid. As h increases the cross-sectional area of the column decreases and the column must spin more rapidly, which is consistent with (2-39b) since the angular velocity of the column is $(\zeta + f)/2$.

Equations 2-35 and 2-38 are linearized about H and U, which is constant. These quantities are related geostrophically:

$$U = -\frac{g}{f}\frac{\partial H}{\partial y} \tag{2-40}$$

where H is the depth of a fluid of constant density as before. If perturbations u, v, and h as well as f are taken to be independent of y, the following system of equations results:

$$\begin{aligned}
\delta\left(\frac{\partial u}{\partial t} + U\frac{\partial u}{\partial x}\right) - fv + g\frac{\partial h}{\partial x} &= 0 \\
\frac{\partial v}{\partial t} + U\frac{\partial v}{\partial x} + fu &= 0 \\
\frac{\partial h}{\partial t} + U\frac{\partial h}{\partial x} + H\frac{\partial u}{\partial x} + v\frac{\partial H}{\partial y} &= 0
\end{aligned} \tag{2-41}$$

Here δ identifies terms that would contribute to dD/dt in the divergence equation ($D = \partial u/\partial x + \partial v/\partial y$). The general divergence equation is obtained by differentiating the u and v components of the equation of motion with respect to x and y. In this case note that u carries the entire divergence since $\partial v/\partial y = 0$. Treating the coefficient H as a constant and assuming harmonic perturbations of the form $u_0 e^{i\mu(x-ct)}$, $v_0 e^{i\mu(x-ct)}$, and $h_0 e^{i\mu(x-ct)}$ transforms (2-41) into the following system:

$$\begin{aligned}
\delta\,(U - c)i\mu u_0 - fv_0 + gi\mu h_0 &= 0 \\
fu_0 + i\mu(U - c)\,v_0 &= 0 \\
i\mu H u_0 + \partial H/\partial y\,v_0 + i\mu(U - c)\,h_0 &= 0
\end{aligned}$$

In order that (2-42) will have nontrivial solutions for u_0, v_0, and h_0 the following condition must be satisfied:

$$\begin{vmatrix} \delta(U - c)i\mu & -f & g\mu i \\ f & (U - c)i\mu & 0 \\ i\mu H & \dfrac{\partial H}{\partial y} & (U - c)i\mu \end{vmatrix} = 0$$

Expansion of this determinant leads to a cubic frequency equation

$$\delta(U - c)^3 - (gH + f^2/\mu^2)(U - c) - \frac{fg}{\mu^2}\frac{\partial H}{\partial y} = 0 \tag{2-43}$$

This equation contains a pair of fast gravity wave solutions and one slow meteorological solution. In order to isolate the fast solutions set $U = 0$ and $\delta = 1$, which gives

$$c = \pm \sqrt{gH + f^2/\mu^2} \tag{2-44}$$

and $c = 0$. These are inertial gravity waves, and when $f = 0$, (2-44) reduces to the formula for shallow-water (gravity) waves (2-31).

If the first term under the radical can be dropped in comparison to the second, inertial oscillations are isolated:

$$\nu = \mu c = \pm f \tag{2-45}$$

These conditions are met if the scale $(1/\mu)$ is large enough or if gH is small. The inertial solutions can be derived directly from the nonlinear equations of motion with the pressure gradient neglected:

$$\frac{du}{dt} = -fv \qquad \frac{dv}{dt} = fu \tag{2-46}$$

These equations can be combined to give

$$\frac{d^2u}{dt^2} + f^2u = 0 \tag{2-47}$$

which has solutions of the form

$$u = u_0 e^{\pm ift} \tag{2-48}$$

so that the period is $2\pi/f = 12/\sin\varphi$ hr.

An artificiality of this analysis is that the pressure is assumed to be constant whereas, in nature, adjustment in the pressure field would be brought about by gravity waves generated by the imbalance between the mass and wind fields. Nevertheless there are a number of instances observed in nature where the inertial effects similar to those described previously are evident. For example, the observed paths of constant-pressure balloons show loops and cusps that are suggestive of an inertial influence. Another phenomenon that has been explained to some degree by an inertial oscillation is the nocturnal boundary-layer jet. Here a diurnal variation in the eddy viscosity can result in a significant nocturnal reduction in the friction force at about 500 m due to the temporal variation of the static stability. The decrease in the friction force, in turn, will set up an ageostrophic wind component which then experiences an inertial oscillation, modified by friction, of course. A classical example of inertial motion was observed in the Baltic Sea by Gustafson and Kullenberg (1936) after a squall provided a sudden impulse. Subsequent current measurements clearly showed an inertial oscillation superimposed on a general northward drift.

The slow meteorological solution to (2-43) may be obtained by setting $\delta = 0$:

$$c = U + \frac{(f/H)\,\partial H/\partial y}{\mu^2 + (f^2/gH)}$$

This expression can be written in terms of the basic state potential vorticity $\bar{q} = f/H$, which gives

$$\frac{\partial \bar{q}}{\partial y} = -\frac{f}{H^2}\frac{\partial H}{\partial y} = \frac{f^2 U}{gH^2} \tag{2-49}$$

The basic state has a nonzero potential vorticity gradient because the free surface height $H(y)$ slopes in the y-direction to satisfy the geostrophic mean flow condition (2-40). With (2-49) the phase velocity can now be written in the following form:

$$c = U - \frac{H\,\partial q/\partial y}{\mu^2 + (f^2/gH)} \tag{2-50}$$

This solution is a type of Rossby wave and it gives phase speeds that are reasonable for observed synoptic disturbances. The formula can be generalized if f is allowed to vary with latitude. In this case the potential vorticity gradient becomes

$$\frac{\partial \bar{q}}{\partial y} = \left(\beta - \frac{1}{H}\frac{\partial H}{\partial y}\right)\Big/H = [\beta + (f^2U/gH)]/H \tag{2-51}$$

where $\beta = df/dy$. This is an example of the rule that Rossby waves propagate in the direction $\mathbf{k} \times \nabla\bar{q}$ relative to the mean flow. The phase speed with the f variation is given by (2-50) with (2-51). This may be verified by using $f = f(y)$ in (2-41) with the v equation of motion replaced a linearized vorticity equation.

The Rossby waves can be isolated in (2-43) by setting $\delta = 0$ in (2-41). This implies that the v component is geostrophic, that is,

$$fv = g \frac{\partial h}{\partial x} \tag{2-52}$$

However, the u component, which is proportional to the divergence, is not evaluated geostrophically.

When the disturbance fields vary in both x and y, it is necessary to replace Equations 2-35a and 2-35b with the vorticity and divergence equations in order to carry out the analysis of this section. It can be shown in this case that the *gravity* waves will be eliminated when the *time derivative of the divergence is neglected in the divergence equation*. This leads to a relation between the rotational part of the wind and the height such as the geostrophic condition (2-52).

It is interesting to compare vorticity and divergence in the two types of waves considered here. This is especially easy in this case because

$$\left|\frac{D}{\zeta}\right| = \left|\frac{\partial u/\partial x}{\partial v/\partial x}\right| \tag{2-53}$$

For the inertial gravity waves ($U = 0$) it can be shown by multiplying (2-42) by $e^{i\mu(x-ct)}$ that

$$v = -\frac{ifu}{\mu c} \tag{2-54}$$

With (2-54) and (2-44) the ratio (2-53) becomes

$$\left|\frac{D}{\zeta}\right|_{I-G} = (1 + \mu^2 gHf^{-2})^{1/2} \tag{2-55}$$

This quantity is always greater than 1 so that the divergence dominates the vorticity in the inertial gravity waves.

For the geostrophic or Rossby solution ($\delta = 0$) it is convenient to write the vorticity and divergence in terms of h. From (2-52) the vorticity can be written

$$\frac{\partial v}{\partial x} = -\frac{\mu^2 g}{f} h \tag{2-56}$$

The following diagnostic equation relating u and h can be derived from (2-41) when $\delta = 0$:

$$\frac{\partial^2 u}{\partial x^2} - (f^2/gH)\, u = \frac{U}{H} \frac{\partial^2 h}{\partial x^2} \tag{2-57}$$

This is the quasi-geostrophic equation for the divergent part of the wind. Differentiating it and introducing the exponential wave form gives

$$\frac{\partial u}{\partial x} = \frac{i\mu Ugh}{gH + (f^2/\mu^2)} \tag{2-58}$$

Now if (2-56) and (2-58) are substituted into (2-53) the ratio becomes

$$\left|\frac{D}{\zeta}\right|_R = \frac{(U\mu/f)}{(\mu^2 gH/f^2) + 1} \tag{2-59}$$

The quantity in the numerator is called the *Rossby number* and for synoptic scale motion it has a value of about 1/10. Since the denominator is greater than 1 it is clear that the divergence is small compared with the vorticity for the Rossby-type waves. This information will be useful in formulating the scale analysis in Chapter 3.

2-7 RESPONSE TO INITIAL CONDITIONS

Sections (2-7) and (2-8) will provide background for the treatment of initialization in Chapter 11. In the previous section two types of wave motion were found: (1) fast inertial gravity waves that have a speed of about 300 m sec^{-1} (for $H = 10$ km); (2) slow Rossby waves that have a speed of about 10 m sec^{-1}. Most weather systems have phase speeds in the Rossby wave range which indicate that the inertial gravity waves have small amplitudes for synoptic-scale motions. When the complete equations ($\delta = 1$) are used for prediction it is important to initialize them in such a way that the inertial gravity waves have small amplitude. This problem can be investigated by summing the solutions of the previous section to represent arbitrary initial conditions. Corresponding to each of the three phase velocities, c_j, $j = 1, 2, 3$, [given approximately by (2-50) and (2-44)], there is a different set of solutions for the velocity components and the height of the free surface, say u_j, v_j and h_j. However, since the system (2-42) is homogeneous, one of the latter quantities is arbitrary in each set and may be specified. Choose $u_j = U - c_j$ and solve two of the equations in (2-42) with $\delta = 1$ for the other amplitudes. The result is

$$u_j = U - c_j$$

$$v_j = if/\mu$$

$$h_j = g^{-1}[(f^2/\mu^2) - (U - c_j)^2] \tag{2-60}$$

The general solution for a particular μ can now be written

$$u = \sum_{j=1}^{3} a_j u_j e^{i\mu(x - c_j t)}$$

$$v = \sum_{j=1}^{3} a_j v_j e^{i\mu(x - c_j t)}$$

$$h = \sum_{j=1}^{3} a_j h_j e^{i\mu(x - c_j t)} \tag{2-61}$$

where the a_j are arbitrary constants.

Suppose the initial values of u, v and h at $t = 0$ are given by the harmonic waves, $u(x,0) = u_0 e^{i\mu x}$, $v(x,0) = v_0 e^{i\mu x}$, $h(x,0) = h_0 e^{i\mu x}$, where u_0, v_0 and h_0 are complex constants. Substitute these initial conditions into (2-61):

$$u_0 = \sum_{j=1}^{3} a_j u_j$$

$$v_0 = \sum_{j=1}^{3} a_j v_j$$

$$h_0 = \sum_{j=1}^{3} a_j h_j \tag{2-62}$$

The phase velocities are approximated as follows:

$$c_1 = U - \frac{U}{1 + (gH\mu^2/f^2)}$$

$$c_2 = U + \sqrt{gH + (f^2/\mu^2)}$$

$$c_3 = U - \sqrt{gH + (f^2/\mu^2)} \tag{2-63}$$

When (2-63) and (2-60) are employed, (2-60) can be solved to give the following a_j:

$$a_1 = \frac{i\mu f^{-1} gHv_0 - gh_0}{U^2 f^4 \mu^{-4} \alpha^{-2} - \alpha}$$

$$a_{2,3} = \mp u_0/2\alpha^{1/2} \mp \frac{if\mu^{-1}(1 \pm U\alpha^{-1/2})v_0 + gh_0}{2(Uf^2\mu^{-2}\alpha^{-1/2} \pm \alpha)} \tag{2-64}$$

where $\alpha \equiv gH + f^2\mu^{-2}$.

Suppose the initial conditions are geostrophic:

$$u = -\frac{g}{f}\frac{\partial h}{\partial y} = 0 \qquad v = \frac{g}{f}\frac{\partial h}{\partial x}$$

which corresponds to

$$u_0 = 0 \qquad v_0 = i\mu f^{-1} gh_0 \tag{2-65}$$

When these conditions are substituted into (2-64) the amplitudes become:

$$a_1 = \frac{\mu^2 f^{-2} g h_0}{1 - U^2 f^4 \mu^{-4} \alpha^{-3}}$$

$$a_{2,3} = \frac{U \alpha^{-3/2} g h_0}{2(1 \pm U f^2 \mu^{-2} \alpha^{-3/2})} \tag{2-66}$$

For synoptic scale disturbances the following inequalities hold:

$$\alpha^{1/2} > f\mu^{-1} >> U \tag{2-67}$$

The Rossby wave contribution to the initial v [i.e., $if\mu^{-1}a_1$ from (2-60) to (2-61)] is in phase with v_0 and has only a slightly larger magnitude, which implies that the initial rotational component is nearly geostrophic. The inertial gravity waves are also present with the initial conditions (2-65) and the ratio of the amplitude of these waves to the Rossby wave amplitude is

$$\frac{a_{2,3}}{a_1} \simeq \frac{U}{(gH)^{1/2}} \frac{f^2}{\mu^2 gH} \tag{2-68}$$

This number is quite small for the conditions (2-67), but for internal gravity waves its value will be much larger.

The inertial gravity waves can be *eliminated* completely if the proper value of u_0 is selected. Setting $a_{2,3}$ equal to zero in (2-64) and using the geostrophic relation for v_0 gives the expression for u_0

$$u_0 = \frac{U g h_0}{gH + f^2 \mu^{-2}} \tag{2-69}$$

where a term that is small compared to α has been dropped in the denominator. The amplitude (2-69) of the initial u, together with the exponential part in (2-61) gives precisely the quasi-geostrophic divergence given in (2-58). The development in this section follows Hinkelmann (1951) and Phillips (1960).

2-8 GEOSTROPHIC ADJUSTMENT

Section 2-7 treated the juxtaposition of two gravity waves and a Rossby wave, all having the same wavelength. The gravity waves cause a periodic oscillation about the geostrophic balance that continues indefinitely unless there is friction. However, if the initial imbalance occurs in a limited portion of an infinite domain, the gravity waves will eventually propagate out of the imbalance region and leave a state of geostrophic balance after a period of adjustment. This process determines the response of a primitive equation model to imperfect initial conditions. In fact, this adjustment process operates continually to keep the atmosphere in a state of approximate geostrophic balance.

The linearized shallow water equations for a resting basic state can be written as follows

$$\frac{\partial u}{\partial t} - fv + g\frac{\partial h}{\partial x} = 0$$

$$\frac{\partial v}{\partial t} + fu = 0 \qquad (2\text{-}70)$$

$$\frac{\partial h}{\partial t} + H\frac{\partial u}{\partial x} = 0$$

These equations can be obtained by setting $U = 0$ in (2-41). As indicated earlier this system has three wave solutions: two inertial gravity waves given by (2-44) and the Rossby type wave (2-50), which in this case is stationary because when H is constant $\partial\bar{q}/\partial y = 0$.

This problem was first treated by Rossby (1938) and later the time evolution was obtained by Cahn (1945). The development in this section, which follows Schoenstadt (1977), employs the spatial Fourier transform, which is defined as

$$\tilde{u}\,(\mu,t) = \int_{-\infty}^{\infty} u(x,t)e^{-i\mu x}\,dx \qquad (2\text{-}71)$$

The inverse transform can be written

$$u(x,t) = \frac{1}{2\pi}\int_{-\infty}^{\infty} \tilde{u}\,(\mu,t)e^{i\mu x}\,d\mu \qquad (2\text{-}72)$$

The equation set (2-70) is transformed by multiplying by $e^{-i\mu x}$ and integrating from $-\infty$ to ∞. When the x-derivative terms are integrated by parts the terms evaluated at infinity are dropped and the transformed ordinary differential equation set may be written:

$$\frac{d\tilde{u}}{dt} = f\tilde{v} - i\mu g\tilde{h}$$

$$\frac{d\tilde{v}}{dt} = -f\tilde{u} \qquad (2\text{-}73)$$

$$\frac{d\tilde{h}}{dt} = -i\mu H\tilde{u}$$

where $\tilde{v}$ and $\tilde{h}$ have the same form as (2-71). The transform of the initial u field is given by

$$\tilde{u}_0 = \tilde{u}(\mu,0) = \int_{-\infty}^{\infty} u(x,0)e^{-i\mu x}\,dx \qquad (2\text{-}74)$$

where $\tilde{v}_0$ and $\tilde{h}_0$ have similar definitions.

The system (2-73) has solutions of the form $e^{-i\mu c_j t}$, which are the same as the shallow-water solutions obtained earlier. In this case $U = 0$ so that the phase speeds become $c_1 = 0$, $c_2 = \mu^{-1}\nu$, $c_3 = -\mu^{-1}\nu$, where

$$\nu = (f^2 + \mu^2 gH)^{1/2} \tag{2-75}$$

The general solution for arbitrary $\tilde{u}_0$, $\tilde{v}_0$, and $\tilde{h}_0$ can be obtained from (2-61) by replacing u by $\tilde{u}$, etc. and setting $U = 0$ in (2-64). The terms can be combined to give the following solution set:

$$\begin{aligned}
\tilde{u}(\mu,t) &= \tilde{u}_0 \cos\nu t + \left(\frac{f\tilde{v}_0 - i\mu g\tilde{h}_0}{\nu}\right)\sin\nu t \\
\tilde{v}(\mu,t) &= \frac{\mu^2 gH\tilde{v}_0 + i\mu gf\tilde{h}_0}{\nu^2} - \frac{f\tilde{u}_0 \sin\nu t}{\nu} + \left(\frac{f^2\tilde{v}_0 - i\mu gf\tilde{h}_0}{\nu^2}\right)\cos\nu t \\
\tilde{h}(\mu,t) &= \left(\frac{f^2\tilde{h}_0 - i\mu Hf\tilde{v}_0}{\nu^2}\right) - \frac{i\mu H\tilde{u}_0 \sin\nu t}{\nu} + \left(\frac{\mu^2 gH\tilde{h}_0 + i\mu Hf\tilde{v}_0}{\nu^2}\right)\cos\nu t
\end{aligned} \tag{2-76}$$

Each transformed field can be written as the sum of a steady-state part $(\ )_S$, and a transient part $(\ )_T$, as follows:

$$\begin{aligned}
\tilde{u}_S(\mu) &= 0 \\
\tilde{v}_S(\mu) &= \frac{i\mu g}{f}\left(\frac{f^2\tilde{h}_0 - i\mu fH\tilde{v}_0}{\nu^2}\right) \\
\tilde{h}_S(\mu) &= \left(\frac{f^2\tilde{h}_0 - i\mu fH\tilde{v}_0}{\nu^2}\right)
\end{aligned} \tag{2-77}$$

and

$$\begin{aligned}
\tilde{u}_T(\mu) &= \tilde{u}_0 \cos\nu t + \frac{f}{\nu}(\tilde{v}_0 - if^{-1}\mu g\tilde{h}_0)\sin\nu t \\
\tilde{v}_T(\mu) &= -\frac{f}{\nu}\tilde{u}_0 \sin\nu t + \frac{f^2}{\nu^2}(\tilde{v}_0 - \mathrm{i}f^{-1}\mu g\tilde{h}_0)\cos\nu t \\
\tilde{h}_T(\mu) &= -\frac{i\mu H}{\nu}\tilde{u}_0 \sin\nu t + \frac{i\mu Hf}{\nu^2}(\tilde{v}_0 - \mathrm{i}f^{-1}\mu g\tilde{h}_0)\cos\nu t
\end{aligned} \tag{2-78}$$

Note that the steady-state solution (2-77) represents a state of geostrophic balance since $\tilde{v}_S = i\mu gf^{-1}h_S$ and $\tilde{u}_S = 0$, as can also be seen by setting $d/dt = 0$ in (2-73). The transient solutions (2-78) are directly proportional to the initial departures from geostrophic balance, which are $(\tilde{v}_0 - i\mu gf^{-1}h_0)$ and $\tilde{u}_0$.

The steady-state solution will be examined in more detail later, but first it is important to show that the transient solutions die away as time increases.

With the use of the inverse transform (2-72) the transient solutions can be written

$$u_T(x,t) = \frac{1}{2\pi}\int_{-\infty}^{\infty} \tilde{u}(\mu,0)\cos\upsilon t\, e^{i\mu x}\, d\mu + \frac{1}{2\pi}\int_{-\infty}^{\infty} \frac{f}{\upsilon}\tilde{d}(\mu,0)\sin\upsilon t\, e^{i\mu x}\, d\mu$$

$$v_T(x,t) = -\frac{1}{2\pi}\int_{-\infty}^{\infty} \frac{f\tilde{u}_0}{\upsilon}\sin\upsilon t\, e^{i\mu x}\, d\mu + \frac{1}{2\pi}\int_{-\infty}^{\infty} \frac{f^2}{\upsilon^2}\tilde{d}(\mu,0)\cos\upsilon t\, e^{i\mu x}\, d\mu \tag{2-79}$$

$$h_T(x,t) = -\frac{i}{2\pi}\int_{-\infty}^{\infty} \frac{\mu H}{\upsilon}\tilde{u}_0\sin\upsilon t\, e^{i\mu x}\, d\mu + \frac{i}{2\pi}\int_{-\infty}^{\infty} \frac{\mu H f}{\upsilon^2}\tilde{d}(\mu,0)\cos\upsilon t\, e^{i\mu x}\, d\mu$$

where

$$d(x,t) = v(x,t) - gf^{-1}\frac{\partial h}{\partial x}(x,t)$$

is the departure from geostrophic balance. Schoenstadt (1977) applied the method of stationary phase to the equation set (2-79). When x is fixed and when $|x| << L_R ft = (gH)^{1/2}t$ the equations reduce to:

$$u_T \sim \frac{1}{(2\pi\alpha)^{1/2}}\left[|\tilde{u}(x/\alpha,0)|\cos(ft+\phi) + |\tilde{d}(x/\alpha,0)|\sin(ft+\psi)\right]$$

$$v_T \sim \frac{1}{(2\pi\alpha)^{1/2}}\left[-|\tilde{u}(x/\alpha,0)|\sin(ft+\phi) + |\tilde{d}(x/\alpha,0)|\cos(ft+\psi)\right] \tag{2-80}$$

$$h_T \sim \frac{1}{(2\pi\alpha)^{1/2}}\frac{(-Hx)}{f\alpha}\left[|\tilde{u}(x/\alpha,0)|\sin(ft+\phi) - |\tilde{d}(x/\alpha,0)|\cos(ft+\psi)\right]$$

where ψ and ϕ are slowly varying phase angles, $L_R = (gH)^{1/2}/f$ is the Rossby radius of deformation and $\alpha = L_R^2 ft$.

The limiting solutions (2-80) show that the transient velocities u_T and v_T die off in proportion to $t^{-1/2}$ for fixed x and h_T dies off as $t^{-3/2}$. This behavior arises because the initial imbalance excites inertial gravity waves that carry energy away from initial region of imbalance. In fact, the energy propagates with the group velocity, which is given by

$$G = \frac{\partial\upsilon}{\partial\mu} = \frac{\partial}{\partial\mu}(f^2 + \mu^2 gH)^{1/2} = \mu gH(f^2 + \mu^2 gH)^{-1/2} \tag{2-81}$$

This expression shows that the short-wave energy moves out with the shallow-water speed $c = \sqrt{gH}$, while the larger scale energy moves more slowly. After the transient waves have propagated away from the initial region of imbalance, only the steady state fields are left. Mathematically this is shown by (2-80) where the solutions damp for fixed x (i.e., as the transient wave energy moves past x).

The final solution is highly dependent on the ratio L_R^2/L^2 where $L = 1/\mu$.

This can be seen by rewriting (2-77) as follows:

$$\tilde{v}_S = \frac{1}{1 + (L_R^2/L^2)}\left(\frac{L_R^2}{L^2}\tilde{v}_0 + i\mu f^{-1}g\tilde{h}_0\right)$$
$$\tilde{h}_S = \frac{1}{1 + (L_R^2/L^2)}\left(\frac{L_R^2}{L^2}\frac{f\tilde{v}_0}{i\mu g} + \tilde{h}_0\right) \tag{2-82}$$

Assume that initially the coriolis force and the pressure gradient have the same order of magnitude, which means that $\tilde{v}_0$ and $i\mu f^{-1}\tilde{h}_0$ are of the same magnitude. Consider first the case $L^2 << L_R^2$, which allows (2-82) to be approximated as

$$\tilde{v}_S = \tilde{v}_0 \qquad \tilde{h}_S = \frac{f\tilde{v}_0}{i\mu g} \tag{2-83}$$

Note that the final wind is equal to the initial wind and the final height is geostrophically related to the initial wind field.

When the condition $L^2 >> L_R^2$ is used (2-82) reduces to:

$$\tilde{v}_S = i\mu f^{-1} g\tilde{h}_0 \qquad \tilde{h}_S = \tilde{h}_0 \tag{2-84}$$

In this case the final fields are determined entirely by the initial height. This behavior can be summarized as follows: *for scales that are smaller than* L_R *the final state is determined by the initial wind and for scales that are larger than* L_R *the final state is determined by the initial mass field.* This result is much more general than might be expected from this simplified analysis. It also applies for a two-dimensional barotropic atmosphere. In a continuously stratified atmosphere the results apply if $L_R = c_g/f$, where c_g is the phase speed of the internal gravity waves. This result can be found by separating the vertical structure into eigenfunctions, as was done by Okland (1970).

With a barotropic atmosphere in midlatitudes and $H \approx 10$ km, $L_R = 3000$ km and $2\pi L_R = 18{,}000$ km. In this case, the synoptic waves with wavelength around 5000 km are clearly "short" waves. However with a stratified atmosphere where the internal wave speed is $c_g \sim 100$ m sec^{-1}, $L_R \sim 1000$ km, which corresponds to the scale of the synoptic waves. Thus both the initial mass and wind fields are important in initializing these waves. Note that in the tropics where f is small most waves are "short," which means that they are primarily determined by the initial wind field.

It is useful to write the final height field in terms of an integral of the initial geostrophic departure. The inverse transform of h_S from (2-77) can be written with the use of (2-72) as

$$h_S(x) = h(x,0) - \frac{1}{2\pi}\int_{-\infty}^{\infty} \frac{Hf\, i\mu}{\upsilon^2}\tilde{d}_0\, e^{i\mu x}\, d\mu \tag{2-85}$$

where d_0 is the initial geostrophic departure. It is now useful to employ the convolution theorem, which may be written:

$$\frac{1}{2\pi}\int_{-\infty}^{\infty} \tilde{F}(\mu)\,\tilde{G}(\mu)\,e^{i\mu x}\,d\mu = \int_{-\infty}^{\infty} F(x')\,G(x-x')\,dx' \tag{2-86}$$

where $\tilde{F}$ and $\tilde{G}$ are the transforms of F and G. Consider the following function whose transform can be written:

$$\int_{-\infty}^{\infty} e^{-|x|/LR}\,e^{-i\mu x}\,dx = \frac{2L_R}{1+\mu^2 L_R^{\,2}} = \frac{2L_R f^2}{\upsilon^2}$$

Now with the use of $G(x) = e^{-|x|/LR}$ and $F(x) = \partial d(x,0)/\partial x$ in (2-86), Equation 2-85 becomes:

$$h_S(x) = h(x,0) - \frac{H}{2L_R f}\int_{-\infty}^{\infty} e^{-|x-x'|/LR}\,\frac{\partial d(x',0)}{\partial x'}\,dx'$$

After integration by parts this solution can be written:

$$h_S(x) = h(x,0) + \frac{H}{2L_R^{\,2} f}\int_{-\infty}^{\infty} \frac{x-x'}{|x-x'|}\,e^{-|x-x'|/LR}\,d(x',0)\,dx' \tag{2-87}$$

This result shows that the influence of an initial geostrophic departure at a particular point dies off in a distance L_R. The steady-state velocity fields can be obtained geostrophically from (2-87) with the relations:

$$v_S(x) = fg^{-1}\,\partial h_S/\partial x \qquad u_S = 0 \tag{2-88}$$

These two sections of this chapter have treated two different responses to ageostrophic initial conditions. In Section 2-6 the initial fields are in the form of a single sinusoidal wave, and the solution oscillates indefinitely about the geostrophic state. In this section the initial imbalance is localized in an infinite region, and the solution approaches a steady state as the gravity waves propagate out of the imbalance region. This process works even faster in two-dimensional domains because the gravity waves spread their energy into a much larger region during the same time period. In general, if the initial imbalance has a scale that is small in comparison with the scale of the region, the adjustment process operates very efficiently, whereas when those scales are comparable, the fields will oscillate for some time. The final state, which is achieved after adjustment, is critically dependent on $(L/L_R)^2$ where $L_R = c_g/f$ with c_g being the phase velocity for the appropriate gravity waves in the system. When the scale of the initial field L is small compared to L_R the final state is determined by the rotational part of the initial wind field whereas when L is large compared to L_R the final state is determined by the initial mass field. It is very important to take into account this adjustment process while developing an initialization procedure for the primitive equations.

CHAPTER 3

Scale Analysis

3-1 INTRODUCTION

A scale analysis, which will be carried out in this chapter, provides a systematic method of comparing the magnitudes of the various terms comprising the hydrodynamical equations governing atmospheric motions. This theory, together with energy considerations, permits the design of consistent dynamical-mathematical models for dynamical analysis and numerical weather prediction. J. Charney introduced this technique to the study of large-scale meteorological dynamics in 1948; further developments have been added since that time, especially by Burger (1958) and Phillips (1963).

The physical variables are assumed to have characteristic values and scales in space and time as follows:

L = characteristic horizontal scale (roughly a quarter wavelength of disturbances)

T = local time scale (roughly a quarter of the local period)

V = characteristic horizontal velocity

As shown in in Figure 3-1 it is assumed that the approximate magnitudes of the derivatives are as follows:

$$\frac{\partial v}{\partial x} \sim \frac{\partial u}{\partial x} \sim \frac{V}{L}, \text{ etc.,} \ \frac{\partial u}{\partial t} \sim \frac{V}{T}$$

In the following development all terms in each equation will be written as a product of the same dimensional combination times a nondimensional coefficient. The relative magnitude of the coefficients determines terms that may be neglected. The analysis also gives the scales for some quantities such as the vertical motion, which were not specified at the beginning of the analysis. This method will be applied to some of the phenomena shown in Figure 2-1 after first analyzing the shallow-water equations.

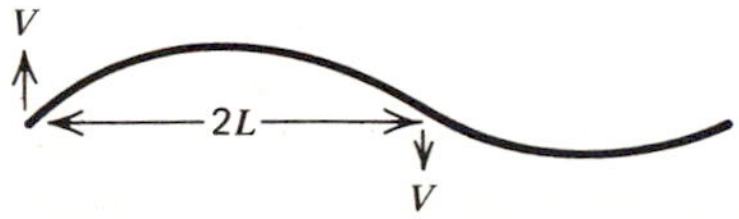

Figure 3-1 Illustrating characteristic length.

3-2 SHALLOW-WATER EQUATIONS

It is convenient to illustrate the scale analysis technique with the shallow-water equations that describe the hydrostatic motion of an incompressible fluid with a free upper surface. As seen in Chapter 2 these equations allow both inertial gravity waves and Rossby waves as do the more complete baroclinic equations. The general shallow-water equations roughly represent motions that have been averaged through the troposphere.

The equations motion [(2-35a) and (2-35b)] may be combined to give

$$\frac{\partial \mathbf{V}}{\partial t} + \mathbf{V} \cdot \nabla \mathbf{V} + \nabla \phi + f\mathbf{k} \times \mathbf{V} = 0 \tag{3-1}$$

where $\phi = gh$. Here it is assumed that the coriolis parameter f is constant; the proper earth geometry will be included in a later section. The continuity equation (2-38) can be written

$$\frac{\partial \phi}{\partial t} + \mathbf{V} \cdot \nabla \phi + \phi \nabla \cdot \mathbf{V} = 0 \tag{3-2}$$

The time scale is given by

$$T = L/C \tag{3-3}$$

where C is an average phase speed for the motions concerned. The synoptic scale features have $C \sim V$, which leads to

$$T = L/V \tag{3-4}$$

which is called the advective time scale. If $L \sim 10^6$ m and $V \sim 10$ msec^{-1}, then (3-4) gives $T \sim 10^5$ sec ($\sim$ 1 day), which is reasonable for the one-quarter period of synoptic disturbances.

The terms in the equation of motion (3-1) with the exception of the pressure gradient force are scaled as follows:

$$\begin{array}{ccccccc} \dfrac{\partial \mathbf{V}}{\partial t} & + & \mathbf{V} \cdot \nabla \mathbf{V} & + \nabla \phi + & f\mathbf{k} \times \mathbf{V} & = & 0 \\ & & & & & & \\ \dfrac{V^2}{L} & & \dfrac{V^2}{L} & & fV & & \\ & & & & & & \\ Ro\, fV & & Ro\, fV & & fV & & \end{array} \tag{3-5}$$

where $Ro = V/fL$ is the Rossby number. Note that the Rossby number is the ratio of the acceleration to the coriolis force. For typical synoptic scale values of $f \sim 10^{-4}$sec^{-1}, $L \sim 10^6$ m, $V \sim 10$ msec^{-1}, the Rossby number becomes $Ro \sim 0.1$. In fact, the Rossby number is small for a wide range of motions in the atmosphere and in the oceans.

When Ro is small, (3-5) shows that the acceleration is small in comparison to the coriolis force. Consequently the coriolis force can only be balanced by the pressure gradient force, which gives

$$\nabla\phi \sim fV \tag{3-6}$$

In order to analyze the continuity equation (3-2), the ϕ field is separated as follows:

$$\phi = \overline{\phi} + \phi' \tag{3-7}$$

where $\overline{\phi}$ is a constant. The scale of ϕ' can be obtained by substituting (3-7) into (3-6), which yields

$$\phi' \sim fVL \tag{3-8}$$

which is known as "geostrophic" scaling.

Introduce the relation (3-7) into (3-2) and analyze the various terms with the use of (3-4) and (3-8):

$$\begin{array}{ccccccccc} \dfrac{\partial\phi'}{\partial t} & + & \mathbf{V}\cdot\nabla\phi' & + & \phi'\nabla\cdot\mathbf{V} & + & \overline{\phi}\nabla\cdot\mathbf{V} & = & 0 \\ fV^2 & & fV^2 & & fV^2 & & \overline{\phi}V/L & & \end{array} \tag{3-9}$$

or

$$Ro\,F\overline{\phi}\frac{V}{L} \qquad Ro\,F\overline{\phi}\frac{V}{L} \qquad Ro\,F\overline{\phi}\frac{V}{L} \qquad \overline{\phi}V/L$$

where $F = f^2L^2/\overline{\phi}$ is a *rotational Froude number*. This number may also be written as follows:

$$F = f^2L^2/\overline{\phi} = L^2/L_R{}^2 \tag{3-10}$$

where $L_R = \overline{\phi}^{1/2}/f$ is the Rossby *radius of deformation*. It was shown in Section 2-7 that L_R is very important in the geostrophic adjustment process.

If terms of order Ro are neglected the equation of motion (3-5) is

$$\nabla\phi + f\mathbf{k}\times\mathbf{V} = 0 \qquad \text{or} \qquad \mathbf{V} = f^{-1}\mathbf{k}\times\nabla\phi \tag{3-11}$$

Thus the wind is geostrophic with the error due to the neglected terms of order Ro. If $F \lesssim 1$ the first approximation to the continuity equation (3-9) is

$$\overline{\phi}\nabla\cdot\mathbf{V} = 0 \tag{3-12}$$

Note that (3-12) is consistent with (3-11) since the divergence of the geostrophic wind is zero when f is constant. The relations (3-11) and (3-12) are purely diagnostic and contain no time derivatives. This is consistent with observations that show that the large-scale atmospheric flow is approximately geostrophic. Consequently, if the complete equations (3-5) and (3-9) are used for prediction, small errors in the initial wind and height fields will lead to large errors in the time tendencies (see Section 2-7). In fact Richardson (1922) applied the surface pressure tendency equation, which is similar to (3-9), to observed data and he obtained a ridiculously large pressure tendency, although little actual change was observed. This difficulty arises because (3-1) and (3-2) describe fast inertial gravity waves as well as the slow Rossby wave type motions (see Section 2-5).

It is desirable to develop a set of prediction equations that use the fact that the wind is nearly geostrophic. In Section 2-5 it was shown that the divergence is small in comparison with the vorticity for linear Rossby waves. This is also implied by the approximations (3-11) and (3-12). Consequently, it is desirable to separate the wind into *rotational* and *divergent* parts as follows:

$$\mathbf{V} = \mathbf{V}_\psi + \mathbf{V}_\chi \qquad \mathbf{V}_\psi = \mathbf{k} \times \nabla\psi \qquad \mathbf{V}_\chi = \nabla\chi \tag{3-13}$$

where ψ is the streamfunction for the rotational part of the wind and χ is the velocity potential for the divergent part of the wind. The vorticity and divergence now become

$$\zeta = \mathbf{k} \cdot \nabla \times \mathbf{V} = \nabla^2\psi \qquad D = \nabla \cdot \mathbf{V} = \nabla^2\chi \tag{3-14}$$

These equations can be solved for ψ and χ if boundary conditions are specified. The vorticity equation is obtained by taking $\mathbf{k} \cdot \nabla \times$ of (3-1), which yields

$$\frac{\partial}{\partial t}\zeta + \mathbf{V} \cdot \nabla\zeta + (f + \zeta)\,\nabla \cdot \mathbf{V} = 0 \tag{3-15}$$

The divergence equation is obtained by taking $\nabla\cdot$ of (3-1) with the result

$$\frac{\partial D}{\partial t} + \nabla \cdot (\mathbf{V} \cdot \nabla\, \mathbf{V}) + \nabla^2\phi - f\zeta = 0 \tag{3-16}$$

Scale the velocity components as follows:

$$\mathbf{V}_\psi \sim V \qquad \mathbf{V}_\chi \sim R_1 V \tag{3-17}$$

where R_1 is a small, nondimensional number that must be determined. Substitute (3-13) into (3-9) and use (3-17):

$$\frac{\partial\phi'}{\partial t} + \mathbf{V}_\psi \cdot \nabla\phi' + \mathbf{V}_\chi \cdot \nabla\phi' + \phi'\nabla \cdot \mathbf{V}_\chi + \overline{\phi}\nabla \cdot \mathbf{V}_\chi = 0$$

$$Ro\, F\overline{\phi}\,\frac{V}{L} \quad Ro\, F\overline{\phi}\,\frac{V}{L} \quad R_1 Ro\, F\overline{\phi}\,\frac{V}{L} \quad R_1 Ro\, F\overline{\phi}\,\frac{V}{L} \quad R_1\,\overline{\phi}\,\frac{V}{L} \tag{3-18}$$

If the last term is to be balanced it is necessary that

$$R_1 \lesssim Ro\, F \tag{3-19}$$

Rewrite the vorticity equation (3-15) with (3-13) and carry out the scale analysis, which gives

$$\frac{\partial \zeta}{\partial t} + \mathbf{V}_\psi \cdot \nabla \zeta + \mathbf{V}_\chi \cdot \nabla \zeta + fD + \zeta D = 0$$

$$\frac{V^2}{L^2} \quad \frac{V^2}{L^2} \quad R_1 \frac{V^2}{L^2} \quad \frac{R_1}{Ro}\frac{V^2}{L^2} \quad R_1 \frac{V^2}{L^2} \tag{3-20}$$

where $\zeta \sim V/L$ and $D \sim R_1 V/L$ have been used. The divergence equation (3-16) is rewritten and scaled as follows:

$$\frac{\partial D}{\partial t} + \nabla \cdot (\mathbf{V}_\psi \cdot \nabla \mathbf{V}_\psi) + \nabla \cdot (\mathbf{V}_\psi \cdot \nabla \mathbf{V}_\chi) + \nabla \cdot (\mathbf{V}_\chi \cdot \nabla \mathbf{V}_\psi)$$

$$R_1 \frac{V^2}{L^2} \quad \frac{V^2}{L^2} \quad R_1 \frac{V^2}{L^2} \quad R_1 \frac{V^2}{L^2} \tag{3-21}$$

$$+ \nabla \cdot (\mathbf{V}_\chi \cdot \nabla \mathbf{V}_\chi) + \nabla^2 \phi' - f\zeta = 0$$

$$R_1^2 \frac{V^2}{L^2} \quad \frac{1}{Ro}\frac{V^2}{L^2} \quad \frac{1}{Ro}\frac{V^2}{L^2}$$

From the vorticity equation (3-20) it is seen that

$$R_1 \lesssim Ro \tag{3-22}$$

in order that the divergence term will be balanced. The ratio of the divergence to the vorticity may now be written:

$$\frac{|D|}{|\zeta|} = R_1 \tag{3-23}$$

where R_1 must satisfy (3-19) and (3-22). This agrees with the linear result (2-59) for Rossby waves if $L = \mu^{-1}$ and $\overline{\phi} = gH$. The divergence is small in comparison to the vorticity as a result of the rotation of the system.

Consider motions which satisfy $F \sim 1$, $Ro << 1$. In this case (3-19) and (3-22) are satisfied by $R_1 = Ro$. Now, drop all terms in (3-18), (3-20) and (3-21), which are order Ro or smaller compared to the largest terms in each equation. This yields the following simplified system of equations:

$$\frac{\partial \phi'}{\partial t} + \mathbf{V}_\psi \cdot \nabla \phi' + \overline{\phi} D = 0 \tag{3-24}$$

$$\frac{\partial \zeta}{\partial t} + \mathbf{V}_\psi \cdot \nabla \zeta + fD = 0 \tag{3-25}$$

$$\nabla^2 \phi' - f\zeta = 0 \tag{3-26}$$

Equation (3-26) shows that the vorticity is geostrophic, and if $\zeta = \nabla^2\psi$ is introduced, a solution for the streamfunction is $\psi = \phi'/f$. The rotational part of the wind then becomes

$$\mathbf{V}_\psi = \mathbf{k} \times \nabla\psi = f^{-1}\mathbf{k} \times \nabla\phi' \tag{3-27}$$

which is the geostrophic wind (3-11). Equations 3-24, 3-25, and 3-26 or 3-27 are called the *quasi-geostrophic equations*. Note that vorticity and advecting wind are geostrophic, but the divergence is not (the geostrophic divergence is zero in this model). Although the divergence is small in comparison with the vorticity (3-23), the divergence terms in (3-24) and (3-25) are of same order of magnitude as the other terms in the equations.

The divergence may be eliminated between (3-24) and (3-25), which yields

$$\left(\frac{\partial}{\partial t} + \mathbf{V}_\psi \cdot \nabla\right)(\zeta - (f/\bar{\phi})\,\phi') = 0 \tag{3-28}$$

This is the *quasi-geostrophic potential vorticity equation,* and it can be shown by expanding and differentiating $g^{-1}\,\bar{\phi}\,q = (\zeta + f)/(1 + \phi'/\bar{\phi})$ that it is a reasonable approximation to the potential vorticity equation (2-39b) for the model. With the use of (3-26) and (3-27), Equation 3-28 can be written in terms of ϕ' only.

A diagnostic equation for the divergence may be obtained by eliminating the time derivatives between (3-24) and (3-25) with the use of (3-26). This equation becomes

$$\nabla^2 D - (f^2/\bar{\phi})\,D = (1/f\bar{\phi})\,\mathbf{k} \times \nabla\phi' \cdot \nabla(\nabla^2\phi') \tag{3-29}$$

which is called the quasi-geostrophic divergence equation. When this equation is linearized as in the previous chapter it reduces to the x-derivative of (2-57). It is especially important to note that the divergence is directly related to the ϕ' field (3-29) or the vorticity through (3-26). This is unusual in fluid dynamical systems; it results from the strong rotation of the system.

A reasonable value of F for cyclone scale motions ($L \sim 10^6$ m, $f \sim 10^{-4}\text{sec}^{-1}$, $\bar{\phi}^{1/2} = 300\ \text{msec}^{-1}$) is $F \sim 0.1$. The preceding analysis with $F \sim 1$ was carried out for comparison with the baroclinic scaling, which will be used in the next section. If $F \sim Ro << 1$, then by (3-19) $R_1 = Ro^2$. The vorticity equation (3-20) for this condition reduces to

$$\frac{\partial\zeta}{\partial t} + \mathbf{V}_\psi \cdot \nabla\zeta = 0 \tag{3-30}$$

which is the nondivergent barotropic vorticity equation. The continuity equation is not needed in this case and the divergence equation again gives the geostrophic relation (3-27).

It is important to note that the prediction equations, (3-28) and (3-30), which were derived in this section, are not sensitive to small errors in the initial conditions because all of the terms are of the same order. This is not the case for the original equations [(3-1) and (3-2)].

3-3 BAROCLINIC EQUATIONS

In this section the scale analysis is extended to the baroclinic equations on a spherical earth. It is convenient to use the following vertical coordinate:

$$Z \equiv -\ell n(p/p_0) \tag{3-31}$$

where p_0 is standard sea-level pressure. The vertical coordinate Z is related to the actual height z, and the geopotential $\phi = gz$ by the equation of state and the hydrostatic equation:

$$RT = p\alpha = -pg\frac{\partial z}{\partial p} = \frac{\partial \phi}{\partial Z} \tag{3-32}$$

One advantage of Z is that it is approximately equal to the actual height divided by the scale height $H = RT/g$, which is about 8 km.

This system is closely related to the pressure coordinate system of Chapter 1 and the vertical derivatives are related as follows:

$$\frac{\partial}{\partial p} = -\frac{1}{p}\frac{\partial}{\partial Z} \tag{3-33}$$

while the other partial derivatives are the same in both systems. The Z-velocity $\dot{Z}$ is related to ω through

$$\dot{Z} = -\dot{p}/p = -\omega/p \tag{3-34}$$

The equation of motion in the Z-system is

$$\frac{\partial \mathbf{V}}{\partial t} + \mathbf{V} \cdot \nabla \mathbf{V} + \dot{Z}\frac{\partial \mathbf{V}}{\partial Z} + \nabla\phi + f\mathbf{k} \times \mathbf{V} = 0 \tag{3-35}$$

The first law of thermodynamics can be written with (3-32) as

$$\frac{\partial}{\partial t}\frac{\partial \phi}{\partial Z} + \mathbf{V} \cdot \nabla \frac{\partial \phi}{\partial Z} + \dot{Z}\frac{\partial}{\partial Z}\left(\frac{\partial \phi}{\partial Z} + \kappa\phi\right) = \kappa Q \tag{3-36}$$

where $\kappa = R\, c_p^{-1}$ and Q is the heat added per unit time. The continuity equation is

$$\nabla \cdot \mathbf{V} + \frac{\partial \dot{Z}}{\partial Z} - \dot{Z} = 0 \tag{3-37}$$

In this scale analysis the nondimensional parameters will turn out to be *Ro*, ε, and L/a, where a is the radius of the earth. The quantity ε is a rotational Froude number, which is inversely proportional to the static stability of the atmosphere, and is analogous to the F used in the last section. For this reason the scales determined in the last section are used here for the various quantities. The derivatives are estimated with

$$\frac{\partial}{\partial t} \sim \frac{V}{L} \qquad \nabla \sim \frac{1}{L} \qquad \frac{\partial}{\partial Z} \sim 1 \tag{3-38}$$

except that $\nabla f \sim \beta = 2\Omega \cos \varphi/a$. This expression for β is derived in (3-56). Z is nondimensional and $\partial/\partial Z \sim 1$ corresponds to a vertical scale of order 8 km, which is reasonable for tropospheric disturbances. The velocity is broken into rotational and divergent parts as in the previous section (See 3-13 and 3-14.) and the geopotential is separated into

$$\phi = \overline{\phi}(Z) + \phi' \tag{3-39}$$

where $\overline{\phi}(Z)$ is taken from a standard atmosphere. The dependent variables are scaled as follows:

$$\mathbf{V}_\psi \sim \mathbf{V} \qquad \mathbf{V}_\chi \sim R_1 V \tag{3-40}$$

$$\dot{Z} \sim R_1\, V/L \tag{3-41}$$

$$\phi' \sim fVL \tag{3-42}$$

The scaling is the same as in the last section with R_1 as yet undetermined. The $\dot{Z}$ scale is obtained from the continuity equation (3-37) with the use of the scale for $\mathbf{V}_\chi$. The ϕ' scaling follows directly from the geostrophic scaling (3-8).

Since it is expected that the divergence will be small in comparison with the vorticity, it is again convenient to replace the equation of motion with the vorticity and divergence equations. The vorticity equation for this system is given below along with the scales for each term:

$$\begin{array}{cccccc}
\dfrac{\partial \zeta}{\partial t} & + \mathbf{V}_\psi \cdot \nabla \zeta & + \mathbf{V}_\chi \cdot \nabla \zeta & + \mathbf{V}_\psi \cdot \nabla f & + \mathbf{V}_\chi \cdot \nabla f & + \dot{Z}\dfrac{\partial \zeta}{\partial Z} \\[2ex]
\dfrac{V^2}{L^2} & \dfrac{V^2}{L^2} & \dfrac{R_1 V^2}{L^2} & \dfrac{(\beta a/f)L/a}{Ro}\dfrac{V^2}{L^2} & \dfrac{(\beta a/f)L/a}{Ro}\dfrac{R_1 V^2}{L^2} & \dfrac{R_1 V^2}{L^2} \\[4ex]
+ fD & + \zeta D & + \mathbf{k} \cdot \nabla \dot{Z} \times \dfrac{\partial \mathbf{V}_\psi}{\partial Z} & + \mathbf{k} \cdot \nabla \dot{Z} \times \dfrac{\partial \mathbf{V}_\chi}{\partial Z} = 0 & & \\[2ex]
\dfrac{R_1}{Ro}\dfrac{V^2}{L^2} & \dfrac{R_1 V^2}{L^2} & \dfrac{R_1 V^2}{L^2} & \dfrac{R_1^2 V^2}{L^2} & &
\end{array} \tag{3-43}$$

where the additional scales are $\zeta \sim V/L$, $D \sim R_1 V/L$, and $Ro = V/fL$ has been used to introduce the common factor V^2/L^2. The divergence equation with the scales for each term is given below:

$$\frac{\partial D}{\partial t} + \nabla \cdot (\mathbf{V}_\psi \cdot \nabla \mathbf{V}_\psi) + \nabla \cdot (\mathbf{V}_\psi \cdot \nabla \mathbf{V}_\chi + \mathbf{V}_\chi \cdot \nabla \mathbf{V}_\psi) + \nabla \cdot (\mathbf{V}_\chi \cdot \nabla \mathbf{V}_\chi) + \nabla \dot{Z} \cdot \frac{\partial \mathbf{V}_\psi}{\partial Z} + \dot{Z} \frac{\partial D}{\partial Z}$$

$$\frac{R_1 V^2}{L^2} \qquad \frac{V^2}{L^2} \qquad \frac{R_1 V^2}{L^2} \qquad \frac{R_1^2 V^2}{L^2} \qquad \frac{R_1 V^2}{L^2} \qquad \frac{R_1^2 V^2}{L^2}$$

$$+ \nabla \dot{Z} \cdot \frac{\partial \mathbf{V}_\chi}{\partial Z} + \nabla^2 \phi' - f\zeta - \mathbf{k} \times \nabla f \cdot \mathbf{V}_\psi - \mathbf{k} \times \nabla f \cdot \mathbf{V}_\chi = 0$$

$$\frac{R_1^2 V^2}{L^2} \qquad \frac{1}{Ro} \frac{V^2}{L^2} \qquad \frac{1}{Ro} \frac{V^2}{L^2} \qquad \frac{(\beta a/f) L/a}{Ro} \frac{V^2}{L^2} \qquad \frac{(\beta a/f) L/a \, R_1}{Ro} \frac{V^2}{L^2} \tag{3-44}$$

The continuity equation (3-37) is scaled so that all terms are of the same order:

$$D + \frac{\partial \dot{Z}}{\partial Z} - \dot{Z} = 0 \tag{3-45}$$

$$\frac{R_1 V}{L} \qquad \frac{R_1 V}{L} \qquad \frac{R_1 V}{L}$$

The first law of thermodynamics (3-36) is scaled as follows:

$$\frac{\partial}{\partial t} \frac{\partial \phi'}{\partial Z} + \mathbf{V}_\psi \cdot \nabla \frac{\partial \phi'}{\partial Z} + \mathbf{V}_\chi \cdot \nabla \frac{\partial \phi'}{\partial Z} + \dot{Z}\,\Gamma(Z) + \dot{Z} \frac{\partial}{\partial Z} \left(\frac{\partial \phi'}{\partial Z} + \kappa \phi' \right) = \kappa Q \tag{3-46}$$

$$fV^2 \qquad fV^2 \qquad R_1 fV^2 \qquad \frac{R_1 fV^2}{Ro\,\varepsilon} \qquad R_1 fV^2$$

where

$$\Gamma(Z) = \frac{\partial}{\partial Z} \left(\frac{\partial \bar{\phi}}{\partial Z} + \kappa \bar{\phi} \right) = R \left(\frac{\partial \bar{T}}{\partial Z} + \kappa \bar{T} \right) = \frac{H^2 g}{T} \left(\frac{g}{c_p} + \frac{1}{H} \frac{\partial \bar{T}}{\partial Z} \right) \tag{3-47}$$

Here the hydrostatic equation (3-32) and $H = R\bar{T}/g$ have been used to rewrite (3-47). Γ is called the static stability because it is proportional to the difference between the dry adiabatic lapse rate and a standard atmosphere lapse rate. The parameter ε, a rotational Froude number, is defined as

$$\varepsilon \equiv f^2 L^2 \Gamma^{-1} \tag{3-48}$$

This quantity can be rewritten in terms of the Richardson's number

$$\varepsilon = 1/(Ro^2 Ri) \tag{3-49}$$

where the Richardson's number is defined as

$$Ri = \Gamma / V^2 \tag{3-50}$$

that is the ratio of static stability to the vertical wind shear squared. In the analysis that follows, the heating term in (3-46) will be dropped, but for any heating rate that might be proposed it can be compared to the other terms in order to see if it will affect the scale analysis.

It is convenient to compute ε from (3-48) by first estimating the Richardson number from (3-50). The use of the following values: $g \sim 10$ msec^{-1}, $\overline{T} \sim 300°$, $g/c_p + H^{-1}\,\partial T/\partial Z \sim 3.5° \times 10^{-3}$ m^{-1}, $H \sim 10^4$ m, $V \sim 10$ msec^{-1} leads to

$$Ri \sim 100 \tag{3-51}$$

3-4 MIDLATITUDE ANALYSIS

Considering the synoptic scale midlatitude disturbances where $L \sim 10^6$ m, the parameters become

$$Ro \sim 0.1 \qquad L/a \sim 0.1 \qquad \varepsilon \sim 1 \qquad \beta a/f \sim 1$$

where $a \sim 6.4 \times 10^6$ m and $f \sim 10^{-4}$ sec^{-1}. With $\varepsilon \sim 1$, the vorticity equation (3-43) and the first law of thermodynamics (3-46) both give

$$R_1 \lesssim Ro$$

Thus it is appropriate to set $R_1 = Ro$. Dropping all terms in (3-43), (3-44) and (3-46) that are of order Ro or less gives the following reduced system of equations:

$$\frac{\partial \zeta}{\partial t} + \mathbf{V}_\psi \cdot \nabla (\zeta + f) + fD = 0 \tag{3-52}$$

$$\nabla^2 \phi' - f\zeta = 0 \tag{3-53}$$

$$\frac{\partial}{\partial t}\frac{\partial \phi'}{\partial Z} + \mathbf{V}_\psi \cdot \nabla \frac{\partial \phi'}{\partial Z} + \Gamma(Z)\dot{Z} = 0 \tag{3.54}$$

In the vorticity equation (3-52) the following terms have been neglected: advection of absolute vorticity by the divergent part of the wind, vertical advection of vorticity, the part of the divergence term that involves ζ and the twisting term. The temperature advection by the divergent part of the wind and the fluctuating part of the stability have been neglected in the first law of thermodynamics (3-54).

It is now convenient to introduce the beta plane approximation in place of the spherical geometry. The cartesian coordinates are defined

$$\mathbf{\nabla} = \mathbf{i}\frac{\partial}{\partial x} + \mathbf{j}\frac{\partial}{\partial y} \qquad \mathbf{V} = u\mathbf{i} + v\mathbf{j}$$

so that x increases to the east and y increases to the north. The spatial variation of f in (3-52) and (3-53) is important only in the advection term

$$\mathbf{V}_\psi \cdot \mathbf{\nabla} f = v_\psi \frac{df}{dy} = v_\psi \beta \tag{3-55}$$

where

$$\beta = \frac{d}{dy}(2\Omega \sin \varphi) = 2\Omega \cos \varphi \frac{d\varphi}{dy} = \frac{2\Omega \cos \varphi}{a} \tag{3-56}$$

To show that the variation of f is unimportant when it is merely a coefficient, expand f in a Taylor series about $y = y_0$:

$$f = f_0 + \beta_0(y - y_0) + = f_0\left[1 + \frac{\beta_0}{f_0}(y - y_0) + \ldots\right] \tag{3-57}$$

Since the analysis treats disturbances of scale L, it is reasonable to restrict the variation of y so that $|y - y_0| \lesssim L$. In middle latitudes $\beta \sim f/a$, so that the second term in (3-57) is bounded by

$$\left|\frac{\beta_0}{f_0}(y - y_0)\right| \lesssim L/a \tag{3-58}$$

Since $L/a \sim 0.1$ it is consistent to use $f = f_0$ except where it is differentiated and to replace β by β_0 in (3-55). The beta plane approximation can be justified by first transforming the equations to a conformal coordinate system and then showing that the spatial variation of the map factor may be neglected. This is reasonable since the map factor is normally a trigonometric function of latitude that can be replaced with a constant when L/a is small. Phillips (1963) carried out a comprehensive scale analysis of the Z equations by writing them in Mercator coordinates and then by expanding all quantities into series in the Rossby number. His analysis showed that the use of cartesian coordinates is appropriate for the parameter range considered here.

The vorticity equation (3-52) may now be written

$$\frac{\partial \zeta}{\partial t} + \mathbf{V}_\psi \cdot \mathbf{\nabla}(\zeta + \beta_0 y) - f_0 e^Z \frac{\partial}{\partial Z}(e^{-Z}\dot{Z}) = 0 \tag{3-59}$$

since $\mathbf{V}_\psi \cdot \nabla(\beta_0 y) = \beta_0 \mathbf{V}_\psi \cdot \nabla y = \beta_0 v_\psi$. A modified form of the continuity equation (3-45) has been used to eliminate D. The divergence equation (3-53) becomes

$$\nabla^2\phi' = f_0\zeta = f_0\nabla^2\psi \tag{3-60}$$

with the use of (3-40). The appropriate solution to this equation is

$$\psi = f_0^{-1}\phi' \tag{3-61}$$

so that the rotational part of the wind and the vorticity become

$$\mathbf{V}_\psi = f_0^{-1}\,\mathbf{k} \times \nabla\phi' \qquad \zeta = f_0^{-1}\,\nabla^2\phi' \tag{3-62}$$

The set, (3-54), (3-59), and (3-62), are the *quasi-geostrophic equations*.

A single equation may be derived by eliminating $\dot{Z}$ between (3-54) and (3-59). Solve (3-54) for $e^{-Z}\dot{Z}$ and differentiate with respect to $\dot{Z}$:

$$\frac{\partial}{\partial Z}(e^{-Z}\dot{Z}) = -\frac{\partial}{\partial t}\frac{\partial}{\partial Z}\left(\frac{e^{-Z}}{\Gamma}\frac{\partial\phi'}{\partial Z}\right) - \mathbf{V}_\psi \cdot \nabla \frac{\partial}{\partial Z}\left(\frac{e^{-Z}}{\Gamma}\frac{\partial\phi'}{\partial Z}\right) \tag{3-63}$$

where the term in $\partial\mathbf{V}_\psi/\partial Z$ was eliminated with the use of (3-62). Substitute (3-63) into (3-59) and collect common terms:

$$\left(\frac{\partial}{\partial t} + \mathbf{V}_\psi \cdot \nabla\right)\left[\zeta + \beta_0 y + e^Z\frac{\partial}{\partial Z}\left(\frac{f_0 e^{-Z}}{\Gamma}\frac{\partial\phi'}{\partial Z}\right)\right] = 0 \tag{3-64}$$

This is the *quasi-geostrophic potential vorticity equation* and it can be compared with (3-28) for the shallow-water equations. With (3-62) this equation can be written entirely in terms of ϕ' as follows:

$$\left[\nabla^2 + e^Z\frac{\partial}{\partial Z}\left(\frac{e^{-Z}}{\Gamma}\frac{\partial}{\partial Z}\right)\right]\frac{\partial\phi'}{\partial t}$$
$$= -\mathbf{k} \times \nabla\phi' \cdot \nabla\left[f_0^{-1}\,\nabla^2\phi' + \beta_0 y + e^Z\frac{\partial}{\partial Z}\left(\frac{f_0 e^{-Z}}{\Gamma}\frac{\partial\phi'}{\partial Z}\right)\right] \tag{3-65}$$

If the distribution of ϕ' is known initially the right hand side may be computed. The operator on the left is elliptic so that (3-65) can be solved for $\partial\phi'/\partial t$ if proper boundary conditions are specified.

The quasi-geostrophic equations also determine Z at any particular time. To see this rewrite the vorticity equation (3-59) and the first law of thermodynamics (3-54) as follows:

$$\frac{\partial\zeta}{\partial t} = \frac{1}{f_0}\nabla^2\frac{\partial\phi'}{\partial t} = -\mathbf{V}_\psi \cdot \nabla(\zeta + \beta_0 y) + f_0 e^Z\frac{\partial}{\partial Z}(e^{-Z}\dot{Z}) \tag{3-66}$$

$$R\frac{\partial T'}{\partial t} = \frac{\partial}{\partial Z}\frac{\partial\phi'}{\partial t} = -\mathbf{V}_\psi \cdot \nabla\frac{\partial\phi'}{\partial Z} - \Gamma(Z)\,\dot{Z} \tag{3-67}$$

Given the vorticity advection, $-\mathbf{V}_\psi \cdot \nabla(\zeta + \beta_0 y)$, and the temperature advection, $-\mathbf{V}_\psi \cdot \nabla(\partial\phi'/\partial Z)$, the $\dot{Z}$ field is uniquely determined such that $\partial\zeta/\partial t$ and $\partial T'/\partial t$ are given geostrophically and hydrostatically by $\partial\phi'/\partial t$. A diagnostic equation for $\dot{Z}$ may be found by taking $\partial/\partial Z$ of (3-66) and subtracting $f_0^{-1}\nabla^2$ of (3-67):

$$\Gamma(Z)\nabla^2\dot{Z} + f_0^2\frac{\partial}{\partial Z}\left(e^Z\frac{\partial}{\partial Z}(e^{-Z}\dot{Z})\right) = f_0\frac{\partial}{\partial Z}[\mathbf{V}_\psi \cdot \nabla(\zeta + \beta_0 y)]$$

$$- \nabla^2[\mathbf{V}_\psi \cdot \nabla(\partial\phi'/\partial Z)] \qquad (3\text{-}68)$$

This is called the *quasi-geostrophic vertical motion equation,* and it is analogous to the quasi-geostrophic divergence equation (3-29) of the last section. The right-hand side can be written entirely in terms of ϕ' with (3-62). If the distribution of ϕ' is given at any time, the equation may be solved for $\dot{Z}$ since the operator on the left is an elliptic operator. When $\dot{Z}$ has been computed from (3-68), the divergence can be obtained from (3-45). Thus it can be seen with the use of (3-62) that the divergence is a function of the vorticity. This is a result of the rotational constraint which is strong when the Rossby number is small.

Equation 3-68 is often used as a diagnostic tool in synoptic studies. If the ϕ' field is known, either in a case study or at some point in a quasi-geostrophic forecast, then the vertical motion can be found by solving (3-68). This vertical motion field can then be related to precipitation and cloud patterns.

In order to solve either (3-65) or (3-68), boundary conditions must be specified at the top of the atmosphere and, also at the lower surface. If $\dot{Z}$ is known, then $(\partial/\partial Z)(\partial\phi'/\partial t)$ can be found from (3-54), for solving (3-65). At the top of the atmosphere ($Z \rightarrow \infty$) the boundary condition is that $\dot{Z}$ remain finite (see 3-34). In order to determine $\dot{Z}$ at the lower boundary it is necessary to relate $\dot{Z}$ to w. Expand $gw = d\phi/dt$, and scale the terms as before:

$$gw = \frac{\partial\phi'}{\partial t} + \mathbf{V}_\psi \cdot \nabla\phi' + \mathbf{V}_\chi \cdot \nabla\phi' + \dot{Z}\frac{\partial\phi'}{\partial Z} + \dot{Z}R\overline{T} \qquad (3\text{-}69)$$

$$fV^2 \qquad fV^2 \qquad R_1 fV^2 \qquad R_1 fV^2 \qquad \frac{R_1}{Ro}MfV^2$$

where $\partial\overline{\phi}/\partial Z = R\overline{T}$ has been used. Here M, which is defined

$$M \equiv R\overline{T}/f^2L^2 \qquad (3\text{-}70)$$

is an inverse rotational Froude number. For the scales considered here $R_1 = Ro$ and

$$M \sim 10 \qquad (3\text{-}71)$$

when $R\overline{T} \sim 10^5$ m^{2}sec^{-2}. Note that $M = F^{-1}$ from Section 3-2 if $\overline{\phi} = R\overline{T}$, which is roughly true for the troposphere. Under these conditions the last term on the right hand side of (3-69) dominates and the equation reduces to

$$gw = R\overline{T}\,\dot{Z} \tag{3-72}$$

This shows that a typical value for the vertical velocity is $w \sim g^{-1}fV^2M \sim 1$ cm sec^{-1}. When (3-72) is applied at the lower boundary $Z = Z_s$, it becomes

$$\dot{Z}_s = (g/R\overline{T})w_s = (g/R\overline{T})\mathbf{V} \cdot \nabla h_s \tag{3-73}$$

where $h_s(x,y)$ is the height of the lower boundary. The vertical motion at the top of the Ekman layer [Charney and Eliassen (1949)], could be added, but Phillips (1963) has shown that it is too small to be important in this analysis. If there are no mountains then (3-73) reduces to $\dot{Z}_s = 0$.

It is convenient to apply (3-73) on a constant Z say $Z = 0$, which corresponds to the pressure surface $p = p_0$. The error in any variable can be found by expanding it into a Taylor series in Z, and the resulting error is Z_s. Clearly this approximation is consistent with the neglect of other terms which are of order 1/10 as long as the smoothed mountains are not higher than $H/10$, or about 1 km.

It will be useful to have the quasi-geostrophic equations in pressure coordinates. With the use of (3-33) and (3-34) the vorticity equation (3-59) and the first law of thermodynamics (3-54) become:

$$\left(\frac{\partial \zeta}{\partial t} + \mathbf{V}_\psi \cdot \nabla\right)(\zeta + \beta_0 y) - f_0 \frac{\partial \omega}{\partial p} = 0 \tag{3-74}$$

$$\frac{\partial^2 \phi}{\partial t \partial p} + \mathbf{V}_\psi \cdot \nabla\,(\partial\phi/\partial p) + \sigma\,(p)\omega = 0 \tag{3-75}$$

where $\sigma = \Gamma/p^2 = (1/p)(d/dp)\,[p(d\overline{\phi}/dp) - \overline{\phi}\,]$. The potential vorticity equation (3-64) can be written:

$$\left(\frac{\partial}{\partial t} + f_0^{-1}\,\mathbf{k} \times \nabla\phi \cdot \nabla\right)\left[f_0^{-1}\,\nabla^2\phi + \beta_0 y + \frac{\partial}{\partial p}\left(\frac{f_0}{\sigma_{(p)}}\frac{\partial \phi}{\partial p}\right)\right] = 0 \tag{3-76}$$

The vertical motion equation (3-68) takes the form:

$$\sigma\nabla^2\omega + f_0^2\,\frac{\partial^2\omega}{\partial p^2} = f_0\,\frac{\partial}{\partial p}(\mathbf{V}_\psi \cdot \nabla(\zeta + \beta y)) - \nabla^2\left(\mathbf{V}_\psi \cdot \nabla\,\frac{\partial \phi'}{\partial p}\right) \tag{3-75}$$

This equation is called the *quasi-geostrophic omega equation*.

3-5 TROPICS

The parameter values $Ro \sim 0.1$, $L/a \sim 0.1$, and $\varepsilon \sim 1$ are appropriate for synoptic scale disturbances in midlatitudes. Synoptic scale tropical disturbances have

$$Ro \sim 1 \qquad L/a \sim 0.1 \qquad \varepsilon \sim 10^{-2} \qquad \beta L/f \sim 1 \tag{3-78}$$

where ε is obtained from (3-49) with $Ri = 100$. In this case $\beta \sim f/L$ because f varies from 0 at the equator to the typical value of f in a distance L. The vorticity equation (3-43) requires that $R_1 \leq Ro \sim 1$, while the first law of thermodynamics (3-46) imposes $R_1 \lesssim Ro\ \varepsilon \sim \varepsilon$. Thus the proper value is

$$R_1 = \varepsilon \tag{3-79}$$

If terms of order $V^2/10L^2$ or less are dropped in (3-43) it reduces to

$$\frac{\partial \zeta}{\partial t} + \mathbf{V}_\psi \cdot \nabla(\zeta + f) = 0 \tag{3-80}$$

and the divergence equation becomes

$$\nabla \cdot (\mathbf{V}_\psi \cdot \nabla \mathbf{V}_\psi) + \nabla^2 \phi' - f\zeta - \mathbf{k} \times \nabla f \cdot \mathbf{V}_\psi = 0 \tag{3-81}$$

This equation is called the *balance equation;* it is often used for initializing primitive equation models. The first law of thermodynamics is not needed in this equation set because the divergence does not occur in (3-80). However, if strong heating occurs in the tropics, the heating term in (3-46) may become larger than fV^2. In this case the vertical motion scaling (3-79) could be modified and the divergence would appear in the vorticity equation. It can be seen that the balance in (3-46) would be between the heating and the vertical motion term.

The scale analysis developed here does not cover all important types of motion in the tropics even if heating is included. Equatorial Kelvin waves and certain mixed Rossby-gravity waves are not properly treated by the advective time scale used and they may also have smaller vertical scales than assumed here, (see Sections 4-12 and 4-13).

3-6 PLANETARY SCALE

The largest scale motions in the atmosphere can be represented with

$$L/a \sim 1 \qquad Ro \lesssim 0.01 \qquad \varepsilon \sim 100 \qquad \beta a/f \sim 1$$

Under these conditions the largest terms in the vorticity equation (3-43) cannot be balanced unless

$$R_1 \sim 1 \tag{3-82}$$

and this scaling is also consistent for the first law of thermodynamics (3-46). Now the dominant terms in (3-43) and (3-44) become

$$(\mathbf{V}_\psi + \mathbf{V}_\chi) \cdot \nabla f + fD = 0 \tag{3-83}$$

$$\nabla^2\phi' - f\zeta - \mathbf{k} \times \nabla f \cdot (\mathbf{V}_\psi + \mathbf{V}_\chi) = 0 \tag{3-84}$$

Note that both of these equations are satisfied exactly when the velocity is geostrophic

$$\mathbf{V} = \mathbf{V}_\psi + \mathbf{V}_\chi = f^{-1}\mathbf{k} \times \nabla\phi' \tag{3-85}$$

In the first law of thermodynamics all of the terms are of the same order. The predictive system for the planetary-scale motions is (3-45), (3-46), and (3-85). The analysis of this section does not include the free, planetary-scale, Rossby waves, which have phase velocities that are much larger than V (see 4-10). However, these large phase velocities for the planetary waves are seldom observed, which indicates that the planetary-scale motions are mainly forced by heating, mountain effects, and perhaps nonlinear interaction with smaller scales. These motions are difficult to forecast and the upper boundary condition may be very important (see Section 7-11).

3-7 BALANCE SYSTEM

It is desirable to develop a more widely applicable set of equations that include all of the terms considered above for the various special cases, and are also more accurate for the synoptic-scale motions. Charney (1962) proposed the *balance system* in which all of the terms that are of order Ro or larger in the synoptic scale analysis are retained. The resulting set of equations can be written:

$$\frac{\partial\zeta}{\partial t} + (\mathbf{V}_\psi + \mathbf{V}_\chi) \cdot \nabla(\zeta + f) + \omega\partial\zeta/\partial p + (f + \zeta)D + \mathbf{k} \cdot \nabla\omega \times \frac{\partial \mathbf{V}_\psi}{\partial p} = 0 \tag{3-86}$$

$$\nabla \cdot (\mathbf{V}_\psi \cdot \nabla\mathbf{V}_\psi) + \nabla^2\phi - f\zeta - \mathbf{k} \times \nabla f \cdot \mathbf{V}_\psi = 0 \tag{3-87}$$

$$\frac{\partial}{\partial t}\frac{\partial\phi}{\partial p} + (\mathbf{V}_\psi + \mathbf{V}_\chi) \cdot \nabla\frac{\partial\phi}{\partial p} + \frac{\omega}{p}\frac{\partial}{\partial p}\left[p\frac{\partial\phi}{\partial p} - \kappa\phi\right] = 0 \tag{3-88}$$

$$D + \partial\omega/\partial p = 0 \tag{3-89}$$

For completeness the other relations are:

$$V_\psi = \mathbf{k} \times \nabla\psi \qquad \mathbf{V}_\chi = \nabla\chi$$
$$\zeta = \nabla^2\psi \qquad D = \nabla^2\chi \tag{3-90}$$

The equations are written in pressure coordinates for convenience in application. In the vorticity equation the only term missing is the portion of the twisting term, which involves the divergent part of the wind. In the divergence equation all terms that depend on the divergent part of the wind have been dropped. The resulting equation, which can be written in terms of ψ and ϕ, is called the *balance equation*. The first law of thermodynamics is complete. Heating and friction terms should be added to this set if they are of the same magnitude as the terms retained, or larger.

The balance system is not sensitive to small errors in the initial state since it was derived with a scale analysis. They do not allow gravity waves because the divergence tendency is neglected in the divergence equation. For synoptic scale motions the largest terms neglected are of order Ro^2. They also contain all of the terms that were obtained in the scale analyses for the tropics and the planetary scales. The only exception is the term $-\mathbf{k} \times \nabla f \cdot \mathbf{V}_\chi$, which was required in the divergence equation for the planetary scale motion. This term could be added to (3-87) without affecting energetic consistency, but the presence of the term will complicate the solution of the equations. The equations also contain the full variation of f, whereas in the quasi-geostrophic equations f is replaced by a constant wherever it is not differentiated. The full variation of f is especially important when a larger forecast area is employed.

Unfortunately the balance system is very difficult to solve due to its highly implicit form. It is not possible to derive a simple potential vorticity equation or an omega equation as with the quasi-geostrophic set. In addition the balance system does not describe some important tropical circulations such as Kelvin waves. As a result the balance system has not been used very much in operational numerical prediction. Normally, when more accuracy is required than can be obtained with the quasi-geostrophic set, the primitive equations are used. However, the balance system can still be helpful in initializing the primitive equations and in understanding certain dynamical processes.

CHAPTER 4

Atmospheric Waves: Part II

4-1 INTRODUCTION

This chapter treats more complicated wave motions than were treated in Chapter 2. Wave disturbances in the atmosphere originate from instabilities of certain flow fields, direct forcing or nonlinear interactions. Barotropic instability results from horizontal shear in a basic wind field, and it is a form of the "hydrodynamic instability" that has been studied in fluid mechanics [Lin (1955)]. Baroclinic instability is related to the vertical shear of the basic wind field or the horizontal temperature gradient through the thermal wind relation. This instability is related to the earth's rotation, and it has not been widely studied except in meteorology and oceanography. Barotropic and baroclinic effects occur together in the atmosphere, but it is easier to study them separately. In the tropics, near the equator, large-scale waves can exist that are quite different from either the Rossby waves or the inertial gravity waves of higher latitudes. The fact that f goes to zero at the equator allows waves of mixed character to exist, and it also tends to trap certain types of disturbances near the equator.

4-2 ROSSBY WAVES

The barotropic vorticity equation for a beta plane may be written

$$\frac{\partial \zeta}{\partial t} + \mathbf{V} \cdot \nabla(\zeta + \beta y) = 0 \tag{4-1}$$

where

$$\nabla \cdot \mathbf{V} = 0 \tag{4-2}$$

Equation 4-1 may be obtained from the quasi-geostrophic potential vorticity equation (3-64) by setting the perturbation temperature $R^{-1}\partial\phi'/\partial Z = 0$ or by letting the static stability Γ be very large. The barotropic vorticity equation is appropriate for a homogeneous fluid that is contained between two rigid horizontal plates, or for a free surface model when $F << 1$ (see Section 3-2). In Section 7-1-1 the equivalent barotropic model will be developed. This model assumes that the geopotential and the temperature are related by a function of pressure only. The result of this assumption is that (4-1) applies at the equivalent barotropic level, which is approximately 500 mb. In fact, operational forecasts made with (4-1) at 500 mb show considerable skill.

To investigate the question of barotropic instability, consider a zonal current that varies only with latitude, that is, $U = U(y)$. Equation 4-1 is linearized by writing: $\zeta = \bar{\zeta} + \zeta'$, $u = U + u'$, $v = v'$, which gives the following form:

$$\frac{\partial \zeta'}{\partial t} + U \frac{\partial \zeta'}{\partial x} + v' \left(\frac{\partial \bar{\zeta}}{\partial y} + \beta \right) = 0 \tag{4-3}$$

where $\bar{\zeta} = -dU/dy$. A stream function can be introduced to satisfy (4-2) by writing $u' = -\partial\psi/\partial y$ and $v' = \partial\psi/\partial x$. With these relations (4-3) becomes

$$\frac{\partial}{\partial t} \nabla^2\psi + U \frac{\partial}{\partial x} \nabla^2\psi + \left(\beta - \frac{d^2U}{dy^2} \right) \frac{\partial \psi}{\partial x} = 0 \tag{4-4}$$

Now consider perturbations of the form $\psi = \Psi(y)e^{i\mu(x-ct)}$ (referred to as normal mode solutions) and substitute into (4-4) giving

$$(U - c) \left(\frac{d^2\Psi}{dy^2} - \mu^2\Psi \right) - \left(\frac{d^2U}{dy^2} - \beta \right) \Psi = 0 \tag{4-5}$$

The current will be taken to be of finite width, centered at $y = 0$ and with rigid boundaries at $y = \pm d$. Since the normal velocities must vanish at these boundaries,

$$v(\pm d) = \frac{\partial \psi}{\partial x}(\pm d) = -i\mu\Psi(\pm d)e^{i\mu(x-ct)} = 0$$

Hence the boundary conditions are fulfilled if

$$\Psi(d) = \Psi(-d) = 0 \tag{4-6}$$

Equation 4-5 subject to the boundary conditions (4-6) constitutes an eigenvalue problem for c.

Before treating the general case $U = U(y)$, it is useful to consider $U =$ constant. In this case (4-5) reduces to

$$\frac{d^2\Psi}{dy^2} - \left(\mu^2 - \frac{\beta}{U - c} \right) \Psi = 0 \tag{4-7}$$

This equation has solutions of the form

$$\Psi_n = A \cos \left[\frac{(2n - 1)\pi y}{2d} \right] \qquad n = 1,2,\ldots \tag{4-8}$$

where $[(2n - 1)\pi/2d]^2 = -\mu^2 + \beta/(U - c)$. Clearly (4-8) satisfies the boundary conditions (4-6). The phase velocity now becomes

$$c = U - \beta/\{\mu^2 + [(2n - 1)\pi/2d]^2\} \tag{4-9}$$

This is a nondivergent Rossby wave with a finite lateral extent and it can be compared with the solutions in section (2-5). Note that the solutions Ψ_n given by (4-8) form a complete set so that they can be summed to represent an arbitrary initial state. For $n = 1$ and $d \to \infty$ this formula reduces to

$$c = U - \beta/\mu^2 \tag{4-10}$$

This formula should be compared to (2-50) when $\partial\bar{q}/\partial y$ is evaluated with (2-51). The combination of (2-50) and (2-51) differs from (4-10) because of the presence of a free surface in the shallow-water equations. These extra terms are unimportant except when the scale is very large in the denominator of (2-50). It was indicated previously that the Rossby waves propagate in the direction $\mathbf{k} \times \nabla\bar{q}$ with respect to the mean flow U [see (2-50)]. For the Rossby waves in this section, $\bar{q} = f/H_0$, where H_0 is a constant, so that $\nabla\bar{q}$ is toward the north and the propagation is to the west relative to the mean flow. The formula (4-10) was first derived by Rossby (1939), although the solution in spherical coordinates had been obtained much earlier [Hough (1898)] as one of the solutions to the Laplace tidal equations. The formula permits a stationary solution for $U > 0$ when the wavelength $\mathcal{L} = \mathcal{L}_s = 2\pi(U/\beta)^{1/2}$. For $\mathcal{L} < \mathcal{L}_s$, the propagation is toward the east, while for $\mathcal{L} > \mathcal{L}_s$ the propagation is toward the west. Synoptic disturbances at 500 mb move with speeds similar to those given by (4-10), but the very long waves do not have the rapid westward propagation indicated by (4-10).

4-3 CONDITIONS FOR BAROTROPIC INSTABILITY

In this section a necessary condition for barotropic instability will be derived, and the energy equations will be developed. For perturbations of the type $\psi = \Psi(y)e^{i\mu(x-ct)}$ to be unstable, the phase velocity must be complex; that is, $c = c_r + ic_i$, and the amplitude function Ψ will also be complex in general. Next multiply (4-5) by the complex conjugate of Ψ, say Ψ^*,

$$(U - c)\left(\Psi^* \frac{d^2\Psi}{dy^2} - \mu^2\Psi^*\Psi\right) - \left(\frac{d^2U}{dy^2} - \beta\right)\Psi^*\Psi = 0 \tag{4-11}$$

The first term may be written in the form

$$\Psi^* \frac{d^2\Psi}{dy^2} = \frac{d}{dy}\left(\Psi^* \frac{d\Psi}{dy}\right) - \frac{d\Psi^*}{dy}\frac{d\Psi}{dy}$$

Also the product of a complex quantity and its conjugate is the square of the absolute value of the quantity; hence,

$$\Psi\Psi^* = |\Psi|^2 \qquad \text{and} \qquad \frac{d\Psi^*}{dy}\frac{d\Psi}{dy} = \left|\frac{d\Psi}{dy}\right|^2$$

Utilizing these results, dividing (4-11) by $(U - c)$, and integrating between $\pm d$ yields

$$\int_{-d}^{d} \left[\frac{d}{dy}\left(\Psi^* \frac{d\Psi}{dy}\right) - \mu^2 |\Psi|^2 - \left|\frac{d\Psi}{dy}\right|^2\right] dy = \int_{-d}^{d} \frac{(d^2U/dy^2 - \beta)\,|\Psi|^2}{(U - c)}\, dy \qquad (4\text{-}12)$$

The boundary conditions require that Ψ vanish at $\pm d$; hence its real and imaginary parts must vanish separately. Thus Ψ^* as well as Ψ is zero at the boundaries, and the first term of the left side of (4-12) integrates to zero, leaving

$$\int_{-d}^{d} \left(\mu^2|\Psi|^2 + \left|\frac{d\Psi}{dy}\right|^2\right) dy = -\int_{-d}^{d} \frac{(d^2U/dy^2 - \beta)(U - c)^*|\Psi|^2}{|U - c|^2}\, dy$$

Note that the right-hand integrand has been multiplied above and below by $(U - c)^*$. Next replace c with $c_r + ic_i$ and take the conjugate as indicated, giving

$$\int_{-d}^{d} \left(\mu^2|\Psi|^2 + \left|\frac{d\Psi}{dy}\right|^2\right) dy = -\int_{-d}^{d} \frac{(d^2U/dy^2 - \beta)(U - c_r)|\Psi|^2}{|U - c|^2}\, dy - ic_i \int_{-d}^{d} \frac{(d^2U/dy^2 - \beta)|\Psi|^2}{|U - c|^2}\, dy$$

Equating real and imaginary parts in this equation requires the coefficient of i to vanish, since the other two integrals are real. Consequently,

$$c_i \int_{-d}^{d} \frac{(d^2U/dy^2 - \beta)|\Psi|^2}{|U - c|^2}\, dy = 0 \qquad (4\text{-}13)$$

If amplified waves exist, $c_i \neq 0$. Therefore (4-13) requires that the integral vanish. For this to occur, it is apparent that the *quantity* $d^2U/dy^2 - \beta$ *must change sign at least once in the region,* $-d < y < d$. Thus a *necessary condition* for *barotropic instability* is that at some value(s) of y, say y_k,

$$\left(\frac{d^2U}{dy^2} - \beta\right)_{yk} = 0 \qquad -d < y_k < d \qquad (4\text{-}14)$$

This theorem, originally derived by Lord Rayleigh (1880) for a nonrotating system, was extended by H. L. Kuo (1951) for meteorological applications to a rotating earth by the addition of the β term. Condition (4-14) may be written in the form

$$\frac{d}{dy}\left(-\frac{dU}{dy} + f\right) = 0 \qquad \text{or} \qquad \frac{d\zeta_a}{dy} = 0 \qquad \text{at } y_k$$

which states that the absolute vorticity must be a maximum or minimum at some point(s) in the basic current.

More information can be gained about barotropic instability by deriving an energy equation for the linear disturbances. Multiply (4-4) by $-\psi$ and integrate with respect to x and y:

$$\int_{-d}^{d} \overline{\left[-\psi\nabla \cdot \frac{\partial}{\partial t}\nabla\psi - U\frac{\psi\partial\nabla^2\psi}{\partial x} - \frac{\partial}{\partial x}\left(\frac{\psi^2}{2}\right)\left(\beta - \frac{d^2U}{dy^2}\right)\right]}\, dy = 0 \qquad (4\text{-}15)$$

where $\overline{(\ )} = L^{-1}\int_0^L (\ )\, dx$. The periodicity condition and the north-south boundary conditions are:

$$\begin{aligned} \psi(x + L,y,t) &= \psi(x,y,t) \\ \psi(x,d,t) &= \psi(x-d,t) = 0 \end{aligned} \qquad (4\text{-}16)$$

If the various terms in (4-15) are integrated by parts and conditions (4-16) are employed, the following energy equation can be derived:

$$\frac{d}{dt}\int_{-d}^{d} \frac{\overline{u'^2 + v'^2}}{2}\, dy = -\int_{-d}^{d} \overline{u'v'}\frac{dU}{dy}\, dy \qquad (4\text{-}17)$$

where $u' = -\partial\psi/\partial y$ and $v' = \partial\psi/\partial x$. The sign of the right-hand side of this equation can be determined by expressing ψ as follows

$$\psi(x,y,t) = \Psi(y,t)\cos[\mu x - \theta(y,t)] \qquad (4\text{-}18)$$

where Ψ is the amplitude and θ is the phase. The momentum flux $\overline{u'v'}$ can then be written

$$\overline{u'v'} = \overline{-\partial\psi/\partial y\ \partial\psi/\partial x} = \Psi^2\partial\theta/\partial y\ \mu\ \overline{\sin^2(\mu x - \theta)} +$$
$$\mu\partial\Psi/\partial y\ \Psi\ \overline{\sin(\mu x - \theta)\cos(\mu x - \theta)}$$

When trigonometric identities are introduced and the condition that L be a multiple of $2\pi\mu^{-1}$ is used, the momentum flux becomes

$$\overline{u'v'} = (\mu/2)\Psi^2\,\partial\theta/\partial y \qquad (4\text{-}19)$$

which shows that the sign of $\overline{u'v'}$ is determined by the phase tilt in latitude $(\partial\theta/\partial y)$ of the wave. With (4-19), the energy equation (4-17) can be written

$$\frac{d}{dt}\int_{-d}^{d}\frac{\overline{u'^2 + v'^2}}{2}\,dy = -\,\mu/2\int_{-d}^{d}\Psi^2\,\frac{\partial\theta}{\partial y}\frac{dU}{dy}\,dy \tag{4-20}$$

This equation shows that a disturbance will grow if it tilts opposite to the wind shear $[(\partial\theta/\partial y)(dU/dy) < 0]$ while it will damp if it tilts in the same sense as the wind shear $[(\partial\theta/\partial y)(dU/dy) > 0]$.

4-4 SOME UNSTABLE PROFILES

In this section, the stability of two wind profiles are considered that approximately represent certain atmospheric mean wind fields. A jet profile is given by

$$U = U_0\,\text{sech}^2(y/y_0) \tag{4-21}$$

and a shear zone profile is given by

$$U = U_0\tanh(y/y_0) \tag{4-22}$$

The jet profile (4-21) is known as the Bickley jet. These wind fields are shown in Figures 4-1 and 4-2. Westerly jets ($U_0 > 0$) similar to (4-21) are almost always present at upper levels in midlatitudes. Easterly jets ($U_0 < 0$) occur in the tropics at certain times of the year, and shear zones similar to (4-22) occur in the intertropical convergence zone.

Clearly, if $\beta = 0$, both wind profiles satisfy the necessary condition for instability (4-14) since the curvature changes sign in Figures 4-1 and 4-2. In general the necessary condition for instability can be written

$$\left(\frac{d^2U}{dy^2}\right)_{\max} > \beta \tag{4-23}$$

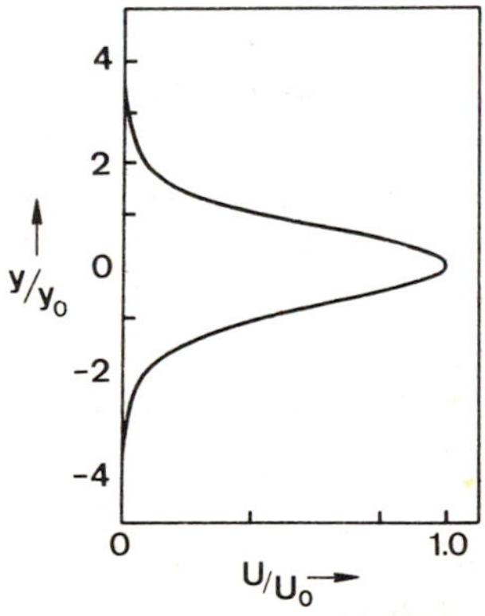

Figure 4.1 $U = U_0\,\text{sech}^2\,y/y_0$.

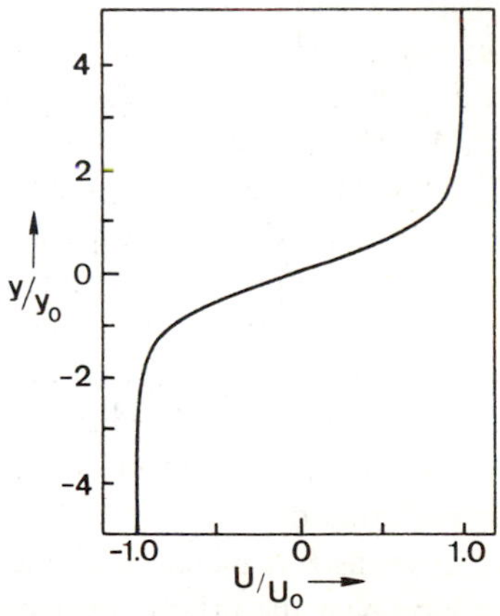

Figure 4.2 $U = U_0\tanh y/y_0$.

This condition may be evaluated for the profiles (4-21) and (4-22) by setting the third derivative to zero and solving for $(d^2U/dy^2)_{max}$. For the Bickley jet the necessary condition for instability is

$$-2 < b < 2/3 \tag{4-24}$$

where

$$b = \beta y_0^2/U_0 \tag{4-25}$$

The condition for the shear zone profile is

$$|b| < 4/(3\sqrt{3}) \tag{4-26}$$

The eigenvalue problem (4-5) has not been solved analytically for (4-21) or (4-22) except that some neutral solutions have been found for certain values of b and μy_0. Kuo (1973) has solved the eigenvalue problem for (4-21) and (4-22) by integrating (4-5) numerically and then searching for the c that satisfies the boundary conditions (4-6).

Figure 4-3 shows the dimensionless eigenvalues c_r/U_0 and $\delta = \mu y_0 \, c_i/U_0$, which were obtained by Kuo (1973) for the Bickley jet (4-21) with the boundaries moved to infinity ($d \rightarrow \infty$). Note that $b > 0$ corresponds to westerly flow while $b < 0$ corresponds to easterly flow. Figure 4-3a shows that the phase velocity for unstable waves is eastward for a westerly jet ($b > 0$) with the speed ranging up to about 50 percent of the maximum jet speed. For easterly flow the phase velocity is westward with the largest phase speeds exceeding 2½ times the maximum jet speed. This is a Rossby wave effect [see (4-9)], and note that for fixed b, c_r becomes more easterly as the longest wavelengths are approached ($\mu \rightarrow 0$). Figure 4-3b shows that the unstable region is confined within $-2 < b < 2/3$ as expected. The easterly jet is actually made more unstable by the presence of β. However, when the beta effect is large enough (through b), the motions are stable. The figure indicates that the most unstable wavelength decreases as $|b|$ increases for both westerlies and easterlies.

Figure 4-4 shows the dimensionless eigenvalues (which were obtained by Kuo (1973)) for the shear layer (4-22). With this profile, as is suggested by (4-26), the phase speeds and growth rates are independent of the direction of the basic current. Figure 4-4a indicates that the unstable waves all propagate towards the west except for the case when $b = 0$, which has $c_r = 0$. The maximum $|c_r|$ is about 90 percent of the maximum wind speed, and $|c_r|$ increases with the wavelength for the fixed b except in the corner near the origin. Figure 4-4b shows that the most unstable wave has a maximum growth rate at $b = 0$, and the growth rate decreases to 0 at $b = 4/(3\sqrt{3})$. The most unstable wavelength decreases as b is increased, which was also true for the Bickley jet. The unstable region near the origin is apparently caused by beta.

It is useful to examine the structure of the barotropically unstable waves.

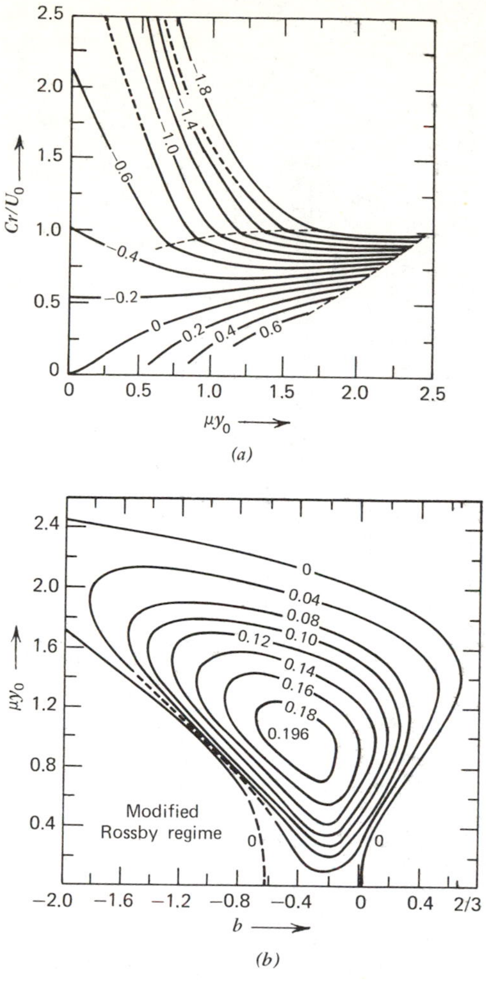

Figure 4.3 Eigenvalues for $U = U_0 \operatorname{sech}^2 (y/y_0)$ from Kuo (1973). (*a*) b as a function of μy_0 and c_r/U_0; (*b*) the growth rate δ as a function of b and the dimensionless wavenumber μy_0. (From H.L. Kuo, *Dynamics of Quasi-geostrophic Flows*. Academic Press, 1973.)

The results that will be shown were computed by Williams et al. (1971) for $U_0 > 0$, $b = 0$ and $d = 5y_0$. Figure 4-5 contains the amplitude and phase for the most unstable wave ($\mu y_0 = 0.9$) with the Bickley jet. The solution is written $\psi = P(y)\cos[\mu(x - c_r t) - \theta(y)]$ where $P(y)$ gives the amplitude structure and θ is the phase angle. In the figure it is seen that the maximum amplitude occurs at $y = 0$ and the amplitude decays smoothly to zero at the boundary. The phase

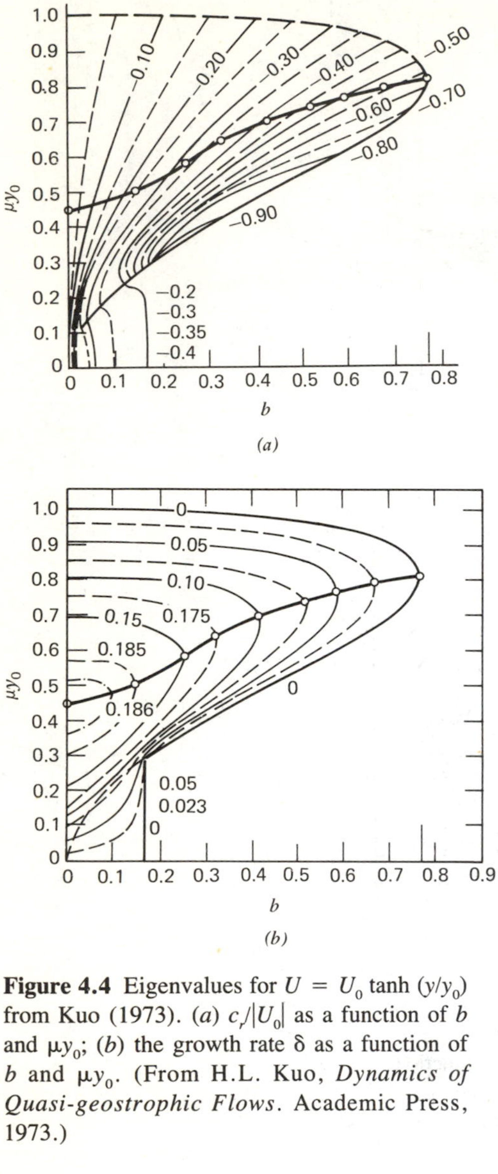

Figure 4.4 Eigenvalues for $U = U_0 \tanh (y/y_0)$ from Kuo (1973). (*a*) $c_r/|U_0|$ as a function of b and μy_0; (*b*) the growth rate δ as a function of b and μy_0. (From H.L. Kuo, *Dynamics of Quasi-geostrophic Flows*. Academic Press, 1973.)

shows that the wave tilts opposite to the shear, and (4-20) states that this phase relation is necessary if the disturbance is to grow. This general phase behavior can be expected for all barotropically unstable jets.

Figure 4-6 contains the amplitude and phase for the most unstable wave ($\mu y_0 = 0.45$) for $U_0 > 0$ and $b = 0$. This figure shows that the maximum amplitude occurs at $y = \pm y_0$, and there is a relative minimum at $y = 0$. The

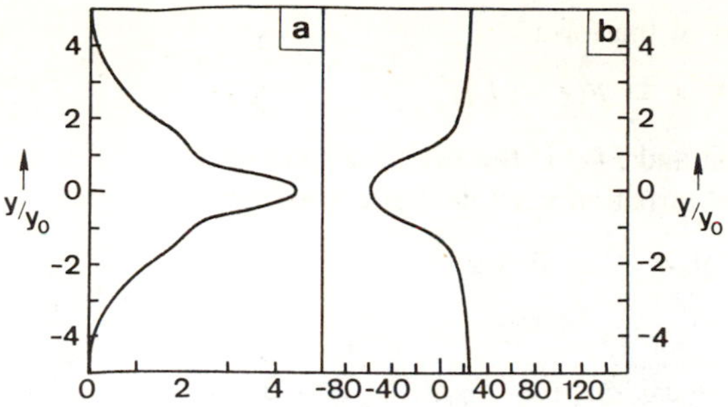

Figure 4.5 Structure of most unstable solution to Bickley jet. (*a*) amplitude P; (*b*) phase θ in degrees.

phast tilt is opposite to the shear, which is again necessary [see (4-29)] if the disturbance is to grow.

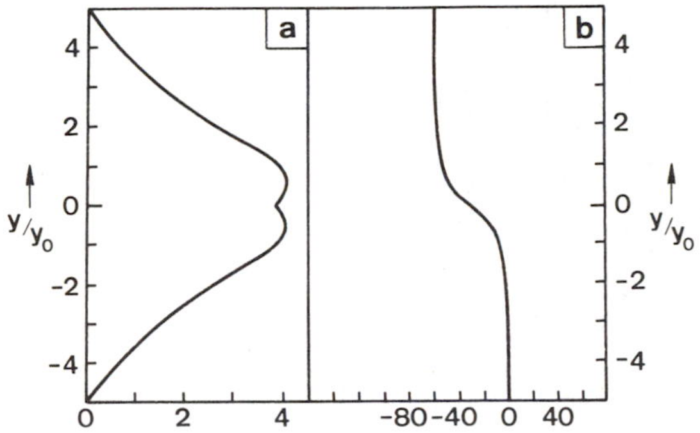

Figure 4.6 Same as Figure 4.5 except that the sheer layer profile (4.22) is used.

4-5 LINEAR SHEAR

It is natural to ask whether instability is possible in a current with linear horizontal shear. Obviously the approach would have to be different from that taken in the preceding treatment, because in the case of linear shear with $\beta = 0$ there are no *normal modes* to (4-5) which satisfy the boundary conditions (4-6).

An alternative approach is to treat the issue as an initial-value problem. To simplify the discussion, disregard the rotational effect of the earth (β term) in (4-4) and assume $U = U_0 + Sy$, in which case (4-4) reduces to

$$\frac{\partial \nabla^2 \psi}{\partial t} + U \frac{\partial \nabla^2 \psi}{\partial x} = 0 \tag{4-27}$$

The solution of this equation is of the form

$$\nabla^2\psi = F(x - Ut)$$

where F is an arbitrary function and $F(x)$ is the perturbation vorticity at $t = 0$.

Next consider an initial-perturbation velocity field consisting simply of

$$v = -v_0 \sin \mu x$$

then

$$\nabla^2\psi = \zeta = -\mu v_0 \cos \mu x \qquad \text{at} \qquad t = 0$$

and at time t,

$$\nabla^2\psi = -\mu v_0 \cos \mu(x - Ut) \tag{4-28}$$

To find the stream function, assume it has the same functional form as the vorticity, that is,

$$\psi = A \cos \mu(x - Ut)$$

Then

$$\nabla^2\psi = -A\mu^2 \cos \mu(x - Ut) - As^2t^2\mu^2 \cos \mu(x - Ut)$$

Equating the right sides of this equation and (4-28) determines the value of A; hence,

$$\psi = \frac{v_0 \cos \mu(x - Ut)}{\mu(1 + S^2t^2)} \tag{4-29}$$

The total velocity components are:

$$u = U - \frac{\partial\psi}{\partial y} = U - \frac{v_0\mu St \sin \mu(x - Ut)}{\mu(1 + S^2t^2)}$$

$$v = \frac{\partial\psi}{\partial x} = -\frac{v_0 \sin \mu(x - Ut)}{1 + S^2t^2}$$

It is apparent that ψ and v are inversely proportional to the square of t, and u varies inversely as the first power of t. Since the perturbation moves with velocity, $U = U_0 + Sy$, the waves become tilted in the direction of the shear as well as being damped with time. Once the waves begin to tilt in the direction of the wind shear, the energy equation (4-20) shows that they will be damped as is seen here. This solution can also be written in terms of a continuous spectrum of normal modes, $c(y') = U(y')$, which have singular vorticity at $y = y'$ and zero vorticity elsewhere [Case (1960)]. The solution is written as an integral of these functions times the initial vorticity.

The normal mode solutions for unstable mean wind fields often do not form a complete set. Hence, they cannot be used to construct a general solution for all reasonable initial conditions, as can be done with the Rossby wave solution (4-8). Case (1960), using the initial value approach, found that in addition to the discrete normal modes obtained from (4-5) and (4-6), continuous modes similar to those described above were also required for a general solution. These continuous modes have phase speeds that are equal to the mean wind at a certain point, and when smooth initial conditions are used they lead to damping which is similar to that obtained above. Thus it can be expected that after a certain period of time the continuous spectrum modes will disappear leaving only the nondamped discrete modes.

4-6 BAROTROPIC EFFECTS IN THE ATMOSPHERE

The analysis in this chapter shows that barotropic instability can occur when the gradient of the absolute vorticity changes sign. The presence of beta tends to stabilize midlatitude westerly jets, although easterly jets may be destabilized under certain conditions by the presence of beta. If no unstable waves are possible, it is likely that disturbances will be damped by the continuous spectrum effects [Case (1960)]. The energy equation shows that a disturbance will be damped if it tilts in the same sense as the mean wind, but that it will be amplified if it tilts in the opposite direction. South of the middle latitude jet most disturbances tilt SW-NE so that they lose energy barotropically to the mean flow. This is also shown by observations of the momentum flux $\overline{u'v'}$. Thus in the mean it appears that midlatitude disturbances are barotropically damped and by losing energy to the mean flow, they help maintain it against friction. However, barotropic instability must occur for short periods when jets become too sharp. In the tropics barotropic instability is more common due to the fact that easterly jets are more unstable and also because the heating (which generates the mean flow) tends to have a smaller horizontal scale.

4-7 BAROCLINIC INSTABILITY

Baroclinic instability, which arises from the vertical wind shear in a rotating atmosphere, was first investigated by Charney (1947) and Eady (1949). The quasi-geostrophic equations may be used to discuss this instability. The potential vorticity equation (3-64) may be written

$$\left(\frac{\partial}{\partial t} + \mathbf{k} \times \nabla\psi^* \cdot \nabla\right) q = 0 \tag{4-30}$$

where

$$q = \nabla^2\psi^* + e^Z \frac{\partial}{\partial Z}\left(\frac{f_0^2 e^{-Z}}{\Gamma} \frac{\partial\psi^*}{\partial Z}\right) + \beta y \tag{4-31}$$

is the *potential vorticity*. Here $\psi^* = f_0^{-1}\phi$ is the geostrophic streamfunction and Γ is the static stability (3-47). The first law of thermodynamics, which is needed for the boundary conditions, takes the form:

$$\left(\frac{\partial}{\partial t} + \mathbf{k} \times \nabla\psi^* \cdot \nabla\right)\frac{\partial\psi^*}{\partial Z} + f_0^{-1}\,\Gamma\,\dot{Z} = 0 \qquad (4\text{-}32)$$

The Z coordinate is convenient for linear instability studies because it is very close to the height coordinate and therefore Γ is constant if the lapse rate $-\partial T/\partial z$ is constant. A constant static stability in pressure coordinates is quite unrealistic.

The potential vorticity equation will be linearized with

$$\psi^*(x,y,Z,t) = \overline{\psi}(y,Z) + \psi(x,y,Z,t) \qquad (4\text{-}33)$$

where $|\psi|/|\overline{\psi}|$ is assumed to be small. The mean wind is given by $U = -\partial\overline{\psi}/\partial y$. When (4-33) is used in (4-30) it reduces to

$$\left(\frac{\partial}{\partial t} + U\frac{\partial}{\partial x}\right)q' + \frac{\partial\psi}{\partial x}\frac{\partial\overline{q}}{\partial y} = 0 \qquad (4\text{-}34)$$

where

$$q' = \nabla^2\psi + e^Z\frac{\partial}{\partial Z}\left(\frac{f_0^2\,e^{-Z}}{\Gamma}\frac{\partial\psi}{\partial Z}\right) \qquad (4\text{-}35)$$

and

$$\frac{\partial\overline{q}}{\partial y} = \beta - \frac{\partial^2 U}{\partial y^2} - e^Z\frac{\partial}{\partial Z}\left(\frac{f_0^2\,e^{-Z}}{\Gamma}\frac{\partial U}{\partial Z}\right) \qquad (4\text{-}36)$$

Equation 4-36 includes both barotropic (second term) and baroclinic (third term) effects. The linearized first law of thermodynamics is

$$\left(\frac{\partial}{\partial t} + U\frac{\partial}{\partial x}\right)\frac{\partial\psi}{\partial Z} - \frac{\partial\psi}{\partial x}\frac{\partial U}{\partial Z} + f_0^{-1}\Gamma\dot{Z} = 0 \qquad (4\text{-}37)$$

where $\dot{Z}$ is the perturbation vertical motion. This equation is required for the vertical boundary conditions.

Now introduce $\psi = \Psi(y,Z)e^{i\mu(x-ct)}$ into (4-34), which gives

$$(U - c)\left[\frac{\partial^2\Psi}{\partial y^2} + e^Z\frac{\partial}{\partial Z}\left(\frac{f_0^2\,e^{-Z}}{\Gamma}\frac{\partial\Psi}{\partial Z}\right) - \mu^2\Psi\right] + \frac{\partial\overline{q}}{\partial y}\Psi = 0 \qquad (4\text{-}38)$$

The first law of thermodynamics becomes

$$(U - c)\frac{\partial\Psi}{\partial Z} - \frac{\partial U}{\partial Z}\Psi + f_0^{-1}\Gamma W = 0 \qquad (4\text{-}39)$$

where $\dot{Z} = W(y,z)e^{i\mu(x-ct)}$. Charney and Stern (1962) and Pedlosky (1964a) have derived a necessary condition for instability similar to (4-14), which depends on $\partial\bar{q}/\partial y$ in the interior and $\partial U/\partial Z$ on the upper and lower boundaries. This theorem is not as useful as (4-14) because in general it has three terms, but it has been used for stratospheric problems [see Holton (1975)].

4-8 BAROCLINIC INSTABILITY WITH LINEAR SHEAR

The simplest baroclinic instability solution with a continuous wind profile was derived by Eady (1949). He made the following simplifying assumptions:

1. $\beta = 0$.
2. Boussinesq ($e^{-Z} \approx$ constant).
3. Static stability constant (Γ = const). (4-40)
4. Solution independent of y ($\partial/\partial y = 0$).
5. Upper boundary condition, lid at $Z = 1$ ($W = 0$).

The wind profile is a linear function of Z:

$$U = SZ \tag{4-41}$$

where S is constant. With the use of (4-40) the mean potential vorticity gradient (4-36) becomes

$$\frac{\partial \bar{q}}{\partial y} = 0 \tag{4-42}$$

and the potential vorticity equation reduces to

$$(U - c)\left(\frac{f_0^2}{\Gamma}\frac{\partial^2 \Psi}{\partial Z^2} - \mu^2 \Psi\right) = 0 \tag{4-43}$$

The solution to this equation may be written

$$\Psi = A \sinh\left(\frac{Z}{\varepsilon^{1/2}}\right) + B \cosh\left(\frac{Z}{\varepsilon^{1/2}}\right) \tag{4-44}$$

where $\varepsilon = f_0^2/\mu^2\Gamma$ [see (3-48)]. The boundary conditions $W = 0$ at $Z = 0,1$ can be written from (4-39) as

$$(U - c)\frac{d\Psi}{dZ} - S\Psi = 0 \qquad \text{at } Z = 0,1 \tag{4-45}$$

Differentiate (4-44) and substitute into (4-45):

$$-c\varepsilon^{-1/2} A - SB = 0 \tag{4-46}$$

$$(S - c)\varepsilon^{-1/2}[A \cosh(\varepsilon^{-1/2}) + B \sinh(\varepsilon^{-1/2})] - S[A \sinh(\varepsilon^{-1/2}) + B \cosh(\varepsilon^{-1/2})] = 0$$

A and B will not be identically zero if the determinant of the coefficients vanishes; this leads to the following equation for the phase velocity:

$$c^2 - Sc + S^2(\varepsilon^{1/2} \coth \varepsilon^{-1/2} - \varepsilon) = 0 \tag{4-47}$$

Solve (4-47) for c and rearrange:

$$\begin{aligned} c &= \frac{S}{2} \pm S[1/4 - (\varepsilon^{1/2} \coth \varepsilon^{-1/2} - \varepsilon)]^{1/2} \\ &= \frac{S}{2} \pm S\varepsilon^{1/2} \left\{ \left[\frac{\varepsilon^{-1/2}}{2} - \tanh\left(\frac{\varepsilon^{-1/2}}{2}\right)\right] \left[\frac{\varepsilon^{-1/2}}{2} - \coth\left(\frac{\varepsilon^{-1/2}}{2}\right)\right]\right\}^{1/2} \end{aligned} \tag{4-48}$$

The quantity under the radical becomes negative when

$$\frac{\varepsilon^{-1/2}}{2} < 1.20 \tag{4-49}$$

In this case c becomes complex and the solution becomes unstable. Using the form (3-48), $\varepsilon = L^2/L_R{}^2$, where $L_R = \Gamma^{1/2}/f_0$, the instability requirement (4-49) can be rewritten as

$$\frac{\mathcal{L}}{2\pi} = L > \frac{L_R}{2.40} \tag{4-50}$$

When this condition is satisfied the growth rate becomes

$$\mu c_i = \pm \frac{S}{L_R} \left\{ \left[\frac{\varepsilon^{-1/2}}{2} - \tanh\left(\frac{\varepsilon^{-1/2}}{2}\right)\right] \left[\coth\left(\frac{\varepsilon^{-1/2}}{2}\right) - \frac{\varepsilon^{-1/2}}{2}\right]\right\}^{1/2} \tag{4-51}$$

Thus the growth rate is directly proportional to the vertical wind shear S and all waves are unstable if $S \neq 0$, provided L satisfies (4-50). The maximum growth rate occurs for

$$L = \frac{L_R}{1.92} \tag{4-52}$$

This analysis indicates that the scale for baroclinic instability is $L \sim L_R$, or that $\varepsilon \sim 1$. Since it is observed that $\varepsilon \sim 1$ for synoptic scale disturbances it is reasonable to conclude that their principal energy source is baroclinic instability.

The phase speed of the unstable waves is

$$c_r = \frac{S}{2} \tag{4-53}$$

which is reasonable due to the vertical symmetry in the model. The unstable eigensolutions have symmetry about $Z = 1/2$ and the vertical structure is qualitatively similar to observed synoptic scale disturbances.

It is important to point out that this form of instability is closely tied to the upper and lower boundary conditions (4-45). If these conditions were replaced by $\Psi = 0$ at these boundaries these unstable waves could not exist.

This problem is an example of the situation mentioned earlier with barotropic instability, where the discrete normal modes do not form a complete set. In this case there is just one pair of solutions for each μ. Pedlosky (1964b) has treated this problem with the initial value approach, and he found continuous spectrum solutions which damp smooth initial disturbances.

Charney (1947) used the same wind profile that Eady used, but also included some effects that Eady left out. Charney included the beta effect, placed the upper boundary at infinity and did not make the Boussinesq approximation. In this case the mean potential vorticity gradient (4-36) becomes

$$\frac{\partial \bar{q}}{\partial y} = \beta + f_0^2 S/\Gamma \tag{4-54}$$

where Γ is constant. For mean westerly flow ($S > 0$) the potential vorticity gradient is a positive constant, whereas with Eady's model this gradient is zero. The eigenvalue problem (4-38) now becomes

$$(SZ - c)\left[\left(\frac{f_0^2}{\Gamma}\right)\left(\frac{d^2\Psi}{dZ^2} - \frac{d\Psi}{dZ}\right) - \mu^2\Psi\right] + (\beta + f_0^2 S/\Gamma)\Psi = 0 \tag{4-55}$$

This equation is much more difficult to solve than (4-43), because $\partial\bar{q}/\partial y$ is not zero. This equation can be transformed into the confluent-hypergeometric equation. An important parameter in the transformed equation is

$$r = \frac{\Gamma(\beta + Sf_0^2/\Gamma)}{f_0^2 S(1 + 4\Gamma f_0^{-2}\mu^2)^{1/2}} \tag{4-56}$$

It is very difficult to solve for c when the confluent hypergeometric functions are substituted into the transformed boundary conditions. This problem has been treated by Gambo (1950), Kuo (1952), Green (1960), and Burger (1962), and Kuo (1973) has provided a review of the problem. Figure 4-7 shows the stability diagram that was obtained by Green (1960) by numerical integration, with a lid at $Z = 1$. The abscissa is the wavelength $1/\mu$, the ordinate is the vertical wind shear S and the isolines are curves of constant growth rate μc_i. The upper thick line is the neutral curve $r = 1$, which was found by Charney, Gambo, and Kuo. The dashed line gives the maximum growth rate. Burger showed that instability occurs for all values of r, except for positive integers that are neutral curves. The thick lines near the abscissa correspond to $r = 2$ and $r = 3$.

This is a very unusual stability problem because the neutral curves do not separate unstable regions from stable or neutral regions. However the growth rates outside of the line marked 0.1 are so small that such waves would not exist in the presence of friction. For the larger values of S, the most unstable portion of the diagram is similar to Eady's result.

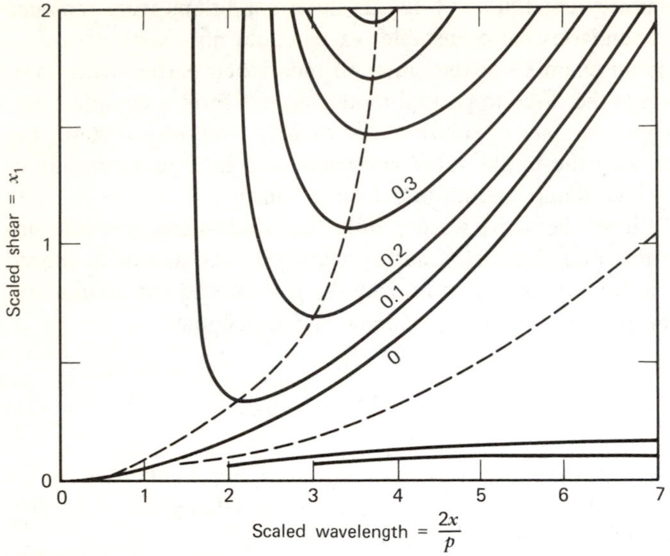

Figure 4.7 Stability diagram for the Charney model with a lid at Z = 1 as computed by Green (1960). (From J.S.A. Green, "A Problem in Baroclinic Stability." *Royal Meteorological Society,* 1960.)

4-9 TWO-LEVEL MODEL

Since the stability properties of the Charney model are so difficult to analyze analytically, it is useful to examine a model which has a greatly simplified vertical structure. The "two-level" model divides the atmosphere into four layers and specifies the wind at two intermediate levels and the vertical motion at the middle level. The mathematical development is very simple, and the results are consistent with Charney's model. This analysis will be carried out in pressure coordinates to simplify application to the troposphere. The vorticity equation (3-74) and the first law of thermodynamics (3-75) may be written:

$$\left(\frac{\partial}{\partial t} + \mathbf{k} \times \nabla\psi^* \cdot \nabla\right)(\nabla^2\psi^* + \beta y) - f_0\, \partial\omega/\partial p = 0 \qquad (4\text{-}57)$$

$$\left(\frac{\partial}{\partial t} + \mathbf{k} \times \nabla\psi^* \cdot \nabla\right) \partial\psi^*/\partial p + (\sigma/f_0)\omega = 0 \qquad (4\text{-}58)$$

In formulating a two-level model it is more convenient to finite difference (4-57) and (4-58), and then combine them to form a finite difference potential vorticity equation directly. With the first procedure the upper and lower boundary conditions can be included automatically.

First, linearize (4-57) and (4-58) by setting:

$$\left.\begin{aligned} \psi^* &= -U(p)y + \psi(x,p,t) \\ \omega &= \omega'(x,p,t) \end{aligned}\right\} \tag{4-59}$$

These equations describe a basic zonal flow $U(p)$, plus a disturbance field that is independent of y. The substitution of (4-59) into (4-57) and (4-58) leads to:

$$\left(\frac{\partial}{\partial t} + U\frac{\partial}{\partial x}\right)\frac{\partial^2\psi}{\partial x^2} + \beta\frac{\partial\psi}{\partial x} - f_0\,\partial\omega'/\partial p = 0 \tag{4-60}$$

$$\left(\frac{\partial}{\partial t} + U\frac{\partial}{\partial x}\right)\frac{\partial\psi}{\partial p} - \frac{dU}{dp}\frac{\partial\psi}{\partial x} + (\sigma/f_0)\omega' = 0 \tag{4-61}$$

These equations are linear even when ψ and ω' are not small.

The vertical structure of the two-level model is shown in Figure 4-8. The boundary condition $\omega' = 0$ is enforced at the surface $p = p_s$ and at the tropopause $p = p_T$. The latter condition is a reasonable approximation because the large static stability in the stratosphere tends to make the vertical motion small.

Now, apply the vorticity equation (4-60) at levels 1 and 3 and use centered finite differences on the last term (see Chapter 5):

$$\left(\frac{\partial}{\partial t} + U_1\frac{\partial}{\partial x}\right)\frac{\partial^2\psi_1}{\partial x^2} + \beta\frac{\partial\psi_1}{\partial x} - f_0\frac{\omega'_2}{\Delta p} = 0 \tag{4-62}$$

$$\left(\frac{\partial}{\partial t} + U_3\frac{\partial}{\partial x}\right)\frac{\partial^2\psi_3}{\partial x^2} + \beta\frac{\partial\psi_3}{\partial x} + f_0\frac{\omega'_2}{\Delta p} = 0 \tag{4-63}$$

The remaining equation is obtained by applying the first law of thermodynamics at level 2:

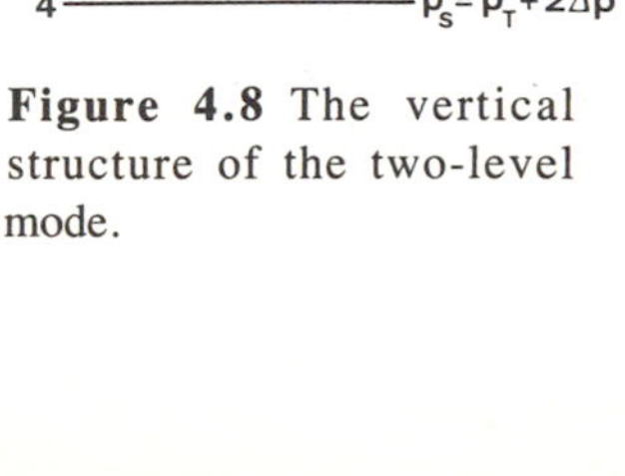

Figure 4.8 The vertical structure of the two-level mode.

$$\left[\frac{\partial}{\partial t} + \left(\frac{U_1 + U_3}{2}\right)\frac{\partial}{\partial x}\right](\psi_1 - \psi_3) - \left(\frac{U_1 - U_3}{2}\right)\left(\frac{\partial\psi_1}{\partial x} + \frac{\partial\psi_3}{\partial x}\right) - \left(\frac{\Delta p\sigma_2}{f_0}\right)\omega'_2 = 0 \quad (4\text{-}64)$$

This equation has been multiplied by $-\Delta p$ and certain quantities have been obtained by averaging the values at levels 1 and 3. Equations 4-62, 4-63 and 4-64 are three equations in the unknowns ψ_1, ψ_3, and ω'_2.

Before solving these equations, it is useful to obtain energy equations which can be used to interpret the solutions. Multiply (4-62) by $-\psi_1$, (4-63) by $-\psi_3$, add and average with respect to x giving:

$$\frac{d}{dt}\left[\frac{\overline{(\partial\psi_1/\partial x)^2 + (\partial\psi_3/\partial x)^2}}{2}\right] = -(f_0/\Delta p)\,\overline{\omega'_2(\psi_1 - \psi_3)} \quad (4\text{-}65)$$

The term on the left is the time rate of change of the disturbance kinetic energy. A potential energy equation is obtained by multiplying (4-64) by $\lambda(\psi_1 - \psi_3)$ and averaging in x:

$$\frac{d}{dt}\left[\frac{\overline{\lambda(\psi_1 - \psi_3)^2}}{4}\right] = \frac{\lambda}{4}(U_1 - U_3)\,\overline{(\psi_1 - \psi_3)\left(\frac{\partial\psi_1}{\partial x} + \frac{\partial\psi_3}{\partial x}\right)} + (f_0/\Delta p)\,\overline{\omega'_2(\psi_1 - \psi_3)} \quad (4\text{-}66)$$

where

$$\lambda = 2f_0^2/(\Delta p^2\sigma_2) \quad (4\text{-}67)$$

Note that $\psi_1 - \psi_3$ is proportional to the vertically averaged perturbation temperature.The left side of (4-66) is the time rate of change of the disturbance available potential energy. In Section 1-11 it was shown that the available potential energy could be approximated by the temperature variance on isobaric surfaces divided by the mean static stability. The last term in (4-65) represents the conversion from disturbance available potential energy to disturbance kinetic energy, since it occurs with opposite sign in (4-66). This term will be positive if the warmer air ($\psi_1 - \psi_3 > 0$) is rising ($\omega_2 < 0$) and the cooler air ($\psi_1 - \psi_3 < 0$) is sinking ($\omega_2 > 0$). This process converts potential energy to kinetic energy since it lowers the center of gravity of the atmosphere. The presence of a geostrophic vertical wind shear $U_1 - U_3$ implies a mean horizontal temperature gradient in the y or north-south direction. The middle term in (4-66) represents the conversion from mean available potential energy (associated with $U_1 - U_3$) to disturbance available potential energy. This term is positive when the northward moving ($(\partial\psi_1/\partial x + \partial\psi_3/\partial x)/2 > 0$) air is warm ($\psi_1 - \psi_3 > 0$), and the southward moving $[(\partial\psi_1/\partial x + \partial\psi_3/\partial x)/2 < 0]$ air is cool $(\psi_1 - \psi_3 < 0)$. If y boundaries are present this process will reduce $U_1 - U_3$.

The following wave solutions will be used in the system of equations:

$$\psi_1 = \Psi_1 e^{i\mu(x-ct)}$$

$$\psi_3 = \Psi_3 e^{i\mu(x-ct)} \tag{4-68}$$

$$\omega'_2 = (\Delta p f_0^{-1})\, W e^{i\mu(x-ct)}$$

Substituting (4-68) into (4-62), (4-63) and (4-64) yield

$$\mu[\beta - \mu^2(U_1 - c)]\Psi_1 + iW = 0 \tag{4-69a}$$

$$\mu[\beta - \mu^2(U_3 - c)]\Psi_3 - iW = 0 \tag{4-69b}$$

$$\mu[U_3 - c]\Psi_1 - \mu[U_1 - c]\Psi_3 + i2W/\lambda = 0 \tag{4-69c}$$

If the amplitudes Ψ_1, Ψ_3, and W are to be nonzero then the determinant of the coefficients of (4-69) must vanish. This condition leads to the following quadratic equation for c:

$$2\mu^2(\mu^2 + \lambda)c^2 + [2\beta(2\mu^2 + \lambda) - 2\mu^2(\mu^2 + \lambda)(U_1 + U_3)]c$$

$$+2\beta^2 - \beta(2\mu^2 + \lambda)(U_1 + U_3) + 2\mu^4 U_1 U_3 + \mu^2\lambda(U_1^2 + U_3^2) = 0$$

The following formula for c can be obtained with the use of the quadratic formula:

$$c = (U_1 + U_3)/2 - \frac{\beta(2\mu^2 + \lambda)}{2\mu^2(\mu^2 + \lambda)} \pm \frac{[\lambda^2\beta^2 - \mu^4(\lambda^2 - \mu^4)(U_1 - U_3)]^{1/2}}{2\mu^2(\mu^2 + \lambda)} \tag{4-70}$$

The solution is unstable when c is complex, which occurs when the quantity under the square root sign in (4-70) becomes negative. In fact, this will occur when μ^4 is less than λ^2 and $(U_1 - U_3)^2$ is sufficiently large. If the radical is real, neutral solutions are found. In a stability diagram with coordinates of wavelength (μ^{-1}) and vertical shear $(U_1 - U_3)$, the unstable region is bounded by the curve defined by the vanishing of the radical. This condition can be written

$$(U_1 - U_3)^2 = \frac{\lambda^2\beta^2}{\mu^4(\lambda^2 - \mu^4)} \tag{4-71}$$

and this curve is given in Figure 4-9 for fixed λ and β. The unstable region is bounded on the short wave side by the asymptote

$$\mu^{-1} = \lambda^{-1/2} = \Delta p \sigma_2^{1/2}/(f_0/\sqrt{2}) \qquad (4\text{-}72)$$

For long waves where $\mu^2 << \lambda$, (4-71) reduces to

$$|U_1 - U_3| = \beta/\mu^2 \qquad (4\text{-}73)$$

At intermediate wavelengths (4-71) has a minimum that can be found by setting its derivative to zero. The minimum

$$(U_1 - U_3)_{\min} = 2\beta/\lambda = \beta \frac{\Delta p^2 \sigma_2}{2f_0^2} \qquad (4\text{-}74)$$

occurs at $\mu^{-1} = 2^{1/4}\lambda^{-1/2}$. The stability properties of the two-level quasi-geostrophic model are the same as those for a quasi-geostrophic model that has two incompressible homogeneous layers [Phillips (1951)] if the parameters are properly equated.

The short-wave cutoff (4-72), is related to the static stability and the long-wave stability is related to the beta effect since (4-73) is similar to the beta term in the Rossby wave formula. The minimum unstable vertical shear is proportional to beta times the static stability. It is interesting to note that this instability disappears when the earth's rotation is set to zero. For the special case $\beta = 0$, the instability requirement can be written

$$\mu^{-1} > \Delta p \sigma_2^{1/2}/(f_0\sqrt{2}) \qquad U_1 \neq U_3 \qquad (4\text{-}75a)$$

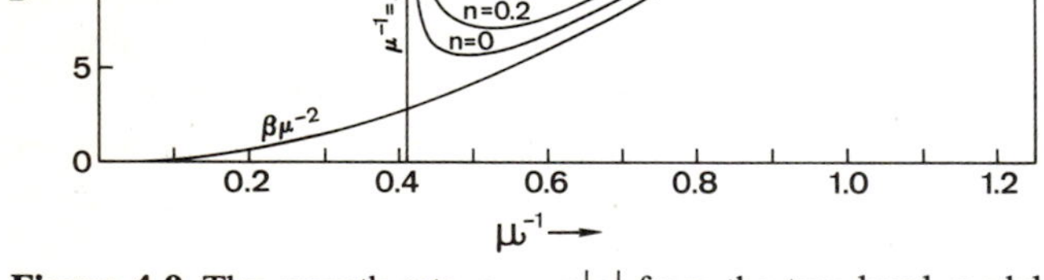

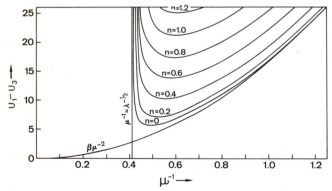

Figure 4.9 The growth rate $n = \mu|c_i|$ from the two-level model as a function of $U_1 - U_3$ and μ^{-1} for $\lambda = 5.88 \times 10^{-12}$ m^{-2} and $\beta = 1.67 \times 10^{11}$ m^{-1}s^{-1}. The units for μ^{-1}, $U_1 - U_3$ and n are 10^6 m, m s^{-1} and 10^{-5} s^{-1}, respectively.

This can be compared with the corresponding condition (4-50) for the Eady solution:

$$\mu^{-1} > \Gamma^{1/2}/(f_0\, 2.4) \qquad S = dU/dZ \neq 0 \tag{4-75b}$$

These conditions clearly have the same general form. For the general case when $\beta \neq 0$, the stability diagram for the two-level model (Figure 4-9) is superficially quite different from the diagram for the Charney continuous model (Figure 4-7). In the latter all of the diagram is unstable except for certain curves where the solution is neutral. However, the growth rates over much of the continuous diagram are very small. If friction were present many of those waves would be damped. When a certain threshold growth rate is specified, the effectively unstable region would be enclosed by one of the lines of constant growth rate in Figure 4-7. These have shapes that are similar to the stability boundary (4-71) in Figure 4-9 for the two-level model. In this sense the two-level model gives the gross behavior of synoptic scale baroclinically unstable waves. The most unstable wavelength, that is about 4000 or 5000 km, is the scale of the observed synoptic scale waves.

4-10 WAVE STRUCTURE

In this section the structure of waves in the two-level model will be determined, and this will allow the terms in the energy equations (4-65) and (4-66) to be evaluated. Equation 4-70 has two solutions that will be indicated by c^+ and c^-, which correspond to the $+$ and $-$ signs in the equation. In Section 2-6 the general solution for the shallow-water equations was written in terms of the three phase speeds and eigensolutions. For the two-level model the general solution is

$$\psi_1 = Re[a^+\Psi_1^{\;+}e^{i\mu(x-c^+t)} + a^-\Psi_1^{\;-}e^{i\mu(x-c^-t)}] \tag{4-76a}$$

$$\psi_3 = Re[a^+\Psi_3^{\;+}e^{i\mu(x-c^+t)} + a^-\Psi_3^{\;-}e^{i\mu(x-c^-t)}] \tag{4-76b}$$

$$\omega'_2 = \Delta p f_0^{-1} Re[a^+W^+e^{i\mu(x-c^+t)} + a^-W^-e^{i\mu(x-c^-t)}] \tag{4-76c}$$

where *Re* indicates the real part of a complex number. Euler's formula

$$e^{ix} = \cos x + i \sin x \tag{4-77}$$

is useful in evaluating (4-76) since any complex number can be written $\Psi = |\Psi|e^{i\theta}$. Equation 4-76c is not required because ω'_2 can be related diagnostically by the omega equation to ψ_1 and ψ_3. The relationship between the amplitudes for c^+ or c^- can be found from the set of equations (4-69). In particular, adding (4-69a) and (4-69b) leads to

$$\Psi_1^{\pm} = -\frac{c^{\pm} - (U_3 - \beta/\mu^2)}{c^{\pm} - (U_1 - \beta/\mu^2)}\Psi_3^{\pm} \tag{4-78}$$

The vertical motion can be found from (4-69b) in the form

$$W^{\pm} = -i\mu^3[c^{\pm} - (U_3 - \beta/\mu^2)]\ \Psi_3^{\pm} \tag{4-79}$$

If the amplitude and phase of ψ_1 and ψ_3 are given initially, a^+ and a^- may be found by using these initial conditions in (4-76a) and (4-76b).

The neutral waves that are outside the unstable region in Figure 4-9 have real c's and the satisfy $c^+ > c^-$. Equation 4-78 shows that $\Psi_1^{\pm}$ and $\Psi_3^{\pm}$ are in phase or 180° out of phase since the coefficient on the right-hand side is entirely real. The vertical motion is 90° out of phase with the streamfunction field as may be seen from (4-79). Because of these phase relationships, the energy conversion terms on the right sides of (4-65) and (4-66) are zero for either of these neutral waves. If the solution sums (4-76a,b,c) are used, the conversions will vary periodically about zero.

For the short neutral waves, terms of the order of β/μ^2 can be dropped in (4-70). This leads to the condition

$$c^{\pm} = (U_1 + U_3)/2 \pm ½\left[\frac{\mu^2 - \lambda}{\mu^2 + \lambda}(U_1 - U_3)^2\right]^{½} \tag{4-80}$$

In this case (4-78) gives

$$\Psi_1^+/\Psi_3^+ > 1 \qquad \Psi_1^-/\Psi_2^- < 1$$

Thus the larger amplitude occurs at the level where the phase speed is nearest to the mean wind speed. By writing $W = |W|e^{-i\theta}$, where θ is the phase at $t = 0$, and by choosing $\Psi_3 > 0$, it can be shown from (4-79) and (4-80) that $\theta = 90°$. This means that there is rising motion ($\omega < 0$) ahead of the trough and sinking motion ($\omega > 0$) behind it. This wave structure is found for the neutral waves of the Eady model from Section 4-8. The general vertical structure found here is similar to that which comes from the equivalent barotropic model (see Section 7-1-1).

When there is no vertical shear, $U_1 - U_3$ can be set to zero in (4-70), which leads to

$$\begin{aligned} c^+ &= (U_1 + U_3)/2 - \beta/(\mu^2 + \lambda) \\ c^- &= (U_1 + U_3)/2 - \beta/\mu^2 \end{aligned} \tag{4-81}$$

The c^- solution is a pure Rossby wave [see (4-10)], since (4-79) and (4-69c) yield $W^- = 0$ and $\Psi_1^- = \Psi_3^-$. The c^+ solution is an internal Rossby wave because (4-78) and (4-79) give $\Psi_1^+ = -\Psi_3^+$ and $W^+ \neq 0$. This behavior can be expected for the longer waves when $(U_1 - U_3)^2$ is sufficiently small.

In the unstable region of Figure 4-9 the phase speeds may be written:

$$c\pm = c_r \pm i\, n/\mu$$

where

$$c_r = (U_1 + U_3)/2 - \beta(2\mu^2 + \lambda)/[2\mu^2(\mu^2 + \lambda)]$$
$$n = [\mu^4(\lambda^2 - \mu^4)(U_1 - U_3)^2 - \lambda^2\beta^2]^{1/2}/[2\mu(\mu^2 + \lambda)] \tag{4-82}$$

The solutions can now be written

$$\psi_{1,3} = Re[a^+\Psi_{1,3}^+\, e^{i\mu(x - c_r t)}\, e^{nt} + a^-\Psi_{1,3}^-\, e^{i\mu(x - c_r t)}\, e^{-nt}] \tag{4-83}$$

Except for the special case $a^+ = 0$, the growing solution will rapidly dominate the damped solution. For this reason it is desirable to examine in detail the structure of the growing solution.

When c is complex the coefficients on the right-hand sides of (4-78) and (4-79) will be complex, and therefore the phase structure of the unstable waves will be different from the structure of the neutral waves, which were discussed earlier. Equations 4-78 and 4-79 are rewritten as follows with the use of (4-82):

$$\Psi_1^\pm = -\frac{\{c_r - [(U_1 + U_3)/2 - \beta/\mu^2]\}^2 - (U_1 - U_3)^2/4 + n^2/\mu^2 \mp in(U_1 - U_3)/\mu}{[c_r - (U_1 - \beta/\mu^2)]^2 + n^2/\mu^2}\Psi_3^\pm \tag{4-84}$$

$$W^\pm = \mu^3\{\pm\, n/\mu - i[c_r - (U_3 - \beta/\mu^2)]\}\,\Psi_3^\pm \tag{4-85}$$

Note that the phase structure of the waves reverses between the growing and damping solutions. These equations can be used to compute the structure of the amplified or damped wave. The perturbation temperature at level 2 may be computed from the integral of the hydrostatic equation as follows:

$$T_2' = f_0\,(\psi_1 - \psi_3)/[R\, \ell n(p_3/p_1)] \tag{4-86}$$

Now as an example the structure of the amplified solution will be computed with the following typical values: $f_0 = 10^{-4}\text{sec}^{-1}$, $\beta = 1.67 \times 10^{-11}\text{m}^{-1}\text{sec}^{-1}$, $\mathcal{L} = 2\pi/\mu = 4000$ km, $\lambda = 5.88 \times 10^{-12}\text{m}^{-2}$, $p_s = 1000$ mb, $\Delta p = 400$ mb, $U_1 - U_3 = 20$ m sec^{-1}, $a^- = 0$, $a^+\Psi_3^+ = 10$ m sec$^{-1}/\mu$. The last relation specifies the amplitude and phase of the growing solution at level 3. The following solutions for ψ_1 and ψ_3 can be found from (4-83) with the use of (4-84) and (4-77):

$$\psi_1 = (14.2 \text{ msec}^{-1})\mu^{-1} \cos[\mu(x - c_r t) + 64°]\, e^{nt}$$
$$\psi_3 = (10 \text{ msec}^{-1})\mu^{-1} \cos[\mu(x - c_r t)]\, e^{nt} \tag{4-87}$$

while the vertical motion is obtained from (4-76c), (4-77) and (4-85) in the form:

$$\omega'_2 = -1.36 \times 10^{-3}\text{mb sec}^{-1}\cos[\mu(x - c_r t) + 116°]\, e^{nt} \tag{4-88}$$

The temperature is obtained by substituting into (4-86), which yields

$$T'_2 = (4.35C)\cos[\mu(x - c_r t) + 108°]\, e^{nt} \tag{4-89}$$

Note that the streamfunction amplitude is given in terms of the v-component amplitude divided by the wavenumber.

The fields given by (4-87), (4-88), and (4-89) are shown in the cross section in Figure 4-10. The upper and lower curves represent ψ_1 and ψ_3, respectively, and show that the disturbance tilts westward with height as is indicated by the trough (T) and ridge (R) lines. It can be seen from (4-87) that the disturbance amplitude is larger at the upper level, and this can be traced to the presence of beta. The maximum and minimum disturbance temperatures are indicated by W and C, respectively. The arrows show the vertical motion extremes at the central level. The hatched areas indicate horizontal convergence and the unhatched areas, horizontal divergence. These fields are required by mass continuity.

Observed synoptic scale disturbances have many features in common with the unstable waves in the two-level model. They tilt westward with height and they have rising motion ahead of the upper level trough. Also, observed systems tend to have maximum rainfall east of the surface low position. In Figure 4-10 it can be seen that the maximum vertical motion is just east of the surface trough position, which is consistent with observed rainfall.

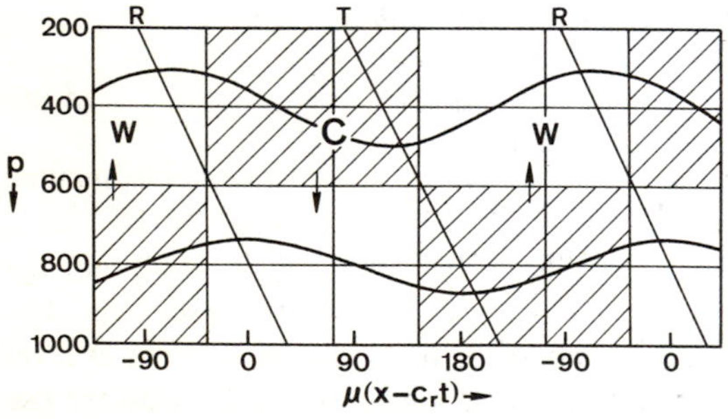

Figure 4-10 Cross section of the unstable wave as given by (4.87), (4.88), and (4.89).

The energy transformations in (4-65) and (4-66) are easily evaluated from Figure 4-10 or from (4-87), (4-88), and (4-89). In the figure it is clear that the warm air is rising and the cold air is sinking so that disturbance available potential energy is being converted into disturbance kinetic energy. The warm air is moving northward since it lies mainly between the trough and ridge and conversely the cold air is moving southward. This converts zonal mean available potential energy to disturbance available potential energy. In an unstable wave where both the kinetic energy and the temperature variance are growing, these positive conversions are required.

Oort (1964) compiled the data for the atmospheric energy diagram, presented in Figure 4-11. In the diagram $\overline{K}$ is the kinetic energy of the zonally averaged wind and $\overline{P}$ is the available potential energy of the zonally averaged temperature field, while K' is the kinetic energy of the departure of the wind from the zonal mean and P' is the available potential energy of the temperature departure from the zonal mean. The data are for the annual mean in the Northern Hemisphere. Simplified forms of the energy conversions $\{\overline{P}\cdot P'\}$ and $\{P'\cdot K'\}$ are given by the first terms on right of (4-66) and (4-65), respectively, while $\{K'\cdot\overline{K}\}$

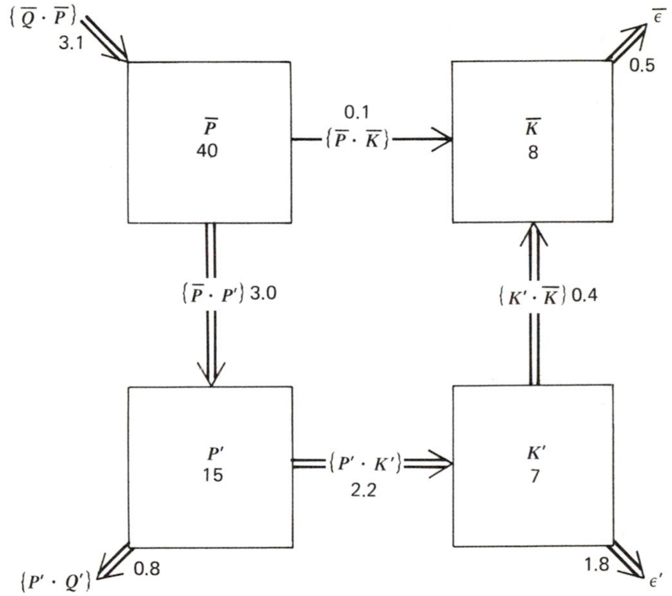

Figure 4.11 The atmospheric energy cycle from the data of Oort (1964). The numbers in the squares give observed annual mean Northern Hemisphere energy values in units of 10^5 joules m^{-2} and the energy exchange arrows are in units of watts m^{-2}. (From A.H. Oort, "On Estimates of the Atmospheric Energy Cycle." *American Meteorological Society,* 1964.)

is analogous to the right side of (4-17). The conversion $\{\bar{P}\cdot\bar{K}\}$ contains $-\bar{\omega}\,\bar{T}$ and it is determined by the mean meridional circulation. Figure 4-11 shows that the zonally averaged heating $\bar{Q}$, which flows into $\bar{P}$, is primarily converted into P' and then into K'. It was just shown that baroclinically unstable waves would cause such energy conversions, and spectral studies show that the transformations are primarily caused by the synoptic scale waves, although the planetary scale waves also contribute. The barotropic transformation from K' to $\bar{K}$ is expected as discussed in Section 4-6. The figure shows that $\{\bar{P}\cdot\bar{K}\}$ is very small. These results strongly suggest that baroclinic synoptic scale waves help keep the general circulation in balance. The kinetic energy produced by these waves helps balance the kinetic energy lost by the atmosphere due to friction. The northward heat flux maintains the thermal balance by transporting heat from low latitudes where there is excess heating to high latitudes where there is excess cooling. The synoptic disturbances also help maintain the kinetic energy of the zonal mean flow through barotropic damping.

Note that the ridge and the trough are in regions of horizontal divergence and convergence, respectively. Equation 4-57 states that the maximum vorticity (which is on the trough line) can only increase if there is horizontal convergence ($\partial\omega/\partial p > 0$) there because the advection is zero. The same argument applies on the ridge where the vorticity is a minimum. Clearly a wave cannot grow unless the difference between the maximum and minimum vorticity increases. In continuous models like Eady's and Charney's, there is convergence along the trough line at all levels in the unstable solution.

Gall (1976) and Simmons and Hoskins (1977) numerically determined the stability properties of zonal wind profiles that represent average northern hemisphere conditions. They found a most unstable wavelength near 2000 km compared with 4000 km for the simple profiles considered in the chapter. These shorter unstable waves have large amplitude only in the lower troposphere, and Staley and Gall (1977) showed that they are very sensitive to the static stability and wind shear in the lower troposphere. Gall, Blakeslee, and Somerville (1979) have shown that friction and finite amplitude effects lead to predominance by the longer waves. However, the shorter waves may still be important in the growth of smaller-scale surface disturbances.

4-11 VERTICAL ENERGY PROPAGATION

The troposphere contains most of the kinetic energy in the atmosphere since it has about 80 percent of the mass. If there were no reflection or absorption, much of this energy could be transported above the tropopause and there would be a very large response. The sound and gravity waves solutions (2-12) show this behavior where the velocity components grow with height in proportion to $\rho^{-1/2}$, so that the energy density is constant within the wave train. However in a nonisothermal atmosphere with a mean wind, the energy propagation may be greatly restricted.

In this section the vertical energy propagation in large-scale midlatitude disturbances will be investigated with the quasi-geostrophic equations. The proper treatment of vertical energy transport is very important for the long waves in numerical prediction models.

Some information on vertical energy transport with a variable mean wind can be obtained following Eliassen and Palm (1960) and Charney and Drazin (1961). If it is assumed that a neutral wave moving with speed c is present, the linearized first law of thermodynamics (4-37) becomes:

$$(U - c)\frac{\partial^2\psi}{\partial x\partial Z} - \frac{\partial\psi}{\partial x}\frac{\partial U}{\partial Z} + f_0^{-1}\,\Gamma\dot{Z} = 0 \qquad (4\text{-}90)$$

Now multiply this equation by ψ and average with respect to x, which gives:

$$\overline{\psi\dot{Z}} = f_0\,\Gamma^{-1}\,(U - c)\,\overline{\frac{\partial\psi}{\partial x}\frac{\partial\psi}{\partial Z}} \qquad (4\text{-}91)$$

The term on the left represents the ''vertical energy flux'' since ψ is proportional to ϕ'. Also $\overline{\partial\psi/\partial x\;\partial\psi/\partial Z}$ represents the northward heat flux. Equation 4-91 shows that the vertical energy flux must vanish at any level where the phase speed is equal to the mean wind speed. The solution near such a singular level may become nonlinear, but the energy does not usually propagate very far past this level. Clearly the vertical structure of $U(Z)$ has a very important influence on the transfer of energy from the lower levels to the upper levels.

More information can be obtained following Charney and Drazin (1961) by examining the quasi-geostrophic potential vorticity equation (4-34). First assume that U is independent of y and substitute $\psi = \Psi(Z)\cos\alpha y\; e^{i\mu(x-ct)}$ into (4-34), which gives:

$$(U - c)\left[e^Z\frac{\partial}{\partial Z}\left(\frac{f_0^2\,e^{-Z}}{\Gamma}\frac{\partial\Psi}{\partial Z}\right) - (\mu^2 + \alpha^2)\,\Psi\right] + \frac{\partial\bar{q}}{\partial y}\,\Psi = 0 \qquad (4\text{-}92)$$

where

$$\frac{\partial\bar{q}}{\partial y} = \beta - e^Z\frac{\partial}{\partial Z}\left(\frac{f_0^2\,e^{-Z}}{\Gamma}\frac{\partial U}{\partial Z}\right)$$

Equation 4-92 can be written in canonical form by introducing a new variable Q, which is defined as

$$Q = f_0\,(e^{-Z}/\Gamma)^{1/2}\,\Psi \qquad (4\text{-}93)$$

When (4-93) is used in (4-92) the equation can be written as follows:

$$\frac{d^2Q}{dZ^2} + n^2Q = 0 \qquad (4\text{-}94)$$

where

$$n^2 = -\frac{\Gamma}{f_0^2}(\mu^2 + \alpha^2) - \Gamma^{1/2} e^{Z/2} \frac{d^2}{dZ^2}(e^{-Z/2}\Gamma^{-1/2}) + \frac{\Gamma\, \partial\bar{q}/\partial y}{f_0^2 (U - c)} \tag{4-95}$$

Equation 4-94 is in the form of the equation for one-dimensional wave propagation in a medium of variable refractive index $n(Z)$. The solution behaves roughly as follows

$n^2 > 0$: $Q(Z)$ oscillates with Z and energy propagation is permitted
$n^2 < 0$: $Q(Z)$ varies exponentially with Z, and energy propagation is inhibited or trapped

This behavior can be more easily understood if a layer of constant U and Γ is considered. In that case (4-95) becomes

$$n^2 = -(\Gamma/f_0^2)\left[\mu^2 + \alpha^2 + \frac{f_0^2}{4\Gamma} - \frac{\beta}{(U - c)}\right] \tag{4-96}$$

where n^2 is now constant in the layer. The solutions to (4-94) are e^{inZ} and e^{-inZ}. Clearly if n is real the solution can propagate vertically and the streamfunction amplitude will vary as $e^{Z/2}$ [see (4-93)]. However if n is imaginary then the solutions will be $e^{+|n|Z}$ and $e^{-|n|Z}$. When the energy source is below the layer, the vertically damped solution must be chosen, since amplitude cannot increase away from the source unless the flow is unstable.

Charney and Drazin (1961) applied (4-96) to forced stationary waves, which could be excited by heating or by mountain forcing. If $c = 0$ in (4-96), the condition for free propagation of energy ($n^2 > 0$) can be written:

$$0 < U < \frac{\beta}{\mu^2 + \alpha^2 + f_0^2/4\Gamma} \tag{4-97}$$

Thus for vertical propagation of stationary waves the mean flow must be westerly, but not too strong. In fact, Charney and Drazin estimated that the maximum value of the right-hand term in (4-97) is 38 m sec^{-1}, and this occurs for the largest scale of motion. If (4-97) is applied to succeeding layers it can be used in an atmosphere with $U(Z)$.

Vertical energy propagation cannot extend very far into the stratosphere during the summer because of the stratospheric easterlies. However, Matsuno (1970) has demonstrated that energy can propagate upward into the polar night jet when the horizontal shear in the mean wind is included. Equation 4-97 favors vertical propagation for the long waves (small μ) and observations in the stratosphere show very little energy in the shorter waves. Also, Charney and Pedlosky (1963) have shown that baroclinically unstable waves are vertically trapped. Holton (1975) provides an extensive treatment of stratospheric dynamics and the interaction with the troposphere. The numerical prediction of long waves in the atmosphere is very dependent on proper handling of the vertical energy propagation, which will be discussed in Section 7-10.

4-12 BAROTROPIC EQUATORIAL WAVES

The structure of some atmospheric motions is significantly modified near the equator. Also the distinction between Rossby waves and inertial gravity waves becomes very blurred with some equatorial wave solutions. The horizontal structure of equatorial waves will be investigated in this section with a barotropic model, and the vertical structure will be treated in the next section.

This analysis follows Matsuno (1966*a*), who employed the shallow-water equations (see Section 2-5) on an equatorial beta plane where $f = \beta y$. When these equations are linearized about a state of no motion, the set can be written:

$$\frac{\partial u}{\partial t} + \frac{\partial \phi}{\partial x} - \beta y v = 0$$

$$\frac{\partial v}{\partial t} + \frac{\partial \phi}{\partial y} + \beta y u = 0 \qquad (4\text{-}98)$$

$$\frac{\partial \phi}{\partial t} + \Phi\left(\frac{\partial u}{\partial x} + \frac{\partial v}{\partial y}\right) = 0$$

where $\phi = gh$ and $\Phi = gH$. Now assume that u, v, and ϕ are proportional to $e^{i(\mu x + \upsilon t)}$ so that the waves propagate in the east-west direction. In this case, the set (4-98) reduces to:

$$i\upsilon u + i\mu\phi - \beta y v = 0$$

$$i\upsilon v + d\phi/dy + \beta y u = 0 \qquad (4\text{-}99)$$

$$i\upsilon\phi + \Phi(i\mu u + dv/dy) = 0$$

where u, v, and ϕ are now only functions of y. By eliminating u and ϕ, the following equation for v can be obtained:

$$\frac{d^2v}{dy^2} + \left(\frac{\upsilon^2}{\Phi} - \mu^2 + \frac{\mu\beta}{\upsilon} - \frac{\beta^2 y^2}{\Phi}\right) v = 0 \qquad (4\text{-}100)$$

This equation can be written in more convenient form by writing: $y = \Phi^{1/4}\beta^{-1/2}\xi$, $\mu = \beta^{-1/2}\Phi^{-1/4}k$, $\upsilon = \Phi^{1/4}\beta^{1/2}\omega$. In terms of these quantities (4-100) becomes:

$$\frac{d^2v}{d\xi^2} + \left(\omega^2 - k^2 + \frac{k}{\omega} - \xi^2\right) v = 0 \qquad (4\text{-}101)$$

This is a form of the Schrödinger equation for a simple harmonic oscillator, and it has solutions when:

$$\omega^2 - k^2 + \frac{k}{\omega} = 2n + 1 \qquad (n = -1, 0, 1, 2, 3 \ldots) \tag{4-102}$$

In this case the solution is

$$v = A\, e^{-\xi^2/2} H_n(\xi) \tag{4-103}$$

where H_n is a Hermite polynomial of order n. The first few terms are $H_0 = 1$, $H_1 = 2\xi$, $H_2 = 4\xi^2 - 2$. The solutions are trapped near the equator by the exponential unless the order of H_n is too large. In any case the solutions must die out in y fast enough that $f = \beta y$ is still valid.

Equation 4-102 is the frequency equation, which may be written

$$\omega^3 - (k^2 + 2n + 1)\,\omega + k = 0 \tag{4-104}$$

This cubic equation normally has three distinct roots corresponding to two inertial gravity waves and one Rossby wave. The solutions can be separated by assuming (1) $\omega^2 \sim k^2$ and (2) $|\omega| << k$ for k large (small x-scale). The solutions then become:

$$(1)\ \omega_{1,2} = \mp\sqrt{k^2 + 2n + 1} \tag{4-105}$$

$$(2)\ \omega_3 = \frac{k}{(k^2 + 2n + 1)} \tag{4-106}$$

When these solutions are written in terms of the dimensional phase velocities ($c = -\upsilon/\mu$) the result is:

$$\begin{aligned} c_{1,2} &= \mp\Phi^{1/2}\left(1 + \frac{\beta(2n+1)}{\mu^2\,\Phi^{1/2}}\right)^{1/2} \\ c_3 &= -\beta/[\mu^2 + \beta(2n+1)] \end{aligned} \tag{4-107}$$

Clearly $c_{1,2}$ are a pair of eastward and westward propagating inertial gravity waves and c_3 is a westward propagating Rossby wave.

Figure 4-12 gives the frequencies obtained by Matsuno (1966) from (4-104) as a function of k for the various n. The figure shows that as long as $n \geq 1$ the three solutions are completely separated. Now consider the case $n = 0$, which allows (4-104) to be written

$$(\omega - k)(\omega^2 + k\omega - 1) = 0$$

The solution $\omega = k$ must be exlcuded since it leads to an indeterminant solution for u. The solution $\omega_1 = -k/2 - \sqrt{(k/2)^2 + 1}$ is an eastward propagating inertial gravity wave. The other solution

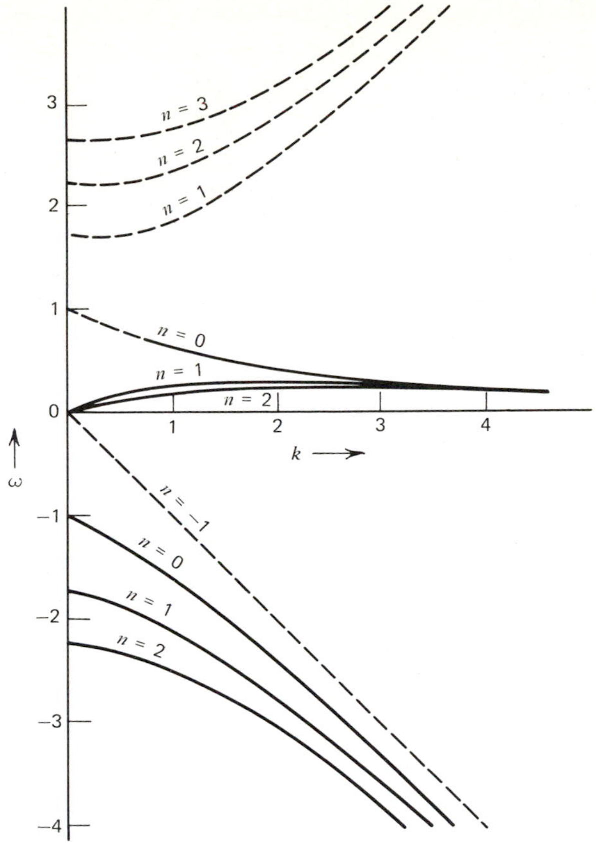

Figure 4.12 Nondimensional frequencies from (4.104) as a function of wavenumber. The lines indicate the following types of waves: thin solid line—eastward propagating inertial gravity wave; thin dashed line—westward propagating inertial gravity wave; thick solid line—Rossby wave; thick dashed line—Kelvin wave. (*After Matsuno, 1966.*) (From T. Matsuno (1966). "Quasi-geostrophic Motions in the Equatorial Area," *Journal Meteorological Society of Japan,* 1966.)

$$\omega_{RG} = -k/2 + \sqrt{(k/2)^2 + 1} \tag{4-108}$$

is called a mixed Rossby gravity wave. Note that as $k \to 0$, $\omega_{RG} \to 1$ which agrees with the limit of the gravity wave solution (4-105), while as $k \to \infty$, $\omega_{RG} \to 0$, which agrees with the limit of the Rossby wave solution (4-106). The structure of the mixed Rossby gravity wave is shown in Figure 4-13*b*.

Another important special case is $n = -1$, which, it turns out, corresponds to $v \equiv 0$. When this condition is used the system (4-99) reduces to

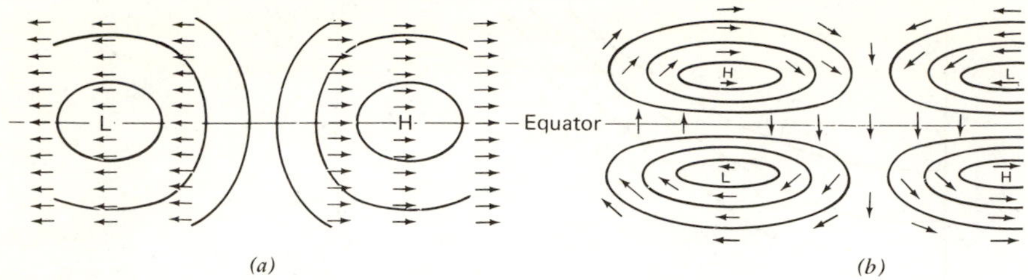

Figure 4.13 Velocity and pressure distributions in the horizontal plane for (*a*) Kelvin waves, and (*b*) mixed Rossby-gravity waves. (*After Matsuno, 1966.*) (From T. Matsuno (1966) "Quasi-geostrophic Motions in the Equatorial Area," *Journal Meteorological Society of Japan,* 1966.)

$$i\nu u + i\mu\phi = 0 \tag{4-109a}$$

$$\frac{d\phi}{dy} + \beta y u = 0 \tag{4-109b}$$

$$i\nu\phi + \Phi i\mu u = 0 \tag{4-109c}$$

Elimination between (4-109a) and (4-109c) gives

$$c = \nu/\mu = \pm\, \Phi^{1/2} \tag{4-110}$$

which is the relation for pure gravity waves. Then (4-109a) and (4-109b) can be solved to give

$$cu = \phi = A\, e^{-\beta y^2/2c} \tag{4-111}$$

Also note from (4-109b) that the u component is exactly geostrophic. The only acceptable solution from (4-110) is $c = \Phi^{1/2}$, since the negative root gives an increasing in y solution, which violates the equatorial beta plane assumption. This solution is an atmospheric Kelvin wave. The structure of the Kelvin wave is given in Figure 4-13*a*. In the ocean Kelvin waves propagate along coast lines as shallow-water waves, and they decay exponentially away from the coast. Note that if $n = -1$ is inserted into (4-104), then $\omega = -k$ is a solution that corresponds to $c = \Phi^{1/2}$. It will be seen later that large-scale forcing along the equator excites Kelvin waves.

4-13 VERTICAL STRUCTURE OF EQUATORIAL WAVES

Lindzen (1967) has determined the vertical structure of the equatorial waves that have the horizontal structure obtained in the last section. This analysis will employ a log-pressure vertical coordinate following Holton (1972a). The linearized equations in Z coordinates (see Section 3-3) can be written:

$$\frac{\partial u}{\partial t} + \frac{\partial \phi}{\partial x} - \beta y v = 0$$

$$\frac{\partial v}{\partial t} + \frac{\partial \phi}{\partial y} + \beta y u = 0 \tag{4-112}$$

$$\frac{\partial u}{\partial x} + \frac{\partial v}{\partial y} + \frac{\partial \dot{Z}}{\partial Z} - \dot{Z} = 0$$

$$\frac{\partial}{\partial t}\frac{\partial \phi}{\partial Z} + \dot{Z}\Gamma = \kappa Q$$

Here all quantities are perturbations except the constant static stability which is given by (3-47). The heating Q will be zero in the following wave analysis.

Now assume wave solutions that vary in x and t according to $e^{i(\mu x + \upsilon t)}$. In this case the system (4-112) can be written:

$$i\upsilon u + i\mu\phi - \beta y v = 0 \tag{4-113}$$

$$i\upsilon v + \partial\phi/\partial y + \beta y u = 0 \tag{4-114}$$

$$i\mu u + \partial v/\partial y + \partial \dot{Z}/\partial Z - \dot{Z} = 0 \tag{4-115}$$

$$i\upsilon \frac{\partial \phi}{\partial Z} + \dot{Z}\Gamma = 0 \tag{4-116}$$

where u, v, ϕ, and Z are functions of only y and Z. First eliminate u between (4-113) and (4-114), which gives

$$(\upsilon^2 - \beta^2 y^2)\, v = i\left(\upsilon \frac{\partial}{\partial y} - \mu\beta y\right)\phi \tag{4-117}$$

Next eliminate u and Z between (4-113), (4-115), and (4-116), which yields

$$\left[\frac{1}{\Gamma}\upsilon^2\left(\frac{\partial^2}{\partial Z^2} - \frac{1}{\partial Z}\right) + \mu^2\right]\phi + i\left(\upsilon\frac{\partial}{\partial y} + \mu\beta y\right) v = 0 \tag{4-118}$$

When ϕ is eliminated between (4-117) and (4-118) the final equation is

$$\mathcal{L}_Z v - \mathcal{M}_y v = 0 \tag{4-119}$$

$$\text{where } \mathcal{L}_Z = \frac{1}{\Gamma}\left(\frac{\partial^2}{\partial Z^2} - \frac{\partial}{\partial Z}\right)$$

$$\mathcal{M}_y = \frac{1}{\upsilon^2 - \beta^2 y^2}\left(\frac{\partial^2}{\partial y^2} - \frac{\mu^2}{\upsilon^2}\beta^2 y^2 + \frac{\mu\beta}{\upsilon}\right) - \frac{\mu^2}{\upsilon^2}$$

Since the operators each contain derivatives with respect to only one variable, the solution can be separated as follows:

$$v(y,Z) = \sum_n \Psi_n(Z)\, V_n(y)$$

where n indicates the various horizontal solutions. For each n (4-119) can be written

$$\frac{\mathcal{L}_Z \Psi_n}{\Psi_n} = \frac{\mathcal{M}_y V_n}{V_n} = -\frac{1}{gh_n} \tag{4-120}$$

where h_n is the separation constant that is known as the "equivalent depth."

The latitudinal structure equation can be written from (4-120) as follows:

$$\frac{d^2V_n}{dy^2} + \left(\frac{\mu\beta}{\upsilon} - \mu^2 + \frac{\upsilon^2}{gh_n} - \frac{\beta^2 y^2}{gh_n}\right) V_n = 0 \tag{4-121}$$

This equation is identical to (4-100), which was derived by Matsuno (1966) for a barotropic atmosphere if $h_n = \Phi/g$. When the following frequency equation is satisfied:

$$\left(\frac{\mu\beta}{\upsilon} - \mu^2 + \frac{\upsilon^2}{gh_n}\right) \frac{(gh_n)^{1/2}}{\beta} = 2n + 1 \tag{4-122}$$

the solution can be written

$$V_n = \exp[-\beta y^2/2(gh_n)^{1/2}] H_n[\beta^{1/2} y/(gh_n)^{1/4}] \tag{4-123}$$

The vertical structure equation from (4-120) takes the form:

$$\frac{d^2\Psi_n}{dZ^2} - \frac{d\Psi_n}{dZ} + \frac{\Gamma}{gh_n}\Psi_n = 0 \tag{4-124}$$

The general solution is

$$\Psi_n = e^{Z/2}\left(C_1 e^{-i\lambda Z} + C_2 e^{i\lambda Z}\right) \tag{4-125}$$

where $\lambda = (\Gamma/gh_n - 1/4)^{1/2}$, is the vertical wave number. The solution will propagate vertically if λ is real and it will be vertically trapped (damped) if λ is imaginary (see Section 4-11). The behavior can be classified in terms of h_n as follows:

$0 < h_n < 4\Gamma/g$: vertical propagation

$\left.\begin{matrix} h_n > 4\Gamma/g \\ h_n < 0 \end{matrix}\right\}$: vertically trapped

For an isothermal atmosphere with $T = 256$ K, the critical value $h = 4\Gamma/g$ is 8.6 km and it will increase as the static stability increases. Lindzen (1967) has shown, by applying the lower boundary condition, that the only free mode solution for the isothermal atmosphere is the Lamb wave, which has $h_n = g^{-1}\gamma RT = 10.5$ km (see Section 2-3). Since this is greater than the critical value, the Lamb wave is vertically trapped, which is consistent with the solution found in Section 2-4. Thus vertically propagating solutions only occur if they are forced in some region of the atmosphere. For example, latent heat released in convective clouds could excite waves that propagate into higher regions.

If observed frequencies and wave numbers are specified, (4-122) gives the equivalent depth that is related to the vertical scale. When μ and υ are sufficiently small and $n \geq 1$, the equation can be written:

$$(gh_n)^{1/2} = \frac{2n+1}{2[(\mu/\upsilon) - (\mu^2/\beta)]} \left(1 \pm \left\{1 - \frac{(4\upsilon^2/\beta)\,[(\mu/\upsilon) - (\mu^2/\beta)]}{(2n+1)^2}\right\}^{1/2}\right) \qquad (4\text{-}126)$$

Here $(gh_n)^{1/2}$ must be positive, otherwise the solution (4-123) would grow rapidly with y. For westerly waves ($\upsilon < 0$) only the negative root is allowed, which is an inertial gravity wave. For easterly waves ($\upsilon > 0$) both roots are allowed; the negative root is an inertial gravity wave while the positive root is a Rossby wave. These solutions correspond exactly with the barotropic solutions derived in the last section provided Φ is replaced by gh_n.

Lindzen (1967) examined the decay of the solutions in y with respect to the equatorial beta plane approximation. Holton (1970) showed that the Rossby wave mode was only valid when $n = 1$.

When vertical propagation occurs, the vertical wavelength becomes

$$L_z = \frac{2\pi H}{\lambda} = 2\pi H/(\Gamma/gh_n - 1/4)^{1/2} \qquad (4\text{-}127)$$

where H is the scale height. Note that the vertical wavelength can be computed from the frequency with the use of (4-126). The latter equation shows that the equivalent depth decreases as the frequency decreases which, from (4-127), implies a decrease in L_z. Holton (1970) noted that the $n = 1$ Rossby mode has L_z ranging from 39 km to 15 km for periods ranging from 7 days to 10 days, respectively. These scales are not unreasonable for observed tropical wave disturbances. However, some of these waves have a structure in y that does not correspond to the $n = 1$ mode. The tropical wave disturbances are apparently driven by latent heat released in the associated cloud clusters. Instability studies of tropical waves with parameterized heating do not explain the observed horizontal scales and they give rather small growth rates. Apparently the scales are determined by other effects that occur before the wave has a large enough amplitude for appreciable latent heating.

The relation between υ and gh_n for the mixed Rossby gravity wave ($n = 0$) can be found from (4-108) by redimensionalizing and by setting $\Phi = gh_0$. The equation can then be written

$$(gh_0)^{1/2} = \upsilon^2/(\beta - \mu\upsilon) \qquad (4\text{-}128)$$

It is clear that the equivalent depth h_0, and through (4-127) the vertical scale L_z, decreases rapidly with decreasing υ for sufficiently small υ. Yanai and Maruyama (1966) have used time series analysis to detect westward propagating waves in the lower stratosphere, which closely resemble the mixed Rossby gravity wave. The horizontal wavelength is about 10,000 km (four waves around the earth) and the period is about five days, which corresponds to a phase speed of about 20 m sec^{-1}. The waves tilt westward with height with a vertical wavelength of 4-8 km. If the values $\mu = 2\pi/(10{,}000 \text{ km})$ and $\upsilon = 2\pi/(\text{five days})$ are used in (4-128) and (4-127), the vertical wavelength in the stratosphere is about 5 km, which is consistent with the observations. It is believed that these waves are forced by latent heat release from convection in the troposphere. However, tropical cloud patterns are seldom observed to move as fast as 20 m sec^{-1}, and it appears that the mixed Rossby gravity waves are excited by 5-day oscillations in the slowly moving cloud patterns. Holton (1972b) has demonstrated, with a numerical model, how this process could work. If a longer period of 10 days or more, which corresponds to moving tropospheric disturbance, is used in (4-128) and (4-127) the vertical scale is *1* km or less. Such solutions have not been observed, although the observations may not have high enough vertical resolution to rule them out. Lindzen (1966) showed that waves are generated most efficiently by heating when the scale of the heating and of the wave are the same, and Chang (1976) and Hayashi (1976) pointed out that latent heating in the tropics has a vertical scale that is comparable to the depth of the troposphere. For this reason it seems unlikely that waves with small vertical wavelengths would be forced.

The Kelvin wave solution, which corresponds to $n = -1$, is obtained by setting $v = 0$ in (4-114) and (4-116). The horizontal structure for u and ϕ is given by (4-111), and the vertical structure is given by (4-122) where $c^2 = gh_{-1}$. The vertical wavelength becomes

$$L_z = 2\pi H/(\Gamma/c^2 - 1/4)^{1/2} \qquad (4\text{-}129)$$

As was pointed out earlier, the only acceptable solution is $c = (gh_{-1})^{1/2}$ since the negative root does not damp with increasing y. Wallace and Kousky (1968) discovered a wave number 1 Kelvin wave in the stratosphere that moves toward the east at about 30 m sec^{-1}. The waves tilt eastward with height and the vertical wavelength is 10-12 km. When $c = 30$ m sec^{-1} is used in (4-129), then $L_z \simeq 10$ km, which is consistent with the observations. Chang (1976) studied the forcing of stratospheric Kelvin waves by tropospheric heat sources, and he found that the forcing is most efficient for wave number 1 even when the sources are distributed randomly. He also found that the most favored vertical wavelength is about twice the scale of the heating. This theory agrees with the numerical solutions that were obtained by Holton (1972b).

In the troposphere, the linear study of stationary forced tropical circulations, carried out by Webster (1972), strongly suggests that the wave number 1 Kelvin wave is important. If an easterly mean flow of 5 m sec^{-1} is present, a steady Kelvin wave solution would be possible if $c = 5$ m sec^{-1}. However if $c = 5$ m sec^{-1} is substituted into (4-129) then $L_z \sim 1$ km, which is not consistent with the vertical scale of the heating. Chang (1977) has shown that the addition of a reasonable linear friction has a large effect on low-frequency equatorial Kelvin waves. He found a solution that has a slow phase speed and a large vertical scale, and which decays rapidly with height. Chang suggested that these solutions might be used to explain the monsoon and Walker circulations and the 40 to 50 days oscillation [Madden and Julian (1971, 1972)] in the troposphere. This friction has little effect on the faster Kelvin waves that are observed in the stratosphere. Chang (1977) suggests that the friction may be caused by momentum transport in tropical convection clouds as reported by many vorticity budget studies of tropical data.

This discussion of equatorial waves does not include the effect of vertical wind shear, which was treated for midlatitude waves in section 4-10. Holton (1975) gives a review of these effects. Holton and Lindzen (1972) have discussed the role of the Kelvin waves and the mixed Rossby gravity waves in the quasi-biennial oscillation.

CHAPTER 5

Numerical Methods

5-1 INTRODUCTION

The previous chapters have presented the fundamental hydrodynamical equations that govern atmospheric motions and also described various types of disturbances, or waves, that characterize these motions—their velocity, pressure and temperature distributions, their growth and decay, and their sources of energy. V. Bjerknes (1904) is recognized as the first to suggest that, given observed initial fields of mass and velocity, it would be possible in principle to determine the mass and velocity distribution at any future time by solving the hydrodynamical equations as an initial value problem. Although these nonlinear partial differential equations do not have, in general, analytic or closed solutions, they can be integrated by numerical methods to yield a forecast of the meteorological variables for a future time. Present numerical weather prediction models, as they are called, show skill over climatological or persistence forecasts for about one week and even longer in some respects.

A pioneering attempt to predict the weather by numerical integration was made by an Englishman, L. F. Richardson (1922), during World War I. Although his procedure was basically sound, there were some flaws that resulted in large errors with respect to the observed fields. Moreover, the enormous computing time required to solve the equations in the general form he used discouraged any immediate further attempts at numerical weather prediction, even to find out why Richardson's forecast went awry. Just after World War II the electronic computer (ENIAC) was installed at Princeton University and Charney, Fjørtoft, and von Neumann (1950) made the first successful numerical forecast at 500 mb with a simple barotropic vorticity model, which was a development by C. G. Rossby in the late 1930s and early 1940s. In fact, there had been considerable progress in both numerical methods and dynamic meteorology between the two wars that made the Princeton numerical forecast more timely than Richardson's effort. This chapter and the next will deal with some numerical methods currently applied to weather prediction.

5-2 FINITE DIFFERENCE METHODS

The most common numerical integration procedure for weather prediction has been the finite-difference method in which the derivatives in the differential equations of motion are replaced by finite difference approximations at a discrete set of points in space and time. The resulting set of equations, with appropriate restrictions, can then be solved by algebraic methods.

Taylor series may be used to establish appropriate finite difference approximations to derivatives as follows:

$$f(x \pm \Delta x) = f(x) \pm f'(x)\Delta x + f''(x)\frac{\Delta x^2}{2!} \pm f'''(x)\frac{\Delta x^3}{3!} \pm \ldots \tag{5-1}$$

where for later convenience, $\Delta x > 0$. Using only the + series and solving for $f'(x)$ gives

$$f'(x) = \frac{f(x + \Delta x) - f(x)}{\Delta x} + R \tag{5-2}$$

where the term of highest order in the remainder R is $-f''(x)\Delta x/2$. When R is dropped in (5-2) the remaining approximation for the derivative $f'(x)$, referred to as a *forward difference* for $\Delta x > 0$, is said to be of *order* Δx, denoted by the symbol $0(\Delta x)$. The latter represents the truncation error of the finite difference approximation.

If the series with the negative sign in (5-2) is subtracted from the positive series, the following *centered* difference approximation for $f'(x)$ results:

$$f'(x) = \frac{f(x + \Delta x) - f(x - \Delta x)}{2\Delta x} + O(\Delta x^2) \tag{5-3}$$

On the other hand, the addition of the two series in (5-1) leads to

$$f''(x) = \frac{f(x + \Delta x) - 2f(x) + f(x - \Delta x)}{\Delta x^2} + O(\Delta x^2) \tag{5-4}$$

In both cases the truncation error is of order Δx^2 giving more accurate approximations than from (5-2), which might have been expected from geometric considerations.

Since wavelike motions are characteristic of the atmosphere it is of interest to apply the centered difference approximations for $f'(x)$ to a simple harmonic function, $f(x) = A \sin(2\pi x/L)$. The ratio of the finite difference approximation, say $f'_D(x)$ to the true value of $f'(x)$ is readily found to be

$$\frac{f'_D(x)}{f'(x)} = \frac{\sin(2\pi\Delta x/L)}{2\pi\Delta x/L} \tag{5-5}$$

Since the ratio $(\sin\alpha)/\alpha$ approaches 1 as α approaches 0, it is evident that the finite difference approximation approaches the true value of $f'(x)$ as $\Delta x/L$ approaches zero. Thus the truncation error will be small when Δx is small compared to L. On the other hand, the error can be extremely bad for relatively small L, for example, for $L = 2\Delta x$, $f'_D(x) = 0$ for all x, regardless of the true value of $f'(x)$.

5-3 THE ADVECTION EQUATION

As an introduction to the basic mathematical concepts involved in the finite-difference method of solving partial differential equations, a simple linear equation with constant coefficients, usually referred to as the advection equation, will be considered, namely,

$$\frac{\partial F}{\partial t} + c\frac{\partial F}{\partial x} = 0 \qquad c > 0 \tag{5-6}$$

This equation is obviously similar in form to a linearized version of the first two terms in the equation of motion, the thermodynamic or vorticity equations, etc.; however c may also be interpreted more generally as a phase velocity, say, of gravity waves propagating in the x-direction. In any event, analytical solutions to this differential equation and to corresponding difference equations are readily found and may be compared to numerical solutions for accuracy.

The initial condition at $t = 0$ will be assumed to be a simple wave

$$F(x,0) = Ae^{i\mu x} \tag{5-7}$$

where $\mu = 2\pi/L$ and L is the wavelength as usual. Equation (5-6) may be solved by the method of separation of variables by letting

$$F(x,t) = G(t)H(x) \tag{5-8}$$

Substituting (5-8) into (5-6) leads immediately to

$$G'(t)/G(t) = -cH'(x)/H(x) = \text{constant} = -k$$

Integration gives $G = A_1e^{-kt}$, $H = A_2e^{kx/c}$, which together with the initial condition (5-7), gives $k = i\mu c$; and thus

$$F(x,t) = Ae^{i\mu(x-ct)} \tag{5-9}$$

In fact, it is easily shown that for an arbitrary initial condition, say, $F(x,0) = G(x)$, the general solution is $G(\xi)$, where $\xi = x - ct$, that is,

$$F(x,t) = G(x - ct) \tag{5-10}$$

It is clear from this result that the solution F will have the same value at all coordinates (x,t) for which

$$x - ct = \text{constant} = a \tag{5-11}$$

and $F = G(a)$ at those pairs of x and t. The lines (5-11) in the (x,t) plane, which have a slope of $1/c$, are the *characteristics* of the advection equation, as shown in Figure 5-1; and the solution is said to propagate along these curves.

Numerical Solution. Next, a numerical solution to this initial value problem will be sought. First let

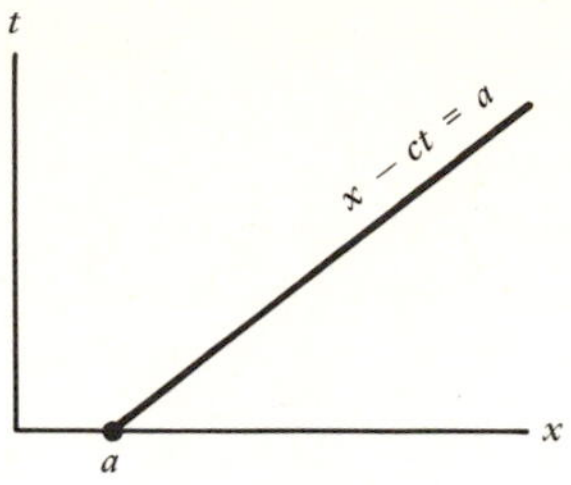

Figure 5.1 The line $x - ct = a$ is a characteristic of the advection equation.

$$x = m\Delta x,\ m = 0,\ \pm 1, \pm 2, \ldots, \text{ and } t = n\Delta t,\ n = 0,1,2, \ldots$$

which replaces the continuous (x,t) space by a *mesh* or *grid* of discrete points. Using second-order finite difference approximation of (5-3) for the derivatives in (5-6) gives

$$\frac{F_{m,n+1} - F_{m,n-1}}{2\Delta t} + c\frac{F_{m+1,n} - F_{m-1,n}}{2\Delta x} = 0$$

or (5-12)

$$F_{m,n+1} = F_{m,n-1} - \frac{c\Delta t}{\Delta x}(F_{m+1,n} - F_{m-1,n})$$

which is referred to as a *three-level* scheme because three time levels are involved.

This equation represents a simple marching procedure, called the *leapfrog scheme,* whereby the value of F at some point $m\Delta x$ and time $(n + 1)\,\Delta t$ is derived from values at previous times n and $n - 1$. Clearly (5-12) cannot be used to calculate $F_{m,1}$ (i.e., for the first time step), since the values are not known at $n = -1$ (i.e., prior to $t = 0$). Hence some other scheme must be used for the first time step, for example, with a forward difference approximation for $\partial F/\partial t$, which will be done later. For the present, the finite difference equation (5-12) will be solved analytically, rather than with a computer, using the method of separation of variables. As a shortcut an exponential solution will be assumed that takes into account the harmonic initial condition as follows:

$$F_{m,n} = B^{n\Delta t}\, e^{i\mu m\Delta x} \tag{5-13}$$

where B may be complex number. Substituting this expression into (5-12) gives

$$(B^{(n+1)\Delta t} - B^{(n-1)\Delta t})\, e^{i\mu m\Delta x} = -\frac{c\Delta t}{\Delta x} B^{n\Delta t}\,(e^{i\mu(m+1)\Delta x} - e^{i\mu(m-1)\Delta x})$$

Canceling the common factor $F_{m,n}$, applying Euler's formula $e^{i\theta} = \cos\theta + i \sin\theta$, and multiplying through by $B^{\Delta t}$ leads to

$$B^{2\Delta t} + 2i\,\sigma\, B^{\Delta t} - 1 = 0 \tag{5-14}$$

where

$$\sigma = \frac{c\Delta t}{\Delta x} \sin \mu\Delta x \tag{5-15}$$

Solving this quadratic gives

$$B^{\Delta t} = -\,i\sigma \pm (1 - \sigma^2)^{1/2} \tag{5-16}$$

Two cases may be considered, $|\sigma| \lesseqgtr 1$.

Stable Case. $|\sigma| \leq 1$ (no exponential growth). In this case the radical is real, and the two values of $B^{\Delta t}$ may be written in the polar form[1] as

$$B_+^{\Delta t} = e^{-i\alpha} \qquad \text{and} \qquad B_-^{\Delta t} = e^{i(\alpha+\pi)} \tag{5-17}$$

where as shown in the adjacent Figure 5-2,

$$\alpha = \arcsin \sigma \tag{5-18}$$

The complete finite difference solution (5-13) then takes the form

$$F_{m,n} = [Me^{-i\alpha n} + Ee^{i(\pi+\alpha)n}]\, e^{i\mu m\Delta x} \tag{5-19}$$

where M and E are arbitrary constants to be determined by the initial conditions. A slightly different notation for later usage is to denote the roots of (5-14) as λ_1 and λ_2, in which case the two solutions to the difference equation are: $\lambda_1^n F_{m,0}$ and $\lambda_2^n F_{m,0}$. Then the general solution becomes

$$M\lambda_1^n F_{m,0} + E\lambda_2^n F_{m,0} \tag{5-20}$$

Returning now to the solution (5-19), it may be noted that at the initial time ($n = 0$) (5-7) and (5-19) yield

$$F_{m,0} = Ae^{i\mu m\Delta x} = (M + E)\, e^{i\mu m\Delta x}$$

hence, $M + E = A$. Also, $e^{\pi i} = -1$, thus

$$F_{m,n} = (A - E)\, e^{i\mu(m\Delta x - \alpha n/\mu)} + (-1)^n\, Ee^{i\mu(m\Delta x + \alpha n/\mu)} \tag{5-21}$$

Comparing this solution, say F_D, of the finite difference equation with the "true" solution, (5-9), of the differential equation reveals some important differences. First, there are two waves in the finite difference solution, F_D, whereas there is only a single wave in the true solution, F. The two waves, or modes, occur because the finite difference equation (5-12) is of second order, which

[1] A polar form of a complex number is: $a + bi = (a^2 + b^2)^{1/2} \exp\,(i \arctan b/a)$.

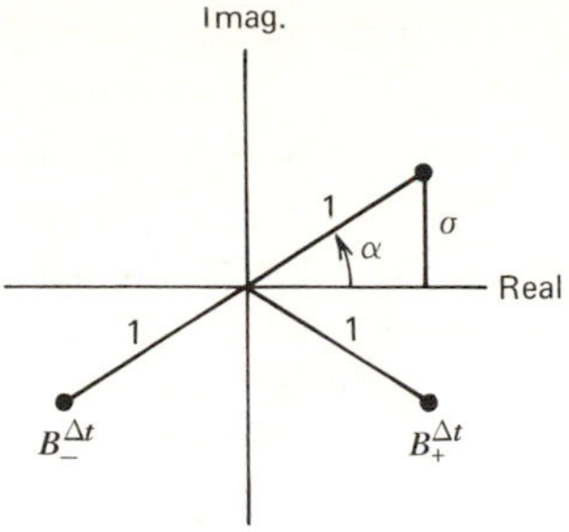

Figure 5.2

leads to two solutions and the two arbitrary constants denoted by M and E in (5-19). One of these, M, was eliminated by means of the initial condition. The latter is sufficient to determine the single constant associated with the solution of the first-order differential equation. Before further comparison of the two solutions, the second constant E will be determined by prescribing the method for making the first time step Δt. The simplest procedure is to take a forward step in time while retaining a centered difference for the $\partial F/\partial x$, that is,

$$\frac{F_{m,1} - F_{m,0}}{\Delta t} + c\,\frac{F_{m+1,0} - F_{m-1,0}}{2\Delta x} = 0 \tag{5-22}$$

Substituting in the initial values, $F_{m,0} = Ae^{i\mu m\Delta x}$, etc. leads to

$$F_{m,1} = A(1 - i\ \sin\alpha)e^{i\mu m\Delta x} \tag{5-23}$$

which is the value assigned to the solution (5-21) for $n = 1$. Thus

$$A(1 - i\ \sin\alpha)e^{i\mu m\Delta x} = (A - E)e^{i\mu m\Delta x - i\alpha} - Ee^{i\mu m\Delta x + i\alpha}$$

Solving this equation for E gives

$$E = -A(1 - \cos\alpha)/2\cos\alpha$$

Thus the second constant of integration has been determined by specifying the solution at $t = \Delta t$ in addition to $t = 0$, the former being calculated by a forward difference approximation with respect to time. Substituting this value of E into (5-21) gives the following complete solution to the difference equation:

$$F_{m,n} = A\,\frac{1 + \cos\alpha}{2\cos\alpha}\,e^{i\mu(m\Delta x - n\alpha/\mu)} + (-1)^{n+1}A\,\frac{1 - \cos\alpha}{2\cos\alpha}\,e^{i\mu(m\Delta x + n\alpha/\mu)} \tag{5-24}$$

Further comparisons of the solution of the difference equation with the true solution may now be made. First note that as $\Delta x \rightarrow 0$, (5-15) shows that $\sigma \rightarrow c\mu\Delta t$; and then for small Δt, (5-18) gives $\alpha = c\mu\Delta t$. Thus, in (5-24) the exponential factor in the first wave becomes exp $i\mu(x - ct)$. Now letting Δt approach zero, gives $\alpha = 0$, $(1 + \cos\alpha)/2\cos\alpha = 1$ and $(1 - \cos\alpha)/2\cos\alpha$

= 0. Thus, as Δx and Δt are allowed to approach zero (while keeping $|\sigma| \leq 1$), the first mode in (5-24) approaches the true solution while the second mode vanishes. Hence the first mode corresponds to the true solution and is commonly referred to as the *physical mode;* while the second, which arises from using a second-order difference equation to approximate a first-order differential equation, is referred to as the *computational mode*. The latter is obviously a spurious mode with respect to (5-6) and is a source of error. Note that the computational mode changes sign at every time step due to the factor $(-1)^{n+1}$ and travels in the opposite direction to the physical mode.

Amplitude. When α is small, the amplitude, $A(1 + \cos\alpha)/2\cos\alpha$, of the physical mode, which is a constant, is nearly the true amplitude A, while the amplitude of the computational mode is small. Moreover, from (5-18) α is small when σ is small; and the latter, according to (5-15), for a given value of $c\Delta t/\Delta x$ will be small when $\mu\Delta x$ is small, that is, when $\Delta x << L$. This might be expected on intuitive grounds, namely, that the numerical results will be more accurate when Δx is small, or more precisely, when there are many gridpoints to resolve a given wavelength than when there are only a few.

Phase Speed. Next the phase speed c_F of the numerical solution will be compared to the true wave speed c. Comparison of (5-9) and (5-24) shows that the expression $n\alpha/\mu$ in the latter is the counterpart of ct in the differential equation.

Now $n\alpha/\mu = n\Delta t\alpha/\mu\Delta t = t\alpha/\mu\Delta t = c_F t$, where

$$c_F = \frac{\alpha}{\mu\Delta t} = \frac{\arcsin[(c\Delta t/\Delta x)\sin\mu\Delta x]}{\mu\Delta t} \tag{5-25}$$

In order to see the effects of truncation error on the phase velocity the sine and arcsine functions above may be expanded in Taylor series. Prior to that a particularly simple special case may be considered, that is, $c\Delta t/\Delta x = 1$, in which case the numerator in (5-25) becomes simply $\mu\Delta x$ and

$$c_F = \mu\Delta x/\mu\Delta t = \Delta x/\Delta t = c$$

Thus there is no error in phase velocity. Note that for this case, $\Delta t/\Delta x = 1/c$, which is precisely the slope of the characteristic (5-11). In the general case, series may be used as follows:

$$\sin \mu\Delta x = \mu\Delta x - (\mu\Delta x)^3/3! + \ldots$$

$$\arcsin \beta = \beta + \beta^3/6 + \ldots, \text{ for } \beta < 1$$

where from (5-25)

$$\beta = (c\Delta t/\Delta x)\,[\mu\Delta x - (\mu\Delta x)^3/6]$$

Substituting the series into (5-25) and simplifying leads to the approximation

$$\frac{c_F}{c} \doteq 1 - \frac{1}{6}\left[1 - \left(\frac{c\Delta t}{\Delta x}\right)^2\right]\left(\frac{2\pi\Delta x}{L}\right)^2 + \ldots . \tag{5-26}$$

To ensure stability for all wavelengths, the condition $|\sigma| \leq 1$, reduces to $|c\Delta t/\Delta x| \leq 1$, which will be assumed in (5-26). If just the first term in both series were used, the result would be $c_F \doteq c$. The inclusion of the second-order terms in the series shows that the time differencing tends to overestimate the phase speed while the space differencing tends to underestimate the phase speed with the latter factor dominating. From (5-26), $c_F \leq c$; that is, the speed of the finite difference wave is always less or at most equal to the true speed in the second-order case. Moreover, as $\Delta x/L$ approaches zero, c_F approaches c, hence waves that are relatively long compared to Δx have little phase speed error. Table 5-1 [constructed form (5-25)] shows c_F as a function of $L = n\Delta x$ (abscissa) and $c\Delta t/\Delta x$ (ordinate) for the second-order leapfrog scheme and also for more accurate fourth-order space differencing, which will be discussed later. The table verifies expectations from (5-26), that is, the accuracy of the phase velocity increases with increasing wavelength. The $2\Delta x$ wavelength, which is the shortest wave resolvable on a grid, is stationary, as can be seen from (5-25), since $\sin[(2\pi/2\Delta x)\Delta x] = 0$. Incidentally, the approximation (5-26) is not satisfactory for short wavelengths because of series truncation.

The phase speed of the analytic solution is a constant c, whereas the phase speed of the numerical wave solution varies with wavelength. This phenomenon, which is obviously a source of error, is referred to as *computational dispersion*. Consequently, an initial field of F containing many wavelengths would be distorted in the numerical solution as time passes, with the shorter waves trailing the longer waves, contrary to the true solution, which has the same phase velocity for all wavelengths in this simple case.

Table 5-1

	$\frac{c\Delta t}{\Delta x}$:	$2\Delta x$	$4\Delta x$	$6\Delta x$	$8\Delta x$	$10\Delta x$	$12\Delta x$
Second order	0.2	0	0.64	0.83	0.91	0.94	0.96
	0.4	0	0.66	0.84	0.92	0.95	0.96
	0.6	0	0.68	0.87	0.93	0.96	0.97
	0.8	0	0.74	0.92	0.96	0.97	0.98
Fourth order	0.2	0	0.86	0.97	0.99	1.00	1.00
	0.4	0	0.89	0.99	1.00	1.01	1.01
	0.6	0	0.98	1.03	1.03	1.02	1.01
	0.8	0	Unstable	1.11	1.07	1.04	1.03

The table gives the ratio of finite difference wave speed to true wave speed, c_F/c, as a function of wavelength in terms of Δx (abscissa) versus $c\Delta t/\Delta x$ (ordinate) for second- and fourth-order space differencing and leapfrog time differencing for the advection equation.

Group Velocity. It also is of interest to compute the group velocity, the rate at which energy is propagated, for the numerical solution of the advection equation. The formula for group velocity is [see, for example, Haltiner and Martin (1957)]

$$G = \frac{d(\mu c)}{d\mu} = -L^2 \frac{d}{dL}\left(\frac{c}{L}\right) \tag{5-27}$$

The true value of the phase velocity is a constant c in our advection-equation example, hence $G = c$, that is, the group velocity equals the phase velocity.

For the numerical case, formula (5-25) gives

$$G_F = \frac{d(\mu c_F)}{d\mu} = \frac{d}{d\mu}\left\{\frac{\mu \arcsin\left[(c\Delta t/\Delta x)\sin \mu\Delta x\right]}{\mu\Delta t}\right\}$$

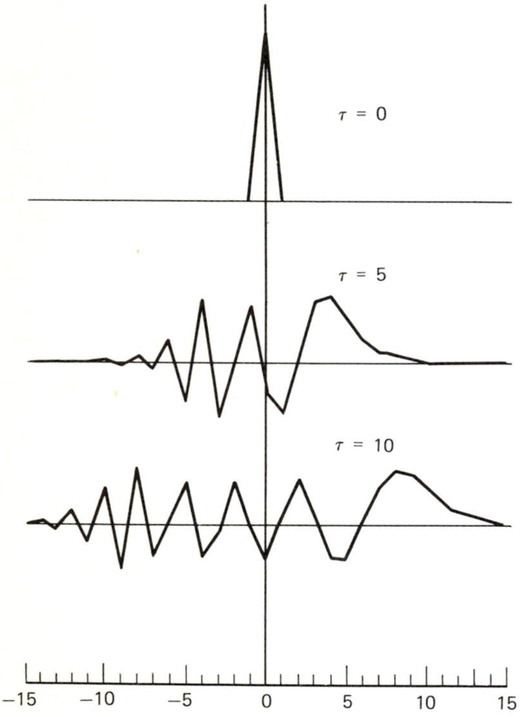

Figure 5.3*a* Solutions of the advection equation, $\partial F_j/\partial t + c(F_{j+1} - F_{j-1})/2\Delta x = 0$, for the initial state and two later nondimensional times. (*After Matsuno, 1966.*) (From T. Matsuno, "False Reflection of Waves at a Boundary Due to Use of Finite Differences." *Journal Meteorological Society of Japan,* 1966.)

or (5-28)

$$G_F = c\frac{\cos \mu\Delta x}{\left[1 - \left(\dfrac{c\Delta t}{\Delta x}\sin \mu\Delta x\right)^2\right]^{1/2}}$$

First note that if $c\Delta t/\Delta x = 1$, $G_F = c$, which is the analytically correct value. Next consider $c\Delta t/\Delta x < 1$, then for low wave number μ(long wavelength), $\mu\Delta x$ is small and again G_F approaches c, the true value. On the other hand, very serious errors occur for short waves, for example, with $c\Delta t/\Delta x < 1$, and

$$L = 4\Delta x \qquad \mu\Delta x = \pi/2 \qquad \text{and} \qquad G_F = 0$$

$$L = 2\Delta x \qquad \mu\Delta x = \pi \qquad \text{and} \qquad G_F = -c$$

Thus energy in the $2\Delta x$ to $4\Delta x$ wavelengths, which may be mostly noise in a numerical prediction model, can propagate rapidly "upstream" away from the source; and for somewhat longer wavelengths G_F is significantly underestimated (O'Brien and Grotjahn, 1976). Figure 5-3 shows rather unusual but interesting cases of two initial states consisting of a triangular and a rectangular pulse. The analytic solutions of the advection differential equation [as shown in the heavy solid line in (*a*)], progress steadily toward the right at the rate of one space unit

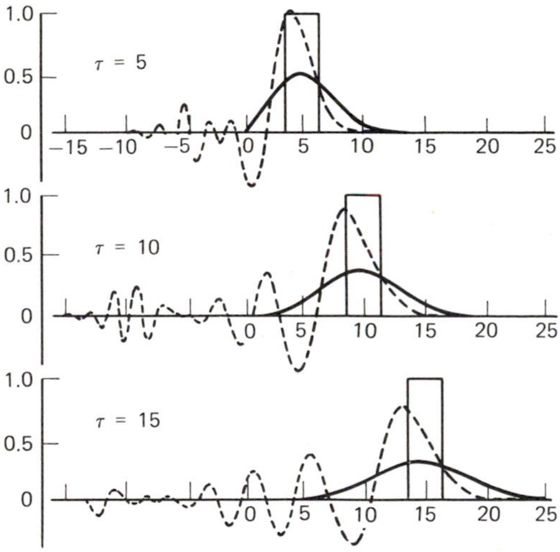

Figure 5.3 ***(b)*** Analytic solutions of the advection equation (heavy solid line), with centered differences (dashed line), and upstream differencing (thin solid line) for three times. *(After Wurtele, 1961.)* (From M. Wurtele, "On the Problem of Truncation Error." *Swedish Geophysical Society,* 1961.)

per unit time. The dashed line shows the solution with centered space differences and the solid curve in (*b*) shows the solution to the upstream-difference equation discussed in Section 5-6-2. The largest wave in the centered-difference solutions dampens and lags behind the true solution somewhat; however another serious source of error is the trailing parasitic waves that either lag the main wave or propagate upstream. Note that the parasitic waves moving at approximately $-c$ have a wavelength of about $2d$, as suggested by (5-28). The solution corresponding to "upstream" differencing in (*b*) shows only a slight phase lag and no parasitic waves; however, there is very rapid damping of the solution.

It is desirable to add a few more remarks about the spurious computational mode. If its value were plotted as a function of time, for example, beginning at an inflection point, its subsequent variation would be similar to that shown in Figure 5-4. The alternating positive and negative values are due to the factor $(-1)^{n+1}$, which gives it the apparent $2\Delta t$ period. On the other hand, the slowly varying or modulated amplitude is a consequence of its propagation at speed $-\alpha/\mu\Delta t$. In actual computation the behavior of the computational mode is superimposed on the physical mode to give the total numerical solution. Since the computational mode is a source of error, it would be desirable to eliminate it, if possible.

Return now to the form (5-20), which is a linear combination of the two independent solutions, and suppose initial values are imposed at $t = 0$ and at $t = \Delta t$ (i.e., at $n = 0$ and $n = 1$) as follows:

$$F_{m,0} = (M\lambda_1^0 + E\lambda_2^0)\,F_{m,0}$$

$$F_{m,1} = (M\lambda_1 + E\lambda_2)\,F_{m,0}$$

Solving the pair of equations for E and M gives

$$E = \frac{(F_{m,1}/F_{m,0}) - \lambda_1}{\lambda_2 - \lambda_1} \qquad \text{and} \qquad M = 1 - E \tag{5-29}$$

In order for the computational mode to vanish, the additional computational condition that would have to be imposed would be

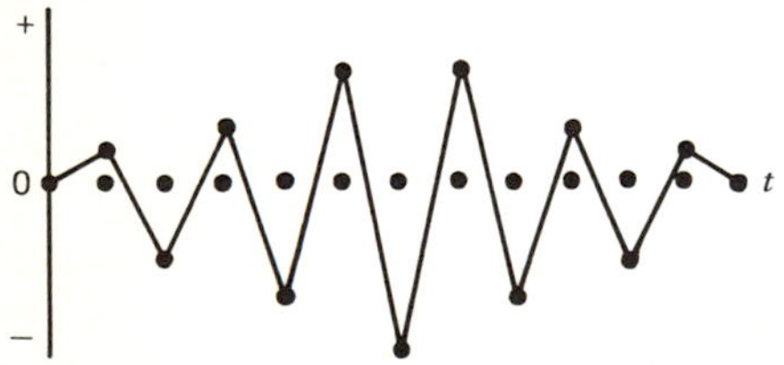

Figure 5.4

$$F_{m,1} = \lambda_1 F_{m,0} = A(\cos\alpha - i\sin\alpha)\, e^{i\mu m\Delta x} \tag{5-30}$$

which differs from (5-23).

This is obviously possible in the simple linear example considered here. However in nonlinear equations where numerical methods are generally mandatory, it is not generally possible to determine the λ's. As a consequence, the value of $F_{m,1}$ is determined by some forward differencing scheme, the most common of which is the Euler scheme (5-22), although this scheme would lead to severe problems if used continuously.

Unstable Case. $|\sigma| > 1$. Now turn back to (5-16) and consider the case $|\sigma| > 1$. Then the quantity $(1 - \sigma^2)^{1/2}$ is imaginary and both roots are pure imaginary.

$$B_{+}^{\Delta t} = -i(\sigma - S), \text{ where } |\sigma| > S \equiv (\sigma^2 - 1)^{1/2} > 0$$

$$B_{-}^{\Delta t} = -i(\sigma + S)$$

If, for example, σ is positive, the magnitude, $R = |B_{-}^{\Delta t}|$ *exceeds 1* and $B_{-}^{\Delta t} = Re^{-i\pi/2}$ will grow exponentially when raised to the *n*th power. If $\sigma < -1$, the other root has a magnitude exceeding 1. In either case the solution

$$F_{m,n} = (MB_{+}^{n\Delta t} + EB_{-}^{n\Delta t})\, e^{i\mu m\Delta x}$$

will amplify with increasing time, which is contrary to the true solution of the differential equation.

This phenomenon of *exponential* amplification of the solution of the difference equation is known as *computational instability* and clearly *must be avoided*. The *condition* for a *stable* solution in this case is $|\sigma| < 1$, that is,

$$\left|\frac{c\Delta t}{\Delta x}\sin\mu\Delta x\right| \leq 1 \tag{5-31}$$

If this condition is to hold for all admissible wavelengths, then the maximum magnitude of $\sin\mu\Delta x = 1$, (at $L = 4\Delta x$), requires that

$$\left|\frac{c\Delta t}{\Delta x}\right| \leq 1 \tag{5-32}$$

which is commonly referred to as the *Courant-Friedrichs-Levy* (CFL) condition for computational stability. The question might be raised as to whether (5-31) would suffice, if the initial condition were a single pure sine wave. The answer is that calculations on a computer invariably result in roundoff errors which introduce other, and eventually, all allowable Fourier components. Hence to prevent instability (5-32) must be imposed.

Figure 5-5 shows an x,t plot of discrete gridpoints. The triangle of large dots represents those (m,n) gridpoints on which the solution for the point (5,3) depends or the *domain of dependence,* or *influence,* when the centered finite difference or *leapfrog* scheme is used on the advection equation. The equation for the left side of the triangle is: $t - (\Delta t/\Delta x)\, x =$ constant. Now suppose that the characteristic through the point (5,3) is the line labeled

$$x - ct = x_0 \qquad \text{(characteristic)}$$

Since it was shown earlier that the solution of the differential equation propagates along characteristics, the true solution at the point (5,3) must be $F(x_0)$. However, in the example illustrated here, the point x_0 lies outside the domain of dependence of the point (5,3); hence the solution obtained from the difference equation cannot give a correct value to the solution of the differential equation. Note that in this case the slope of the triangle side exceeds that of the characteristic, that is,

$$\frac{\Delta t}{\Delta x} > \frac{1}{c} \qquad \text{or} \qquad \frac{c\Delta t}{\Delta x} > 1$$

which violates the computational stability criterion (5-32); so a satisfactory solution to the difference equation cannot be expected.

Another interesting feature of Figure 5-5 is that the lattice of points in the domain of dependence on which the solution to the difference equation for a given point depends consists only of alternate points, except for $t = 0$. This peculiarity can lead to the separation of the solutions at adjacent points, primarily due to the computational mode that "flip-flops" at every time step.

5-4 SOME BASIC CONCEPTS

Having studied the numerical solution to a simple, but important, linear partial differential equation, it is now desirable to discuss some basic, general concepts related to the solution of partial differential equations by numerical methods.

First, if a *difference equation* is substituted for a *differential equation,* intuitively it would seem necessary that if a desirable result is to be obtained, the former should approach the latter as the finite difference increments are reduced to zero.

Definition A difference equation is said to be *consistent* or *compatible* when it approaches the corresponding differential equation as the finite difference increments, Δt, Δx, etc. approach zero.

Since the difference equation is only an approximation to the differential equation, the accuracy of the former may be measured by taking the difference between the two, which is called the *truncation error Tr,*

$$Tr = \text{difference eq} - \text{differential eq} \qquad \text{(5-33)}$$

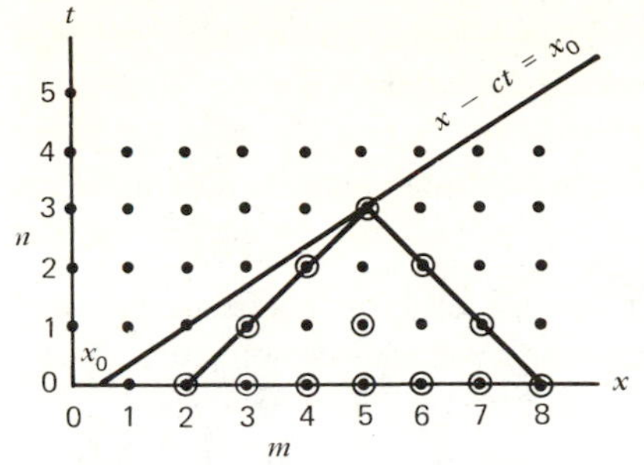

Figure 5.5 Illustrates the domain of dependence of the finite difference solution at $n = 3$ and $m = 5$.

As an example, consider the advection equation previously examined for which

$$Tr = \frac{F_{m,n+1} - F_{m,n-1}}{2\Delta t} + c\frac{F_{m+1,n} - F_{m-1,n}}{2\Delta x} - \left(\frac{\partial F}{\partial t} + c\frac{\partial F}{\partial x}\right)_{m,n} \tag{5-34}$$

To interpret the significance of truncation error, it is necessary to expand the first two terms in Taylor series.

$$F_{m,n\pm 1} = F_{m,n} \pm \frac{\partial F}{\partial t}\frac{\Delta t}{1!} + \frac{\partial^2 F}{\partial t^2}\frac{\Delta t^2}{2!} \pm \frac{\partial^3 F}{\partial t^3}\frac{\Delta t^3}{3!} \pm \cdots$$

Similar series can be written for $F_{m\pm 1,n}$. When these series are substituted into (5-34), the result is

$$Tr = \frac{\partial^3 F}{\partial t^3}\frac{\Delta t^2}{6} + c\frac{\partial^3 F}{\partial x^3}\frac{\Delta x^2}{6} + \text{higher powers of } \Delta t \text{ and } \Delta x \tag{5-35}$$

or sometimes simply as, $Tr = O(\Delta t^2) + O(\Delta x^2)$. Nevertheless, the size of the coefficients is also important.

It is evident that the difference equation approximation in (5-34) is *consistent* with the differential equation, that is,

$$Tr \rightarrow O \text{ as } \Delta t,\ \Delta x \rightarrow 0 \tag{5-36}$$

It is quite clear from the previous example that consistency alone is not sufficient to guarantee that the solution of the difference equation will be a good approximation to the solution of the differential equation, which is, after all, the real goal. Again, from intuitive considerations, it would be reasonable to expect that an acceptable solution to the difference equation over some specified interval of space and time would approach the solution of the differential equation as the finite difference increments Δt, Δx, etc., approach zero.

Definition A finite-difference solution is said to be *convergent* if, for a fixed time interval, $T = n\Delta t$, it *approaches the solution of the differential equation* as the increments Δt, Δx, etc. approach zero.

Definition If a *difference scheme* gives a *convergent solution for any initial conditions,* the *scheme is* also said to be *convergent.*

The next definition concerns the stability of a difference system and may be expressed in several ways. In simple terms, any numerical scheme that allows a growth of error that eventually "swamps" the true solution is unstable. The preceding statement is rather vague, however, and a more specific mathematical definition is desirable. Several usable definitions follow.

Definition I According to Richtmyer and Morton (1967) the difference scheme is *stable* if its solutions remain uniformly bounded functions of the initial state for all sufficiently small Δt (that is, $0 < \Delta t \leq \tau$, and $n\,\Delta t = T$).

Definition II When the corresponding differential solution is bounded, a finite difference scheme is *unstable* if, for a fixed spatial grid and homogeneous boundary conditions, there exist initial disturbances for which the finite-difference solution becomes unbounded as n goes to infinity. In general this is a more stringent requirement than Definition I.

Definition III A set of difference equations is *stable* if the cumulative effect of all round-off errors remains negligible as n increases.

The question of convergence is difficult to investigate because it involves derivatives of the true solution for which the upper and lower bounds are not known. On the other hand, stability is generally not as difficult to ascertain; and fortunately, there is an important theorem by Lax that relates consistency and stability to convergence.

Lax Equivalence Theorem (Richtmyer and Morton, 1967)
Given a properly posed, linear initial-value problem and a finite difference approximation that satisfies the *consistency* condition, *stability* (according to Definition I) is the *necessary* and *sufficient* condition for *convergence*.

In the example of the leapfrog scheme applied to the advection equation discussed earlier, the difference equation is consistent and was shown to be stable for $c\Delta t/\Delta x \leq 1$. It was further shown to converge for a particular initial state. On the other hand, when $c\Delta t/\Delta x > 1$, convergence is not possible for all initial states (e.g., all wavelengths).

5-5 STABILITY ANALYSIS

There are several methods of stability analysis. Obviously, when an analytical solution of the difference equation can be found, such as in the application of the leapfrog scheme to the advection equation, the solution can be examined directly. However in many cases other methods are required.

5-5-1 The Matrix Method

In the matrix method the solution of the difference system at every gridpoint at the time $(n + 1)\Delta t$ is assumed to be expressible in terms of the values at time $n\Delta t$ as follows:

$$\mathbf{U}_{n+1} = A\,\mathbf{U}_n \tag{5-37}$$

where $\mathbf{U}$ is a vector representing all of the dependent variables (perhaps augmented) at all of the gridpoints and A is a matrix representing the difference system.

As an example, consider the following parabolic differential and corresponding difference equations

$$\frac{\partial F}{\partial t} = K\frac{\partial^2 F}{\partial x^2} \tag{5-38}$$

and

$$\frac{F_{m,n+1} - F_{m,n}}{\Delta t} = K\frac{F_{m+1,n} - 2F_{m,n} + F_{m-1,n}}{\Delta x^2} \tag{5-39}$$

or

$$F_{m,n+1} = rF_{m-1,n} + (1 - 2r)\,F_{m,n} + rF_{m+1,n} \qquad r = K\,\Delta t/\Delta x^2 \tag{5-40}$$

If, for simplicity, the boundary values are taken to be $F_{0,n} = F_{J,n} = 0$, then (5-40) can be written in the matrix form (5-37).

$$\begin{bmatrix} F_{1,n+1} \\ F_{2,n+1} \\ \cdot \\ \cdot \\ \cdot \\ F_{J-1,n+1} \end{bmatrix} = \begin{bmatrix} 1-2r & r & 0 & 0\ldots & 0 \\ r & 1-2r & r & 0\ldots & 0 \\ 0 & r & 1-2r & r\ldots & 0 \\ & & & & \\ & & & & \\ 0 & 0 & \ldots\ldots\ldots & \ldots\ldots\ldots & 1-2r \end{bmatrix} \begin{bmatrix} F_{1,n} \\ F_{2,n} \\ \cdot \\ \cdot \\ \cdot \\ F_{J-1,n} \end{bmatrix} \tag{5-41}$$

It follows from (5-41) that

$$\mathbf{F}_n = A\,\mathbf{F}_{n-1} = A\,(A\mathbf{F}_{n-2}) = \ldots.\, A^n\,\mathbf{F}_0 \tag{5-42}$$

where $\mathbf{F}_0$ is the vector representing the initial conditions. The matrix A is referred to as the *amplification* matrix.

It is apparent from (5-42) that the question of computational stability is related to the properties of the matrix A, which will now be discussed as needed. The so-called eigenvalues (or characteristic values) λ_k of A are the roots of the characteristic equation

$$|A - \lambda I| = 0 \tag{5-43}$$

where I is the identity matrix and the bars denote a determinant. In the example (5-41), the determinant is of order $J - 1$, hence the characteristic equation has the same order and there are $J - 1$ eigenvalues. Associated with each eigenvalue is an eigenvector $\mathbf{v}_k$, which satisfies the equation

$$A\mathbf{v}_k = \lambda_k \mathbf{v}_k \qquad k = 1,2, \ldots \tag{5-44}$$

When the eigenvectors form a complete, linearly independent set, an arbitrary initial condition, such as $\mathbf{F}_0$ in (5-42), can be expressed as a linear combination of the eigenvectors:

$$\mathbf{F}_0 = \sum_k C_k \mathbf{v}_k \tag{5-45}$$

where C_k are constants. A sufficient condition for the matrix A to have a complete set of eigenvectors is that the eigenvalues be nonzero and differ from one another. However, under certain circumstances, a repeated eigenvalue may also lead to a complete set of linearly independent vectors. Also, real symmetric matrices, Hermitian matrices and normal matrices lead to linearly independent sets. In any event, for the examples considered here and usually those of common interest, the sufficiency condition is fulfilled. Assuming this to be the case, substitution of (5-45) into (5-42) and use of (5-44) gives

$$\mathbf{F}_0 = \sum_{k=1} C_k A^n \mathbf{v}_k = \sum_k C_k A^{n-1} A\mathbf{v}_k = \sum_k C_k A^{n-1} \lambda_k \mathbf{v}_k \ldots$$

Repeating this procedure leads to

$$F_n = \sum_{k-1} C_k \lambda_k^n \mathbf{v}_k \tag{5-46}$$

It is evident from (5-46) that the solution $\mathbf{F}_n$ will remain bounded, as required by Definitions I and II for a *stable* difference scheme, if the eigenvalues have magnitudes less or equal to one, that is,

$$|\lambda_k| \leq 1 \text{ for all } k \tag{5-47}$$

In general, a particular nonzero eigenmode will *amplify*, remain *neutral*, or *dampen* according to whether its associated eigenvalue has a magnitude *greater*, *equal*, or *less than* one,

$$|\lambda_k| \begin{array}{l} > 1, \text{ amplify} \\ = 1, \text{ neutral} \\ < 1, \text{ dampen} \end{array} \tag{5-48}$$

Strictly speaking, however, the condition (5-47) is more stringent than required for stability according to Definition I. The eigenvalues may be permitted to exceed one by a term having a magnitude no larger than order Δt, that is,

$$|\lambda_k| \leq 1 + 0\,(\Delta t) \tag{5-49}$$

This condition will permit exponential growth of the solution, but the solution remains bounded for a fixed time interval, say T. Such amplification may be fitting and proper for the physical-mathematical system, for example, with baroclinic instability. Further discussion of this case will be given later.

Returning to (5-47), note that a difference system may fail to meet this stability condition by having one (or more) eigenvalues exceed 1 in magnitude, yet if that eigenmode (vector) were not present in the initial state $\mathbf{F}_0$, in theory the solution $\mathbf{F}_n$ would not amplify. However in actual practice, round-off errors occur, hence all modes are soon present and the numerical solution would grow exponentially. A second related point is that if some modes are considered to be undesirable "noise," it may be feasible to filter them from the initial state with the aim of eliminating them from the solution. The elimination may be only temporary, however, since there may be physical or mathematical mechanisms within the difference system, as well as round-off errors, that regenerate the undesirable modes causing them to reappear. If this happens, steps can be taken to suppress them during the integration procedure, perhaps by diffusion terms, or by periodically applying explicit space or time filters. Another possibility is to judiciously choose a differencing scheme that will selectively dampen certain modes.

To consider the matter of error growth further, suppose that errors were to appear at some time, say $t = 0$ for convenience, and assume for simplicity that no further errors are subsequently introduced. If $\mathbf{F}'_0$ represents the contaminated value, the contaminated solution after n time steps, according to (5-42), will be

$$F'_n = A^n \mathbf{F}'_0 \tag{5-50}$$

If the error after n time steps is defined to be

$$\boldsymbol{\epsilon}_n = \mathbf{F}_n - \mathbf{F}'_n$$

it follows from (5-42) to (5-50) that

$$\boldsymbol{\epsilon}_n = A^n \boldsymbol{\epsilon}_0 \tag{5-51}$$

which is precisely the same form as (5-42). Next, $\boldsymbol{\epsilon}_0$ can be expressed in the same manner as (5-45) and $\boldsymbol{\epsilon}_n$ is similar to (5-46):

$$\boldsymbol{\epsilon}_n = \Sigma_k E_k \lambda_k^n \mathbf{v}_k \tag{5-52}$$

Thus the evolution of errors parallels that of the finite difference solution, mode by mode. Since this holds for round-off errors as well as other types, Definition III is a useful practical definition for stability. Although computational stability according to Definitions I and II is unrelated to round-off error, from a pragmatic point of view Definition III is appropriate since actual computation invariably involves round-off error. Moreover, the same condition for the computational stability of a difference scheme results whether couched in terms of the difference solution or error growth.

Return now to the example used in this section for illustration and express the matrix in (5-41) as the sum of the identity matrix I and a tridiagonal matrix M as follows:

$$A = I + rM$$

where

$$M = \begin{bmatrix} -2 & 1 & 0 & \cdots & 0 \\ 1 & -2 & 1 & \cdots & \\ 0 & 1 & -2 & 1 \; \cdot\cdot & \\ \cdots\cdots & \cdots\cdots & \cdots\cdots & \cdots\cdots & \\ \cdots\cdots & \cdots\cdots & \cdots\cdots & 1 & -2 \end{bmatrix}$$

It can be shown that if an arbitrary matrix A is a rational function of a second matrix M, then the eigenvalues of A are the same rational function of the eigenvalues of M, that is,

$$\text{if } A = f(M) \qquad \text{then} \qquad \alpha_k = f(\beta_k)$$

where α_k and β_k are the eigenvalues of A and M, respectively. Also the eigenvalues of a tridiagonal matrix of order $J - 1$, with elements a, b, and c in that order, are

$$\beta_k = b + 2\sqrt{ac}\cos\frac{k\pi}{J} \qquad k = 1,2\ldots J-1$$

Using the foregoing results gives the following eigenvalues for the matrix A:

$$\lambda_k = 1 - 4r\sin^2\frac{k\pi}{2J} \qquad k = 1,2\ldots J-1$$

It is readily seen that

$$|\lambda_k| \leq 1, \text{ provided } r \leq \tfrac{1}{2}, \text{ that is, } K\Delta t/\Delta x^2 \leq \tfrac{1}{2}$$

which is the stability condition for the difference equation (5-39) corresponding to the diffusion equation (5-38).

When the boundary values are not zero or conditions are imposed on the derivatives at the boundaries, the procedure is the same, however the column vectors and the matrix must be augmented. A very important feature of this method is that *boundary conditions can be included* in the analysis. Similarly, if more than two time levels are involved or when there is a system of equations to be solved, the matrix must be augmented accordingly. Some examples will be given later in connection with the von Neumann method of stability analysis.

5-5-2 Von Neumann Method

The von Neumann method is less general than the matrix method just described because the boundary conditions cannot be included, but it is much simpler to apply. It consists of replacing the spatial variation by a single Fourier component. This is sufficient for linear equations with constant coefficients since separate solutions are additive. The method will be illustrated on the *leapfrog* scheme applied to the advection equation (5-6), which must be placed in the form (5-37). However, since there are three time levels in (5-12), it is convenient to introduce a new variable, $G_{m,n} = F_{m,n-1}$. Then (5-12) may be written in the system

$$\begin{aligned} F_{m,n+1} &= G_{m,n} - \frac{c\Delta t}{\Delta x}(F_{m+1,n} - F_{m-1,n}) \\ G_{m,n+1} &= F_{m,n} \end{aligned} \tag{5-53}$$

Next, let

$$F_{m,n} = B_n^{(1)}\, e^{i\mu m\Delta x} \qquad G_{m,n} = B_n^{(2)}\, e^{i\mu m\Delta x}$$

Substituting these forms into (5-53) and canceling the common exponential factor leads to a pair of equations that can be put in vector form as follows:

$$\begin{bmatrix} B_{n+1}^{(1)} \\ B_{n+1}^{(2)} \end{bmatrix} = \begin{bmatrix} -2i\sigma & 1 \\ 1 & 0 \end{bmatrix} \begin{bmatrix} B_n^{(1)} \\ B_n^{(2)} \end{bmatrix} \tag{5-54a}$$

or

$$\mathbf{B}_{n+1} = A\mathbf{B}_n = A^2\mathbf{B}_{n-1} \cdot\cdot\cdot\cdot\cdot\cdot A^{n+1}\mathbf{B}_0 = \sum_{k=1}^{2} \lambda_k^{n+1}\, b_k v_k \tag{5-54b}$$

where the λ_k are the eigenvalues of the 2×2 matrix A; σ is defined by (5-15) and the b_k are constants. The eigenvalues are found by solving the equation

$$\begin{vmatrix} -2i\sigma - \lambda & 1 \\ 1 & -\lambda \end{vmatrix} = 0$$

or

$$\lambda^2 + 2i\sigma\lambda - 1 = 0 \tag{5-55}$$

The coefficients of this equation are identical to those in (5-14), hence the pair of eigenvalues is given by (5-16). As described earlier, a necessary *condition* for *computational stability* is that $|\lambda| \leq 1$ for all eigenvalues. Moreover, from the previous analysis of the roots of (5-55), that is, the right side of (5-16), it is clear that the difference scheme is stable if $|\sigma| \leq 1$, as given by (5-31); and the guarantee of stability for all admissible wavelengths is $c\Delta t/\Delta x \le 1$, as given by (5-32). In fact

$$|\lambda_k| \equiv 1 \qquad k = 1,2 \tag{5-56}$$

thus both modes corresponding to the λ's are *neutral*. Note that if the exponential factor is retained when passing from (5-53) to (5-54) the result is similar in form to (5-54) except that the vector **B** is replaced by a vector consisting of components F and G.

The more general criterion for stability given by (5-49), which fulfills the requirements of Definition I—that the solutions of the difference equation remain uniformly bounded functions of the initial state for a finite time T and for sufficiently small Δt and $N\Delta t = T$, will nevertheless, permit exponential growth. To show this, assume

$$\lambda = 1 + a\Delta t \tag{5-57}$$

where a is a constant. Then

$$\lambda^N = (1 + a\Delta t)^N = \left(1 + \frac{aT}{N}\right)^N \qquad N\Delta t = T$$

$$= 1 + N\left(\frac{aT}{N}\right) + \frac{N(N-1)}{2!}\left(\frac{aT}{N}\right)^2 + \ldots\ldots.$$

As N increases indefinitely with decreasing Δt, the series approaches

$$\lambda^N = 1 + aT + \frac{(aT)^2}{2!} + \ldots\ldots\ldots = e^{aT}$$

Thus, as seen from the various expressions for the solution, (5-20), (5-42), (5-46), or (5-54), those modes associated with eigenvalues of the form (5-57) will display exponential growth. However, within a finite time interval T, the solutions to the difference equation are bounded as $N \to \infty$; and thus the difference scheme is computationally stable in accordance with Definition I.

Even though the differential system may not call for growth, a small amount of growth with a convergent scheme may be practically acceptable, particularly if the scheme has other desirable features, for example, damping of a computational mode. In situations when exponential growth is in accordance with the physics, such as baroclinic or barotropic instability, (5-57) is certainly appropriate.

To pursue this discussion regarding the eigenvalues somewhat further, assume that

$$\lambda = 1 + f(\Delta t) \tag{5-58}$$

where f is an arbitrary function of Δt. Now take the log of (5-58), expand the log in a series and multiply by N giving

$$N \ln \lambda = N \ln[1 + f(\Delta t)] \doteq N[f(\Delta t) + \ldots]$$

Now revert to the exponential form after dropping terms of higher order

$$\lambda^N \doteq e^{Nf(\Delta t)}$$

Next consider some examples. First assume $f(\Delta t) = a\Delta t^2$, then

$$\lambda^N = e^{aN\Delta t^2} = e^{aT\Delta t}$$

If $N \to \infty$ and $\Delta t \to 0$, then $\lambda^N \to 1$ and no amplification takes place in the limit, although for a finite Δt some growth will occur for $a > 0$. On the other hand, if $f(\Delta t) = a\Delta t^{1/2}$, then

$$\lambda^N = e^{aN\Delta t^{1/2}} = e^{aT/\Delta t^{1/2}}$$

In this case as $N \to \infty$ and $\Delta t \to 0$, λ^N is unbounded and fails the stability requirement of Definition I.

The von Neumann condition (5-49) on the eigenvalues is certainly necessary for stability of the difference system, but may not be sufficient if the eigenvectors do not form a complete set. Sufficient conditions for a complete set, and thus for stability are somewhat more involved and may be found in standard texts on matrix theory or numerical solutions for partial differential equations, such as Richtmyer and Morton (1967).

5-5-3 The Energy Method

The last method of stability analysis to be mentioned here is the so-called *energy* method, which may or may not have anything to do with physical forms of energy. This method provides a sufficient condition for stability and is also applicable to nonlinear equations. If the true solution is known to be bounded, then the finite difference solution should be examined for boundedness. If it can be determined that the sum $\sum_m (u_{m,n})^2$, over all gridpoints for any time n, is bounded, then every $u_{m,n}$ is also bounded and stability is established. This method is usually considerably more difficult to apply than the von Neumann method, but it sometimes is usable on systems where the von Neumann method is inapplicable. In this text, except for a simple example, we confine the discussion henceforth to the von Neumann method, which is applicable to a wide variety of linear problems and serves as a useful guide to nonlinear problems.

5-6 EXAMPLES OF THE VON NEUMANN METHOD

In this section further examples of stability analysis will be given including iterative schemes, two space dimensions, multiple equations, etc.

5-6-1 Euler Scheme

First consider the two-level forward difference scheme called the *Euler scheme,* which was used to determine the computational boundary condition (5-22) for the leapfrog scheme,

$$F_{m,n+1} = F_{m,n} - \frac{c\Delta t}{2\Delta x}(F_{m+1,n} - F_{m-1,n}) \tag{5-59}$$

It is readily shown that the truncation error is of order, $O(\Delta t) + O(\Delta x^2)$ (student exercise). Assuming a solution of the form

$$F_{m,n} = B^{n\Delta t} e^{i\mu m\Delta x} \tag{5-60}$$

and substituting into (5-59) gives

$$B^{\Delta t} = 1 - \sigma i = (1 + \sigma^2)^{1/2} e^{-i\theta}$$

where σ is given by (5-15) and $\theta = \arctan \sigma$. After utilizing the initial condition, (5-60) becomes

$$F_{m,n} = A\left[1 + \left(\frac{c\Delta t}{\Delta x}\right)^2 \sin^2 \mu\Delta x\right]^{n/2} e^{i\mu(m\Delta x - n\theta/\mu)}$$

It is immediately apparent that the Euler scheme gives exponential growth for almost all wavelengths.[2] Consequently, it is of little consolation to note that no computational mode in time appears, the reason being that the difference equation is first order in time as is the differential equation.

In order to facilitate other stability analyses, it is convenient to note that for a solution of the form (5-60), the centered difference may be expressed in the form

$$F_{m+1,n} - F_{m-1,n} = (2i \sin \mu\Delta x) F_{m,n} \tag{5-61}$$

5-6-2 Uncentered Differencing, Von Neumann Method

As a slight variation from the Euler scheme, assume the forward time difference but a backward space difference to approximate the advection equation, that is,

$$F_{m,n+1} = F_{m,n} - (c\Delta t/\Delta x)(F_{m,n} - F_{m-1,n}) \tag{5-62}$$

With $c > 0$, the space derivative may be described as "upstream," and for $c < 0$, "downstream," especially when $c = U$ is the mean wind velocity. Assuming the usual solution form, (5-13) gives

[2] Strictly speaking if one were able to fix μ, then the scheme would be stable and convergent; however, in practice this is not feasible for reasons of round-off error alone, which can introduce arbitrarily large wave numbers.

$$F_{m,n+1} = [1 - \sigma(1 - e^{-i\mu\Delta x})] F_{m,n} \qquad \sigma = c\Delta t/\Delta x$$

The eigenvalue for this single element matrix is just the element

$$\lambda = 1 - \sigma + \sigma \cos \mu\Delta x - \sigma i \sin \mu\Delta x$$

and

$$\begin{aligned} |\lambda|^2 &= (1 - \sigma + \sigma \cos \mu\Delta x)^2 + \sigma^2 \sin^2 \mu\Delta x \\ &= 1 - 2\sigma(1 - \cos \mu\Delta x)(1 - \sigma), \text{ a parabola in } \sigma \end{aligned}$$

Note that when: $\sigma = 0$ or $\sigma = 1$, $|\lambda| = 1$ neutral

$\sigma < 0$ or $\sigma > 1$, $|\lambda| > 1$ amplified

$0 < \sigma < 1$, $|\lambda| < 1$ damped

Thus with *upstream* differencing, $c > 0$, *damped or neutral solutions* are the norm, provided $0 \leq c\Delta t/\Delta x \leq 1$. On the other hand, with *downstream* differencing ($c < 0$), $\sigma < 0$, and the solutions are *amplified* (*computationally unstable*). (For stability with $c < 0$, the space differencing would involve points m and $m + 1$.)

If F is taken as temperature and c, the wind velocity, it would be natural to look upstream when forecasting temperature changes by advection, rather than downstream. The numerical solution bears this out, although there is erroneous damping (Figure 5-3*b*). Upstream differencing is sometimes used for moisture advection, despite the damping, because negative values of moisture will not be produced, as may happen with central differencing (Figure 5-3).

Energy Method. The upstream case is a particularly easy one to illustrate the energy method which is also applicable to nonlinear equations. For this purpose F is assumed to be cyclic so that $F_{-1,n} = F_{M,n}$, and $x = m\Delta x$, $m = 0,1, \ldots M$. The solution is assumed to be bounded initially and it will be shown that the following relationship holds (with the proper restriction on σ):

$$\sum_m F^2_{m,n+1} \leq \sum_m F^2_{m,n} \tag{5-63}$$

This condition will ensure that the sum of the squares of $F_{m,n}$ does not increase with n. Moreover, it is evident that the individual $F_{m,n}$ must be also bounded if the sum of the squares of all $F_{m,n}$ is bounded. Thus (5-63) is a *sufficient* condition for *computational stability*.

First square both sides of (5-62), collect terms and then sum over m giving

$$\sum F^2_{m,n+1} = \sum_m [(1 - \sigma)^2 F^2_{m,n} + 2\sigma(1 - \sigma) F_{m,n} F_{m-1,n} + \sigma^2 F^2_{m-1,n}] \tag{5-64}$$

Two relationships will be derived for use in (5-64). The first follows directly from the cyclic continuity:

$$\sum_{m=0}^{M} F_{m-1,n}^2 = \sum_{m=0}^{M} F_{m,n}^2$$

The second relationship derives from the foregoing result and the simple fact that the square of a real quantity is positive as follows:

$$(F_{m,n} - F_{m-1,n})^2 = \underset{\text{a}}{F_{m,n}^2} - \underset{\text{b}}{2F_{m,n}F_{m-1,n}} + \underset{\text{c}}{F_{m-1,n}^2} \geq 0$$

Transposing the middle term (b) summing, then combining the first and last sums (a and c) gives

$$\sum_m F_{m,n}^2 \geq \sum_m F_{m,n} F_{m-1,n}$$

Now return to (5-64) and make use of these two relationships successively to give

$$\begin{aligned}\sum F_{m,n+1}^2 &= \sum_m \{[(1-\sigma)^2 + \sigma^2] F_{m,n}^2 + 2\sigma(1-\sigma) F_{m,n} F_{m-1,n}\} \\ &\leq \sum_m [(1-\sigma)^2 + \sigma^2 + 2\sigma(1-\sigma)] F_{m,n}^2 = \sum_m F_{m,n}^2 \end{aligned} \qquad (5\text{-}65)$$

The substitution leading to the inequality is, of course, valid only if the coefficient $2\sigma(1 - \sigma)$ is positive. The latter follows if $0 < \sigma \leq 1$, which is precisely the condition for computational stability of upstream differencing derived earlier in this section. The last equality holds because the coefficient of $F_{m,n}^2$ is exactly 1. Thus (5-63) has been established. The proof of (5-63) is considerably more complicated for most differencing schemes.

5-6-3 Trapezoidal Implicit Scheme

Both the forward and central time differencing schemes discussed previously have problems associated with them in addition to truncation error, the Euler scheme being unstable and the leapfrog, though conditionally stable, having a computational mode. The next technique, a trapezoidal scheme, avoids the two foregoing problems but, as will be seen, has another complication. This procedure uses only two time levels and thus avoids the computational mode, while using central differences for the space derivative centered at $[n + (1/2)]\Delta t$ by averaging values at n and $n + 1$ as follows

$$\frac{F_{m,n+1} - F_{m,n}}{\Delta t} = -\frac{c}{2}\left(\frac{F_{m+1,n+1} - F_{m-1,n+1}}{2\Delta x} + \frac{F_{m+1,n} - F_{m-1,n}}{2\Delta x}\right) \qquad (5\text{-}66)$$

Using (5-61) on the central differences easily leads to

$$F_{m,n+1} = \left(\frac{1 - i(c\Delta t/2\Delta x)\sin\mu\Delta x}{1 + i(c\Delta t/2\Delta x)\sin\mu\Delta x}\right) F_{m,n} \equiv \lambda F_{m,n}$$

The eigenvalue λ is again just the coefficient of $F_{m,n}$, the amplification matrix. Since the magnitude of the ratio of two complex numbers is just the ratio of their magnitudes, it follows immediately that

$$|\lambda| \equiv 1, \text{ \textit{unconditionally stable} for all } \Delta x \text{ and } \Delta t$$

By expanding in series about the time $n + \frac{1}{2}$, it may be shown that the implicit scheme has a truncation error of second order in t and x [i.e., $O(\Delta t)^2 + O(\Delta x)^2$].

The complication referred to earlier is that (5-66) no longer provides a simple marching process. Suppose the calculations have been completed for all gridpoints m at time n and it is desired to proceed to time $n + 1$. Then (5-66) may be solved for $F_{m,n+1}$, but the quantity, $F_{m+1,n+1}$, which is not yet known, appears on the right side. This means that a system of simultaneous equations for the F's must be solved, rather than simply progressing one at a time as in the leapfrog scheme (5-12). The latter is referred to as an *explicit* scheme and (5-66), an *implicit* scheme. The number of simultaneous equations will essentially equal the number of gridpoints, perhaps many thousands, and this involves inverting, in one form or another, a large matrix, which is very time consuming even with a high-speed computer. Consequently, implicit methods have been little used in meteorology; however some semiimplicit techniques are feasible.

The equation following (5-66) may be written

$$F_{m,n} = \lambda F_{m,n-1} = \ldots = \lambda^n F_0 \equiv A\lambda^n e^{i\mu m\Delta x}$$

$$= Ae^{i\mu(m\Delta x - 2n\theta/\mu)}$$

where

$$\theta = \arctan\left[(c\Delta t/2\Delta x)\sin\mu\Delta x\right]$$

It is readily seen that

$$c_F = 2\theta/\Delta t\mu$$

Now when $L = 2\Delta x$, $\mu\Delta x = \pi$ and $\theta = 0$; hence $c_F = 0$. For large L, $\mu\Delta x << 1$ and $\sin\mu\Delta x \doteq \mu\Delta x$. Thus $\theta \doteq \arctan(c\mu\Delta t/2)$. Continuing, for small $c\mu\Delta t/2$, $\theta \doteq c\mu\Delta t/2$ and $c_F \doteq c$; whereas for large $c\mu\Delta t/2$, $\theta \doteq \pi/2$; and $c_F = \pi/\Delta t\mu$, which does not depend on c. It may be inferred that for large Δt, which will not create instability with this scheme, c_F will be in serious error. Thus the *implicit scheme,* although *unconditionally stable,* has serious errors in the phase velocity not only for short waves as in the leapfrog scheme, but also for relatively large $c\Delta t/\Delta x$. The implications will be discussed later in connection with geostrophic adjustment when semiimplicit schemes are used with the primitive equations for the purpose of increasing the permissible size of Δt.

5-6-4 Euler Backward Scheme

The Euler backward scheme, sometimes referred to under the name *Matsuno,* who introduced it to meteorological usage, attempts to attain a trapezoidal character while avoiding the implicit character of the preceding scheme. This is accomplished by resorting to a trial forward step followed by a "backward" step as follows:

$$F^*_{m,n+1} = F_{m,n} - \frac{c\Delta t}{2\Delta x}(F_{m+1,n} - F_{m-1,n}) \tag{5-67a}$$

$$F_{m,n+1} = F_{m,n} - \frac{c\Delta t}{2\Delta x}(F^*_{m+1,n+1} - F^*_{m-1,n+1}) \tag{5-67b}$$

The von Neumann method may now be applied by assuming a solution of the form $F_{m,n} = A_n e^{i\mu m\Delta x}$ where A_n provides the time variation. Making use of (5-61) and $\sigma = (c\Delta t/\Delta x) \sin \mu\Delta x$ gives

$$F^*_{m,n+1} = (1 - \sigma i) F_{m,n} \tag{5-68}$$

and substituting (5-68) into (5-67b) gives

$$F_{m,n+1} = F_{m,n} - i\sigma(1 - i\sigma) F_{m,n}$$

or

$$F_{m,n+1} = (1 - \sigma^2 - \sigma i) F_{m,n}$$

It is evident that the scheme will be stable if

$$|1 - \sigma^2 - \sigma i| = (1 - \sigma^2 + \sigma^4)^{1/2} \leq 1 \tag{5-69}$$

which holds provided $|\sigma| \leq 1$. To insure stability for all μ requires

$$\left|\frac{c\Delta t}{\Delta x}\right| \leq 1 \tag{5-70}$$

This is the same condition as for the leapfrog scheme. However the leapfrog scheme gave neutral solutions; whereas in the Euler backward scheme the solutions are damped, except when the equality holds in (5-69). Moreover, the damping is wave-number dependent, since σ depends on μ. For $L = 2\Delta x$, $\sigma = 0$; hence there is no damping. Similarly for a fixed $c\Delta t/\Delta x$, $\sin \mu\Delta x$ decreases with large L; hence σ decreases and damping diminishes. Maximum damping takes place in between with $\sigma = 0.707$, which would occur, for example, with the combination $L = 4\Delta x$ and $c\Delta t/\Delta x = 0.707$, or other similar pairs. If c represents wave speed and c_g is the speed of the fastest gravity wave and Δt and Δx are chosen so that $c_g \Delta t/\Delta x$ is slightly less than unity for stability; then $c_m \Delta t/\Delta x << 1$ for the slower meteorological waves, which, therefore, experience little damping.

The damping characteristics may be seen from another viewpoint by writing $c = L/T = \upsilon/\mu$, where T is the period and υ the frequency, from which it follows that $\sigma = \upsilon\Delta t\,(\sin \mu\Delta x)/\mu\Delta x$. Since $(\sin \mu\Delta x)/\mu\Delta x < 1$, Δt must be chosen so that $\upsilon\Delta t < 1$ to guarantee computational stability for all wavelengths. In the limiting case as $\mu\Delta x$ approaches zero, $(\sin \mu\Delta x)/\mu\Delta x$ approaches 1 and $\sigma \rightarrow \upsilon\Delta t$; hence very low frequency waves such as meteorological waves give a small σ and experience little damping. On the other hand, high-frequency waves (e.g., external gravity waves), are generally strongly damped, except for the frequency where $\sigma = \upsilon\Delta t = 1$, which is undamped. Internal gravity waves may have low frequencies comparable to meteorological waves and would not be damped much either. Thus the damping characteristics of the Euler backward differencing scheme are rather complex. It should also be mentioned that filters may be applied directly to the data to remove short wavelengths or high frequencies or both, as will be discussed in Section 5-7-3 and Chapter 11.

The Euler backward or Matsuno scheme has been used for initializing numerical prediction models to dampen spurious inertial gravity noise generated during the early stages of a numerical forecast or whenever data are inserted into a model. (See Section 11-4.)

Also note that the Euler backward scheme has no computational mode, thus eliminating that source of error. However, it has the serious drawback of taking twice as long as the leapfrog scheme because of the two steps or iterations required for each Δt forward in time [see (5-67)]. Since computer time is a critical factor, especially in operational forecasting, this scheme is mainly used, if at all, during an initialization procedure and/or periodically during a forecast to eliminate the computational mode arising with the leapfrog scheme.

5-6-5 Fourth-Order Space Differencing

In view of the significant truncation errors associated with the centered difference (leapfrog) scheme as reflected in the errors in phase velocities given in Table 5-1, it is desirable to consider higher-order differences. Toward this end consider the following fourth-order, space-centered scheme for the advection equation (5-6)

$$\frac{F_{m,n+1} - F_{m,n-1}}{2\Delta t} = -c\left(a\frac{F_{m+1,n} - F_{m-1,n}}{2\Delta x} + b\frac{F_{m+2,n} - F_{m-2,n}}{4\Delta x}\right) \qquad (5\text{-}71)$$

Since each of the terms with coefficients a and b are valid approximations for $\partial F/\partial x$, it is clear that (5-71) will be a consistent scheme provided that $a + b = 1$. A second equation relating a and b may be derived by requiring that the second-order truncation errors vanish. This implies that the sum of the Taylor series term $a(\partial^3F/\partial x^3)\Delta x^3/3!(2\Delta x)$, and a similar term, $b(\partial^3F/\partial x^3)\,(2\Delta x)^3/3!(4\Delta x)$, from series expansions for $F_{m\pm1,n}$ and $F_{m\pm2,n}$ must vanish. Thus $a + 4b = 0$, as well as $a + b = 1$, giving

$$a = \tfrac{4}{3} \qquad b = -\tfrac{1}{3} \tag{5-72}$$

The resulting truncation error is

$$\frac{\Delta t^2}{6}\frac{\partial^3F}{\partial t^3} - c\,\frac{\Delta x^4}{30}\frac{\partial^5F}{\partial x^5} = O(\Delta t^2) + O(\Delta x^4) \tag{5-73}$$

The stability will be investigated next. As a variation on previous approaches, assume a solution of the form

$$F_{m,n} = Ae^{i\alpha n\Delta t + i\mu m\Delta x} \tag{5-74}$$

Substitution of (5-74) into (5-71) leads to

$$\sin\alpha\Delta t = -\frac{c\Delta t}{\Delta x}\left(\tfrac{4}{3}\sin\mu\Delta x - \tfrac{1}{6}\sin 2\mu\Delta x\right) \tag{5-75}$$

If α is real, neutral solutions result with no damping or amplification, as evident from (5-74). The condition for a real α is that the right side of (5-75) have magnitude less or equal to 1, otherwise α is complex. To insure stability for all wavelengths, it is necessary to find the maximum magnitude of the terms in parens on the right side of (5-75). Taking the derivative of this quantity with respect to $\mu\Delta x$ and setting it to zero gives

$$\tfrac{4}{3}\cos\mu\Delta x - \tfrac{1}{3}\cos 2\mu\Delta x = 0 \tag{5-76}$$

Next replace $\cos 2\mu\Delta x$ by $(2\cos^2\mu\Delta x - 1)$ and solve the quadratic for $\cos\mu\Delta x$. Choosing the real root yields

$$\cos\mu\Delta x = -0.225 \qquad \text{and} \qquad \mu\Delta x = 103^\circ$$

and

$$\tfrac{4}{3}\sin 103^\circ - \tfrac{1}{6}\sin 206^\circ = 1.37$$

Using this value in (5-75) gives the following criterion necessary to maintain stability for all wave numbers

$$|c\Delta t/\Delta x| \le 0.73 \tag{5-77}$$

It is evident that (5-77) is more stringent than (5-32), and, for a given c and Δx, the Δt would have to be 27 percent smaller for fourth-order differencing versus second-order. Also several additional terms have to be calculated for (5-71). The overall result is a considerable increase in computing time, which is the price paid for the smaller truncation error. However, as reflected in the smaller phase speed errors shown in Table 5-1, fourth-order differencing can be very worthwhile. The tabular values were calculated from a formula similar to (5-25), that is,

$$c_F = \frac{1}{\mu\Delta t} \arcsin\left[\frac{c\Delta t}{\Delta x} {}^4/_3 \sin \mu\Delta x - {}^1/_6 \sin 2\mu\Delta x)\right] \tag{5-78}$$

Note that the minimum resolvable wavelength of 2Δx is *stationary* as in the second-order scheme. Also there are two values of (5-75) for $\alpha\Delta t < 2\pi$, one of which is the physical mode and the other, a computational mode due to time differencing. Moreover, the need for more points in computing differences can complicate formulation of boundary conditions; and, in addition, computational modes in space may appear. Nevertheless, it should be noted that there is more gain in accuracy by using fourth-order differencing than by reducing the grid size, *per unit increase* in computing time. An unfortunate result of fourth-order differencing is the high negative group velocity of the two-gridlength wave. Since the $2\Delta x$ wavelength remains stationary while the phase velocity of the $4\Delta x$ wave is closer to c than in the second-order case, the group velocity (see 5-27) of the $2\Delta x$ wave is strongly negative. This is easily verified by substitution of (5-78) into (5-27) giving

$$G_{F4} = c\,\frac{{}^4/_3 \cos \mu\Delta x - {}^1/_3 \cos 2\mu\Delta x}{\{1 - [(c\Delta t/\Delta x)({}^4/_3 \sin \mu\Delta x - {}^1/_6 \sin 2\mu\Delta x)]^2\}^{1/2}}$$

For $L = 2\Delta x$, $G_{F4} = -5c/3$; while for other wavelengths, the group velocity depends on the value of $(c\Delta t/\Delta x)$, which is limited to being ≤ 0.73 for stability. For $c\Delta t/\Delta x = 0.70$ and $L = 4\Delta x$, $G_F \approx c$. It can be concluded therefore that fourth-order differencing can lead to more rapid spreading of noise opposite to the phase velocity in the very short wavelengths from any source in the model, physical or computational.

An implicit fourth-order scheme for computing first-order derivatives is the Padé (or compact) differencing (see, for example, Navon and Riphagen 1979); which for the x-direction is as follows:

$$\frac{1}{6}\left[\left(\frac{\partial u}{\partial x}\right)_{i+1} + 4\left(\frac{\partial u}{\partial x}\right)_i + \left(\frac{\partial u}{\partial x}\right)_{i-1}\right] = \frac{u_{i+1} - u_{i-1}}{2\Delta x}$$

Here the determination of $(\partial u/\partial x)_i$, $i = 1 \ldots .$, involves the solution of a linear system with only a tri-diagonal coefficient matrix. Another advantage is that fewer fictitious boundary points are needed than with (5-71) which involves 5 points. With explicit time differencing this benefit is somewhat offset by the need to invert a matrix, however, the compact scheme is more accurate than the 5-point scheme even though both have fourth-order accuracy. For implicit time schemes, which inevitably require matrix inversion anyway, the added matrix inversion may be of little consequence.

When applied to the advection equation the compact fourth-order scheme is exactly equivalent to the finite element method with piecewise linear basis functions (See Section 6-7) which is shown to be considerably more accurate than the 5-point fourth-order scheme (Table 6-1).

5-6-6 Oscillation Equation

In the von Neumann method the spatial variation of the dependent variable is assumed to be represented by a Fourier component, say $F = B(t) \exp(i\mu x)$. If this is substituted into the advection equation, $\partial F/\partial t + c\partial F/\partial x = 0$, and the common factor eliminated the result is

$$\frac{dB}{dt} = -ci\mu B$$

1st order
1st degree

or, if a centered finite difference approximation is used for the x variation, the equation becomes

$$\frac{dB}{dt} = -(ci \sin \mu\Delta x/\Delta x)\, B$$

In either case, the result is an ordinary differential equation, called the *oscillation* equation, which, together with its solution, may be written as

$$\frac{dB}{dt} = i\omega B \qquad B = B_0 e^{i\omega t}$$

The parameter ω is the frequency and $2\pi/\omega$ is the period T of the oscillation. This equation may now be examined for numerical solutions. Consider the two-level scheme

$$B_{n+1} - B_n = i\omega\Delta t\,(aB_{n+1} + bB_n) \tag{5-79}$$

where a and b are both positive; and solve for B_{n+1}, giving

$$B_{n+1} = \left(\frac{1 + ib\omega\Delta t}{1 - ia\omega\Delta t}\right) B_n \tag{5-80}$$

It is evident from (5-79) that for consistency $a + b = 1$. For stability the magnitude of the eigenvalue, $(1 + ib\omega\Delta t)/(1 - ia\omega\Delta t)$, must be ≤ 1. Using the polar form for the numerator and denominator gives

$$|\lambda|^2 = \frac{1 + (b\omega\Delta t)^2}{1 + (a\omega\Delta t)^2}$$

from which it follows that for *stability*, $b \leq a$. Consider some choices for a and b.

$a = 0, b = 1$	forward differencing, amplifying (unstable)
$a = 1, b = 0$	backward implicit, damping (stable)

$a = b = ½$ trapezoidal implicit, neutral (stable)

Using (5-61) the leapfrog scheme (5-12) may be written in a similar form

$$B_{n+1} = B_{n-1} + 2i\omega\Delta t B_n$$

where $\omega = -\sin \mu\Delta x/2\Delta x$. Introducing the notation $D_n = B_{n-1}$ leads to the matrix equation

$$\begin{bmatrix} B \\ \\ D \end{bmatrix}_{n+1} = \begin{bmatrix} 2i\omega\Delta t & 1 \\ \\ 1 & 0 \end{bmatrix} \begin{bmatrix} B \\ \\ D \end{bmatrix}_n \tag{5-81}$$

The equation for the eigenvalues of the matrix in this form is

$$\lambda^2 - 2i\omega\Delta t\lambda - 1 = 0$$

The eigenvalues are easily found to be $\lambda = +i\omega\Delta t \pm \sqrt{1 - \omega^2\Delta t^2}$ and

$$|\lambda| = 1, \text{ if } |\omega\Delta t| \leq 1: \textit{conditionally stable}$$

The two values of λ give two modes, one physical and one computational, as in (5-16). If $|\omega\Delta t| > 1$, or $2\pi\Delta t > T$, (T = period), the numerical solution will be unstable.

5-6-7 Two-Dimensional Advection Equation

Consider next the equation

$$\partial F/\partial t + \mathbf{V}_s \cdot \nabla F = 0 \text{ where } \mathbf{V}_s = U\mathbf{i} + V\mathbf{j} = \text{const.} \tag{5-82}$$

Let $\Delta x = \Delta y = d$, $x = jd$, $y = kd$, $t = n\Delta t$, and apply centered differences

$$F_{j,k,n+1} - F_{j,k,n-1} = \\ -\frac{U\Delta t}{d}(F_{j+1,k,n} - F_{j-1,k,n}) - \frac{V\Delta t}{d}(F_{j,k+1,n} - F_{j,k-1,n}) \tag{5-83}$$

Following the von Neumann method, substitute solutions of the form

$$F_{j,k,n} = B_n e^{i(pjd+qkd)}$$

into (5-83) and simplify, leading to

$$B_{n+1} = B_{n-1} - \frac{2i\Delta t}{d}(U \sin pd + V \sin qd)B_n \tag{5-84}$$

Next define $D_n = B_{n-1}$, place (5-84) in matrix form, and find the eigenvalues. The procedure parallels equations (5-53) and (5-55) except that σ is replaced by $(\Delta t/d)(U \sin pd + V \sin qd)$ in (5-55). The eigenvalues are

$$\lambda = -i(\Delta t/d)\,(U \sin pd + V \sin qd) \pm \sqrt{1 - (\Delta t/d)^2\,(U \sin pd + V \sin qd)^2}$$

The eigenvalues will have magnitude 1 provided

$$(\Delta t/d)\,|U \sin pd + V \sin qd| \leq 1 \tag{5-85}$$

Next place $U = V_s \cos\theta$ and $V = V_s \sin\theta$ in the above equation, giving

$$(V_s \Delta t/d)|\cos\theta \sin pd + \sin\theta \sin qd| \leq 1$$

Since the wave numbers p and q are independent, take the maximum values of one for $\sin pd$ and $\sin qd$, and maximize the sum, $\cos\theta + \sin\theta$, which is $\sqrt{2}$, occurring at $\theta = \pi/4$. The result is the linear computational stability criterion for the leapfrog scheme applied to the two-dimensional advection equation, that is,

$$V_s\,\Delta t\,\sqrt{2}/d \leq 1 \qquad \text{or} \qquad V_s\,\Delta t \leq 0.707d \tag{5-86}$$

Note that with two dimensions the maximum value of Δt required for stability is almost 30 percent smaller than for one dimension, other things being equal. The reason for the decrease in the maximum Δt required for stability may be seen in Figure 5-6. Here a wave propagating from SW to NE has an effective distance of $d/\sqrt{2}$ between gridpoints. Basically, the stability criterion says that the wave cannot move more than the effective distance between gridpoints during time Δt without incurring computational instability.

5-6-8 External Gravity Waves, Leapfrog Scheme

To illustrate the procedure for a stability analysis when there are two equations, consider the one-dimensional system for gravity waves

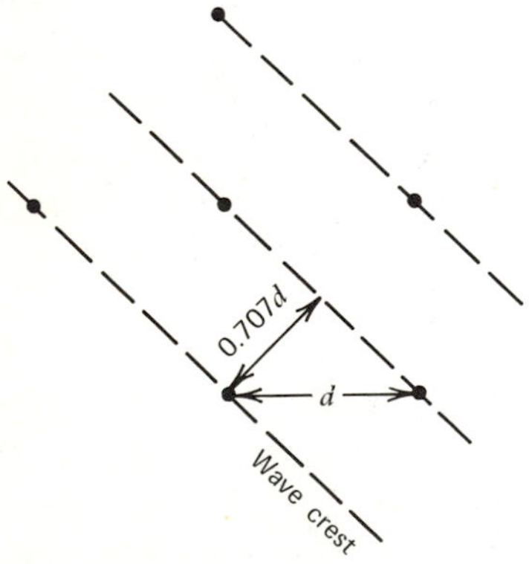

Figure 5.6

$$\frac{\partial u}{\partial t} + U\frac{\partial u}{\partial x} + \frac{\partial \phi}{\partial x} = 0 \qquad \Phi\frac{\partial u}{\partial x} + \frac{\partial \phi}{\partial t} + U\frac{\partial \phi}{\partial x} = 0 \tag{5-87}$$

The central difference equations with $\Delta x = d$ are

$$\begin{aligned} &\frac{u_{m,n+1} - u_{m,n-1}}{2\Delta t} + U\frac{u_{m+1,n} - u_{m-1,n}}{2d} + \frac{\phi_{m+1,n} - \phi_{m-1,n}}{2d} = 0 \\ &\Phi\frac{u_{m+1,n} - u_{m-1,n}}{2d} + \frac{\phi_{m,n+1} - \phi_{m,n-1}}{2\Delta t} + U\frac{\phi_{m+1,n} - \phi_{m-1,n}}{2d} = 0 \end{aligned} \tag{5-88}$$

Next substitute into (5-88) a solution of the form

$$u = Ae^{i(\alpha n\Delta t + \mu m d)} \qquad \phi = Be^{i(\alpha n\Delta t + \mu m d)} \tag{5-89a}$$

giving the homogeneous pair of equations

$$\begin{aligned} &A\left(\frac{\sin \alpha\Delta t}{\Delta t} + U\frac{\sin \mu d}{d}\right) + B\frac{\sin \mu d}{d} = 0 \\ &A\left(\Phi\frac{\sin \mu d}{d}\right) + B\left(\frac{\sin \alpha\Delta t}{\Delta t} + U\frac{\sin \mu d}{d}\right) = 0 \end{aligned} \tag{5-89b}$$

Using the procedure for obtaining the frequency equations in the analytical case, that is, setting the determinant of the coefficients of A and B to zero, as required for a nontrivial solution, leads to

$$\sin \alpha\Delta t = -(\Delta t/d)(U \pm \Phi^{1/2}) \sin \mu d \tag{5-90}$$

Since the solutions of the differential system (5-87) are neutral, a real α is desired. If the right side of (5-90) is to have magnitude less than 1 for all wave numbers, then

$$|\sin \mu d\,(U \pm \Phi^{1/2})(\Delta t/d)| \leq 1 \tag{5-91}$$

Stability for all wave numbers requires $|c\Delta t/d| \leq 1$, where $c = U \pm \Phi^{1/2}$ is the speed of external gravity waves.

The same result can be obtained by the von Neumann procedure, in which case the amplification matrix is 4×4, giving a quartic equation for the eigenvalues. Fortunately, however, the quartic is biquadratic, which readily leads to (5-90) (student exercise). When the usual situation of two dimensions in space is involved, the right side of (5-91) becomes $\sqrt{2}/2 = 0.707$ as in (5-86).

5-6-9 Staggered Grid

Consider the same problem with the staggered grid shown in Figure 5-7, where the same spacing d has been maintained but one variable has been moved over a distance $d/2$. Although the number of gridpoints is doubled the number of variables to be computed remains the same. The centered difference equations are:

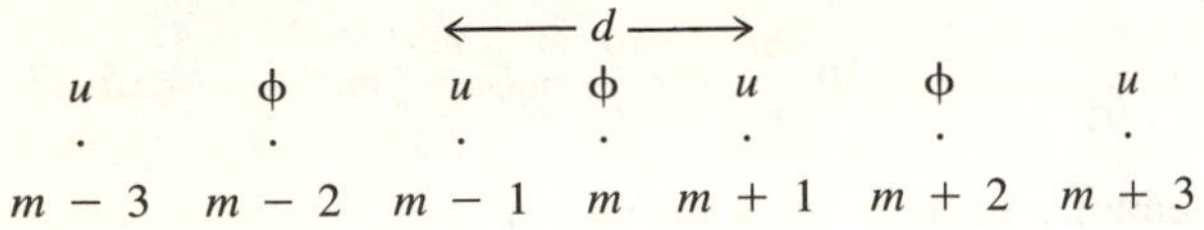

Fig. 5.7 Staggered grid of two variables.

$$\frac{u_{m+1,n+1} - u_{m+1,n-1}}{2\Delta t} + U\frac{u_{m+3,n} - u_{m-1,n}}{2d} + \frac{\phi_{m+2,n} - \phi_{m,n}}{d} = 0$$
$$\Phi\frac{u_{m+1,n} - u_{m-1,n}}{d} + \frac{\phi_{m,n+1} - \phi_{m,n-1}}{2\Delta t} + U\frac{\phi_{m+2,n} - \phi_{m-2,n}}{2d} = 0 \qquad (5\text{-}92)$$

To examine the effect of staggering on the stability and phase velocity substitute solutions of the form (5-89a) with d replaced by $d/2$ into the foregoing equations and follow the previous procedure. The resulting stability criterion, analogous to (5-91) is:

$$\left|\sin(\mu d/2)\,(U\cos\mu d \pm \Phi^{1/2})\,(\Delta t/d)\right| \leq 1/2 \qquad (5\text{-}93)$$

Note that the pressure force and the divergence have been evaluated over a distance d in the staggered case (5-92) as compared to $2d$ in the unstaggered case (5-88). However the advection terms are evaluated over $2d$ in both cases. The stability condition (5-93) for staggered case requires a maximum Δt of about half the value given by (5-91) for the unstaggered case (assuming $U/\Phi^{1/2}$ is small), which implies a near *doubling* of *computation* time.

Regarding the effect of truncation error on phase speed, (5-89), (5-90) show that the phase speeds, $-\alpha/\mu$, with the staggered and unstaggered grids are, respectively,

$$(1/\mu\Delta t)\arcsin[(\Delta t/d)(\sin\mu d)(U \pm \Phi^{1/2})] \text{ unstaggered}$$
$$(1/\mu\Delta t)\arcsin\{(\Delta t/d)[U\sin\mu d \pm 2\,\Phi^{1/2}\sin(\mu d/2)]\}\text{: staggered} \qquad (5\text{-}94)$$

whereas the true velocity is $(U \pm \Phi^{1/2})$. Both grids have the same truncation error with respect to the advection term, but the staggered grid gives more accurate gravity wave propagation since $(\sin\mu d)/\mu d < [\sin(\mu d/2)/(\mu d/2)] < 1$ (student exercise). This results in a better treatment of the geostrophic adjustment process with staggered grids and should predict the structure of the smaller scale features more accurately (as discussed in Section 7-3), which may be worthwhile despite the extra computing time.

5-7 FORWARD-BACKWARD SCHEME, PRESSURE AVERAGING, AND SEMI-IMPLICIT METHODS

The preceding examples brought out some significant problems associated with numerical weather prediction using equations that permit both meteorological modes and inertial gravity waves. The latter are important primarily for the "geostrophic adjustment" process (Section 2-7) by which real and spurious imbalances between the wind and mass fields created by observation errors, mountains, point heat sources, objective analysis schemes, etc. are eliminated. Generally no attempt is made to forecast the gravity waves, if only for lack of initial data to resolve them. However, the inertial gravity waves (and the Lamb wave) impose a stringent computational stability condition on Δt, and require a much smaller Δt than needed to maintain a high degree of numerical accuracy for the meteorological waves with respect to time truncation error. By far the largest truncation error for the meteorological waves is associated with space truncation. In other words, the time step in primitive equation models is more than two orders of magnitude less than the period of ordinary meteorological waves, while the scale of short synoptic waves is less than one order of magnitude greater than the space increment. Also it may be seen from Table 5-1 that when $c\Delta t/\Delta x$ is small, the phase errors are considerably greater than when $c\Delta t/\Delta x$ is nearly 1. Moreover, the size of Δt is dictated by high speed gravity or Lamb waves, hence

$$1 \gtrsim c_g \Delta t/\Delta x >> c_{\text{met}} \Delta t/\Delta x \tag{5-95}$$

There have been and continue to be various attempts to circumvent the stringent stability requirement on Δt imposed by the high-speed gravity-type waves. In this section, several schemes are described. One basic concept is to treat those terms in the equations that govern the propagation of the gravity waves implicitly, that is, the pressure force in the momentum equations and the divergence term in the continuity equation, while the advection and other terms are treated explicitly. It may be recalled that an implicit scheme applied to the advection equation [see (5-66)] is unconditionally stable, placing no limit on the size of Δt.

5-7-1 Forward-Backward Scheme

To illustrate this scheme in the simplest fashion omit the advection term in (5-87). Next predict the ϕ field first by forward differencing; then apply backward differencing to the momentum equation as follows:

$$\begin{aligned} \phi_{m,n+1} &= \phi_{m,n} - (\Phi \Delta t/2d)\,(u_{m+1,n} - u_{m-1,n}) \\ u_{m,n+1} &= u_{m,n} - (\Delta t/2d)\,(\phi_{m+1,n+1} - \phi_{m-1,n+1}) \end{aligned} \tag{5-96}$$

Following the von Neumann method, let $\phi = D_n\, e^{i\mu m\Delta x}$ and $u = B_n\, e^{i\mu m\Delta x}$ and substitute these into (5-96). The resulting matrix equation is

$$D_{n+1} = D_n - \Phi\, \sigma i B_n \tag{5-97}$$

$$B_{n+1} = B_n - \sigma i D_{n+1} = B_n - \sigma i(D_n - \Phi\, \sigma i B_n) \tag{5-98}$$

where $\sigma = (\Delta t/d) \sin \mu d$ and the last form is obtained by substitution from (5-97). In matrix form the pair becomes

$$\begin{bmatrix} B_{n+1} \\ \\ D_{n+1} \end{bmatrix} = \begin{bmatrix} 1 - \Phi\sigma^2 & -\sigma i \\ \\ -\Phi\sigma i & 1 \end{bmatrix} \begin{bmatrix} B_n \\ \\ D_n \end{bmatrix} \tag{5-99}$$

The equations for the eigenvalues and their solutions are, respectively,

$$\begin{gathered} (1 - \lambda)^2 - \Phi\sigma^2 (1 - \lambda) + \Phi\sigma^2 = 0 \\ \lambda = \{2 - \Phi\sigma^2 \pm [\Phi\sigma^2 (\Phi\sigma^2 - 4)]^{1/2}\}/2 \end{gathered} \tag{5-100}$$

If $\Phi\sigma^2 \leq 4$, the quantity under the radical is 0 or negative and the magnitude of $|\lambda|^2$ is exactly 1. On the other hand, $\Phi\sigma^2 > 4$ will give a $|\lambda|$ greater than 1. Hence the stability condition becomes

$$|(\Delta t/d)\, \Phi^{1/2} \sin \mu d| \leq 2 \tag{5-101}$$

Thus it has been found that this scheme permits a Δt that is twice as large as that of the leapfrog scheme (see 5-91 with $U = 0$). The advection term was not included here and, unfortunately, centered space differencing would be unstable. However, Gadd (1978) has successfully used the forward-backward method with a modified form of the Lax-Wendroff advection scheme (Section 5-7-5). The procedure is very efficient because large time steps can be taken with the advection terms.

5-7-2 Pressure Averaging

Another somewhat similar scheme by Shuman (1971) and Brown and Campana (1978), which also permits a larger Δt than the leapfrog scheme, is the following

$$\frac{\phi_{m,n+1} - \phi_{m,n-1}}{2\Delta t} + U \frac{\phi_{m+1,n} - \phi_{m-1,n}}{2d} + \Phi \frac{(u_{m+1,n} - u_{m-1,n})}{2d} = 0 \tag{5-102a}$$

$$\frac{u_{m,n+1} - u_{m,n-1}}{2\Delta t} + U \frac{u_{m+1,n} - u_{m-1,n}}{2d} + \frac{1}{2d} [(1 - 2a) (\phi_{m+1,n} - \phi_{m-1,n}) + a (\phi_{m+1,n+1} - \phi_{m-1,n+1} + \phi_{m+1,n-1} - \phi_{m-1,n-1})] = 0 \tag{5-102b}$$

In this system the values of ϕ at time $n + 1$ from the first equation are used in the second equation as in the previous example. Note, however, that the only variation from the ordinary leapfrog scheme is the averaging of the pressure force over times, $n+1,n$ and $n-1$, in the second equation. If the parameter a is zero (5-102) reduces to the leapfrog scheme. To simplify the analysis, the advection terms will be neglected for the present, that is, take $U = 0$. Next assume solutions of the form, $u_{m,n} = A \exp[i(\mu md + \alpha n\Delta t)]$ and $\phi_{m,n} = B \exp[i(\mu md + \alpha n\Delta t)]$, and substitute into (5-102), giving a pair of homogeneous equations in A and B. Setting the determinant equal to zero for a nontrivial solution gives

$$\sin^2 \alpha\Delta t = S[1 - 2a(1 - \cos \alpha\Delta t)] \tag{5-103}$$

where

$$S = \Phi\,(\Delta t/d)^2 \sin^2 \mu d \tag{5-104}$$

For a real α the right side of (5-103) must be ≥ 0; hence the coefficient of S must be ≥ 0. To gain some insight take the minimum value of $\cos \alpha\Delta t$ of -1, which yields

$$(1 - 4a) \geq 0 \qquad \text{or} \qquad a \leq 1/4, \text{ required for stability} \tag{5-105}$$

The equality gives the familiar 1-2-1 averaging of the pressure force at times, $n + 1$, n and $n - 1$. Next place the maximum value of a, $a = 1/4$, in (5-103) and substitute $1 - \cos^2 \alpha\Delta t$ for $\sin^2 \alpha\Delta t$, giving

$$2 \cos^2 \alpha\Delta t + S \cos \alpha\Delta t + S - 2 = 0, \text{ or}$$

$$\cos \alpha\Delta t = [(S \pm (S - 4)]/4$$

For a real α, the right side must have magnitude ≤ 1, hence for stability

$$S \leq 4 \text{ or } \sqrt{S} \leq 2 \tag{5-106}$$

Then from (5-104), the *stability* requirement in one dimension corresponding to the maximum values of $a = 1/4$ and $|\sin \mu d| = 1$, is

$$\Phi^{1/2}\,(\Delta t/d) \leq 2$$

Comparison of this result to (5-91) shows that the Shuman pressure-averaging technique permits a maximum of doubling the permissible time step for computational stability. The curve labeled $\sigma_1 = U(\Delta t/d) \sin \mu d = 0$ in Figure 5-8 from Schoenstadt and Williams (1976) shows S as a function of a. Note that S drops very sharply as a decreases from its maximum permitted value of 1/4.

When the advection terms are included ($U \neq 0$), the value of S again decreases significantly. Additional curves are shown in Figure 5-8 for other values of σ_1. In a typical NWP model σ_1 may be of the order of a few tenths giving a value of S of about 1.5 to 2.5 for $a = 1/4$, which, in turn, would permit Δt to be 25 to 50 percent larger than in the simple leapfrog scheme.

5-7-3 Time Averaging

Time averaging or filtering has been used in other ways in numerical integration. To gain some appreciation of its effects, consider the simple wave form

$$F = A\, e^{i2\pi t/T} = A\, e^{i\omega t}$$

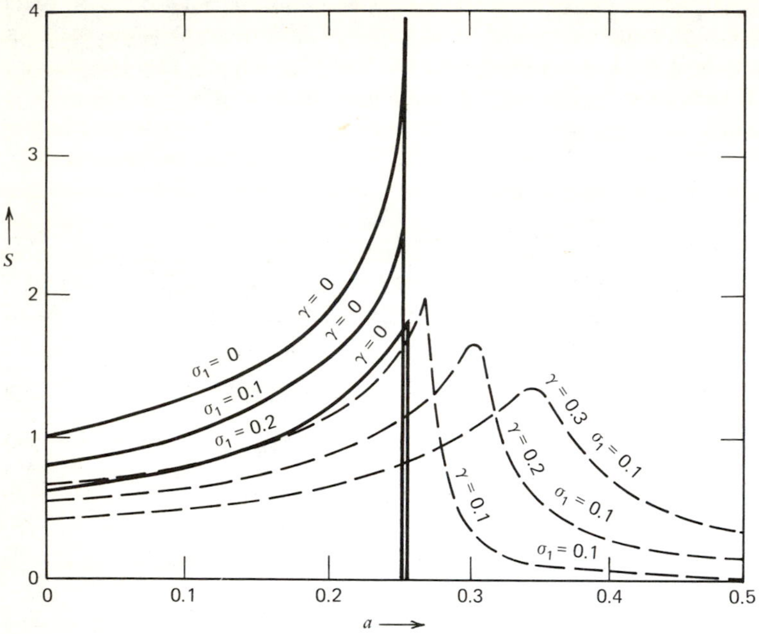

Figure 5.8

Now take the time average of F according to the formula

$$\begin{aligned}\overline{F}(t) &= (1 - 2\gamma)\,F(t) + \gamma[F(t + \Delta t) + F(t - \Delta t)] \\ &= F(t) + \gamma[F(t + \Delta t) - 2F(t) + F(t - \Delta t)]\end{aligned} \tag{5-107}$$

The result of averaging F is

$$\begin{aligned}\overline{F}(t) &= A\{(1 - 2\gamma)\,e^{i2\pi t/T} + \gamma[e^{i2\pi(t+\Delta t)/T} + e^{i2\pi(t-\Delta t)/T}]\} \\ &= F(1 - 2\gamma + 2\gamma \cos 2\pi\Delta t/T)\end{aligned}$$

The ratio, $\overline{F}/F = R$, is called the *response function*. If $\gamma = 1/4$, the simple 1-2-1 average results, and

$$R(1/4) = 0.5(1 + \cos 2\pi\Delta t/T)$$

It is evident that the averaging reduces the amplitude but not the phase of F. Consider a few examples:

$T = 2\Delta t \quad R = 0 \qquad T = 4\Delta t \quad R = 0.5 \qquad T >> \Delta t \quad R \doteq 1$

Thus, the averaging operator (5-107) with $\gamma = 1/4$ removes or filters $2\Delta t$ waves and reduces the amplitude of $4\Delta t$ waves by one-half, but has little effect on long-period waves. As such, (5-107) may be described as a low-pass filter, meaning that high frequencies tend to be removed. In this connection, note that the computational mode associated with the leapfrog scheme has essentially a $2\Delta t$ period, hence the 1-2-1 filter will effectively remove this "noise."

A filter of the form (5-107) may be used in connection with the leapfrog scheme [Robert (1966), Asselin (1972)] as follows. Assume the average $\overline{F}_{n-1}$ has been computed and stored for the time $(n - 1)\,\Delta t$ as well as the unaveraged value of F_n for time $n\Delta t$. Then the prediction equation is used to compute the tendency $(\partial F/\partial t)_n$ using the unaveraged values F_n (also F_{n-1}, as needed), from which the predicted values F_{n+1} are obtained from:

$$F_{n+1} = \overline{F}_{n-1} + 2\Delta t\,(\partial F/\partial t)_n$$

Next an average value of $\overline{F}_n$ is computed as follows:

$$\overline{F}_n = F_n + \gamma(F_{n+1} - 2F_n + \overline{F}_{n-1}) \tag{5-108}$$

At this point $\overline{F}_n$ is stored in place of $\overline{F}_{n-1}$ and the prediction procedure is repeated.

As might be expected the time filter does effect the computational stability criterion. When there is no pressure averaging ($a = 0$) and S meets the stability criterion, the solutions will be damped and the damping increases with increasing γ. The critical value of S for stability, which is always less than 1, decreases as γ increases, requiring a progressively smaller Δt.

When pressure averaging is included similar effects on computational stability are observed except that the time averaging extends the stable region significantly beyond $a = 1/4$. As before, the inclusion of the advection term reduces the stable region. Figure 5-8 contains several additional curves combining pressure averaging and time averaging with $\sigma_1 = 0.1$.

Despite the advantage of immediately suppressing $2\Delta t$-wave, values of γ less than 0.25 are preferable primarily because the stability condition requires a progressively small Δt as γ increases. Moreover, repeated use of an even weak filter eventually dampens the higher meteorological frequencies.

Filtering (or smoothing) is highly desirable both in time and space to remove high frequency and short wavelength noise that is generated due to various sources, such as, mountains, point sources of heat, injection of observations, differencing schemes, boundaries, etc. Some differencing schemes, such as the Euler-backward scheme, have inherent damping at high frequencies; in other cases, a diffusion term may be added, more or less arbitrarily, to the equations to dampen noise. This need not be entirely artificial since diffusion through turbulent eddies of various scales is constantly occurring in the atmosphere even though the viscosity of air is extremely small so that molecular viscosity is insignificant in those scales of motion of primary interest to the meteorologist.

A final comment is in order with the pressure-averaging technique. In the example given here, the shallow-water equations were used and the geopotential and wind velocity were the only dependent variables. In baroclinic primitive equation models temperature is usually one of the prognostic variables. In this case temperature and surface pressure are predicted first, the former with the thermodynamic equation and the latter with the continuity equation. Then these two predicted variables, say, at time $n + 1$, are used in the hydrostatic equation to determine the geopotential field at time $n + 1$. Finally the horizontal velocity components are predicted with the momentum equations wherein the pressure force is now averaged using ϕ at times $n - 1$, n, and $n + 1$, as done in (5-102b).

5-7-4 Semi-Implicit Method

The semi-implicit method (Kwizak and Robert, 1971) goes a step nearer to a fully implicit scheme by treating implicitly those terms in the equations of motion that are primarily responsible for the propagation of gravity waves. Again the shallow-water equations will be used to illustrate the method, but in two dimensions this time:

$$u_{n+1} = u_{n-1} - \frac{\Delta t}{d}\overline{\mathbf{V}} \cdot \boldsymbol{\nabla} u_n - \frac{\Delta t}{2d}[\boldsymbol{\nabla}_x (\phi_{n-1} + \phi_{n+1})] \tag{5-109}$$

$$v_{n+1} = v_{n-1} - \frac{\Delta t}{d}\overline{\mathbf{V}} \cdot \boldsymbol{\nabla} v_n - \frac{\Delta t}{2d}[\boldsymbol{\nabla}_y (\phi_{n-1} + \phi_{n+1})] \tag{5-110}$$

$$\phi_{n+1} = \phi_{n-1} - \frac{\Delta t}{d}\overline{\mathbf{V}} \cdot \boldsymbol{\nabla} \phi_n - \Phi\frac{\Delta t}{2d}[\boldsymbol{\nabla} \cdot (\mathbf{V}_{n-1} + \mathbf{V}_{n+1})] \tag{5-111}$$

$$\text{where } \overline{\mathbf{V}} = U\mathbf{i} + V\mathbf{j} \qquad \mathbf{V} = u\mathbf{i} + v\mathbf{j} \qquad \boldsymbol{\nabla} = \nabla_x\mathbf{i} + \nabla_y\mathbf{j} \tag{5-112}$$

$$\nabla_x A_n = A_{j+1,k,n} - A_{j-1,k,n} \qquad x = jd \qquad y = kd \qquad t = n\Delta t, \text{ etc.}$$

The foregoing system is termed *semi-implicit* because the advection terms, which are linearized here, are treated in explicit fashion. When these nonlinear terms are allowed their full variability, more sophisticated differencing must be used to avoid nonlinear instability, that will be discussed later. The next step is to eliminate u_{n+1} and v_{n+1} from Equation 5-111 to produce an equation for ϕ_{n+1} involving variables only at times n and $n - 1$. To accomplish this apply the operators $\boldsymbol{\nabla}_x$ and $\boldsymbol{\nabla}_y$ to (5-109) and (5-110), respectively, and substitute the right sides for $\boldsymbol{\nabla}_x u_{n+1}$ and $\boldsymbol{\nabla}_y v_{n+1}$ into (5-111), with the result

$$\phi_{n+1} = \phi_{n-1} - \frac{\Delta t}{d}\overline{\mathbf{V}} \cdot \boldsymbol{\nabla}\phi_n - \frac{\Phi\Delta t}{2d}\boldsymbol{\nabla} \cdot \mathbf{V}_{n-1}$$

$$- \Phi\frac{\Delta t}{2d}\left\{\boldsymbol{\nabla} \cdot \mathbf{V}_{n-1} - \frac{\Delta t}{d}\boldsymbol{\nabla} \cdot [(\overline{\mathbf{V}} \cdot \boldsymbol{\nabla}\, \mathbf{V}_n + \tfrac{1}{2}\, \boldsymbol{\nabla} (\phi_{n-1} + \phi_{n+1})]\right\}$$

Rearranging and defining, $\nabla_F^2 A = A_{i+2,j} + A_{i-2,j} + A_{i,j+2} + A_{i,j-2} - 4A_{i,j}$, gives

$$\begin{aligned} \nabla_F^2\phi_{n+1} - \frac{4d^2}{\Phi\,\Delta t^2}\phi_{n+1} &= -\nabla_F^2\phi_{n-1} + \frac{4d^2}{\Phi\,\Delta t^2}\phi_{n-1} \\ &+ \frac{4}{\Phi}\frac{d}{\Delta t}\overline{\nabla}\cdot\nabla\phi_n - \frac{4d}{\Delta t}\nabla\cdot\mathbf{V}_{n-1} - 2\nabla\cdot(\overline{\mathbf{V}}\cdot\nabla\mathbf{V}_n) \end{aligned} \tag{5-113}$$

This equation is of the Helmholtz type elliptic equation

$$\nabla_F^2\,\phi_{n+1} - B\phi_{n+1} = F(x,y) \tag{5-114}$$

Here F and B are known and (5-114) can be solved for ϕ_{n+1} by various methods over a given region given the values on the boundaries. The relaxation method begins with a first guess and then uses an iterative procedure to correct successive approximations. More recently direct elimination methods have been devised that are much faster, but are not quite as widely applicable as the relaxation method. Both techniques will be discussed in a later section. Whatever the method of solution, when the ϕ's at time $n + 1$ are calculated they are used in the momentum equations for the implicit differencing of the pressure force term, as has been done to the velocity divergence in the continuity equation. The consequences of this implicit treatment are (1) a less stringent stability criterion permitting a much larger Δt, two to four times as large depending on the particular form of the equations; but also (2) a considerable decrease in the speed of the gravity waves that impedes the geostrophic adjustment process.

5-7-5 Lax Wendroff Scheme

The Lax Wendroff scheme (Richtmyer and Morton, 1967) is similar to the two-step Euler backward scheme with a forward diffusing step, $\Delta t/2$, and central in space first estimate, followed by a leapfrog step. Applied to the advection equation (5-6) the scheme is

$$\begin{aligned} F^*_{m+\frac{1}{2},n+\frac{1}{2}} &= \tfrac{1}{2}\,(F_{m+1,n} + F_{m,n}) - (c\,\Delta t/2d)\,(F_{m+1,n} - F_{m,n}) \\ F_{m,n+1} &= F_{m,n} - (c\,\Delta t/d)\,(F^*_{m+\frac{1}{2},n+\frac{1}{2}} - F^*_{m-\frac{1}{2},\,n+\frac{1}{2}}) \end{aligned} \tag{5-115}$$

The first step is referred to as diffusing and by itself is stable but strongly damping. To gain some insight into the result of the two steps, substitute the * value into the second equation with suitable indices. The result is

$$\begin{aligned} F_{m,n+1} = F_{m,n} &- (c\,\Delta t/2d)\,(F_{m+1,n} - F_{m-1,n}) + \\ &(c^2\Delta t^2/2)\,(F_{m+1,n} - 2F_{m,n} + F_{m-1,n})/d^2 \end{aligned} \tag{5-116}$$

The last term, an approximation for $(c^2\Delta t^2/2)\,\partial^2 F/\partial x^2$, is recognizable as a diffusion term and appears to be a dissipative term added to the original differential equation that controls what would otherwise be the unstable Euler scheme. However, this is not quite the case, for (5-116) is readily seen to be *consistent* with the advection equation by dividing 5-116 by Δt and letting d and Δt go to zero. The truncation error, as well as the consistency, may also be seen by differentiating the advection equation with respect to t and then substituting from the original equation as follows:

$$\frac{\partial^2 F}{\partial t^2} = -c\frac{\partial}{\partial t}\frac{\partial F}{\partial x} = -c\frac{\partial}{\partial x}\frac{\partial F}{\partial t} = -c\frac{\partial}{\partial x}\left(-c\frac{\partial F}{\partial x}\right) = c^2\frac{\partial^2 F}{\partial x^2}$$

Now expand F in a Taylor series and substitute for $\partial^2 F/\partial t^2$ as follows:

$$F_{n+1} = F_n + \Delta t\, \partial F/\partial t + (\Delta t^2/2)\, \partial^2 F/\partial t^2 + \dots$$
$$\frac{\partial F}{\partial t} \doteq (F_{n+1} - F_n)/\Delta t - (c^2 \Delta t/2)\, \partial^2 F/\partial x^2 \qquad (5\text{-}117)$$

Equating the right side of (5-117) to a central difference approximation for $\partial F/\partial x$ and rearranging gives (5-116), and also shows that the Lax Wendroff scheme is second order in both time and space. Some other good features of the scheme are the absence of a temporal computational mode and the damping characteristic which is most pronounced at the $2d$ wavelength. The principal drawback is obviously the two-step feature, which requires twice the computer time than the leapfrog scheme because the stability condition is the same as for the leapfrog scheme, namely, $|c\Delta t/d| \leq 1$ (for one space dimension).

5-8 A SUMMARY OF SOME DIFFERENCE SCHEMES

In the preceding pages a number of difference schemes has been analyzed in varying detail, the purpose being to describe numerical analysis techniques and to acquaint the reader with some of the most commonly used schemes and some pitfalls.

Kurihara (1965) investigated a variety of differencing schemes as applied to the linear system

$$\frac{\partial u}{\partial t} + U\frac{\partial u}{\partial x} = fv - \frac{\partial \phi}{\partial x}$$
$$\frac{\partial v}{\partial t} + U\frac{\partial v}{\partial x} = -fu$$
$$\frac{\partial \phi}{\partial t} + U\frac{\partial \phi}{\partial x} = -gH\frac{\partial u}{\partial x} \qquad (5\text{-}118)$$

If h represents u, v, or ϕ, the system (5-118) may be written as

$$\frac{\partial h}{\partial t} = F_1 + F_2 = F \tag{5-119}$$

where $F_1 = -U\,\partial h/\partial x$ and F_2 is the right side of (5-118). Table 5-2 gives a summary of the characteristics of ten different integration schemes.

The separation of F into the parts, F_1 and F_2, is prompted by the fact that the slow, low-frequency meteorological waves are primarily associated with the nonlinear advective terms while the linear terms represented by F_2 are responsible for the high-frequency inertial gravity oscillations. The latter fast-moving waves are more likely to be the cause of computational instability and also are usually suppressed as undesirable noise in a meteorological forecast, except as necessary to effect "geostrophic adjustment" by removing noncyclostrophic imbalances between the wind and pressure. The implicit methods can successfully eliminate the computational instability and permit larger Δt's, but only at the expense of time-consuming inversion of large matrices in the gridpoint method. However, the two- or three-step iterative methods listed in Table 5-2 are also quite useful in suppressing noise and are simple to apply. Since (5-119) is a linear equation, the use of more than two time levels results in the appearance of a computational mode.

Note that a combination of several of the schemes may be more effective than a single scheme. For example, after applying the leapfrog method (1) for a sizable number of time steps because of its simplicity, method 4 could be used for a few steps to dampen the computational mode, and then method 3 for a few steps to suppress the noise before finally returning to the leapfrog method. The Euler backward scheme, method 2, has also been used for a few steps to restart after many leapfrog steps in order to eliminate the computational mode and suppress noise.

Lilly (1965) examined a number of time integration schemes as applied to a spectral form of the simplified barotropic vorticity equation. The time variation of the amplitudes of the Fourier components are expressible as a system of nonlinear ordinary differential equations as follows:

$$\frac{dA_i}{dt} = F_i\,(A_1, A_2, \ldots, t)$$

Of the eight schemes applied to a four-component system, the best overall—considering simplicity, efficiency, and accuracy—appeared to be the Adams-Bashforth scheme as follows

$$A_i^{n+1} = A_i^n + \Delta t\,(\tfrac{3}{2}F_i^n - \tfrac{1}{2}F_i^{n-1}) \tag{5-120}$$

Since there are three time levels present, this scheme has a computational mode; however, it tends to damp, which is favorable. On the other hand, the physical

Table 5-2 Properties of Various Methods (Kurihara, 1965)

Method	Difference equation	Number of time levels	Computational stability	Physical mode: Amplitude	Physical mode: Phase	Computational mode: Amplitude
Implicit:						
(*A*) Backward	$h^{r+1} - h^r = \Delta t F^{r+1}$	2	Absolutely stable	Highly selective damping	Retardation	None
(*B*) Trapezoidal	$h^{r+1} - h^r = \Delta t(F^{r+1} + F^r)/2$	2	Absolutely stable	No change	Little retardation	None
(*C*) Partly	$h^{r+1} - h^r = \Delta t F_1^r + \frac{\Delta t}{2}(F_2^{r+1} + F_2^r)$	2	Unstable for meteorological wave and one gravity wave			None
(*D*) Partly	$h^{r+1} - h^{r-1} = 2\Delta t F_1^r + 2\Delta t F_2^{r+1}$	3	(Very weak) unstable for meteorological wave	Damping of gravity wave and weak amplifying of meteorological wave		Damping
Explicit:						
(*O*) Forward	$h^{r+1} - h^r = \Delta t F^r$	2	Unstable			None
(1) Leapfrog (centered)	$h^{r+1} - h^{r-1} = 2\Delta t F^r$	3	Conditionally stable ($b < 1$)	No change	Moderate acceleration	No change
Iterative:						
(2) Euler-backward	$h^* - h^r = \Delta t F^r$ $h^{r+1} - h^r = \Delta t F^*$	2	Conditionally stable ($b < 1$)	Moderately selective damping	Large acceleration	None
(3) Modified Euler-backward	$h^* - h^r = \frac{\Delta t}{2} F^r$ $h^{**} - h^r = \Delta t F^*$ $h^{r+1} - h^r = \Delta t F^{**}$	2	Conditionally stable ($b < \sqrt{2}$).	Highly selective damping	Moderate acceleration	None
(4) Leapfrog-trapezoidal	$h^* - h^{r-1} = 2\Delta t F^r$	3	Conditionally stable ($b < \sqrt{2}$)	Little damping	Little error	Very effective damping (in particular of meteorological wave)
(5) Leapfrog-backward	$h^* - h^{r-1} = 2\Delta t F^r$ $h^{r+1} - h^r = \Delta t F^*$	3	Conditionally stable ($b < 0.8$)	Moderately selective damping	Moderate acceleration	Damping

[a]In ''difference equation,'' F_1 and F_2 represent nonlinear and linear terms, respectively, and $F = F_1 + F_2$. ''Number of time levels'' means what is associated with each marching step. In ''computational stability,'' $b = \mu c \Delta t$, where c is an appropriate phase velocity. Under ''physical mode,'' retardation or acceleration means a fictitious change of phase velocity resulting only from finite differencing in time. (From Kurihara, 1965.)

mode tends to amplify; but the rate of erroneous amplification is small if Δt is relatively small, especially for the longer wavelengths. Thus the Adams-Bashforth scheme is suitable unless the period of integration is lengthy.

Young (1968) analyzed the properties of 13 time-differencing schemes applied to a system of first-order differential equations representing a simple linear and a nonlinear baroclinic model of the atmosphere, which can be represented in the form

$$\frac{dX_i}{dt} = f_i\,(X_1, X_2, \ldots\ldots X_M; t) \tag{5-121}$$

He compared the numerical solutions to the exact analytical solution and found that the best results were obtained from the following methods:

$$\begin{aligned} A.\quad \hat{X}_{n+\frac{1}{2}} &= X_n + f_n\,\Delta t/2 \\ \overline{X}_{n+\frac{1}{2}} &= X_n + \tfrac{1}{2}\,(f_n + f_{n+\frac{1}{2}})\,\Delta t/2 \\ X_{n+1} &= X_n + \bar{f}_{n+\frac{1}{2}}\,\Delta t \end{aligned} \tag{5-122}$$

B. Kutta Scheme

$$\begin{aligned} \hat{X}_{n+\frac{1}{2}} &= X_n + f_n\,\Delta t/2 \\ X_{n+\frac{1}{2}} &= X_n + \hat{f}_{n+\frac{1}{2}}\,\Delta t/2 \\ \overset{*}{X}_{n+1} &= X_n + \bar{f}_{n+\frac{1}{2}}\,\Delta t \\ X_{n+1} &= X_n + \tfrac{1}{6}\,(f_n + 2\hat{f}_{n+\frac{1}{2}} + 2\bar{f}_{n+\frac{1}{2}} + \overset{*}{f}_{n+1})\,\Delta t \end{aligned} \tag{5-123}$$

$$C.\quad \hat{X}_{i,n+\frac{1}{2}} = X_{i,n} + f_i\,(\hat{X}_{1,n+\frac{1}{2}}, \ldots \hat{X}_{i-1,n+\frac{1}{2}}, X_{i,n}, \ldots X_{M,n})\,\Delta t/2$$

$$X_{j,n+1} = \hat{X}_{j,n+\frac{1}{2}} + f_j\,(X_{M,n+1} \ldots X_{j-1,n+1}, \hat{X}_{j,n+\frac{1}{2}} \ldots, \hat{X}_{1,n+\frac{1}{2}})\,\Delta t/2 \tag{5-124}$$

where n refers to the time step, $t = n\Delta t$.

While very accurate compared to the other schemes, these iterative schemes require more computer time than single-step schemes. Haltiner (1959) used the Runge-Kutta scheme for solution of the first numerical moist convection model with very good results; however the number of gridpoints was small compared to the typical multilevel prediction models so that computation time was not an issue.

The differencing schemes summarized here certainly do not comprise an exhaustive list, which is not the purpose of this text. For more detail, refer to the articles cited and to texts on numerical integration of differential equations.

5-9 PARABOLIC EQUATIONS

The diffusion equation (5-38), which was used to illustrate the full matrix method, is an example of a parabolic equation. Assuming the dependent variable is known at an initial time over a given region and at the boundaries of the region for all future time, the problem is to find the solution over the interior of the region for future times. The numerical methods of solution here are similar to those used for hyperbolic equations. A simpler equation will be considered first which, together with its analytic solution, is the following:

$$\partial F/\partial t = aF \qquad F = F_0\, e^{at} \tag{5-125}$$

where a is a constant. Note that the diffusion equation (5-38) reduces to this form if the solution is assumed to be continuous and harmonic in x, say, $F = F_1\,(t)\, e^{i\mu x}$. Also if F is thought of as velocity and $a = -\,C_D$, (5-125) represents a form of simple linear frictional drag.

Consider now the consistent *forward difference* approximation

$$\begin{aligned} F_n - F_{n-1} = a\Delta t\, F_{n-1} \qquad \text{or} \qquad F_n &= (1 + a\Delta t)\, F_{n-1} \\ &= (1 + a\Delta t)^n\, F_0 \end{aligned} \tag{5-126}$$

Because of the simple form of this solution, it can be analyzed directly for convergence. Assume a time interval, $T = n\Delta t$, and expand $(1 + a\Delta t)^n$ as was done for (5-57), that is,

$$(1 + a\Delta t)^n = (1 + aT/n)^n = 1 + aT + n(n - 1)\,(aT/n)^2/2! + \ldots$$

As Δt tends toward zero, n approaches ∞, and the series reduces to

$$(1 + a\Delta t)^n = 1 + aT + (aT)^2/2 + \ldots = e^{aT}$$

Thus the numerical solution F_n converges toward the true solution, $F_0\, e^{aT}$, over a fixed time interval T as Δt is made smaller and smaller. In terms of the von Neumann stability analysis the eigenvalue is $(1 + a\Delta t)$ which provides for exponential growth if $a > 0$.

When $a < 0$, the solution is damped and again the solution converges. In this case, when considering a simple marching process in time for a fixed Δt, care must be taken in choosing Δt so that $|a\Delta t| < 1$; for if the quantity $(1 + a\Delta t) \leq 0$, the solution will either remain zero (for the equality case), and when less than zero, the solution will oscillate between positive and negative values.

Next consider the *central differencing* scheme with linear damping as follows:

$$(F_{n+1} - F_{n-1})\,/2\Delta t = -\,C_D\, F_n \tag{5-127}$$

Placing (5-127) in matrix form gives

$$\begin{bmatrix} F \\ G \end{bmatrix}_{n+1} = \begin{bmatrix} -2C_D\Delta t & 1 \\ 1 & 0 \end{bmatrix} \begin{bmatrix} F \\ G \end{bmatrix}_n$$

where $F_{n-1} = G_n$.

The characteristic equation for the eigenvalues is easily found to be

$$\lambda^2 + 2\Delta t\, C_D \lambda - 1 = 0$$

and

$$\lambda = -C_D\,\Delta t \pm \sqrt{1 + (C_D\,\Delta t)^2}$$

The positive root is of the form $\lambda = 1 + a\Delta t + O(\Delta t^2)$, and corresponds to the physical solution; however the negative root will alternate between plus and minus values due to a coefficient $(-1)^n$ and will amplify exponentially. Consequently, *central differencing* will *not* give a *convergent solution* and should not be used.

Suppose the equation is of a mixed parabolic and hyperbolic type, for example, a momentum equation with advection and linear drag (or diffusion) such as

$$\frac{\partial u}{\partial t} + U\frac{\partial u}{\partial x} = -C_D\, u \tag{5-128}$$

If centered differencing is used on the first two terms, the drag term must be treated in a forward sense with respect to time if the scheme is to be stable, that is,

$$(u_{m,n+1} - u_{m,n-1})/2\Delta t = -U\,(u_{m+1,n} - u_{m-1,n})/2\Delta x - C_D\, u_{m,n-1} \tag{5-129}$$

Thus, relative to the time derivative, the advection term is centered at time n; whereas the friction term is forward with a step of $2\Delta t$.

If a diffusion term of the form $K\,\partial^2 u/\partial x^2$ appears on the right side of (5-128) and u is assumed to be periodic in x, that is, $u = A(t) \exp i\mu x$, then $K\,\partial^2 u/\partial x^2 = -K\,\mu^2 u$. Thus an explicit diffusion term behaves somewhat like the linear drag term except that it is scale dependent with a coefficient that increases with the square of the wave number.

In general, explicit diffusion terms can discriminate different space scales whatever their frequency. On the other hand, a time-differencing scheme can implicitly achieve selective damping as a function of frequency and therefore can distinguish between waves of different frequency even of the same wavelength [e.g., (5-67)]. A combination of explicit and implicit damping is the best means of filtering small-scale, high-frequency waves. Still another method of removing "noise" from geophysical variables is to apply filters directly to the variables, for example, to initial data, or periodically during a numerical integration as in Section 5-7-3, or to the final product for "cosmetic" reasons. There is a discussion of some filters in Chapter 11.

The explicit scheme (5-39) used for the diffusion equation (5-38) required a relatively small Δt; however there are other schemes that have certain advantages. For example, an explicit second-order scheme that is *always stable* is that by *Dufort and Frankel*

$$\frac{F_{m,n+1} - F_{m,n-1}}{2\Delta t} = K\frac{F_{m+1,n} - F_{m,n+1} - F_{m,n-1} + F_{m-1,n}}{\Delta x^2} \tag{5-130}$$

where it is *required* for consistency that Δt go to zero faster than Δx. The truncation error is

$$T = O(\Delta t^2) + O(\Delta x^2) + O[(\Delta t/\Delta x)^2]$$

Although (5-130) appears to be implicit because of the term $F_{m,n+1}$ on the right side, this term may be transposed to the left side and coupled with the like term in the time derivative. Such schemes are sometimes referred to as *pseudo-implicit.*

Additional terms may be present in the differential equation, such as,

$$\frac{\partial F}{\partial t} = K\,\partial^2 F/\partial x^2 + a\,\partial F/\partial x + bF \tag{5-131}$$

for which a somewhat generalized difference scheme is

$$\frac{F_{m,n+1} - F_{m,n}}{\Delta t} = K\frac{\theta\nabla_x^2 F_{m,n+1} + (1-\theta)\nabla_x^2 F_{m,n}}{\Delta x^2} + \frac{a\nabla_x F_{m,n}}{2\Delta x} + bF_{m,n} \tag{5-132}$$

where $0 \le \theta \le 1$. When $\theta = 0$, the scheme is explicit; whereas $\theta \ne 0$ gives an implicit scheme. With $a = 0$, $b = 0$, and $\theta = \frac{1}{2}$, the scheme reduces to *Crank-Nicholson* implicit scheme which is always stable; whereas with $\theta = 0$, the scheme is conditionally stable, requiring $K\Delta t/\Delta x^2 \le \frac{1}{2}$, as derived earlier in Section 5-5-1.

More generally the stability condition is as follows:

$$K\Delta t/\Delta x^2 \le 1/(2 - 4\theta) \qquad \text{if } 0 \le \theta < \tfrac{1}{2} \text{ and} \tag{5-133}$$

$$\text{no restriction on } \Delta t, \text{ if } \tfrac{1}{2} \le \theta \le 1$$

With these conditions, the eigenvalues fulfill the von Neumann condition, $|\lambda| \le 1 + O(\Delta t)$. The stability proof for this case and many other schemes, including iterative methods for solving the implicit schemes, are given in Richtmyer and Morton (1967).

As a brief indication of the nature of the *iterative methods,* consider the following procedure, known as the *Gauss-Seidel* iteration. As applied to the implicit form of (5-132), with $\theta = \frac{1}{2}$ and $a = b = 0$, this technique obtains an explicit improved estimate, say, $(k + 1)$, of $F_{m,n+1}$ from the kth estimate as follows:

$$F^{k+1}_{m,n+1} = \frac{1}{1+2r}F_{m,n} + \frac{r}{(1+2r)}\left(F^{k+1}_{m-1,n+1} + F^{k}_{m+1,n+1} + \nabla_x^2 F_{m,n}\right) \qquad r = K\Delta t/2\Delta x^2 \tag{5-134}$$

Note that the $(k + 1)$ term on the right side is at point $m - 1$, presumably already calculated.

5-10 ELLIPTIC EQUATIONS

Elliptic partial differential equations arise in science and engineering most often in connection with steady-state problems or *diagnostic* equations, a term that is used in NWP to describe relationships between meteorological variables in the absence of time derivatives. However, in some instances, a time derivative is the dependent variable sought in an elliptic equation such as in the vorticity equation for filtered models where the lead term is $\nabla^2 (\partial\psi/\partial t)$. The best-known elliptic equations are the Poisson and Helmholtz types, which in two dimensions are, respectively,

$$\nabla^2 G = F_1\,(x,y) \qquad \nabla^2 G - H_1 G = F_1\,(x,y) \tag{5-135}$$

where $F_1\,(x,y)$ is a known "forcing" function and H_1 is a known positive coefficient. In order to solve the equation over a region, (1) the dependent variable G, (2) its normal derivative, or (3) a combination of the two must be known on the boundary curve C enclosing the region. The first boundary specification is referred to as a *Dirichlet* condition; the second, a *Neumann* condition; and the third is a mixture of the two.

5-10-1 Relaxation Method

In the past the most common method of solution used by meteorologists has been the successive approximation *relaxation method* (SOR) in which an initial guess of the solution is made and then progressively improved until an acceptable level of accuracy is reached. To illustrate this method consider a rectangular region covered by a grid of equally spaced points separated by a distance d over which a solution to a Helmholtz equation is sought with known values of G on the boundary. The simplest finite difference approximation for the Laplacian ∇^2 at some point (i,j) is

$$\nabla^2 G_{i,j} \doteq \frac{G_{i-1,j} + G_{i+1,j} + G_{i,j-1} + G_{i,j+1} - 4G_{i,j}}{d^2} \equiv \frac{\nabla_F^2 G_{i,j}}{d^2} \tag{5-136}$$

Substituting this expression into the Helmholtz equation (5-135) gives

$$\nabla_F^2 G_{i,j} - HG_{i,j} = F_{i,j} \tag{5-137}$$

where $H = H_1 d^2$ and $F = F_1 d^2$. Now assume an initial estimate or "guess" of T is made, followed by another, etc., and let $G_{i,j}^m$ represent the mth estimate. Then the *residual* $R_{i,j}^m$ for the mth estimate is defined as follows:

$$G_{i-1,j}^m + G_{i+1,j}^m + G_{i,j-1}^m + G_{i,j+1}^m - (4 + H)\,G_{i,j}^m - F_{i,j} = R_{i,j}^m \tag{5-138}$$

The objective of the subsequent iterations is to reduce the residuals to some acceptably small value although the exact solution with the $R_{i,j} \equiv 0$ everywhere will not be reached. Given the mth estimate $G^m_{i,j}$, an improved value $G^{m+1}_{i,j}$, which will temporarily reduce the residual $R^m_{i,j}$ to zero, may be obtained by changing only $G^m_{i,j}$ to $G^{m+1}_{i,j}$ in (5-138) and setting the next residual to zero as follows:

$$G^m_{i-1,j} + G^m_{i+1,j} + G^m_{i,j-1} + G^m_{i,j+1} - (4 + H)\, G^{m+1}_{i,j} - F_{i,j} = 0$$

Next subtract this equation from (5-138) and solve for $G^{m+1}_{i,j}$ given

$$G^{m+1}_{i,j} = G^m_{i,j} + R^m_{i,j}/(4 + H)$$

or more generally, (5-139)

$$G^{m+1}_{i,j} - G^m_{i,j} = -\,(R^{m+1}_{i,j} - R^m_{i,j})/(4 + H)$$

Intuitively, this procedure seems to be a step in the right direction and so it can be shown. However, since the residual at any point is dependent on the four surrounding points, it is evident that when the residual at a neighboring point, say $(i,j + 1)$, is reduced to zero in similar fashion by correcting the value, $G^m_{i,j+1}$, the residual at point (i,j) will depart from zero again. To determine the amount consider the mth residual at $(i,j + 1)$

$$G^m_{i+1,j+1} + G^m_{i-1,j+1} + G^m_{i,j+2} + G^m_{i,j} - (4 + H)\, G^m_{i,j+1} - F_{i,j+1} = R^m_{i,j+1}$$

Now calculate the new residual, say, $R^{m*}_{i,j+1}$ at $(i,j + 1)$ when the new estimate, $G^{m+1}_{i,j}$ from (5-139) is used instead of $G^m_{i,j}$; the result is

$$G^m_{i+1,j+1} + G^m_{i-1,j+1} + G^m_{i,j+2} + [G^m_{i,j} + R^m_{i,j}/(4 + H)]$$
$$- (4 + H)\, G^m_{i,j+1} - F_{i,j+1} = R^{m*}_{i,j+1}$$

Subtracting the foregoing equation from the preceding one gives

$$R^{m*}_{i,j+1} = R^m_{i,j+1} + R^m_{i,j}/(4 + H)$$

Thus, reducing the residual at a given point (i,j) to zero increases the residuals at the four surrounding points by an amount exactly equal to the correction to $G^m_{i,j}$. When the $(m + 1)$th approximation is calculated over the entire grid in accordance with (5-139), the procedure is known as *simultaneous relaxation*. With $H \geq 0$, this relaxation method always converges, although it may do so slowly. In fact, the effect of a new guess on surrounding residuals suggests that overcorrection would be a good strategy to hasten convergence as discussed below.

Sequential Relaxation. Several improvements to simultaneous relaxation will yield more rapid convergence. As with the Gauss-Seidel method (5-134), using new values of T at preceding points as they are obtained, say, $G^{m+1}_{i-1,j}$ and

$G_{i,j-1}^{m+1}$ instead of $G_{i-1,j}^{m}$ and $G_{i,j-1}^{m}$ in (5-139) when calcuating the residual $R_{i,j}^{m}$ for determining $G_{i,j}^{m+1}$ by (5-139), gives faster convergence and is known as *sequential relaxation*.

Also, as suggested above or when a few steps of the relaxation method are done manually, it is quickly seen that if the residuals have the same sign over at least several adjacent gridpoints, it pays to *overrelax,* that is, to add a larger correction than given by (5-139), (the latter just making the residual zero) as follows:

Overrelaxation

$$G_{i,j}^{m+1} = G_{i,j}^{m} + \alpha R_{i,j}^{m}/(4 + H) \qquad 1 \leq \alpha \leq 2 \qquad \text{(SOR)(5-140)}$$

The optimal value of the overrelaxation coefficient depends on the specific form of the coefficients of the equation and the error distribution. However, a theoretical estimate may be made for a simplified equation, which then can be made more precise by numerical experiments. Frankel (see Richtmyer and Morton, 1967) showed that for the Poisson equation ($H = 0$) with sequential overrelaxation (SOR) the optimum value of $\omega = \alpha/4$ for maximum rate of convergence is given by the smaller root of

$$\omega^2 t_m^2 - 4\omega + 1 = 0$$

where $t_m = \cos(\pi/M) + \cos(\pi/N)$ and M and N are the number of grid intervals in the x- and y-directions on a rectangular grid. For large M and N

$$\omega_{\text{opt}} \rightarrow \tfrac{1}{2} - \frac{\pi}{2\sqrt{2}}\left(\frac{1}{M^2} + \frac{1}{N^2}\right)^{1/2}$$

If M and N are very large the second term is small and ω_{opt} approaches ½ or α in (5-140) approaches 2. The overrelaxation coefficient may be very sensitive and small changes can, on occasion, radically change the rate of convergence. The SOR method is very flexible and can be used under a wide range of conditions, including irregular boundaries, interior boundary points, three dimensions, etc. Proofs of convergence, etc. may be found in the standard numerical methods texts for partial differential equations.

5-10-2 Direct Methods

The SOR method is quite general; however it takes considerable computer time and has been replaced by faster, accurate, direct methods in most problems. The *block-cyclic reduction method* was introduced by Buneman (1969) and has been used by numerous investigators, including Sweet (1973), Rosmond and Faulkner (1976), Rosmond (1975), Faulkner (1976), and Leslie and McAlvaney (1973). The following example of this method is taken from Rosmond and Faulkner (1976). Consider the equation

$$\frac{\partial^2\psi}{\partial y^2} + K_1(x)\frac{\partial^2\psi}{\partial x^2} + K_2(x)\frac{\partial\psi}{\partial x} - K_3(x)\psi = F(x,y) \qquad (5\text{-}141)$$

which is approximated by the difference form

$$\frac{\nabla_y^2 \psi_{i,j}}{\Delta y^2} + K_{1i} \frac{\nabla_x^2 \psi_{i,j}}{\Delta x^2} + \frac{K_{2i} \nabla_x \psi_{i,j}}{\Delta x} - K_{3i} \psi_{i,j} = F_{i,j}$$

$$i = 1, \ldots M; j = 1, \ldots N$$

or

$$A_i \psi_{i-1,j} + B_i \psi_{i,j} + C_i \psi_{i+1,j} - \psi_{i,j+1} - \psi_{i,j-1} = G_{i,j} \tag{5-142}$$

where

$$A_i = s^2 (½ \Delta x K_{2i} - K_{1i}) \qquad s = \Delta y / \Delta x \qquad G_{i,j} = -\Delta y^2 F_{i,j}$$

$$B_i = 2 + s^2 (\Delta x^2 K_{3i} + 2K_{1i}) \qquad C_i = -s^2 (½ \Delta x K_{2i} + K_{1i})$$

This system of simultaneous equations for the ψ's may be written in matrix form as

$$D \boldsymbol{\psi} = \mathbf{G} \tag{5-142a}$$

Here $\boldsymbol{\psi}$ and $\mathbf{G}$ are column vectors consisting of MN elements and D is a sparse matrix of $(MN)^2$ elements. Most of the elements of D are zeros except for three consecutive elements near the main diagonal in each row and a negative one M spaces away on either side.

Schematically this matrix equation may be represented in the form

$$\begin{bmatrix} (E) & (-I) & & & 0 \\ (-I) & (E) & (-I) & & 0 \\ 0 & (-I) & (E) & (-I) & \\ & & & & \\ & & (-I) & (E) & (-I) \\ & & & (-I) & (E) \end{bmatrix} \begin{bmatrix} \boldsymbol{\psi}_1 \\ \boldsymbol{\psi}_2 \\ \cdot \\ \cdot \\ \cdot \\ \boldsymbol{\psi}_N \end{bmatrix} = \begin{bmatrix} \mathbf{g}_1 \\ \mathbf{g}_2 \\ \cdot \\ \cdot \\ \cdot \\ \mathbf{g}_N \end{bmatrix} \tag{5-143}$$

where E is an $M \times M$ matrix, $\boldsymbol{\psi}_j$ and $\mathbf{g}_j$ are column vectors consisting of M elements (e.g., $\psi_{1j}, \psi_{2j}, \ldots \psi_{Mj}$ and I is the $M \times M$ unit matrix):

$$E = \begin{bmatrix} B_1 & C_1 & 0 & & & 0 \\ A_2 & B_2 & C_2 & & & \\ 0 & A_3 & B_3 & C_3 & & \\ 0 & & \cdots & & & \\ & & A_i & B_i & C_i & 0 \\ & & \cdots & & & \\ & & & A_{M-1} & B_{M-1} & C_{M-1} \\ & & & 0 & A_M & B_M \end{bmatrix} \quad \boldsymbol{\psi}_j = \begin{bmatrix} \psi_{1,j} \\ \psi_{2,j} \\ \cdot \\ \cdot \\ \cdot \\ \psi_{M,j} \end{bmatrix} \quad \mathbf{g}_j = \begin{bmatrix} g_{1,j} \\ g_{2,j} \\ \cdot \\ \cdot \\ \cdot \\ g_{M,j} \end{bmatrix} \tag{5-144}$$

The $g_{i,j}$ are equal to $G_{i,j}$ except for $g_{1,j}$, $g_{M,j}$, $g_{i,1}$, and $g_{i,N}$, which include boundary values of ψ: $\psi_{0,j}$, $\psi_{M+1,j}$, $\psi_{i,0}$, $\psi_{i,N+1}$ for Dirichlet boundary conditions.

Thus the large matrix D is represented as a much smaller matrix with elements that are themselves matrices. As a consequence the system of equations (5-142) or (5-142a) may be written as

$$E\boldsymbol{\psi}_j - I\boldsymbol{\psi}_{j-1} - I\boldsymbol{\psi}_{j+1} = \mathbf{g}_j \qquad j = 1,2, \ldots ,N \tag{5-145}$$

Some examples by the reader with (5-145) will show that it gives the same values as (5-142) provided that $g_{i,j}$ is properly related to $G_{i,j}$ where boundary values are involved. For example, for $i = 1$ (5-142) gives

$$A_1\psi_{0,j} + B_1\psi_{1,j} + C_1\psi_{2,j} - \psi_{1,j+1} - \psi_{1,j-1} = G_{1,j} \tag{5-146}$$

where $\psi_{0,j}$ is a boundary value. Furthermore, take $j = 1$, and this relationship becomes

$$A_1\psi_{0,1} + B_1\psi_{1,1} + C_1\psi_{2,1} - \psi_{1,2} - \psi_{1,0} = G_{1,1} \tag{5-146a}$$

On the other hand, for $i = j = 1$, (5-143) gives

$$B_1\psi_{1,1} + C_1\psi_{2,1} - \psi_{1,2} = g_{1,1} \tag{5-147}$$

Comparison of (5-146a) and (5-147) shows that $g_{1,1}$ is related to $G_{1,1}$ as follows:

$$g_{1,1} = G_{1,1} - A_1\psi_{0,1} + \psi_{1,0}$$

If $j \neq 1$ and $j \neq N$, (5-144) yields

$$B_1\psi_{1,j} + C_1\psi_{2,j} - \psi_{1,j-1} - \psi_{1,j+1} = g_{1,j}$$

and comparing with (5-146) gives

$$g_{1,j} = G_{i,j} - A_1\psi_{0,j}$$

In general, these relationships must be developed for the $g_{i,j}$ whenever any one of the following indices occur: $i = 1, i = M, j = 1, j = N$.

Equation 5-143 is just a convenient compact form for the system (5-142a); the next step involves using this format to provide a fast, direct method of solution. In order to illustrate the method of cyclic reduction, an example with $N = 7$ [Rosmond and Faulkner (1976)] will be presented, for which (5-143) becomes

$$\begin{bmatrix} E & -I & 0 & 0 & 0 & 0 & 0 \\ -I & E & -I & 0 & 0 & 0 & 0 \\ 0 & -I & E & -I & 0 & 0 & 0 \\ 0 & 0 & -I & E & -I & 0 & 0 \\ 0 & 0 & 0 & -I & E & -I & 0 \\ 0 & 0 & 0 & 0 & -I & E & -I \\ 0 & 0 & 0 & 0 & 0 & -I & E \end{bmatrix} \begin{bmatrix} \boldsymbol{\psi}_1 \\ \boldsymbol{\psi}_2 \\ \boldsymbol{\psi}_3 \\ \boldsymbol{\psi}_4 \\ \boldsymbol{\psi}_5 \\ \boldsymbol{\psi}_6 \\ \boldsymbol{\psi}_7 \end{bmatrix} = \begin{bmatrix} \mathbf{g}_1 \\ \mathbf{g}_2 \\ \mathbf{g}_3 \\ \mathbf{g}_4 \\ \mathbf{g}_5 \\ \mathbf{g}_6 \\ \mathbf{g}_7 \end{bmatrix} \tag{5-148}$$

Now multiply each even row by E and add to each the odd rows immediately above and below giving the following result:

$$\begin{bmatrix} E & -I & 0 & 0 & 0 & 0 & 0 \\ 0 & E^2-2I & 0 & -I & 0 & 0 & 0 \\ 0 & -I & E & -I & 0 & 0 & 0 \\ 0 & -I & 0 & E^2-2I & 0 & -I & 0 \\ 0 & 0 & 0 & -I & E & -I & 0 \\ 0 & 0 & 0 & -I & 0 & E^2-2I & 0 \\ 0 & 0 & 0 & 0 & 0 & -I & E \end{bmatrix} \begin{bmatrix} \boldsymbol{\psi}_1 \\ \boldsymbol{\psi}_2 \\ \boldsymbol{\psi}_3 \\ \boldsymbol{\psi}_4 \\ \boldsymbol{\psi}_5 \\ \boldsymbol{\psi}_6 \\ \boldsymbol{\psi}_7 \end{bmatrix} = \begin{bmatrix} \mathbf{g}_1 \\ \mathbf{g}_1 + \mathbf{g}_3 + E\mathbf{g}_2 \\ \mathbf{g}_3 \\ \mathbf{g}_3 + \mathbf{g}_5 + E\mathbf{g}_4 \\ \mathbf{g}_5 \\ \mathbf{g}_5 + \mathbf{g}_7 + E\mathbf{g}_6 \\ \mathbf{g}_7 \end{bmatrix} \qquad (5\text{-}149$$

Next obtain the product of the fourth row of the matrix and the vector and equate it to the fourth element of the vector on the right of (5-149) giving

$$(E^2 - 2I)\boldsymbol{\psi}_4 - I(\boldsymbol{\psi}_2 + \boldsymbol{\psi}_6) = \mathbf{g}_3 + \mathbf{g}_5 + E\mathbf{g}_4 \qquad (5\text{-}150)$$

Note that this equation involves only even numbered $\boldsymbol{\psi}$'s. Similar equations involving even numbered $\boldsymbol{\psi}$'s are obtained by expanding rows 2 and 6 in (5-149). Consequently, a reduced matrix equation involving only the even-numbered $\boldsymbol{\psi}$'s is obtained as follows:

$$\begin{bmatrix} E^2-2I & -I & 0 \\ -I & E^2-2I & -I \\ 0 & -I & E^2-2I \end{bmatrix} \begin{bmatrix} \boldsymbol{\psi}_2 \\ \boldsymbol{\psi}_4 \\ \boldsymbol{\psi}_6 \end{bmatrix} = \begin{bmatrix} \mathbf{g}_1 + \mathbf{g}_3 + E\mathbf{g}_2 \\ \mathbf{g}_3 + \mathbf{g}_5 + E\mathbf{g}_4 \\ \mathbf{g}_5 + \mathbf{g}_7 + E\mathbf{g}_6 \end{bmatrix} \qquad (5\text{-}151)$$

Observe that (5-151) is similar in form to (5-149). To simplify the notation, define $E^2 - 2I \equiv E^{(1)}$ and $\mathbf{g}_j + \mathbf{g}_{j+2} + E\mathbf{g}_{j+1} = \mathbf{g}_{j+1}^{(1)}$, in which case (5-151) may be written as

$$\begin{bmatrix} E^{(1)} & -I & 0 \\ -I & E^{(1)} & -I \\ 0 & -I & E^{(1)} \end{bmatrix} \begin{bmatrix} \boldsymbol{\psi}_2 \\ \boldsymbol{\psi}_4 \\ \boldsymbol{\psi}_6 \end{bmatrix} = \begin{bmatrix} \mathbf{g}_2^{(1)} \\ \mathbf{g}_4^{(1)} \\ \mathbf{g}_6^{(1)} \end{bmatrix} \qquad (5\text{-}152)$$

The reduction process may now be repeated to give a matrix with just one element.

$$[(E^{(1)})^2 - 2I]\,\boldsymbol{\psi}_4 = \mathbf{g}_2^{(1)} + \mathbf{g}_6^{(1)} + E^{(1)}\mathbf{g}_4^{(1)} \qquad (5\text{-}153)$$

or

$$E^{(2)}\,\boldsymbol{\psi}_4 = \mathbf{g}_4^{(2)} \qquad (5\text{-}154)$$

$$\begin{aligned} \text{where} \quad & E^{(2)} = (E^{(1)})^2 - 2I = (E^2 - 2I)^2 - 2I \\ \text{and} \quad & \mathbf{g}_4^{(2)} = \mathbf{g}_2^{(1)} + \mathbf{g}_6^{(1)} + E^{(1)}\mathbf{g}_4^{(1)} \end{aligned} \qquad (5\text{-}155)$$

Equation 5-154 is a fourth-order polynomial in E that must be factored in order to solve for ψ_4. First note that (5-155) is of the form

$$E^{(r+1)} = (E^{(r)})^2 - 2I \qquad (5\text{-}156)$$

In the trigonometric identity, $\cos 2\theta = 2\cos^2\theta - 1$, let $\theta = 2^r\beta$ and further multiply through by 2 giving

$$2\cos(2^{r+1}\beta) = [2\cos(2^r\beta)]^2 - 2 \qquad (5\text{-}157)$$

By identifying $E^{(r)} = 2\cos(2^r\beta)$, (5-156) is seen to be of the same form as (5-157). Moreover, $2\cos(2^r\beta)$ is recognizable as the Chebyshev polynomial of order 2^r, for which the zeros are

$$\alpha_j^{(r)} = 2\cos\left(\pi\frac{2j-1}{2^{r+1}}\right) \qquad j = 1,2,\ldots 2^r \qquad (5\text{-}158)$$

By analogy, $E^{(r)}$ is expressible as a product of linear factors

$$E^{(r)} = \prod_{j=1}^{2^r}\left[E - 2\cos\left(\pi\frac{2j-1}{2^{r+1}}\right)I\right] = 0 \qquad (5\text{-}159)$$

With this result (5-154) may be written with $r = 2$ as (superscript omitted)

$$(E - \alpha_4 I)\,\psi_4^{(4)} = \mathbf{g}_4^{(2)}$$

$$\text{where} \qquad \psi_4^{(4)} = (E - \alpha_1 I)(E - \alpha_2 I)(E - \alpha_3 I)\,\psi_4 \qquad (5\text{-}160)$$

Equation 5-160 can be solved by Gaussian elimination for $\psi_4^{(4)}$. Then the procedure can be repeated with

$$(E - \alpha_3 I)\,\psi_4^{(3)} = \psi_4^{(4)}$$

$$\text{where} \qquad \psi_4^{(3)} = (E - \alpha_1 I)(E - \alpha_2 I)\,\psi_4$$

Repetition of the process results in four Gaussian eliminations, the last being

$$(E - \alpha_1 I)\,\psi_4 = \psi_4^{(2)}$$

the solution of which gives ψ_4.

Now return to (5-152) with ψ_4 to obtain ψ_2 from the equation obtained by expanding the first row of (5-152):

$$E^{(1)}\,\psi_2 = \mathbf{g}_2^{(1)} + \psi_4$$

Here, $E^{(1)} = E^2 - 2I$, is a second-order polynomial in E whose roots are given by (5-158) with $r = 1$. Two Gaussian eliminations are needed in order to obtain ψ_2 and similarly two more to obtain ψ_6 from its equation gotten by expanding the third row of (5-152).

Having obtained $\boldsymbol{\psi}_2$, $\boldsymbol{\psi}_4$, and $\boldsymbol{\psi}_6$, the vectors with odd indices $\boldsymbol{\psi}_1$, $\boldsymbol{\psi}_3$, $\boldsymbol{\psi}_5$, and $\boldsymbol{\psi}_7$ can be determined. For example, expanding the first row of (5-148) gives

$$E\boldsymbol{\psi}_1 - \boldsymbol{\psi}_2 = \mathbf{g}_1 \qquad \text{or} \qquad E\boldsymbol{\psi}_1 = \mathbf{g}_1 + \boldsymbol{\psi}_2$$

With $\boldsymbol{\psi}_2$ known, the Gauss elimination technique can be used to find $\boldsymbol{\psi}_1$. Similarly, the other odd-numbered vectors can be obtained, thus completing the solution of (5-148), and therefore the system (5-142). This system, with $N = 7 = 2^3 - 1$, requires 12 Gaussian eliminations. Generally a system with $N = 2^k - 1$ requires $k\,(N + 1)/2$ eliminations.

As developed here, the block-cyclic reduction method applies only to systems with $N = 2^k - 1$; however, Sweet (1973) has devised methods that permit N's of the form $N = 2^k3^m5^n - 1$, when k, m, and n are arbitrary positive integers and later developed an algorithm for an arbitrary N. Moreover the foregoing method is unstable for large N (see Section 5-10-4).

5-10-3 Gaussian Elimination

At this point a brief outline of the Gaussian elimination method as applied here may be appropriate. A series of equations of the form $(E - \alpha I)\boldsymbol{\psi} = \mathbf{g}$ had to be solved [see (5-160), etc.] where E is an $M \times M$ tridiagonal matrix. The expanded system may be written as

$$\begin{aligned}
b_1\psi_1 + c_1\psi_2 \qquad\qquad\qquad\qquad &= g_1 \\
a_2\psi_1 + b_2\psi_2 + c_2\psi_3 \qquad\qquad &= g_2 \\
a_3\psi_2 + b_3\psi_3 + c_3\psi_4 \qquad &= g_3 \\
\cdots \qquad\qquad & \\
a_M\psi_{M-1} + b_M\psi_M &= g_M
\end{aligned}$$

Now divide the first equation by b_1, divide the second equation by a_2 and subtract, which eliminates ψ_1 from the second equation, leaving a result of the form

$$b_2^{(1)}\,\psi_2 + c_2^{(1)}\,\psi_3 = g_2^{(1)}$$

Then repeat the foregoing procedure with this equation and the third equation of the system above, and so on. When the last equation is reached the procedure eliminates ψ_{M-1}, leaving an equation in just ψ_M, which can then be determined directly. Then the steps are reversed and ψ_{M-1}, ψ_{M-2}, etc. are successively calculated on up to ψ_1, completing the solution of the tridiagonal system of equations. What makes the direct method so effective is the factoring of the matrices $E^{(r)}$ into tridiagonal products which can be inverted rapidly and accurately by Gauss elimination.

5-10-4 Buneman Variant

When the vectors $\mathbf{g}_j$ are calculated in direct fashion as indicated in the foregoing section, Busbee et al. (1970) have shown that increasingly severe round-off errors and instability develop as N gets large. Faulkner (1976) found that the errors were unacceptable for $N \geq 31$ even with double precision arithmetic on an IBM 360/67. Buneman (1969) alleviated this problem by alternatively calculating the $\mathbf{g}_j^{(r)}$. As seen by (5-150) and (5-152), these vectors are of the form

$$\mathbf{g}_j^{(r+1)} = \mathbf{g}_{j-h}^{(r)} + \mathbf{g}_{j+h}^{(r)} + E^{(r)}\,\mathbf{g}_j^{(r)} \qquad h = 2^r \tag{5-161}$$

Buneman expressed $\mathbf{g}_j^{(r)}$ in the form

$$\mathbf{g}_j^{(r)} = E^{(r)}\,\mathbf{P}_j^{(r)} + \mathbf{q}_j^{(r)} \tag{5-162}$$

Substituting this into (5-161) and using (5-156) leads to

$$[(E^{(r)})^2 - 2I]\,\mathbf{P}_j^{(r+1)} + \mathbf{q}_j^{(r+1)} = E^{(r)}\,(\mathbf{P}_{j-h}^{(r)} + \mathbf{P}_{j+h}^{(r)})$$
$$+ \mathbf{q}_{j-h}^{(r)} + \mathbf{q}_{j+h}^{(r)} + (E^{(r)})^2\,\mathbf{P}_j^{(r)} + E^{(r)}\,\mathbf{q}_j^{(r)}$$

Note that if the following relations are fulfilled for $\mathbf{P}_j$ and $\mathbf{q}_j$ then (5-161) and (5-162) will hold, as well as the foregoing equation:

$$\mathbf{P}_j^{(r+1)} = \mathbf{P}_j^{(r)} + (E^{(r)})^{-1}\,(\mathbf{P}_{j-h}^{(r)} + \mathbf{P}_{j+h}^{(r)} + \mathbf{q}_j^{(r)}) \tag{5-163a}$$

$$\mathbf{q}_j^{(r+1)} = \mathbf{q}_{j-h}^{(r)} + \mathbf{q}_{j+h}^{(r)} + 2\mathbf{P}_j^{(r+1)} \tag{5-163b}$$

It is evident that $\mathbf{P}_j^{(r)}$ and $\mathbf{q}_j^{(r)}$ may be successively determined recursively from (5-163a,b). First the following series of matrix equations is successively solved:

$$E^{(r)}\,(\mathbf{P}_j^{(r+1)} - \mathbf{P}_j^{(r)}) = \mathbf{P}_{j-h}^{(r)} + \mathbf{P}_{j+h}^{(r)} + \mathbf{q}_j^{(r)} \qquad r = 0,1,\,.\,.\,.\,k$$

where (5-164)

$$E^{(0)} = E \qquad \mathbf{P}_j^{(0)} = 0 \qquad \mathbf{q}_j^{(0)} = \mathbf{g}_j^{(0)} = \mathbf{g}_j$$

Equation 5-164 is solved in the same fashion as (5-154) for the difference $(\mathbf{P}_j^{(r+1)} - \mathbf{P}_j^{(r)})$, after which $\mathbf{P}_j^{(r+1)}$ is obtained by adding it to $\mathbf{P}_j^{(r)}$, which was obtained in the previous cycle, that is,

$$\mathbf{P}_j^{(r+1)} = (\mathbf{P}_j^{(r+1)} - \mathbf{P}_j^{(r)}) + \mathbf{P}_j^{(r)} \tag{5-165}$$

Having obtained $\mathbf{P}_j^{(r+1)}$, $\mathbf{q}_j^{(r+1)}$ is obtained directly from (5-163b). With the $\mathbf{P}$ and $\mathbf{q}$'s available, equations of the form (5-154) can be written, by virtue of (5-162), as

$$E^{(r)}\,\boldsymbol{\psi}_j = \mathbf{g}_j^{(r)} = E^{(r)}\,\mathbf{P}_j^{(r)} + \mathbf{q}_j^{(r)}$$

or

$$E^{(r)}\,(\boldsymbol{\psi}_j - \mathbf{P}_j^{(r)}) = \mathbf{q}_j^{(r)}$$

This equation is now solved for the difference $(\boldsymbol{\psi}_j - \mathbf{P}_j^{(r)})$ which, in turn, is added to $\mathbf{P}_j^{(r)}$, previously calculated, to give $\boldsymbol{\psi}_j$, that is,

$$\boldsymbol{\psi}_j = (\boldsymbol{\psi}_j - \mathbf{P}_j^{(r)}) + \mathbf{P}_j^{(r)} \tag{5-166}$$

The preceding example of the cyclic reduction method assumed Dirichlet boundary conditions. Cyclic or Neumann boundary conditions can also be treated. For example, in the cyclic case, consider

$$\psi_{i,N+1} = \psi_{i,1} \qquad \psi_{i,0} = \psi_{i,N}$$

In this case D is an $N \times N$ matrix with $N = 2^k$

$$D = \begin{bmatrix} E & -I & & & 0 & -I \\ -I & E & -I & & & 0 \\ . & . & . & . & . & . \\ 0 & 0 & . & -I & E & -I \\ -I & 0 & . & 0 & -I & E \end{bmatrix} \tag{5-167}$$

The coefficient matrix E for a Poisson equation with Neumann or periodic boundary conditions (the resulting matrix of the system) is singular. Hence the solution can be determined only within an arbitrary constant that must be specified.

With Neumann conditions at the boundaries, $\partial\psi/\partial y$ may be written as

$$\left(\frac{\partial\psi}{\partial y}\right)_N = \frac{\psi_{i,N+1} - \psi_{i,N-1}}{2\Delta y} \qquad \left(\frac{\partial\psi}{\partial y}\right)_1 = \frac{\psi_{i,2} - \psi_{i,0}}{2\Delta y} \tag{5-168}$$

In this case D is a singular $N \times N$ matrix ($N = 2^k + 1$) of the form:

$$D = \begin{bmatrix} E & -2I & & & & \\ -I & E & -I & & & \\ . & . & . & . & & \\ & & & -I & E & -I \\ & & & & -2I & E \end{bmatrix} \tag{5-169}$$

which can be reduced by the cyclic reduction method (see Adams et al (1978)).

In the SOR method, diagonal dominance is necessary and is enhanced when $K_3 > 0$ in (5-141). On the other hand $K_3 < 0$ diminishes the diagonal dominance, and if sufficiently negative the SOR method will not converge. Fortunately, the direct method is almost insensitive to diagonal dominance of the system.

Rosmond (1975) has presented subroutines for direct solution of the three-dimensional equation

$$\frac{\partial^2\psi}{\partial x^2} + \frac{\partial^2\psi}{\partial y^2} + K_1(z)\frac{\partial^2\psi}{\partial z^2} + K_2(z)\frac{\partial\psi}{\partial z} - K_3(z)\,\psi = G(x,y,z) \qquad (5\text{-}170)$$

The method consists of using cyclic reduction to reduce the three-dimensional equations to a series of two-dimensional Helmholtz equations, which are, in turn, reduced to one-dimensional tridiagonal systems solvable by Gaussian elimination. The method is limited by the requirement that the number of grid intervals in two coordinate directions must be $2^k \pm 1$ depending on the type of boundary conditions.

5-10-5 Helmholtz Equation on a Sphere

Faulkner (1976) has extended cyclic reduction technique just described to solve the Helmholtz equation

$$\nabla^2\psi - h\psi = \mathrm{F} \qquad (5\text{-}171)$$

where both the Helmholtz coefficient h and the forcing function F vary with latitude φ and longitude λ. Somewhat like the SOR technique, the procedure begins with a first "guess" and then iterates using cyclic reduction to reach an approximate solution, which is very accurate and much faster than SOR.

In spherical coordinates (5-171) may be written as

$$\left[\cos\varphi\,\frac{\partial}{\partial\varphi}\left(\frac{\partial\psi}{\partial\varphi}\cos\varphi\right) + \frac{\partial^2\psi}{\partial\lambda^2}\right]/(r\cos\varphi)^2 - h\psi = F \qquad (5\text{-}172)$$

and in finite difference form as

$$[\cos\varphi_{i+1/2}\,(\psi_{i+1,j} - \psi_{i,j}) - \cos\varphi_{i-1/2}\,(\psi_{i,j} - \psi_{i-1,j})]\cos\varphi_i/d_i$$

$$+ (\psi_{i,j+1} - 2\psi_{i,j} + \psi_{i,j-1})\,s/d_i - h_{i,j}\,\psi_{i,j} = F_{i,j} \qquad (5\text{-}173)$$

$i = 1, \ldots M;\ j = 1, \ldots N$

r = radius	$\Delta\lambda = 2\pi/N$
$d_i = (r\Delta\varphi\cos\varphi_i)^2$	$\Delta\varphi = \pi/(M+1)$
$s = (\Delta\varphi/\Delta\lambda)^2$	$\varphi_i = (\pi/2) - i\Delta\varphi$
i = 0, and $M + 1$ at poles	$\lambda = j\Delta\lambda$

At the North and South Poles, respectively, the equations are

$$4(\overline{\psi}_1 - \psi_0) - (h_0\psi_0 + F_0)d_0 = 0$$
$$4(\overline{\psi}_M - \psi_{M+1}) - (h_{M+1}\,\psi_{M+1} + F_{M+1})\,d_0 = 0 \qquad (5\text{-}174)$$

where $\overline{\psi}_1 = \sum_1^N \psi_{i,j}$ and $\overline{\psi}_M = \sum_1^N \psi_{M,j}$ are zonal averages one gridpoint from the poles. Equation 5-173 defines the solution everywhere but at the poles, where there is singularity.

In the case of a Poisson equation, $h \equiv 0$ in (5-171), and the system (5-172, 5-173) is singular. This is resolved by setting $\psi_0 = 0$ and generating a solution, say Ψ, at the South Pole by setting F to zero in (5-173) and treating Ψ as independent of longitude. The reduced system of equations coupled with the equation (5-174) defines a value of Ψ_i at each latitude including the south polar value. Ψ_i is added to $\psi_{i,j}$ to give the complete solution.

When the coefficient h varies with latitude the reduction equations do not apply directly and the Helmholtz equation must be solved iteratively. Also the system is no longer singular and two independent polar values must be found. The procedure uses a zonally averaged value of h on the left side of (5-173) and adds an appropriate correction to the forcing function on the right side, which is updated after each iteration. The details may be found in Faulkner (1976). Convergence of the iterative routines is satisfactory, the errors being less than 10^{-10} times the solution except for a few cases.

The National Center for Atmospheric Research (NCAR), Boulder, Col., and the Naval Environmental Prediction Research Facility (NEPRF), Monterey, Ca., have a variety of programs for the direct solution of Poisson and Helmholtz equations.

5-10-6 Reduction of a Three-Dimensional Elliptic Equation to Two-Dimensional Equations

A three-dimensional elliptic equation may be transformed into a set of two-dimensional equations under appropriate conditions as follows.

Consider the Poisson equation

$$\nabla_3^2\,\phi \equiv \nabla^2\phi + \partial^2\phi/\partial z^2 = F$$

Now write the vertical derivative in a finite difference form,

[e.g., $\partial^2\phi/\partial z^2 = (\phi_{k+1} - 2\phi_k + \phi_{k-1})/\Delta z^2$], which gives

$$\nabla^2\boldsymbol{\phi} + M\boldsymbol{\phi} = \mathbf{F} \qquad (5\text{-}175)$$

where $\boldsymbol{\phi}$ and $\mathbf{F}$ are column vectors and $\mathbf{M}\boldsymbol{\phi}$ is the product

$$\frac{1}{\Delta z^2}\begin{bmatrix} -2 & 1 & 0 & 0 & \cdots\cdots & 0 \\ 1 & -2 & 1 & 0 & \cdots\cdots & 0 \\ & & & & & 0 \\ 0 & 1 & -2 & 1 & \cdots\cdots & \\ & & \cdots & \cdots & \cdots & \\ 0 & & & & 0 & 1 \quad -2 \end{bmatrix}\begin{bmatrix} \phi_1 \\ \phi_2 \\ \cdot \\ \cdot \\ \cdot \\ \cdot \\ \cdot \\ \cdot \\ \cdot \\ \cdot \\ \cdot \\ \phi_K \end{bmatrix}$$

Nonzero upper and lower boundary values of the arbitrary variable ϕ are incorporated into the forcing function $\mathbf{F}$. Next the eigenvectors of the matrix M are expressed as a linearly independent, orthogonal set, $\mathbf{E}_j$, $j = 1, 2 \ldots K$, which is frequently feasible in typical problems encountered in meteorology. More specifically, real symmetric, Hermitian or normal matrices are sufficient for the purpose. Now (5-175) is multiplied by the matrix E^{-1}, which is the inverse of a matrix E made up of the column vectors $\mathbf{E}_j$. The result is

$$\nabla^2\boldsymbol{\phi}_j' + E^{-1}ME\boldsymbol{\phi}' = \mathbf{F}' \tag{5-175a}$$

where

$$E = \begin{bmatrix} E_{11} \; E_{12} & \ldots & E_{1K} \\ E_{21} \; \ldots & & \\ \cdot & & \\ \cdot & & \\ \cdot & & \\ \cdot & & \\ \cdot & & \\ E_{K1} & & E_{KK} \end{bmatrix} \qquad \begin{aligned} \boldsymbol{\phi}' &= E^{-1}\boldsymbol{\phi} \\ \mathbf{F}' &= E^{-1}\mathbf{F} \end{aligned}$$

In accordance with (5-47) the eigenvectors are related to the eigenvalues by the relations

$$\mathbf{E}_j^{-1}M\mathbf{E}_j = \lambda_j \qquad j = 1, 2, \ldots K$$

or

$$E^{-1}ME = [\lambda]$$

where $[\lambda]$ is a diagonal matrix of the K eigenvalues. Thus (5-175) can be written

$$\nabla^2\boldsymbol{\phi}' + [\lambda]\,\boldsymbol{\phi}' = \mathbf{F}'$$

This vector equation is equivalent to K separate two-dimensional Helmholtz equations, one for each level, for the K elements of $\boldsymbol{\phi}'$, which are functions of two-dimensional fields of ϕ. Thus the three-dimensional elliptic equation has been transformed into K two-dimensional equations. While it is possible to solve a three-dimensional elliptic equation by relaxation or other methods, there may be considerable savings in storage and/or computation time by the method outlined here.

5-11 NONLINEAR INSTABILITY AND ALIASING

Earlier discussions of computational instability dealt with linear equations with constant coefficients. Methods of analyzing the stability of a difference scheme were described and stability criteria for commonly used schemes were derived and discussed. However, the actual equations used in numerical preduction models are nonlinear and often other coefficients are not constant. The nonlinearity does not lessen the linear stability requirement and, in fact, as might be expected (Murphy's law), it introduces added complications in the quest for accurate numerical solutions. The existence of a phenomenon, which is referred to as *nonlinear instability,* was first noted by Phillips (1956) in his pioneering attempt to simulate the general circulation of the atmosphere by integrating a simplified set of equations describing the atmosphere from an initial state of rest. Phillips (1959) discovered the cause of the instability to be *aliasing,* a phenomenon whereby a wave generated by a nonlinear interaction (from the advection term) that is too short ($< 2d$) to be represented on the grid is falsely represented (aliased) as a longer wavelength. Repeated aliasing over many time steps may give rise to a rapid growth of energy (instability) through feedback into the wavelength band, $2d$ to $4d,$ which destroys the validity of the numerical forecast or simulation. Arakawa (1966) devised a differencing scheme to prevent this instability, which will be described a bit later.

For the present, in order to gain some insight into this phenomenon consider an extremely simple, but surprisingly realistic, atmospheric prediction equation:

$$\frac{\partial \zeta}{\partial t} = -\mathbf{V} \cdot \nabla \zeta = -\nabla \cdot (\zeta \mathbf{V}) \qquad \mathbf{V} = \mathbf{k} \times \nabla \psi \qquad \zeta = \nabla^2 \psi \qquad (5\text{-}176)$$

If the Gauss divergence theorem (see A-13) is applied to (5-176) over a region and there is no flux at the boundaries or the region is closed, the right side of (5-176) vanishes. Hence, $\partial \bar{\zeta}/\partial t = 0$, where the bar represents the integral over the region, and thus it is seen that the total (or mean) vorticity is conserved. If (5-176) is multiplied by ζ, the result can be easily put in the form

$$\frac{\partial(\zeta^2/2)}{\partial t} = -\tfrac{1}{2} \nabla \cdot (\zeta^2 \mathbf{V}) \qquad (5\text{-}177)$$

Application of the Gauss divergence theorem again shows that the total or *mean square vorticity,* called *enstrophy,* is also conserved. Finally, multiply (5-176) by ψ giving

$$\psi\partial(\nabla^2\psi)/\partial t = -\psi\nabla \cdot (\zeta\mathbf{V})$$

Now modify each term as follows:

$$\psi\partial(\nabla \cdot \nabla\psi)/\partial t = \psi\nabla \cdot \nabla \frac{\partial\psi}{\partial t} = \nabla \cdot \left(\psi\nabla \frac{\partial\psi}{\partial t}\right) - \nabla\psi \cdot \nabla \frac{\partial\psi}{\partial t}$$

$$\psi\nabla \cdot (\zeta\mathbf{V}) = \nabla \cdot (\psi\zeta\mathbf{V}) - \zeta\mathbf{V} \cdot \nabla\psi$$

Substituting the last equations in the prior one gives

$$\nabla\psi \cdot \nabla \frac{\partial\psi}{\partial t} = \nabla \cdot \left(\psi\nabla \frac{\partial\psi}{\partial t}\right) + \nabla \cdot (\psi\zeta\mathbf{V}) - \zeta\mathbf{V} \cdot \nabla\psi \tag{5-178}$$

The term $-\zeta\mathbf{V} \cdot \nabla\psi$ vanishes identically since $\mathbf{V}$ is $\perp$ to $\nabla\psi$; also $\nabla\psi\cdot\nabla\partial\psi/\partial t = \frac{1}{2}\,\partial\nabla\psi\cdot\nabla\psi/\partial t$ where $\nabla\psi\cdot\nabla\psi$ is twice the kinetic energy. When the Gauss theorem is applied, the right side of (5-178) vanishes, leaving

$$\overline{\partial/(\nabla\psi\cdot\nabla\psi)\partial t} = 0 \tag{5-179}$$

which states that the *mean kinetic energy* is *conserved* over a closed region.

Thus it has been shown that over a closed region, *the model* (5-176) conserves *mean kinetic energy, mean vorticity,* and *mean enstrophy*. These properties hold for the differential system, and it would be desirable, perhaps necessary, to have the properties also maintained when the differential equation is replaced by a difference equation and solved numerically.

Suppose there is a rectangular region of dimensions, L_x and L_y, over which the streamfunction ψ is continuously represented by a double Fourier series of the form

$$\psi = \sum_{\substack{m=0\\n=1}}^{\infty} \left(a_{m,n} \cos \frac{2\pi mx}{L_x} + b_{m,n} \sin \frac{2\pi mx}{L_x}\right) \sin \frac{\pi ny}{L_y} \tag{5-180}$$

where the coefficients $a_{m,n}$ and $b_{m,n}$ are functions of time. If this series is used to calculate the product $-\mathbf{V} \cdot \nabla\zeta$ in (5-176) together with the trigonometric identities to recover a series of the same form, it will be found that when a trigonometric term from the $\mathbf{V}$ series with wave numbers m_1, n_1 is multiplied by a term from the $\nabla\zeta$ series with wave numbers m_2,n_2, the result involves the following four pairs of wave numbers:

$$\begin{array}{ll} m_1 + m_2\,,\ n_1 + n_2 & \quad m_1 - m_2\,,\ n_1 + n_2 \\ m_1 + m_2\,,\ n_1 - n_2 & \quad m_1 - m_2\,,\ n_1 - n_2 \end{array} \tag{5-181}$$

[Note that negative combinations in (5-181) can be made positive by changes of the sign of the coefficient.] It is evident from this result that the term $\mathbf{V} \cdot \nabla\zeta$ causes the transfer of vorticity and energy between different wave numbers. This *nonlinear interaction* therefore results in the exchange of energy within the total spectrum and indeed may develop wave components which previously did not exist.

Note that the terms of the trigonometric series (5-180) are the orthogonal characteristic functions of the following equation for a rectangular region:

$$\nabla^2\psi_{m,n} + \mu^2_{m,n}\,\psi_{m,n} = 0 \tag{5-182}$$

where the eigenvalues of (5-182) are $\mu^2_{m,n} = (2\pi m/L_x)^2 + (\pi n/L_y)^2$. Because of the orthogonality, the mean kinetic energy and mean enstrophy, which are conserved over the closed region, may be shown to be

$$\begin{aligned} \overline{K} &= \tfrac{1}{2}\,\overline{\Sigma(\nabla\psi_{m,n})^2} = \overline{\Sigma K_{m,n}} = \tfrac{1}{2}\,\overline{\Sigma\,\mu^2_{m,n}\,\psi^2_{m,n}} \\ \overline{\zeta^2} &= \overline{\Sigma(\nabla^2\psi_{m,n})^2} = \overline{\Sigma\,\mu^2_{m,n}\,K_{m,n}} = \overline{\Sigma\,\mu^4_{m,n}\,\psi^2_{m,n}} \end{aligned} \tag{5-183}$$

Since these quantities are *conserved,* so *also is their ratio,* $\overline{\zeta^2}/\overline{K} = 2\overline{\mu}^2$, where μ *is an average wave number*.

To simplify the notation consider just three wave numbers in one dimension, $\mu_1 > \mu_2 > \mu_3$; then

$$K_1 + K_2 + K_3 = C_1, \text{ a constant}$$

$$\mu_1^2K_1 + \mu_2^2K_2 = \mu_3^2K_3 = C_2, \text{ a constant}$$

It is evident that if there were only two wave components; say K_1 and K_2, both would have to be constant and no exchange would take place (just solve the pair of equations for K_1, K_2). So consider three components and eliminate K_1 from the first equation and K_3 from the second, for example, with the following result:

$$(\mu_1^2 - \mu_2^2)K_2 + (\mu_1^2 - \mu_3^2)K_3 = \mu_1^2\,C_1 - C_2$$

$$(\mu_1^2 - \mu_3^2)K_1 + (\mu_2^2 - \mu_3^2)K_2 = C_2 - \mu_3^2\,C_1$$

Since the right-hand numbers are constant and the coefficients of the K's are positive, it follows that if K_2 decreases, then K_1 and K_3 must increase, and vice versa, or symbolically,

$$K_1 \leftarrow K_2 \rightarrow K_3 \qquad \text{or} \qquad K_1 \rightarrow K_2 \leftarrow K_3 \tag{5-184}$$

Thus it is seen that energy is not transferred in just one direction of the wave number spectrum, as illustrated for the case of three waves. When more waves are present, the transfer processes are much more complex; however as derived by Fjørtoft (1953), (5-183) shows that energy cannot flow consistently in one direction (e.g., cascading toward higher wave numbers), but rather such transfer is limited and the higher the wave number, the more it is limited. The foregoing are properties of the continuous differential equations, properties that would certainly be desirable to maintain when the differential system is replaced by a difference system.

5-11-1 Discrete Mesh

Now suppose the continuous region is discretized as follows:

$$x = id \qquad i = 0, \ldots . I \qquad Id = L_x$$

$$y = jd \qquad j = 0, \ldots . J \qquad Jd = L_y$$

Assuming that ψ vanishes at $y = 0$ and at L_y and also is cyclic in x as in (5-180), there are $I(J - 1)$ arbitrary values of ψ that can be used to determine the coefficients of the following finite Fourier series:

$$\psi_{i,j} = \sum_{m=0}^{I/2} \sum_{n=1}^{J-1} \left(a_{m,n} \cos \frac{2\pi mid}{Id} + b_{m,n} \sin \frac{2\pi mid}{Id} \right) \sin \frac{\pi njd}{Jd} \qquad (5\text{-}185)$$

This series appears to have $(2 + I)(J - 1)$ coefficients; however $\sin(2\pi mi/I)$ vanishes at $m = 0$ and $m = I/2$, hence $2(J - 1)$ of the b's, namely, $b_{0,n}$ and $b_{I/2,n}$, may be taken to be zero. Thus the number of coefficients exactly equals the number of arbitrary gridpoint values of ψ.

Therefore, instead of an infinite series, as in (5-180), only a finite series can be obtained from a finite set of gridpoint values. The maximum wave number in the x-direction is $I/2$, which corresponds to the *shortest wavelength, 2d,* representable on a finite grid. Now if nonlinear interactions occur between two wave numbers m_1 and m_2 and the sum $(m_1 + m_2)$ *exceeds* I/2, the resulting wave cannot be resolved and will be falsely represented in terms of a permissible wave number. This *misrepresentation,* known as *aliasing,* may be determined by letting $m_1 + m_2 = I - s$. Now consider the cosine term in (5-185), for example, which becomes $\cos[2\pi(I - s)i/I] = \cos 2\pi i \cos(2\pi is/I) + \sin 2\pi i \sin(2\pi is/I) = \cos(2\pi is/I)$ where the last equality is valid only for integer values of i. A similar result may be obtained for the sine term. Thus if nonlinear interaction produces a wave number $(m_1 + m_2) > I/2$, it will falsely appear as

$$s = I - (m_1 + m_2) \qquad (5\text{-}186)$$

Figure 5-9 illustrates an example of aliasing where a $(4d/3)$ wave is misrepresented as a $4d$ wave.

Next suppose that the resulting wave number s turns out to be one of the original waves, say m, then

$$m_1 = I - (m_1 + m_2) \qquad \text{or} \qquad 2m_1 = I - m_2$$

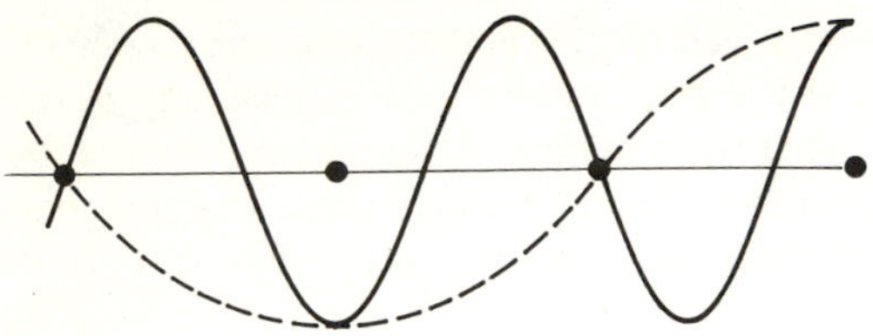

Figure 5.9 Aliasing.

The bounds on m_1 for feedback to occur may be obtained by letting m_2 take on the extreme values, $I/2$ and 0, with the result

$$I/4 \leq m_1 < I/2, \textit{ for feedback} \tag{5-187}$$

The feedback through aliasing explains how nonlinear instability can develop if energy is falsely generated and persistently channeled toward the short resolvable wavelengths, $2d$ to $4d$, which is what Phillips observed in his general circulation experiments. In a paper published in 1959, he used the simple barotropic model (5-176) to show that the *leapfrog-centered space-differencing scheme* did indeed lead to nonlinear instability with a catastrophic rise in kinetic energy in these short wavelengths. This is clearly contrary to the results of Fjørtoft showing that total kinetic energy is conserved and also there is no cascade of energy toward short wavelengths in the continuous case, that is, the *average wave number is also conserved.* Obviously a mere reduction in grid size d and/or the time increment Δt will not eliminate this difficulty. Phillips did show that the instability could be controlled by periodically removing wavelengths $4d$ and smaller by using a Fourier analysis to isolate them. In fact, application of a space filter, for example, $\overline{A} = (1 + k\nabla^2)^n A$, inclusion of an artificial diffusing term such as $\upsilon\nabla^2 A$, or the use of a selective dissipative finite difference scheme may control nonlinear instability; however, such methods are not very satisfying and affect longer waves as well.

Arakawa (1966) devised an elegant method for eliminating nonlinear instability, which will be illustrated for the case of nondivergent winds with (5-176). The latter may be written in Jacobian form as

$$\partial\zeta/\partial t = -J(\psi,\zeta)$$

With the continuous case (5-176), multiplication by ζ and ψ, respectively, and integration over the domain led to the conservation laws. Therefore each of the products, $\overline{\zeta J(\psi,\zeta)}$, $\overline{\psi J(\psi,\zeta)}$, will be examined with several different finite difference Jacobians to determine if they conserve kinetic energy or enstrophy (Arakawa, 1966).

As a guide to the formulation of the Jacobian note that the analytic Jacobian may be expressed alternatively as

$$J(\psi,\zeta) = \frac{\partial\psi}{\partial x}\frac{\partial\zeta}{\partial y} - \frac{\partial\psi}{\partial y}\frac{\partial\zeta}{\partial x} = \frac{\partial}{\partial x}\left(\psi\frac{\partial\zeta}{\partial y}\right) - \frac{\partial}{\partial y}\left(\psi\frac{\partial\zeta}{\partial x}\right)$$
$$= \frac{\partial}{\partial y}\left(\zeta\frac{\partial\psi}{\partial x}\right) - \frac{\partial}{\partial x}\left(\zeta\frac{\partial\psi}{\partial y}\right)$$

The corresponding finite difference Jacobians in terms of the adjoining nine-point stencil are

$$\begin{aligned} J^{++} &= [(\psi_1 - \psi_3)(\zeta_2 - \zeta_4) - (\psi_2 - \psi_4)(\zeta_1 - \zeta_3)]/4d^2 \\ J^{+x} &= [(\psi_1(\zeta_5 - \zeta_8) - \psi_3(\zeta_6 - \zeta_7) - \psi_2(\zeta_5 - \zeta_6) + \psi_4(\zeta_8 - \zeta_7)]/4d^2 \\ J^{x+} &= [\zeta_2(\psi_5 - \psi_6) - \zeta_4(\psi_8 - \psi_7) - \zeta_1(\psi_5 - \psi_8) + \zeta_3(\psi_6 - \psi_7)]/4d^2 \end{aligned} \tag{5-188}$$

The symbols + and x refer to the points in the stencil in Figure 5-10 used in the derivatives of ψ and ζ in that order.

Consider now the gain in the square vorticity at point zero due to the value at point 1, and vice versa. The results, excluding the factor $4d^2$, are

$$\begin{aligned} \zeta_0\, J_0^{++} &\sim -\zeta_0\,\zeta_1(\psi_2 - \psi_4) + \text{other terms} \\ \zeta_1\, J_1^{++} &\sim \zeta_1\,\zeta_0(\psi_5 - \psi_8) + \text{other terms} \end{aligned} \tag{5-189}$$

Since the terms do not cancel and no other opportunity for the product $\zeta_0\,\zeta_1$ occurs over the grid, the sum $\overline{\zeta\, J^{++}}$ cannot vanish in general, and $\overline{\zeta^2}$ will not be conserved (i.e., $\overline{\partial\zeta^2/\partial t} \neq 0$). Similarly,

$$\begin{aligned} \zeta_0\, J_0^{+x} &\sim \zeta_0\,\zeta_5(\psi_1 - \psi_2) + \ldots \\ \zeta_5\, J_5^{+x} &\sim \zeta_5\,\zeta_0(\psi_2 - \psi_1) + \ldots \\ \zeta_0\, J_0^{x+} &\sim -\zeta_0\,\zeta_1(\psi_5 - \psi_8) + \ldots \\ \zeta_1\, J_1^{x+} &\sim \zeta_1\,\zeta_0(\psi_2 - \psi_4) + \ldots \end{aligned} \tag{5-190}$$

6	2	5
3	0	1
7	4	8

Figure 5.10

From (5-189) and (5-190) it is clear that

$$J^{+x} \text{ and } \tfrac{1}{2}(J^{++} + J^{x+}) \textit{ conserve } \overline{\zeta^2} \tag{5-191}$$

A similar examination of the finite difference approximations of $\psi J(\psi,\zeta)$ shows that

$$J^{x+} \text{ and } \tfrac{1}{2}(J^{++} + J^{+x}) \text{ conserve } \overline{K} = \tfrac{1}{2}\,\overline{V^2} \tag{5-192}$$

By combining (5-191) and (5-192) it is seen that the *Arakawa Jacobian,*

$$\tfrac{1}{3}(J^{++} + J^{+x} + J^{x+}) \text{ conserves both } \overline{\zeta^2} \text{ and } \overline{K} \tag{5-193}$$

Consequently, it also conserves the *mean wave number*. As a result, these conservation properties *prevent nonlinear instability*. *Aliasing is still present* in the form of phase errors but the latter also result from linear finite-difference truncation errors.

The conservation properties discussed here for the Arakawa Jacobian have been established for the time continuous case, but not for time differencing. For example, with the leapfrog time differencing scheme and the Arakawa Jacobian, it would follow that

$$\overline{\zeta_{0,n}\,(\zeta_{0,n+1} - \zeta_{0,n-1})} = 2\Delta t\,\overline{\zeta_{0,n}\,J_{0,n}} = 0, \text{ and hence}$$

$$\overline{\zeta_{0,n}\,\zeta_{0,n+1}} = \overline{\zeta_{0,n}\,\zeta_{0,n-1}}$$

However, for strict conservation of mean square vorticity the result should be

$$\overline{\zeta^2_{0,n+1}} = \overline{\zeta^2_{0,n}} = \overline{\zeta^2_{0,n-1}}, \text{ etc.}$$

Now if $\zeta_{0,n} = (\zeta_{0,n+1} + \zeta_{0,n-1})/2$ the above property holds; but it would take a rather complex scheme to achieve this property. The desired result is achieved in practice if ζ varies smoothly between successive time steps, but this is not always the case and occasional smoothing and restarting is necessary to avoid solution decoupling at adjacent time steps.

5-11-2 Primitive Equations Considerations

The previous section dealt with a filtered model and advection with nondivergent winds only. In primitive equation models the velocity components are not separated into rotational and divergent parts, although of course this is feasible if considered advantageous. Consider first the following nonlinear advection equation and its corresponding kinetic energy equation:

$$\frac{\partial u}{\partial t} = -u\frac{\partial u}{\partial x}; \qquad \frac{\partial(u^2/2)}{\partial t} = -u^2\frac{\partial u}{\partial x} = -\frac{1}{3}\frac{\partial u^3}{\partial x} \tag{5-194}$$

Integration of the latter with respect to x gives

$$\int_0^L \frac{\partial(u^2/2)}{\partial t}\,dx = -\frac{1}{3}(u_L^3 - u_0^3) \tag{5-195}$$

If $u_0 = u_L$, including the case of zero flux at the boundaries, the right side vanishes and $\partial(u^2/2)/\partial t = 0$ (i.e., kinetic energy is conserved). If the interval, 0 to L, is divided into equal segments with endpoints given by $x_j = jd$, $j = 0$ to J, the right side of (5-195) may be written as a sum of

$$\int_0^L \frac{\partial(u^2/2)}{\partial t}\,dx = -⅓[(u_1^3 - u_0^3) + (u_2^3 - u_1^3)\ldots$$
$$+ (u_j^3 - u_{j-1}^3) + (u_{j+1}^3 - u_j^3)\ldots + (u_J^3 - u_{J-1}^3)]$$

The purpose here is to bring out the fact that when discretization occurs there will be a summing over the domain (instead of an integral). For conservation to occur, the successive terms in the sum must be of the form $(A_{j+1} - A_j)$, so that the intermediate terms cancel, as suggested above, leaving only the values at the boundaries, which must be accounted for separately.

Next several finite difference approximations for (5-194) will be examined for the conservation property. First, consider centered space differencing (time differencing will be ignored here)

$$\frac{\partial u_j}{\partial t} = -u_j\frac{(u_{j+1} - u_{j-1})}{2d} \tag{5-196}$$

Multiplying by u_j and forming the sum (integral)

$$\int_0^L \frac{\partial(u^2/2)}{\partial t}\,dx = -½\sum_{j=1}^{J-1}(u_j^2\,u_{j+1} - u_j^2\,u_{j-1}) \tag{5-197}$$

where, for convenience, $u_J = u_0 = 0$.
It is apparent that these terms are not of the form $(A_{j+1} - A_j)$ which would cancel when summed, that is, lowering the index j by 1 in $u_j^2\,u_{j+1}$ does not give $u_j^2\,u_{j-1}$. Thus ordinary centered differences, although consistent and linearly stable for appropriate Δt, do not conserve kinetic energy.

Another possibility would be to use the flux difference from:

$$\frac{\partial u_j}{\partial t} = -\frac{\partial(u_j^2/2)}{\partial x} = -(u_{j+1}^2 - u_{j-1}^2)/4d \tag{5-198}$$

Multiplication by u_j and summing leads to $-\Sigma(u_{j+1}^2\ u_j\ -\ u_j\ u_{j-1}^2)/4$, which again is not of the form, $(A_{j+1}\ -\ A_j)$; hence (5-198) is not energy conserving either. Perhaps these results are not too surprising when one considers the sums as numerical approximations of the energy integral. In this light another possibility would be to use the difference form

$$\frac{\partial u_j}{\partial t} = -\frac{1}{6d}(u_{j+1} + u_j + u_{j-1})(u_{j+1} - u_{j-1})$$

Multiplying by u_j and summing leads to

$$-\tfrac{1}{6}\ \Sigma[u_j^2\ u_{j+1} + u_j\ u_{j-1}^2) - (u_{j-1}^2\ u_j + u_{j-1}\ u_j^2)]$$

for the right side, which is of the form $(A_j\ -\ A_{j-1})$. Thus all terms except those due to the boundaries cancel, making the scheme energy conserving for interior points. While this finite difference form is too simple for more complex systems, it does suggest the use of some kind of averaging technique to achieve the conservation property.

The foregoing examples introduce the subject of energy conserving difference schemes. Considering the manner in which the energy equations of Chapter 1 are derived, it becomes evident that some kind of flux form involving the continuity equation should be considered and total energy conservation should also be a prime target. The latter must be considered within the framework of a complete prediction model to be considered later; however some simple models can be used to illustrate the basic concept of the Arakawa technique and others. Consider the advection equation in the (x,p) plane and the continuity equation as follows:

$$\frac{\partial F}{\partial t} = -u\frac{\partial F}{\partial x} - \omega\frac{\partial F}{\partial p} \qquad \frac{\partial u}{\partial x} + \frac{\partial \omega}{\partial p} = 0 \tag{5-199}$$

The first equation may be put in flux form by multiplying the continuity equation by F and adding it to the advection equation, giving

$$\frac{\partial F}{\partial t} = -\frac{\partial(uF)}{\partial x} - \frac{\partial(\omega F)}{\partial p} \equiv -\mathcal{L}(F) \tag{5-200}$$

The finite difference approximation for the operator $\mathcal{L}$ is defined as follows:

$$\mathcal{L}(F)_{i,k} = \frac{1}{d}\left[\frac{(u_{i+1,k} + u_{i,k})}{2}\frac{(F_{i+1,k} + F_{i,k})}{2} - \frac{(u_{i,k} + u_{i-1,k})}{2}\frac{(F_{i,k} + F_{i-1,k})}{2}\right]$$
$$+ \frac{1}{\Delta p}\left[\omega_{i,k+1}\left(\frac{F_{i,k+1} + F_{i,k}}{2}\right) - \omega_{i,k}\left(\frac{F_{i,k} + F_{i,k-1}}{2}\right)\right] \tag{5-201}$$

where $x = id$, $p = k\Delta p$ and variables u and ω are staggered in the vertical as shown in Figure 5-11.

↑	$k-1$	—	u,F
	k	—	ω
Δp	k	—	u,F
	$k+1$	—	ω
↓	$k+1$	—	u,F

Figure 5.11 Nonstaggered horizontal and vertically staggered variables in a p-coordinate system.

u,ω,F	u,ω,F	u,ω,F	
·	·	·	$\leftarrow d \rightarrow$ ·
$i-1$	i	$i+1$	

Now it will be shown that the operator $\mathscr{L}$ conserves the square of F, where F may represent velocity u, vorticity ζ or some other physical quantity. Thus $\mathscr{L}$ will make no contribution to the time rate of mean kinetic energy $\partial(u^2/2)/\partial t$ or $\partial(\zeta^2/2)/\partial t$, etc. For this purpose multiply $\mathscr{L}\,(F)_{i,k}$ in (5-201) by $F_{i,k}$, which would correspond to $-\partial(F^2_{i,k}/2)/\partial t$ in (5-200). The result, after canceling several terms, is

$$F_{i,k}\,\mathscr{L}(F)_{i,k} = \frac{1}{4d}(F_{i,k}F_{i+1,k}u_{i+1,k} + F^2_{i,k}u_{i+1,k} + F_{i,k}F_{i+1,k}u_{i,k}$$

$$- F_{i,k}F_{i-1,k}u_{i,k} - F^2_{i,k}u_{i-1,k} - F_{i,k}F_{i-1,k}u_{i-1,k}) \qquad (5\text{-}202)$$

$$+ \frac{1}{2\Delta p}(F_{i,k}F_{i,k+1}\omega_{i,k+1} + F^2_{i,k}\omega_{i,k+1} - F^2_{i,k}\omega_{i,k} - F_{i,k}F_{i,k-1}\omega_{i,k})$$

The continuity equation in (5-199) is approximated by central differences and then multiplied by $(-\tfrac{1}{2}F^2_{i,k})$, giving

$$0 = -\tfrac{1}{2}F^2_{i,k}\left(\frac{u_{i+1,k} - u_{i-1,k}}{2d} + \frac{\omega_{i,k+1} - \omega_{i,k}}{\Delta p}\right) \qquad (5\text{-}203)$$

Adding (5-202) and (5-203) yields

$$F_{i,k}\,\mathscr{L}\,(F)_{i,k} = \frac{1}{4d}[(u_{i+1,k} + u_{i,k})F_{i+1,k}F_{i,k} - (u_{i,k} + u_{i-1,k})F_{i,k}F_{i-1,k}]$$

$$+ \frac{1}{2\Delta p}(\omega_{i,k+1}F_{i,k+1}F_{i,k} - \omega_{i,k}F_{i,k}F_{i,k-1}) \qquad (5\text{-}204)$$

Inspection of (5-204) shows that the first part in brackets on the right side of (5-204) is of the form $(A_{i+1} - A_i)$ and will cancel term by term when summed with respect to i (except for boundary fluxes). The second term is of the form, $(B_{i,k+1} - B_{i,k})$, which will similarly cancel when summed with respect to the vertical index k, again except for boundary fluxes. If the latter are zero the result is

$$\Sigma\partial(F^2/2)/\partial t = -\Sigma F_{i,k}\,\mathcal{L}(F)_{i,k} = 0 \tag{5-205}$$

Thus the quantity F^2 (as well as F) will be conserved in the mean over the domain of integration when the right side of (5-200) is approximated by the difference scheme (5-201). When $F = u$, the first equation in (5-199) is just local time tendency of u plus advection terms in the u-momentum equation. Hence scheme (5-201) will conserve kinetic energy, $u^2/2$, and prevent nonlinear instability. Although the derivations have included only one horizontal coordinate, the results apply equally well when both x- and y-direction are considered. When applied to the thermodynamic equation, the finite difference approximation for the advection terms (5-201) will conserve $\overline{T}$ and $\overline{T^2}$, and $\overline{\theta}$ and θ^2.

Note that staggering in the vertical resulted in a simpler difference form that nevertheless conserved F^2. Staggering the variables in the horizontal also provides a simpler conserving finite difference form as follows:

$$\frac{\partial(uF)_{i,k}}{\partial x} = \frac{1}{d}\left[\left(\frac{F_{i,k} + F_{i+1,k}}{2}\right)u_{i+½,k} - \left(\frac{F_{i,k} + F_{i-1,k}}{2}\right)u_{i-½,k}\right] \tag{5-206}$$

$$\left(\frac{\partial u}{\partial x}\right)_{i,k} = \frac{u_{i+½} - u_{i-½}}{d} \tag{5-207}$$

F	u	F	u	F
·	·	·	·	·
$i-1$	$i-½$	i	$i+½$	$i+1$

$\longleftarrow d \longrightarrow$

When these expressions are used in $\mathcal{L}(F)$ and the continuity equation, as in 5-202 and 5-203, respectively, together with the same form of vertical differencing, it is easily shown that the combined horizontal and vertical advections conserve the square of F (student exercise).

Total energy (kinetic and potential) conservation in a fairly comprehensive numerical prediction model will be considered later in Chapter 7.

CHAPTER 6

GALERKIN METHODS

6-1 INTRODUCTION

In Chapter 5 finite difference methods for solving partial differential equations were developed. These methods specify the dependent variables at certain grid-points in space and time, and the derivatives in the equations are evaluated using Taylor series approximations. The Galerkin procedure, discussed in this chapter, represents the dependent variables with a sum of functions that have a prescribed spatial structure. The coefficient associated with each function is normally a function of time. This procedure transforms a partial differential equation into a set of ordinary differential equations for the coefficients. These equations are usually solved with finite differences in time. The two most useful Galerkin methods are the spectral method and the finite element method. The spectral method, which employs orthogonal functions, has been used in meteorological problems for a number of years. The finite element method employs functions that are zero except in a limited region where they are low-order polynomials. This method, which was developed in engineering, has only recently been introduced into meteorology and oceanography.

The Galerkin procedure can be illustrated with the following equation:

$$\mathcal{L}(u) = f(x) \tag{6-1}$$

where $\mathcal{L}$ is a differential operator, u is the dependent variable, and $f(x)$ is a specified forcing function. Suppose that (6-1) is to be solved in the domain $a \leq x \leq b$ and that appropriate boundary conditions are provided. Consider a series of linearly independent functions $\varphi_j(x)$ that will be called *basis functions*. The next step is to approximate $u(x)$ with a finite series as follows:

$$u(x) \simeq \sum_{j=1}^{N} u_j \varphi_j(x) \tag{6-2}$$

where u_j is the coefficient for jth basis function. The error in satisfying the differential equation (6-1) with the N terms of the sum (6-2) is

$$e_N = \mathcal{L}\left(\sum_{j=1}^{N} u_j \varphi_j\right) - f(x) \tag{6-3}$$

The Galerkin procedure requires that the error be orthogonal to each basis function in the following sense:

$$\int_a^b e_N \varphi_i \, dx = 0 \qquad i = 1, \ldots, N \tag{6-4}$$

The final form is obtained by substituting (6-3) into (6-4):

$$\int_a^b \varphi_i \mathcal{L} \left(\sum_{j=1}^{N} u_j \varphi_j \right) dx - \int_a^b \varphi_i f(x) dx = 0 \qquad i = 1, \ldots, N \tag{6-5}$$

This reduces the problem to N algebraic equations that relate the unknown coefficients u_j to the "transforms" of the forcing function. This procedure is quite general and can be applied to more dependent and independent variables.

6-2 EXAMPLE WITH SPECTRAL AND FINITE ELEMENT METHODS

Now the spectral method and the finite element method will be applied to the following simple form of (6-1):

$$\frac{d^2u}{dx^2} = f(x) \qquad 0 \leq x \leq \pi \tag{6-6}$$

The boundary conditions are

$$u(0) = u(\pi) = 0 \tag{6-7}$$

For the spectral method the following basis functions are particularly appropriate:

$$\varphi_j = \sin jx \qquad j = 1, \ldots, N \tag{6-8}$$

because they are orthogonal on the interval $0 \leq x \leq \pi$ and they satisfy the boundary conditions (6-7). With these basis functions

$$\mathcal{L} \left(\sum_{j=1}^{N} (u_j \varphi_j) \right) = \sum_{j=1}^{N} (-j^2) \, u_j \varphi_j$$

and (6-5) becomes

$$- \sum_{j=1}^{N} j^2 u_j \int_0^{\pi} \varphi_i \varphi_j \, dx = \int_0^{\pi} \varphi_i f(x) dx \qquad i = 1, \ldots, N \tag{6-9}$$

The product of the basis functions can be written

$$\int_0^{\pi} \sin ix \sin jx \, dx$$

$$= \tfrac{1}{2} \int_0^{\pi} [\cos (i - j)\, x - \cos (i + j)\, x] dx = (\pi/2)\delta_{ij} \qquad (6\text{-}10)$$

where δ_{ij} is the Kronecker delta, which satisfies $\delta_{ij} = 1$ if $i = j$ and $\delta_{ij} = 0$ if $i \neq j$. Equation 6-10 is merely the orthogonality condition that arises since the integral vanishes except when $i = j$. With the use of (6-10), the solution to (6-9) becomes

$$u_i = - \frac{2}{i^2 \pi} \int_0^{\pi} \varphi_i f \, dx \qquad (6\text{-}11)$$

Each coefficient is proportional to the finite Fourier transform of the forcing term so that if $f(x)$ can be completely represented with the finite set of basis functions the solution is exact. In this example both the error in the solution and the error in the differential equation are orthogonal to the basis functions, so that all of the error is outside of the description (6-2). This is because $\mathcal{L}(\varphi_i)$ is proportional to φ_i so that if the error is orthogonal to $\mathcal{L}(\varphi_i)$ it will also be orthogonal to φ_i. This will also be true when certain other linear equations are treated with the spectral method, but it will not generally be true with nonlinear equations.

Now consider the same differential equation (6-6) with the finite element method. Divide the interval $0 \leq x \leq \pi$ into $N + 1$ segments such that $(N + 1)\, \Delta x = \pi$. In this example the basis functions are chosen to be tent-shaped, piecewise linear functions, which are also called chapeau functions, as shown in Figure 6-1. As can be seen from the figure, $\varphi_j(x)$ has a maximum of 1 at $x = j\Delta x$, which is called the *nodal point*. The basis function decreases linearly to zero at $x = (j \pm 1)\Delta x$, and it is zero everywhere else. Mathematically $\varphi_j(x)$ is defined as follows:

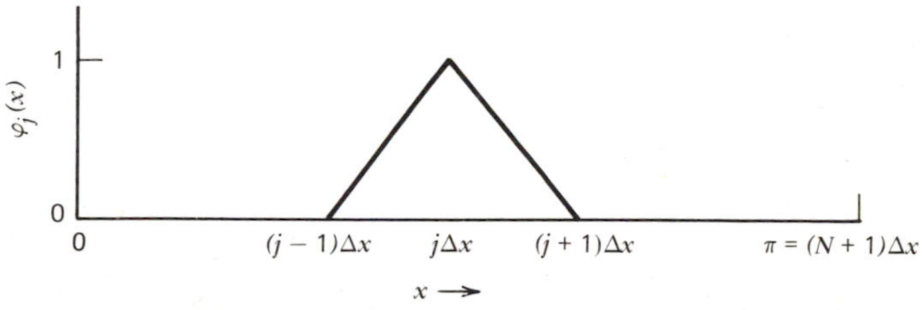

Figure 6.1 Piecewise linear basis function.

$$\varphi_j(x) = \begin{cases} 0, \; x > (j+1)\Delta x & \text{or} \quad x < (j-1)\Delta x \\ [x - (j-1)\Delta x]/\Delta x & (j-1)\Delta x \le x \le j\Delta x \\ [(j+1)\Delta x - x]/\Delta x & j\Delta x \le x \le (j+1)\Delta x \end{cases} \tag{6-12}$$

Note that the coefficient u_j is actually the value of the function at $x = j\Delta x$ since $\varphi_j(j\Delta x) = 1$ and $\varphi_i(j\Delta x) = 0$ for $i \neq j$. These elements are not quite orthogonal, but only adjacent elements interact, and the boundary conditions (6-7) are automatically satisfied.

Equation 6-5 now becomes

$$\sum_{j=1}^{N} u_j \int_0^{\pi} \varphi_i \frac{d^2\varphi_j}{dx^2}\, dx - \int_0^{\pi} \varphi_i f(x) dx = 0$$

This form of the equation is not appropriate because it involves a second derivative of the piecewise linear basis function. However, this problem can be avoided by integrating the first term by parts as follows:

$$\sum_{j=1}^{N} u_j \int_0^{\pi} \left[\frac{d}{dx}\left(\frac{\varphi_i \, d\varphi_j}{dx} \right) - \frac{d\varphi_i}{dx}\frac{d\varphi_j}{dx} \right] dx - \int_0^{\pi} \varphi_i f(x) dx = 0$$

The first term vanishes because all of the φ's are zero at $x = 0, \pi$. The Galerkin equation now becomes

$$-\sum_{j=1}^{N} u_j \int_0^{\pi} \frac{d\varphi_i}{dx}\frac{d\varphi_j}{dx} = \int_0^{\pi} \varphi_i f(x) dx \qquad i = 1, \ldots, N \tag{6-13}$$

Note that differentiating (6-12) gives:

$$\frac{d\varphi_j}{dx} = \begin{cases} 0 \quad , x > (j+1)\Delta x & \text{or } x < (j-1)\Delta x \\ 1/\Delta x \; , (j-1)\Delta x < x < j\Delta x & \\ -1/\Delta x \; , j\Delta x < x < (j+1)\Delta x & \end{cases} \tag{6-14}$$

The left-hand side of (6-13) is easily evaluated since only three terms in the sum are different from zero:

$$-\sum_{j=1}^{N} u_j \int_0^{\pi} \frac{d\varphi_i}{dx}\frac{d\varphi_j}{dx}\, dx = \frac{u_{i-1}\,\Delta x - 2u_i\,\Delta x + u_{i+1}\,\Delta x}{\Delta x^2} \tag{6-15}$$

The right-hand integral in (6-13) may be evaluated if $f(x)$ is approximated in terms of the basis functions:

$$f(x) \simeq \sum_{j=1}^{N} f_j \varphi_j \tag{6-16}$$

so that the integral becomes

$$\int_0^{\pi} \varphi_i f(x) dx = \sum_{j=1}^{N} f_j \int_0^{\pi} \varphi_i \varphi_j \, dx = \sum_{j=1}^{N} f_j \int_{(i-1)\Delta x}^{(i+1)\Delta x} \varphi_i \varphi_j \, dx$$

If $\xi = x - i\Delta x$ is introduced the integral can be expanded into three integrals:

$$\int_0^{\pi} \varphi_i f(x) dx = -f_{i-1} \int_{-\Delta x}^{0} \frac{\xi(\xi + \Delta x)}{\Delta x^2} d\xi + 2f_i \int_{-\Delta x}^{0} \frac{(\xi + \Delta x)^2}{\Delta x^2} d\xi + f_{i+1} \int_0^{\Delta x} \frac{\xi(\Delta x - \xi)}{\Delta x^2} d\xi \tag{6-17}$$

When these terms have been evaluated, (6-17) and (6-15) can be substituted into (6-13), which gives

$$\frac{u_{i+1} - 2u_i + u_{i-1}}{\Delta x^2} = \frac{f_{i+1} + 4f_i + f_{i-1}}{6} \tag{6-18}$$

This equation applies for $2 \leq i \leq N - 1$ and the equations for $i = 1$ and $i = N$ are obtained by removing any terms in $i = 0$ or $i = N + 1$. Equation 6-18 may be solved by Gaussian elimination (see Section 5-10-3).

Since each coefficient in this finite element expansion represents the solution at a certain point in space, it is convenient to compare (6-18) with finite difference forms of (6-6). The centered difference form of this equation is

$$\frac{u_{i+1} - 2u_i + u_{i-1}}{\Delta x^2} = f_i \tag{6-19}$$

where $u_i = u(i\Delta x)$. The finite element equation (6-18) and the finite difference equation (6-19) are the same, except that the forcing term in (6-18) appears in a weighted average. When these equations are solved with an $f(x)$, which is sinusoidal, the finite element form is considerably more accurate for the shorter wavelengths.

In this example it appears that the spectral method is superior because the solution error is actually orthogonal to the basis functions. This is not generally true with the finite element method because $\mathcal{L}(u_i)$ depends on u_{i-1}, u_i, and u_{i+1}. Each increase in N will normally change all of the solutions u_i, whereas with the spectral method the original N amplitudes are not changed because they are already exact. However if the variation of f should require fine resolution in only a small area, the finite element method can easily be applied by letting Δx vary. In this case the spectral method would require more components because its spatial resolution is uniform. The finite element method can be used to design better finite difference equations, for example, with variable space increments.

6-3 TIME DEPENDENCE

In the previous sections the Galerkin procedure has been applied to one-dimensional equations that are independent of time. The treatment of time variation is important for most meteorological prediction problems. Consider the following simplified equation:

$$\frac{\partial u}{\partial t} + \mathcal{L}(u) = 0 \tag{6-20}$$

where the operator $\mathcal{L}$ may be nonlinear. Approximate $u(x,t)$ with a finite series as follows:

$$u(x,t) \simeq \sum_{j=1}^{N} u_j(t)\, \varphi_j(x) \tag{6-21}$$

where the coefficients $u_j(t)$ are functions of time and the basis functions $\varphi_j(x)$ are functions of x. Usually the Galerkin procedure is not applied to the time dependence because it is more convenient to use finite differences in time.

The Galerkin form of (6-20) is obtained by substituting (6-21) into (6-20), multiplying by $\varphi_i(x)$ and integrating over the domain as follows:

$$\sum_{j=1}^{N} \frac{du_j}{dt} \int_a^b \varphi_i \varphi_j\, dx + \int_a^b \varphi_i\, \mathcal{L}\left(\sum_{j=1}^{N} u_j\, \varphi_j\right) dx = 0 \qquad i = 1, \ldots, N \tag{6-22}$$

This process gives N coupled ordinary differential equations in the coefficients $u_j(t)$. This set can be solved by introducing finite differences in time.

The importance of energy conserving finite difference schemes was discussed in Section 5-11. The Galerkin method leads naturally to energy conservation in equations with quadratic energy invariants. To show this multiply (6-20) by u and integrate with respect to x:

$$\int_a^b \frac{\partial(u^2/2)}{\partial t}\, dx = -\int_a^b u\, \mathcal{L}(u)\, dx \tag{6-23}$$

For an energy conserving system, (see Section 5-11-2), the operator must satisfy the condition

$$\int_a^b \psi\, \mathcal{L}(\psi)\, dx = 0 \tag{6-24}$$

where ψ is any reasonable function that satisfies the boundary conditions. In this case (6-23) becomes

$$\frac{d}{dt}\int_a^b u^2/2\, dx = 0 \tag{6-25}$$

which shows the energy conservation for the exact equation. To demonstrate that the same result holds for the finite sum (6-21), multiply the ith equation of (6-22) by u_i and sum from $i = 1$ to $i =$ N:

$$\int_a^b \left(\sum_{i=1}^N u_i\, \varphi_i\right) \frac{\partial}{\partial t}\left(\sum_{j=1}^N u_j\, \varphi_j\right) dx = -\int_a^b \left(\sum_{i=1}^N u_i\, \varphi_i\right) \mathcal{L}\left(\sum_{j=1}^N u_j\, \varphi_j\right) dx \tag{6-26}$$

The integral on the right vanishes from (6-24) if $\psi = \Sigma\, u_j\, \varphi_j = \Sigma\, u_i\, \varphi_i$. Therefore (6-26) can be written

$$\int_a^b \frac{\partial}{\partial t}\left(\sum_{i=1}^N u_i\, \varphi_i\right)^2 /2\, dx = 0 \tag{6-27}$$

which expresses the energy conservation for the Galerkin approximation to the spatial variation. As with finite difference equations, the actual degree of energy conservation will depend on the time differencing that is used in (6-22).

6-4 BAROTROPIC VORTICITY EQUATION WITH FOURIER BASIS FUNCTIONS

In this section the spectral method will be applied to the barotropic vorticity equation on the beta plane. Fourier basis functions are appropriate for the beta plane when the fields are periodic in x and y. The development of this section closely follows Lorenz (1960a). The barotropic vorticity equation may be written:

$$\frac{\partial}{\partial t}\nabla^2\psi + \mathbf{k} \times \nabla\psi \cdot \nabla(\nabla^2\psi) + \beta\, \partial\psi/\partial x = 0 \tag{6-28}$$

where ψ is the streamfunction. Suppose that the fields are periodic in both x and y so that

$$\psi(x + 2\pi/k, y + 2\pi/\ell, t) = \psi(x,y,t) \tag{6-29}$$

With the beta plane geometry and the periodicity condition, the appropriate orthogonal basis functions are of the form:

$$\varphi_{mn}\,(x,y) = e^{i(mkx + n\ell y)} \tag{6-30}$$

These functions are eigensolutions of the equation:

$$\nabla^2\varphi + b\varphi = 0 \tag{6-31}$$

where the eigenvalues are given by

$$b = (m^2k^2 + n^2\ell^2) \tag{6-32}$$

The streamfunction can be approximated in terms of these basis functions as follows:

$$\psi(x,y,t) \simeq \sum_m \sum_n C_{mn}(t)\, e^{i(mkx + n\ell y)}$$

where only a finite number of terms are included.

In order for ψ to be real the coefficients must satisfy the condition

$$C_{mn} = C^*_{-m-n}$$

where ( )* indicates the complex conjugate. This can be shown by considering only the m,n and $-m, -n$. It is convenient to introduce the wave-number vector $\mathbf{M} = mk\mathbf{i} + n\ell\mathbf{j}$ and the radius vector $\mathbf{R} = x\mathbf{i} + y\mathbf{j}$. The approximation for ψ can now be written

$$\psi(x,y,t) \simeq \sum_{\mathbf{M}} C_{\mathbf{M}}(t)\, e^{i\mathbf{M}\cdot\mathbf{R}} \tag{6-33}$$

With the use of (6-31) or (6-33) the vorticity can be written

$$\nabla^2\psi \simeq -\sum_{\mathbf{M}} (\mathbf{M}\cdot\mathbf{M})\, C_{\mathbf{M}}(t)\, e^{i\mathbf{M}\cdot\mathbf{R}} \tag{6-34}$$

The quantities that are required in the nonlinear term in (6-28) may be written:

$$\begin{aligned} \nabla\psi &\simeq \sum_{\mathbf{H}} i\mathbf{H}\, C_{\mathbf{H}}\, e^{i\mathbf{H}\cdot\mathbf{R}} \\ \nabla(\nabla^2\psi) &\simeq -\sum_{\mathbf{L}} i\mathbf{L}(\mathbf{L}\cdot\mathbf{L})\, C_{\mathbf{L}}\, e^{i\mathbf{L}\cdot\mathbf{R}} \end{aligned} \tag{6-35}$$

The wave number vectors $\mathbf{H}$ and $\mathbf{L}$ are introduced because the sums must be multiplied together and rearranged.

Now substitute the various sums [(6-33), (6-34), and (6-35)] into (6-28) which gives:

$$\begin{aligned} -\sum_{\mathbf{L}} (\mathbf{L}\cdot\mathbf{L}) \frac{d}{dt} C_{\mathbf{L}}\, e^{i\mathbf{L}\cdot\mathbf{R}} &+ \sum_{\mathbf{L}}\sum_{\mathbf{H}} (\mathbf{L}\cdot\mathbf{L})\, \mathbf{k}\cdot\mathbf{H}\times\mathbf{L}\, C_{\mathbf{H}}\, C_{\mathbf{L}}\, e^{i(\mathbf{H}+\mathbf{L})\cdot\mathbf{R}} \\ &+ i\beta \sum_{\mathbf{L}} L_x\, C_{\mathbf{L}}\, e^{i\mathbf{L}\cdot\mathbf{R}} = e_N \end{aligned} \tag{6-36}$$

where e_N is the error in satisfying the equation.

The Galerkin method for this equation is similar to the method used in (6-22), except that the equation must be multiplied by the complex conjugate of the basis function since the basis function is complex. To carry out this process multiply (6-36) by $e^{-i\mathbf{M}.\mathbf{R}}$, integrate over the periodic domain and require that e_N be orthogonal to each basis function, which gives

$$\int_0^{2\pi/k}\int_0^{2\pi/\ell}\left\{-\sum_{\mathbf{L}}(\mathbf{L}\cdot\mathbf{L})\frac{d}{dt}C_{\mathbf{L}}\,e^{i(\mathbf{L}-\mathbf{M})\cdot\mathbf{R}}+i\beta\sum_{\mathbf{L}}L_x C_{\mathbf{L}}\,e^{i(\mathbf{L}-\mathbf{M})\cdot\mathbf{R}}\right.$$
$$\left.+\sum_{\mathbf{L}}\sum_{\mathbf{H}}(\mathbf{L}\cdot\mathbf{L})\,\mathbf{k}\cdot\mathbf{H}\times\mathbf{L}\,C_{\mathbf{H}}C_{\mathbf{L}}\,e^{i(\mathbf{H}+\mathbf{L}-\mathbf{M})\cdot\mathbf{R}}\right\}dydx=0$$

for each $\mathbf{M}$ in the original sum (6-33). Each integral of the exponential function will vanish except when the exponent is zero. This leads to the following equation for each $\mathbf{M}$:

$$\frac{dC_{\mathbf{M}}}{dt}=\frac{imk\beta C_{\mathbf{M}}}{\mathbf{M}\cdot\mathbf{M}}+\sum_{\mathbf{H}}\frac{(\mathbf{M}-\mathbf{H})\cdot(\mathbf{M}-\mathbf{H})\,\mathbf{k}\cdot\mathbf{H}\times\mathbf{M}}{\mathbf{M}\cdot\mathbf{M}}C_{\mathbf{M}-\mathbf{H}}C_{\mathbf{H}} \qquad (6\text{-}37)$$

In the first two terms the contribution occurs for $\mathbf{L}=\mathbf{M}$ and in the last term for $\mathbf{L}=\mathbf{M}-\mathbf{H}$.

Equation 6-37 represents N ordinary differential equations, where N is the number of terms in the sum (6-33). The last term in the equation gives the interaction between different waves that comes from the nonlinear advection term in (6-28). In particular wave $\mathbf{M}$ is affected by the interaction of waves $\mathbf{H}$ and $\mathbf{M}-\mathbf{H}$ as was discussed in Section 5-11. When the last term is dropped (6-37) becomes a set of linear uncoupled equations that can be solved to give the Rossby wave solution.

In Section 6-3 it was pointed out that the Galerkin procedure preserves energy type invariants that arise from quadratic nonlinearities in the original equations. Equation 6-28 conserves both kinetic energy and mean square vorticity or enstrophy. The kinetic energy for the region can be written:

$$K=\int_0^{2\pi/k}\int_0^{2\pi/\ell}\frac{\nabla\psi\cdot\nabla\psi}{2}\,dydx$$
$$=\tfrac{1}{2}\sum_{\mathbf{H}}\sum_{\mathbf{M}}i^2\,\mathbf{H}\cdot\mathbf{M}\,C_{\mathbf{H}}C_{\mathbf{M}}\int_0^{2\pi/k}\int_0^{2\pi/\ell}e^{i(\mathbf{H}+\mathbf{M})\cdot\mathbf{R}}\,dydx$$

where the $\nabla\psi$ product was obtained from (6-35) with different summations. The integral on the right is nonzero only when $\mathbf{H}=-\mathbf{M}$ so that the energy can be written

$$K=\tfrac{1}{2}\sum_{\mathbf{M}}\mathbf{M}\cdot\mathbf{M}C_{\mathbf{M}}C_{-\mathbf{M}}=\tfrac{1}{2}\sum_{\mathbf{M}}\mathbf{M}\cdot\mathbf{M}|C_{\mathbf{M}}|^2 \qquad (6\text{-}38)$$

where the condition $C_{-\mathbf{M}}=C^*_{\mathbf{M}}$ has been used in the last step.

The energy form in (6-38) is conserved ($dK/dt = 0$) by both the original vorticity equation (6-28) and the spectral form (6-37). The conservation for (6-28) was demonstrated in Section 5-11, and the conservation for (6-38) follows from the development in Section 6-3. An equation for the rate of change of energy in wave **M** can be obtained by differentiating $C_{\mathbf{M}} C_{-\mathbf{M}}$ with respect to t and by using (6-37). The resulting equation shows that the energy in wave **M** changes in proportion to $C_{\mathbf{M}}$ times the amplitudes of pairs of interacting waves. Thus if $C_{\mathbf{M}}$ is maintained at zero, the energy flow out of the other waves to it must be zero. This shows in another way that energy will be conserved in any set of waves that might be selected for sum (6-33). Since interactions outside of this set are neglected, aliasing cannot occur in a spectral model. This automatically eliminates the nonlinear computational instability which occurs with finite difference equations (see Section 5-11).

The set of ordinary differential equations (6-37) can be integrated numerically with a variety of schemes (e.g., Table 5-2). In fact Baer and Platzman (1961) noted that the linear term in (6-37) can be treated exactly so that the only time differencing errors come from the nonlinear terms. The spectral method is much more accurate than most finite difference methods for the same number of degrees of freedom. In particular the linear advection that was examined in Chapter 5 is treated exactly by the spectral method provided that the initial field is resolved. Finite difference methods experience false dispersion since the short waves move too slowly. The spectral method has no aliasing because interactions involving shorter waves outside of the truncated set are excluded. On the other hand, the finite differencing falsely reflects interactions with shorter waves back onto longer waves. With the Arakawa Jacobian finite difference forms (see Section 5-11-1), this aliasing does not produce spurious energy, but it does cause phase errors in the interacting waves. In spectral models the most important error involves the neglect of interactions with wave components which are outside of the original set. The neglect of these interactions causes an error in the waves that are represented by the basis functions. Thus although the error in the original equation is orthogonal to the basis functions, the error in the solution will occur in the scales described by the basis functions.

When the spectral method is applied to a vorticity equation such as (6-28), a Poisson equation for $\partial\psi/\partial t$ does not have to be solved since the basis functions are eigensolutions of (6-31). The Poisson equation must be solved at each time step with finite difference methods. The biggest drawback to this form of the spectral equations is in calculating the nonlinear term which appears as the sum in (6-37). The coefficient preceding $C_{\mathbf{M}-\mathbf{H}}\, C_{\mathbf{H}}$ is called the interaction coefficient and it is usually computed just once and stored for use during the integration of the equation. The problem is that if there are N degrees of freedom the number of operations needed to compute the nonlinear terms goes as N^2 for this spectral model as compared with N for most finite difference methods. Thus for high resolution (large N), this form of the spectral method requires relatively larger amounts of computer time than finite difference methods. In Section 6-6 a method of calculating these *nonlinear* terms more efficiently is presented. However the present method is very convenient for low-order models. Lorenz (1960a) obtained some very interesting nonlinear solutions with a three-component system. It can be seen from (6-37) that at least three waves are required for nonlinear interaction because the sum is zero unless there are at least two other waves.

In this section the spectral equations will be formulated for barotropic motion on the sphere. The barotropic vorticity equation in spherical coordinates can be written:

$$\frac{\partial}{\partial t}\nabla^2\psi - \frac{1}{a^2}\left[\frac{\partial\psi}{\partial\mu}\frac{\partial\nabla^2\psi}{\partial\lambda} - \frac{\partial\psi}{\partial\lambda}\frac{\partial\nabla^2\psi}{\partial\mu}\right] + \frac{2\Omega}{a^2}\frac{\partial\psi}{\partial\lambda} = 0 \qquad (6\text{-}39)$$

where

$$\nabla^2 = \frac{\partial}{\partial\mu}\left[(1-\mu^2)\frac{\partial}{\partial\mu}\right] + \frac{1}{1-\mu^2}\frac{\partial^2}{\partial\lambda^2} \qquad (6\text{-}40)$$

In these equations λ is the longitude and $\mu = \sin\varphi$, where φ is the latitude. The spectral method was first applied in spherical coordinates by Silberman (1954) and the development of this section follows Platzman (1960).

The appropriate orthogonal basis functions are

$$Y_{m,n}(\mu, \lambda) = P_{m,n}(\mu)\, e^{im\lambda} \qquad (6\text{-}41)$$

where $P_{m,n}$ denotes associated Legendre functions of the first kind, which are defined by

$$P_{m,n}(\mu) = \left[\frac{(2n+1)(n-m)!}{(n+m)!}\right]^{1/2}\frac{(1-\mu^2)^{m/2}}{2^n\, n!}\frac{d^{n+m}}{d\mu^{n+m}}(\mu^2-1)^n \qquad (6\text{-}42)$$

These basis functions are spherical harmonics that satisfy the equation

$$\nabla^2 Y_{m,n} + b\, Y_{m,n} = 0 \qquad (6\text{-}43)$$

where the eigenvalues are given by

$$b = n(n+1)/a^2 \qquad (6\text{-}44)$$

Here $|m|$ is the planetary wavenumber and $n - |m|$ is the number of zeros between the poles. Also n must be greater than or equal to $|m|$. These basis functions are orthogonal so that

$$\frac{1}{4\pi}\int_0^{2\pi}\int_{-1}^{1} Y_{m,n}\, Y^*_{m',n'}\, d\mu d\lambda = \begin{cases} 1 \text{ for } (m',n') = (m,n) \\ 0 \text{ for } (m',n') \neq (m,n) \end{cases} \qquad (6\text{-}45)$$

The streamfunction can be approximated as follows:

$$\psi(x,y,t) = a^2 \sum_{m=-M}^{M} \sum_{n=|m|}^{|m|+J} \psi_{m,n}(t)\, Y_{m,n}(\lambda,\mu) \tag{6-46}$$

where J may be a function of m.

Since ψ must be real $\psi_{m,n}$ must satisfy

$$\psi_{-m,n} = (-1)^m \psi^*_{m,n} \tag{6-47}$$

This condition was derived with the use of the relation $P_{-m,n} = (-1)^m P_{m,n}$. The coefficients $\psi_{m,n}$ can be obtained from the transform:

$$\psi_{n,m}(t) = \frac{1}{4\pi a^2} \int_0^{2\pi} \int_{-1}^{1} \psi(\lambda,\mu,t)\, Y^*_{m,n}\, d\mu d\lambda \tag{6-48}$$

The vorticity has the following expansion:

$$\nabla^2\psi \simeq -\sum_{m=-M}^{M} \sum_{n=|m|}^{|m|+J} n(n+1)\, \psi_{m,n}(t)\, Y_{m,n} \tag{6-49}$$

which follows from (6-43) and (6-44).

The Galerkin method is applied by substituting (6-46) and (6-49) into (6-39), multiplying by $Y^*_{m,n}$ and integrating with respect to μ and λ. When the orthogonality conditions (6-45) are employed this equation reduces to:

$$\frac{d\psi_{m,n}}{dt} = \frac{2\Omega mi}{n(n+1)} \psi_{m,n} - \frac{1}{n(n+1)} F_{m,n} \tag{6-50}$$

The nonlinear terms $F_{m,n}$ may be written

$$F_{m,n} = -\sum_{m_1=-M}^{M} \sum_{n_1=|m_1|}^{|m_1|+J} \sum_{m_2=-M}^{M} \sum_{n_2=|m_2|}^{|m_2|+J} i\psi_{m_1,n_1}\, \psi_{m_2,n_2}\, L(m,n;m_1,n_1;m_2,n_2) \tag{6-51}$$

where the interaction coefficients are given by (6-52)

$$L(m,n;m_1,n_1;m_2,n_2) = \begin{cases} \tfrac{1}{2}[n_1(n_1+1) - n_2(n_2+1)] \\ \displaystyle\int_{-1}^{1} P_{m,n}\,[m_1 P_{m_1,n_1} \frac{dP_{m_2,n_2}}{d\mu} \\ \displaystyle - m_2 P_{m_2,n_2} \frac{dP_{m_1,n_1}}{d\mu}]\, d\mu \text{ for } m = m_1 + m_2 \\ = 0 \qquad \text{for } m \neq m_1 + m_2 \end{cases}$$

In obtaining this result the subscripts 1 and 2 were used for expansions (6-48) and (6-49), respectively. This form for the interaction coefficients comes from the fact that $F_{m,n}$ changes sign when ψ_{m_1,n_1} and ψ_{m_2,n_2} are interchanged.

Equation 6-50 has the same form as the prediction equation (6-37) for the Fourier basis function. However the spherical coordinate equation has more complicated interaction coefficients because of the integral involving the Legendre functions. It can be shown by the same method as before that energy is conserved, and Platzman (1960) has also shown that mean square vorticity is conserved. The spectral method applied to spherical (global) prediction has the advantage that there is no polar problem such as occurs with finite difference models (see Section 7-6). The only major disadvantage in solving (6-50) is in the large number of terms that come from the nonlinear terms. This problem will be treated in the next section.

6-5 TRANSFORM METHOD

In this section a newer method for handling the nonlinear terms in (6-50) will be presented, which avoids the use of interaction coefficients [see (6-51) and (6-52)]. This method was formulated independently by Orszag (1970) and Eliasen, Machenhauer, and Rasmussen (1970), and it has been reviewed by Bourke, McAvaney, Puri, and Thurling (1977). The problem with the interaction coefficient method for computing nonlinear terms is that it requires multiplication of two series (together), which is very time consuming. The transform method sums the series at certain spatial grid points and these fields are multiplied together at each point to form the nonlinear terms. Then the nonlinear terms must be transformed back to spectral space. The usefulness of this process is enhanced by the existence of efficient transform methods. In spherical coordinates the fast Fourier transform is used in longitude and the Legendre integrals in latitude are evaluated by Gaussian quadrature. This method is far superior to the interaction coefficient method for the sphere if there are very many components in the system.

The nonlinear terms that must be transformed may be rewritten as follows:

$$F(\mu,\lambda) = \frac{1}{a^2}\left(\frac{\partial\psi}{\partial\mu}\frac{\partial\nabla^2\psi}{\partial\lambda} - \frac{\partial\psi}{\partial\lambda}\frac{\partial\nabla^2\psi}{\partial\mu}\right)$$
$$= \frac{1}{a^2}\left[\frac{\partial}{\partial\lambda}\left(\frac{\partial\psi}{\partial\mu}\nabla^2\psi\right) - \frac{\partial}{\partial\mu}\left(\frac{\partial\psi}{\partial\lambda}\nabla^2\psi\right)\right] \tag{6-53}$$

It is now convenient to define the following quantities, which are the λ and φ velocity components multiplied by $\cos\varphi$:

$$U \equiv \frac{-\cos^2\varphi}{a}\frac{\partial\psi}{\partial\mu} \qquad V \equiv \frac{1}{a}\frac{\partial\psi}{\partial\lambda} \tag{6-54}$$

Note that these components vanish at the poles.

When these velocities are introduced into (6-53) it can be written as follows:

$$F(\mu,\lambda) = -\frac{1}{a}\left[\frac{1}{1-\mu^2}\frac{\partial}{\partial\lambda}(U\nabla^2\psi) + \frac{\partial}{\partial\mu}(V\nabla^2\psi)\right] \tag{6-55}$$

The velocity components (6-54) can be computed from (6-46) at longitude-latitude grid points, and the vorticity can be obtained at the same points using (6-49). The details of the process will be given later. The products $U\nabla^2\psi$ and $V\nabla^2\psi$ can be calculated at each gridpoint and the resulting products can be Fourier analyzed in λ to give the following relations:

$$\begin{aligned} U\nabla^2\psi &= a \sum_{m=-M}^{M} A_m(\mu)\, e^{im\lambda} \\ V\nabla^2\psi &= a \sum_{m=-M}^{M} B_m(\mu)\, e^{im\lambda} \end{aligned} \tag{6-56}$$

The transform of $F(\mu,\lambda)$ is given by

$$F_{m,n} = \frac{1}{4\pi}\int_0^{2\pi}\int_{-1}^{1} e^{-im\lambda} P_{m,n} F(\mu,\lambda)\, d\mu d\lambda \tag{6-57}$$

The λ integration in (6-57) can be carried out by substituting (6-56) into (6-55) and by inserting the result in (6-57), which gives:

$$F_{m,n} = -½\int_{-1}^{1}\left(\frac{im}{1-\mu^2} A_m P_{m,n} + \frac{dB_m}{d\mu} P_{m,n}\right) d\mu$$

The second term can be integrated by parts, which gives

$$F_{m,n} = -½\int_{-1}^{1}\left(\frac{im}{1-\mu^2} A_m P_{m,n} - B_m \frac{dP_{m,n}}{d\mu}\right) d\mu \tag{6-58}$$

where the condition $B_m = 0$ at $\mu = \pm 1$ was used to simplify the integral. This condition follows since V is equal to the actual velocity times $\cos\varphi$. The form of $F_{m,n}$ given by (6-58) is superior to the earlier form because only the known function $P_{m,n}$ is differentiated.

The integrand in (6-58) is a polynomial in μ and the integral can be evaluated following Eliasen et al. (1970) by the Gaussian quadrature formula. If the integrand is denoted by $Q(\mu)$, the formula gives the following expression for $F_{m,n}$:

$$F_{m,n} = ½\sum_{k=1}^{K} G_k^{(K)}\, Q(\mu_k) \tag{6-59}$$

In (6-59) the summation is carried over K values of μ_k, where the μ_k's are roots of the Legendre polynomial $P_{O,K}$ and $G_k^{(K)}$ are the corresponding Gauss coefficients. The formula is exact for any polynomial of degree smaller than or equal to $2K - 1$ [see Gerald (1978)]. Thus apart from round-off errors, no approximation is introduced by computing the integral when a sufficiently high value of K is used. The maximum degree of $Q(\mu)$ can be most easily obtained from (6-52).

Before discussing this process for treating the nonlinear terms in more detail, it is necessary to determine the relation between J, m and M, which must be defined in the sum (6-46). In rhomboidal truncation $J = M$, so that each latitudinal mode has the same number of waves in longitude. With triangular truncation $J = M - |m|$, so all basis functions that have the same scale, that is, the same eigenvalue, $b = n(n + 1)/a^2$, are either retained or dropped. Thus the mode with the smallest latitudinal scale has the largest longitudinal scale. The terms rhomboidal and triangular refer to the areas enclosed in m,n space. Most meteorological models use the rhomboidal truncation in part because it gives better longitudinal resolution. In the remainder of this development, the rhomboidal truncation will be used.

In order to construct the fields (6-56) it is necessary to obtain U and V from ψ. First expand U and V into these sums:

$$U = \frac{1}{a} \sum_{m=-M}^{M} \sum_{n=|m|}^{|m|+M+1} U_{m,n} Y_{m,n}$$
$$V = \frac{1}{a} \sum_{m=-M}^{M} \sum_{n=|m|}^{|m|+M} V_{m,n} Y_{m,n} \tag{6-60}$$

The following relations will be useful in evaluating (6-54):

$$(\mu^2 - 1) \frac{\partial Y_{m,n}}{\partial \mu} = n\, D_{m,n+1} Y_{m,n+1} - (n + 1)\, D_{m,n} Y_{m,n-1}$$
$$\frac{\partial Y_{m,n}}{\partial \lambda} = im\, Y_{m,n} \tag{6-61}$$

where $D_{m,n} \equiv [(n^2 - m^2)/(4n^2 - 1)]^{1/2}$. The final expressions for $U_{m,n}$ and $V_{m,n}$ can be obtained by substituting (6-46) and (6-60) into (6-54), using (6-61) and by applying the orthogonality condition (6-45):

$$U_{m,n} = (n - 1)\, D_{m,n}\, \psi_{m,n-1} - (n + 2)\, D_{m,n+1}\, \psi_{m,n+1}$$
$$V_{m,n} = im\, \psi_{m,n} \tag{6-62}$$

Note that the expansion for U as given in (6-60) must extend one degree above that defined for ψ, since nonzero values of $U_{|m|,|m|+M+1}$ are implied by nonzero values of $\psi_{|m|,|m|+M}$.

The quantities U, V, and $\nabla^2\psi$ can now be evaluated at points

$$\lambda_j = 2\pi j/N \qquad \varphi_k = \arcsin \mu_k$$

where $j = 1, \ldots, N$ and $k = 1, \ldots, K$. The φ_k's are called the Guassian latitudes. Consider for example $V(\lambda_j, \mu_k)$, which can be written:

$$V(\lambda_j, \mu_k) = \sum_{m=-M}^{M} e^{im\lambda_j} \left[\sum_{n=|m|}^{|m|+M} im\, \psi_{m,n} P_{m,n}(\mu_k) \right] \tag{6-63}$$

with the use of (6-41), (6-46), and (6-62). Similar expressions can be written for $U(\lambda_j, \mu_k)$ and $\nabla^2\psi(\lambda_j, \mu_k)$. The outer summation can be carried out very efficiently with the use of the fast Fourier transform method, which was developed by Cooley and Tukey (1965). The number of operations required for the fast Fourier method applied over N points is of order $N \log_2 N$, while for the direct method order N^2 operations are required. The fast Fourier transform method is clearly much faster than the direct method for larger values of N. The next step is to compute $U\nabla^2\psi$ and $V\nabla^2\psi$ at each gridpoint. After these products have been computed, the Fourier transforms must be calculated to give A_m and B_m for use in (6-56). For example, using the discrete Fourier transform:

$$A_m(\mu_k) = \frac{1}{aN} \sum_{j=1}^{N} e^{-im\lambda_j} (U\nabla^2\psi)_{jk} \tag{6-64}$$

where $-M \leq m \leq M$. A similar expression is obtained for $B_m(\mu_k)$. The fast Fourier transform can also be used here to save time.

It is important to choose N large enough to avoid aliasing when the products are transformed back to wave number space as in equation (6-64). Orszag [(1969), (1970)] suggested that $N = 4M$ would be needed, but later Orszag (1971a) and Machenhauer and Rasmussen (1972) showed that $N = 3M + 1$ was adequate to provide alias-free transforms.

Now that $A_m(\mu_k)$ and $B_m(\mu_k)$ are known, $F_{m,n}$ can be computed exactly from (6-59) if the degree of the polynomials is less than or equal to $2K - 1$. The maximum degree can be determined from (6-52) by noting the $P_{m,n}$ is a polynomial of degree n and by considering these selection rules for the interactions: $m = m_1 + m_2$, $|n_1 - n_2| < n < |n_1 + n_2|$. The conclusion that is given in Bourke et al. (1977) is that the maximum degree is $5M - 1$, so that the number of Gaussian latitudes is $K \geq M/2$.

This method of computing $F_{m,n}$ is more efficient than the interaction coefficient method and it requires much less computer storage. The number of calculations required for the interaction coefficient method is of order (M^5) while for the transform method it is of order $(25\, M^3)$ [see Bourke et al. (1977)]. It will be shown in the next section that the transform method is more efficient for even a moderate value of M and this advantage increases rapidly with M.

6-6 SPECTRAL MODEL OF SHALLOW-WATER EQUATIONS

In this section the spectral method will be extended to the primitive equations and it will be demonstrated that semi-implicit differencing can be applied with little extra effort. The shallow-water equations in spherical coordinates will be used to demonstrate the procedure following Eliasen et al. (1970) and Bourke (1972). The equation of motion and the continuity equation can be written:

$$\frac{\partial \mathbf{V}}{\partial t} = -(\zeta + f)\,\mathbf{k} \times \mathbf{V} - \nabla\left(\phi' + \frac{\mathbf{V}\cdot\mathbf{V}}{2}\right) \tag{6-65}$$

$$\frac{\partial \phi'}{\partial t} = -\nabla \cdot \phi' \mathbf{V} - \bar{\phi} D \tag{6-66}$$

This form of the equation of motion will simplify the derivation of the vorticity and divergence equations. Note that the geopotential has been split into a mean $\bar{\phi}$, and a departure ϕ', which will facilitate the implementation of semi-implicit time differencing.

The velocity is broken into rotational and divergent parts as follows:

$$\mathbf{V} = \mathbf{k} \times \nabla\psi + \nabla\chi = (U/\cos\varphi)\,\mathbf{i} + (V/\cos\varphi)\,\mathbf{j} \tag{6-67}$$

The modified components U and V will also be used here. Now form the vorticity and divergence equations by taking $\nabla \cdot$ and $\mathbf{k} \cdot \nabla \times$ of (6-65), which gives:

$$\frac{\partial \zeta}{\partial t} = -\nabla \cdot (\zeta + f)\,\mathbf{V} \tag{6-68}$$

$$\frac{\partial D}{\partial t} = \mathbf{k} \cdot \nabla \times [(\zeta + f)\,\mathbf{V}] - \nabla^2\left(\phi' + \frac{\mathbf{V}\cdot\mathbf{V}}{2}\right) \tag{6-69}$$

The vorticity and divergence become

$$\zeta = \nabla^2\psi \qquad D = \nabla^2\chi \tag{6-70}$$

In spectral models it is convenient to replace the equation of motion by the vorticity and divergence equations because the relations (6-70) are simplified when spherical harmonics are used as basis functions, and because the equations only contain scalars. This form of the equations is also more convenient for application of semi-implicit differencing.

The vorticity equation (6-68) and the divergence equation (6-69) can now be expanded with the use of (6-67) and (6-70) to give:

$$\frac{\partial}{\partial t}\nabla^2\psi = -\frac{1}{a\cos^2\varphi}\left[\frac{\partial}{\partial\lambda}(U\nabla^2\psi) + \cos\varphi\frac{\partial}{\partial\varphi}(V\nabla^2\psi)\right]$$

$$- 2\Omega(\sin\varphi\,\nabla^2\chi + V/a) \tag{6-71}$$

$$\frac{\partial}{\partial t}\nabla^2\chi = \frac{1}{a\cos^2\varphi}\left[\frac{\partial}{\partial\lambda}(V\nabla^2\psi) - \cos\varphi\frac{\partial}{\partial\varphi}(U\nabla^2\psi)\right]$$

$$+ 2\Omega(\sin\varphi\nabla^2\psi - U/a) - \nabla^2\left(\frac{U^2+V^2}{2\cos^2\varphi} + \phi'\right) \tag{6-72}$$

Similarly the continuity equation (6-66) becomes:

$$\frac{\partial\phi'}{\partial t} = -\frac{1}{a\cos^2\varphi}\left[\frac{\partial}{\partial\lambda}(U\phi') + \cos\varphi\frac{\partial}{\partial\varphi}(V\phi')\right] - \bar{\phi}\nabla^2\chi \tag{6-73}$$

The two components of (6-67) can be written:

$$U = -\frac{\cos\varphi}{a}\frac{\partial\psi}{\partial\varphi} + \frac{1}{a}\frac{\partial\chi}{\partial\lambda} \tag{6-74}$$

$$V = \frac{1}{a}\frac{\partial\psi}{\partial\lambda} + \frac{\cos\varphi}{a}\frac{\partial\chi}{\partial\varphi} \tag{6-75}$$

Equations 6-71, 6-72, and 6-73 are the predictive equations for ψ, χ, and ϕ' and (6-74) and (6-75) are diagnostic expressions for U and V. The nonlinear terms in these equations are in a convenient form for the transform method which was presented in the last section, since the multiplication can be performed at the gridpoints before differentiation.

Each of the dependent variables is approximated in terms of the spherical harmonic basis functions (6-41) as follows:

$$\psi \simeq a^2 \sum_{m=-M}^{M}\sum_{n=|m|}^{|m|+M} \psi_{m,n} Y_{m,n} \qquad \chi \simeq a^2 \sum_{m=-M}^{M}\sum_{n=|m|}^{|m|+M} \chi_{m,n} Y_{m,n} \tag{6-76}$$

$$\phi' \simeq a^2 \sum_{m=-M}^{M}\sum_{n=|m|}^{|m|+M} \phi_{m,n} Y_{m,n} \tag{6-77}$$

$$U \simeq a \sum_{m=-M}^{M}\sum_{n=|m|}^{|m|+M+1} U_{m,n} Y_{m,n} \qquad V \simeq a \sum_{m=-M}^{M}\sum_{n=|m|}^{|m|+M+1} V_{m,n} Y_{m,n} \tag{6-78}$$

These expansions are for the rhomboidal wavenumber truncation. Equations 6-74 and 6-75 are transformed in the same manner as Equations 6-54 were in the last section and the result is

$$U_{m,n} = (n-1)\,D_{m,n}\,\psi_{m,n-1} - (n+2)\,D_{m,n+1}\,\psi_{m,n+1} + im\chi_{m,n}$$

$$V_{m,n} = -(n-1)\,D_{m,n}\,\chi_{m,n-1} + (n+2)\,D_{m,n+1}\,\chi_{m,n+1} + im\psi_{m,n} \tag{6-79}$$

where $D_{m,n} = [(n^2 - m^2)/(4n^2 - 1)]^{1/2}$

Note that the expansions for U and V must extend one degree above the expansions for ψ and χ.

The quantities needed for the nonlinear terms are obtained by evaluating the sums in (6-76), (6-77), and (6-78) at equally spaced points in longitude and at Gaussian latitudes. The required products are computed at each point and the products are then Fourier transformed in longitude as follows:

$$U\nabla^2\psi = a \sum_{m=-M}^{M} A_m e^{im\lambda} \qquad V\nabla^2\psi = a \sum_{m=-M}^{M} B_m e^{im\lambda} \tag{6-80}$$

$$V\phi' = a^3 \sum_{m=-M}^{M} C_m e^{im\lambda} \qquad V\phi' = a^3 \sum_{m=-M}^{M} D_m e^{im\lambda} \tag{6-81}$$

$$\frac{U^2 + V^2}{2} = a^2 \sum_{m=-M}^{M} E_m e^{im\lambda} \tag{6-82}$$

The spectral equations are formed by substituting (6-76), (6-77), (6-78), (6-80), (6-81), and (6-82) into the system (6-71) to (6-73) and multiplying each equation by $Y^*_{m,n}$ and integrating over the domain. With the use of the orthogonality condition (6-45) the equations finally reduce to the following set:

$$-n(n+1)\frac{\partial\psi_{m,n}}{\partial t} = \frac{1}{2}\int_{-1}^{1}\frac{1}{1-\mu^2}\left(imA_m P_{m,n} - B_m \frac{dP_{m,n}}{d\mu}\right)d\mu$$
$$+ 2\Omega[n(n-1)D_{m,n}\chi_{m,n-1} + (n+1)(n+2)D_{m,n+1}\chi_{m,n+1} - V_{m,n}] \tag{6-83}$$

$$-n(n+1)\frac{\partial\chi_{m,n}}{\partial t} = \frac{1}{2}\int_{-1}^{1}\frac{1}{1-\mu^2}\left(imB_m P_{m,n} + A_m \frac{dP_{m,n}}{d\mu}\right)d\mu$$
$$- 2\Omega[n(n-1)D_{m,n}\psi_{m,n-1} + (n+1)(n+2)D_{m,n+1}\psi_{m,n+1} + U_{m,n}]$$
$$+ n(n+1)(E_{m,n} + \phi_{m,n}) \tag{6-84}$$

$$\frac{\partial\phi_{m,n}}{\partial t} = -\frac{1}{2}\int_{-1}^{1}\frac{1}{1-\mu^2}\left(imC_m P_{m,n} - D_m \frac{dP_{m,n}}{d\mu}\right)d\mu$$
$$+ \overline{\phi}n(n+1)\chi_{m,n} \tag{6-85}$$

where

$$E_{m,n} = \frac{1}{2}\int_{-1}^{1}\frac{E_m}{1-\mu^2}P_{m,n}\,d\mu \tag{6-86}$$

The integrals are evaluated by the Gaussian quadrature formula as before, but this time $(5M + 1)/2$ Gaussian latitudes are required. As before the required number of longitudinal gridpoints is $3M + 1$.

Bourke (1972) compared the efficiency of the transform method to the interaction coefficient method for this model. Figure 6-2 shows the computer time required per time step for the two methods as a function of the truncation number M. The figure shows clearly that even for $M = 15$ the transform method is an order of magnitude faster than the interaction coefficient method. In fact, the interaction coefficient method becomes almost intractable for M much larger than 15. At $M = 15$ there are over 500,000 interaction coefficients.

The system (6-83) to (6-85) is very convenient for the application of semi-implicit time differencing. All terms are evaluated explicitly except that $\phi_{m,n}$ in (6-84) and $\chi_{m,n}$ in (6-85) are treated implicitly. These two equations are easily solved for $\phi_{m,n}$ $(t + \Delta t)$, and equations (6-83) and (6-84) can then be solved explicitly. In contrast, semi-implicit finite difference models require the solution of a Helmholtz equation for $\phi(t + \Delta t)$ at every time step (see Section 5-7-2). Thus in spectral primitive equation models a much longer time step can be used with almost the same computational effort per time step.

The introduction of the transform method and semi-implicit differencing have made the spectral primitive equation models competitive with finite dif-

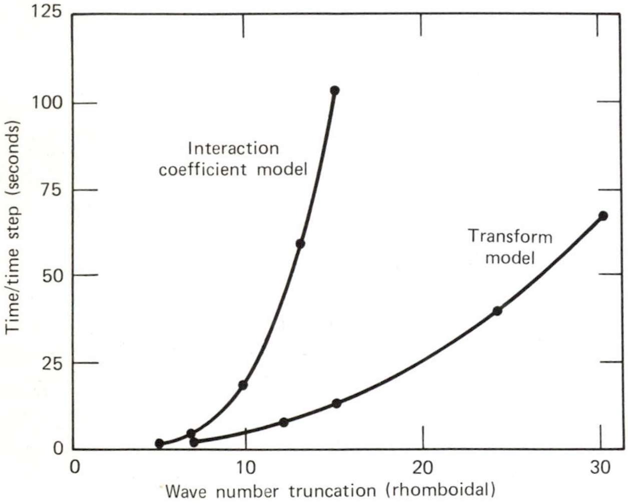

Figure 6.2 Computation time per time step(s) as a function of spectral resolution obtained by Bourke (1972). Integrations of a global spectral model employing a transform method and employing the interaction coefficient method are compared. (From W. Bourke, "An Efficient, One-level, Primitive-equation Spectral Model, 1972." *Americal Meteorological Soc.*)

ference models for global prediction. The procedures used in this section are easily extended to baroclinic models as will be discussed in Section 7-8. Comparisons have shown that as good or better forecasts can be made with global spectral models than with finite difference models which use the same amount of computer time [Doron et al. (1974) and Daley, Girard, Henderson, and Simmonds (1976)].

Energy is not exactly conserved in this model even with continuous time variation. This is because the kinetic energy for the shallow water equations is proportional to $\phi \mathbf{V} \cdot \mathbf{V}$, which is a cubic energy form, and consequently the analysis of Section 6-3 does not apply. However, the nonlinear terms are computed very accurately in spectral models and experience shows that the energy is in fact very nearly conserved. Bourke (1972) integrated the model that was developed in this section for 116 days, and obtained an energy change of only 2 percent.

6-7 ADVECTION EQUATION WITH FINITE ELEMENTS

In this section the finite element method with linear elements will be applied to the advection equation

$$\frac{\partial u}{\partial t} + c\frac{\partial u}{\partial x} = 0 \tag{6-87}$$

This equation was treated extensively in Chapter 5 with various finite difference schemes. The Galerkin equation is obtained by setting $\mathscr{L} = c\,(\partial/\partial x)$ in (6-22) which gives

$$\sum_{j=1}^{N} \frac{du_j}{dt} \int_a^b \varphi_i \, \varphi_j \, dx + c \sum_{j=1}^{N} u_j \int_a^b \varphi_i \frac{\partial \varphi_j}{\partial x} dx = 0 \qquad i = 1, \ldots, N \tag{6-88}$$

The linear basis functions $\varphi_j(x)$ are defined by (6-12) and a typical one is shown in Figure 6-1. In this application u is periodic so that the basis functions must satisfy $\varphi_0 = \varphi_N$ and $\varphi_1 = \varphi_{N+1}$.

The first term in (6-88) can be evaluated from (6-17), which is of the same form with du_j/dt in place of f_j, and the second term can be computed with the use of (6-14). The resulting equation with $i = m$ can be written:

$$\frac{1}{6}\left(\frac{du_{m+1}}{dt} + 4\frac{du_m}{dt} + \frac{du_{m-1}}{dt}\right) + c\frac{u_{m+1} - u_{m-1}}{2\Delta x} = 0 \tag{6-89}$$

The advection term is the same as is obtained from centered differencing, but the time derivative appears as a weighted average over three points. It will be seen later that this greatly increases the accuracy of the solution.

Now apply leapfrog time differencing which gives the following equation:

$$\frac{1}{12\Delta t}[u_{m+1,n+1} - u_{m+1,n-1} + 4(u_{m,n+1} - u_{m,n-1}) + u_{m-1,n+1} - u_{m-1,n-1}]$$

$$+ \frac{c}{2\Delta x}(u_{m+1,n} - u_{m-1,n}) = 0 \tag{6-90}$$

The stability and phase error can be investigated by substituting $u_{m,n} = A \exp[i(\mu\Delta xm + \alpha\Delta tn)]$ into (6-90). This yields

$$\sin\alpha\Delta t = -(c\Delta t/\Delta x)(3\sin\mu\Delta x)/(2 + \cos\mu\Delta x) \tag{6-91}$$

The solution is stable [that is, $|\sin\alpha\Delta t| \leq 1$] if

$$(3c\Delta t/\Delta x)[\sin\mu\Delta x/(2 + \cos\mu\Delta x)]_{\max} \leq 1$$

The bracketed term is a maximum when $\mu\Delta x = 120°$, so that the stability condition becomes

$$|c\Delta t/\Delta x| \leq 1/\sqrt{3} \tag{6-92}$$

This criterion is considerably more restrictive than the CFL condition that arises from the leapfrog finite difference scheme. However, it will be shown that (6-90) gives even better phase speed than the fourth-order leapfrog scheme for which the computational stability criterion is $|c\Delta t/\Delta x| \leq 0.73$ (see Section 5-6-5). Thus it is not unreasonable that the leapfrog finite element scheme would have a more restrictive computational stability criteria.

The finite element formula with leapfrog time differencing is actually implicit, since the new value $u_{m,n+1}$ cannot be obtained explicity from the earlier time values. Thus it seems reasonable to use a fully implicit form which does not have the time-step restriction (6-92). Consider the following time difference approximation to (6-89):

$$\frac{1}{6\Delta t}(u_{m+1,n+1} - u_{m+1,n} + 4(u_{m,n+1} - u_{m,n}) + u_{m-1,n+1} - u_{m-1,n})$$

$$+ \frac{c}{4\Delta x}(u_{m+1,n+1} - u_{m-1,n+1} + u_{m+1,n} - u_{m-1,n}) = 0 \tag{6-93}$$

This fully implicit scheme can be shown to be neutral for all time steps, and it should require about the same effort per time step as (6-90). For this reason implicit time differencing schemes are often desirable when finite elements are used.

The phase speed for the leapfrog scheme is given by

$$c_F = -\alpha/\mu = \frac{1}{\mu\Delta t}\arcsin\left(\frac{c\Delta t}{\Delta x}\frac{3\sin\mu\Delta x}{2 + \cos\mu\Delta x}\right) \tag{6-94}$$

If $\Delta t/\Delta x$ and μ are fixed, this expression approaches c as $\Delta t \to 0$, which shows that the solution converges. If Δt is small in comparison to $\Delta x/c$, this formula reduces to

$$c_F = \frac{c}{\mu\Delta x}\frac{3\sin\mu\Delta x}{2+\cos\mu\Delta x} = \frac{c}{\mu\Delta x}\frac{\sin\mu\Delta x}{[1 - \tfrac{2}{3}\sin^2(\mu\Delta x/2)]} \tag{6-95}$$

Table 6-1 contains c_F/c from (6-95) for typical values of L.

Table 6-1 c_F/c for the FEM Solution and for Fourth-Order Space-Differenced Scheme for Various Wavelengths L

L	$2\Delta x$	$3\Delta x$	$4\Delta x$	$6\Delta x$
FEM	0	0.83	0.96	0.99
Fourth order	0	0.61	0.85	0.96

The table also includes the ratio for the fourth-order scheme from the limit of (5-78) for small Δt. The finite element formula (6-95) can be expanded in $\mu\Delta x$, which leads to an error that is of order $(\mu\Delta x)^4$. Table 6-1 shows that although the linear finite element equation and the fourth-order finite difference equation have the same order of truncation error, the finite element equation is much more accurate. At $L = 3\Delta x$ the finite element solution gives only 17 percent error in phase speed, while the fourth-order finite difference gives 39 percent. However for $L = 2\Delta x$, $c_F = 0$, which indicates that the finite element computational group velocity is very large for this wavelength. This can be shown by differentiating as follows:

$$G = \frac{d(\mu c_F)}{d\mu} = \frac{(2\cos\mu\Delta x + 1)}{(\cos\mu\Delta x + 2)^2} \tag{6-96}$$

When $L = 2\Delta x$, ($\mu\Delta x = \pi$), this formula gives $G = -3c$, which is much larger than the $-(5/3)c$ that occurs with fourth-order differencing. This suggests that small-scale noise will propagate very rapidly in finite element models. This tendency toward noisiness has been observed in various finite element models. The degree of accuracy indicated above for the finite element model has been verified by Cullen (1973) in a two-dimensional advective problem. Note that although the FEM gives a solution for all values of x in the range considered, the high accuracy is only obtained at the nodal points since the fields are assumed to be linear between nodal points. In the next section this method is applied to the barotropic vorticity equation.

6-8 BAROTROPIC VORTICITY EQUATION WITH FINITE ELEMENTS

In this section the finite element method is applied to the nonlinear barotropic vorticity equation in a two-dimensional domain. The basis functions will be linear functions on triangular elements. The barotropic vorticity equation can be written

$$\frac{\partial \eta}{\partial t} = -\mathbf{k} \times \nabla\psi \cdot \nabla\eta \tag{6-97}$$

where

$$\eta = f(y) + \nabla^2\psi \tag{6-98}$$

is the absolute vorticity.

Following Fix (1975) both ψ and η are expanded in terms of the basis functions $\varphi_j(x,y)$ as given below:

$$\psi(x,y,t) \simeq \sum_{j=1}^{N} \varphi_j(t)\, \psi_j(x,y) \tag{6-99}$$

$$\eta(x,y,t) \simeq \sum_{j=1}^{N} \eta_j(t)\, \varphi_j(x,y) \tag{6-100}$$

When the Galerkin method is applied to (6-98) the following is obtained:

$$\sum_{j=1}^{N} \psi_j(t) \int\!\!\int \varphi_i \nabla^2 \varphi_j \, dA = -\int\!\!\int \varphi_i(x,y) f(y)\, dA + \sum_{j=1}^{N} \eta_j(t) \int\!\!\int \varphi_i(x,y)\, \varphi_j(x,y)\, dA$$

for $i = 1, \ldots, N$. Since linear basis functions will be used it is necessary to integrate the left-hand side by parts, which gives:

$$\sum_{j=1}^{N} \psi_j \int\!\!\int \nabla\varphi_i \cdot \nabla\varphi_j dA = \int\!\!\int \varphi_i f(y) dA - \sum_{j=1}^{N} \eta_j \int\!\!\int \varphi_i \varphi_j dA \tag{6-101}$$

for $i = 1,2, \ldots, N$.

The boundary terms that arise from the integration by parts were set to zero by assuming that either ψ is periodic in space or that there is no flow normal to the boundaries (i.e., $\mathbf{k} \times \nabla\psi \cdot \mathbf{n} = 0$, where $\mathbf{n}$ is a unit vector normal to the boundary). Now apply the Galerkin method to the vorticity equation (6-97), which leads to the following form:

$$\sum_{j=1}^{N} \frac{d\eta_j}{dt} \int\!\!\int \varphi_i \varphi_j \, dA = -\sum_{j=1}^{N} \sum_{k=1}^{N} \psi_j \eta_k \int\!\!\int \varphi_i \mathbf{k} \times \nabla\varphi_j \cdot \nabla\varphi_k \, dA \tag{6-102}$$

for $i = 1, \ldots, N$. This equation is of the same form that was obtained with the spectral model, but the nonlinear term requires much less effort because the only φ's which interact are those that are physically adjacent.

The equations (6-101) and (6-102) conserve both mean square vorticity (enstrophy) and kinetic energy. The enstrophy conservation can be shown by multiplying (6-102) by η_i and summing over i. When the summations are taken under the integrals, the form (6-26) is found. Since the integral of $\eta\mathbf{k} \times \nabla\psi \cdot \nabla\eta$ vanishes, the conservation of $\eta^2/2$ follows directly. The kinetic energy change can be examined by first differentiating (6-101) and substituting the result into (6-102), which gives:

$$-\sum_{j=1}^{N} \frac{d\psi_j}{dt} \iint \nabla\varphi_i \cdot \nabla\varphi_j \, dA$$

$$= -\sum_{j=1}^{N}\sum_{k=1}^{N} \psi_j\eta_k \iint \varphi_i \mathbf{k} \times \nabla\varphi_j \cdot \nabla\varphi_k dA \qquad (6\text{-}103)$$

for $i = 1,2, \ldots ,N$. Multiply this equation by $-\psi_i$ and sum over i. The resulting equation is again of the same form as (6-26) and the left-hand side is the derivative of the total kinetic energy. Since the integral of $\psi\mathbf{k} \times \nabla\psi \cdot \nabla\eta$ is zero, the energy is conserved. These results are not dependent on the particular basis functions that are employed.

The systems of equations (6-101) and (6-102) can be written in matrix forms which are more convenient for solution. Let $\boldsymbol{\psi}$ and $\boldsymbol{\eta}$ be column vectors of the values of ψ_i and η_i, respectively. Then (6-101) takes the form:

$$K\boldsymbol{\psi} = \mathbf{Q} \qquad (6\text{-}104)$$

where the elements of the matrix K are

$$K_{ij} = \iint \nabla\varphi_j \cdot \nabla\varphi_i \, da \qquad (6\text{-}105)$$

and $\mathbf{Q}$ is a column vector of the right-hand side of (6-101). Similarly, system (6-102) becomes

$$M\frac{d\boldsymbol{\eta}}{dt} = \mathbf{J} \qquad (6\text{-}106)$$

where the elements of M are

$$M_{ij} = \iint \varphi_i\varphi_j \, dA \qquad (6\text{-}107)$$

and $\mathbf{J}$ is a column vector of the right-hand side of (6-102).

The solution procedure will be illustrated for the case where leapfrog time differencing is used in (6-105), which leads to the equation:

$$M\Delta\boldsymbol{\eta} = 2\Delta t \, \mathbf{J}_n \qquad (6\text{-}108)$$

where $\Delta\boldsymbol{\eta} = \boldsymbol{\eta}_{n+1} - \boldsymbol{\eta}_{n-1}$. The matrices K and M are computed initially and stored for later use. The equations can be integrated beginning with $\psi_{j,n}$, $\eta_{j,n-1}$ and $\eta_{j,n}$. The right-hand side of (6-108) can be computed from $\psi_{j,n}$ and $\eta_{j,n}$, and that equation can then be solved for $\Delta\eta_j$. This increment can be added to $\eta_{j,n-1}$ to obtain $\eta_{j,n+1}$. With these values the right-hand side of (6-104) can be computed, and (6-104) can be solved for $\psi_{j,n+1}$, and the process can be continued. In this procedure it is necessary to invert the matrices K and M during each time step. These matrices are very sparse since only adjacent elements interact. In some cases direct methods, such as those discussed in Section 5-10-4, can be used, but iterative methods are much more flexible.

Cullen (1973) has shown that the two-dimensional advective stability criterion for linear elements is

$$\frac{|c|\Delta t}{d} \leq 1/\sqrt{6} \tag{6-109}$$

where d is the distance between nodal points. This is consistent with the one-dimensional result (6-92), because the step from one to two dimensions is usually achieved by replacing the grid size with $d/\sqrt{2}$. In this application $|c|$ would correspond to the maximumm velocity in the domain. Since the condition (6-108) is rather restrictive for Δt and since two matrices must be inverted per time step it may be worth while to use a fully implicit form similar to (6-93).

A natural generalization of the tent function in one dimension to two dimensions is a basis function which is composed of triangular elements. On each triangle the function varies linearly from 0 at two vertices to 1 at the third, which is the nodal point for the basis function. Figure 6-3 shows how a typical basis function φ_j is constructed on a rectangular grid of nodal points. This function is the sum of the six plane surfaces that are associated with each triangle. The basis functions can be equally well constructed when the nodal points are irregularly located, and it is not necessary to have six triangular elements in the construction.

The elements in the matrix equations (6-104) and (6-106) are obtained by evaluating the integrals in equations (6-101) and (6-106). These integrals can be reduced to a series of integrals over triangles such as are shown in Figure 6-3. Within each triangle any point is affected by only the three basis functions that have nodal points at the three vertices of the triangle. Zienkiewicz (1971) and Desai and Abel (1972) describe a convenient procedure for evaluating the integrals over each triangle. This involves introducing triangular coordinates that vary linearly across each triangle in the same manner as the basis functions. The integrals can then be evaluated quite generally.

A rigorous mathematical analysis of the finite element method is given in the book by Strang and Fix (1973). The stability and convergence of the method are discussed in considerable detail. Most finite element applications are based on a variational formulation rather than the Galerkin approach that has been used here, although the Galerkin method is most appropriate when time dependence is included. Pinder and Gray (1977) developed the finite element method with the Galerkin approach and gave applications in hydrology, which has similar equations to those that occur in numerical weather prediction.

The finite element method has been applied to atmospheric prediction with the primitive equations in shallow water form. Cullen (1974) and Hinsman

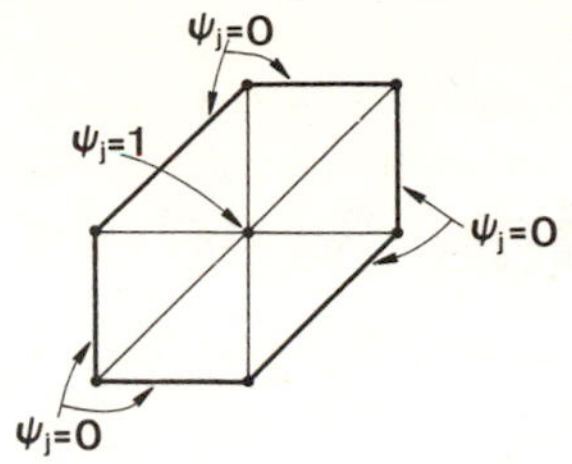

Figure 6.3 Construction of the basis function ς_j on a rectangular array of nodal points.

(1975) carried out global forecasts with these equations using linear basis functions on triangles as discussed in this section. The elements were efficiently arranged so that the area of each element was almost the same over different parts of the globe. Most global finite difference models have a large variation in grid size between the equator and the pole and, consequently, are not very efficient.

Staniforth and Mitchell (1977) reformulated the shallow-water equations in terms of the vorticity and divergence as was done in Section 6-6 for the spectral model. In this form semi-implicit time differencing can be applied easily, which allows a much larger time step. This is very important since the finite element method generally requires more computer time per time step. Staniforth and Mitchell also found very little noise generation in their forecasts, whereas many finite element primitive equation models tend to generate small scale noise if no smoothing is used [Cullen (1975)].

The finite element method when applied to meteorological equations gives very accurate phase propagation and also handles nonlinearities very well. The main drawback to the use of the method is the requirement that an equation solver must be applied to invert a large matrix at every time step for each variable. The development of flexible exact solvers for these matrices is of great importance. The finite element method can easily be applied to variable resolution problems, but some finite element models do tend to produce noise probably as a result of the large spurious group velocity for the shortest wave. However, the formulation of Staniforth and Mitchell (1977) seems to reduce this problem considerably. Schoenstadt (1978) has shown that noise is generated in finite element models where all variables are carried at the same nodal points. When the variables are staggered at different nodal points or when the vorticity and divergence equation are used this problem can be avoided. The general procedure used by Staniforth and Mitchell (1977) appears to be superior because semi-implicit differencing can be easily implemented, and the forecasts are not noisy.

CHAPTER 7

Numerical Prediction Models

7-1 FILTERED MODELS

7-1-1 Quasi-Geostrophic Equivalent Barotropic Model

The vorticity and divergence equations governing the quasi-geostrophic filtered models, which are characterized by the absence of gravity waves and a balance between the wind and pressure fields (3-74, 3-60, 3-62), are:

$$\frac{\partial \zeta}{\partial t} + \mathbf{V}_\psi \cdot \nabla(\zeta + f) = f_0 \frac{\partial \omega}{\partial p} \text{ (a)}$$

$$f_0 \nabla^2 \psi = \nabla^2 \phi \quad \text{or} \quad \mathbf{V} = \frac{1}{f_0} \mathbf{k} \times \nabla \phi \text{ (b)} \qquad (7\text{-}1)$$

Here the wind field is assumed to be of the simple form,

$$\mathbf{V}(x,y,p,t) = \widetilde{A(p)}\, \mathbf{V}(x,y,t), \text{ where } (\overline{}) = \frac{1}{p_0} \int_0^{p_0} (\quad)\, dp \qquad (7\text{-}2)$$

and p_0 is the surface pressure that will be assumed to be 1000 mb. Integrating (7-2) shows that $\overline{A} = 1$. Substituting $\mathbf{V}$ into the vorticity equation (7-1) and integrating in the vertical leads to

$$\frac{\partial \overline{\zeta}}{\partial t} + \overline{A^2}\, \overline{\mathbf{V}} \cdot \nabla \overline{\zeta} + \overline{\mathbf{V}} \cdot \nabla f = f_0\, \omega(p_0)/p_0 \equiv f_0 \omega_0 / p_0 \qquad (7\text{-}3)$$

Next multiplying (7-3) by $\overline{A^2}$ gives

$$\frac{\partial \zeta^*}{\partial t} + \mathbf{V}^* \cdot \nabla(\zeta^* + f) = \overline{A^2} f_0 \omega_0 / p_0 \qquad (7\text{-}4)$$

where $\mathbf{V}^* = \overline{A^2}\, \overline{\mathbf{V}}$, etc. To evaluate the boundary condition at p_0 note that

$$gw = \frac{d(gz)}{dt} = \frac{\partial \phi}{\partial t} + \mathbf{V} \cdot \nabla \phi + \omega \frac{\partial \phi}{\partial p}$$

Using the hydrostatic equation, $\partial\phi/\partial p = -\alpha$, and solving for ω gives the general relation

$$\omega = \rho\left(\frac{\partial\phi}{\partial t} + \mathbf{V}\cdot\nabla\phi - gw\right) \tag{7-5}$$

If the surface terrain is not level, the vertical velocity w_s at terrain level may be expressed in terms of the surface horizontal wind component V_{sn} normal to terrain contours z_s and the terrain height gradient, $|\nabla z_s| = |\partial z_s/\partial n|$, as $|w_s| = V_{sn}|\nabla z_s|$, or

$$w_0 \doteq w_s = \mathbf{V}_s\cdot\nabla z_s \doteq \mathbf{V}_0\cdot\nabla z_s \tag{7-6}$$

Evaluating (7-5) at p_0 and using (7-6) gives

$$\omega_0 \doteq \rho_0\left[\frac{\partial\phi}{\partial t} + \mathbf{V}_0\cdot\nabla(\phi - \phi_s)\right] \tag{7-7}$$

where $\phi_s = gz_s$. Strictly speaking, $\partial\phi/\partial t$ and $\mathbf{V}_0\cdot\nabla\phi$ should be evaluated on the pressure surface intersecting the terrain at the point in question; however for practical purposes the 1000-mb pressure level is used.

For the quasi-geostrophic case $\mathbf{V}\cdot\nabla\phi = 0$. Also for the present assume that the surface is level. Then (7-7) simplifies to

$$\omega_0 = \rho_0\,\partial\phi_0/\partial t = \rho_0 A_0\,\partial\overline{\phi}/\partial t = (\rho_0 A_0/\overline{A^2})\,\partial\phi^*/\partial t \tag{7-8}$$

Substituting from (7-7) and (7-8) into (7-4) and dropping the * leads to the prediction equation

$$\frac{\partial\zeta}{\partial t} + \mathbf{V}\cdot\nabla(\zeta + f) = M'\frac{\partial\phi}{\partial t} \qquad M' = f_0A_0/R\overline{T}_0 \tag{7-9}$$

The foregoing equation has only one dependent variable ϕ since both $\mathbf{V}$ and ζ are related geostrophically to ϕ. As a prediction equation (7-9) should be applied at the level p^*, which is assumed to be the same everywhere over the forecast region. From climatological data in middle latitudes $A(p^*) = \overline{A^2} \doteq 1.25$, which gives $p^* \doteq 500$ mb. Had the assumed atmosphere been barotropic, $A(p)$ would be identically *one* and the same equation would apply at all levels. Consequently p^* has been called the equivalent barotropic level and (7-9) the *equivalent barotropic vorticity* equation. Except for taking $\omega_0 = 0$, and thus $M' = 0$ in (7-9), this equation was used in the first modern numerical weather forecast by Charney, Fjørtoft, and von Neumann (1950).

A source of error in hemispheric models with $M' = 0$ is the rapid retrogression of ultralong waves, numbers 1, 2, and 3, which in the real atmosphere may move either west or east at rather slow speeds. A simple linear perturbation analysis of (7-9) gives a phase speed of $c = (U - \beta L^2/4\pi^2)/(1 + M'f_0L^2/4\pi^2)$. This reduces to the familiar Rossby wave speed when $M' =$

0 and gives rapid retrogression for large L (Wolff, 1958, Cressman, 1958). A suitably chosen $M' \neq 0$ will obviously reduce the erroneous retrogression and improves forecasts somewhat; however the ultralong waves are not forecast correctly. Due to the rather slow phase speeds of meteorological waves, the CFL criterion permits a Δt of 0.5 to 1 hr for a grid distance of about 400 km. Simple centered differences were commonly used in short range forecasts with filtered models since nonlinear instability did not become a problem for these periods. The centered difference form of (7-9) may be written in the notation of Section 5-10 as a Helmholtz equation.

$$\left(\frac{m_{ij}^{2}}{d^2}\nabla_{\mathrm{F}}^2 - M'\right)\left(\frac{\partial\phi}{\partial t}\right)_{i,j} = -\frac{m_{ij}^{2}}{4d^2}\mathrm{JJ}_{i,j}(\phi, \eta) \tag{7-10}$$

where $\mathrm{JJ}(A,B) = (A_{i+1,j} - A_{i-1,j})(B_{i,j+1} - B_{i,j-1})$
$- (A_{i,j+1} - A_{i,j-1})(B_{i+1,j} - B_{i-1,j})$

To solve the equation over a limited region of the earth, $\partial\phi/\partial t$ must be known on the boundaries. In Northern Hemisphere forecasts on a polar stereographic projection the boundaries are near the equator where $\partial\phi/\partial t$ is small. Hence $\partial\phi/\partial t$ is assumed to vanish at the lateral boundaries. Nevertheless such fictitious boundary conditions eventually propagate errors inward and corrupt the forecast. Studies with a GCM global baroclinic PE model indicated that random errors of 0.5°C near the equator will significantly affect the middle latitudes near the same longitude in about one week and the other side of the hemisphere in about two weeks or so. In any event, when the tendency has been calculated, the geopotential may be extrapolated forward in time (e.g., by the leapfrog scheme).

$$\phi_{i,j,n+1} = \phi_{i,j,n-1} + 2\Delta t\left(\frac{\partial\phi}{\partial t}\right)_{i,j,n} \tag{7-11}$$

7-1-1-1 Energetics of the Barotropic Model. To obtain a kinetic energy equation for the model, multiply by $\psi = \phi/f_0$ and for simplicity, let $M' = 0$, giving

$$\begin{aligned}\psi\frac{\partial}{\partial t}\nabla^2\psi &= -\psi\nabla\cdot(\zeta + f)\,\mathbf{V}\\ &= -\nabla\cdot\psi(\zeta + f)\,\mathbf{V} + (\zeta + f)\,\mathbf{V}\cdot\nabla\psi\end{aligned} \tag{7-12}$$

Also

$$\psi\frac{\partial}{\partial t}\nabla\cdot\nabla\psi = \psi\nabla\cdot\frac{\partial}{\partial t}\nabla\psi = \nabla\cdot\left(\psi\frac{\partial}{\partial t}\nabla\psi\right) - \nabla\psi\cdot\frac{\partial}{\partial t}\nabla\psi \tag{7-13}$$

Now substitute from (7-13) into the left side of (7-12) and apply the Gauss divergence theorem (A-13) over the forecast area, which is assumed to be a global surface or a region with zero-flux boundaries.

The term $\mathbf{V} \cdot \nabla\psi$ vanishes identically since $\mathbf{V} = \mathbf{k} \times \nabla\psi$ and the integrals for the form $\nabla \cdot (\quad)$ also vanish, hence (7-12) reduces to

$$\int \frac{\partial}{\partial t}\left(\frac{\nabla\psi \cdot \nabla\psi}{2}\right) d\sigma = 0 \qquad \text{or} \qquad \frac{d}{dt}\int \frac{V^2}{2}\, d\sigma = 0 \tag{7-14}$$

where $d\sigma$ is an element of area. Thus the total kinetic energy per unit mass over the forecast region is conserved. Any increase or decrease in perturbation kinetic energy must be compensated by an opposite change in the KE of the mean flow. There are no transformations between potential and kinetic energy, hence no baroclinic development, a serious limitation of the equivalent barotropic model.

7-1-2 Quasi-Geostrophic Multilevel Baroclinic Model

By lifting the restriction imposed on the wind field (7-2) and letting the geostrophic wind direction vary freely with height, a baroclinic model may be developed. The vorticity and divergence equations are identical to (7-1). In addition to complete the system, the first law of thermodynamics must be introduced along with the hydrostatic relation (1-59) to replace temperature. Thus substituting $-R^{-1}\,\partial\phi/\partial \ell np = T$ into (1-57b) gives

$$\frac{\partial}{\partial t}\frac{\partial\phi}{\partial p} + \mathbf{V} \cdot \nabla \frac{\partial\phi}{\partial p} + \sigma\omega = -Q \tag{7-15}$$

where Q represents any diabatic heating and σ is a static stability parameter. The latter is, at most, a function of p for the quasi-geostrophic case in accordance with scale analysis (Section 3-4):

$$\sigma = \frac{\partial\phi}{\partial p}\frac{\partial \ell n\theta}{\partial p} \tag{7-16}$$

The two dependent variables ϕ and ω are typically staggered in the vertical with $\omega = 0$ at $p = 0$ and $\omega = \omega_0$ at p_0 as shown in Figure 7-1. Equations 7-1 and 7-15 form a closed system; however, to solve the prediction equation (7-1a) for the tendency, $\partial\psi/\partial t = (1/f_0)\,(\partial\phi/\partial t)$, the vertical velocity ω is needed. A *diagnostic* equation for ω may be obtained by eliminating the time derivatives between (7-1a) and (7-15) by operating on (7-15) with ∇^2 and on (7-10) with $\partial/\partial p$ and subtracting one equation from another. The result is the *ω-equation* (3-75)

$$\sigma_S \nabla^2\omega + f_0^2 \frac{\partial^2\omega}{\partial p^2} = f_0 \frac{\partial}{\partial p}[\mathbf{V} \cdot \nabla(\zeta + f)] - \nabla^2\left(\mathbf{V} \cdot \nabla \frac{\partial\phi}{\partial p}\right) - \nabla^2 Q \tag{7-17}$$

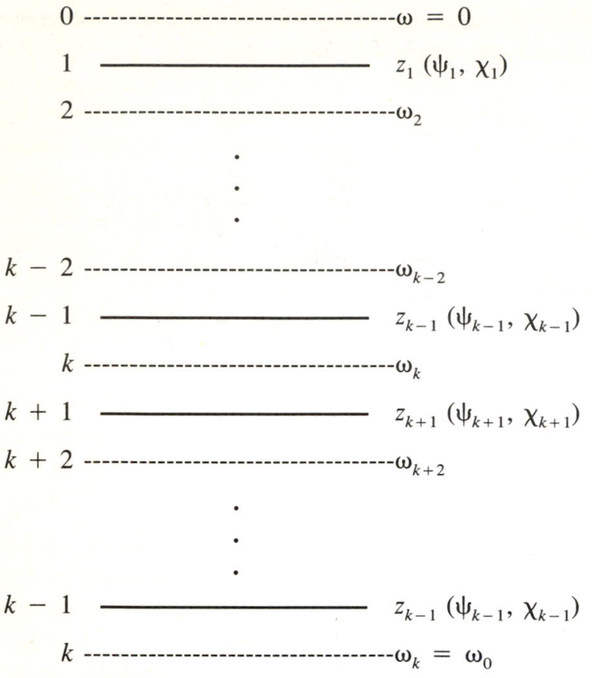

Figure 7.1 Vertical indexing and specification of the dependent variables for a multilevel, baroclinic, filtered model.

where $\sigma_S(p)$ is the standard stability parameter. The elliptic equation (7-17) is solved at the even levels such as level k in Figure 7-1. With centered differences and using the notation of (7-10), (7-17) may be written as

$$\frac{m_{i,j}^2\,\sigma_k\,\nabla_F^2\,\omega_{i,j,k}}{d^2} + \frac{f_0^2}{\Delta p^2}(\omega_{i,j,k+2} - 2\omega_{i,j,k} + \omega_{i,j,k-2}) =$$

$$\frac{m_{i,j}^2}{8d^2\Delta p^2}[\mathrm{JJ}\,(\phi_{i,j,k+1}, \zeta_{i,j,k+1} + f_{i,j}) - \mathrm{JJ}\,(\phi_{i,j,k-1}, \zeta_{i,j,k-1} + f_{i,j})$$

$$-\frac{m_{i,j}^2}{16d^4 f_0^2\,\Delta p}\nabla_F^2\,[m_{i,j}^2\,\mathrm{JJ}\,(\phi_{i,j,k+1} + \phi_{i,j,k-1}, \phi_{i,j,k+1} - \phi_{i,j,k-1})] - \frac{m_{i,j}^2}{d^2}\nabla_F^2 Q_{i,j,k} \tag{7-18}$$

Since the ϕ field is not available at the k level, the average of the $k - 1$ and $k + 1$ has been used to approximate z_k for $\mathbf{V}_k$ in the finite difference approximation of $\mathbf{V} \cdot \boldsymbol{\nabla}(\partial\phi/\partial p)$ in (7-18). This three-dimensional elliptic equation can be solved by relaxation or direct methods provided ω is known on the surfaces enclosing the region over which the forecast is made. Normally, ω is taken to be *zero* at the *lateral boundaries* as well as at $p = 0$. At $p = p_0$, ω_0 may be determined from (7-7). However, note that ϕ is not forecast at the lowest level in the model and hence must be extrapolated from levels above when needed for calculating wind or vorticity. Another difficulty is that the earth's surface, which really constitutes the lower boundary, is not a pressure surface and presents a problem when applying the lower boundary condition. As an approximation the lower boundary condition is applied at the lowest pressure level of the model, usually 1000 mb, or perhaps 850 or 700 mb over high terrain. The difficulties associated with the lower boundary condition when pressure is the vertical coordinate led N. Phillips (1957) to introduce the "σ" vertical coordinate, namely, pressure normalized by surface pressure, that is, p/p_S or, as an alternative, $(p-p_T)/(p_S - p_T)$, where p_T is a constant upper pressure, for example, a pressure near the average tropopause level. The σ coordinate system is described in Section 1-9.

7-1-3 Linear Balanced Model

The governing equations for the linear balanced model are the vorticity, divergence (balance), thermodynamic, and continuity equations:

$$\frac{\partial}{\partial t}\nabla^2\psi + \mathbf{V}_\psi \cdot \nabla(\zeta + f) + \mathbf{V}_\chi \cdot \nabla f = f\frac{\partial\omega}{\partial p} \tag{7-19}$$

$$f\nabla^2\psi + \nabla f \cdot \nabla\psi = \nabla^2\phi \tag{7-20}$$

$$\frac{\partial}{\partial t}\left(\frac{\partial\phi}{\partial p}\right) + \mathbf{V} \cdot \nabla\frac{\partial\phi}{\partial p} + \sigma\omega = -Q \tag{7-21}$$

$$\nabla^2\chi + \frac{\partial\omega}{\partial p} \tag{7-22}$$

The dependent variables are the streamfunction ψ for the rotational wind component $\mathbf{V}_\psi$, the potential function χ for the divergent wind component $\mathbf{V}_\chi$, the vertical velocity ω and the geopotential ϕ. To obtain a diagnostic equation for ω, the time derivatives between (7-19) and (7-21) must be eliminated. It is first necessary to differentiate (7-20) with respect to time and use the result to eliminate $\partial\nabla^2\psi/\partial t$ from (7-19), giving

$$\frac{\partial}{\partial t}\nabla^2\phi - \nabla f \cdot \nabla\frac{\partial\psi}{\partial t} + \mathbf{V}_\psi \cdot \nabla(\zeta + f) + \mathbf{V}_\chi \cdot \nabla f = f\frac{\partial\omega}{\partial p} \tag{7-23}$$

Now proceed as in the quasi-geostrophic system to operate on the foregoing equation with $\partial/\partial p$ and on (7-21) with ∇^2 to eliminate the first two terms yielding the ω-equation

$$\nabla^2 (\sigma\omega) + f^2 \frac{\partial \omega}{\partial p} = f \frac{\partial}{\partial p} [\mathbf{V}_\psi \cdot \nabla(\zeta + f)] - \nabla^2 \left(\mathbf{V} \cdot \nabla \frac{\partial \phi}{\partial p} \right)$$

$$+ f \nabla f \cdot \frac{\partial \mathbf{V}_\chi}{\partial p} - \nabla f \cdot \nabla \frac{\partial^2 \psi}{\partial p \partial t} \qquad (7\text{-}24)$$

where σ varies in space and time, but is directly computable from the ϕ or T fields. The foregoing equation is not strictly diagnostic since a time derivative appears in the last term. Moreover $\mathbf{V}_\chi$ appears explicitly in the third term on the right as well as part of $\mathbf{V}$ in the term involving thermal advection. Consequently, the system must be solved iteratively as follows:

Step 1: Given an initial ϕ field solve (7-20) for ψ at all odd levels (see Fig. 7-1), which provides $\mathbf{V}_\psi = \mathbf{k} \times \nabla\psi$ and $\zeta = \nabla^2\psi$.

Step 2: Solve the ω-equation (7-24) omitting the last term as well as $\mathbf{V}_\chi$ to give a first estimate, $\omega^{(1)}$.

Step 3: Solve the continuity equation (7-22) for $\chi^{(1)}$ using $\omega^{(1)}$, for example,

$$\frac{m_{i,j}^2}{d^2} \nabla_F^2 \chi_{i,j,k+1}^{(1)} = -\frac{\omega_{i,j,k+2}^{(1)} - \omega_{i,j,k}^{(1)}}{2\Delta p} \qquad (7\text{-}25)$$

which gives $\mathbf{V}_\chi^{(1)} = \nabla\chi^{(1)}$

Step 4: Solve equation (7-19) for $(\partial\psi/\partial t)^{(1)}$ using $\mathbf{V}_\chi^{(1)}$ and $\omega^{(1)}$.

Step 5: Return to step 2 and obtain a second estimate $\omega^{(2)}$ using $\mathbf{V}_\chi^{(1)}$ and $(\partial\psi/\partial t)^{(1)}$.

Step 6: Repeat steps 2 and 3 and continue iterations until convergence is obtained, that is, until ω, χ, and $\partial\psi/\partial t$ are changing negligibly (within preassigned error limits).

Step 7: Next the actual prediction is made, for example, with the leapfrog scheme:

$$\psi_{n+1} = \psi_{n-1} + 2\Delta t \left(\frac{\partial \psi}{\partial t} \right)_n \qquad (7\text{-}26)$$

Step 8: Solve (7-29) for ϕ_{n+1} using ψ_{n+1}.

This completes the solution for a single time step, after which steps 2 through 8 may be repeated to advance another Δt, and so forth, until the forecast is complete. Unfortunately, the iterative procedure requiring repeated solutions of elliptic equations is very time consuming on a computer and that reduces the advantages of this model for operational purposes.

7-1-4 Nonlinear Balanced Model

The forecasting procedure for the nonlinear balanced model is very similar to the foregoing method for the linear balance system except that the nonlinear balance equation and the associated vorticity equation and ω-equation are as follows:

$$\frac{\partial \zeta}{\partial t} + \mathbf{V} \cdot \nabla \eta + \omega \frac{\partial \zeta}{\partial p} - \eta \frac{\partial \omega}{\partial p} + \mathbf{k} \cdot \nabla \omega \times \frac{\partial \mathbf{V}_\psi}{\partial p} = 0 \qquad (7\text{-}27)$$

$$\nabla \cdot (f \nabla \psi) + 2 \left[\frac{\partial^2 \psi}{\partial x^2} \frac{\partial^2 \psi}{\partial y^2} - \left(\frac{\partial^2 \psi}{\partial x \partial y} \right)^2 \right] = \nabla^2 \Phi \qquad (7\text{-}28)$$

$$\begin{aligned} \nabla^2(\sigma\omega) + f^2 \frac{\partial^2 \omega}{\partial p^2} &= f \frac{\partial}{\partial p} J(\psi,\eta) + \frac{\alpha}{\theta} \nabla^2 J(\psi,\theta) - 2 \frac{\partial^2}{\partial t\, \partial p} J\left(\frac{\partial \psi}{\partial x}, \frac{\partial \psi}{\partial y}\right) \\ &\quad - f \frac{\partial}{\partial p} (\zeta \nabla^2 \chi) + f \frac{\partial}{\partial p}\left(\omega \frac{\partial \zeta}{\partial p}\right) + f \frac{\partial}{\partial p}\left(\nabla \omega \cdot \nabla \frac{\partial \psi}{\partial p}\right) \\ &\quad - f \frac{\partial}{\partial p} (\nabla \chi \cdot \nabla \eta) - \frac{\alpha}{\theta} \nabla^2 (\nabla \chi \cdot \nabla \theta) - \nabla f \cdot \nabla \frac{\partial^2 \psi}{\partial p\, \partial t} \end{aligned} \qquad (7\text{-}29)$$

The additional complexity of this system increases the computer time required for the iterative method of solution considerably. In fact, it is doubtful whether the complete system has ever been used operationally. Several abbreviated versions have been used by NMC and various other weather services. Specifically, the ω-equation has been simplified and the iterative procedure eliminated in order to meet operational requirements. As a consequence, strict consistency with respect to scale analysis and integral constraints is not maintained. However, for short- and medium-range forecasts, especially with filtered models, some such approximations need not lead to trouble and the balanced models can perform better than the quasi-geostrophic models.

On the other hand, in making a choice between filtered and PE models, the approximations made in filtered equations and their higher order must be weighed against the greater accuracy and simpler form of the first-order momentum equations which have the complication of permitting inertial-gravity waves. In the latter half of the 1960s, the PE models became operationally feasible and have prevailed since that time. A great deal of research and development through the 1960s and 1970s have contributed to improved numerical methods and better representation of the physics of atmospheric processes.

7-2 PRIMITIVE EQUATION MODELS

Most primitive equation models currently use the vertical coordinate $\sigma = p/p_S$, which will be used in this section in developing a vertical differencing scheme that conserves energy and certain other integral properties of the continuous equations. Lorenz (1960b) first imposed energy conservation in the formulation of a balanced model in pressure coordinates. The development here follows Arakawa and Lamb (1977) who introduced the following more general sigma system in order to obtain better resolution in the stratosphere:

$$\sigma = (p - p_I)/\pi \tag{7-30}$$

where

$$\pi = \begin{cases} \pi_U \equiv p_I - p_T, \text{ for } p_T \leq p \leq p_I \\ \pi_L \equiv p_S - p_I, \text{ for } p_I \leq p \leq p_S \end{cases}$$

Here p_I and p_T are constants. Thus σ, which varies from 1 at p_S to -1 at p_T, behaves like the standard σ described in Section 1-9-1 below p_I and like the p-coordinate above p_I (see Figure 7-2). The standard σ-system is recovered by setting $p_I = p_T = 0$.

The following basic equations with this σ-coordinate are obtainable from (1-64), (1-65), (1-67), and (1-57) by merely replacing p_S with π:

$$\frac{d\mathbf{V}}{dt} + \nabla\phi + \sigma\alpha\nabla\pi + f\mathbf{k} \times \mathbf{V} = \mathbf{F} \tag{7-31}$$

$$\frac{\partial\phi}{\partial\sigma} = -\pi\alpha \tag{7-32}$$

$$\frac{\partial\pi}{\partial t} + \nabla \cdot \pi\mathbf{V} + \pi\, \partial\dot{\sigma}/\partial\sigma = 0 \tag{7-33}$$

$$c_p\, dT/dt - \alpha\omega = Q \tag{7-34}$$

where $\mathbf{F}$ is the friction, Q is the heating, and $\omega = \pi\dot{\sigma} + \sigma(\partial\pi/\partial t + \mathbf{V} \cdot \nabla\pi)$. Note that some of the terms in the equations are zero in the upper region where π is constant.

The following forms of the hydrostatic equation can be derived from (7-32):

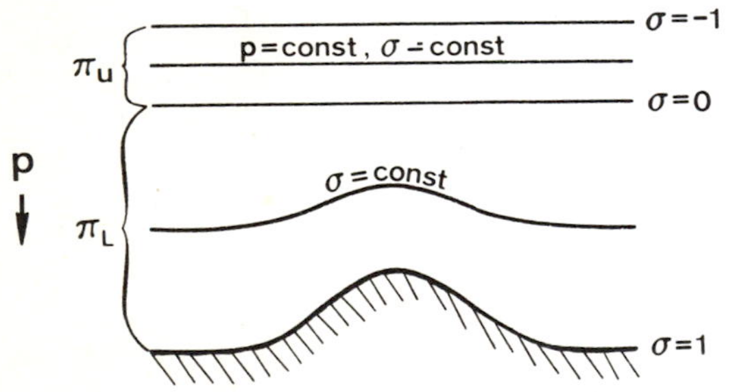

Figure 7.2 Definition of the layers of the model in terms of the vertical σ coordinate.

$$\delta(\phi\sigma) = -(\pi\sigma\alpha - \phi)\delta\sigma \tag{7-35a}$$

$$\delta\phi = -RT\,\delta\,\ell n p \tag{7-35b}$$

$$= -c_p\,\theta\,\delta(p/p_0)^\kappa \tag{7-35c}$$

$$= c_p \frac{d\,\ell n\,\theta}{d\,(1/\theta)}\,\delta(p/p_0)^\kappa \tag{7-35d}$$

$$\delta(c_pT + \phi) = (p/p_0)^\kappa\,c_p\,\delta\theta \tag{7-35e}$$

where $\theta = T(p_0/p)^\kappa$ is the potential temperature and δ indicates a differential in the vertical. These relations will be helpful later in imposing constraints on the finite difference equations.

7-2-1 Constraints from Continuous Equations

The total derivative of an arbitrary scalar can be written

$$\frac{dA}{dt} = \frac{\partial A}{\partial t} + \mathbf{V}\cdot\nabla A + \dot{\sigma}\frac{\partial A}{\partial \sigma} \tag{7-36}$$

which is the advective form of dA/dt. The flux form can be found by multiplying (7-36) by π and (7-33) by A and adding:

$$\pi\frac{dA}{dt} = \frac{\partial}{\partial t}(\pi A) + \nabla\cdot(\pi A\mathbf{V}) + \frac{\partial}{\partial\sigma}(\pi\dot{\sigma}A) \tag{7-37}$$

In Section 1-10 it was shown that the domain averaged potential plus kinetic energy will be conserved if there is no heating or friction. This result will now be rederived in the σ system so that the vertical differencing can be arranged so as to maintain this constant in the difference equations. First the dot product of $\pi\mathbf{V}$ with (7-31) gives

$$\pi\frac{d}{dt}\left(\frac{V^2}{2}\right) = -\pi\mathbf{V}\cdot(\nabla\phi + \sigma\alpha\nabla\pi) + \pi\mathbf{V}\cdot\mathbf{F} \tag{7-38}$$

The left side of this equation can be written in flux form by setting $A = \mathbf{V}^2/2$ in (7-37), which allows the equation to be rewritten as follows:

$$\frac{\partial}{\partial t}\left(\frac{\pi}{2}V^2\right) + \nabla\cdot\left(\frac{\pi}{2}\mathbf{V}\,V^2\right) + \frac{\partial}{\partial\sigma}\left(\frac{\pi}{2}\dot{\sigma}\,V^2\right)$$
$$= -\mathbf{V}\cdot[\pi\nabla\phi + \sigma\alpha\pi\nabla\pi] + \pi\mathbf{V}\cdot\mathbf{F} \tag{7-39}$$

The rate of kinetic energy production by the pressure gradient force can be rewritten as follows with the use of (7-33), (7-32), and (7-35a):

$$
\begin{aligned}
-\mathbf{V}\cdot(\pi\nabla\phi + \sigma\alpha\pi\nabla\pi) &= -\nabla\cdot(\pi\phi\mathbf{V}) + \phi\nabla\cdot\pi\mathbf{V} - \sigma\alpha\pi\mathbf{V}\cdot\nabla\pi \\
&= -\nabla\cdot(\pi\phi\mathbf{V}) - \phi[\partial\pi/\partial t + \partial(\pi\dot{\sigma})/\partial\sigma] - \sigma\pi\alpha\mathbf{V}\cdot\nabla\pi \\
&= -\nabla\cdot(\pi\phi\mathbf{V}) - \frac{\partial}{\partial\sigma}(\pi\dot{\sigma}\phi) + (\sigma\pi\alpha - \phi)\frac{\partial\pi}{\partial t} \\
&\qquad - \pi\alpha\left[\sigma\left(\frac{\partial\pi}{\partial t} + \mathbf{V}\cdot\nabla\pi\right) + \pi\dot{\sigma}\right] \\
&= -\nabla\cdot(\pi\phi\mathbf{V}) - \frac{\partial}{\partial\sigma}\left(\pi\phi\dot{\sigma} + \phi\sigma\frac{\partial\pi}{\partial t}\right) - \pi\sigma\omega
\end{aligned}
\tag{7-40}
$$

The first law of thermodynamics (7-34) can be put in flux form with (7-37) which gives:

$$
\frac{\partial}{\partial t}(\pi\, c_p T) + \nabla\cdot(\pi c_p T\mathbf{V}) + \frac{\partial}{\partial\sigma}(\pi c_p T\dot{\sigma}) = \pi\,(Q + \alpha\omega) \tag{7-41}
$$

The equation for total energy is found by substituting (7-40) into (7-39) and adding the result to (7-41). Integration of this equation from $\sigma = -1$ to $\sigma = 1$ yields:

$$
\begin{aligned}
&\frac{\partial}{\partial t}[p_s\phi_s + \int_{-1}^{1}\pi(\tfrac{1}{2}V^2 + c_pT)\,d\sigma] + \nabla\cdot\int_{-1}^{1}\pi\mathbf{V}\,(V^2/2 + c_pT + \phi)d\sigma \\
&\qquad = \int_{-1}^{1}\pi(\mathbf{V}\cdot\mathbf{F} + Q)\,d\sigma
\end{aligned}
\tag{7-42}
$$

with the use of the conditions, $\dot{\sigma} = 0$, $\partial\pi/\partial t = \partial p_s/\partial t$ at $\sigma = 1$, and $\dot{\sigma} = 0$, $\partial\pi/\partial t = 0$ at $\sigma = -1$. When the global integral of (7-42) is carried out the divergence term vanishes and total energy is conserved if $\mathbf{F} = 0$ and $Q = 0$. Equation 7-42 corresponds to (1-92), which was derived in pressure coordinates. The vertical differencing will be designed so that total energy conservation will be maintained.

Other useful constraints that involve the potential temperature will be derived. When there is no heating each air parcel conserves potential temperature so that $d\theta/dt = 0$ (see 1-9b). In fact any well behaved function of θ, say $g(\theta)$, will be conserved following a parcel of air. With the use of (7-37), this can be written

$$
\frac{\partial}{\partial t}[\pi g(\theta)] + \nabla\cdot(\pi g(\theta)\,\mathbf{V}) + \frac{\partial}{\partial\sigma}(\pi g(\theta)\,\dot{\sigma}) = 0 \tag{7-43}
$$

When this equation is integrated from $\sigma = -1$ to $\sigma = 1$,

$$
\frac{\partial}{\partial t}\int_{-1}^{1}\pi g(\theta)\,d\sigma + \nabla\cdot\int_{-1}^{1}\pi g(\theta)\,\mathbf{V}\,d\sigma = 0 \tag{7-44}
$$

and after horizontal integration, (7-44) shows that the global mean $g(\theta)$ is conserved. Although this is true for any function with the continuous equations, Arakawa and Lamb (1977) point out that only two functions can be conserved for adiabatic flow when the vertical variation is discrete. One function should be $g(\theta) = \theta$ since global conservation of θ is desirable. The earlier UCLA general circulation model [Arakawa (1972)] used $g(\theta) = \theta^2$ for the second constraint, while the new model [Arakawa and Lamb (1977)] uses $g(\theta) = \ell n\theta$. They state that the former choice is appropriate for the troposphere where θ is more normally distributed, but when the stratosphere is also present the θ distribution is more skewed so that $\ell n\theta$ is a better choice. They also argue that when $g(\theta) = \ell n\theta$, it is easier to properly describe the relationship between static stability changes and energy conversion, which was derived by Lorenz (1960b).

7-2-2 Vertical Differencing

For the vertical differencing the atmosphere is divided into K layers by $K - 1$ levels of constant σ. The layers are identified with odd k and the levels that divide the layers with even k. The distribution of variables is shown in Figure 7-3. The increment in σ is given by $\Delta\sigma_k = \sigma_{k+1} - \sigma_{k-1}$ and the following sums hold:

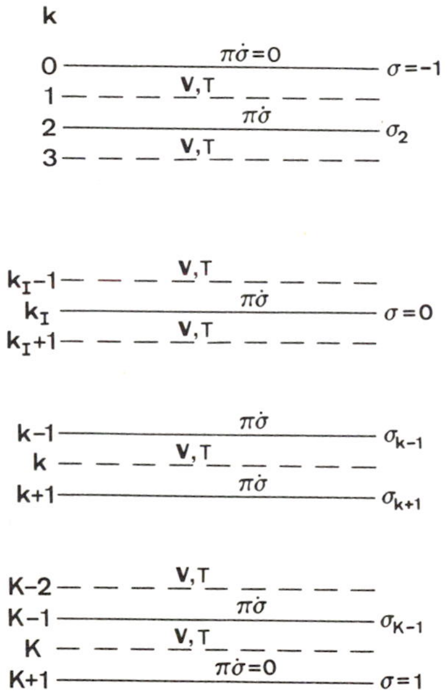

Figure 7.3 The vertical structure of the model.

$$\sum_{k=1}^{k_I-1}{}' \Delta\sigma_k = 1 \qquad \sum_{k=k_I+1}^{K}{}' \Delta\sigma_k = 1$$

where Σ' indicates summation over odd k.

The continuity equation (7-33) is finite differenced vertically as follows:

$$\frac{\partial \pi_k}{\partial t} + \nabla \cdot (\pi_k \mathbf{V}_k) + \frac{1}{\Delta\sigma_k}[(\pi\dot{\sigma})_{k+1} - (\pi\dot{\sigma})_{k-1}] = 0 \qquad (7\text{-}45)$$

Note that $\pi_k = \pi_U$ for $k < k_I$ and $\pi_k = \pi_L$ for $k > k_I$. When (7-45) is summed from $k = 1$ to $k = K$ and the boundary conditions $\dot{\sigma}_0 = \dot{\sigma}_{K+1} = 0$ are employed, the following surface pressure tendency equation is obtained:

$$\frac{\partial \pi_L}{\partial t} = -\sum_{k=1}^{K}{}' \nabla \cdot (\pi_k \mathbf{V}_k)\, \Delta\sigma_k \qquad (7\text{-}46)$$

The $\dot{\sigma}$'s can be obtained by summing (7-45) down to the required level and using (7-46) if $k > k_I$.

For any variable A, which is carried at odd k, the flux form of (7-37) can be written:

$$\pi_k \frac{dA_k}{dt} = \frac{\partial(\pi_k A_k)}{\partial t} + \nabla \cdot (\pi_k A_k \mathbf{V}_k)$$
$$+ \frac{1}{\Delta\sigma_k}[(\pi\dot{\sigma})_{k+1}\hat{A}_{k+1} - (\pi\dot{\sigma})_{k-1}\hat{A}_{k-1}] \qquad (7\text{-}47a)$$

where $\hat{A}$ is defined by an interpolation of A from adjacent layers. This form guarantees that the global average of A will be conserved by advective effects. Equation 7-47a can be rewritten with the use of (7-45), which gives the expression.

$$\pi_k \frac{dA_k}{dt} = \pi_k \left(\frac{\partial}{\partial t} + \mathbf{V}_k \cdot \nabla\right) A_k$$
$$+ \frac{1}{\Delta\sigma_k}[(\pi\dot{\sigma})_{k+1}(\hat{A}_{k+1} - A_k) + (\pi\dot{\sigma})_{k-1}(A_k - \hat{A}_{k-1})] \qquad (7\text{-}47b)$$

When (7-47b) is divided by the π_k it gives the advective form of dA/dt which is consistent with the flux form (7-47a).

Since the choice of $\hat{A}$ is arbitrary, as long as it is consistent, it is possible to satisfy an additional constraint. Now, require that the global integral of $F(A)$ be conserved by advective effects. Let $F_k \equiv F(A_k)$ and $F'_k \equiv dF(A_k)/dA_k$. Multiply (7-47b) by F'_k, which gives

$$\left(\frac{\pi dF}{dt}\right)_k = \pi_k \left(\frac{\partial}{\partial t} + \mathbf{V}_k \cdot \boldsymbol{\nabla}\right) F_k$$

$$+ \frac{1}{\Delta\sigma_k} [(\pi\dot{\sigma})_{k+1} F'_k (\hat{A}_{k+1} - A_k) + (\pi\dot{\sigma})_{k-1} F'_k (A_k - \hat{A}_{k-1})] \qquad (7\text{-}48)$$

With the use of (7-45), (7-48) can be rewritten as follows:

$$\left(\frac{\pi dF}{dt}\right)_k = \frac{\partial}{\partial t}(\pi_k F_k) + \boldsymbol{\nabla} \cdot (\pi_k F_k \mathbf{V}_k)$$

$$+ \frac{1}{\Delta\sigma_k} \{\pi\dot{\sigma}_{k+1} [F'_k (\hat{A}_{k+1} - A_k) + F_k]$$

$$- (\pi\dot{\sigma})_{k-1} [-F'_k (A_k - A_{k-1}) + F_k]\} \qquad (7\text{-}49)$$

This equation will be in flux form if

$$\hat{F}_{k+1} = F'_k (\hat{A}_{k+1} - A_k) + F_k$$

$$\hat{F}_{k-1} = -F'_k (A_k - \hat{A}_{k-1}) + F_k$$

Now replace k by $k + 2$ in the second equation and eliminate $\hat{F}_{k+1}$, which gives

$$\hat{A}_{k+1} = \frac{(F'_{k+2} A_{k+2} - F_{k+2}) - (F'_k A_k - F_k)}{F'_{k+2} - F'_k} \qquad (7\text{-}50)$$

This is a finite difference analogue of the identity

$$A = d(F'A - F)/dF'$$

When $F(A) = A^2$, for example, (7-50) gives

$$\hat{A}_{k+1} = \tfrac{1}{2} (A_k + A_{k+2}) \qquad (7\text{-}51)$$

This constraint, which leads to conservation of A^2, was first derived by Lorenz (1960b).

The equation of motion (7-31) is written in flux form (7-37) and differenced as follows:

$$\frac{\partial}{\partial t}(\pi_k \mathbf{V}_k) + \boldsymbol{\nabla} \cdot (\pi_k \mathbf{V}_k \mathbf{V}_k) + \frac{1}{\Delta\sigma_k} [(\pi\dot{\sigma})_{k+1} \hat{\mathbf{V}}_{k+1} - (\pi\dot{\sigma})_{k-1} \hat{\mathbf{V}}_{k-1}]$$

$$= - \pi_k \boldsymbol{\nabla}\phi_k - \sigma_k \alpha_k \pi_k \boldsymbol{\nabla}\pi_k - f\mathbf{k} \times \pi_k \mathbf{V}_k + \pi_k F_k \qquad (7\text{-}52)$$

If $A = \mathbf{V}$ and $F(A) = A^2$, then (7-51) shows that the advective terms will conserve kinetic energy if

$$\hat{\mathbf{V}}_{k+1} = \tfrac{1}{2} (\mathbf{V}_k + \mathbf{V}_{k+2}) \qquad (7\text{-}53)$$

The rate of working by the pressure gradient force is found by taking $\mathbf{V}_k \cdot$ the pressure gradient terms in (7-52) and by following the procedure used in (7-40) with the result:

$$
\begin{aligned}
&- \mathbf{V}_k \cdot (\pi_k \nabla \phi_k + \sigma_k \alpha_k \pi_k \nabla \pi_k) = -\nabla \cdot (\pi_k \phi_k \mathbf{V}_k) \\
&- \phi_k \left\{ \frac{1}{\Delta\sigma_k} [(\pi\dot{\sigma})_{k+1} - (\pi\dot{\sigma})_{k-1}] + \partial \pi_k/\partial t \right\} - \pi_k (\sigma\alpha)_k \mathbf{V}_k \cdot \nabla \pi_k \\
&= -\nabla \cdot (\pi_k \phi_k \mathbf{V}_k) - \frac{1}{\Delta\sigma_k} [(\pi\dot{\sigma})_{k+1} \hat{\phi}_{k+1} - (\pi\dot{\sigma})_{k-1} \hat{\phi}_{k-1}] \\
&+ \frac{1}{\Delta\sigma_k} [(\pi\dot{\sigma})_{k+1} (\hat{\phi}_{k+1} - \phi_k) + (\pi\dot{\sigma})_{k-1} (\phi_k - \hat{\phi}_{k-1})] \\
&\qquad - \phi_k \frac{\partial \pi_k}{\partial t} - \pi_k (\sigma\alpha)_k \mathbf{V}_k \cdot \nabla \pi_k \\
&= -\nabla \cdot (\pi_k \phi_k \mathbf{V}_k) - \frac{1}{\Delta\sigma_k} [(\pi\dot{\sigma})_{k+1} \hat{\phi}_{k+1} \\
&\qquad - (\pi\dot{\sigma})_{k-1} \hat{\phi}_{k-1}] + [\pi_k (\sigma\alpha)_k - \phi_k] \, \partial \pi_k/\partial t \\
&- \pi_k \left\{ (\sigma\alpha)_k \left(\frac{\partial}{\partial t} + \mathbf{V}_k \cdot \nabla \right) \pi_k - \frac{1}{\pi_k \Delta\sigma_k} [(\pi\dot{\sigma})_{k+1} (\hat{\phi}_{k+1} - \phi_k) \right. \\
&\qquad \left. + (\pi\dot{\sigma})_{k-1} (\phi_k - \hat{\phi}_{k-1})] \right\} \\
&= -\nabla \cdot (\pi_k \phi_k \mathbf{V}_k) - \frac{1}{\Delta\sigma_k} \left\{ \left[(\pi\dot{\sigma})_{k+1} + \sigma_{k+1} \frac{\partial \pi_k}{\partial t} \right] \hat{\phi}_{k+1} \right. \\
&\left. - \left[(\pi\dot{\sigma})_{k-1} + \sigma_{k-1} \frac{\partial \pi_k}{\partial t} \right] \hat{\phi}_{k-1} \right\} - \pi_k (\omega\alpha)_k
\end{aligned}
\tag{7-54}
$$

Here $(\omega\alpha)_k$ is defined by

$$
(\omega\alpha)_k \equiv (\sigma\alpha)_k \left(\frac{\partial}{\partial t} + \mathbf{V}_k \cdot \nabla \right) \pi_k - \frac{1}{\pi_k \Delta\sigma_k} [(\pi\dot{\sigma})_{k+1} (\hat{\phi}_{k+1} - \phi_k) + (\pi\dot{\sigma})_{k-1} (\phi_k - \hat{\phi}_{k-1})] \tag{7-55}
$$

The following expression was used:

$$
\pi_k (\sigma\alpha)_k = \phi_k - (\hat{\phi}_{k+1} \sigma_{k+1} - \hat{\phi}_{k-1} \sigma_{k-1})/\Delta\sigma_k \tag{7-56}
$$

which can be obtained from (7-35a). Note that $\hat{\phi}_{k+1}$ has not yet been specified.

The first law of thermodynamics will be developed in terms of θ and then rewritten in terms of T. The finite difference version of (7-43) for $g(\theta) = \theta$ is given by

$$\frac{\partial}{\partial t}(\pi_k \theta_k) + \nabla \cdot (\pi_k \theta_k \mathbf{V}_k) + \frac{1}{\Delta\sigma_k}[(\pi\dot{\sigma})_{k+1}\,\hat{\theta}_{k+1} - (\pi\dot{\sigma})_{k-1}\,\hat{\theta}_{k-1}] = 0 \qquad (7\text{-}57)$$

Here

$$\theta_k \equiv T_k/P_k \qquad (7\text{-}58)$$

where P_k corresponds to $(p/p_0)^\kappa$ for layer k. The actual form will be given later but it will depend on π_k, σ_{k-1}, and σ_{k+1}. This form of the first law of thermodyanmics clearly conserves the global mean θ. The earlier version of the UCLA general circulation model conserved θ^2 so that from (7-51) $\hat{\theta}_{k+1} = (\theta_{k+1} + \theta_k)/2$. In the present UCLA model the global integral of $\ell n\theta$ is conserved. Equation 7-50 with $A = \theta$ and $F(A) = \ell n\theta$ gives

$$\hat{\theta}_{k+1} = \frac{\ell n\,\theta_k - \ell n\,\theta_{k+2}}{(1/\theta_{k+2}) - (1/\theta_k)} \qquad (7\text{-}59)$$

From (7-48) the advective form of (7-57) is

$$\pi_k \left(\frac{\partial}{\partial t} + \mathbf{V}_k \cdot \nabla\right) \theta_k + \frac{1}{\Delta\sigma_k}[(\pi\dot{\sigma})_{k+1}(\hat{\theta}_{k+1} - \theta_k) + (\pi\dot{\sigma})_{k-1}(\theta_k - \hat{\theta}_{k-1})] = 0 \qquad (7\text{-}60)$$

When (7-58) is introduced into (7-60) it becomes

$$\pi_k \left(\frac{\partial}{\partial t} + \mathbf{V}_k \cdot \nabla\right) T_k - \pi_k \frac{T_k}{P_k}\frac{\partial P_k}{\partial \pi_k}\left(\frac{\partial}{\partial t} + \mathbf{V}_k \cdot \nabla\right)\pi_k + \frac{1}{\Delta\sigma_k}[(\pi\dot{\sigma})_{k+1}(P_k\,\hat{\theta}_{k+1} - T_k) + (\pi\dot{\sigma})_{k-1}(T_k - P_k\,\hat{\theta}_{k-1})] = 0 \qquad (7\text{-}61)$$

This equation can be combined with (7-45) to yield the flux form:

$$\frac{\partial}{\partial t}(c_p \pi_k T_k) + \nabla \cdot (c_p \pi_k T_k \mathbf{V}_k) + \frac{c_p}{\Delta\sigma_k}[(\pi\dot{\sigma})_{k+1}\,\hat{T}_{k+1} - (\pi\dot{\sigma})_{k-1}\,\hat{T}_{k-1}]$$
$$= \pi_k \frac{c_p\,T_k}{P_k}\frac{\partial P_k}{\partial \pi_k}\left(\frac{\partial}{\partial t} + \mathbf{V}_k \cdot \nabla\right)\pi_k + \frac{1}{\Delta\sigma_k}[(\pi\dot{\sigma})_{k+1}\,c_p\,(\hat{T}_{k+1} - P_k\,\hat{\theta}_{k+1}) + (\pi\dot{\sigma})_{k-1}\,c_p(P_k\,\hat{\theta}_{k-1} - \hat{T}_{k-1})] \qquad (7\text{-}62)$$

Here $\hat{T}_{k+1}$ will be specified later. According to (7-41) the total energy will be conserved under adiabatic frictionless conditions if the right side of (7-61) is equal to $\pi_k\,(\omega\alpha)_k$, which is given by (7-55). The first terms will be equal if

$$(\sigma\alpha)_k = \frac{c_p T_k}{P_k} \frac{\partial P_k}{\partial \pi_k} \tag{7-63}$$

This is necessary for $k > k_{\mathrm{I}}$ since otherwise the terms are not present. The elimination of $(\sigma\alpha)_k$ between (7-56) and (7-62) gives

$$\phi_k - \frac{1}{\Delta\sigma_k}(\hat{\phi}_{k+1}\,\sigma_{k+1} - \hat{\phi}_{k-1}\,\sigma_{k-1}) = \pi_{\mathrm{L}} \frac{c_p T_k}{P_k} \frac{\partial P_k}{\partial \pi_k} \tag{7-64}$$

for $k > k_{\mathrm{I}}$. On equating the other terms in $(\omega\alpha)_k$ the following conditions are obtained:

$$c_p\,(\hat{T}_{k+1} - P_k\,\hat{\theta}_{k+1}) = \phi_k - \hat{\phi}_{k+1} \tag{7-65a}$$

$$c_p\,(P_k\,\hat{\theta}_{k-1} - \hat{T}_{k-1}) = \hat{\phi}_{k-1} - \phi_k \tag{7-65b}$$

When (7-58) is used, (7-65a) and (7-65b) can be rewritten as follows:

$$(c_p\,\hat{T}_{k+1} + \hat{\phi}_{k+1}) - (c_p\,T_k + \phi_k) = P_k c_p(\hat{\theta}_{k+1} - \theta_k) \tag{7-66a}$$

$$(c_p\,T_k + \phi_k) - (c_p\,\hat{T}_{k-1} + \hat{\phi}_{k-1}) = P_k c_p(\theta_k - \hat{\theta}_{k-1}) \tag{7-66b}$$

where $\hat{\theta}_{k+1}$ is given by (7-59). The equations (7-66a) and (7-66b) correspond to (7-35e). Now replace k by $k + 2$ in (7-66b), add the result to (7-66a) and use (7-58), which leads to

$$\phi_{k+2} - \phi_k = -c_p(P_{k+2} - P_k)\,\hat{\theta}_{k+1} \tag{7-67}$$

This hydrostatic relation is a finite difference form of (7-35c). When $\hat{\theta}_{k+1}$ is eliminated from (7-67) with (7-59) the final form is

$$\phi_{k+2} - \phi_k = c_p \frac{\ell n\theta_{k+2} - \ell n\theta_k}{[(1/\theta_{k+2}) - (1/\theta_k)]}(P_{k+2} - P_k) \tag{7-68}$$

which corresponds to (7-35d). This equation is used to compute ϕ_k for odd k, however, another condition is needed to determine ϕ_k in addition to (7-68). Now multiply (7-64) by $\Delta\sigma_k$ and sum from $k = k_{\mathrm{I}+1}$ to $k = K$, which gives

$$\sum_{k=k_{\mathrm{I}}+1}^{K}{}' \phi_k\,\Delta\sigma_k - \phi_{\mathrm{S}} = \sum_{k=k_{\mathrm{I}}+1}^{K}{}' \pi_{\mathrm{L}} \frac{c_p T_k}{P_k} \frac{\partial P_k}{\partial \pi_k} \Delta\sigma_k \tag{7-69}$$

where $\phi_{K+1} = \phi_{\mathrm{S}}$. However the first sum can be rewritten as follows:

$$\sum_{k=k_{\mathrm{I}}+1}^{K}{}' \phi_k\,\Delta\sigma_k = \phi_k + \sum_{k=k_{\mathrm{I}}+1}^{K-2}{}' \sigma_{k+1}\,(\phi_k - \phi_{k-2}) \tag{7-70}$$

Combining (7-69) and (7-70) gives the following expression for ϕ_K:

$$\phi_K = \phi_S + \sum_{k=k_I+1}^{K}{}' \pi \frac{c_p T_k}{P_k} \frac{\partial P_k}{\partial \pi_k} - \sum_{k=k_I+1}^{K-2}{}' \sigma_{k+1} (\phi_k - \phi_{k-2}) \qquad (7\text{-}71)$$

Equations 7-68 and 7-71 can be used to determine ϕ for all odd levels. In the equation of motion (7-52) $\sigma_k \alpha_k$ is computed from (7-63). The first law of thermodynamics (7-62) can be rewritten in the following form:

$$\frac{\partial}{\partial t}(\pi_k T_k) + \nabla \cdot (\pi_k T_k \mathbf{V}_k) + \frac{1}{\Delta\sigma_k}[(\pi\dot{\sigma})_{k+1} P_k \hat{\theta}_{k+1} - (\pi\dot{\sigma})_{k-1} P_k \hat{\theta}_{k-1}]$$

$$= \frac{(\pi_k \alpha_k \sigma_k)}{c_p}\left(\frac{\partial}{\partial t} + \mathbf{V}_k \cdot \nabla\right) \pi_k + \pi_k Q_k / c_p \qquad (7\text{-}72)$$

where (7-63) was used on the right side and the heating term has been added.

This prediction system will be complete when P_k is specified. In the upper region where $k < k_I$ Arakawa and Lamb (1977) chose

$$P_k = [(p_{k-1}\, p_{k+1})^{1/2} / p_0]^{\kappa} \qquad (7\text{-}73)$$

which allows the proper vertical energy propagation when the p_k's are spaced in proportion to $\ell n p$. For $k > k_I$ the earlier versions of the UCLA model used

$$P_k = [\tfrac{1}{2}(p_{k-1} + p_{k+1})/p_0]^{\kappa} \qquad (7\text{-}74)$$

However, Phillips (1974) pointed out that when (7-74) is used in (7-68) and (7-71), the resulting ϕ's are not very accurate. This is because (7-71) applies the accumulated errors of the upper levels to the calculation of ϕ_K. Phillips suggested the following form

$$P_k = \frac{1}{1+\kappa} \frac{1}{p_0^{\kappa}} \frac{p_{k+1}^{1+\kappa} - p_{k-1}^{1+\kappa}}{p_{k+1} - p_{k-1}} \qquad (7\text{-}75)$$

Tokioka (1978) has shown that (7-75) is exact for an isentropic atmosphere. He also showed that the best choice of P_k, for an atmosphere where $T_k(p_0/p_k)^a$ is constant with height, is given by

$$P_k = \frac{1}{p_0^{\kappa}} \left(\frac{1}{1+a} \frac{p_{k+1}^{1+a} - p_{k-1}^{1+a}}{p_{k+1} - p_{k-1}} \right)^{\kappa} \qquad (7\text{-}76)$$

Another problem with the hydrostatic equation used here is that $\phi_{k+2} - \phi_k$ depends on both T_{k+2} and T_k. This causes some difficulty when it is necessary to determine the temperatures from the geopotentials as may be required during initialization. Tokioka (1978) has suggested that this problem can be avoided if ϕ is specified on the even levels.

Other approximations for the hydrostatic equation have been used successfully in numerical prediction models [for example, see Shuman and Hovermale (1968)]. However, it is felt that the energy conserving schemes similar to those developed in this section will be superior for somewhat longer forecasts.

7-3 STAGGERED GRID SYSTEMS

In discussing previous models, it may be recalled that $\dot{\sigma}$ and the other dependent variables are staggered in the vertical direction, which leads to considerable savings in storage space and computation time. Similarly, when computing horizontal derivatives by means of finite differences at some gridpoint, much of the data come from adjacent points, which suggests that it would be more efficient if the variables are staggered in the horizontal as well, and perhaps even alternating the position of variables with successive time steps. Also staggered schemes can reduce the problem of solution separation that occurs with leapfrog time differencing on a nonstaggered grid.

Winninghoff (1968) [see also Arakawa and Lamb (1977) and Mesinger and Arakawa (1976)] compared five different arrangements of the dependent variables, as shown in Figure 7-4 with the shallow-water equations for dispersion and geostrophic adjustment properties.

Schoenstadt (1978) carried out a more extensive investigation of geostrophic adjustment with one-dimensional versions of grids A through D. The analysis parallels the development of the continuous theory in Section 2-8. When spatial finite differences are introduced into (2-70) and the resulting equations are Fourier transformed in x, the equation set can be written:

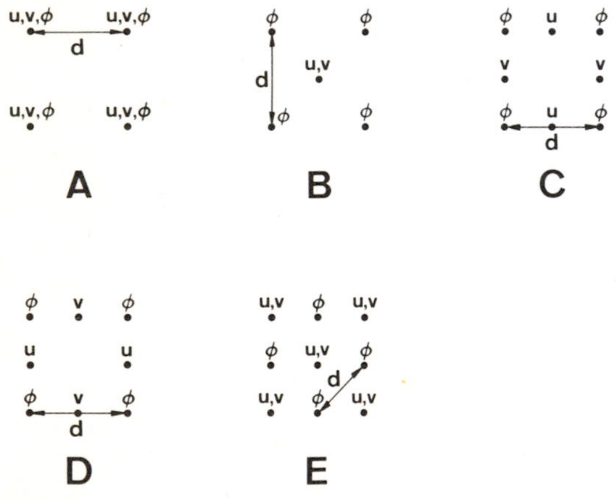

Figure 7.4 The five grids that were analyzed by Winninghoff (1968) and Arakawa and Lamb (1977).

$$\frac{d\tilde{u}}{dt} = f\beta(\mu)\tilde{v} - ig\sigma(\mu)\tilde{h}$$

$$\frac{d\tilde{v}}{dt} = -f\beta(\mu)\tilde{u} \tag{7-77}$$

$$\frac{d\tilde{h}}{dt} = -iH\sigma(\mu)\tilde{u}$$

where, $\tilde{u}$, $\tilde{v}$, and $\tilde{h}$ are the transformed variables, and β and σ are determined for each grid. For example, $\beta = 1$ and $\sigma = (\sin \mu d)/d$ for grid *A*, and $\beta = \cos(\mu d/2)$ and $\sigma = (\sin \mu d/2)/(d/2)$ for grid *C*. The system (7-77) can be solved for arbitrary initial conditions using the same procedure as was applied to (2-73). In fact, the solutions to (7-77) can be obtained from (2-77) and (2-78) by substituting $\sigma \rightarrow \mu$, $f\beta \rightarrow f$ and $\hat{\upsilon} \rightarrow \upsilon$. Thus the new frequency is given by

$$\hat{\upsilon} = (f^2\beta^2 + \sigma^2 gh)^{1/2} \tag{7-78}$$

which may be compared with the differential frequency (2-75). The time evolution of the finite difference solution can be obtained in terms of the appropriate Fourier integral of (2-77) and (2-78). This type of solution was obtained by Winninghoff (1968), Arakawa and Lamb (1977), and Schoenstadt (1978) for certain initial conditions. However, considerable information can be obtained from (7-78) and the expressions for $\tilde{u}$, $\tilde{v}$, and $\tilde{h}$ for the various grid arrangements.

Figure 7-5 shows the finite difference phase velocity ($\hat{\upsilon}/\mu$) and group velocity ($d\hat{\upsilon}/d\mu$) as functions of $\mu d/\pi$ for grids *A* through *D*. The phase velocities

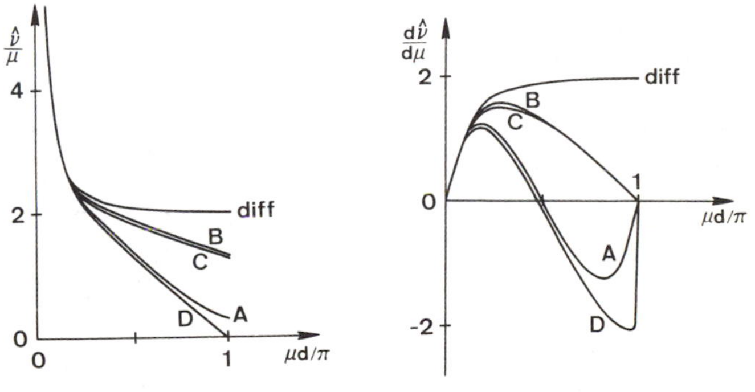

Figure 7.5 The phase velocity $c = \hat{\upsilon}/\mu$ and the group velocity $d\hat{\upsilon}/d\mu$ from Schoenstadt (1978) as functions of $\mu d/\pi$ for the four grids as indicated. The differential solution is also included. These results use the values: $gH = 10^4\ m^2\ sec^{-2}$, $f = 10^{-4}\ sec^{-1}$, $d = 500$ km.

are all less than the differential value and the error is largest for the shortest wave ($\mu = \pi/d$) and for grids A and D. The group velocities are also too slow for the short waves, and they become spuriously negative for grids A and D. Since the energy propagates with the group velocity, grids B and C should give the fastest geostrophic adjustment. Grids A and D are very poor and they may be noisy because the short waves propagate energy in the wrong direction.

It is especially important to determine the errors in the steady geostrophic flow that is left after the gravity waves have propagated out of the region. The steady finite difference solutions that can be obtained from (2-77) are:

$$\tilde{v}_s = ig\left(\frac{f\beta\sigma}{\hat{\upsilon}^2}\tilde{h} - iH\frac{\sigma^2}{\hat{\upsilon}^2}\tilde{v}_0\right) \tag{7-79a}$$

$$\tilde{h}_s = f^2\frac{\beta^2}{\hat{\upsilon}^2}\tilde{h}_0 - ihf\frac{\beta\sigma}{\hat{\upsilon}^2}\tilde{v}_0 \tag{7-79b}$$

The difference between the finite difference solutions (7-79) and the differential solutions (2-77) is determined by the behavior of the ratios $\beta/\hat{\upsilon}$, $\sigma\beta/\hat{\upsilon}^2$, and $\sigma^2/\hat{\upsilon}^2$. Schoenstadt (1978) has computed these ratios as functions of $\mu d/\pi$, and the results are shown in Figure 7-6 for the various grids. The figure shows that grid A is by far the poorest, especially as the wavelength approaches $2d$. For example when $\mu = \pi/d$, $\beta/\hat{\upsilon}$ is about 5 times too large for grid A so that from (7-79b) the height is 25 times too large! This demonstrates the well-known difficulty of noise generation in the pressure field for unstaggered grids. That is, the velocity change at a central point is related to the pressure at the adjacent points, but not at the central point so that the proper geostrophic adjustment cannot occur on the smallest scale. The staggered grids can take advantage of this relationship between the variables, and Figure 7-6 shows that they are all better than the unstaggered grid.

Considering the group velocity accuracy from Figure 7-5 and the amplitude behavior in Figure 7-6, the two best grids are B and C. Schoenstadt (1978) argues that grid C is better than grid B because $\beta/\hat{\upsilon}$ and $\beta\sigma/\hat{\upsilon}^2$ actually go to zero as $\mu \rightarrow \pi/d$. This is the smallest scale the grid can resolve and it will be poorly forecast. Schoenstadt also examined fourth-order differencing and finite elements with linear basic functions, and he found that grid A remains poor for the short waves. Arakawa and Lamb (1977) have examined the various grids in two dimensions, as shown in Figure 7-4, and they conclude that grid C is superior unless the grid size is larger than the Rossby radius of deformation $L_R = (gh)^{1/2}/f$. In this case scheme B is better. They provide a detailed description of the UCLA general circulation model which employs scheme C.

It was shown in Section 5-6-9 that staggered grids require half the time step that is required for unstaggered grids. However, the extra computer time required is well spent with grids C and B because they give better structure for the shorter waves as may be seen in Figure 7-6. These waves may arise from

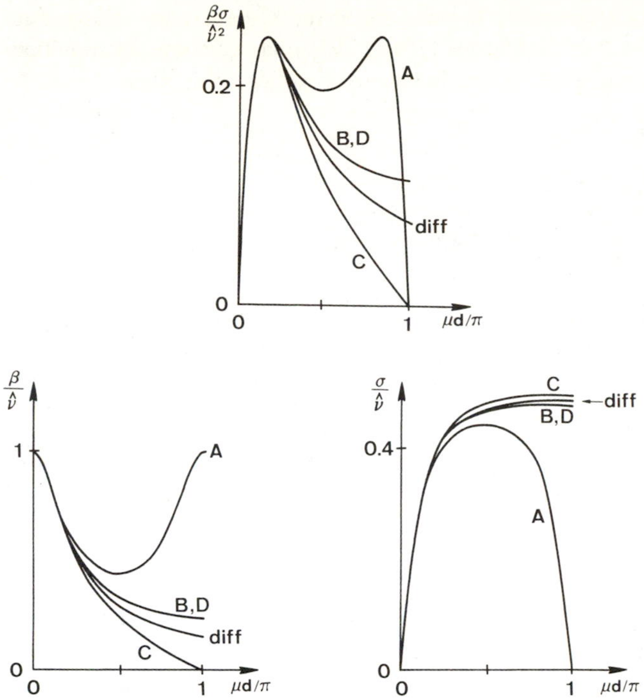

Figure 7.6 The quantities $\beta/\hat{\upsilon}$, $\sigma/\hat{\upsilon}$ and $\beta\sigma/\hat{\upsilon}^2$ as functions of $\mu d/\pi$. This figure uses the same constants as Figure 7-5.

geostrophic adjustment after initialization, from smaller scale heating, from nonlinear interaction or from mountain effects. In any case their structure will be better simulated with schemes *C* or *B* than scheme *A*. To obtain similar small-scale structure with scheme *A,* a smaller grid size would be required as well as additional smoothing. Thus the proper staggered grids should give better forecasts for a given amount of computer time.

Eliassen (1956) proposed a grid staggered in both space and time for a baroclinic PE model as shown in Figure 7-7. This scheme has excellent geostrophic adjustment properties because the arrangement of variables at each time

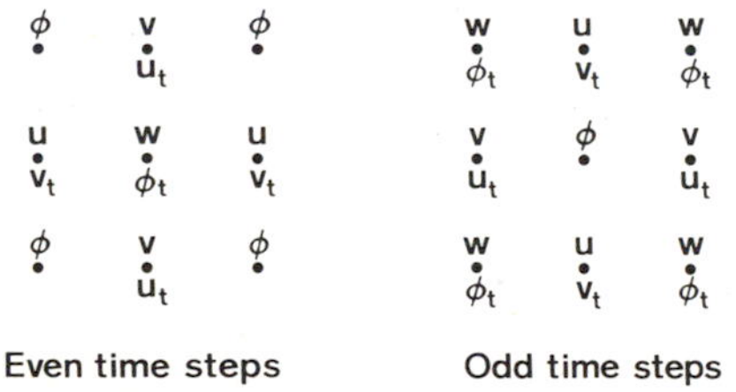

Figure 7.7

is optimal for the principal terms. An analysis of the scheme may be found in Mesinger and Arakawa (1976). Phillips (1962, 1979) has developed a modified version of the Eliassen scheme, which has many excellent properties.

7-4 EXAMPLE OF A STAGGERED PRIMITIVE EQUATION MODEL

In this section the finite difference equations will be given for a spatially staggered model with the vertical structure that was derived in Section 7-2. The difference equations are a simplification of those developed by Arakawa and Lamb (1977) and do not include certain terms that Arakawa and Lamb (1977) used to achieve enstrophy conservation when the flow is nondivergent. A more general enstrophy conserving scheme will be presented in Section 7-5.

7-4-1 Equations in Curvilinear Coordinates

The equations will be developed in the orthogonal curvilinear coordinates ξ and η. The actual distances in the ξ and η direction are given by

$$(dS)_\xi = (1/m)d\xi \qquad (dS)_\eta = (1/n)d\eta \tag{7-80}$$

u and v are the corresponding velocity components, respectively.

With the use of the vector expressions given in Section A-3 in the appendix, the vertically differenced equations (7-45), (7-52), and (7-72) from Section 7-2 can be written in curvilinear coordinates as follows:

$$\frac{\partial}{\partial t}\left(\frac{\pi}{mn}\right) + \frac{\partial}{\partial \xi}\left(\frac{\pi u_k}{n}\right) + \frac{\partial}{\partial \eta}\left(\frac{\pi v_k}{m}\right) + \frac{\pi}{\Delta\sigma_k}(\dot{\sigma}_{k+1} - \dot{\sigma}_{k-1}) = 0 \tag{7-81}$$

$$\begin{aligned}\frac{\partial}{\partial t}\left(\frac{\pi u_k}{mn}\right) &+ \frac{\partial}{\partial \xi}\left(\frac{\pi u_k u_k}{n}\right) + \frac{\partial}{\partial \eta}\left(\frac{\pi v_k u_k}{m}\right) + \frac{\pi}{2\Delta\sigma_k}[\dot{\sigma}_{k+1}(u_k \\ &+ u_{k+2}) - \dot{\sigma}_{k-1}(u_k + u_{k-2})] \\ &- \left[\frac{f}{mn} + v_k\frac{\partial}{\partial \xi}\left(\frac{1}{n}\right) - u_k\frac{\partial}{\partial \eta}\left(\frac{1}{m}\right)\right]\pi v_k \\ &+ \frac{1}{n}\left(\frac{\pi\partial\phi_k}{\partial \xi} + \sigma_k\alpha_k\,\pi\frac{\partial \pi}{\partial \xi}\right) = \frac{\pi(F_\xi)_k}{mn}\end{aligned} \tag{7-82}$$

$$\begin{aligned}\frac{\partial}{\partial t}\left(\frac{\pi v_k}{mn}\right) &+ \frac{\partial}{\partial \xi}\left(\frac{\pi v_k u_k}{n}\right) + \frac{\partial}{\partial \eta}\left(\frac{\pi v_k v_k}{m}\right) \\ &+ \frac{\pi}{2\Delta\sigma_k}[\dot{\sigma}_{k+1}(v_k + v_{k+2}) - \dot{\sigma}_{k-1}(v_k + v_{k-2})]\end{aligned}$$

$$+ \left(\frac{f}{mn} + v_k \frac{\partial}{\partial \xi} \frac{1}{n} - u_k \frac{\partial}{\partial \eta} \frac{1}{m} \right) \pi u_k + \frac{1}{m} \left(\pi \frac{\partial \phi_k}{\partial \eta} + \sigma_k \alpha_k \pi \frac{\partial \pi}{\partial \eta} \right) = \frac{\pi (F_\eta)_k}{mn} \tag{7-83}$$

$$\frac{\partial}{\partial t} \left(\frac{\pi}{mn} T_k \right) + \frac{\partial}{\partial \xi} \left(\frac{\pi u_k T_k}{n} \right) + \frac{\partial}{\partial \eta} \left(\frac{\pi v_k T_k}{m} \right) + \frac{\pi P_k}{\Delta \sigma_k} (\dot{\sigma}_{k+1} \hat{\theta}_{k+1} - \dot{\sigma}_{k-1} \hat{\theta}_{k-1})$$

$$= \frac{\pi \alpha_k \sigma_k}{c_p} \left[\frac{\partial}{\partial t} \left(\frac{\pi}{mn} \right) + \frac{u_k}{n} \frac{\partial \pi}{\partial \xi} + \frac{v_k}{m} \frac{\partial \pi}{\partial \eta} \right] + \frac{\pi}{c_p mn} Q_k \tag{7-84}$$

In addition (7-53) was used in the vertical advection terms, and $k_I = 1$, which excludes the upper layer.

7-4-2 Horizontal Differencing

It was pointed out in Section 7-3 that the unstaggered grid is not as desirable for the primitive equations because of its poor geostrophic adjustment properties. Arakawa and Lamb (1977) have shown the grid C (see Figure 7-4) is the superior grid arrangement in two dimensions. This model uses grid C as shown in Figure 7-8. In the figure the grid is centered on a π point where T and $\dot{\sigma}$ are computed, and the intermediate fluxes G and F are also indicated. The finite difference form of the continuity equation (7-81) is written

$$\frac{\partial}{\partial t} \Pi_{i,j} + F_{i+1/2,j,k} - F_{i-1/2,j,k} + G_{i,j+1/2,k} - G_{i,j-1/2,k} + \frac{1}{\Delta \sigma_k} (\dot{S}_{i,j,k+1} - \dot{S}_{i,j,k-1}) = 0 \tag{7-85}$$

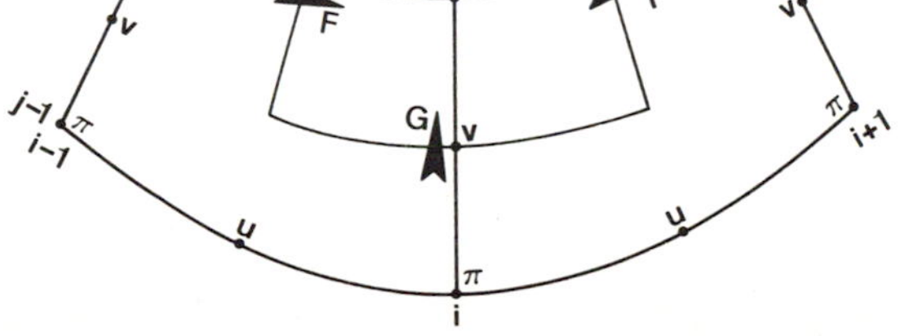

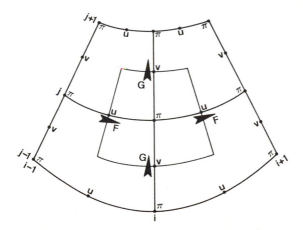

Figure 7.8 The grid centered on the π point.

where

$$\Pi_{i,j} \equiv \Delta\xi\Delta\eta\pi_{i,j}/(mn)_{i,j}$$

$$\dot{S}_{i,j,k} \equiv \Pi_{i,j}\,\dot{\sigma}_{i,j,k}$$

$$F_{i+½,j,k} \equiv ½\,\overline{\left(\frac{u\Delta\eta}{n}\right)}_{i+½,j,k}\,\overline{(\pi_{i,j} + \pi_{i+1,j})}$$

$$G_{i,j+½,k} \equiv ½\left(\frac{v\Delta\xi}{m}\right)_{i,j+½,k}(\pi_{i,j+1} + \pi_{i,j}) \tag{7-86}$$

Equation 7-85 has been multiplied by $\Delta\xi\Delta\eta$ where $\xi = i\Delta\xi$ and $\eta = j\Delta\eta$. The bar indicates Fourier smoothing, which will be discussed later.

Figure 7-9 shows the grid centered on a u point and it includes the required fluxes for the u prediction equation. Equation 7-82 is written in finite difference form as follows:

$$\frac{\partial}{\partial t}(\Pi^u_{i,j}\,u_{i,j,k}) + [F_{i+½,j}\,(u_{i+1,j} + u_{i,j}) - F^u_{i-½,j}\,(u_{i,j} + u_{i-1,j})$$

$$+ G^u_{i,j+½}\,(u_{i,j+1} + u_{i,j}) - G^u_{i,j-½}\,(u_{i,j} + u_{i,j-1})]_k$$

$$+ \frac{1}{2\Delta\sigma_k}[\dot{S}^u_{k+1}\,(u_{k+2} + u_k) - \dot{S}^u_{k-1}\,(u_k + u_{k-2})]_{i,j}$$

$$= [\pi_{i+½,j}\,C_{i+½,j}\,(v_{i+½,j+½} + v_{i+½,j-½})$$

$$+ \pi_{i-½,j}\,C_{i-½,j}\,(v_{i-½,j+½} + v_{i-½,j-½})]_k$$

$$- \frac{\Delta\eta}{2n_{i,j}}\,[\overline{(\pi_{i+½,j} + \pi_{i-½,j})\,(\phi_{i+½,j} - \phi_{i-½,j})}$$

$$\overline{+\,\sigma\,((\pi\alpha)_{i+½,j} + (\pi\alpha)_{i-½,j})}\;\overline{(\pi_{i+½,j} - \pi_{i-½,j})}]_k + \left(\frac{\Pi F_\xi}{mn}\right)_{i,j,k} \tag{7-87}$$

where

$$\Pi^u_{i,j} = ⅛\,[\Pi_{i+½,j+1} + \Pi_{i-½,j+1} + \Pi_{i-½,j-1} + \Pi_{i+½,j-1}$$

$$+ 2\,(\Pi_{i+½,j} + \Pi_{i-½,j})] \tag{7-88a}$$

$$F^u_{i+½,j,k} = ⅛\,[F_{i+1,j+1} + F_{i,j+1} +$$

$$2\,(F_{i,j} + F_{i+1,j}) + F_{i+1,j-1} + F_{i,j-1}]_k \tag{7-88b}$$

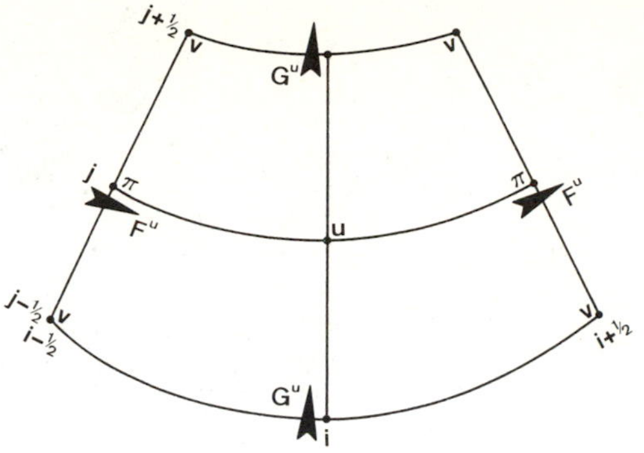

Figure 7.9 The grid centered on a μ point.

$$G^u_{i,j+\frac{1}{2},k} = \tfrac{1}{8}\left[\, 2\left(G_{i+\frac{1}{2},j+\frac{1}{2}} + G_{i-\frac{1}{2},j+\frac{1}{2}}\right) + G_{i+\frac{1}{2},j+\frac{3}{2}} + G_{i-\frac{1}{2},j+\frac{3}{2}} + G_{i+\frac{1}{2},j-\frac{1}{2}} + G_{i-\frac{1}{2},j-\frac{1}{2}}\right]_k \qquad \text{(7-88c)}$$

$$C_{i,j,k} = \left(\frac{f\Delta\xi\Delta\eta}{mn}\right)_{i,j} - \left(u_{i+\frac{1}{2},j} + u_{i-\frac{1}{2},j}\right)_k \left[(1/m)_{i,j+\frac{1}{2}} - (1/m)_{i,j-\frac{1}{2}}\right] \Delta\xi/2 + \left(v_{i,j+\frac{1}{2}} + v_{i,j-\frac{1}{2}}\right)_k \left[(1/n)_{i+\frac{1}{2},j} - (1/n)_{i-\frac{1}{2},j}\right] \frac{\Delta\eta}{2} \qquad \text{(7-88d)}$$

and $\dot{S}^u$ is computed from $\dot{S}$ in the same way that Π^u is computed from Π.

In a similar manner to (7-87), the v-equation (7-83) is approximated as follows:

$$\frac{\partial}{\partial t}\left(\Pi^v_{i,j}\, v_{i,j,k}\right) + \tfrac{1}{2}\left[F^v_{i+\frac{1}{2},j}\left(v_{i+i,j} + v_{i,j}\right) - F^v_{i-\frac{1}{2},j}\left(v_{i,j} + v_{i-1,j}\right)\right.$$

$$\left. + G^v_{i,j+\frac{1}{2}}\left(v_{i,j+1} + v_{i,j}\right) - G^v_{i,j-\frac{1}{2}}\left(v_{i,j} + v_{i,j-1}\right)\right]_k$$

$$+ \frac{1}{2\Delta\sigma_k}\left[\dot{S}^v_{k+1}\left(v_{k+2} + v_k\right) - \dot{S}^v_{k-1}\left(v_k + v_{k-2}\right)\right]_{i,j}$$

$$= -\tfrac{1}{4}\left[\pi_{i,j-\frac{1}{2}}\, C_{i,j-\frac{1}{2}}\left(u_{i+\frac{1}{2},j-\frac{1}{2}} + u_{i-\frac{1}{2},j-\frac{1}{2}}\right) + \pi_{i,j+\frac{1}{2}}\, C_{i,j+\frac{1}{2}}\right.$$

$$\left.\left(u_{i+\frac{1}{2},j+\frac{1}{2}} + u_{i-\frac{1}{2},j+\frac{1}{2}}\right)\right]_k$$

$$- \frac{\Delta\xi}{2m_{i,j}}\left[\left(\pi_{i,j+\frac{1}{2}} + \pi_{i,j-\frac{1}{2}}\right)\left(\phi_{i,j+\frac{1}{2}} - \phi_{i,j-\frac{1}{2}}\right)\right.$$

$$\left. + \sigma\left((\alpha\pi)_{i,j+\frac{1}{2}} + (\alpha\pi)_{i,j-\frac{1}{2}}\right)\left(\pi_{i,j+\frac{1}{2}} - \pi_{i,j-\frac{1}{2}}\right)\right]_k + \left(\frac{\Pi F_\eta}{mn}\right)_{i,j,k} \qquad \text{(7-89)}$$

where

$$\Pi^v_{i,j} = \tfrac{1}{8}\,[\Pi_{i+1,j+1/2} + \Pi_{i-1,j+1/2} + \Pi_{i-1,j-1/2} + \Pi_{i+1,j-1/2} + 2\,(\Pi_{i,i+1/2} + \Pi_{i,j-1/2})] \quad \text{(7-90a)}$$

$$F^v_{i+1/2,j,k} = \tfrac{1}{8}\,[F_{i+3/2,j+1/2} + 2\,(F_{i+1/2,j+1/2} + F_{i+1/2,j-1/2}) + F_{i-1/2,j+1/2} + F_{i+3/2,j-1/2} + F_{i-1/2,j-1/2}]_k \quad \text{(7-90b)}$$

$$G^v_{i,j+1/2,k} = \tfrac{1}{8}\,[G_{i+1,j+1} + G_{i+1,j} + 2\,(G_{i,j+1} + G_{i,j}) + G_{i-1,j+1} + G_{i-1,j}]_k \quad \text{(7-90c)}$$

and $\dot{S}^v$ is computed from $\dot{S}$ in the same way that Π^v is computed from Π.

The first law of thermodynamics (7-84) is differenced as (see Figure 7-8) as follows:

$$\begin{aligned}
&\frac{\partial}{\partial t}(\Pi_{i,j}\,T_{i,j,k}) + \tfrac{1}{2}\,[F_{i+1/2,j}(T_{i+1,j} + T_{i,j}) - F_{i-1/2,j}(T_{i,j} + T_{i-1,j}) \\
&\quad + G_{i,j+1/2}(T_{i,j+1} + T_{i,j}) - G_{i,j-1/2}(T_{i,j} + T_{i,j-1})]_k \\
&\quad + \frac{P_{i,j,k}}{\Delta\sigma_k}(\dot{S}_{k+1}\,\hat{\theta}_{k+1} - \dot{S}_{k-1}\,\hat{\theta}_{k-1})_{i,j} = \frac{1}{c_p}\Bigg\{(\pi\sigma\alpha)_{i,j,k}\frac{\partial \Pi_{i,j}}{\partial t} \\
&\quad + \tfrac{1}{4}\Bigg[\left(\frac{\overline{u\Delta\eta}}{n}\right)_{i+1/2,j}[(\pi\sigma\alpha)_{i+1,j} + (\pi\sigma\alpha)_{i,j}]\,(\pi_{i+1,j} - \pi_{i,j}) \\
&\quad + \left(\frac{\overline{u\Delta\eta}}{n}\right)_{i-1/2,j}[(\pi\sigma\alpha)_{i,j} + (\pi\sigma\alpha)_{i-1,j}]\,(\pi_{i,j} - \pi_{i-1,j}) \\
&\quad + \left(\frac{\overline{v\Delta\xi}}{m}\right)_{i,j+1/2}[(\pi\sigma\alpha)_{i,j+1} + (\pi\sigma\alpha)_{i,j}]\,(\pi_{i,j+1} - \pi_{i,j}) \\
&\quad + \left(\frac{\overline{v\Delta\xi}}{m}\right)_{i,j-1/2}[(\pi\sigma\alpha)_{i,j} + (\pi\sigma\alpha)_{i,j-1}]\,(\pi_{i,j} - \pi_{i,j-1})\Bigg]_k \\
&\quad + \Pi_{i,j}\,Q_{i,j,k}\Bigg\}
\end{aligned} \quad \text{(7-91)}$$

The prediction equation for $\Pi_{i,j}$ is found by summing (7-85) in the vertical and employing the boundary conditions on $\dot{\sigma}$. A diagnostic equation for $\dot{S}_{i,j,k}$ is obtained by forming a partial sum of (7-85) and eliminating $\partial\Pi_{i,j}/\partial t$. The system is completed with the formulas (7-68), (7-71), (7-63) and (7-59) for ϕ, $\sigma\alpha$, and $\hat{\theta}$.

When this model is applied to global prediction, with $\xi = \lambda$ (longitude) and $\eta = \varphi$ (latitude), the scale factors become $m = 1/a \cos \varphi$ and $\eta = 1/a$. The special differencing required near the pole will be discussed in Section 7-6. Spherical grids would require an unreasonably small time step if left unmodified because of the convergence of the meridians. Arakawa and Lamb (1977) handle this problem by smoothing certain terms that were indicated with an over bar, that control east-west gravity wave propagation. The description of this smoothing will be given in Section 7-6. Other polar smoothing procedures were discussed by Williamson (1976).

Arakawa and Lamb (1977) use leapfrog time differencing with an Euler-backward step (see Section 5-6-4) after every five time steps, with heating introduced at that time. Monaco and Williams (1975) have successfully tested the model described in this section, which is a simplified version of the model developed by Arakawa and Lamb (1977).

7-4-3 Energy Conservation

The finite difference equations developed in this section conserve total energy in the absence of heating and friction, when the time variation is continuous. In Section 7-2 total energy conservation was demonstrated for continuous horizontal variation and finite differences in the vertical. Thus, it is only necessary to demonstrate that the horizontal differences give the proper contributions to the various energy integrals.

First it is desirable to show that the finite difference advections do not change the mass integral of the kinetic energy, since there is no change with the continuous equations (see 7-39). This was demonstrated for an unstaggered grid in pressure coordinates in Section 5-11-2. Consider for example, the v-component, which must satisfy the following equation if only advection is considered:

$$\frac{1}{g}\int\int\int \frac{\partial}{\partial t}\pi v^2/2 \,\frac{d\sigma d\xi d\eta}{mn} = \frac{1}{g}\int\int\int \left[\frac{v\partial(\pi v)}{\partial t} - \frac{v^2}{2}\frac{\partial \pi}{\partial t}\right]\frac{d\sigma d\xi d\eta}{mn} = 0$$

In finite difference form this requirement becomes

$$\Delta K = \frac{1}{g}\sum_{i,j,k}\left[v_{i,j,k}\frac{\partial}{\partial t}(\Pi_{i,j}\, v_{i,j,k}) - \frac{v_{i,j,k}^2}{2}\frac{\partial \Pi^v_{i,j,k}}{\partial t}\right] = 0 \tag{7-92}$$

Now differentiate (7-90a) with respect to t and use (7-90b) and (7-90c), which gives:

$$\frac{\partial \Pi^v_{i,j}}{\partial t} + F^v_{i+½,j,k} - F^v_{i-½,j,k} + G^v_{i,j+½,k} - G^v_{i,j-½,k} + \frac{1}{\Delta\sigma_k}(\dot{S}^v_{i,j,k+1} - \dot{S}^v_{i,j,k-1}) = 0 \tag{7-93}$$

This equation corresponds to the left side of (7-89) with $v_{i,j,k} = 1$. In fact, the formula for $\Pi^v_{i,j}$ is obtained by requiring that the left side of (7-89) be equal to the appropriate average of the continuity equation (7-85) at surrounding points. Equation 7-92 for ΔK is evaluated as follows from (7-93) and from (7-89) with the right side set to 0 as follows:

$$
\begin{aligned}
g\Delta K = \sum_{i,j,k} \Bigg\{ & - \frac{v_{i,j,k}}{2} [F^v_{i+\frac{1}{2},j} (v_{i+1,j} + v_{i,j}) - F^v_{i-\frac{1}{2},j} (v_{i,j} + v_{i-1,j}) \\
& + G^v_{i,j+\frac{1}{2}} (v_{i,j+1} + v_{i,j}) - G^v_{i,j-\frac{1}{2}} (v_{i,j} + v_{i,j-1})]_k \\
& - \frac{v_{i,j,k}}{2\Delta\sigma_k} [\dot{S}^v_{k+1} (v_{k+2} + v_k) - \dot{S}^v_{k-1} (v_k + v_{k-2})]_{i,j} \\
& + \frac{v^2_{i,j,k}}{2} (F^v_{i+\frac{1}{2},j} - F^v_{i-\frac{1}{2},j} + G^v_{i,j+\frac{1}{2}} - G^v_{i,j-\frac{1}{2}})_k \\
& + \frac{v^2_{i,j,k}}{2\Delta\sigma_k} (\dot{S}^v_{k+1} - \dot{S}^v_{k-1})_{i,j} \Bigg\} \\
= \sum_{i,j,k} \Bigg[\Bigg(& - \frac{v_{i,j}\, v_{i+1,j}\, F^v_{i+\frac{1}{2},j}}{2} + \frac{v_{i,j}\, v_{i-1,j}\, F^v_{i-\frac{1}{2},j}}{2} \\
& - v_{i,j}\, v_{i+1,j}\, G^v_{i,j+\frac{1}{2}} + v_{i,j}\, v_{i,j-1}\, G^v_{i,j-\frac{1}{2}} \Bigg)_k \\
& + (-v_k\, v_{k+2}\, \dot{S}^v_{k+1} + v_k\, v_{k-2}\, \dot{S}^v_{k-1})_{i,j} \Bigg]
\end{aligned}
\tag{7-94}
$$

The terms in (7-94) are in flux form so that contributions from adjacent points cancel and the sums will vanish with appropriate boundary conditions. This same result can be obtained for the u equation (7-87), which proves that the advection terms conserve kinetic energy.

In the continuous equations the coriolis force cannot change the kinetic energy because $\mathbf{V} \cdot f\mathbf{k} \times \mathbf{V} = 0$ everywhere. When the coriolis terms in (7-87) and (7-89) are multiplied by u and v, respectively, and added, it can be seen that the energy production at point (i,j) is canceled by contributions from points $(i \pm \frac{1}{2}, j \pm \frac{1}{2})$.

The last step in demonstrating energetic consistency involves showing that the energy conversion between kinetic and potential energy is correct. The rate of working by the north-south pressure gradient force can be written:

$$
g^{-1}\sum_{i,j,k}\left(-\frac{v_{i,j,k}\,\Delta\xi}{2\,m_{i,j}}\{(\pi_{i,j+1/2}+\pi_{i,j-1/2})(\phi_{i,j+1/2}-\phi_{i,j-1/2})\right.
$$

$$
\left.+[(\sigma\alpha\pi)_{i,j+1/2}+(\sigma\alpha\pi)_{i,j-1/2}](\pi_{i,j+1/2}-\pi_{i,j-1/2})\}_k\right)
$$

$$
=g^{-1}\sum_{i,j,k}\left(\phi_{i,j+1/2,k}(G_{i,j+1}-G_{i,j})_k-\frac{\Delta\xi}{4}\left\{\frac{v_{i,j}}{m_{i,j}}[(\sigma\alpha\pi)_{i,j+1/2}\right.\right.
$$

$$
+(\sigma\alpha\pi)_{i,j-1/2}](\pi_{i,j+1/2}-\pi_{i,j-1/2})
$$

$$
\left.\left.+\frac{v_{i,j+1}}{m_{i,j+1}}[(\sigma\alpha\pi)_{i,j+3/2}+(\sigma\alpha\pi)_{i,j+1/2}](\pi_{i,j+3/2}-\pi_{i,j+1/2})\right\}_k\right) \tag{7-95}
$$

where G was introduced from (7-86) and the various terms have been recollected. The terms are now centered on π points. The same development can be carried out with the east-west pressure gradient and the result can be added to (7-95). Then the mass divergence can be eliminated with the continuity equation (7-85). The remaining portion of the derivation involves only vertical differences that were worked out previously in equation (7-54). Since the horizontal differences in (7-95) correspond to those used in the first law of thermodynamics (7-91), the total energy is conserved.

Many other primitive equation prediction models have been developed that have been integrated stably (see Joint Organizing Committee, 1974). However, it appears that models with properly staggered grids and energy conservation should be superior for the longer forecast periods. In the next section a new potential enstrophy conserving scheme will be presented which promises to give better forecasts, especially near mountains.

7-5 POTENTIAL ENSTROPHY CONSERVING SCHEME

The various UCLA general circulation models developed by A. Arakawa conserve enstrophy (mean square absolute vorticity) when the horizontal motion is nondivergent, and they also conserve total energy when the heating and friction are zero. Enstrophy conservation is important since the atmosphere is quasi-nondivergent (see Chapter 3). Arakawa (1966) argued that conservation of energy and enstrophy in a barotropic model precludes false transfer of energy to small scales (see Section 5-11-1). The baroclinic model described by Arakawa and Lamb (1977) conserves enstrophy when the motion is nondivergent by adding momentum advection terms that are not present in the model described in the previous section.

Arakawa and Lamb (1978) have developed a new finite difference model that is designed to conserve potential vorticity as well as total energy. They argue that this is especially important when small-scale, high topography is present as is the case with many mountain ranges. Consider the motion of a homogeneous fluid that is described by the shallow-water equations (see Section 2-5). Each fluid parcel conserves the potential vorticity, $q = (\zeta + f)/h$, where h is the depth of the fluid. Near high mountains there are large gradients in h and truncation errors usually prevent q from being conserved. The new scheme is designed to conserve the domain average of q^2 and as nearly as possible to conserve q for parcels. The scheme will be developed here for the shallow-water equations, but the results can be generalized to baroclinic models. Sadourny (1975) has formulated a scheme that is similar in some respects.

The shallow-water equations from Section 2-5 may be expressed as

$$\frac{\partial \mathbf{V}}{\partial t} + \mathbf{V} \cdot \nabla \mathbf{V} + f\mathbf{k} \times \mathbf{V} + g\nabla (h + h_S) = 0 \tag{7-96a}$$

$$\frac{\partial h}{\partial t} + \nabla \cdot h\mathbf{V} = 0 \tag{7-96b}$$

where h_S is the height of the lower boundary and h is the fluid depth. The components of the momentum equation (7-96a) can be written in the following vector invariant form (see Equation A-9)

$$\frac{\partial u}{\partial t} - v(f + \zeta) + \frac{\partial}{\partial x}[\tfrac{1}{2}(u^2 + v^2) + g(h + h_S)] = 0 \tag{7-97a}$$

$$\frac{\partial v}{\partial t} + u(f + \zeta) + \frac{\partial}{\partial y}[\tfrac{1}{2}(u^2 + v^2) + g(h + h_S)] = 0 \tag{7-97b}$$

7-5-1 Continuous Integral Constraints

The total energy equation can be formed from (7-97a) and (7-97b) (student exercise), that is,

$$\frac{\partial}{\partial t}\left[\frac{h}{2}(V^2 + gh) + ghh_S\right] + \nabla \cdot \left\{h\left[\frac{V^2}{2} + g(h + h_S)\right]\mathbf{V}\right\} = 0 \tag{7-98}$$

When this equation is integrated over a closed domain, the result is

$$\frac{d}{dt}\int\int\left[\left(\frac{h}{2}\right)(V^2 + gh) + ghh_S\right]dxdy = 0 \tag{7-99}$$

which expresses the energy conservation for the shallow-water equations (analogous to 1-92).

The conservation of potential vorticity, obtained in Section 2-5, can be written

$$\frac{\partial q}{\partial t} + \mathbf{V} \cdot \nabla q = 0 \tag{7-100}$$

where $q = (\zeta + f)/h$. The following equation for the potential enstrophy ($q^2/2$) can be derived by multiplying (7-96b) by $q^2/2$ and (7-100) by hq and adding:

$$\frac{\partial}{\partial t}(\tfrac{1}{2}\, hq^2) + \nabla \cdot (\tfrac{1}{2}\, q^2\, h\mathbf{V}) = 0 \tag{7-101}$$

When this equation is integrated over the domain the result is

$$\frac{d}{dt}\int\int \tfrac{1}{2}\, hq^2\, dxdy = 0 \tag{7-102}$$

which demonstrates conservation of potential enstrophy for the differential system. A finite difference scheme will be designed to maintain (7-99) and (7-102).

Additional constraints can be found by considering the special case where the mass flux $h\mathbf{V}$ is nondivergent, that is, $\nabla \cdot h\mathbf{V} = 0$. In this special case high mountains could be present and $\nabla \cdot \mathbf{V}$ could be quite large. Now define

$$\mathbf{V}^* \equiv h\mathbf{V} = \mathbf{k} \times \nabla\psi^* \tag{7-103}$$

Equation 7-100 can be written:

$$\frac{\partial}{\partial t}(hq) + J(\psi^*, q) = 0 \tag{7-104}$$

where J is the usual Jacobian and where $\partial h/\partial t = 0$ from (7-96b) was used. The constraints

$$\int\int qJ(\psi^*, q)\, dxdy = 0 \tag{7-105a}$$

$$\int\int \psi^* J(\psi^*, q)\, dxdy = 0 \tag{7-105b}$$

give conservation of mean potential enstrophy and mean kinetic energy, respectively. This will be achieved later with the *Arakawa Jacobian,* which is given by (5-193).

7-5-2 Difference Equations

The finite difference scheme uses grid *C,* which is superior for geostrophic adjustment and was also used in Section 7-4. The arrangement of variables is shown in Figure 7-10 and the vorticity is included because it will play an important role in the new difference scheme.

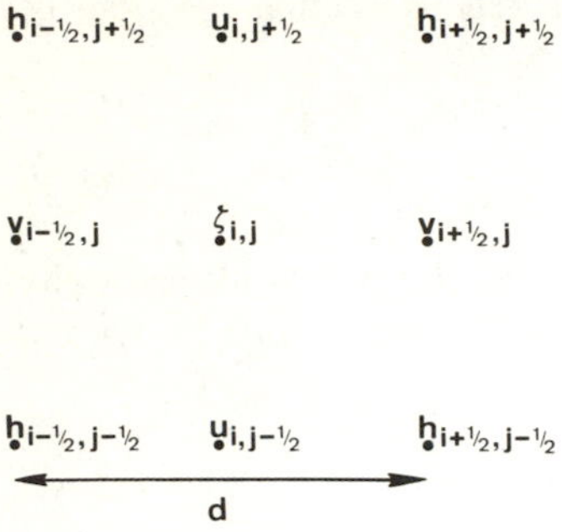

Figure 7.10 Arrangement of variables on staggered grid.

The equation of continuity (7-96b) is differenced as follows:

$$\frac{\partial h_{i+\frac{1}{2},j+\frac{1}{2}}}{\partial t} + \frac{1}{d}\left(\overset{*}{u}_{i+1,j+\frac{1}{2}} - \overset{*}{u}_{i,j+\frac{1}{2}} + \overset{*}{v}_{i+\frac{1}{2},j+1} - \overset{*}{v}_{i+\frac{1}{2},j}\right) = 0 \qquad (7\text{-}106)$$

where $\overset{*}{u}_{i+1,j+\frac{1}{2}} \equiv (h^u\, u)_{i+1,j+\frac{1}{2}}$, $\overset{*}{v}_{i+\frac{1}{2},j} \equiv (h^v\, v)_{i+\frac{1}{2},j}$. The quantities h^u and h^v are functions of h that will be specified later. The equations of motion (7-97a) and (7-97b) are written in general form as follows:

$$\frac{\partial}{\partial t} u_{i,j+\frac{1}{2}} - \alpha_{i,j+\frac{1}{2}}\, \overset{*}{v}_{i+\frac{1}{2},j+1} - \beta_{i,j+\frac{1}{2}}\, \overset{*}{v}_{i-\frac{1}{2},j+1} - \gamma_{i,j+\frac{1}{2}}\, \overset{*}{v}_{i-\frac{1}{2},j}$$

$$- \delta_{i,j+\frac{1}{2}}\, \overset{*}{v}_{i+\frac{1}{2},j} + \varepsilon_{i+\frac{1}{2},j+\frac{1}{2}}\, \overset{*}{u}_{i+1,j+\frac{1}{2}} - \varepsilon_{i-\frac{1}{2},j+\frac{1}{2}}\, \overset{*}{u}_{i-1,j+\frac{1}{2}}$$

$$+ \frac{1}{d}\left(K_{i+\frac{1}{2},j+\frac{1}{2}} - K_{i-\frac{1}{2},j+\frac{1}{2}} + \Phi_{i+\frac{1}{2},j+\frac{1}{2}} - \Phi_{i-\frac{1}{2},j+\frac{1}{2}}\right) = 0 \qquad (7\text{-}107)$$

$$\frac{\partial}{\partial t} v_{i+\frac{1}{2},j} + \gamma_{i+1,j+\frac{1}{2}}\, \overset{*}{u}_{i+1,j+\frac{1}{2}} + \delta_{i,j+\frac{1}{2}}\, \overset{*}{u}_{i,j+\frac{1}{2}} + \alpha_{i,j-\frac{1}{2}}\, \overset{*}{u}_{i,j-\frac{1}{2}}$$

$$+ \beta_{i+1,j-\frac{1}{2}}\, \overset{*}{u}_{i+1,j-\frac{1}{2}} + \phi_{i+\frac{1}{2},j+\frac{1}{2}}\, \overset{*}{v}_{i+\frac{1}{2},j+1} - \phi_{i+\frac{1}{2},j-\frac{1}{2}}\, \overset{*}{v}_{i+\frac{1}{2},j-1}$$

$$+ \frac{1}{d}\left(K_{i+\frac{1}{2},j+\frac{1}{2}} - K_{i+\frac{1}{2},j-\frac{1}{2}} + \Phi_{i+\frac{1}{2},j+\frac{1}{2}} - \Phi_{i+\frac{1}{2},j-\frac{1}{2}}\right) = 0 \qquad (7\text{-}108)$$

where α, β, γ, δ, ε, and ϕ are functions of q, K is a function of the u and v, and $\Phi = g(h + h_S)$. The pairs of terms involving ε and ϕ give more generality to the scheme and they vanish because of their form as the grid size approaches zero. Note that the indices of all quantities are counted with respect to the ζ point in the center of Figure 7-10. Constraints will be imposed to determine the various undefined coefficients in (7-107) and (7-108).

A domain averaged kinetic energy equation is formed by multiplying (7-107) by $u^*_{i,j+½}$ and (7-108) by $v^*_{i+½,j}$, adding and summing over the entire domain which yields:

$$\sum_{u \text{ points}} \frac{\partial}{\partial t}\left(\frac{h^u u^2}{2}\right)_{i,j+½} + \sum_{v \text{ points}} \frac{\partial}{\partial t}\left(\frac{h^v v^2}{2}\right)_{i+½,j}$$

$$- \sum_{u \text{ points}} \left(\frac{u^2}{2}\frac{\partial h^u}{\partial t}\right)_{i,j+½} - \sum_{v \text{ points}} \left(\frac{v^2}{2}\frac{\partial h^v}{\partial t}\right)_{i+½,j}$$

$$- \frac{1}{d} \sum_{h \text{ points}} (K_{i+½,j+½} + \Phi_{i+½,j+½}) (u^*_{i+1,j+½} - u^*_{i,j+½}$$

$$+ v^*_{i+½,j+1} - v^*_{i+½,j}) = 0 \qquad (7\text{-}109)$$

Use was made of the following relations between two variables A and B defined on staggered grid points:

$$\sum_{A \text{ points}} A_{i,j}(B_{i+½,j} - B_{i-½,j}) = - \sum_{B \text{ points}} B_{i+½,j}(A_{i+1,j} - A_{i,j}) \qquad (7\text{-}110)$$

and a similar result with respect to the j index. Note that all terms involving α, β, δ, ε, and ϕ cancel in (7-109) as is the case when the kinetic energy equation is formed from the continuous equations (7-97a) and (7-97b).

The finite difference vorticity equation is formed from (7-107) and (7-108) as follows:

$$\frac{\partial \zeta_{i,j}}{\partial t} = \frac{1}{d}\frac{\partial}{\partial t}(u_{i,j-½} - u_{i,j+½} + v_{i+½,j} - v_{i-½,j})$$

$$= -\frac{1}{d}[-\alpha_{i,j-½}\, v^*_{i+½,j} - \beta_{i,j-½}\, v^*_{i-½,j} - \gamma_{i,j-½}\, v^*_{i-½,j-1}$$

$$- \delta_{i,j-½}\, v^*_{i+½,j-1} + \alpha_{i,j+½}\, v^*_{i+½,j+1} + \beta_{i,j+½}\, v^*_{i-½,j+1} + \gamma_{i,j+½}\, v^*_{i-½,j}$$

$$+ \delta_{i,j+½}\, v^*_{i+½,j} + (\gamma u^*)_{i+1,j+½} + (\delta u^*)_{i,j+½} + (\alpha u^*)_{i,j-½} + (\beta u^*)_{i-1,j-½}$$

$$- (\gamma u^*)_{i,j+½} - (\delta u^*)_{i-1,j+½} - (\alpha u^*)_{i-1,j-½} - (\beta u^*)_{i,j-½}$$

$$+ \varepsilon_{i+½,j-½}\, u^*_{i+1,j-½} - \varepsilon_{i-½,j-½}\, u^*_{i-1,j-½} - \varepsilon_{i+½,j+½}\, u^*_{i+1,j+½}$$

$$+ \varepsilon_{i-½,j+½}\, u^*_{i-1,j+½} + \phi_{i+½,j+½}\, v^*_{i+½,j+1} - \phi_{i+½,j-½}\, v^*_{i+½,j-1}$$

$$- \phi_{i-½,j+½}\, v^*_{i-½,j+1} + \phi_{i-½,j-½}\, v^*_{i-½,j-1}\,] \qquad (7\text{-}111)$$

This equation will be required for many of the constraints that will be enforced on the difference equations.

7-5-3 Constraints Enforced

The constraints that are used to determine the difference scheme are listed below.

1. For the special case $\nabla \cdot \mathbf{V}^* = 0$ the stream function ψ^* can be defined so that

$$u^*_{i,j+1/2} = d^{-1}\,(\psi^*_{i,j} - \psi^*_{i,j+1}),\; v^*_{i+1/2,j} = d^{-1}\,(\psi^*_{i+1,j} - \psi^*_{i,j}) \qquad (7\text{-}112)$$

   When these relations are used in the right side of (7-110), the difference forms of (7-105a) and (7-105b) can be enforced. These conditions are satisfied by requiring that the right side of (7-110) correspond to the *Arakawa Jacobian,* which is given by (5-193).
2. It can be seen from (7-100) that if q is constant everywhere, then it cannot change in time. The finite difference equations are required to satisfy this condition in this case. This is important because if high mountains are present there will be large variations in $\zeta + f$ and $h,$ which could cause large errors with most difference schemes.
3. It is required that the potential enstrophy be conserved for general divergent flow as indicated by (7-102).
4. Finally total energy conservation according to (7-99) is required with the use of (7-109) and another equation for the potential energy change.

The application of these constraints involves extensive algebra that can be found in Arakawa and Lamb (1978) and will not be repeated here. The resulting expressions are given below:

$$\begin{aligned}
\varepsilon_{i+1/2,j+1/2} &= {}^1/_{24}\,(q_{i+1,j+1} + q_{i,j+1} - q_{i,j} - q_{i+1,j})\\
\phi_{i+1/2,j+1/2} &= {}^1/_{24}\,(-q_{i+1,j+1} + q_{i,j+1} + q_{i,j} - q_{i+1,j})\\
\alpha_{i,j+1/2} &= {}^1/_{24}\,(2q_{i+1,j+1} + q_{i,j+1} + 2q_{i,j} + q_{i+1,j})\\
\beta_{i,j+1/2} &= {}^1/_{24}\,(q_{i,j+1} + 2q_{i-1,j+1} + q_{i-1,j} + 2q_{i,j})\\
\gamma_{i,j+1/2} &= {}^1/_{24}\,(2q_{i,j+1} + q_{i-1,j+1} + 2q_{i-1,j} + q_{i,j})\\
\delta_{i,j+1/2} &= {}^1/_{24}\,(q_{i+1,j+1} + 2q_{i,j+1} + q_{i,j} + 2q_{i+1,j})
\end{aligned} \qquad (7\text{-}113)$$

where the potential vorticity is given by

$$q_{i,j} = \frac{f + d^{-1}(u_{i,j-1/2} - u_{i,j+1/2} + v_{i+1/2,j} - v_{i-1/2,j})}{(h_{i+1/2,j+1/2} + h_{i-1/2,j+1/2} + h_{i-1/2,j-1/2} + h_{i+1/2,j-1/2})/4} \tag{7-114}$$

The quantities h^u and h^v are defined as follows:

$$\begin{aligned} h^u_{i,j+1/2} &= 1/2\,(h_{i+1/2,j+1/2} + h_{i-1/2,j+1/2}) \\ h^v_{i+1/2,j} &= 1/2\,(h_{i+1/2,j+1/2} + h_{i+1/2,j-1/2}) \end{aligned} \tag{7-115}$$

The kinetic energy term is written

$$K_{i+1/2,j+1/2} = 1/4\,(u^2_{i+1,j+1/2} + u^2_{i,j+1/2} + v^2_{i+1/2,j+1} + v^2_{i+1/2,j}) \tag{7-116}$$

Arakawa (1978) has tested this scheme with flow in a channel over a narrow, high mountain range. The long-term integrations showed that the new scheme gave a good solution for a coarse grid size while the old model [Arakawa and Lamb (1977)] gave a very poor solution that was improved only when the grid size was greatly reduced.

The new scheme is actually simpler than the older scheme, partially because it is not written in flux form. The scheme does not exactly conserve momentum, but its additional conservative properties are much more important especially when mountains are present. Arakawa and Lamb (1978) describe how the scheme can be applied to a baroclinic atmosphere on the globe. Sadourny (1975) has developed a similar scheme, which does not have all of the constraints that were used in the model described in this section. Burridge and Haseler (1977) have developed and tested a baroclinic model based on the difference equations that were developed by Sadourny (1975). Although neither of these models have been extensively tested or compared, this new approach to model formulation is very promising.

7-6 SPHERICAL GRIDS

The most natural coordinates for representing large-scale meteorological phenomena on the earth are the spherical polar coordinates λ, φ together with an appropriate vertical coordinate, as described in Chapter 1. Nevertheless, most past numerical prediction models dealing with a hemisphere or less have used cartesian coordinates on a conformal map of a section of the earth projected on a plane. The most popular map for either the northern or southern hemisphere has been the polar stereographic projection; however, distortion becomes severe if the projection is extended into the opposite hemisphere. Also artificial boundary conditions placed in the equatorial region give rise to errors that eventually propagate into higher latitudes. Some experiments with a global model with and without an equatorial wall showed significant differences in the middle and high latitudes in a week or so. Of course, two polar stereographic projections can be matched at the equator but this is rather awkward compared to spherical coordinates.

On the other hand, spherical coordinates have some peculiarities, for example, the poles are singular points and velocity components are not defined there. This is not a serious problem, however since with staggered grids the poles are mass points not motion points. When taking derivatives near the poles, as shown in Figure 7-11, scalars may be treated directly as follows: Let $\lambda_i = i\Delta\lambda$, $i = 1,2, \ldots ,2N$. Then if A is a scalar

$$\left(\frac{\partial A}{\partial \varphi}\right)_2 = \frac{A_3 - A_1}{2\Delta\varphi} \tag{7-117}$$

On the other hand, with vector components a sign change must be made. For example, if the meridional wind components at points 1 and 3 are v_1 and v_3 then the meridional derivative at point 2, after reversing the sign at 3 would be

$$\left(\frac{\partial v}{\partial \varphi}\right)_2 = \frac{(-v_3) - v_1}{2\Delta\varphi} \tag{7-118}$$

If both v_1 and v_3 were poleward and therefore positive, convergence would be expected and obtained from (7-118) by the sign change. A similar result would be obtained if point 2 is a meridional velocity point and a divergence computation is needed at the pole P.

A more troublesome problem in the finite difference method, which *does not* exist in the spectral method, is that the convergence of the meridians results in an ever decreasing distance between gridpoints, $\Delta x = a \cos\varphi \, \Delta\lambda$ as the poles are approached for a fixed $\Delta\lambda$. Consequently, the computational stability condition requires an ever smaller Δt [e.g., see (5-32)], which is usually unacceptable. Various methods have been used to overcome this difficulty. One technique is to abruptly change the spacing $\Delta\lambda$ between gridpoints at certain latitudes, perhaps by skipping every other point. However, this leads to complications with the differencing scheme and may cause some irregularity in fields where such a transition is made. Following Arakawa and Lamb (1977), the convergence of meridians problem will be examined with linearized shallow-water system:

$$\frac{\partial u}{\partial t} = -\frac{1}{a\cos\varphi}\frac{\partial \phi}{\partial \lambda} \qquad \frac{\partial v}{\partial t} = -\frac{1}{a}\frac{\partial \phi}{\partial \varphi} \tag{7-119}$$

$$\frac{\partial \phi}{\partial t} = -\frac{\overline{\Phi}}{a\cos\varphi}\left[\frac{\partial u}{\partial \lambda} + \frac{\partial}{\partial \varphi}(v\cos\varphi)\right] \tag{7-120}$$

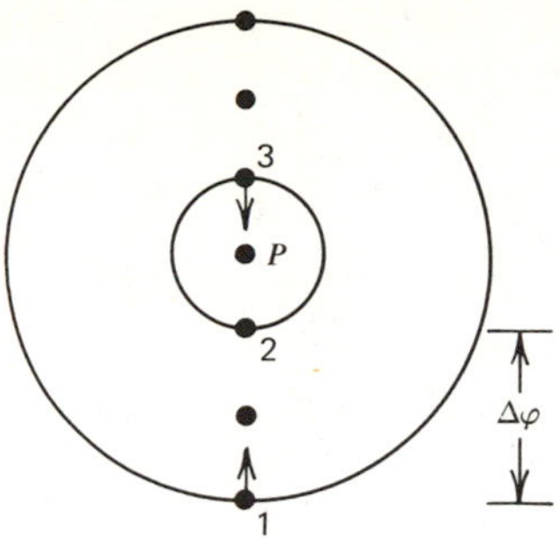

Figure 7.11 Illustrating treatment of a polar point.

As shown in Figure 7-12 only the surface pressure p_s is carried at the pole P and $\partial p_s/\partial t$ is computed from the meridional mass flux at the v points ($P - 1$). The momentum equations are not solved at the pole so the singular point is avoided. Nevertheless at $P - 1$, the east west distance between points separated by a constant $\Delta\lambda$ reaches a minimum for the grid. Here an inordinately small Δt is required to maintain computational stability compared to elsewhere on the grid for the same $\Delta\lambda$. To avoid instability Arakawa and Lamb (1977) and others longitudinally average certain terms in the dynamical equations that govern the propagation of gravity waves. To illustrate this method, semidiscrete analogues for the simple dynamical system (7-119)-(7-120) may be written:

$$\frac{\partial u_{i+1/2,j}}{\partial t} + \frac{1}{a\cos\varphi}\frac{1}{\Delta\lambda}(\delta_\lambda\phi)_{i+1/2,j} = 0 \qquad (7\text{-}121)$$

$$\frac{\partial v_{i,j+1/2}}{\partial t} + \frac{1}{a}\frac{1}{\Delta\varphi}(\delta_\varphi\phi)_{i,j+1/2} = 0 \qquad (7\text{-}122)$$

$$\frac{\partial \phi_{i,j}}{\partial t} + \frac{gH}{a\cos\varphi}\left[\frac{1}{\Delta\lambda}(\delta_\lambda u) + \frac{1}{\Delta\varphi}\delta_\varphi(v\cos\varphi)\right]_{i,j} = 0 \qquad (7\text{-}123)$$

Now substitute solutions of the following form into (7-121 to 7-123)

$$\begin{aligned} u_{i+1/2,j} &= R_e\{\hat{u}_j\, e^{i[\mu(i+1/2)\Delta\lambda+\sigma t]}\} \\ v_{i,j+1/2} &= R_e\{\hat{v}_{j+1/2}\, e^{i(\mu i\Delta\lambda+\sigma t)}\} \\ \phi_{i,j} &= R_e\{\hat{\phi}_j\, e^{i(\mu i\Delta\lambda+\sigma t)}\} \end{aligned} \qquad (7\text{-}124)$$

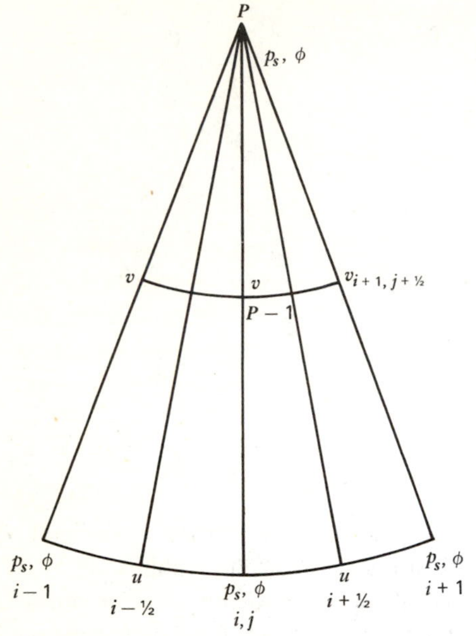

Figure 7-12 Illustrating treatment of a polar point with spherical coordinates.

where $\hat{i} = \sqrt{-1}$. The result is

$$\hat{i}\sigma\hat{u}_j \qquad + \frac{\hat{i}}{a \cos \varphi_j}\left(\frac{\sin \mu\Delta\lambda/2}{\mu\Delta\lambda/2}\right) S_j(\mu)\,\hat{\phi}_j = 0 \tag{7-125}$$

$$\hat{i}\sigma\hat{v}_{j+½} + \frac{1}{a\Delta\varphi}(\hat{\phi}_{j+1} - \hat{\phi}_j) \qquad = 0 \tag{7-126}$$

$$\hat{i}\sigma\hat{\phi}_j \qquad + \frac{gH}{a \cos \varphi_j}\left\{\hat{i}\left[\frac{\sin(\mu\Delta\lambda/2)}{\mu\Delta\lambda/2}\right] S_j(\mu)\,\hat{u}_j\right\} \tag{7-127}$$

$$+ \frac{1}{\Delta\varphi}[(\hat{v}\cos\varphi)_{j+½} - (\hat{v}\cos\varphi)_{j-½})] = 0$$

where $S_j(\mu)$ is a longitudinal smoothing operator applied to the divergence term in the continuity equation, and the longitudinal pressure gradient. Eliminating $\hat{u}$ and $\hat{v}$ in the foregoing equations gives the discrete analog of the meridional structure equation for $\hat{\phi}$

$$C^2 \left[\frac{\mu}{a \cos \varphi_j} \frac{\sin (\mu\Delta\lambda/2)}{(\mu\Delta\lambda/2)} S_j(\mu) \right]^2 \hat{\phi}_j +$$

$$\frac{C^2}{(a\Delta\varphi)^2} \left[(\hat{\phi}_j - \hat{\phi}_{j-1}) \frac{\cos \varphi_{j-1/2}}{\cos \varphi_j} - (\hat{\phi}_{j+1} - \hat{\phi}_j) \frac{\cos \varphi_{j+1/2}}{\cos \varphi_j} \right] = \sigma^2 \hat{\phi}_j \tag{7-128}$$

where $C^2 = gH$. For a given wave number μ with the boundary condition, $\hat{\phi} = 0$, at the poles, the possible values of σ^2 are the obtainable eigenvalues of the matrix equation (7-128) for all j's between the poles. When μ is large, the maximum eigenvalue is nearly the maximum diagonal component, which is approximately the maximum value of the coefficient of $\hat{\phi}_j$ in (7-128). Thus the maximum value of σ for a given latitude is

$$\sigma_{\max} \doteq \frac{2C}{a\Delta\lambda} \frac{S_j(\mu)}{(\cos \varphi_j)_{\min}} \sin \left(\frac{\mu\Delta\lambda}{2} \right) \tag{7-129}$$

The computational stability condition is of the form [see Section 5.6.6]

$$|\sigma| \Delta t \leq \varepsilon \tag{7-130}$$

where ε is a constant (e.g., $\varepsilon = 1$ for the leapfrog scheme). Now take $S_j = 1$, corresponding to no smoothing for the present, then the stability condition (7-130) with the use of (7-129) becomes

$$\frac{C\Delta t}{a\Delta\lambda} \leq \frac{\varepsilon}{2} (\cos \varphi_j) \tag{7-131}$$

Here $\sin(\mu\Delta\lambda/2)$ has been taken to be one to insure stability for all wave numbers. Since $\cos \varphi_j$ is small near the poles, Δt would have to be very small to maintain stability.

Arakawa's method, which permits a larger Δt, smooths the longitudinal pressure gradient in the momentum equation. If the amplitudes of these derivatives are reduced according to each wave number by the factor

$$S_j(\mu) = \frac{a\Delta\lambda \cos \varphi_j}{d \sin(\mu\Delta\lambda/2)} \tag{7-132}$$

where d is a specified constant length, then (7-128) becomes

$$\frac{C^2}{d^2} \hat{\phi}_j + \frac{C^2}{(a\Delta\varphi)^2} \left[(\hat{\phi}_j - \hat{\phi}_{j-1}) \frac{\cos \varphi_{j-1/2}}{\cos \varphi_j} - (\hat{\phi}_{j+1} - \hat{\phi}_j) \frac{\cos \varphi_{j+1/2}}{\cos \varphi_j} \right] = \sigma^2 \hat{\phi}_j \tag{7-133}$$

In this form the dependence on cos φ_j is eliminated in the first term and the CFL stability criterion depends on the constant d. If d is taken to be $a\Delta\varphi$, S_j in (7-132) becomes

$$S_j(\mu) = \frac{\Delta\lambda \cos \varphi_j}{\Delta\varphi \sin(\mu\Delta\lambda/2)} \tag{7-134}$$

The smoothing need be performed only at the higher latitudes where cos φ_j becomes small. Thus (7-132) is utilized only when $S_j(\mu) < 1$, otherwise $S_j(\mu)$ is taken to be 1. To apply the smoothing operator, the zonal pressure gradient and zonal mass flux are expanded into a Fourier series around each latitude circle φ_j. Then the amplitude of each wave component is reduced by the factor $S_j(\mu)$. In practice the Fourier decomposition may be used at the highest several latitudes and a simpler smoother is applied at lower latitudes to save computer time.

As contrasted with some of the other schemes, the Arakawa's technique does not smooth or truncate Fourier expansions of the fields of the meteorological variables but rather, their gradients. On the other hand, the truncation method eliminates those waves at each latitude φ_j, which would result in computational instability as the pole is approached. In this case $S_j(\mu)$ may be treated as a Kronecker delta and applied to the Fourier expansion of the relevant meteorological variables at each latitude φ_j. When a given wave number μ gives a frequency σ in (7-129) that would lead to computational instability, the wave is dropped from the series. The remaining Fourier components are reassembled to form the field. As a result there is increasing smoothing (elimination of short waves) as the pole is approached, but it must be remembered that with the fixed $\Delta\lambda$, the waves eliminated are of very short wave length in the higher latitudes.

While the two schemes differ in principle, one truncating the series, the other longitudinal smoothing of the pressure gradient and horizontal divergence, there appears to be no great difference in the results. These methods are not completely satisfactory and further research is needed in this area.

7-7 FINE MESH MODELING

The smallest wavelength resolvable on any grid is twice the grid size, and short wavelengths ($< 6d$) are poorly handled as discussed in Chapter 5. Large-scale operational models, covering a hemisphere or the entire globe, have a grid distance of the order of several hundred kilometers. As a consequence, to be reasonably well-handled by a finite difference model, the wavelength of a disturbance should be roughly eight gridlengths (i.e., about 2000 km or more). Over much of the globe data are relatively sparse and probably do not warrant a smaller grid size. However, over the populated continental areas data are much more dense and a reduced grid size can resolve smaller disturbances or features and lessen truncation errors in phase speed prediction. Also a better representation of nonlinear transfers is achieved with a shorter gridlength because of less aliasing, which holds regardless of data density, and less diffusion is needed to control small-scale noise. Where large-scale forcing is present, a fine mesh grid may simulate the generation of fronts through nonlinear transfer of energy. If some kind of forcing is present, such as orography, a small gridlength can resolve smaller scales of motion not representable with a coarser grid. Of course, a price is paid in additional computing time with a smaller gridlength. As shown in Chapter 5 halving the horizontal grid distance over a given domain increases the computation by a factor of 8. Consequently, it may be impractical to decrease the gridlength over the entire globe or even a hemisphere. An alternative is to superimpose a fine mesh (FM) over one or more limited areas of the larger coarse mesh (CM). This introduces the problem of providing for boundary conditions on the periphery of the fine mesh during the course of the integration period, unless the increased resolution is effected in some sort of continuous fashion, for example, in a finite element model by smoothly decreasing the size of the elements.

7-7-1 One-Way Influence

If there were no coarse mesh, the boundary values would be held constant and the fine mesh would have to be chosen large enough to avoid contamination of the forecasts by the propagation of errors inward from the boundaries that would adversely affect the interior area of interest during the period of the forecast. With an FM nested within the CM the simplest procedure is simply to interpolate in an appropriate fashion from the predicted CM variables to the FM boundaries at each time step of the CM and carry out the prediction on the FM with these boundary values. The CM points falling in the interior of the FM are ignored in the FM calculations and the FM calculations have no influence on the CM prediction, which is entirely independent of the FM and is normally completed prior to beginning the FM forecast. Because of the different gridlength in the two meshes the truncation errors are different and smaller in the FM. As a consequence, troughs, ridges, and the like, move with different speeds in the two meshes, especially the shorter scales where the CM resolution is poor. As a result, discontinuities or distortions tend to develop between the two forecasts along the boundaries of the FM. Despite these problems associated with the boundaries, such models have produced useful forecasts in the interior of the fine-mesh region. Implicit in the one-way influence approach is the assumption that the small-scale phenomena have no significant influence on the larger-scale system treated in the coarse mesh, in particular, on the boundary conditions furnished the FM model as well as outside the fine mesh area. Of course, this is not generally true since there is a two-way exchange between scales not just in one way. For example, baroclinic disturbances may feed the zonal flow, and tropical cyclones significantly affect the surrounding large-scale flow through the upward flux of heat and moisture.

7-7-2 Boundary Conditions

In any limited region the boundary values should be specified in such a manner as to make the problem well posed, that is, the solution should depend continuously on the boundary conditions so that small changes in the boundary values produce only small changes in the solution. Unfortunately, as has been shown by Sundström (1973), the usual set of "primitive" differential equations on which NWP models are based are ill posed for any specification of the boundary conditions because of the hydrostatic approximation. In addition, the finite difference formulations are frequently of higher order and create new problems by requiring extra "computational" boundary conditions. Despite these adverse circumstances, successful forecasts have been made with nested models by including viscous terms in the equations to dampen unwanted small-scale perturbations and by smoothing the predictions near the boundaries where the gravity-wave noise arises. Shapiro (1977) has summarized the results of various attempts to establish acceptable boundary specifications for prediction systems.

Elvius and Sundström (1973) recommended that boundary conditions for a limited area be specified in such a way that gravity waves are controlled, rather than how well the quasi-geostrophic waves are handled. They proposed that the boundary conditions required by the corresponding linearized differential equations be specified *a priori* and the computational boundary conditions arising from higher-order difference equations be obtained by interpolation and/or extrapolation from the interior. For the barotropic system over a closed region and also for the open region where flow is permitted through the boundaries, they propose, first, that the tangential velocity be specified at inflow boundary points. If either the normal velocity or the geopotential alone is also prescribed at the boundaries, gravity waves will be reflected back into the limited area and noisy, perhaps unstable, solutions are created. On the other hand, a proper combination of normal velocity and geopotential corresponding to the ingoing characteristic for gravity waves, $(\phi - \phi^{1/2} V_n)$, will permit gravity waves approaching the boundary from the interior to pass out of the region without reflection.

For a baroclinic system a correct set of boundary conditions, if such existed, would have to specify the normal velocity and temperature in a way that gravity waves could pass freely out of the region. Unfortunately, a multilevel model has more than one eigenvalue. Orlanski (1976) proposed that a separate radiation condition be utilized for each gravity wave component as determined from values at gridpoints near the boundary. On the other hand, Sundström recommended the application of the barotropic boundary conditions by prescribing the tangential velocity at inflow points and computing it at outflow points by an appropriate extrapolation from the interior. Also the normal velocity and temperature corresponding to the first inward external gravity mode should be prescribed everywhere. The combination corresponding to the first outward external gravity wave is calculated by extrapolation from the interior, which is approximately the barotropic parts of the normal velocity and temperature. The remaining baroclinic part of the normal velocity and temperature are specified at all boundary points. The foregoing is an overspecification and will give rise to internal gravity wave noise, but the problem is less severe and possibly can be controlled by artificial viscosity.

Miyakoda and Rosati (1977) used the radiation conditions, $\partial\phi/\partial t + c\partial\phi/\partial n = 0$, to calculate the boundary values that would eliminate or reduce the noise from false reflection of waves at the boundaries. At an eastern boundary, for example, the estimate of c is first obtained from radiation condition as follows:

$$(\phi^{n}_{J-1} - \phi^{n-2}_{J-1})/2\Delta t = -c\,[\tfrac{1}{2}(\phi^{n}_{J-1} + \phi^{n-2}_{J-1}) - \phi^{n-1}_{J-2}]/\Delta x \qquad (7\text{-}135)$$

With this value of c, the foregoing difference equation is used again, but with the space and time indices increased by 1, which leads to the boundary value, ϕ^{n+1}_{J}, for *outward* propagation ($c > 0$); that is,

$$\phi^{n+1}_{J} = [(1 - c\Delta t/\Delta x)/(1 + c\Delta t/\Delta x)]\,\phi^{n-1}_{J} + [(2c\Delta t/\Delta x)/(1 + c\Delta t/\Delta x)]\,\phi^{n}_{J-1} \qquad (7\text{-}136)$$

This formula is applied when $0 \leq c\Delta t/\Delta x \leq 1$. When $c\Delta t/\Delta x > 1$, which can result in instability, c is set equal to $\Delta x/\Delta t$. But when $c < 0$, corresponding to *inward* propagation, the coarse mesh solutions are prescribed at the boundary. A propagation speed is computed separately for other variables and every FM boundary gridpoint; however adjustments are made to maintain hydrostatic equilibrium. Note that the boundary value determinations are based on propagation speeds, not merely inflow or outflow. Although the method was moderately successful with p-coordinates, some adverse effects developed with mountains along the interface. Error contamination is rapid if the interface values are inaccurate.

Williamson and Browning (1973) used a global CM model to specify the velocity components and temperature at the inflow points of a nested FM model, and the outflow boundary points were determined from interior values based on CM trajectories that end at the boundary points at the prescribed time. The predominant two-gridlength noise appearing near the boundaries was controlled by explicit smoothing.

Perkey and Kreitzberg (1976) used an empirical weighted average for the FM boundary values, for example,

$$\phi^{(\tau)}_{j} = \phi^{\tau-1}_{j} + W_j \left.\frac{\partial\phi}{\partial\tau}\right|_{FM} \Delta t + (1 - W_j) \left.\frac{\partial\phi}{\partial t}\right|_{CM} \Delta t \qquad (7\text{-}137)$$

where $W_j = 0$, for $j = J$; $W_j = 0.4$, for $j = J - 1$

$W_j = 0.7$, for $j = J - 2$; $W_j = 0.9$, for $j = J - 3$

Thus the boundary values J are determined solely by the CM, the interior points near the boundary are determined by both the CM and FM, and four points inward the values are determined solely by the FM. If the CM is not global, and there is no coarser mesh, then $(\partial\phi/\partial t)_{\text{CM}} = 0$; and the foregoing formula provided a "sponge" to absorb impinging waves. This is usually augmented by heavy viscous damping near the boundary with a diffusion term such as $K\nabla^2$ ( ) or $K\nabla^4$ ( ), or explicit smoothing of the dependent variables.

Shapiro (1977) supplied the boundary values for a nested FM model by interpolating all prognostic variables from a CM eight-level dry, inviscid primitive equation model. Despite the overspecification, the results, after smoothing, were comparable to those with the more sophisticated methods that approximated well-posed boundary conditions. Both linear and higher-order interpolation schemes strongly damped two- and three-gridlength waves, but the linear scheme damped moderately long waves as well. Higher-order interpolation gave smoother solutions. Light smoothing was applied every 200 minutes to both the FM (every 50 time steps) and the CM (every 10 steps) models. Shapiro extended the higher-order interpolation, which restored the amplitude over linear interpolation, in order to minimize the phase errors resulting from interpolation as well. Two-point linear interpolation in one dimension is defined as

$$f_{i+r}^{(0)} = rf_{i+1} + (1 - r)f_i \qquad 0 \le r \le 1 \tag{7-138}$$

(The domain has been scaled so that $\Delta x = 1$).

If f_i is expressed in terms of Fourier components of the form $A_n \sin(nx_n + \phi_n)$ and f_{i+r} by $A_n \sin[n(x_i + \Delta x) + \phi_n]$, then the interpolated value is represented by components of the form

$$A_n^{(0)} \sin[n(x_i + r\Delta x) + \phi_n - d_n]$$

where

$$A_n^{(0)} = \left[1 - 4\,r(1 - r)\sin^2\frac{n\Delta x}{2}\right]^{1/2} A_n \tag{7-139}$$

and

$$d_n = \tan^{-1}\left\{\frac{(1 - r)\sin n\,r\Delta x - r\sin[n(1 - r)\Delta x]}{(1 - r)\cos n\,r\Delta x + r\cos[n(1 - r)\Delta x]}\right\}$$

The ratio $A_n^{(0)}/A_n = \rho_n^{(0)}$ gives the amplitude damping and d_n, the phase shift resulting from the interpolation. The inverse, $[\rho_n^{(0)}]^{-1}$, which will restore the amplitude, can be expressed as an infinite series. When applied to $f_{i+r}^{(0)}$, the result is

$$f_{i+r}^{(h)} = \left[1 + \tfrac{1}{2}(-s\delta^2) + \frac{1\cdot 3}{2\cdot 4}(-s\delta^2)^2 + \cdots + \frac{1\cdot 3 \cdots (2h-1)}{2\cdot 4 \cdots 2h}(-s\delta^2)^h\right] f_{i+r}^{(0)} \qquad (7\text{-}140)$$

where $s = r(1 - r)$ and $\delta^2 f_i = f_{i+1} - 2f_i + f_{i-1}$ and f_{i+r} is given by (7-130). The amplitude response of this interpolation operator involving $(2h + 1)$ points approaches one as h approaches infinity and is maximum for any value of h. For a finite h, the restoration of a function F_j can be expressed in the form:

$$R^{(h)}(F_j) = \sum_{h=0}^{h} \left\{ \left(\frac{s}{4}\right)^h \binom{2h}{h}^2 F_j + \left(\frac{s}{4}\right)^h \binom{2h}{h} \sum_{k=0}^{h-1} (-1)^h \binom{2h}{k} [F_{j+(h-k)} + F_{j-(h-k)}] \right\} \qquad (7\text{-}141)$$

where $\binom{n}{m} = n!/m!\,(n - m)!$, are the binomial coefficients. When F_j is taken to be $f_{i+r}^{(0)}$, then $R^{(h)}(F_j) = f_{i+r}^{(h)}$ is an interpolation operator which for any restoration level h maximizes the restoration of amplitude damped by the linear interpolation $f_{i+r}^{(0)}$.

Shapiro makes use of the fact that when $r = \tfrac{1}{2}$, there is no phase shift (see 7-139) to alter the amplification operator for the purpose of reducing the phase shift error. Applied to a nested FM area the scheme gives satisfactory results when compared to the same FM grid distance over the entire CM region. He also found that without more information over the FM area, the nested solution will not differ appreciably from a solution obtained on the CM alone.

Camerlengo and O'Brien (1979) compared several outflow boundary conditions for any variable ψ including an extrapolation method by Kreiss,

$$\psi_J^{n+1} - \psi_{J-1}^n = \psi_{J-1}^n - \psi_{J-2}^{n-1}, \qquad (7\text{-}142)$$

Orlanski's radiation boundary condition described earlier, and their modification of the Orlanski technique to several cases involving Kelvin and Rossby type waves in an ocean basis. They adapted Orlanski's method to a staggered grid and simplified the procedure somewhat by setting the phase velocity to $\Delta x/\Delta t$ at a zonal outflow boundary while keeping it zero at an inflow boundary. A similar procedure was used for $\Delta y/\Delta t$ at a meridional outflow boundary. At inflow points the value ψ_B^{n+1} is set equal to ψ_B^{n-1}, based on leapfrog time differencing and no surrounding coarse mesh.

In general Kreiss' extrapolation was unsatisfactory while both other methods gave much better results. Camerlengo and O'Brien's modified radiation condition continued to simulate the outflow of the Kelvin wave after the Orlanski procedure had broken down, but there was increasing reflection of the Rossby wave. The authors concluded that their modification gave overall improvement but does not have the long-time stability that a perfect boundary condition should have.

FM models using the various methods described here can produce better forecasts with more detail than a CM model alone; however the FM forecasts eventually degrade to the level of the CM forecasts because of imperfect boundary conditions.

7-7-3 Two-Way Interaction

In the preceding section the solution from a CM model was used to provide the boundary conditions for integration of a nested FM model. As a consequence, the CM solution affected the FM solution, but not vice versa; hence this was referred to as a *one-way influence*. In order to have a *two-way interaction,* the FM solution must influence the CM solution as well, which requires the simultaneous integration of the FM and CM models.

An obvious way to avoid artificial boundaries between a nested region of high resolution and the larger CM region is to vary the grid distance continuously between the two regions. This could be accomplished by a nonlinear coordinate, however, finite difference approximations become more complicated, particularly if uniform accuracy is to be achieved. Varying phase speed errors can cause distortion in the shape of pressure systems and erroneous nonlinear interactions. In addition, the Δt required for stability corresponds to the smallest value for the entire grid which may be wasteful.

Harrison (1973) utilized movable, interacting, doubly, and triply nested meshes in a numerical simulation of a migrating tropical storm. His procedure may be illustrated for one dimension with the help of Figure 7-13, predictions at the CM points 4 and 10 utilize FM predicted values at FM points 6 and 8, respectively. On the other hand, CM points 4 and 10 provide FM boundary values that are used for predictions at the FM interior points 5 and 9. For example, with the simple advective equation, $\partial u/\partial t + U\partial u/\partial x$, the central space difference equations for CM point 4 and FM point 5 are:

$$\frac{\partial u_4}{\partial t} = -\frac{U}{2d}(u_6 - u_3); \quad \frac{\partial u_5}{\partial t} = -\frac{U}{d}(u_6 - u_4) \qquad (7\text{-}143)$$

The procedure consists of first making a prediction for the entire region using the CM points (dots) for the CM time step, say, Δt, for $n\Delta t$ to $(n +$

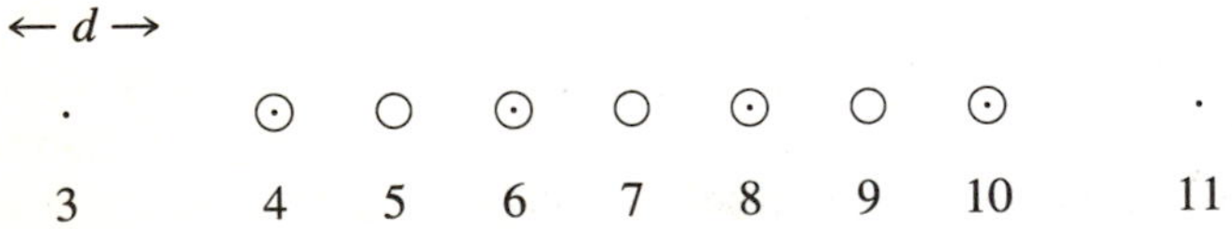

Figure 7-13 *FM* grid (circles) superimposed on a *CM* grid (dots).

1)Δt. Then a prediction to $(n + 1)\Delta t$ on the FM using the smaller time steps ($\Delta t/2$ in this example) appropriate to the FM gridlength. Since the value of u_4 at $(n + \frac{1}{2})\Delta t$ is needed for the prediction at FM point 5, u_4 is linearly interpolated between the CM values at $n\Delta t$ and $(n + 1)\Delta t$. The earlier CM predictions at points 6 and 8 are replaced with FM-predicted values. Thus the FM predictions affect CM predictions, as well as vice versa, and the two grids interact.

Integration over a two-dimensional grid requires interpolation in space, as well as time, along the boundary of the FM, which then consists of CM prediction points plus intermediate FM boundary points along which the CM variables must be interpolated to provide boundary values for predictions on the FM grid (student exercise). After the FM forecast is brought up to time $(n + 1)\Delta t$, another CM forecast step is taken and so forth. This procedure is stable but some noise is generated near the FM boundary; however it can be removed by including a weak diffusion term. The fluxes across the boundaries behave satisfactorily, although a more complex differencing scheme can be used to insure conservation by flux divergence terms.

Phillips and Shukla (1973) considered the two strategies of one-way action using a history tape from CM integrations for FM boundary conditions and a two-way interaction similar to the one just described. By a heuristic argument based on the method of characteristics, they inferred that the two-way interaction procedure would give a more faithful reproduction of the transmission of information into and out of the fine-mesh region. This was verified by integrations with the shallow-water equations, which also showed that the Lax-Wendroff two-step scheme gave a somewhat larger error at 12 hr than did the leapfrog scheme, but the reverse was true at 24 and 48 hr.

Sobel (1976) showed that a two-way interaction scheme gave better results than one-way in a case where a large-scale wave exists in the CM and the FM contains a long and a short wave. Jones (1977) used a triply nested interacting grid with spacings of 10, 30, and 90 km to simulate a hurricane. The treatment of the boundaries permits mass to flow freely at the interfaces and the spiral bands extended smoothly across the interfaces. In real forecasting, obtaining the data to initialize a nested model will be a problem.

7-7-4 Initialization on a Bounded Region

The previous sections have dealt primarily with the proper specification of boundary conditions on a limited area in order to make a problem well posed. Although the discussion of objective analysis and initialization is to be covered in more detail in Chapter 11, it may be appropriate to discuss some aspects of analysis over a limited area here.

If only the geopotential is known over a grid of points, a good approximation to the rotational wind component may be obtained through the solution of a form of the balance equation (7-20 or 7-28) for the streamfunction, provided the equation is elliptic and that either ψ or its normal derivative is known on the boundary. If the balance equation is not elliptic in some parts of the region, the geopotential field must be altered in order to insure ellipticity, but with an obvious sacrifice. The boundary value of ψ around a limited area may be approximated geostrophically outside the tropics, but other estimates are also feasible.

On the other hand given the wind field, **V**, the geopotential field ϕ may be obtained by solving a balance equation with the Neumann or Dirichlet boundary conditions, assuming the stream function can be determined. The latter may be obtained from the known (observed) wind field by calculating the vorticity ζ_0 from the known wind field and then solving the Poisson equation

$$\nabla^2 \psi = \mathbf{k} \cdot \nabla \times \mathbf{V}_0 = \zeta_0 \tag{7-144}$$

with proper boundary conditions. Similarly if there is information in the wind field about the large-scale divergence, the potential function χ for the divergent wind is obtainable from

$$\nabla^2 \chi = \nabla \cdot \mathbf{V}_0 = D_0 \tag{7-145}$$

However, it is generally believed that large-scale divergence is difficult to determine because of the "noise" from errors in the observations and small-scale phenomena.

In order to explore the boundary conditions further, let **t** and **n** be unit vectors tangent and normal to the boundaries. Then the tangential and normal wind components at the boundary, say V_{t0} and V_{n0} may be expressed in terms of ψ and χ as follows:

$$V_{t0} = \mathbf{t} \cdot (\mathbf{k} \times \nabla\psi + \nabla\chi) = \frac{\partial\psi}{\partial n} + \frac{\partial\chi}{\partial s} \tag{7-146}$$

$$V_{n0} = n \cdot (\mathbf{k} \times \nabla\psi + \nabla\chi) = \frac{\partial\psi}{\partial s} + \frac{\partial\chi}{\partial n} \tag{7-147}$$

It is not evident how $\partial\psi/\partial n$ and $\partial\chi/\partial n$ can be calculated from these equations in order to provide Neumann conditions for the solution of (7-146) and (7-147). Since the divergent wind component is generally an order of magnitude less than the rotational wind component, χ may be set to zero everywhere as a first approximation, or simply place $\partial\chi/\partial n = 0$ along the boundary. In this case (7-140) may be integrated around the boundary of the region to give $\psi(s)$, that is,

$$\psi(s) - \psi(s_0) = \int_{s_0}^{s} \frac{\partial\psi}{\partial s}\, ds = -\int V_{n0}\, ds \tag{7-148}$$

However, because of divergent wind components in the observed winds, whether actual or because of errors, the cyclic integral around the region will not vanish in general (i.e., $\oint V_{n0}\,ds \neq 0$), and ψ would be discontinuous. To avoid the discontinuity, the constant $L^{-1} \oint V_{n0}\,ds$, where L is the length of the curve encircling the region, may be added to the right side giving

$$\frac{\partial \psi}{\partial s} = -V_n^{(0)} + L^{-1} \oint V_{n0}\,ds \tag{7-149}$$

Upon integration from s_0 to s_1, the expression for $\psi(s_1)$

$$\psi(s_1) - \psi(s_0) = -\int_{s0}^{s} V_{n0}\,ds + \frac{(s_1 - s_0)}{L} \oint V_{n0}\,ds \tag{7-150}$$

but cyclic integration of (7-149) will clearly give zero in the right side insuring that ψ is continuous. After solving for ψ over the region $\partial\psi/\partial n$ is available and presumably one could integrate (7-146) to determine χ along the boundary and then solve (7-145) for χ. Next one could return to (7-147) with the value of $\partial\chi/\partial n$ and recalculate ψ on the boundary, etc. The iteration scheme might be expected to give increasingly better values of ψ and χ, however there is no guarantee of convergence. In any event, it would be a rather lengthy procedure and it would seem better to simply take a somewhat larger region than needed and then disregard a few outside rows of gridpoints where inaccurate boundary values would produce the greatest errors.

The preceding discussion concerned the use of the balance equation for determining ϕ and involved the prior determination of ψ. This step is not necessary to get ϕ. In fact, Saha and Suryanarayana (1971) got somewhat better results by using winds directly in the divergence equation after neglecting the local time derivative and terms involving w, as follows:

$$\nabla^2\phi = \eta\zeta + \mathbf{k} \cdot \nabla\eta \times \mathbf{V} - \nabla^2 (\mathbf{V}^2/2) \tag{7-151}$$

7-8 BAROCLINIC SPECTRAL MODELS

Baroclinic spectral transform models have been successfully applied by Machenhauer and Daley (1972), Hoskins and Simmons (1975), Gordon and Stern (1974), Daley et al. (1976) and Bourke et al. (1977). A semi-implicit baroclinic spectral model will be developed in this section, but the horizontal transform method will not be presented explicitly since the procedure is the same as was presented in Section 6-7 for the shallow-water equations. This particular development follows Hoskins and Simmons (1975) and Lubeck, Rosmond, and Williams (1977).

The vorticity and divergence equations in sigma coordinates (see Section 1-9-1) can be written:

$$\frac{\partial \zeta}{\partial t} = -\nabla \cdot (\zeta + f)\,\mathbf{V} - \mathbf{k} \cdot \nabla \times (RT\nabla q + \dot{\sigma}\partial \mathbf{V}/\partial \sigma) \tag{7-152}$$

$$\frac{\partial D}{\partial t} = \mathbf{k} \cdot \nabla \times (\zeta + f)\,\mathbf{V} - \nabla \cdot (RT\nabla q + \dot{\sigma}\partial \mathbf{V}/\partial \sigma) - \nabla^2 (\phi + \mathbf{V} \cdot \mathbf{V}/2) \tag{7-153}$$

where $q = \ell n\, p_s$. The adiabatic first law of thermodynamics is

$$\frac{\partial T}{\partial t} = -\mathbf{V} \cdot \nabla T - \sigma^{\kappa}\dot{\sigma}\frac{\partial}{\partial \sigma}(T\sigma^{-\kappa}) + \kappa T\,(\partial q/\partial t + \mathbf{V} \cdot \nabla q) \tag{7-154}$$

and the continuity equation is

$$\frac{\partial q}{\partial t} = -D - \mathbf{V} \cdot \nabla q - \partial \dot{\sigma}/\partial \sigma \tag{7-155}$$

The first law of thermodynamics (7-154) is written in this form for convenience in applying the vertical differencing introduced by Arakawa and Lamb (1977). The hydrostatic equation is

$$\frac{\partial \phi}{\partial \sigma^{\kappa}} = -\frac{R}{\kappa}T\sigma^{-\kappa} \qquad \text{or} \qquad \frac{\partial \phi}{\partial \sigma} = -\frac{RT}{\sigma} \tag{7-156}$$

The velocity components are obtained from the vorticity and divergence by introducing a streamfunction and a velocity potential as described in Section 6-7.

An equation for $\dot{\sigma}$ is obtained by first integrating (7-155) with respect to σ, and applying the boundary conditions $\dot{\sigma}(0) = \dot{\sigma}(1) = 0$, which gives

$$\frac{\partial q}{\partial t} = -(\overline{D} + \overline{G}) \tag{7-157}$$

where $\overline{(\quad)} = \int_0^1 (\quad)\, d\sigma$ and $G = \mathbf{V} \cdot \nabla q$. Now substitute $\partial q/\partial t$ from (7-157) into (7-155) and integrate from 0 to σ, which leads to

$$\dot{\sigma} = (\overline{D} + \overline{G})\sigma - \int_0^{\sigma} (D + G)\, d\sigma \tag{7-158}$$

In order to apply semi-implicit differencing it is necessary to divide the temperature as follows:

$$T = T^*(\sigma) + T'(\sigma,\lambda,\varphi,t) \tag{7-159}$$

where T^* represents an appropriately averaged temperature. The equations can be conveniently written in spherical coordinates by defining the following operator:

$$\alpha(a,b) \equiv \frac{1}{\cos^2\varphi}\frac{\partial a}{\partial \lambda} + \frac{1}{\cos\varphi}\frac{\partial b}{\partial \varphi} \tag{7-160}$$

With the use of (7-159) and (7-160) the basic equations can be written as follows:

$$\frac{\partial \zeta}{\partial t} = -\alpha(A,B) \tag{7-161}$$

$$\frac{\partial D}{\partial t} = \alpha(B, -A) - \nabla^2(a^2 E + \phi + RT^* q) \tag{7-162}$$

$$\frac{\partial T'}{\partial t} = -\alpha(UT', VT') + DT' - \sigma^\kappa \dot{\sigma}\frac{\partial}{\partial \sigma}(T\sigma^{-\kappa}) + \kappa T(G - \overline{G} - \overline{D}) \tag{7-163}$$

$$\frac{\partial q}{\partial t} = -(\overline{D} + \overline{G}) \tag{7-164}$$

where

$$A = (\zeta + f)\,U + \dot{\sigma}\partial V/\partial\sigma + (RT'/a^2)\cos\varphi\,\frac{\partial q}{\partial \varphi}$$

$$B = (\zeta + f)\,V - \dot{\sigma}\partial U/\partial\sigma - (RT'/a^2)\partial q/\partial\lambda$$

$$G = \frac{U}{\cos^2\varphi}\frac{\partial q}{\partial \lambda} + \frac{V}{\cos\varphi}\frac{\partial q}{\partial \varphi}$$

$$E = (U^2 + V^2)/2\cos^2\varphi$$

$$\mathbf{V} = (U/\cos\varphi)\,\mathbf{i} + (V/\cos\varphi)\mathbf{j}$$

The variables are staggered in σ so that ζ, D, U, V, and T are carried at odd values of k where $\sigma = \hat{\sigma}_k$ and and $\dot{\sigma}$ is carried at even values of k where $\sigma = \sigma_k$. This model uses a form of the vertical differencing that was derived by Arakawa and Lamb (1977), and which was discussed in Section 7-2. This version of the vertical differencing conserves total energy and the first and second powers of the potential temperature:

$$\left(\dot{\sigma}\frac{\partial X}{\partial \sigma}\right)_k = \frac{1}{2\Delta\sigma_k}[(X_{k+2} - X_k)\,\dot{\sigma}_{k+1} + (X_k - X_{k-2})\,\dot{\sigma}_{k-1}] \tag{7-165}$$

where $\Delta\sigma_k = (\sigma_{k+1} - \sigma_{k-1})/2$. Following Arakawa and Lamb (1977), the hydrostatic equation (7-156) is differenced as follows:

$$\phi_{k+1} - \phi_k = -\frac{c_p}{2}\{[1 - (\hat{\sigma}_k/\hat{\sigma}_{k+1})^\kappa]\,T_{k+1} + [(\hat{\sigma}_{k+1}/\hat{\sigma}_k)^\kappa - 1]\,T_k\} \tag{7-166}$$

A further condition on ϕ can be obtained by integrating (7-156) by parts from $\sigma = 0$ to $\sigma = 1$, which gives:

$$\int_0^1 \phi \, d\sigma - \phi_S = R \int_0^1 T d\sigma \tag{7-167}$$

The finite difference form of this equation is

$$\sum_k \phi_k(\Delta\sigma_k) - \phi_S = R \sum_k T_k(\Delta\sigma_k) \tag{7-168}$$

where this summation is over odd k and ϕ_S is a surface value.

Equations 7-166 and 7-168 can be combined to give the matrix equation:

$$\boldsymbol{\phi} = C\,\mathbf{T} + \boldsymbol{\phi}_S \tag{7-169}$$

where C is a square matrix and the other quantities are now column vectors. The finite difference form of the surface pressure tendency equation (7-164) is

$$\frac{\partial q}{\partial t} = -\sum_k (G_k + D_k)\,\Delta\sigma_k \tag{7-170}$$

which can be written in matrix form as

$$\frac{\partial q}{\partial t} = -\,\mathbf{N}^T(\mathbf{G} + \mathbf{D}) \tag{7-171}$$

where $\mathbf{N}^T$ is the transpose of a constant column vector. Similarly the finite difference form of (7-158) can be written

$$\dot{\boldsymbol{\sigma}} = Z(\mathbf{G} + \mathbf{D}) \tag{7-172}$$

The next-to-the-last term in the first law of thermodynamics (7-163) is differenced as follows:

$$\sigma^{\kappa}\dot{\sigma}\frac{\partial}{\partial\sigma}(T\sigma^{-\kappa}) = \frac{1}{2\Delta\sigma_k}\left\{\dot{\sigma}_{k+1}\left[T_{k+1}\left(\frac{\hat{\sigma}_k}{\hat{\sigma}_{k+1}}\right)^{\kappa} - T_k\right] + \dot{\sigma}_k\left[T_k - T_{k-1}\left(\frac{\hat{\sigma}_k}{\hat{\sigma}_{k-1}}\right)^{\kappa}\right]\right\} \tag{7-173}$$

For the purpose of the semi-implicit formulation, the temperature is separated according to (7-159). The matrix Y is defined such that its elements are obtained from

$$\frac{T^*_{k+1}(\hat{\sigma}_k/\hat{\sigma}_{k+1})^{\kappa} - T^*_k}{2(\Delta\sigma)_k}\dot{\sigma}_{k+1} + \frac{T^*_k - (\hat{\sigma}_k/\hat{\sigma}_{k-1})^{\kappa}\,T^*_{k-1}}{2(\Delta\sigma)_k}\dot{\sigma}_k \tag{7-174}$$

The vertically averaged divergence can be written $\overline{D} = \mathbf{N}^T \mathbf{D}$ and with the use of (7-172), the vector form of the term can be written:

$$\mathbf{S} = Q\,\mathbf{D} + \mathbf{R}$$

where $Q = YZ + \kappa\, \mathbf{T}^*\mathbf{N}^T$, $\mathbf{R}$ contains terms in T' or terms that affect gravity wave propagation and the elements of $\mathbf{S}$ are $[\sigma^\kappa\, \sigma\, \partial(T\sigma^{-\kappa})/\partial\sigma]_k$.

Equations 7-162, 7-163, 7-172, and 7-169 may now be written:

$$\frac{\partial}{\partial t}\mathbf{D} + \nabla^2(\boldsymbol{\phi}' + R\mathbf{T}^* q) = \mathbf{F}_D \tag{7-175}$$

$$\frac{\partial \mathbf{T}}{\partial t} - Q\mathbf{D} = \mathbf{F}_T \tag{7-176}$$

$$\frac{\partial q}{\partial t} + \mathbf{N}^T\,\mathbf{D} = -\,\mathbf{N}^T\,\mathbf{G} \tag{7-177}$$

$$\boldsymbol{\phi}' = C\mathbf{T} \tag{7-178}$$

where $\phi' = \phi - \phi_S$ and $\mathbf{F}_D$ and $\mathbf{F}_T$ represent terms that have not been explicitly separated out.

The time differencing now follows the semi-implicit differencing, which is given in Section 5-7-4 for the shallow-water equations. When the terms on the left of (7-175) to (7-177) are evaluated implicitly, and (7-178) is used, the difference equations become:

$$\mathbf{D}_{k+1} + \Delta t\nabla^2(C\mathbf{T}_{n+1} + R\mathbf{T}^*\, q_{n+1}) = \mathbf{D}_{n-1} - \tag{7-179}$$

$$\Delta t\nabla^2(C\mathbf{T}_{n-1} + R\mathbf{T}^*\, q_{n-1}) + 2\Delta t(\mathbf{F}_D)_n$$

$$\mathbf{T}_{n+1} - \Delta t Q\mathbf{D}_{n+1} = \mathbf{T}_{n-1} - \Delta t Q\mathbf{D}_{n-1} - 2\Delta t(\mathbf{F}_T)_n \tag{7-180}$$

$$q_{n+1} + \Delta t\,\mathbf{N}^T\,\mathbf{D} = q_{n-1} - \Delta t\,\mathbf{N}^T\,\mathbf{D}_{n-1} - 2\Delta t\,\mathbf{N}^T\,\mathbf{G}_n \tag{7-181}$$

Now the following equation for $\mathbf{D}_{n+1}$ can be found by substituting (7-180) and (7-181) into (7-179):

$$B\,\mathbf{D}_{n+1} = B\,\mathbf{D}_{n-1} + 2\Delta t(\mathbf{F}_D)_n -$$

$$2\Delta t\,\nabla^2(C\mathbf{T}_{n-1} + R\mathbf{T}^* q_{n-1} + C(\mathbf{F}_T)_n - R\mathbf{T}^*\,\mathbf{N}^T\mathbf{G}_n) \tag{7-182}$$

where the matrix operator B is

$$B \equiv \Delta t^2(CQ - R T^*\mathbf{N}^T)\nabla^2 + I \tag{7-183}$$

and I is the identity matrix. In the spectral method the Laplacian in (7-183) is replaced by a constant for each spherical harmonic (see Equation 6-43). Equation 7-182 can then be solved for by inverting B. This can be done by Gauss elimination of or by expanding $\mathbf{D}_{n+1}$ in terms of the eigenvectors of (7-183). Equations 7-180 and 7-181 can be solved for $\mathbf{T}_{n+1}$ and q_{n+1}, respectively, and ζ_{n+1} can be obtained by writing (7-161) in leapfrog form. It has been found that the semi-implicit method takes less than 5 percent more computer time, per time step, than the explicit formulation and a Δt four to six times larger can be used with the semi-implicit equations. The efficient use of the semi-implicit method helps to make spectral models competitive with finite difference models.

The semi-implicit method can be applied to multilevel finite difference models also. The development is similar to that given in this section, except that (7-175) is obtained by spatially differencing the finite difference primitive equations. Equation 7-182 must be solved with a three-dimensional inversion method or by breaking down the vertical structure into eigenfunctions. In the latter case a two-dimensional Poisson equation must be solved for each eigenfunction.

7-9 ISENTROPIC COORDINATE MODELS

Eliassen and Raustein (1968, 1970) integrated the primitive equations with potential temperature as the vertical coordinate with idealized initial data and real data forecasts have been made by Bleck (1974, 1977). The basic equations with potential temperature as the vertical coordinate were given in Section 1-9-2. If the motion is adiabatic ($d\theta/dt = 0$) the equation of motion may be written

$$\frac{\partial \mathbf{V}}{\partial t} + \mathbf{V} \cdot \nabla_\theta \mathbf{V} = -\nabla_\theta M - f\mathbf{k} \times \mathbf{V} \tag{7-184}$$

where $M = c_p T + \phi$ is the Montgomery streamfunction. The hydrostatic equation is

$$\frac{\partial M}{\partial \theta} = \Pi \tag{7-185}$$

where $\Pi = c_p(p/p_0)^\kappa$ is the Exner function. The continuity equation with ($d\theta/dt = 0$) can be written from Equation (1-74)

$$\frac{\partial}{\partial t}\left(\frac{\partial p}{\partial \theta}\right) = -\nabla_\theta \cdot \left(\frac{\partial p}{\partial \theta}\mathbf{V}\right) \tag{7-186}$$

The upper boundary is assumed a coordinate surface by setting θ constant at $p = 0$. When (7-186) is finite differenced the predicted Δp can be stepped downward from the top to give p at any level. A prediction equation is also required for $\theta = \theta_S$ at the lower boundary. Since the pressure is then known as a function of θ, (7-185) can be integrated from the lower boundary upward and M can be calculated at the surface. However, there is a problem at the earth's surface, since θ_S has a large variation there. In fact one or more θ surfaces may intersect the lower surface. The situation is illustrated in Figure 7-14, where the earth's surface is indicated by S. In order to compute a centered difference of $\partial\Pi/\partial x$ at the point (x_1,θ_1) it is necessary to determine the value $\Pi(x_2, \theta_1)$, which is below the earth's surface. Eliassen and Raustein (1968, 1970) developed prediction equations for the required variables at the surface, which could be used to extrapolate to the values below the surface.

The conservation of θ along the surface can be expressed as

$$\frac{\partial\theta_s}{\partial t} + \mathbf{V}_\theta \cdot \nabla\theta_s = 0 \tag{7-187}$$

This equation is used to predict the location of the lower boundary in theta coordinates. The equation of motion at the surface can be obtained by setting $\sigma = 1$ in (1-72) and by using the definition of Π which gives:

$$\frac{\partial\mathbf{V}_s}{\partial t} + \mathbf{V}_s \cdot \nabla\mathbf{V}_s = -\nabla\phi_s - \theta_s\nabla\Pi_s - f\mathbf{k} \times \mathbf{V}_s \tag{7-188}$$

Also Π_s can be predicted since (7-185) can be applied to the layer between θ_s and the next θ surface in the atmosphere. Eliassen and Raustein obtained Π_1 in Figure 7-14 by linearly extrapolating between Π_2 and Π_s, and the same method was used for the velocity components. However, Bleck (1974) and Shapiro (1975) point out that this extrapolation may become too sensitive when the earth's surface is just below θ_2. They suggest an extrapolation, which also uses Π_1 to define intermediate values $\overline{\Pi}$, $\overline{\theta}$, which are used in the extrapolation. The formulas are given by Shapiro (1975). This extrapolation is also used for the velocity components.

The numerical forecasts that have been made with these models are stable and they only require a small amount of smoothing. These isentropic models simulate upper level fronts very well [Shapiro (1975)], and they have also been

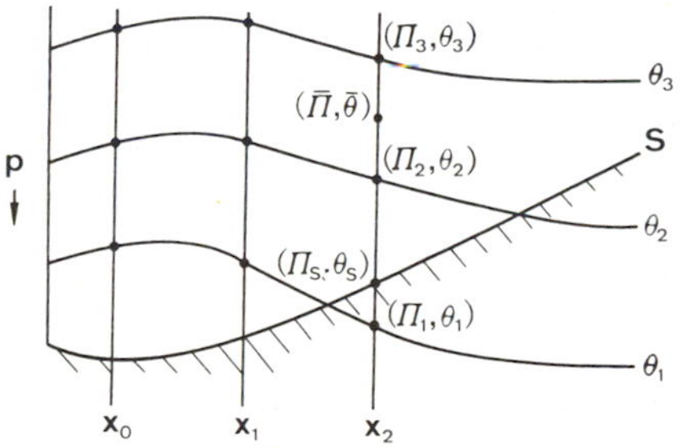

Figure 7-14 Illustration of the vertical extrapolation for the evaluation of finite differences near the surface where an isentropic surface intersects the earth's surface.

applied to cyclogenesis in the lee of a high mountain range [Bleck (1977)]. Gall (1972) has formulated a model that forecasts moisture and includes latent heating. This requires the addition of vertical advection terms in the equations. The main problems with isentropic models occur near the lower boundary where extrapolations cause some noise and where the lapse rate may be adiabatic in the boundary layer. Bleck (1978) compared several hybrid coordinate systems that are isentropic in the upper atmosphere and similar to a sigma system near the earth's surface, and found that some of the methods were promising.

7-10 UPPER BOUNDARY CONDITIONS

The exact upper boundary condition in pressure coordinates is $\omega = 0$ at $p = 0$. However, Lindzen et al. (1968) have shown that when this condition is imposed in a finite difference model with a constant Δp there may be false reflection of energy that also spuriously affects the fields at lower levels. The largest errors can be expected with the long waves which, as was shown in Section 4-11, propagate energy more easily to upper levels in the atmosphere.

Kirkwood and Derome (1977) examined the boundary condition $\omega = 0$ at $p = 0$ in a linearized finite difference midlatitude model of forced stationary planetary waves. The perturbations were assumed to be quasi-geostrophic and they were superimposed on an isothermal atmosphere with a vertical profile of the mean zonal wind. A reference model was developed with $\ell n p$ as the vertical coordinate. The model had 200 levels and a radiation condition at the top, which prevented the reflection of energy from the upper computational level. The finite difference model in p coordinates used a constant Δp and the boundary condition $\omega = 0$ at $p = 0$. In the first experiment with a constant $\overline{u} = 20$ m sec^{-1} the reference solution produced a vertically propagating wave in agreement with (4-97). However, the finite difference solutions with $\omega = 0$ at $p = 0$ were very poor, even with 101 levels, because energy was spuriously reflected by the upper boundary condition. When $\overline{u}$ was increased so that the correct solution became trapped, the high-resolution model (101 levels) was very accurate, but the lower-resolution model (11 levels) still had a 50 percent error in amplitude. The addition of Newtonian cooling improved the $\omega = 0$ at $p = 0$ numerical models because it damped the waves before the false reflection occurred. Although the model treated by Kirkwood and Derome (1977) was very simple, it can be expected that similar errors would occur in a model with more complicated vertical propagation.

Kirkwood and Derome (1977) pointed out that if a numerical prediction model produces a steady-state long-wave solution that is very different from the real atmosphere's solution, then a rapidly moving Rossby wave will be excited. The resulting large errors in the long waves will also affect cyclone movement and formation. In order to reduce this type of error, it is necessary to have adequate vertical resolution for the long waves in the stratosphere, and some mechanism to prevent false reflection of energy from the top of the model. As an approximation to radiative transfer, Newtonian cooling will help, and, according to Dickinson (1969), it should be used to simulate observed wave behavior. Tokioka (1978) and Arakawa and Lamb (1977) have examined vertical differencing schemes with respect to vertical energy propagation. They conclude that in a pressure coordinate model, the levels should be spaced in equal increments of $\ell n p$. This corresponds to nearly equal increments in height, which is reasonable since the vertically propagating waves have a nearly constant vertical wavelength. Also following Arakawa and Lamb (1977) it is probably better to shift from σ-coordinates to p-coordinates at the top of the troposphere. In tropical forecast models that include the stratosphere care must be taken to resolve vertical propagation properly.

7-11 MOUNTAIN EFFECTS

Mountain ranges and other surface topographic features have a large effect on the weather in surrounding regions. In fact all scales of motion including the planetary scale are affected by surface topography. However, mountain effects are not well treated by numerical models because of the lower boundary condition itself and the required smoothing of surface topography.

The kinematic lower boundary condition for ω, which was developed in Sections 3-4 and 7-1-1, cannot be applied at mean sea-level pressure if the mountains are very high. If the boundary condition is applied at the correct pressure, noise may be generated by the "interior" boundary condition. The sigma system (Section 1-9-1), which was developed by Phillips (1957), avoids this problem since the lower boundary becomes a coordinate surface. However the pressure gradient force

$$\nabla_p \phi = \nabla_\sigma \phi + \frac{RT}{p_s} \nabla p_s \tag{7-189}$$

is more complicated. In fact, near high mountains the two terms on the right are very large and the pressure gradient is a small difference between two large terms. Kurihara (1968) treated this problem by interpolating back to isobaric surfaces and then computing $\nabla_p \phi$ directly. Corby, Gilchrist, and Newson (1972) suggest a finite difference form of (7-189), which contains horizontal averages. Phillips (1974) separated ϕ and T into standard values as functions of p and departures, and p_s was divided into a constant value as a function of elevation and a time-dependent portion. This formulation greatly reduces the magnitude of the terms on the right side of (7-189) and hence the error, and they cancel exactly for the standard atmosphere, for which ϕ is constant on a p surface. Experience has shown that otherwise properly formulated models will bring themselves into adjustment near the mountains after a period of integration. Hence it is important that the initialization procedure take into account the actual differencing scheme that is used.

Since surface topography has many features with smaller scales than the grid size it is necessary to smooth topographic heights before use in a model. A linear-smoothing operator applied to a typical mountain range will reduce the maximum heights and increase the width of the mountain range. Charney (1966) has pointed out that this process may cause a large error in the simulation of airflow past the mountain range. For example, consider a high narrow mountain range that is sufficiently high that some of the air must flow around it. After this mountain range has been smoothed it will be much lower and broader so that the air can easily flow over the range and very little air will go around. Thus the numerical solution computed with the smoothed topography will be qualitatively different than a solution obtained with the unsmoothed topography. This error, which results from the use of smoothed topography, will affect the largest scales of motion because of the spacing of mountain ranges around the earth.

This is an important problem for future research. One approach would be to use the potential enstrophy scheme developed by Arakawa and Lamb (1978) as presented in Section 7-5, and smooth the topography in such a way that the heights of major mountain ranges are nearly maintained. It may even be necessary to introduce a fine mesh around the mountains as discussed in Section 7-7.

CHAPTER 8

Boundary Layer Representations

8-1 INTRODUCTION

With respect to the short-range numerical prediction of synoptic-scale, middle-latitude disturbances, the effects of surface friction and heat flux are generally of second order. However, for longer periods the inclusion of these phenomena is essential. Nevertheless, improvement can be expected even in short-range forecasts when these processes are included in NWP models and they may be quite important in some instances. Moreover, if information is desired within the planetary boundary layer (PBL), for example, the surface wind, then the boundary layer must be simulated in some fashion since it will usually lie partly or entirely below the first level in the prediction model at which velocity is calculated.

Basically there are *two* approaches that may be used to represent the PBL in a numerical prediction model. An obvious way is to provide sufficient levels near the earth's surface to *resolve* the *boundary layer* adequately. Then the evolution of the meteorological variables is explicitly predicted by including the necessary closure assumptions and terms representing momentum, heat, and moisture fluxes in the hydrodynamical equations, as will be discussed in Sections 8-9 and 8-10. The accuracy of such a simulation will obviously depend on how well the turbulent fluxes are specified. Pure molecular analogy may not be entirely satisfactory especially with an unstable surface layer because convective plumes will develop that transport heat and moisture differently than Fickian diffusion. This suggests that a complete treatment of the boundary layer should be combined with the treatment of convection; however, such an approach is complex. Stable cases also present difficult problems. In any case it is not known at this time whether the turbulent fluxes can be predicted accurately enough level by level to provide a good structure throughout the PBL, especially since data is generally insufficient to provide initial conditions. Regardless of the various difficulties, the foregoing explicit method of resolving the boundary layer is time consuming on a computer and there are many other demands for more computer time, for example, increasing horizontal and the vertical resolution in the upper troposphere and lower stratosphere. Moreover, for large-scale NWP models the exchange of energy between the PBL and the atmosphere above may be more important than details within the PBL.

The *second approach* is to represent, or parameterize, not only the small-scale turbulent fluxes but also the entire vertical structure of the PBL in terms of one or two layers. From this parameterization key variables such as the wind, temperature, etc., at any desired level, as well as the momentum, heat and moisture fluxes from the surface, etc., may be extracted. Such a parameterization assumes the boundary layer to be quasi-stationary, implying that the response of the PBL to large-scale forcing is very rapid. The parameterization approach gives a less detailed representation than the first approach, but it is far cheaper in computer time and it may be sufficiently accurate for many models, considering grid size, initial data, etc.

The procedure that is followed here for pedagogical purposes is first to consider simple ways of introducing friction and then proceed with some further refinement. However, a complete combined treatment of the PBL and convection would be too lengthy to include in this text. Nevertheless it is hoped that the basic concepts involved will become clear to the reader.

8-2 REYNOLDS EQUATIONS

Boundary layer processes are a consequence of the interaction between the atmosphere and the earth's surface and take place mainly in a layer about 1 km in depth. Above this layer vertical transports of heat, moisture, and momentum result principally from large-scale vertical velocities, cumulus convection, and gravity waves; whereas in the PBL the fluxes are mainly a consequence of small-scale turbulence and convection. Hence it is desirable to utilize the Reynolds formulation of the equations of motion (e.g., see Haltiner and Martin, 1957), wherein the meteorological variables, save density, are expressed as the sum of a short time τ (or space) mean and a fluctuation, for example, $u = \overline{u} + u'$ such that $u' = 0$. The averaging period must be large compared to the periods of turbulent fluctuations but small compared to the variations of the mean motion, with a spectral gap between. When these expressions are substituted into the instantaneous equations of motion, the latter, after averaging and simplifications, may be expressed in the form

$$\frac{d\overline{u}}{dt} = -\frac{1}{\rho}\frac{\partial \overline{p}}{\partial x} + f\overline{v} + \frac{1}{\rho}\frac{\partial}{\partial x}(-\rho\overline{u'u'}) + \frac{1}{\rho}\frac{\partial}{\partial y}(-\rho\overline{u'v'}) + \frac{1}{\rho}\frac{\partial}{\partial z}(-\rho\overline{u'w'}) \tag{8-1}$$

Similar equations apply to the y- and z-directions; however the latter contains a buoyancy term as well. The nine covariances constitute the Reynolds stress tensor. In particular, the *covariances,* $-\rho\overline{u'u'}$, $-\rho\overline{u'v'}$, $-\rho\overline{u'w'}$ represent the *eddy fluxes* of *x-momentum* in the negative x, y, and z directions, respectively, and are frequently referred to as *eddy stresses,* which will be denoted by the symbols τ_{xx}, τ_{yx}, and τ_{zx}. Although the eddy stresses are of the same order of magnitude, the vertical variation is considerably greater (especially in the PBL) than the horizontal variations, which are therefore usually neglected. Thus the vector equation for the mean horizontal motion may be written in the usual form with the addition of an eddy stress term, that is,

$$\frac{d\mathbf{V}}{dt} = -\frac{1}{\rho}\nabla p - f\mathbf{k} \times \mathbf{V} + \frac{1}{\rho}\frac{\partial \tau}{\partial z} \tag{8-2a}$$

where

$$\tau = \tau_{zx}\,\mathbf{i} + \tau_{zy}\,\mathbf{j} \equiv \frac{1}{\rho}\frac{\partial}{\partial z}(-\rho\overline{u'w'})\,\mathbf{i} + \frac{1}{\rho}\frac{\partial}{\partial z}(-\rho\overline{v'w'})\,\mathbf{j}$$

The bars representing the means have been omitted to simplify the notation. Within the PBL, the acceleration term is often small compared to the others and is therefore usually omitted, giving

$$f\mathbf{k} \times (\mathbf{V} - \mathbf{V}_g) = \frac{1}{\rho}\frac{\partial \boldsymbol{\tau}}{\partial z} \tag{8-2b}$$

where $f\mathbf{k} \times \mathbf{V}_g = -\nabla p/\rho$.

In any event, the stress terms are additional dependent variables and the so-called *closure problem* is concerned with establishing a closed system of equations either by expressing the stresses directly in terms of the average flow variables (first-order closure); or by providing additional equations for the eddy stresses (momentum fluxes) derived from the equations of motion in order to complete the system. The derived equations contain triple- and higher-order correlations that may be assumed to be related to the second order or lower terms (referred to as *second-order closure*), as will be discussed at the end of this chapter.

In addition to the momentum flux, the upward turbulent fluxes of sensible heat, water vapor, and latent heat are, respectively,

$$\begin{aligned} H_S &= \rho c_p\,\overline{w'T'} \qquad \text{or} \approx \rho c_p\,\overline{w'\theta'} \\ E_w &= \rho\overline{w'q'} \qquad H_L = \rho L_v\,\overline{w'q'} \end{aligned} \tag{8-3}$$

8-3 BULK FORMULAS

The simplest way that the stress term in (8-2a) has been handled in a numerical prediction model has been to evaluate the derivative, $\rho^{-1}\,\partial\tau/\partial z = -g\,\partial\boldsymbol{\tau}/\partial p$, at the first level above the surface where the velocity is predicted, say $\mathrm{K} - 1$. In central finite difference form, for example, the friction force then becomes

$-g(\boldsymbol{\tau}_K - \boldsymbol{\tau}_{K-2})/2\Delta p$, where Δp is the pressure difference between equally spaced levels. The surface stress $\boldsymbol{\tau}_K$ shall be written as $\boldsymbol{\tau}_s$ henceforth. Since Δp is usually quite large, $\boldsymbol{\tau}_{K-2}$ is usually above the PBL and therefore very small and may be neglected there, as well as at higher levels. Consequently the only level at which a stress term appears is at the first level above the surface.

Now the system may be closed by expressing $\boldsymbol{\tau}_s$ in terms of other model variables. A common way is to assume that the surface stress is parallel to the surface wind $\mathbf{V}_s$ and proportional to a "drag" coefficient C_D as follows:

$$\boldsymbol{\tau}_s = \rho_s C_D V_s \mathbf{V}_s \qquad \text{or} \qquad \boldsymbol{\tau}_s = \rho_s C_D' \mathbf{V}_s \tag{8-4}$$[1]

The first form involving the square of the wind speed is a much better empirical relationship in general. In either case the surface wind velocity $\mathbf{V}_s$ may be estimated by frictional modifications to the surface geostrophic wind obtained from the sea-level pressure field or by extrapolation from one or more upper levels. Though obviously a very simple procedure this can be rather hazardous, however, because of baroclinicity and surface layer stratification. Alternatively, $(\tau_s/\rho)^{1/2}/V_g$ has been related to the surface Rossby number V_g/fz_0 and the static stability, which permits a determination of τ_s from V_g, f, ρ, and z_0, the surface roughness.

In vorticity (filtered type) prediction models the effect of surface friction may be roughly approximated through the lower boundary condition on the "vertical velocity" $\omega = dp/dt$. In pressure coordinates (8-2b) may be written as

$$0 = -\nabla\phi - f\mathbf{k} \times \mathbf{V} - g\, \partial\boldsymbol{\tau}/\partial p \tag{8-5}$$

Applying the operator, $\mathbf{k} \cdot \nabla \times$, to (8-5) and neglecting the variation of f gives

$$f\nabla \cdot \mathbf{V} = -g\mathbf{k} \cdot \nabla \times \partial\boldsymbol{\tau}/\partial p$$

Now replace $\nabla \cdot \mathbf{V}$ by $-\partial\omega/\partial p$ from the continuity equation and integrate from the "top" of the friction layer to the surface, which leads to

$$f(\omega_F - \omega_s) = -g\mathbf{k} \cdot \nabla \times \boldsymbol{\tau}_s \tag{8-6}$$

Here F denotes the top of the friction layer and s, the surface. If the surface stress is approximated by the second of the formulas in (8-4) and $\rho_s C_D$ is treated as a constant, (8-6) reduces to

$$\mathbf{k} \cdot \nabla \times \boldsymbol{\tau}_s = \rho_s C_D \zeta_s$$

where ζ_s is the vorticity. Thus from (8-6)

$$\omega_F = \omega_s - gf^{-1} \rho_s C_D \zeta_s \tag{8-7}$$

[1] In the second form C_D would have dimensions of velocity.

Utilizing the identity $gw = d\phi/dt = \partial\phi/\partial t + \mathbf{V} \cdot \nabla\phi + \omega\partial\phi/\partial p$ and replacing $\partial\phi/\partial p$ by means of the hydrostatic equation leads to

$$\omega = \rho\partial\phi/\partial t + \rho\mathbf{V} \cdot \nabla\phi - g\rho w \tag{8-8}$$

With level terrain the surface vertical velocity is zero, $w_s = 0$; however if the terrain is sloping, $w_s = \mathbf{V}_s \cdot \nabla h_s$, where h_s is the terrain height. Using this result and applying (8-8) at the surface gives, $\omega_s = \rho_s(\partial\phi/\partial t + \mathbf{V} \cdot \nabla\phi)_s - g\rho_s w_s$ and ω_F in (8-7) becomes

$$\omega_F = \rho_s[\partial\phi_0/\partial t + \mathbf{V}_s \cdot (\nabla\phi_0 - \nabla\phi_s)] - gf^{-1}\, \rho_s\, C_D\, \zeta_s \tag{8-9}$$

with $\phi_s = gh_s$. The geopotential of the pressure surface intersecting the terrain surface at the point in question is ϕ_0 and presumably $\nabla\phi_0$ is evaluated on this pressure surface. In practice, these terms, as well as $\mathbf{V}_s$, ζ_s, and ρ_s, are normally evaluated on the lowest pressure surface in the model at which ϕ is predicted, or are extrapolated from upper levels. Alternatively, the term in brackets in (8-9) may be replaced by $\partial p_s/\partial t + \mathbf{V}_s \cdot \nabla p_s$, where p_s is the pressure at terrain height. Further refinements may be obtained by varying the value of C_D and by using the more accurate form for τ_s (8-4a).

An alternate method for computing the surface stress is a theory or empirical relation between the surface Rossby number, $Ro = V_g/fz_0$, and u_*/V_g e.g., from (8-62):

$$\ell\text{n}\, Ro + \ell\text{n}\, \frac{u_*}{V_g} = k\left(A + \sqrt{\left(\frac{V_g}{u_*}\right)^2 + B}\right)$$

where V_g is the geostrophic wind; $u_* = (\tau_s/\rho)^{1/2}$, the friction velocity; z_0, the roughness parameter, which is a measure of surface roughness; $k \doteq 0.4$, the von Karman constant. A and B are numbers that depend on the static stability parameter, $\mu = u_*f/L$, L is the Monin-Obukhov length and the baroclinicity as measured by the horizontal temperature gradient. Stress direction can be similarly estimated. The geostrophic wind, horizontal temperature gradient and static stability can all be estimated from a large scale NWP model.

To complete this simplified procedure for incorporating boundary fluxes in numerical prediction models, some bulk formulas may be used for the surface sensible heat flux H_s and water vapor flux (evaporation) E_w, for example,

$$H_s = \rho c_p\, C_H\, V_s\, (T_s - T_a) \tag{8-10}$$

$$E_w = \rho C_E\, V_s\, (q_s - q_a) \tag{8-11}$$

where C_H and C_E are empirical coefficients; V_s, the surface wind speed; T_s, the surface water temperature; T_a, the air temperature over the water at, say, anemometer level; q_s, the saturation specific humidity corresponding to the surface water temperature and q_a, the specific humidity of the surface air over the water.

8-4 EDDY VISCOSITY, *K*-THEORY

Early treatments of the planetary boundary layer considered the turbulent flux of momentum to be analogous to molecular diffusion. Substituting K for ordinary molecular viscosity gives

$$-\rho\overline{u'w'} = \tau_{zx} = \rho K_x \frac{\partial u}{\partial z} \tag{8-12}$$

Analogous to the mean free path of molecules, a mixing length ℓ may be introduced that represents the mean distance that a turbulent eddy with excess momentum u' travels before blending with the environment. From a dimensional argument it is then easily shown that K is proportional to $\ell u'$ and with $u' \doteq \ell \partial u/\partial z$, the eddy viscosity becomes (see, for example, Haltiner and Martin, 1957).

$$K_x = \ell^2 \frac{\partial u}{\partial z} \tag{8-13}$$

Similar expressions hold for τ_{zy} and K_y.

Thus as an alternative to the earlier bulk formula, the surface eddy stress can be estimated by a finite difference approximation from the NWP output as follows:

$$\tau_{sx} = \rho_s K_x \frac{u_1 - u_s}{\Delta z}$$

where the subscript 1 denotes the first prediction level above the surface. As an approximation the surface velocity u_s may be extrapolated from aloft or set to zero to get a value of τ_{sx}. A similar expression may be used for τ_{sy} and together could be used in place of (8-4). The eddy viscosity coefficient K is sometimes taken as a constant or empirically related to height and the static stability as calculated from the NWP model output. In either case, the K theory is referred to as a *first-order closure* scheme since the eddy stresses have been expressed directly in terms of the mean motion.

8-5 COMBINED PRANDTL AND EKMAN LAYERS

As a step toward greater sophistication in parameterizing the PBL, a two-layer model can be developed consisting of a *constant-flux surface (Prandtl) layer* superposed with a *spiral (Ekman) layer*. But first it is of interest to integrate (8-2b) from z_0 where $\mathbf{V} = 0$ to the "top" of the PBL H, where the stress $\boldsymbol{\tau}$ becomes negligible,

$$\int_{z_0}^{H} -\mathbf{k} \times (\mathbf{V} - \mathbf{V}_g)\, dz = \frac{\boldsymbol{\tau}_s}{\rho f} = \frac{\tau_s\, \mathbf{t}_s}{\rho f} \equiv \frac{u_*^2}{f}\, \mathbf{t}_s$$

Here the variation of ρ has been ignored, $u_*^2 = \tau_s/\rho$ is the *friction velocity* and $\mathbf{t}_s$ is a unit vector in the direction of the surface stress. Now if the integral is made nondimensional by dividing the velocities by the scaling velocity u_* and z by the length parameter, u_*/f, to give $zf/u_* = \xi$, the result is

$$\int_{\xi_0}^{\xi_T} -\mathbf{k} \times (\mathbf{V}^* - \mathbf{V}_g^*)\, d\xi = \mathbf{t}_s$$

where $\mathbf{V}^* = \mathbf{V}/u_*$, $\xi_T = Hf/u_*$ and $\xi_0 = fz_0/u_*$, the inverse of the surface friction Rossby number. Since the right side of the last equation is merely a unit vector in the direction of the surface stress, the nondimensionalization or *scaling* has achieved a universality in the sense that the magnitude of the *integral* of the nondimensional wind velocity deficit with respect to the nondimensional vertical coordinate is a *constant,* independent of geostrophic wind, surface stress and latitude (invalid near the equator). This suggests that the scaling parameters u_* and u_*/f are of importance in PBL considerations.

Blackadar and Tennekes (1968) have shown more generally that if W represents the scaling for the velocity deficit, the equation of motion becomes formally independent of z_0/H provided the height scaling is $H = u_*^2/fW$. In the foregoing case with $W = u_*$, the height scaling was with u_*/f. An alternate scaling for the velocity deficit is V_g. Neither scaling is fully satisfactory over the entire PBL.

8-5-1 Prandtl Layer (Neutral Stratification)

Except possibly for an extremely thin viscous layer at the surface, which can be ignored here, the atmosphere boundary layer is turbulent. Moreover in a layer of 50 m, more or less, upward from the surface, the turbulent fluxes are nearly constant and wind structure depends on the static stability and roughness. For a surface layer of neutral static stability, the mixing length may be approximated by a linear function of the distance from the surface, that is, $\ell = kz$, where k is the von Karman constant. Placing the x-axis along the surface stress in (8-12) leads to the conventional form of the wind profile:

$$\rho(kz)^2\,(\partial u/\partial z)^2 = \tau_s \qquad \text{or} \qquad \frac{\partial u}{\partial z} = \frac{u_*}{kz} \tag{8-14}$$

where $u_*^2 = \tau_s/\rho$; and from (8-13)

$$K = (kz)^2 \frac{\partial u}{\partial z} = kzu_* \tag{8-15}$$

Integration of (8-14) leads to the well-known logarithmic wind profile for the *neutral, constant-flux, surface layer*

$$u = \frac{u_*}{k} \ell n \frac{z}{z_0} \tag{8-16}$$

where the boundary integration constant, z_0, called the *roughness length,* is the level at which the mean wind is presumed to vanish. The *von Karman constant, k,* has been evaluated variously from 0.35 to 0.41. It is clear from (8-16) that u_* and z_0 are appropriate velocity and height scale factors for the neutral surface layer.

If a typical surface weather observation is available including the wind u_a at anemometer level, say $z_a \sim 10$ m, (8-16) with $u_*^2 = \tau_S/\rho$ can be written in the form (8-4) as follows:

$$\tau_S = \rho C_D u_a^2 \qquad \text{where} \qquad C_D = k^2 [\ell n(z_a/z_0)]^{-2} \tag{8-17}$$

Thus one wind observation and estimates of ρ and z_0 can provide an estimate of the surface stress under neutral conditions for an aerodynamically rough sea surface.

If the sea is aerodynamically smooth, there is a laminar sublayer of thickness, $\delta = \upsilon/ku_*$; in which $u(z) = u(0) + u_*^2 z/\upsilon$, where υ is the molecular kinematic viscosity of air. The surface wind $u(0)$ can be taken to be the surface ocean current speed.

With $u(0) = 0$, the friction velocity is given by the implicit relation

$$u_*^2 = k^2 u_a^2 [1 + \ell n (ku_* z_a/\upsilon)]^{-2} \tag{8-18}$$

The solution for u_* gives the surface stress $\tau_s = \rho u_*^2$ and the drag coefficient if desired.

8-5-2 Ekman Layer

Above the surface layer the pressure and coriolis and friction forces are of the same order of magnitude and the acceleration, as mentioned earlier, is one order less; hence (8-2b) may be integrated using the expression for $\boldsymbol{\tau}$ in terms of the eddy viscosity as given by (8-12),

$$\boldsymbol{\tau} = \rho \left(K_x \frac{\partial u}{\partial z} \mathbf{i} + K_y \frac{\partial v}{\partial z} \mathbf{j} \right) \tag{8-19}$$

To simplify matters, take $K_x = K_y = K =$ constant, $\rho =$ constant, and substitute (8-19) into (8-2b) giving

$$f\mathbf{k} \times (\mathbf{V} - \mathbf{V}_g) = K\, \partial^2 \mathbf{V}/\partial z^2 \tag{8-20}$$

To solve this differential equation it is convenient to introduce the complex variable and write the velocity and the ageostrophic velocity, respectively, as

$$u + iv \qquad \text{and} \qquad (u + iv) - (u_g + iv_g) \equiv W$$

Separating the x- and y-components of the vector equation (8-20), then multiplying the y-component by $i = \sqrt{-1}$ and again adding the two equations gives

$$K\frac{\partial^2 W}{\partial z^2} - ifW = 0 \tag{8-21}$$

Note that $\mathbf{V}_g$ is assumed to be constant (barotropic condition) so that $\partial \mathbf{V}_g/\partial z = 0$. The solution of this equation is easily verified to be

$$W = c_1 e^{-(1+i)Bz} + c_2 e^{(1+i)Bz} \tag{8-22}$$

where $B = (f/2K)^{1/2}$ and c_1 and c_2 are arbitrary constants. The assumption that $\mathbf{V}$ approaches $\mathbf{V}_g$ as z becomes large, requires that $c_2 = 0$. Furthermore, in order to have continuity in the wind velocity at the boundary between the Prandtl and Ekman layers, $W(h)$, denoted by W_h, must equal the wind at the top of the Prandtl layer. Expressing c_1 in (8-22) in terms of W_h leads to

$$W = W_h\, e^{-(1+i)B(z-h)} \tag{8-23}$$

In addition, for the sake of continuity, the stress at the bottom of the Ekman layer shall be required to parallel the surface stress. Since the stress is parallel to the wind shear, $\partial(u + iv)/\partial z = \partial W/\partial z$ at the base of the Ekman layer must be parallel to $(u + iv)$ at the top of the surface layer. Differentiating (8-23) and noting that $-(1 + i) = \sqrt{2}\exp(-3i\pi/4)$, leads to

$$\left(\frac{\partial W}{\partial z}\right)_h = -W_h B(1 + i) = W_h B\sqrt{2}\, e^{-3i\pi/4} \tag{8-24}$$

It is clear from (8-24) that the angle between W_h and $(\partial W/\partial z)_h$ is $3\pi/4$ (De Moivre's theorem).

Figure 8-1 shows the relationships between the wind vector at level h and the geostrophic wind. The x-axis has been placed parallel to the geostrophic wind. The cross-isobar angle is denoted as α_s and the wind vector in the surface layer is everywhere parallel to $(u + iv)_h$ with the speed varying according to (8-1b).

Applying the law of sines in Figure 8-1 gives

$$\frac{|W_h|}{\sin\alpha_s} = \frac{V_g}{1/\sqrt{2}} = \frac{|u + iv|_h}{\sin(\pi/4 - \alpha_s)} \qquad \text{or} \qquad |W_h| = \sqrt{2}\, V_g \sin\alpha_s \tag{8-25}$$

$$|u + iv|_h = \sqrt{2}\, V_g \sin\left(\frac{\pi}{4} - \alpha_s\right) = V_g(\cos\alpha_s - \sin\alpha_s) \tag{8-26}$$

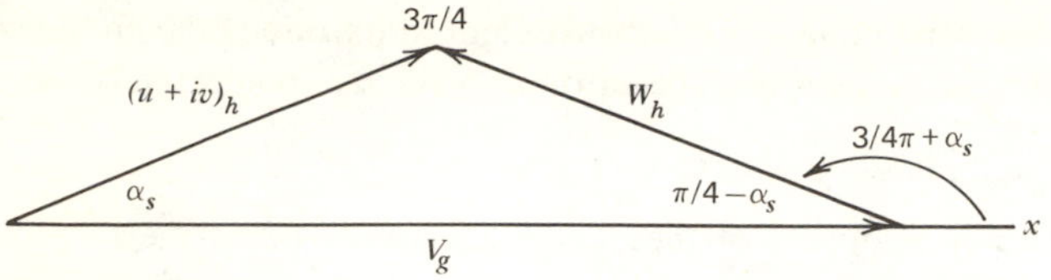

Figure 8-1 Illustrating the relationship between surface and geostrophic winds.

It follows from Figure 8-1 and (8-25) that $W_h = \sqrt{2}\, V_g \sin \alpha_s \exp i\, [(3\pi/4) + \alpha_s]$. Substituting this result into (8-23) gives the solution for the wind $(u + iv)$ in the Ekman spiral layer

$$u + iv = V_g + \sqrt{2}\, V_g \sin \alpha_s\, e^{-B(z-h)}\, e^{i[(3\pi/4) + \alpha_s - B(z-h)]}, \; z \geq h \qquad (8\text{-}27)$$

From (8-17) the solution for the wind in the Prandtl layer in complex form is

$$u + iv \equiv \frac{u_*}{k} \ell n \frac{z}{z_0} e^{i\alpha_s} \qquad z \leq h \qquad (8\text{-}28)$$

In order for the two solutions to match, the wind velocities must be equal at $z = h$; hence from (8-27) and (8-28), or more directly from (8-26) and (8-28),

$$(u_*/k)\, \ell n\, (h/z_0) = V_g\, (\cos \alpha_s - \sin \alpha_s) \qquad (8\text{-}29)$$

Also the coefficient of eddy viscosity (8-15) at level h should equal the constant value in the Ekman layer; thus

$$K = ku_*h \qquad (8\text{-}30)$$

Thus the constant B in (8-22) may be expressed as $B = (f/2ku_*h)^{1/2}$. Earlier it was required that the stress direction in the Ekman solution at level h, which is in the direction of the wind shear, be the same as the wind and stress direction in the Prandtl layer. If it is further required that the stresses in the two solutions match at level h, then, from (8-19) and (8-24),

$$|\tau| = \left| \rho K \frac{\partial(u + iv)}{\partial z} \right| = \left| \rho K \frac{\partial W}{\partial z} \right| \equiv \rho K\, |W_h|\, B\sqrt{2}$$

Substituting for $|W_h|$ from (8-25) and $B = (f/2K)^{1/2}$ and equating the result to the stress in the surface layer ρu_*^2 gives

$$\sqrt{2fK}\, V_g \sin \alpha_s = u_*^2 \qquad (8\text{-}31)$$

Examination of the solutions (8-27) and (8-28) shows that the following parameters are needed to give the wind in the PBL based on the two matching solutions:

$$\mathbf{V}_g,\ z_0,\ h,\ \alpha_s,\ K,\ u_*$$

The wind in the free atmosphere at the top of the PBL would be available by explicit prediction in a numerical prediction model and would be appropriate for V_g. Moreover, the roughness parameter z_0 depends on the character of the underlying surface and can be specified, at least over land. Over the sea, z_0 depends on the sea state, which in turn is a function of the wind; but presumably it could be estimated from the wind speed or u_*. Charnock (1955) proposed the following empirical formula, $gz_0 = \alpha u_*^2$, where $\alpha \doteq 0.014$. Of the remaining four variables one more must be specified, say h, the thickness of the surface layer. A constant value of h can be chosen or perhaps an estimate can be made through an empirical relationship relating h to other parameters predicted by an NWP model.

In any event, with V_g, z_0, h given, the remaining quantities K, u_*, and α_s can be computed from (8-29), (8-30), and (8-31). An obvious limitation to this parameterization scheme is the necessity of specifying the depth of the Prandtl surface layer h, which should be one of the quantities determined by the parameterization and therefore predicted in a numerical model. In fact, more sophisticated models in which various physical processes are interrelated do include a prediction equation for the height of the boundary layer.

8-6 NONNEUTRAL SURFACE LAYER

The previous model of the PBL combined a neutral surface layer and the Ekman spiral layer. When the surface layer is stable or unstable, the similarity theory of Monin and Obukhov suggests that the vertical shear in the surface layer may be represented by a modification of (8-14), namely,

$$\frac{\partial u}{\partial z} = \frac{u_*}{kz}\phi_m\left(\frac{z}{L}\right) \qquad (8\text{-}32)$$

where ϕ_m is an empirical function to be described later and L is the *Monin-Obukhov* length, which depends on the turbulent fluxes as follows:

$$L = \frac{\overline{T}}{gk^2}\frac{u_*^2}{T_{*v}} \qquad T_{*v} = -\overline{w'\theta'}/u_* \qquad (8\text{-}33)$$

The length L arises from the ratio of the generation of mechanical turbulence by Reynolds' stresses to the production of turbulent kinetic energy by buoyancy forces. L may be interpreted as the height at which the magnitudes of mechanical and thermal production of turbulence are equal.

The vertical gradient of potential temperature in the surface layer has a form similar to (8-32).

$$\frac{\partial\theta}{\partial z} = \frac{T_*}{kz}\phi_h\left(\frac{z}{L}\right) \tag{8-34}$$

The functions ϕ_m and ϕ_h represent the modifications to the velocity and temperature profiles due to nonneutral stability conditions. According to (8-14), it would be expected that ϕ_m is unity for neutral stability. Also the heat flux vanishes, that is, $T_* = 0$, and $z/L = 0$, for neutral stability.

Next write (8-32) in the form

$$du = \frac{u_*}{k}\left[\frac{dz}{z} - (1 - \phi_m)\frac{dz/L}{z/L}\right] \tag{8-35}$$

Integration of (8-35) from z_0, where $u_0 = 0$, to an arbitrary level z gives

$$u = \frac{u_*}{k}\left[\ell\text{n}\frac{z}{z_0} - \psi_m\left(\frac{z}{L}\right)\right] \tag{8-36}$$

$$\psi_m\left(\frac{z}{L}\right) = \int_{z_0/L}^{z/L}[1 - \phi_m(\xi)]\,d\ell\text{n}\xi,\ \xi = z/L \tag{8-37}$$

Note that z_0/L is usually small, otherwise ψ_m would depend on z_0/L as well.

In a similar fashion, the vertical temperature profile may be obtained from (8-34). If there is a constant flux of sensible heat, as well as momentum, T_* is constant and the resulting temperature distribution in the constant-flux surface layer is given by

$$\theta - \theta_0 = \frac{T_*}{k}\left[\ell\text{n}\frac{z}{z_0} - \psi_h\left(\frac{z}{L}\right)\right] \tag{8-38}$$

The functions ϕ_m and ϕ_h are shown in Figures 8-2 and 8-3, after Businger et al. (1971). The integral of $(1 - \phi_m)$, namely, ψ_m, is shown in Figure 8-4 [Paulson (1970)].

The coefficient of eddy viscosity K, as defined earlier in (8-12) by the relation $\tau/\rho = K\,\partial u/\partial z$, and the mixing length for the nonneutral surface layer become

$$K = ku_*z/\phi_m(z/L) \qquad \ell = kz/\phi(z/L) \tag{8-39}$$

which follows from (8-32) (8-13) and the definition $u_*^2 = \tau/\rho$. Thus, analogous to wind shear, the nonneutral K is representable in terms of the neutral-layer K modified by $\phi_m(z/L)$ [see (8-15)].

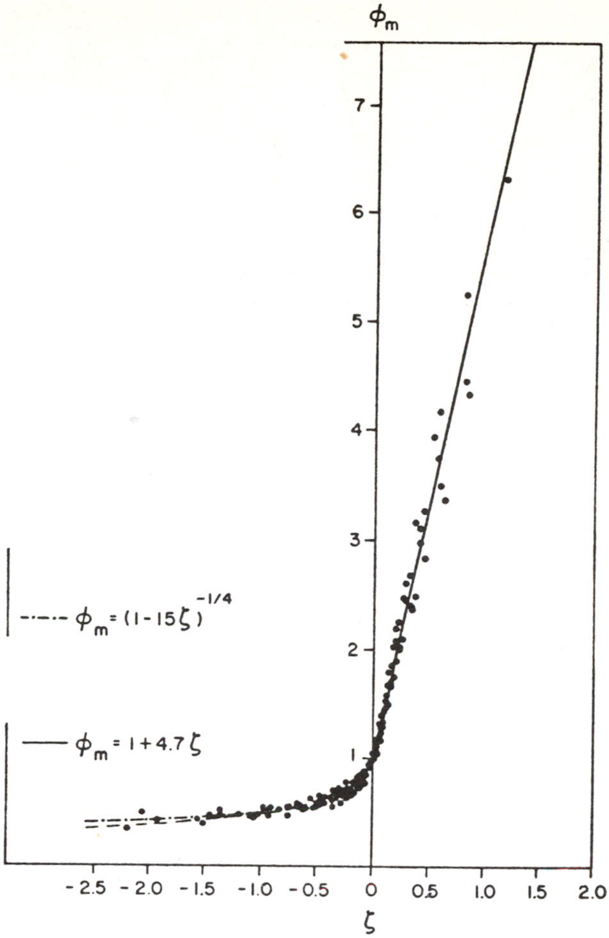

Figure 8-2 Overland results on nondimensional wind shear versus ζ = z/L (Businger et al., 1971). (From J. Businger, et al. ''Flux Profile Relationships in the Atmospheric Surface Layer.'' *American Meteorological Society*, 1971.)

Carefully conducted experiments during situations reasonably well approximating the assumptions of stationarity and horizontal homogeneity underlying the Monin-Obukhov theory verify that the nondimensional wind shear (kz/u_*) $\partial u/\partial z$ is a function of z/L only.

The curves shown in Figure 8-2 and 8-3 are based on overland data and have been fitted with empirical functions for stable and unstable layers as follows:

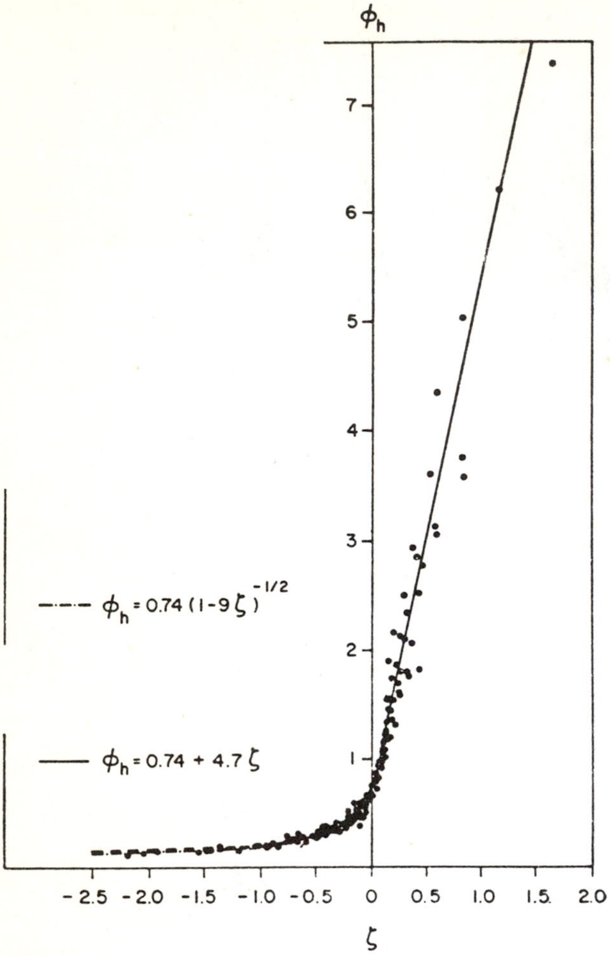

Figure 8-3 Temperature gradients versus $\zeta = z/L$ (Businger et al., 1971). (From J. Businger, et al. "Flux Profile Relationships in the Atmospheric Surface Layer." *American Meteorological Society,* 1971.)

UNSTABLE: $(z/L) < 0$ STABLE: $(z/L) > 0$

$$\phi_m\left(\frac{z}{L}\right) = \left(1 - 15\frac{z}{L}\right)^{-1/4} \qquad \phi_m\left(\frac{z}{L}\right) = 1.00 + 4.7\frac{z}{L}$$

$$\phi_h\left(\frac{z}{L}\right) = 0.74\left(1 - 9\frac{z}{L}\right)^{-1/2} \qquad \phi_h\left(\frac{z}{L}\right) = 0.74 + 4.7\frac{z}{L} \tag{8-40}$$

The scale length L is a measure of the height above the ground where

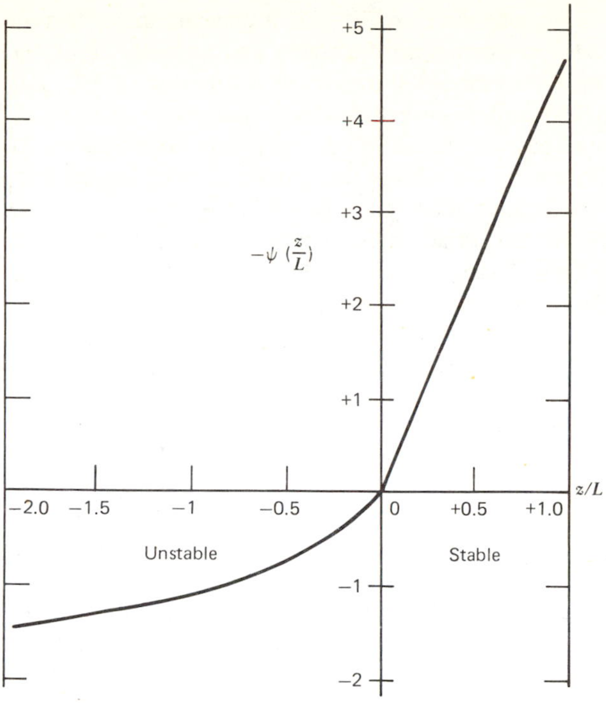

Figure 8-4 The function $\psi\,(z/L) = z/L\,(1 - \phi\,(\xi))d\xi/\xi$ for $\phi_m = 1 + 4.7\,z/L$ (stable) and for $\phi_m = (1 - 15\,z/L)^{-1/4}$ (unstable). (*After Paulson, 1970.*)

buoyant forces become comparable to the mechanical or shear related forces in generating turbulence. This height is lower for the unstable atmosphere and increases as L increases (algebraically) and becomes positive for the stable atmosphere. If the profile expressions (8-32) and (8-34) are solved for u_* and T_* and inserted into the definition for L in (8-33), the following result may be obtained

$$\frac{z}{L} = \frac{g}{T}\frac{\partial\theta/\partial z}{(\partial u/\partial z)^2}\frac{\phi_m^2}{\phi_h} = Ri\,\frac{\phi_m^2}{\phi_h}$$

where Ri is the well-known Richardson number

$$Ri = \frac{g}{T}\frac{\partial\theta/\partial z}{(\partial u/\partial z)^2} \tag{8-41}$$

Since ϕ_m and ϕ_n are functions of z/L only, it is clear that Ri is a unique function of z/L and vice versa. Where direct flux measurements are not available, Ri is often used as a measure of stability. However, it has the disadvantage of varying with height in the surface layer, whereas $L = Tu_*^2/gkT_*$ is constant there. Nevertheless, Ri will be used later to distinguish the stable and unstable cases for application in NWP models. Figure 8-5 shows Ri as a function of z/L. For unstable conditions (8-40) and Figure 8-5 show that $Ri \approx 0.95\ z/L$. On the other hand, for large positive values of z/L (very stable conditions), Ri approaches the value 0.21, which is a critical Richardson number for the cessation of turbulence. For moderately stable air, $z/L \approx Ri/(1 - 5\,Ri)$.

A bulk formula (8-17) for the surface stress (momentum flux) was derived for a neutral surface layer from (8-16). A similar form can be obtained for the nonneutral case from (8-36) as follows:

$$\tau_S = \rho u_a^2 k^2 [\ell n (z_a/z_0) - \psi_m (z_a/L)]^{-2} \equiv \rho C_D u_a^2 \qquad (8\text{-}42)$$

which assumes as before that $u(z_0) = 0$ and $z_a \sim 10$ m. The identity defines C_D if desired. The function ψ_m may be obtained with the use of (8-40) provided the stability parameter L is known. A rough estimate of the static stability can be obtained from air-sea temperature differences and perhaps the cloud type. For this purpose Ri may be more convenient to estimate than L. Figure 8-5 relates Ri and L, which is constant in the surface layer.

Garrett (1977) has given a review of empirically determined drag coefficients over oceans and finds that observations of wind profiles and stress are consistent with Charnock's (1955) relation, $\alpha u_*^2 = gz_0$, where $\alpha \doteq 0.014$ for aerodynamically rough flow. This result may be approximated in the range $4 < V_{10} < 21$ m/sec by a neutral drag coefficient

$$C_{DN} = 0.51 \times 10^{-3}\, V_{10}^{\ 0.46}$$

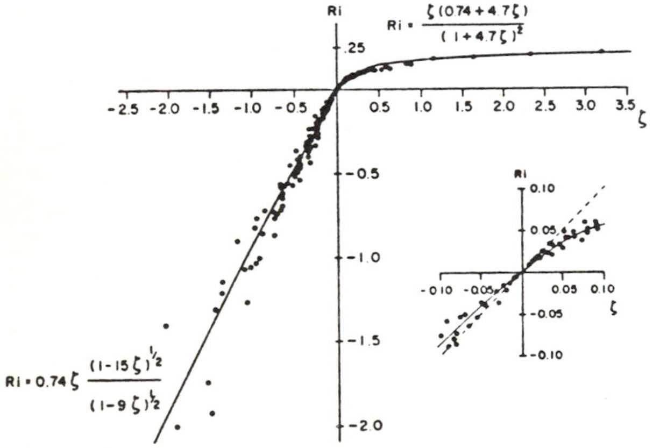

Figure 8-5 Richardson number *Ri(z)* as a function of $\zeta = z/L$, Businger (1971). (From J. Businger, et al. "Flux Profile Relationships in the Atmospheric Surface Layer." *American Meteorological Society*, 1971.)

or the linear form

$$\doteq 10^{-3}\,(0.75 + 0.67V_{10})$$

In terms of the geostrophic wind, the 10-m wind speed V_{10} under neutral conditions is approximated by $V_{10} = 0.94\ V_g^{0.8}$. Also included are curves of the ratio of the nonneutral drag coefficient to the neutral value, that is, C_D/C_{DN}, as a function of z/L, for two values of z_0. The relationship is not linear; moreover the curve for $z_0 = 10$ cm has a greater slope than the one for $z_0 = 0.1$ cm. The ratio C_D/C_{DN} *exceeds 1 for unstable air* and is *less than 1 for stable* air, and further its range is larger for $z_0 = 10$ cm than for $z_0 = 0.1$ cm. A *rough* linear approximation that indicates the general nature of the variation with stability is $C_D/C_{DN} = 1 - 3z/4L$, for $z_0 = 10$ cm; and $1 - 6z/10L$ for $z_0 = 0.10$ m.

Over land form drag due to uneven topography is important as well as frictional drag and contributes about 20 percent. For high mountains the *geostrophic drag coefficient* C_g, used with the geostrophic wind, that is, with $\tau_S = \rho C_g V_g^2$, is about 5×10^{-3} to 9×10^{-3}; over low relief topography (0.5 to 1 km), about 2 to 3×10^{-3}; and for flat land, 1 to 2×10^{-3}. The average value of C_g is about 2×10^{-3} to 3×10^{-3}, which corresponds to C_{DN} (10 m) $\approx 10^{-2}$ and an effective roughness coefficient $z_0 \approx 0.2$ m.

In a similar fashion to (8-42) the upward sensible heat flux, $H_S = \rho c_p\,(\overline{w'\theta'}) = \rho c_p k u_* T_*$, can be obtained from (8-38) and an expression for C_H from (8-10) as follows:

$$H_S = \rho c_p k u_*\,(\theta_S - \theta_a)\,[\ell n\,(z_a/z_0) - \psi_h\,(z_a/L)]^{-1} \equiv \rho c_p\, C_H\, u_a\,(\theta_S - \theta_a)$$

where $\theta_s \doteq T_S$, $\theta_a \doteq T_a$.

Finally it is possible to treat evaporation and latent heat flux in an analogous fashion

$$E_w = -\,k\rho u_* q_* \qquad H_L = k\rho u_* L_v q_* = \rho u_a L_v C_E (q_S - q_{10})$$

The goal of the preceding discussions was to indicate methods of estimating fluxes of momentum, heat, and water vapor from a typical surface synoptic observation or prediction. If wind, temperature, and humidity are known at two levels within the surface layer, the surface fluxes can be determined without the need to estimate static stability, etc. This will be considered in Section 8-7-2. A final note relating to this section is that buoyancy may be significantly affected by water vapor in the air, for example, over the sea when the humidity and its vertical gradient may be large, in which case it is appropriate to introduce virtual temperatures as suggested earlier.

8-6-1 Matching Ekman Spiral

The solution for the wind velocity in a nonneutral surface layer can be easily matched with the Ekman solution for the spiral layer as was done earlier for the surface layer of neutral stability. Although the applicability of this combination, especially for the unstable case, is not as satisfactory as some other approaches to be described shortly, because of its simplicity the matching procedure will be briefly described. For this purpose the velocity stress and coefficient of eddy viscosity at the top of the surface layer must equal the corresponding quantities at the bottom of the spiral layer. The Ekman solution (8-27) remains unchanged. However, the nonneutral solution corresponding to (8-28) is

$$(u + iv) = \frac{u_*}{k}\left[\ell n \frac{z}{z_0} - \psi_m\left(\frac{z}{L}\right)\right] e^{i\alpha_s} \qquad z \leq h$$

which must equal (8-26) at level h for continuity of velocity; thus

$$\frac{u_*}{k}\left[\ell n \frac{z}{z_0} - \psi_m\left(\frac{z}{L}\right)\right] = V_g\,(\cos\alpha_s - \sin\alpha_s) \tag{8-43}$$

Similarly, the constant coefficient of eddy viscosity in the spiral layer must equal that at the top of the surface layer; thus from (8-39)

$$K = u_* kh/\phi_m\left(\frac{h}{L}\right) \tag{8-44}$$

Equation 8-31 remains unchanged in form. The foregoing set of equations, together with the Ekman solution, will define a PBL that is applicable to stable, neutral, or unstable conditions in the surface layer. However an additional variable, L, (or Ri) must be determined. According to (8-33), two new quantities T_* and $\overline{T}$ are needed. The latter can be approximated with sufficient accuracy with a mean value. If (8-38) is evaluated at h, then

$$\theta_h - \theta_0 = \frac{T_*}{k}\left[\ell n \frac{h}{z_0} - \psi_h\left(\frac{h}{L}\right)\right] \tag{8-45}$$

T_* is a constant in the surface layer and can be calculated iteratively from (8-45) (since L involves T_*) provided h, z_0, and $(\theta_h - \theta_0)$ are known. The temperature θ_h can be extrapolated from upper temperatures in the prediction model. Over the sea the surface temperature of the ocean, which generally changes rather slowly, can be used to determine θ_0. However, over land θ_0 is determined from an equation that expresses the balance between the solar radiation, terrestrial radiation, the turbulent flux of latent and sensible heat, and heat conduction into the soil.

O'Brien (1970) proposed a simple empirical formula based on physical reasoning for the coefficient of eddy viscosity $K(z)$ in the Ekman layer above a nonneutral surface layer of depth h where $K(h)$ is given by (8-44). At the top z_T of the Ekman layer, $K = K_T$ and its derivative $(\partial K/\partial z)_T = K'_T$ is taken to be zero. In addition the eddy viscosity and its derivative are assumed to be continuous across the boundary between the surface and Ekman layers. Then a polynomial is fitted to the values of K and K' at h and z_T, and any intervening points if desired. In the simplest case with just the two levels h and z_T, the resulting polynomial is

$$K(z) = K_T + [(z - z_T)^2/\Delta z^2] \{K_h - K_T + (z - h) [K_h' + 2(K_h - K_T)/\Delta z]\}$$

where $\Delta z = (z_T - h)$. The formula requires the specification if h, z_T and K_T while K_h and K_h' come from the surface layer. O'Brien states that despite its simplicity and ease of calculation, this formulation appears to give satisfactory results in numerical models.

8-7 SIMILARITY SOLUTIONS FOR THE ENTIRE PBL

For a neutral, barotropic layer (also stationary and horizontally homogeneous), similarity theory shows that the boundary layer structure scales with u_*/f, as suggested in Section 8-5. However, in regard to the nonneutral case there is diversity of opinion, especially during unstable conditions. More recent investigations and numerical studies suggest that a more appropriate scale height for the PBL is the height above the surface of the inversion base z_i (Deardorff, 1972; Wyngaard et al., 1974). Most of the velocity and temperature changes are confined to the relatively thin surface layer above which there ia a *well-mixed convective* layer through the remainder of the PBL where turbulence is governed mainly by thermal convection rather than forced mechanical mixing. The distribution of the properties in the convective boundary layer may be expected therefore to depend on the dimensionless parameters, z/z_i, z_i/L, and u_*/fz_i, since they involve the surface heat flux, surface stress, and latitude as well as z_i. In this formulation with an NWP model it is necessary to predict the depth of the PBL.

8-7-1 Deardorff Mixed Layer Model

Deardorff (1972) developed a parameterization of the PBL for use in general circulation models (GCM) of the atmosphere. His formulation includes a predictive equation for the entire depth of the PBL, denoted by $(h - z_s)$, which contains the effects of penetrative convection and vertical motion with unstable conditions. With stable conditions the depth is not predicted but is assumed to be proportional to the Monin-Obukhov length L.

Deardorff's procedure begins with an estimate of the *vertically averaged mean wind velocity, potential temperature,* and *specific humidity* within the PBL by interpolation and/or extrapolation from levels within the GCM or NWP model. The *second* major step consists of calculating the *surface fluxes* of *momentum, heat,* and *moisture* using a bulk Richardson number and differences between the mean values obtained in the first step and surface values. *Finally* the *direction of the surface wind velocity* is estimated from the surface pressure gradient obtained from the GCM together with the PBL structure.

To obtain the velocity V_m (and also, θ_m and q_m) at the mid PBL level, $\frac{1}{2}(h + z_s)$, where h and z_s are the heights of the top and bottom of the PBL above mean sea level, Deardorff simply extrapolates from the two lowest levels of the GCM, z_1 and z_3, that carry velocity. For example, the X-component toward east becomes

$$U_m = U_1 + (U_3 - U_1)\left(\frac{h + z_s}{2} - z_1\right)/(z_3 - z_1)$$

If h exceeds z_4, $(h + z_s)/2$ is replaced by z_2. As pointed out by Deardorff, when the PBL is low and capped by a strong inversion the foregoing extrapolation formula may not be satisfactory.

The surface fluxes of sensible heat and moisture are related to the gradients of θ and $\overline{q}$ near typical anemometer levels and to the friction velocity u_*. The fluxes at anemometer level a are assumed to equal those at the surface. The extrapolated value of the mixed layer wind $|\mathbf{V}_m|$ is used as a first estimate of the wind speed at anemometer level, but is subsequently refined if needed.

The gradients of dimensionless wind, temperature and specific humidity are treated as functions of $(z - z_s)/L$, where L is the Monin-Obukhov length as defined earlier, except that the flux of virtual potential temperature is used. The latter is related to the flux of potential temperature by the equation

$$\overline{w'\theta_v'} \doteq \overline{w'\theta'} + 0.61\,\theta\,\overline{w'q'} \qquad (8\text{-}46)$$

The thermal stability of the PBL is designated as follows:

$$\begin{matrix}\text{UNSTABLE} \\ \text{NEUTRAL} \\ \text{STABLE}\end{matrix} \quad (\overline{w'\theta_v'})_a \begin{cases} > 0 & & > 0 \\ = 0, & \text{corresponding to } (\theta_{vs} - \theta_{vm}) & = 0 \\ < 0 & & < 0 \end{cases}$$

where $\theta_{vs} = \theta_s\,(1 + 0.61\,q_s)$ and a represents ''anemometer'' level. The surface values θ_s and q_s are determined from sea surface temperature, or over land from an equation for surface thermal energy balance.

8-7-2 Surface Layer

The *surface-layer* velocity and potential temperature gradients are given by (8-32) and (8-34) with (8-40) from Businger et al. (1971). The neutral and unstable cases may be treated together. When these equations are integrated as in (8-36) the results for the values of u_a and θ_{va} at ''anemometer'' level z_a in the *neutral* or *unstable* case are

$$\frac{u_a}{u_*} = \frac{1}{k}\left\{\ell n\left(\frac{z_r}{z_0}\right) - \left[\ell n\left(\frac{1+\mu^2}{2}\right) + 2\ell n\left(\frac{1+\mu}{2}\right) - 2\tan^{-1}\mu + \frac{\pi}{2}\right]\right\} \tag{8-47}$$

UNSTABLE:

$$\frac{(\theta_{va} - \theta_{vs})u_*}{(-\overline{w'\theta_v'})_a} = \frac{0.74}{k}\left[\ell n\left(\frac{z_r}{z_0}\right) - 2\ell n\left(\frac{1+\eta^2}{2}\right)\right] \tag{8-48}$$

where

$$\mu = \left(1 - \frac{15z_r}{L}\right)^{1/4} \qquad \eta = \left(1 - \frac{9z_r}{L}\right)^{1/4} \qquad z_r = z_a - z_s$$

The direction of u_a, yet undetermined, is represented by the x-axis in Figure 8-6. For the *stable* case the results of integrating (8-35) and (8-34) with (8-40) are more easily seen to be

$$\frac{u_a}{u_*} = \frac{1}{k}\left(\ell n\frac{z_r}{z_0} + \frac{4.7z_r}{L}\right) \tag{8-50}$$

STABLE:

$$\frac{(\theta_{va} - \theta_{vs})u_*}{(-\overline{w'\theta_v'})_a} = \frac{0.74}{k}\left[\ell n\left(\frac{z_r}{z_0}\right) + 6.35\frac{z_r}{L}\right] \tag{8-51}$$

The value of 0.74 is the *ratio* of the eddy diffusivities of *momentum* K_M and *heat* K_H for neutral stratification. For land surfaces z_0 lies between extremes of roughly 10^{-3}m and 1 m with a typical value of about 1 cm. Over the sea the range may be roughly similar; however the magnitude is generally one or two orders less than over land. A value of 0.01 cm is typical.

Upper Mixed Layer. In the remainder of the PBL, velocity and temperature (obtained as deviations with respect to their values at level a) are assumed to be functions of $(h - z_s)/L$ but not $(h - z_s)/z_0$. In the *unstable* case h and z_i are taken to be identical, while in the neutral and stable cases h is considered to be proportional to u_*/f. For the *neutral* and *unstable* cases Deardorff chooses the level z_a to be

$$z_a = z_s + 0.025\,(h - z_s) \tag{8-52}$$

Next the velocity and potential temperature deficits from the GCM values and the corresponding values at the level a are obtained by considering three values of the stability factor, $-(h - z_s)/L$: 0, 4.5 and 45.5, based on a three-dimensional PBL model:

$$\frac{u_m - u_a}{u_*} = 8.4\left[1 - \frac{50(h - z_s)}{L}\right] - 0.16$$

UNSTABLE: for $(\overline{w'\theta_v'}) > 0$

(8-53)

$$\frac{(\theta_{vm} - \theta_{va})u_*}{(-\overline{w'\theta_v'})_a} = 7.3\left[1 - \frac{5.8\,(h - z_s)}{L}\right] - 0.47$$

For the *stable* case Clarke's (1970a) observations for $u_*/fL = 210$ were used to calculate the stability parameter $(h - z_s)/L$. Using a value of $(h - z_s)$ of $0.35u_*/f$ for the neutral case, the value of $(h - z_s)$ for the stable case was estimated to be $0.23\ u_*/f$. The latter value, coupled with $u_*/fL = 210$, gives $(h - z_s)/L \doteqdot 48$ for the *stable* case; and it is assumed that the functional dependence of the deficits is linear in $(h - z_s)/L$ between the neutral case and the foregoing value. The final results for the *stable* case are:

STABLE: $\left\{ (\overline{w'\theta_v'})_a < 0 \right\}$

$$\frac{u_m - u_a}{u_*} = 8.4 + \frac{0.6\,(h - z_s)}{L}; \qquad \frac{\theta_{vm} - \theta_{va}}{(-\overline{w'\theta_v'})_a} = 7.3 + \frac{0.6\,(h - z_s)}{L} \qquad (8\text{-}54)$$

8-7-3 Matching Solutions for the Surface and Mixed Layers

Deardorff then matches the solutions for the surface layer [(8-47) to (8-51)] with those of the mixed or upper layer of the PBL [(8-53) to (8-54)] by requiring continuity of u_a and θ_v at anemometer level z_a. The results are of the form

$$u_* = u_m C_u = u_m/F \qquad (8\text{-}55)$$

$$(-\overline{w'\theta_v'})_a = (\theta_{vm} - \theta_{vs})C_\theta\, u_* = (\theta_{vm} - \theta_{vs})u_*/G \qquad (8\text{-}56)$$

where F and G are functions $(h - z_s')/z_0$ and $(h - z_s)/L$.

The C_u and C_θ defined previously are referred to as the *friction* and *heat transfer coefficients*. Equations 8-55 and 8-56 may be looked on as implicit equations in u_* and L, which together represent the momentum flux and heat flux. A more convenient approach begins by combining (8-55) and (8-56) and introducing the bulk Richardson number as follows:

$$Ri_B = \frac{g(h - z_s)(\theta_{vm} - \theta_{vs})}{\theta_{vm}\, u_m^2} = \frac{(h - z_s)}{kL}\frac{G}{F^2} = \frac{(h - z_s)}{kL}\frac{C_u^2}{C_\theta} \tag{8-57}$$

Now if $(h - z_s)/z_0$ and $(h - z_s)/L$ were specified, C_u, C_θ, and Ri_B could be calculated by means of (8-55), (8-56), and (8-57). Instead L is effectively eliminated and Deardorff provides graphs relating C_u and C_θ to $(h - z_s)/z_0$ and Ri_B. These are done separately for the stable and unstable cases with the latter including the neutral stability case by letting $L \to \infty$. Thus with known h, z_0, and Ri_B, C_u and C_θ can be calculated. For application in computerized numerical models, Deardorff provided numerical approximations to the graphs, which may be found in his article. Instead, some more recent results are presented in Section 8-7-4.

These approximations (or the graphs) together with (8-56) permit the calculation of the momentum and heat fluxes. Needed are the height of the inversion h, which is predicted; the roughness coefficient z_0, which is a characteristic of the surface, and the other ingredients for the bulk Richardson number, that is, u_m, θ_{vm}, and θ_{vs} from the NWP model. The fluxes of momentum and heat at a and z_s are:

$$-\overline{\rho u'w'} = \tau = \rho u_*^2 = \rho u_m^2 C_u^2 \qquad H = c_p\,(\overline{\rho w'\theta'})_a$$
$$= \rho c_p(\theta_s - \theta_m) u_m C_u C_\theta \tag{8-58}$$

The vertical flux of virtual potential temperature obtained from C_θ can be partitioned into kinematic sensible heat and moisture fluxes using (8-46) as follows:

$$(\overline{w'\theta'})_a = (\theta_s - \theta_m)\,(\overline{w'\theta_v'})_a\,/\,(\theta_{vs} - \theta_{vm}) \tag{8-59}$$

and

$$(\overline{w'q'})_a = (q_s - q_m)\,(\overline{w'\theta_v'})_a\,/\,(\theta_{vs} - \theta_{vm}) \tag{8-60}$$

where s denotes a mean surface value around a gridpoint and m the mean value in the PBL as before.

Note also that when Ri_B has been estimated from the output of an NWP model, $(h - z_s)/L$ may be determined from (8-57); and knowing $(h - z_s)$, L may be calculated. Deardorff also treats the limiting case of free convection, which will not be included here to avoid excessive detail. The calculated fluxes can be used in direct fashion by, for example, for τ_s, H_s, and E_s in (8-4), (8-10), and (8-11), instead of empirical bulk expressions. The direction of the surface stress will be considered in Section 8-7-4.

8-7-4 Surface Wind Direction

Deardorff computes the cross isobar angle of the surface wind from the horizontal gradient of pressure at z_s, $(\nabla_H p)_s$, and the mean PBL wind $\mathbf{V}_m$, both obtained from the GCM output.

Figure 8-6 illustrates some of the parameters. The model coordinates are X, Y, towards East and North; and the x-coordinate is in the direction of the surface layer wind and stress. Some pertinent relationships, apparent from the figure are

$$\psi = \arctan (V_m/U_m) \qquad \psi_x = \psi_p - \psi_r$$

$$\psi_p = \arctan - \frac{\partial p/\partial Y}{\partial p/\partial X} \qquad \psi_r = |\psi_p - \psi_x| = \arccos \frac{-\partial p/\partial x}{|\nabla_H p_s|} \leq \frac{\pi}{2}$$

$$u_m = |\mathbf{V}_m| \cos (\psi_x - \psi)$$

The angles ψ_p and ψ are known from the GCM or NWP model.
It is desired to find the angle ψ_r that will give the direction of the surface stress and wind. To accomplish this, Deardorff uses the familiar approximation for the balance of forces in the surface layer, $(\partial p/\partial x)_s \doteq (\partial \tau_{zx}/\partial z)_a$, which represents the dominant terms, since $v_a = 0$.

A further approximation for the vertical shear of the stress gives:

$$-\left(\frac{1}{\rho}\frac{\partial p}{\partial x}\right) = \frac{c u_*^2}{h - z_s} \qquad c = 1.0 + 1.8 \exp [0.2 (h - z_s)/L]$$

Here L may be taken to be ∞ for the neutral and stable cases giving $c = 2.8$ in those cases. The figure suggests that the direction of the x-axis and thus surface wind and stress would be more nearly in the direction of the geostrophic

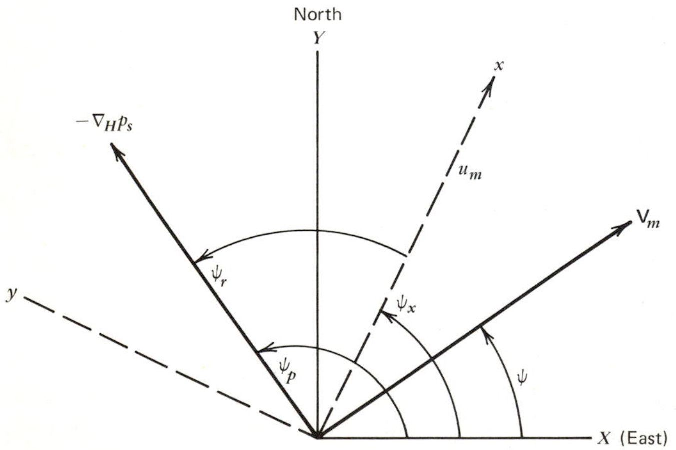

Figure 8-6 Coordinate axes and angles relevant to the determination of the surface cross-isobar angle.

wind than the opposite, which is generally valid, except possibly for low latitudes where unrealistic results may occur because of very weak pressure gradients and nongeostrophic conditions. To avoid such problems, Deardorff suggests the expression $\psi_x = \psi_p \pm \psi_r$ where the + or − sign is chosen to minimize the angle between the direction of $\mathbf{V}_m$ and ψ_x. Having determined ψ_x, the value of u_m^2 can be calculated from $\mathbf{V}_m$. If it differs by more than 15 percent from the value previously assumed to determine Ri_B, the latter is recalculated and also revised values of the fluxes and ψ should be obtained. Iterations are usually not necessary in the unstable cases and can sometimes be avoided in the stable case by initially estimating u_m as 95 percent of $|\mathbf{V}_m|$. Deardorff gives other suggestions for avoiding iterative oscillations that may otherwise occur.

8-7-5 Modified Transfer Coefficients

Yamada (1976) developed improved empirical functions with respect to the observations for calculating the momentum and heat fluxes. The deficits of velocity and temperature for the *outer* layer are first expressed in terms of universal profile functions for u, v, and θ_v of the form $(u - \hat{u})/u_* = F_u[(z/h), (h/L)]$, etc. The choices of $\hat{u}$ and h (PBL thickness) were left open initially. Then matching the *outer* (Ekman) layer with an *inner* (surface) layer of the form (8-36) and (8-38) leads to

$$\begin{aligned} \ell n(h/z_0) - k\hat{u}/u_* &= A(h/L) \\ -(\mathrm{sign}\, f)\, k\hat{v}/u_* &= B(h/L) \\ C(h/L) &= \ell n(h/z_0) - (k/Pr_0)\,(\hat{\theta}_v - \theta_{v0})/T_* \end{aligned} \tag{8-61}$$

where the F's have been absorbed into the functions A, B, and C; and Pr_0 is the Prandtl number for neutral stability. Using the foregoing equations to obtain the geostrophic drag and heat transfer coefficients gives

$$C_D = u_*/\hat{V} = k\{[\ell n(h/z_0) - A]^2 + B^2\}^{-1/2} \tag{8-62}$$

$$C_H = T_*/(\hat{\theta}_v - \hat{\theta}_{v0}) = (k/Pr_0)\,[\ell n(h/z_0) - C]^{-1} \tag{8-63}$$

$$\sin\alpha_s = -B\,(\mathrm{sign}\, f)\, u_*/k\hat{V} \tag{8-64}$$

where the subscript 0 refers to the level z_0, $\hat{V} = (u^2 + v^2)^{1/2}$ and α_s is angle between the surface wind and $\hat{V}$. When the similarity functions A, B, and C and h/z_0 are known the drag and heat transfer cofficients and the surface wind angle can be determined.

Yamada obtained the least scatter with respect to observational data for A, B, and C as functions of h/L when the vertical average of the geostrophic wind $\langle\mathbf{V}_g\rangle \equiv h^{-1}\int_{z0}^{h} \mathbf{V}_g\, dz$ is used for $\hat{\mathbf{V}}$, and somewhat more scatter when A, B, and C were scaled with $\hat{V} = V_h$ or when A, B, and C were expressed as functions of u_*/fL. He also used the vertical average $\langle\theta_v\rangle$ for θ_v.

Although the geostrophic wind profiles are not generally available, $<\mathbf{V}_g>$ may be obtained from the actual winds by integrating the equation of mean motion from z_0 to h,

$$f\mathbf{k} \times (\mathbf{V} - \mathbf{V}_g) = \frac{1}{\rho}\frac{\partial \boldsymbol{\tau}}{\partial z} \tag{8-65}$$

This leads to $<u_g> = <u>$ and $<v_g> = <v> - u_*^2/fh$, which provide appropriate values for $\hat{u}$ and $\hat{v}$.

Since a *bulk* Richardson number is more easily obtained from an NWP model than L, the vertically averaged velocities and potential temperature can be substituted into (8-65) for Ri_B, which can then be expressed in terms of the functions A, B, and C as follows:

$$Ri_B \equiv \frac{gh\,(\hat{\theta}_v - \theta_{v0})}{\hat{\theta}_v\,|\hat{V}|^2} = Pr_0 \frac{h}{L} \frac{\ell n\,(h/z_0) - C}{\{[\ell n(h/z_0) - A]^2 + B^2\}} \tag{8-66}$$

Assuming the similarity functions A, B, and C are known empirical functions of h/L, (8-66) is an implicit equation for h/L given h/z_0 and Ri_B. For the unstable case the approximation, $h/L \doteq Ri_B(0.75/k)\ell n(h/z_0)$, is fairly good (Yu and Madala, 1977). Unfortunately no such simple explicit relationship apparently holds for the stable case, hence (8-66) must be solved.

Yamada's similarity formulas for A, B, and C are

$$\text{STABLE:}\quad \begin{aligned} A &= \begin{cases} 1.855 - 0.380\,h/L & \text{for } 0 \leq h/L \leq 35 \\ -2.94\,(h/L - 19.94)^{1/2} & \text{for } 35 < h/L \end{cases} \\ B &= \begin{cases} 3.020 + 0.300\,h/L & \text{for } 0 \leq h/L \leq 35 \\ 2.85\,(h/L - 12.47)^{1/2} & \text{for } 35 < h/L \end{cases} \\ C &= \begin{cases} 3.665 - 0.829\,h/L & \text{for } 0 \leq h/L \leq 18 \\ -4.32\,(h/L - 11.21)^{1/2} & \text{for } 18 < h/L \end{cases} \end{aligned} \tag{8-67}$$

$$\text{UNSTABLE:}\quad \begin{aligned} A &= 10.0 - 8.145\,(1.0 - 0.008376\,h/L)^{-1/2} \\ B &= 3.020\,(1.0 - 3.290\,h/L)^{-1/2} \\ C &= 12.0 - 8.335\,(1.0 - 0.03106\,h/L)^{-1/2} \end{aligned} \tag{8-68}$$

The height h is taken to be the *height of the surface inversion layer for stable* conditions and the *height of the mixed layer for unstable* conditions. For near-neutral stability $h \doteq u_*/|f|$, but it is much larger for unstable conditions. Yamada avoids the need to compute L by effectively replacing it with Ri_B and presents graphs for the geostrophic drag and heat transfer coefficients, C_D and C_H in (8-62) and (8-63), which are similar in form to Deardorff's.

Yu and Madala (1977) pointed out that when the first level of a GCM or NWP model is within the constant flux layer, only surface-layer similarity theory is needed to compute the surface fluxes. On the other hand, because of the coarse vertical resolution in many models, the first interior level is well above surface layer; hence to calculate the boundary fluxes, the entire PBL must be parameterized (for example, Deardorff's scheme). Continuing Yamada's work, Yu and Madala calculated the surface fluxes based on the Rossby number similarity theory, which assumes that the PBL height is uniquely determined by u_*/f and L, and with the generalized similarity theory, which utilizes the PBL height h instead of u_*/f. They found that the two theories were equally valid under unstable conditions; but under stable conditions, the Rossby number similarity performed better than the generalized theory. Despite these results, they recommend the generalized theory for global models, simply because the determination of the boundary layer height by u_*/f is obviously not valid in the tropics. They also demonstrated feasibility of the Newton-Rapheson method for calculating h/L from the bulk Richardson number Ri_B and z_0 and thence the similarity functions A, B, C, and D (for moisture), a procedure that would be useful in numerical modeling.

8-8 A PREDICTION EQUATION FOR *h*

Smeda (1977) developed a modification to Deardorff's 1972 prediction equation for the depth h of the PBL, which begins with the approximate heat balance equation $\partial(\overline{w'\theta'})/\partial z = -d\theta/dt$. Next let $\Delta\theta = \theta^+ - \theta^-$ be the difference in θ between the stable layer above h and the convective layer below, thus

$$\partial\Delta\theta/\partial t = \partial\theta^+/\partial t - \partial\theta^-/\partial t \tag{8-69}$$

Neglecting horizontal advection, the thermodynamic equation for θ^+ may be written

$$\frac{\partial\theta^+}{\partial t} = -\frac{\partial}{\partial z}(\overline{w'\theta'})^+ + \left(\frac{dh}{dt} - w_h\right)\frac{\partial\theta^+}{\partial z} \tag{8-70}$$

where an increase in h tends to increase θ^+ as base of the inversion slides upward along the $p - \theta$ curve. Assuming little turbulence in the stable layer gives $(\overline{w'\theta'})^+ = 0$ in (8-70). In the convective layer, the lapse rate should be nearly dry adiabatic, hence

$$\partial\theta^-/\partial z \approx 0, \text{ thus } \partial\theta^-/\partial t \doteq -\partial(\overline{w'\theta'})^-/\partial z \tag{8-71}$$

Substituting (8-71) and (8-70) into (8-69) gives

$$\frac{\partial\Delta\theta}{\partial t} = \left(\frac{dh}{dt} - w_h\right)\frac{\partial\theta^+}{\partial z} + \frac{\partial(\overline{w'\theta'})^-}{\partial z} \tag{8-72}$$

It is further assumed that $\partial\Delta\theta/\partial t$ is small compared to the terms on the right side of (8-72), which leads to

$$\frac{\partial h}{\partial t} = -\mathbf{V} \cdot \nabla h + w_h - \frac{\partial \overline{(w'\theta')}^-}{\partial z} \Bigg/ \frac{\partial \theta^+}{\partial z}$$

where $dh/dt = \partial h/\partial t + \mathbf{V} \cdot \nabla h$. Using a linear approximation,

$$\partial \overline{(w'\theta')}^- / \partial z = [\overline{(w'\theta')}_h - \overline{(w'\theta')}_0]/h$$

and following Deardorff by letting $(w'\theta')_h \doteq -0.2\,(w'\theta')_0$ leads to

$$\text{UNSTABLE: } \frac{\partial h}{\partial t} = -\mathbf{V} \cdot \nabla h + w_h + 1.2\,\overline{(w'\theta')}_0 \Bigg/ \left[h \frac{\partial \theta^+}{\partial z} + 9 w_* \theta_m / gh \right] \tag{8-73}$$

The term involving $w_* = [gh/\theta_m\,\overline{(w'\theta')}_0]^{1/3}$ is an empirical correction added by Deardorff to account for effect of convection as the PBL grows through an upper neutral layer after overcoming a surface inversion. w^* is a convective velocity scale for the mixed layer. It governs the asymptotic entrainment rate referred to as free entrainment [Deardorff (1976)]. According to Smeda, (8-73) is applicable to a wide range of stratifications.

The same approach for the stable case was abandoned in favor of an empirical, although similar, form which does not involve heat flux, but rather u_*, f, and h:

$$\text{STABLE: } \frac{\partial h}{\partial t} = -\mathbf{V} \cdot \nabla h + (c_1\, u_*^2/hf)\,[1 - c_2\,(hf/u_*)^\alpha] \tag{8-74}$$

where $c_1 = 0.06$, $c_2 = 3.3$, and $\alpha = 3$. Equations 8-73 and 8-74 utilize various large-scale parameters and require the calculation of Ri, u_*, and $\overline{w'\theta'}$ as described earlier.

8-8-1 Further Comments on PBL Parameterization

The PBL parameterization by Deardorff utilizes the numerical output values within and above the boundary layer together with the surface roughness and the thickness of the boundary layer to diagnose the profiles of the mean variables from which the fluxes are then calculated. Randall (1975) has stated that although qualitatively the answers are correct, significant quantitative errors may occur because separate conservation equations are not carried for the boundary-layer thermodynamic energy, momentum, and moisture. When included, the PBL and the NWP model systems of prognostic equations must be mutually consistent so that they do not produce independent solutions that separate. Moreover, the character of the PBL controls evaporation and the vertical distribution of moisture which, in turn, affect the formation of stratus and convective clouds. Recognizing these interrelationships, the Arakawa-Randall

(A-R) PBL parameterization is designed to interact with the Arakawa-Schubert cumulus parameterization described in Chapter 9. Also the structure of the PBL is strongly influenced by the presence of low-level stratus or fog, which may occur over extensive areas, for example, off the west coasts of the continents.

The unstable, unsaturated PBL, which may have cumulus clouds above, is well mixed with respect to potential temperature θ and moisture q with a sharp decrease in q and an increase in θ at the top. On the other hand, an unstable PBL may be topped by a saturated layer of stratus or stratocumulus, within which the lapse rate is nearly moist adiabatic. The A-R parameterization also permits discontinuities at the top of the PBL.

The stable PBL, which is usually accompanied by cooling at the surface, is not well mixed because of the suppression of turbulence and θ increases markedly with height. While the depth of an *unstable* PBL is about 1 km and may be as much as several kilometers, the *stable* PBL is usually not deeper than several hundred meters and may be less than 50 m, perhaps with a ground inversion.

Randall develops equations for the mean temperature, specific humidity, and momentum for the boundary layer and for the discontinuities in these quantities at the top of the PBL. He uses a modified form of Deardorff's method based on similarity theory to determine the surface fluxes from the large-scale model output and the surface properties. The surface fluxes are presented in terms of the transfer coefficients C_u and C_θ as functions of the Richardson number Ri_B, the depth of the PBL and the surface roughness, although these quantities are computed somewhat differently than in Deardorff's method. Fluxes between the tops of the surface layer and the PBL are interpolated. The presence of stratus in the PBL and cumulus above the PBL are taken into account.

The many details involved are too extensive to be included in this text. However, it may be said that the incorporation of this scheme into the UCLA GCM has resulted in an improved simulation of many inportant features of the observed PBL, the global distribution of stratus and, through interaction with the cumulus parameterization, the distribution of cumulus clouds.

8-9 A HIGH-RESOLUTION MODEL

8-9-1 The Coefficient of Eddy Viscosity

In the introduction it was indicated that providing sufficient levels to resolve the PBL explicitly in a large-scale NWP model may possibly be inadvisable because of additional computer time, more detail than warranted considering a large horizontal grid distance, or lack of data for initial conditions. Also as computer capability increases, perhaps there may be a greater pay-off by treating other features of a model in more sophisticated fashion.

On the other hand, under some circumstances explicit treatment of the PBL may be desirable, in a model with high vertical resolution or for example, in studies of air pollution, diffusion of contaminants, etc., particularly when the wind distribution needs to be known in more detail at some future time. This could be accomplished with a fine-mesh (FM) model superimposed on the coarse-mesh (CM) model.

Blackadar (1978) has given a review of high-resolution explicit boundary-layer models from which his choice will be given here. The basic equations for such a system using the eddy viscosity approach are

$$\frac{d\mathbf{V}}{dt} = -\frac{1}{\rho}\nabla p - fk \times \mathbf{V} + \frac{\partial}{\partial z}\left(K_m \frac{\partial \mathbf{V}}{\partial z}\right) \tag{8-75}$$

$$\frac{d\theta}{dt} = -\frac{1}{\rho c_p}\frac{\partial R_N}{\partial z} + \frac{\partial}{\partial z}\left(K_h \frac{\partial \theta}{\partial z}\right) \tag{8-76}$$

$$\nabla \cdot \mathbf{V} = 0 \tag{8-77}$$

$$\frac{dC}{dt} = S + \frac{\partial}{\partial z}\left(K \frac{\partial C}{\partial z}\right) \tag{8-78}$$

where R_N is the radiative heat flux, C a contaminant, S a source or sink of C, and the other symbols are as used earlier in the text.

The principal problem here is to express the K's in terms of other variables or known quantities. Empirical methods based on observational data suggest the following form:

$$K = \ell^2 s\, F(Ri) \tag{8-79}$$

where $s = [(\partial u/\partial z)^2 + (\partial y/\partial z)^2]^{1/2}$ and ℓ is a mixing length that characterizes the energy containing turbulence. For the surface layer $\ell = kz$ and $F = \phi_m^{-2}$. Above the surface layer Blackadar (1962) has suggested

$$\ell = kz/(1 + kz/\lambda) \tag{8-80}$$

where the parameter λ has been expressed principally in two scalings

$$\text{(a) } \lambda = 0.00027V_g/f \qquad \text{and} \qquad \text{(b) } \lambda = 0.0063u_*/f \tag{8-81}$$

However, as the atmosphere becomes more convective, the scale length should shift from u_*/f to the depth of the mixed layer h.

Regarding stability, a simple function that appears to fit the empirical data quite well (Panofsky, Blackadar, and McVehil (1960)) for negative Ri is the following:

$$\text{UNSTABLE:} \qquad F(Ri) = (1 - 18Ri)^{1/2} \tag{8-82}$$

For *stable* conditions the observational data shows wide scatter, but K_m should approach zero as Ri approaches the critical value Ri_c, which is in the range 0.20 to 0.25. Dyer's (1974) summary of nighttime stable cases leads to

$$\text{STABLE:} \qquad F(Ri) = (1 - 5Ri)^2 \tag{8-83}$$

implying a critical value of 0.2.

Zilitinkevich and Laikhtman (1965) depart from the foregoing essentially empirical approach and utilize the turbulent kinetic energy equation. It is first assumed that

$$K_m = C_1 \ell_z b \qquad \text{and} \qquad K_h = \alpha_T K_m \tag{8-84}$$

where $b^2 = u'^2 + v'^2 + w'^2$, ℓ_z is a length parameter and α_T is assumed constant. The turbulent energy equation, neglecting turbulent transport of energy, may be written

$$K_m s^2 - \alpha_T K_m \frac{g}{\theta} \frac{\partial \bar{\theta}}{\partial z} - \varepsilon = 0 \tag{8-85}$$

where the dissipation rate ε was assumed to be of the form

$$\varepsilon = C_3\, b^3/\ell_z \tag{8-86}$$

Substitution of (8-86) into (8-85) and absorbing C_1^3/C_3 into the definition ℓ_z leads to

$$K_m = \ell_z^2\, s\,(1 - \alpha_T Ri)^{1/2} \tag{8-87}$$

which is similar to the empirical forms (8-79), (8-82), and (8-83). However observational data for the unstable case lead to values of α_T in the range 1.3 to 2, which gives too large a critical value Ri_c.

Blackadar (1974) also used turbulence theory to develop the following expressions for the eddy coefficients in terms of the vertical wind shear, Richardson number, and a mixing length:

$$\text{UNSTABLE: } K_m = \ell^2 s\,(1 - 21Ri)^{1/2} \qquad K_h = \ell^2 s\,(1 - 87Ri)^{1/2} \tag{8-88}$$

$$\text{STABLE:} \qquad K_m = K_h = 1.1\left(\frac{Ri_c - Ri}{Ri_c}\right)\ell^2 s, \text{ if } Ri < Ri_c;\ \text{O, if } Ri \geq R_c \tag{8-89}$$

These simple formulas apply to slightly negative (unstable) Ri as well as $Ri > 0$. These results do not, however, indicate the nature of the parameter ℓ. Near the ground the size of the eddies is limited by the distance from the surface, so that $\ell \sim z$ is appropriate, but aloft empirical evidence must be used. For stable conditions ℓ may be taken to be the Monin L, which is roughly 10 to 50 m. For unstable conditions, the problem is more difficult, but accuracy need not be greater than ability to verify uncertainties in initial state and boundary conditions [see (8-80)].

The foregoing schemes, where the eddy fluxes are written in terms of eddy coefficients K_m, K_h and the latter are expressed directly in terms of mean-flow parameters, are known as *first-order closure* schemes even though turbulence theory may have been used in their derivations.

Second-order closure schemes are based on equations for the turbulent fluxes or second-order moments derived from the Reynolds equations [e.g., (8-1)], and will be discussed in the last section. For the present the application of the K theory to a prediction model will be pursued a bit further with respect to the surface boundary including the determination of surface temperature, some finite difference forms, and the calculation of surface fluxes.

8-9-2 Surface Temperature

Over water the surface temperature can be assumed to be constant as a boundary condition during short-range forecasts. However the land surface temperature may vary considerably over a period of 12 to 24 hr, hence its variation is computed for the lower-boundary condition. Through the latter, certain effects of solar and terrestrial radiation, sensible heating, etc. may be taken into account. Similarly the moisture budget equation is needed at the surface to account for evapotranspiration, etc.

In order, to calculate the land surface temperature θ_g, Blackadar (1977) considers a soil slab of uniform properties receiving a periodic input of heat from above, that is,

$$H = S + 1 - \sigma\theta_g^4 - H_T = \hat{H} \cos \omega t \tag{8-90}$$

where S is the incoming short wave solar radiation; I, the downward long wave radiation; σ, the Stefan Boltzman constant; and H_0, the upward turbulent heat flux. Below is a substrate of constant temperature θ_m, which is the mean temperature of the slab; and in practice θ_m is taken to mean surface air temperature of the recent past.

The predictive equation for θ_g is

$$C_g \frac{\partial \theta_g}{\partial t} = H - \kappa_m C_g(\theta_g - \theta_m) \tag{8-91}$$

Here C_g, the heat capacity of the slab of soil per unit area and $\kappa_m (\theta_g - \theta_m)/C_g$, the heat transfer from the substrate below to the slab, are determined in such a way that the slab temperature and phase will be the same as the surface temperature of a real soil layer of thermal conductivity λ and heat capacity per unit volume C_s.

Toward this end the heat diffusion equations, $\partial T/\partial t = (\lambda/C_s)\, \partial^2 T/\partial z^2$, is solved subject to the conditions that T approaches a constant T_0 at infinite depth; and at the surface $z = 0$, the flux is continuous, that is, $\lambda \partial T/\partial z = \hat{H} \cos \omega t$. The solution is found to be

$$T = T_0 + [\hat{H}/(\lambda C_s \omega)^{1/2}] [\exp \beta z] [\cos(\omega t - \pi/4 + \upsilon z)] \tag{8-92}$$

where $\upsilon = \beta = (C_s \omega/2\lambda)^{1/2}$ and ω is the angular velocity of the earth.

The solution for T must equal the surface temperature θ_g at $z = 0$, and hence must satisfy (8-91). This leads to the following results:

$$T_0 = \theta_m \qquad \kappa_m = \omega \qquad \text{and} \qquad C_g = (\lambda C_s/2\omega)^{1/2} \tag{8-93}$$

Thus the solution of (8-91) with the foregoing values κ_m and C_g will give an appropriate value of θ_g. Since the differential equations involved are linear, the form of (8-90) is not limited to a single harmonic.

8-9-3 Some Prediction Model Details

The prediction equation for the mean-motion acceleration, $\partial u/\partial t$, has a term of the form $\partial(K\partial u/\partial z)/\partial z$, which is placed in finite difference form at level i as follows: $[K_{i+1} (u_{i+2} - u_i) - K_{i-1} (u_i - u_{i-2})]/\Delta z^2$, where $\Delta z = z_{i+1} - z_{i-1}$. At the lowest prediction level (odd numbers) in the model, say 1, the surface fluxes must be used and the foregoing term becomes

$$[K_2 (u_3 - u_1) - u_*^2 u_1/V_1]/(\Delta z)^2 \tag{8-94}$$

where $V_1 = (u_1^2 + v_1^2)^{1/2}$. The factor u_1/V_1 will yield the component of surface stress $u_*^2 = \tau_s/\rho$ in the x-direction and a similar term applies in the y-direction.

The thermodynamic equation for $\partial\theta/\partial t$ at level 1 has a similar term for surface heat flux, namely,

$$[K_2 (\theta_3 - \theta_1)/\Delta z + H_0/c_p \rho \Delta z]/\Delta z \tag{8-95}$$

Needed for evaluating these terms are u_*, V_1 and H_0. For this purpose, similarity theory is used from level 1 down to a level, $z_a \doteq 1$ m, to determine the temperature profile. Below z_a it is assumed that temperature changes are governed by radiative flux divergences as well as turbulence. The similarity wind profile is assumed to hold down to z_0 where the wind speed is zero. The air temperature at level z_a is predicted by the equation

$$\partial\theta_a/\partial t = a(\theta_g - \theta_a) - bH_0/\rho c_p z_a \tag{8-96}$$

which asumes that the radiative cooling rate is proportional to $(\theta_g - \theta_a)$ and that this is counteracted by turbulent heat flux. Blackadar used $a = 8.3 \times 10^{-4}$ sec^{-1} and $b = 0.2$. The shear V_1 (from z_0 to z_1) and $(\theta_1 - \theta_a)$ determine u_* and $T_* = -H_0/c_p k \rho u_*$ by an iterative process using values from the previous time step as a first guess. A first estimate of a bulk Richardson number is calculated as follows:

$$Ri = (gz_1/\bar{\theta}V_1^2)(\theta_1 - \theta_0) \doteq (gz_1/\bar{\theta}V_1^2)[\theta_1 - \theta_a + T_* \ell n(z_a/z_0)] \quad (8\text{-}97)$$

using the latest values of θ_1, θ_a, V_1, and T_*. [Note from (b) or (c) below, that $\theta_a - \theta_0 \doteq T_* \ell n(z_a/z_0)$.] Three cases are then considered:

(a) $Ri > 0.2$: Turbulent momentum and heat fluxes are set to zero.

(b) $0 \le Ri \le 0.2$: Calculate $1/L = z_1^{-1}[Ri/(1 - 5Ri]\ell n(z_1/z_0)$

$u_* = kV_1/[\ell n(z_1/z_0) - \psi_m]$, (see 8-36)

$T_* = (\theta_1 - \theta_a)/[\ell n(z_1/z_a) - \psi_h]$ (see 8-38)

where $\psi_m \doteq \psi_h \doteq -5z_1/L$ (integrate (8-37) with (8-40))

(c) $Ri < 0$: Using last estimate of L calculate $x = (1 - 16z_1/L)^{1/4}$

then $\psi_h = 2\ell n(1 + x^2/2)$

$\psi_m = (\psi_h + \pi)/2 + 2\ell n[(1 + x)/2] - 2\tan^{-2} x$

$u_* = kV_1/[\ell n(z_1/z_0) - \psi_m]$

$T_* = (\theta_1 - \theta_a)/[\ell n(z_1/z_a) - \psi_h]$

$1/L = (Ri/z_1)[\ell n(z_1/z_0) - \psi_m]^2/[\ell n(z_1/z_0) - \psi_h]$

With the new values of u_* and T_*, a new estimate of Ri_B may be calculated and the entire procedure may be repeated, although once was sufficient according to Blackadar. With the final values of u_* and T_*, the surface heat flux H_0 is obtained (see 8-33) from

$$H_0 = -k\, c_p \rho\, u_* T_* \quad (8\text{-}98)$$

This model was used with actual data for several nocturnal situations. After initial adjustment, the variables evolved smoothly and the predicted values agreed quite well with observations.

8-10 MEAN TURBULENT FIELD CLOSURE MODELS (SECOND-ORDER CLOSURE)

The eddy viscosity method has long been used to simulate boundary layer flows. Patterned after molecular viscosity, the eddy stresses are assumed to be proportional to the product of an eddy coefficient and the vertical wind shear as discussed earlier. The eddy coefficients, in turn, can be expressed in terms of a mixing length and the shear. In the constant-flux surface layer the well-known Prandtl hypothesis, relating the mixing length to the distance from the surface, leads to a simple form for the coefficient of eddy viscosity under neutral stability, and more recently under nonneutral conditions by means of the Monin-Obukhov (M-O) similarity theory through the introduction of the M-O length L (or the Richardson number). This extension to stratified conditions depends heavily on empirical functions. Moreover, the extension of the eddy viscosity theory to the remainder of the PBL above the surface layer is faced with the difficulty of determining an appropriate form for the mixing length. Although the essentially empirical formulas discussed in the previous sections give acceptable results for many applications, such *first-order closure* methods, as they are called, are not fully satisfactory nor very elegant.

During the last decade, or so, various turbulent energy, or second-order closure models have been under development with increasing sophistication. The basic concept consists of deriving equations for the turbulent fluxes, $\rho\overline{u'w'}$, etc., from the original governing equations. Mellor and Yamada (1974) made an important contribution by providing a hierarchy of closure models that were ordered systematically in terms of a succession of consistent simplifying assumptions. Following Mellor (1973) the Boussinesq equations for the mean flow may be expressed in the convenient form

$$\frac{\partial U_j}{\partial t} + \frac{\partial}{\partial x_k}(U_k U_j + \overline{u_k u_j}) + \varepsilon_{jkl} f_k U_l = -\frac{\partial P}{\partial x_j} - g_j \beta\Theta + \upsilon\nabla^2 U_j \qquad (8\text{-}99)$$

$$\frac{\partial U_i}{\partial x_i} = 0 \qquad (8\text{-}100)$$

$$\frac{\partial \Theta}{\partial t} + \frac{\partial}{\partial x_k}(U_k \Theta + \overline{u_k \theta}) = \alpha\nabla^2\Theta \qquad (8\text{-}101)$$

where the upper- and lower-case letters denote the mean and turbulent variables, respectively; a repeated index implies summation over 1,2,3; $P = p/\rho$ is the kinematic pressure, $g_j = (0,0,-g)$; $f_j = (0, f_y, f)$ are the components of the earth's vorticity; $\beta = (\partial\rho/\partial T)_p/\rho$ is the coefficient of thermal expansion in the buoyancy term; the overbar represents an ensemble average; υ is the kinematic viscosity; and α the thermal diffusivity. The alternating tensor $\varepsilon_{jk\ell}$ vanishes unless j, k, and ℓ are different, is 1 for an even number of permutations, and -1 for odd permutations.

The equations for the fluctuating components of velocity and potential temperature are obtained by subtracting the foregoing equations for the mean flow from the equations for the total flow (e.g., $U_j + u_j$). The results are

$$\frac{\partial u_j}{\partial t} + \frac{\partial}{\partial x_k}(U_k u_j + U_j u_k + u_k u_j - \overline{u_k u_j}) + \varepsilon_{jkl} f_k u_l$$
$$= -\frac{\partial p}{\partial x_j} - g_j \beta\theta + \upsilon\nabla^2 u_j \qquad (8\text{-}102)$$

$$\frac{\partial u_i}{\partial x_i} = 0 \qquad (8\text{-}103)$$

$$\frac{\partial \theta}{\partial t} + \frac{\partial}{\partial k_k}(\Theta u_k + U_k\theta + u_k\theta - \overline{u_k\theta}) = \alpha\nabla^2\theta \qquad (8\text{-}104)$$

Next the equations for covariances appearing in (8-99) and (8-101) may be obtained from (8-102) to (8-104) by forming the appropriate products and sums, e.g., $u_i\, \partial u_j/\partial t + u_j\, \partial u_i/\partial t = \partial(u_i u_j)/\partial t$, and then taking the ensemble average. Simplification leads to

$$\frac{\partial \overline{u_i u_j}}{\partial t} + \frac{\partial}{\partial x_k}\left(U_k\, \overline{u_i u_j} + \overline{u_k u_i u_j} - \upsilon \frac{\partial}{\partial x_k}\, \overline{u_i u_j}\right) + \frac{\partial}{\partial x_j}\, \overline{p u_i}$$

$$+ \frac{\partial}{\partial x_i}\, \overline{p u_j} + f_k\, (\varepsilon_{jkl}\, \overline{u_l u_i} + \varepsilon_{ikl}\, \overline{u_l u_j})$$

$$= - \overline{u_k u_i}\, \frac{\partial U_j}{\partial x_k} - \overline{u_k u_j}\, \frac{\partial U_i}{\partial x_k} - \beta(g_j \overline{u_i \theta} + g_i \overline{u_j \theta})$$

$$+ \overline{p\left(\frac{\partial u_i}{\partial x_j} + \frac{\partial u_j}{\partial x_i}\right)} - 2\nu\, \overline{\frac{\partial u_i}{\partial x_k}\, \frac{\partial u_j}{\partial x_k}} \tag{8-105}$$

$$\frac{\partial \overline{u_j \theta}}{\partial t} + \frac{\partial}{\partial x_k}\left(u_k \overline{\theta u_j} + \overline{u_k u_j \theta} - \alpha u_j\, \frac{\overline{\partial \theta}}{\partial x_k} - \upsilon \theta\, \frac{\overline{\partial u_j}}{\partial x_k}\right)$$

$$+ \frac{\partial}{\partial x_j}\, \overline{p\theta} + \varepsilon_{jkl} f_k\, \overline{u_l \theta}$$

$$= - \overline{u_j u_k}\, \frac{\partial \Theta}{\partial x_k} - \overline{\theta u_k}\, \frac{\partial U_j}{\partial x_k} - \beta\, g_j\, \overline{\theta^2} + p\, \frac{\overline{\partial \theta}}{\partial x_j}$$

$$- (\alpha + \upsilon)\, \overline{\frac{\partial u_j}{\partial x_k}\, \frac{\partial \theta}{\partial k_k}} \tag{8-106}$$

$$\frac{\partial \overline{\theta^2}}{\partial t} + \frac{\partial}{\partial x_k}\left(U_k\, \overline{\theta^2} + \overline{u_k \theta^2} - \alpha\, \frac{\partial \overline{\theta^2}}{\partial x_k}\right) = - 2\overline{u_k \theta}\, \frac{\partial \Theta}{\partial x_k} - 2\alpha\, \overline{\frac{\partial \theta}{\partial x_k}\, \frac{\partial \theta}{\partial x_k}} \tag{8-107}$$

The last equation is needed because of the appearance of $\overline{\theta^2}$ in (8-106). By varying i and j from 1 to 3 it is seen that there is a total of 10 covariances such as $\overline{u_i u_j}$, $\overline{u_j^2}$, $\overline{u_j \theta}$, etc. in (8-105) to (8-107) and an equal number of equations. Even assuming the mean quantities to be known this set does not form a closed system because of the triple moments such as $\overline{u_k u_i u_j}$ and other terms appearing in the system. Moreover the system is very complex. It is possible to develop equations for the triple moments in an attempt to close the system; however, as might be expected, fourth-order correlations then make their appearance. Thus at some point, it is clearly necessary to express the higher-order moments in terms of the next lower ones. In *second-order closure* methods the triple moments in (8-105) to (8-107) are expressed in terms of second-order terms or lower. The system is still too complex for practical applications and further simplifying assumptions are necessary to make the system more tractable.

Using earlier research results and observation, Mellor (1973) and Mellor and Yamada (1974) developed a hierarchy of models for the PBL based upon organized analytical simplifications and closure assumptions for the triple moments. An important contribution was made by Rotta (1951) who suggested that the energy redistribution turbulence term $\overline{p(\partial u_i/\partial x_j + \partial u_j/\partial x_i)}$ could reasonably be approximated by $-(b/3\ell_1)(\overline{u_i u_j} - \frac{1}{3}\delta_{ij}b^2) + Cb^2(\partial U_i/\partial x_j + \partial U_j/\partial x_i)$ where b^2 is twice the turbulent kinetic energy. Other terms involving p are treated in similar fashion or neglected. The dissipative term $2\upsilon\overline{(\partial u_i/\partial x_k)(\partial u_j/\partial x_k)}$ is approximated by $2b^3\delta_{ij}/3\Lambda_1$ following Kolmogorov's (1942) hypothesis of local, small-scale isotropy. Similarly $2\alpha\overline{(\partial\theta/\partial x_k)(\partial\theta/\partial x_k)}$ is approximated by $2b\overline{\theta^2}/\Lambda_2$. A triple moment approximation is the following:

$$\overline{u_k u_i u_j} = -b\lambda_1\left(\frac{\partial\overline{u_i u_j}}{\partial x_k} + \frac{\partial\overline{u_i u_k}}{\partial x_j} + \frac{\partial\overline{u_j u_k}}{\partial x_i}\right)$$

and similar, although simpler, approximations are made for $\overline{u_k\theta^2}$ and $\overline{u_k u_j\theta}$. The intention here is only to give the flavor of Mellor's procedure for closing and simplifying the system (8-105) to (8-107). The models developed for the PBL were labeled level 4 through level 1. When compared to some actual data the level 4 model performed little better than the considerably less complex level 3 model. However, level 3 displayed significantly better results than the level 2 model. The last requires the solution of no differential, only algebraic equations, and can be expressed in a traditional eddy coefficient format involving the Richardson number. The level 3 model can be reduced to the following system consisting of only two differential and several algebraic equations:

$$\frac{Db^2}{Dt} - \frac{\partial}{\partial x_k}\left(\frac{5}{3}b\lambda_1\frac{\partial b^2}{\partial x_k}\right) = -2\overline{u_k u_i}\frac{\partial U_i}{\partial x_k} - 2\beta g_k\overline{u_k\theta} - 2\frac{b^3}{\Lambda_1} \tag{8-108}$$

$$\overline{u_i u_j} = \frac{\delta_{ij}}{3}b^2 - \frac{3\ell_1}{b}\left[(\overline{u_k u_i} - C_1 b^2\delta_{ki})\frac{\partial U_j}{\partial x_k} + (\overline{u_k u_j} - C_1 b^2\delta_{kj})\frac{\partial U_i}{\partial x_k} - \tfrac{2}{3}\delta_{ij}\overline{u_k u_l}\frac{\partial U_l}{\partial x_k}\right]$$
$$- 3\frac{\ell_1}{a}(g_j\overline{u_i\theta} + g_i\overline{u_j\theta} - \tfrac{2}{3}\delta_{ij}g_l\overline{u_l\theta}) \tag{8-109}$$

$$\frac{D\overline{\theta^2}}{Dt} - \frac{\partial}{\partial x_k}\left(b\lambda_2\frac{\partial\overline{\theta^2}}{\partial x_k}\right) = -2\overline{u_k\theta}\frac{\partial\Theta}{\partial x_k} - 2\frac{b}{\Lambda_2}\overline{\theta^2} \tag{8-110}$$

$$\overline{u_j\theta} = -3\frac{\ell_2}{b}\left(\overline{u_ju_k}\frac{\partial\Theta}{\partial x_k} + \overline{\theta u_k}\frac{\partial U_j}{\partial x_k} + \beta g_j\overline{\theta^2}\right) \tag{8-111}$$

where b^2 is twice the turbulent kinetic energy, $b^2 = \overline{u_1^2} + \overline{u_2^2} + \overline{u_3^2}$. The reduction of (8-105) to (8-107) to this form is rather lengthy and the reader is referred to the Mellor and Yamada 1974 article for the details, as well as the definition of the various constants involved. It is clear that when $\overline{b^2}$ and $\overline{\theta^2}$ have been obtained by solution of their differential equations, the covariances $\overline{u_iu_j}$, $\overline{u_j\theta}$ can be calculated for use in the larger-scale or mean-motion equations. For further comparison to boundary layer data Yamada and Mellor (1975) add a differential equation similar to (8-110) for mixing ratio $\overline{q}$, $\overline{q^2}$, and one for $\overline{q\theta_v}$. They concluded that fairly accurate thermal wind and mean vertical wind data are required to obtain realistic simulations for winds and temperature; and advection terms improved prediction of the velocity field.

For tests with the GFDL GCM Miyakoda and Sirutis (M-S) (1977) utilized a somewhat simplified version of the level 3 model, referred to as level 2.5, in which some additional terms were omitted from (8-108) to (8-110). Equation 8-110 is reduced to an algebraic equation by dropping the terms on the left side, which is similar to simplifications already made in (8-109) and (8-111). In addition, horizontal gradients are dropped in favor of vertical gradients, except in the turbulent energy equation. The covariances, $\overline{u_1u_3}$, $\overline{u_2u_3}$ and $\overline{u_j\theta}$ may be couched in terms of eddy coefficients, including moisture flux, as follows:

$$\begin{pmatrix} -\overline{u_iu_3} \\ -\overline{u_2u_3} \end{pmatrix} \equiv \begin{pmatrix} \tau_x/\rho \\ \tau_y/\rho \end{pmatrix} = K_M \begin{pmatrix} \partial U/\partial z \\ \partial V\partial z \end{pmatrix} \tag{8-112}$$

$$\begin{pmatrix} \overline{u_3\Theta} \\ \overline{u_3q} \end{pmatrix} = \begin{pmatrix} H/\rho \\ E/\rho \end{pmatrix} = -K_H \begin{pmatrix} \partial\Theta/\partial z \\ \partial q/\partial z \end{pmatrix} \tag{8-113}$$

where

$$\begin{aligned} K_m = \ell_1 \Bigg[&(1-3C)\,b^5 + 3\ell_2\,\{(\Lambda_2 - 3\ell_2)\,b^3 \\ &- 3(4\ell_1 + \Lambda_2)\,c\cdot b^3\}\frac{g}{\Theta_0}\frac{\partial\Theta}{\partial z}\Bigg] \div \left[b^4 + 6\ell_1^2\,b^2\left|\frac{\partial \mathbf{V}}{\partial z}\right|^2 + 3\ell_1\ell_2\frac{g}{\Theta_0}\frac{\partial\Theta}{\partial z}\right. \\ &\times \left\{6\ell_1(\Lambda_1 - 3\ell_2)\left|\frac{\partial \mathbf{V}}{\partial z}\right|^2 + \left(7 + \frac{\Lambda_2}{\ell_1}\right)b^2 \right. \\ &\left.\left. + 9\,\ell_2\,(4\,\ell_1 + \Lambda_2)\frac{g}{\Theta_0}\frac{\partial\Theta}{\partial z}\right\}\right] \end{aligned} \tag{8-114}$$

$$K_H = \ell_2\left[b^3 - 6\ell_1 K_M\left|\frac{\partial \mathbf{V}}{\partial z}\right|^2\right] \div \left[b^2 + 3\ell_2\,(4\ell_1 + \Lambda_2)\frac{g}{\Theta_0}\frac{\partial\Theta}{\partial z}\right] \tag{8-115}$$

where ℓ is the mixing length. Their turbulent energy equation has the form

$$\frac{D}{Dt}\left(\frac{b^2}{2}\right) = \frac{\partial}{\partial z}\left[\frac{5}{3}\lambda_1 b \frac{\partial}{\partial z}\left(\frac{b^2}{2}\right)\right] + \frac{\tau_x}{\rho}\frac{\partial U}{\partial z} + \frac{\tau_y}{\rho}\frac{\partial V}{\partial z} + \frac{g}{\theta_0}\overline{w'\theta_v'} - \frac{b^3}{\Lambda_1} \qquad (8\text{-}116)$$

where $D/Dt \equiv (\partial/\partial t) + U(\partial/\partial x) + V(\partial/\partial y)$, and θ_v is the virtual potential temperature. The various parameters have values as follows:

$$\ell_j = A_j\ell \qquad \Lambda_j = \nabla B_j\ell \qquad j = 1{,}2$$

$$(A_1, A_2, B_1, B_2, C) = (0.92, 0.74, 16.6, 10.1, 0.08)$$

$$\Theta_0 = 272.5K \qquad \lambda_1 = \lambda_2 = \lambda_3 = 0.23\ell \qquad p\overline{w'\theta_v'} = -(H + 0.61E)$$

The mixing length definition follows Blackadar (1962):

$$\ell = kz/(1 + kz/\ell_0) \qquad \ell_0 = 0.10\int_0^{z_T} bz\rho dz \div \int_0^{z_T} b\rho dz \qquad (8\text{-}117)$$

Equation 8-116 is solved subject to the boundary condition

$$b^2 = B_1^{2/3}\,\mathbf{V}_*^2 \text{ at } z = z_0$$

where $\mathbf{V}_*$ is the friction velocity. Despite the fact that this turbulence closure model could be used throughout the entire PBL, M-S used the Monin-Obukhov similarity solutions in their ''interfacial'' (surface) layer, extending from height zero to 18 m and the turbulence model in the remainder of the PBL and above. Their turbulence closure model similar to those of Wyngaard and Cote (1974), Sommeria (1976) and Schemm and Lipps (1976), who used grid size d instead of ℓ. M-S suggest that d should be used if $\ell > d$, and $\ell < d$, which occurs only near the surface.

When applied to the GFDL GCM, the M-S turbulence model showed considerable improvement over their previous PBL parameterization which used simpler functional forms for K_M and K_H. It is important that K_M and K_H become small or even zero if the stratification is sufficiently stable. It also should be noted that the level 2.5 model does not allow counter gradient heat flux unless horizontal advection of temperature by the mean flow fields is included. When the turbulence model is applied to any turbulent layers, a high vertical resolution is required if the vertical gradients are large and variable. Over the sea the roughness coefficient may vary considerably from the values used by M-S which are,

$$z_0 = 16.82 \text{ cm over land} \qquad z_0 = 0.032V_*^2/g \text{ over sea}$$

The foregoing coefficient 0.032 may vary from 0.003 for calm seas to 0.077 for fully rough seas. The simple bulk transfer formulas may be acceptable over the sea rather than Monin-Obukhov forms since the fluxes depend primarily on sea roughness rather than stability.

Miyakoda and Sirutis (1977) compared several parameterization schemes in the GFDL GCM denoting the combinations as the A_2, E_4, and F_2 models. The following heat budget equation was employed at the surface with the first and last terms sometimes omitted.

$$\frac{\partial(\Delta \cdot CT_s)}{\partial t} = S^{\downarrow}(1 - a) + R^{\downarrow} - R^{\uparrow} - H_s - L_v E_s + H_{\text{SOIL}} \qquad (8\text{-}118)$$

where T_s is the ground surface temperature; L_v, the latent heat of vaporization Δ is the thickness of the soil layer.

$S^{\downarrow}$ is solar radiation, a is the earth's albedo, R is terrestrial long-wave radiation, $H_s = c_p(\overline{w'\theta'})$ and $E_s = \overline{w'q'}$ provide for the upward fluxes of sensible heat and water vapor, C is the heat capacity of the soil, and H_{SOIL} is the upward heat flux in the soil at the surface. The nonsteady heat equation above, the Arakawa-Randall mixed layer parameterization along with the Arakawa-Schubert (1974) cumulus parameterization (described in Chapter 9) constituted the F_2 *model*. The A_2 *model* neglected the first and last terms in (8-118), used bulk formulas for surface drag and fluxes of heat and moisture, dry and moist convective adjustment (described in Chapter 9) above the 18-m level together with the eddy viscosity formulations:

$$\begin{pmatrix} \dfrac{\tau_x}{\rho} \\[2ex] \dfrac{\tau_y}{\rho} \end{pmatrix} = \ell^2 \left|\frac{\partial \mathbf{V}}{\partial z}\right| \begin{pmatrix} \dfrac{\partial U}{\partial z} \\[2ex] \dfrac{\partial V}{\partial z} \end{pmatrix}; \; \ell = \begin{cases} kz, & z \le z_K = 75 \text{ m} \\[1ex] \dfrac{kz_K(z_A - z)}{z_A - z_K} & z_K < z < z_A \\[1ex] 0 & z > z_A = 2.5 \text{ km} \end{cases} \qquad (8\text{-}119)$$

$$E/\rho = -\ell^2 \frac{\partial \mathbf{V}}{\partial z}\frac{\partial \bar{q}}{\partial z}$$

The E_4 *model* used the heat balance equation including heat flux in the soil, a Monin-Obukhov surface layer with the level 2.5 turbulence in the rest of the PBL and the free atmosphere. Moist convective adjustment is used above the 18-m level.

Thirty-day integrations were undertaken to compare the various models. Although only the overall effects of the combined parameterizations can be differentiated, some inferences can be drawn regarding the boundary layer parameterizations. The magnitude of momentum changes in the lower two km by the mixed-layer parameterization in the F_2 model was very much less than with the turbulence closure model. Although dominantly positive, the effective eddy coefficient K_M was often negative in the mixed-layer model, which casts some doubt on K theory. However, the model tested was an early version from which some errors have been removed and improvements made. Data taken in tropical regions do show that the PBL is well mixed, lending support to the mixed-layer theory. Despite considerable progress with PBL parameterizations, more tests with numerical models that can be verified with adequate observations are needed. Some further comments in these tests will be made at the end of Chapter 9.

CHAPTER 9

Inclusion of Moisture

9-1 MOISTURE CONSERVATION EQUATION

The most important immediate effect of moisture on the dynamics of atmospheric motions is the release of latent heat. In addition, water vapor and clouds have a very prominent role in the reflection, absorption, and emission of solar and terrestrial radiation. Some of these processes are more important in the long-range forecasts and seasonal or climate modeling than in short-range forecasting. In any case, most clouds are a sub-grid-scale phenomena horizontally and/or vertically with respect to large-scale NWP models. This is unfortunate since to the person on the street, sky condition and precipitation in the form of rain, sleet, ice, and snow are probably of greatest interest together with temperature extremes and high winds.

When the air is dry a complete system of equations includes two equations for the horizontal components of motion, the hydrostatic equation, continuity equation, thermodynamic equation, and the equation of state—six equations and six unknowns. When moisture is included, one or more equations for the moisture budget are needed, and modifications of the thermodynamic equation must be made. The equation for water vapor may be obtained in a similar manner to the derivation of the continuity equation for the conservation of mass as illustrated in Figure 1-1 (p. 5), except that the partial density of water vapor ρ_v replaces ρ. The flux of water vapor across the $\delta y \delta z$ face is $\rho_v u \delta y \delta z$ and the flux divergence for the volume $\delta x \delta y \delta z$ in the x-direction is $-[\partial(\rho_v u \delta y \delta z)/\partial x]\delta x$. The foregoing term plus similar terms for the y- and z-directions add up to the expression, $-\nabla_3 \cdot (\rho_v \mathbf{V}_3)\, \delta x \delta y \delta z$. Hence the time rate of change of water vapor *per unit volume,* $\partial \rho_v/\partial t$, is given by

$$\partial \rho_v/\partial t = -\nabla_3 \cdot (\rho_v \mathbf{V}_3) + S \tag{9-1}$$

where S are sources or sinks of water vapor per unit volume per unit time. If ρ_v is replaced by its equivalent ρq, where q is the specific humidity, and the product of q and the continuity equation (1-6) is subtracted from (9-1), the result is

$$\partial q/\partial t = -\mathbf{V}_3 \cdot \nabla_3 q + S/\rho \tag{9-2}$$

A sink of water vapor is condensation or sublimation from saturated air, in which case

$$S/\rho = dq_s/dt \tag{9-3}$$

where q_s is the saturation humidity given by the approximate formula

$$q_s = 0.622e_s/(p - 0.378e_s) \doteq 0.622\, e_s/p \tag{9-4}$$

Here e_s is the saturation vapor pressure, which is related to temperature by the Clausius-Clapeyron equation

$$\frac{de_s}{e_s} = \frac{LdT}{R_vT^2} \tag{9-5}$$

Differentiation of (9-4) and substitution from (9-5) leads to

$$\frac{1}{q_s}\frac{dq_s}{dt} = \frac{L}{R_vT^2}\frac{dT}{dt} - \frac{1}{p}\frac{dp}{dt} \tag{9-6}$$

Assuming no other heat sources, that condensation takes place as a result of saturated adiabatic expansion the condensate precipitates (irreversible case), the thermodynamic equation is

$$-\frac{Ldq_s}{dt} \doteq c_p\frac{dT}{dt} - \frac{RT}{p}\frac{dp}{dt} \tag{9-7}$$

Elimination of dT/dt between (9-6) and (9-7) gives an expression for dq_s/dt in terms of $dp/dt = \omega$ as follows:

$$\frac{dq_s}{dt} = \frac{q_sT}{p}\left(\frac{LR - c_pR_vT}{c_pR_vT^2 + q_sL^2}\right)\omega \equiv F\omega \tag{9-8}$$

where the identity defines F. Combining (9-2), (9-3), and (9-8) gives a moisture conservation equation which allows for condensation from saturated expanding air

$$\frac{\partial q}{\partial t} = -\mathbf{V}\cdot\nabla q - \omega\frac{\partial q}{\partial p} - \delta F\omega + S_j/\rho \tag{9-9}$$

where the Kronecker δ has been introduced and

$$\delta = 1\text{: for } \omega < 0 \text{ and } q \geq q_s$$

$$\delta = 0 \text{ for } \omega \geq 0 \text{ or } q < q_s$$

Alternatively, condensation may be assumed to begin at some critical relative humidity less than 100 percent, or the rate of condensation may be assumed to be a function of the relative humidity, perhaps linear.

9-1-1 Modified Thermodynamic Equation

The S_j/ρ represent other possible sources or sinks of moisture, such as, horizontal diffusion $\nabla \cdot (A\,\nabla q)$, vertical diffusion $\partial(K\partial q/\partial z)/\partial z$, and evaporation from liquid water either at the surface or from precipitation falling through unsaturated air.

The expression for dq_s/dt in (9-8) may also be used in the thermodynamic equation (9-7) giving

$$c_p \frac{dT}{dt} - \frac{RT}{p}\omega = -\delta LF\omega + Q \tag{9-10}$$

where Q represents other sources of heat energy, for example, from conduction, turbulence, evaporation, etc.

If all of the condensate from the saturated expansion is assumed to fall instantly as precipitation, the precipitation P per unit area in a time period Δt is

$$P = \int_t^{t+\Delta t} \int_0^{\infty} - \frac{dq_s}{dt} \rho dz dt = - \int_t^{t+\Delta t} \int_0^{p_0} \frac{\delta F\omega}{g} dp dt$$

9-1-2 Equivalent Potential Temperature and Static Energy

It is appropriate at this time to describe other thermodynamic parameters that are used in connection with the expansion (or compression) of saturated air. Consider first a parcel consisting of one gram of dry air plus m_{s0} grams of saturated water vapor at temperature T and total pressure p undergoing reversible saturated expansion, that is, with condensed liquid remaining with the gas. Then it is easily shown (see Haltiner and Martin, 1957, p. 31) that

$$c_{pd} \ell n\, T - R_d \ell n(p - e_s) + m_s L/T - c_\ell m_{s0} \ell n T = \text{const}$$

or

$$d\{\ell n[T(P - e_s)^{-R_d/c_{pd}} \exp(m_s L/c_{pd} T) - T^{c_\ell m_{s0}/c_{pd}})]\} = 0 \tag{9-11}$$

where the symbols have their usual meanings. Thus the quantity in braces is conserved during reversible saturated expansion. If heat sources other than latent heat are involved, including turbulent dissipation, the right side of (9-11) must include such terms. If the condensate drops out (irreversible case), m_{s0} is replaced by m_s in the last exponential factor.

This last term in the brackets is relatively small in either case and is often neglected, in which case (9-11) can be integrated to the form

$$\theta_e \equiv T[p_{00}/(p - e_s)]^{R_d/c_{pd}} \exp(m_s L/c_{pd}T) \doteq \text{const} \tag{9-12}$$

where $p_{00} = 1000$ mb and $\theta_e\, p_{00}{}^{-R_d/c_{pd}}$ is the constant of integration.

The quantity θ_e, referred to by C. G. Rossby as the *equivalent potential temperature,* is approximately conserved during the saturated "adiabatic" process, as is *wet-bulb potential temperature* θ_{sw}. With respect to static stability of saturated air, the criteria are usually expressed in the form

$$-\frac{\partial\theta_e}{\partial p} \text{ or } -\frac{\partial\theta_{sw}}{\partial p} \begin{matrix} > \\ = 0 \\ < \end{matrix} \begin{matrix} \text{Stable} \\ \text{Neutral} \\ \text{Unstable} \end{matrix}$$

or

$$-\frac{\partial\theta}{\partial p} \begin{matrix} > \\ = \\ < \end{matrix} \frac{L\theta}{Tc_p}\frac{\partial q_s(T)}{\partial p} \tag{9-13}$$

The second form follows from:

$$-L\,dq = c_p dT - RT\,d\ell np \qquad \text{and} \qquad d\ell n\,\theta = d\ell nT - (R/c_p)\,d\ell np$$

The *static energy,* a stability parameter of more recent use, may be introduced by approximating $-(RT/p)dp$ in (9-7) with gdz, *which considers only the vertical displacements,* giving the result

$$c_p dT + gdz + L\,dq_s = 0$$

or

$$dh^* \equiv d\,(c_p T + gz + Lq_s) = 0 \tag{9-14}$$

where the value of c_p for dry air is used. Thus *saturation moist static energy* h^* is nearly conserved during the irreversible saturated-adiabatic expansion. Similarly for dry adiabatic expansion the *dry static energy* s is conserved

$$s = c_{pd}T + gz \qquad \textit{Dry static energy} \tag{9-15}$$

Thus dry static energy s can be used as a stability parameter in a similar manner as the potential temperature.

For an unsaturated parcel with specific humidity q,

$$h = s + Lq \qquad \textit{Moist static energy} \qquad ((9\text{-}16)$$

will be conserved during both *dry* and subsequent *saturated* "adiabatic" expansion. Obviously h is conserved during the dry adiabatic phase since q is unchanged, while above the condensation level h continues to be conserved because the decrease in Lq with condensation is compensated by an increase in s.

It is apparent from the preceding discussion that the standard static stability criteria for a layer of unsaturated or saturated air may be expressed in terms of the vertical gradient of s and h, respectively, and for conditional instability as well. Remember, however, that environmental air is usually entrained into a cumulus updraft that modifies the latter's temperature and moisture content, so the processes are more complex than the adiabatic cases.

9-2 CONVECTIVE ADJUSTMENT

If the lapse rate becomes unstable during a numerical forecast, intense vertical velocities may develop in some models that could ruin the large-scale forecast. In any case, persistent unstable lapse rates are not characteristic of the atmosphere and tend to be removed by convection (except near the ground during daytime heating). Nevertheless, sub-grid-scale phenomena, such as convection, turbulence, etc., triggered by unstable lapse rates can exert a significant influence on the larger scales being explicitly simulated through the transport of heat, moisture, and momentum, and therefore cannot be disregarded.

In this section a simplified treatment of large-scale stable condensation and dry and moist convection, which is used in the Geophysical Fluid Dynamics Laboratory (GFDL) general circulation model (Manabe et al., 1965) will be discussed. The technique consists of first predicting the large-scale variables of temperature and moisture for a time step Δt, neglecting condensation and ignoring the development of any unstable lapse rates. Then the vertical profiles of temperature and moisture at each grid point are examined for superadiabatic lapse rates and/or supersaturation. In the unsaturated case, if the lapse rate exceeds the dry adiabatic value γ_d, it is restored to γ_d. If the air is saturated and $\gamma > \gamma_m$, γ is restored to the moist adiabatic lapse rate γ_m. Specifically, the T and q fields are adjusted by amounts δT and δq to a neutral lapse rate and saturation in accordance with the following procedures.

9-2-1 Case A. Dry Convection, $q < q_s$

$$A_1\colon \gamma \leq \gamma_d, \textit{ Stable} \quad , \delta T = \delta q = 0$$

$$A_2\colon \gamma > \gamma_d, \textit{ Unstable}, \delta q = 0, \delta T \neq 0 \tag{9-17}$$

In case A_2 in any layer for which $\gamma > \gamma_d$ the vertical temperature profile is adjusted to a neutral (or slightly stable) lapse rate, $\gamma = \gamma_d = g/c_p$, subject to the condition that the total potential energy is conserved, that is,

$$\int_{zB}^{zT} c_p \delta T \rho dz = \frac{c_p}{g} \int_{p_T}^{p_B} \delta T dp = 0 \tag{9-18}$$

Here the subscripts B and T represent the bottom and top of the unstable layer. The physical process implied here is that dry convection develops when the lapse rate exceeds the dry adiabatic value; then the convection transports heat upward until a neutral lapse rate is established. Thus potential energy is converted to kinetic energy which, in turn, is eventually dissipated into heat energy. The final result is a redistribution of temperature with total energy conserved. In practice the integral in (9-18) is numerically integrated. For example, if a single layer in the model is affected, say between levels k and $k + 1$, the requirement of a neutral lapse rate and (9-18) reduce to simply

$$(T_k + \delta T_k)\left(\frac{1000}{p_k}\right)^{R/c_p} = (T_{k+1} + \delta T_{k+1})\left(\frac{1000}{p_{k+1}}\right)^{R/c_p} \qquad \text{and} \qquad \delta T_k = -\delta T_{k+1} \tag{9-19}$$

which can be solved for δT_k and δT_{k+1}. At each gridpoint the vertical column of air is checked, layer by layer, for superadiabatic lapse rates and adjusted. If two successive layers are unstable or if a layer becomes unstable as a consequence of adjustment of the adjacent layer, both layers are treated simultaneously to produce a neutral lapse rate in the combined layers. It is apparent that an iterative procedure is required wherein a column is checked for unstable lapse rates, adjustments are made, and adjacent layers are rechecked with further adjustments, if necessary, until the column is everywhere stable or neutral. In operational application the unstable layers may be made slightly stable rather than merely neutral. Care must be taken to account for any saturation or supersaturation that may develop, as will be discussed in the next section.

A somewhat simpler procedure simply uses the mean potential temperature for any superadiabatic lapse rates and omits the requirement for conservation of potential energy. A final point is that the foregoing procedure is not applied to the thin surface (Prandtl) friction layer in which the heat flux is parameterized as discussed in Chapter 8.

9-2-2 Case B. Moist Adjustment $q \geq q_s$

Case B$_1$: $\gamma < \gamma_m$, $q > q_s$, Stable, Large-Scale Condensation. In this case the lapse rate is less than the moist-adiabatic lapse, γ_m; thus any excess moisture should be condensed isobarically with the latent heat warming the air. The process is just the reverse of the wet-bulb process. The temperature and specific humidity adjustment, δT and δq, must bring the air to a saturated state in accordance with the equations

$$-L\delta q = c_p \delta T \qquad \text{and} \qquad q + \delta q = q_s(T + \delta T, p) \tag{9-20}$$

This system, which is implicit since q_s is a function of T and p, can be solved readily on hygrometric or thermodynamic diagrams (see Haltiner and Martin,

1957). It is somewhat more troublesome to solve numerically, but the following iterative procedure is feasible. The second equation in (9-20) may be approximated by the first two terms of a series as follows:

$$q + \Delta q = q_s(T + \delta T) \doteq q_s(T) + \left(\frac{\partial q_s}{\partial T}\right)_p \Delta T \tag{9-21}$$

where q is the initial supersaturated value; T, the initial temperature; and Δq and ΔT are first estimates of δq and δT.

Next, write $q_s \doteq 0.622 e_s/p$, take the differential, $p dq_s = 0.622 de_s$, and substitute from the Clausius-Clapeyron equation (9-5)

$$de_s = (Le_s/R_v T^2)\, dT \tag{9-22}$$

to give

$$dq_s = 0.622(Le_s/R_v p T^2)\, dT = (Lq_s/R_v T^2)\, dT$$

This result may be substituted into (9-21) and rearranged to give

$$\Delta q = \frac{q_s - q}{1 + L^2 q_s / c_p R_v T^2} \tag{9-23}$$

Having calculated a first estimate of Δq, the corresponding ΔT is simply $-L\Delta q = c_p \Delta T$. These two values give a first estimate, say T_1 and q_1, of the adjusted values of temperature and specific humidity. The procedure may now be repeated until the sums of the corrections, $\delta q = \Sigma \Delta q_j$, $\delta T = \Sigma \Delta T_j$, yield a pair of values that satisfy (9-20) with sufficient accuracy.

Case B$_2$: $\gamma \geq \gamma_m$, $q \geq q_s$, Unstable, Moist Convection. In this case the air is unstable and moist convection with condensation takes place. Here the latent heat of condensation is distributed over the unstable layer in such a way that the final lapse rate is moist neutral (i.e., $\gamma = \gamma_m$). It follows that the wet-bulb potential temperature θ_{sw} is constant in the vertical after the convective adjustment has taken place [i.e., $\partial\theta_{sw}(T + \delta T, q + \delta q, p)/\partial p = 0$].

As before, the air is just saturated at each level, $q + \delta q = q_s(T + \delta T, p)$, and all of the latent heat released by condensation is used to warm the air in the layer (but not level by level) (i.e., $\int_{pT}^{pB} c_p\, \delta T dp = - \int_{pT}^{pB} L \delta q dp$). This implicit system must be solved numerically by successive approximations to yield the proper δT and δq at each level.

In summary, the convective adjustment procedure, used effectively for many years in the GFDL GCM, first predicts specific humidity and temperature excluding condensation and then adjusts the temperature and humidity in accordance with the first law of thermodynamics to eliminate superadiabatic lapse rates and supersaturation. In the condensation cases, the precipitation is given by the integral: $P = - \int_0^\infty \delta q \rho dz = - \frac{1}{g} \int_0^{p_0} \delta q dp$

9-3 MODELING CLOUD PROCESSES

In Section 9-2-2 a simplified model was presented for large-scale precipitation where the complex processes associated with condensation and precipitation were ignored completely by assuming that all condensation products immediately fell as rain. A more sophisticated model by Sundquist (1977) follows earlier papers by Kessler (1969) and Ogura and Takahashi (1971). A system of bulk equations governing the condensation and precipitation processes may be written in symbolic form as follows:

$$\partial\theta/\partial t = A(\theta) + (\theta/Tc_p)[L_vS_1 + L_sS_4 - L_vS_6 - L_vS_7 - L_sS_8 + L_f(S_3 - S_5)] \tag{9-24}$$

$$\partial q/\partial t = A(q) - (S_1 + S_4) + (S_6 + S_7 + S_8) \tag{9-25}$$

$$\partial m_c/\partial t = A(m_c) + S_1 - S_2 - S_6 - \partial(\omega_c m_c)/\partial p \tag{9-26}$$

$$\partial m_r/\partial t = A(m_r) + S_2 - S_3 + S_5 - S_7 - \partial(\omega_r m_r)/\partial p \tag{9-27}$$

$$\partial m_i/\partial t = A(m_i) + S_3 + S_4 - S_5 - S_8 - \partial(\omega_i m_i)/\partial p \tag{9-28}$$

where q, m_c, m_r, m_i are the mixing ratios of water vapor, cloud droplets, raindrops and ice crystals, respectively; $A(q) = -\nabla \cdot (q\mathbf{V}) - \partial(q\omega)/\partial p$, etc.; the ω's are fall velocities of condensates; L_v, L_s, and L_f are latent heats of vaporization, sublimation, and fusion; and the source/sink terms are given by the following rates:

S_1 : condensation	S_5 : melting of ice crystals
S_2 : conversion of droplets to raindrops	S_6 : evaporation of droplets
S_3 : production of ice crystals by freezing raindrops	S_7 : evaporation of raindrops
S_4 : sublimation of vapor to ice crystals	S_8 : evaporation of ice crystals

To form a closed set, the preceding system must be either (1) augmented by an additional equation for each of the S's and ω's (assuming no new dependent variables are introduced); or (2) be closed by expressing the S's in terms of θ, q, and the m's, which constitutes a parameterization scheme.

The rate of precipitation P is the downward flux of water mass, which at a level p is

$$P(p) = g^{-1}\,[(\omega + \omega_r)m_r + (\omega + \omega_i)m_i] \tag{9-29}$$

By summing (9-27) and (9-28) and integrating from the top of the cloud p_t, where the mass of liquid and solid water vanishes to an arbitrary level p, $P(p)$ is expressible as

$$P(p) = \frac{1}{g}\int_{Pt}^{p} \{(S_2 + S_4) - (S_7 + S_8) - \partial(m_r + m_i)/\partial t - \nabla \cdot [(m_r + m_i)\mathbf{V}]\}\, dp \tag{9-30}$$

Next consider each of the source terms.

S_1: As described earlier, the degree of supersaturation required for condensation is at most slightly over 100 percent, hence for practical purposes condensation can be assumed to occur at 100 percent. Furthermore, assuming that the relative humidity is approximately steady, the condensation rate S_1 is proportional to water vapor convergence and thus proportional to the rate of change of q.

S_2: Following Kessler (1969), Sundquist assumes that the conversion from droplets to drops consists of two parts, the relative motion between droplets and the collection resulting from a raindrop falling through a cloud. The final result, averaged over all droplet sizes, is

$$S_2 = k_1 (m_c - \alpha') + k_2 (m_c m_r^{7/8}) \tag{9-31}$$

where the values of k_1 and α' are functions of ω, and $k_2 = 2.2 \text{ sec}^{-1}$. S_2 has also been assumed to be proportional to cloud water content.

S_3: Since there is no separate equation for small ice particles, only raindrops may freeze and the glaciation process is assumed to be proportional to m_r.

$$S_3 = k_3 m_r \tag{9-32}$$

where $k_3 = 0$ for $T > 269$ K and reaches a maximum value for $T < 248$ K.

S_4: In a manner similar to that for S_2, an equation for S_4 is derived as follows:

$$S_4 = k_4 \rho_a^{-1/2} s_i m_i^{1/2};\; k_4 \rho_a^{-1/2} = \begin{cases} 4 \times 10^{-5}, & T \doteq 265 \text{ K} \\ 0.5 \times 10^{-5}, & T = 250 \text{ K} \end{cases} \tag{9-33}$$

Here ρ_a is the air density and s_i is the supersaturation with respect to ice. The value of k_4 reflects the fact that sublimation does not become pronounced until the temperature equals 260 K.

S_5: The relationship for S_5 is analogous to that for S_4 except that the rate of melting is proportional to the temperature excess above the freezing point with the result

$$S_5 = 10^{-4} (T - 273) m_i^{1/2} \tag{9-34}$$

where the numerical constants are based on Ogura and Takahashi (1971).

S_6: Since evaporation of small droplets and ice crystals proceeds very rapidly when exposed to subsaturation, it is assumed that they evaporate immediately for purposes of NWP modeling.

S_7 and S_8: Evaporation from raindrops or ice is treated, following Kessler (1969), by considering the diffusion of water vapor away from them and assuming the Marshall-Palmer size distribution, which leads to the result:

$$S_7 = 6 \times 10^{-2} q_s S(\rho_a m_r)^{13/20} \tag{9-35}$$

In order to solve the system of equations the fall velocities for the hydrometeors are needed. The average fall velocity of raindrops according to Kessler is $V_r = 12(\rho m_r)^{1/8}$. A similar expression may be derived for the fall velocity for ice crystals. The mean fall velocity for cloud droplets with a log-normal distribution is $v_c = 1.2 \times 10^8 \gamma_0^2 e^{2\sigma^2}$. These velocities are readily converted to ω's with multiplication by $-g\rho$, thereby closing the cloud physics subsystem, which, of course, must be coupled with the large-scale prediction system that provides **V**, ω, etc.

In practice, the sequence of events may proceed as follows. First large-scale moisture increases the humidity in excess of 100 percent at which time condensation S_1 begins, but the other S_i are zero. When the mixing ratio of cloud droplets exceeds α', the S_2 mechanism begins. Then S_3 may begin at or below an appropriate temperature and eventually S_4, etc. Further details are omitted since it is intended to present only the basic concepts here. The purpose of such sophistication is to obtain a more accurate disposition of the water substance in its several forms and the distribution of latent heat release. This would be especially valuable in weather modification studies.

9-3-1 Nonconvective Condensation

Sundquist (1977) applied a simpler version of the preceding cloud physics to nonconvection condensation and precipitation. Clouds are assumed to fill the volume between certain coordinate levels in the vertical, but they cover only a portion a per unit area while the fraction $b = (1 - a)$ is cloud free. No distinction is made between liquid and ice crystals.

The conservation equation for the water content of the cloud is

$$\partial m/\partial t = -\nabla \cdot (m\mathbf{V}) + aQ_c/L - bE_c/L - P - \partial[(\omega + \omega_c)m]/\partial p \tag{9-36}$$

where m is the mixing ratio of cloud water, Q_c is the heating rate due to condensation, $-E_cL^{-1}$ is the moisture loss due to evaporation of cloud droplets in the clear area, P is conversion of droplets to raindrops, L is the latent heat of condensation, ω is the large-scale vertical velocity and ω_c is the fall velocity of the cloud droplets.

The net heating Q is given by

$$Q = aQ_c - b(E_c + E_r) \tag{9-37}$$

where $-(E_c + E_r)$ is the heat loss due to vaporization of droplets and drops entering the clear portions of the grid area. Substituting (9-37) into (9-36) gives

$$\partial m/\partial t = -\nabla \cdot (m\mathbf{V}) + Q/L - P + bE_r/L - \partial[(\omega + \omega_c)]/\partial p = 0 \qquad (9\text{-}38)$$

The thermodynamic and vapor conservation equations are

$$\partial\theta/\partial t = A(\theta) + \theta Q/Tc_p \qquad (9\text{-}39a)$$

$$\partial q/\partial t = A(q) - Q/L \qquad (9\text{-}39b)$$

where $-A(\alpha) = \mathbf{V} \cdot \nabla\alpha + \omega\partial\alpha/\partial p$ and q is the specific humidity. Assuming the vertical flux convergence term vanishes implies that the large-scale vertical velocity balances the average fall velocity of the droplets, which is probably a reasonable assumption for nonconvective clouds.

Bearing in mind that q does not have to be the saturation value for condensation in the unit area, put $q = rq_s$, where r is the relative humidity and differentiate:

$$\frac{\partial q}{\partial t} = q_s\frac{\partial r}{\partial t} + r\frac{\partial q_s}{\partial t} = q_s\frac{\partial r}{\partial t} + \frac{rq_s}{T\theta}\frac{L}{R_v}\frac{\partial\theta}{\partial t} \qquad (9\text{-}40)$$

where from the definitions of q and θ and the Clausius-Clapeyron equation,

$$\partial q_s/\partial t = Lq_s/T\theta R_v \qquad (9\text{-}41)$$

Substituting (9-40) into (9-39b) and then eliminating $\partial\theta/\partial t$ leads to an expression for Q/L

$$\frac{Q}{L} = \left[A(q) - q_s\frac{\partial r}{\partial t} - \frac{rq_sL}{T\theta R_v}A(\theta)\right]\left(1 + \frac{rq_sL^2}{R_vT^2c_p}\right)^{-1} \qquad (9\text{-}42)$$

To close the system, (9-37) to (9-40), an expression for $\partial r/\partial t$ is needed. Consider the integrated rate of change of q over the clear area and assume that the advection of q is the same over the whole grid area together with $(E_c + E_r)$, which gives

$$\overline{\partial q/\partial t} = b[A(q) + (E_c + E_r)L^{-1}] \qquad (9\text{-}43)$$

Next it is assumed that the change in the vapor in b is partly accounted for in maintaining the value r_b in b, with a changing q_s and the remainder is used for forming cloud of water content m in a part of b. For the latter, the humidity may be raised from q_b to q_s plus m in that fraction Δb which reduces the size of b. Omitting lesser effects due to variations in m, q_b, and q_s, the specific humidity rate of increase due to the new cloud is $(q_s - q_b + m)\,\partial b/\partial t$. Introducing $r_b = q_b/q_s$ and equating it to (9-43) gives

$$[q_s(1 - r_b) + m]\frac{\partial b}{\partial t} = -b[A(q) + (E_c + E_r)L^{-1}] \qquad (9\text{-}44)$$

An expression for $\partial b/\partial t$ is obtainable by differentiating $r = (1 - b)r_s + br_b$, thus, $\partial r/\partial t = -\partial b/\partial t + r_b\, \partial b/\partial t$, which may be used in (9-44) to give

$$\frac{\partial r}{\partial t} = \frac{(1 - r)}{q_s(1 - r_b) + m}\left[A(q) + \frac{E_c + E_r}{L}\right] \tag{9-45}$$

This expression for $\partial r/\partial t$ may now be used in (9-42) for Q/L which, in turn, is used in (9-37). Next, Sundquist assumes that the evaporation of raindrops E_r, which takes place in a cloud-free region as rain falls from above, is proportional to the rate of precipitation and the degree of subsaturation $(1 - r_b)$, with the result

$$E_r(p) = L\, k_r(g/\Delta p)\,(1 - r_b)\,\tilde{P}\,(p - \Delta p/2) \tag{9-46}$$

where $\tilde{P}\,(p - \Delta p/2)$ is the integrated precipitation rate at the level $(p - \Delta p/2)$ and k_r may depend on height and possibly precipitation content. In layers with no clouds the subsaturation is simply $(1 - r)$. A specific representation of the evaporation of cloud droplets will not be presented; however, it would be related to the diffusion process and cloud coverage.

The next consideration is the conversion of cloud droplets to raindrops which will be obtained diagnostically by assuming that the precipitation is proportional to the predicted cloud water content m, that is,

$$P = m\, c_0\, \{1 - \exp[-(m/m_r)^2]\} \tag{9-47}$$

where c_0 and m_r are parameters. The latter may be taken to be a typical value of cloud water content at which precipitation begins. Sundquist used $m_r = 0.5 \times 10^{-3}$ and $c_0 = 10^{-4}$/sec.

As contrasted to the convective adjustment scheme where precipitation occurs immediately upon condensation, in this method the development of precipitation with no initial clouds is very slow initially but increases rapidly after about 5 hr. Experiments with the Sundquist model show promise of improved simulation of large-scale precipitation but more testing is required. In passing it should be mentioned that GFDL and NCAR general circulation models assume that precipitation occurs in the form of snow when freezing level is at or below the level of 350 m and 1.5 km, respectively.

9-4 CUMULUS PARAMETERIZATION

9-4-1 Introduction

The horizontal space scale and time scale of deep cumulus clouds are two or more orders smaller than those of synoptic weather systems, while their vertical scales are similar. Hence, an individual cloud might not be expected to have much influence on a large-scale system; however clouds are frequently organized in groups with a scale comparable to that of synoptic systems. Consequently, the cumulative effect of a large number of individual clouds may have significant effect on the large-scale system through the transfer of heat, moisture, and momentum. While the release of latent heat in middle-latitude systems is not essential to the mechanisms of baroclinic and barotropic instability, it can markedly affect the intensity of systems, especially the smaller disturbances. Moreover, cloud cover and rainfall are very important weather phenomena to earth inhabitants. There are, of course, certain phenomena of a much larger scale than individual cumulus that depend entirely, or almost so, on organized latent heat release for their source of energy, the tropical cyclone being a prime example.

In this section several schemes for determining the statistical effects of many cumuli on large-scale synoptic systems, a procedure known as *cumulus parameterization,* will be examined. The convective adjustment scheme described earlier is a simple type of parameterization scheme. Observations show that cumulus clouds and their effects on the environment vary from cloud to cloud but some common features of deep cumulus may be described with the aid of Figure 9-1. In the updraft, condensation takes place whereas evaporation occurs in the downdraft, particularly below the cloud base where evaporation of falling rain produces cooling which is a stabilizing influence. Evaporation also takes place where cloud air is detrained into the environment aloft and to some extent along the edges of the cloud through turbulent mixing with the environment.

The net latent heat released to the air at any level depends on the differences between the condensation and evaporation and between any freezing and melting at that level. However, the resultant overall diabatic heating from latent heat during the life cycle of the cloud depends only on the precipitation that reaches the ground. Nevertheless, the vertical distribution of such latent heat release in many cumuli can have an important influence on the development of large-scale weather systems.

If in the mean, condensation exceeds evaporation at any level, there will be heating and the water vapor content of the air will decrease, and conversely. By and large, condensation exceeds evaporation aloft so that the latent heat tends to warm and dry the air, while at low levels the opposite is true with net evaporation and cooling, especially between the cloud base and the ground where there is no condensation. Note, however, that the decreasing water vapor aloft by the excess of mean condensation over evaporation may be more than offset by eddy flux convergence of water vapor by the cumulus elements. Freezing of liquid water in the cold upper parts of the cloud and melting at lower levels transports latent heat of fusion upward across the freezing level and contributes in a secondary way to stabilizing the atmosphere.

The environmental air entrained into the updraft on the forward side of a moving thunderstorm is drier and cooler than the warm, moist updraft and

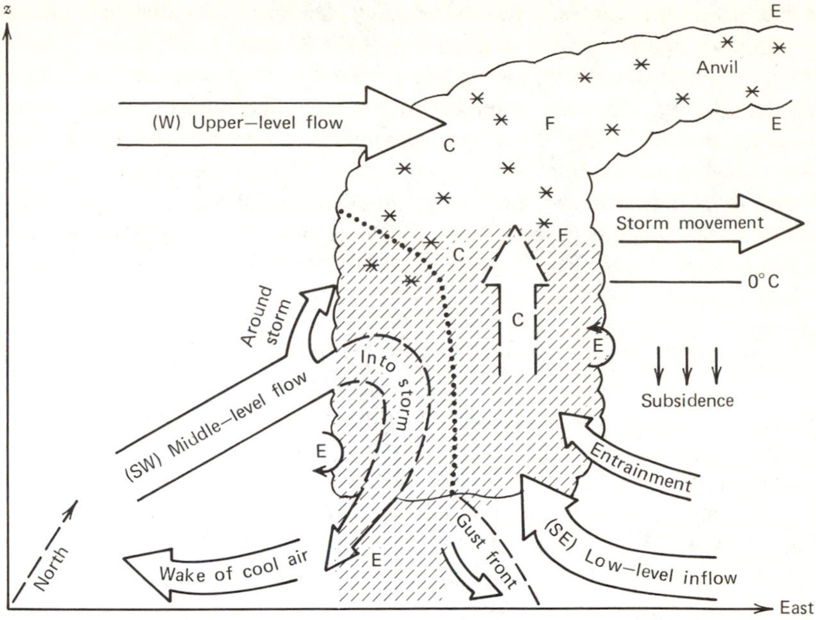

Figure 9-1 Schematic diagram of a mature thunderstorm. (*After Anthes, 1978.*) *C* refers to condensation; *E*, evaporation; and *F*, freezing. Letters in arrows refer to wind direction. (From R. A. Anthes, H. Orville, and D. Rayword. Chapter XIX of *The Thunderstorm: A Social Scientific and Technological Documentary*. E. Kessler, ed. University of Oklahoma Press, 1978.)

therefore tends to cool the updraft. Nevertheless water vapor is added to the updraft by the increasing of the vertical mass flux. Typically, the resultant of the condensation-evaporation, freezing-melting mechanisms, and vertical fluxes in deep cumulus clouds is to warm and moisten the middle and upper troposphere while cooling and drying the lower troposphere. In the total vertical column, *cumulus clouds heat* and *dry* the *atmosphere* provided that *precipitation reaches* the *ground*.

9-4-2 Kuo Method

In 1965 Kuo proposed a parameterization scheme for the statistical effects of deep cumulus convection on a tropical cyclone in the form of latent heat released through condensation and the resulting changes in the large-scale temperature and humidity distributions. He assumed that cumulus convection occurs in deep layers of conditionally unstable stratification over areas of mean low-level convergence. The base of the clouds is taken to be the condensation level of surface air, the vertical distribution of temperature T_s and mixing ratio q_s are those of a moist adiabat, and the top of the cloud occurs where the moist adiabat from the condensation level crosses the environmental sounding. Finally, the cumulus clouds are assumed to dissolve immediately by mixing with the environmental air, imparting to it heat and moisture. Kuo argues that entrainment need not be included explicitly, since the complete mixing with the environment assumed after dissolution of the cloud implies the same total heat transfer to the environment whether entrainment is occurring or not. Kuo further assumes that the total rate of moisture accession M_t per unit horizontal area is given by the convergence of moisture in the column of atmosphere above the unit area plus the surface evaporation, thus

$$M_t = -g^{-1}\int_0^{p_0} \nabla \cdot (q\mathbf{V})\, dp + \rho_0 C_d V_0 (q_s - q_a) \tag{9-48}$$

where q_s is the saturation value corresponding to sea-surface temperature and q_a is the air value just over the sea. This vapor is used to make cloud columns (T_c, q_c) from environmental air (T_e, q_e). Part of the vapor W_1 will condense and precipitate, raising the temperature from T_e to T_c; and the remainder W_2 will increase the specific humidity of the cloud column from q_e to q_c, that is,

$$W_1 = (c_p/L)\int_{p_t}^{p_b} (T_c - T_e)\frac{dp}{g};\; W_2 = \int_{p_t}^{p_b} (q_c - q_e)\frac{dp}{g} \tag{9-49}$$

where p_t and p_b are the top and bottom of the cloud. Hence the total amount of water vapor needed to create the cloud over a unit area is given by the sum of the two integrals

$$W = W_1 + W_2 \doteq g^{-1}\int_0^{p_0} [(c_p/L)(T_c - T_e) + (q_c - q_e)]\, dp \tag{9-50}$$

where $p_b - p_t$ is approximated by p_0 for deep clouds.

Next the rate of cloud production per unit time, C, is assumed to be proportional to the convergence of vapor plus evaporation for the column divided by the amount of water vapor necessary to produce the model cloud as follows:

$$C = \frac{M_t}{W} = \frac{-g^{-1}\int_0^{p_0} \nabla \cdot (q\mathbf{V})\, dp + \rho_0 C_D V_0 (q_s - q_a)}{g^{-1}\int_0^{p_0} [(c_p/L)(T_c - T_e) + q_c - q_e]\, dp} \tag{9-51}$$

The product $C\Delta t$ gives the total production of cloud air during time Δt. As a consequence, the rate of accession of latent heat per unit time, Q, by the mean air at temperature $T = T_e$ at level p is given by

$$\begin{aligned} Q(p) &= C\, c_p[T_c(p) - T(p)] \qquad && T < T_c \quad \text{and} \quad M_t > 0 \\ &= 0 && T \geq T_c \quad \text{or} \quad M_t \leq 0 \end{aligned} \tag{9-52}$$

Now assume the large-scale forecast is made for a time step Δt giving a temperature T^* without the effects of cumuli. Then applying the parameterization scheme gives a temperature $T(t + \Delta t)$

$$T(t + \Delta t) = T^* + C\Delta t(T_c - T^*) \tag{9-53}$$

The corresponding equation for q after application of parameterization is

$$q(t + \Delta t) = q^* + C\Delta t(q_c - q^*) \tag{9-54}$$

The precipitation is that part of the moisture used in warming the air from T^* to T. Therefore the *rate of precipitation* per unit time per unit volume in the column is $Cc_p(T_c - T^*)/L$, which can be summed in the vertical.

A parameterization scheme for cumulus requires additional computer time but need not necessarily be applied at every time step (because the large-scale processes of evaporation and moisture convergence vary slowly). If the scheme is applied, for example, every four time steps, the computed temperature and moisture changes for $4\Delta t$ can be linearily apportioned to the four succeeding steps.

In a 1974 paper Kuo states that the important warming by compression in the descending region of cumulus clouds is automatically accounted for in his scheme. He also introduces a division of the convergence of moisture into a fraction bM_t of the total which increases the humidity of the air, and a fraction $(1 - b)M_t$, which is condensed and precipitates as rain or is carried away with the latent heat warming the air. Kuo suggests that b would be much less than one in regions of low-level convergence in the tropics, but leaves its evaluation to empirical data. Anthes (1977) proposed that b depend on the mean relative humidity of the air in such a way that moistening is greater when the air is drier. But no satisfactory theoretical determination for b is available. Kuo also discussed shallow cumulus created by heat and moisture fluxes associated with a warm surface and unrelated to large-scale convergence. Here the thickness and intensity of the stable layer above the surface mixed layer are the most important factors determining the thickness of the low clouds.

9-5 PARAMETERIZATIONS INVOLVING CLOUD MODELS

In the last decade, or so, more sophisticated schemes involving more detailed cloud physics have been devised [Arakawa (1968), Pearce and Riehl (1968), Ooyama (1971), Arakawa and Schubert (1974), and Anthes (1977)]. Several examples are considered in some detail to illustrate this approach.

As an extension of the Kuo scheme, Anthes (1977) begins by defining a running integral average, $\overline{\alpha} = (\Delta x \Delta y)^{-1} \int \alpha dx dy$ over a horizontal area Δx by Δy (often taken as the grid size) centered over a point (x,y) and then expresses the pertinent variables as $\alpha = \overline{\alpha} + \alpha'$. Because the $\overline{\alpha}$ and α' vary continuously with respect to x and y, $\overline{\alpha'}$ will not vanish exactly. Replacing θ by $\theta + \theta'$ and applying the averaging operator to the thermodynamic equation gives, after use of the continuity equation and some simplifications,

$$\frac{\partial\overline{\theta}}{\partial t} + \overline{\nabla \cdot \overline{\mathbf{V}}\overline{\theta}} + \overline{\nabla \cdot \mathbf{V}'\theta'} + \frac{\partial\overline{\overline{\omega}\overline{\theta}}}{\partial p} + \frac{\partial\overline{\omega'\theta'}}{\partial p} +$$

$$\left[\overline{\nabla \cdot \overline{\mathbf{V}}\theta'} + \frac{\partial\overline{\overline{\omega}\theta'}}{\partial p} + \overline{\nabla \cdot \mathbf{V}'\overline{\theta}} + \frac{\partial\overline{\omega'\overline{\theta}}}{\partial p}\right] = Q/\pi c_p \tag{9-55}$$

where $\pi = (p/1000 \text{ mb})^{R/c_p}$ and Q includes various sources of heat. The terms in the brackets do not vanish because of the way the mean is defined; however they may be expected to be near zero if the size of the area over which the mean is defined is large compared to the scale of the cloud disturbances being parameterized. Assuming this to be the case, these terms are neglected, as well as the horizontal perturbation products in comparison to the vertical perturbation terms, reducing (9-55) to

$$\frac{d\overline{\theta}}{dt} = \frac{1}{\pi c_p}[L_{v\ell}\,(\overline{C - E}) - L_{i\ell}\,\overline{M} + L_{vi}\,\overline{S} + Q_R] - \frac{\partial\overline{\omega'\theta'}}{\partial p} \tag{9-56}$$

Here the condensation $\overline{C}$, evaporation $\overline{E}$, melting $\overline{M}$, sublimation $\overline{S}$, with corresponding latent heats and a radiative term have been specifically indicated, but their covariances with π are neglected. According to Anthes and Kuo the term in brackets includes the horizontal mixing of warm cloud air and compensating subsidence around the clouds. The moisture equations are:

$$\frac{d\overline{q}}{dt} = -(\overline{C - E}) - \overline{S} - \frac{\partial\overline{\omega'q'}}{\partial p} \tag{9-57}$$

$$\frac{d\overline{q}_\ell}{dt} = (\overline{C - E}) + \overline{M} - \overline{P}_\ell - \frac{\partial\overline{\omega'q_\ell'}}{\partial p} \tag{9-58}$$

$$\frac{d\overline{q}_i}{dt} = \overline{S} - \overline{M} - \overline{P}_i - \frac{\partial\overline{\omega'q_i'}}{\partial p} \tag{9-59}$$

Here $\overline{P}_\ell$ represents the liquid precipitation fallout and $\overline{P}_i$ is the frozen precipitation fallout. Except for the eddy fluxes, the sum of (9-57) to (9-59) gives the rate of change of total water at any level which equals the precipitation fallout:

$$d\,(\overline{q} + \overline{q}_\ell + \overline{q}_i)/dt = -(\overline{P}_\ell + \overline{P}_i) \tag{9-60}$$

With regard to the eddy flux term, let a represent the fractional convective cloud cover, then the average of any quantity, say α, will be given by

$$\bar{\alpha} = a\bar{\alpha}^c + (1 - a)\,\bar{\alpha}^b \tag{9-61}$$

where the c and b represent the cloud and clear areas, respectively. Then

$$\overline{\omega'\alpha'} = a\overline{(\omega_c - \bar{\omega})\,(\alpha_c - \bar{\alpha})}^c + (1 - a)\,\overline{(\omega_b - \bar{\omega})\,(\alpha_b - \bar{\alpha})}^b \tag{9-62}$$

Now substitute from (9-61) for $\bar{\alpha}^b$ into (9-62) and make the following approximations in (9-62):

$$\overline{\alpha_c\omega_c}^c = \bar{\alpha}_c^c\bar{\omega}_c^c \qquad \text{and} \qquad \overline{\alpha_b\omega_b}^b = \bar{\alpha}_b^b\,\bar{\omega}_b^b \tag{9-63}$$

which neglect turbulent fluxes within the cloud itself and within the environment. After simplification, the expression of the eddy flux becomes

$$\overline{\omega'\alpha'} = a\,(\bar{\omega}^c - \bar{\omega})\,(\bar{\alpha}_c^c - \bar{\alpha})/(1 - a) \tag{9-64}$$

Because this term is maximum in the middle troposphere, the flux divergence produces diabatic cooling and drying in the lower troposphere and the reverse in the upper troposphere, resulting in a net stabilization of the atmosphere.

The parameterization scheme must determine: (1) the total condensation rate in the grid volume, (2) the vertical distribution of cloud scale heating, (3) the mean properties of temperature, moisture and momentum in the clouds and (4) the percent of convective cloud cover. For this purpose Anthes uses a single deep convective cloud model as a closure method for the parameterization. Following Kuo's scheme, the model requires conditional instability and a minimum critical value of total horizontal moisture convergence M_t. A fraction, $(1 - d)M_t$, is condensed and precipitated, while the fraction dM_t either does not condense or it condenses and re-evaporates (for simplicity assumed to occur at the same level).

With the foregoing definitions, the net total mean condensation of all kinds is

$$(p_b - p_t)\,\langle\bar{C}^*\rangle \equiv \int_{pt}^{pb} \bar{C}^*\,dp = (1 - d)\,gM_t \tag{9-65}$$

where the identity sign defines the operator $\langle\ \ \rangle$, M_t is the moisture convergence (9-48) and p_b and p_t are the pressures at the cloud base and top. The total heating rate Q resulting from condensation in a column equals the latent heat released, that is,

$$(1/g)\int_0^{po} Q dp = (1/g)\int_0^{po} c_p\pi(d\theta/dt)\,dp = -L(1 - d)M_t \tag{9-66}$$

Considering a single cloud Anthes approximates the net local condensation rate in the cloud C_c^* by

$$C_c^* = -\omega_c\, \partial q_c/\partial p + \partial q_c/\partial t_e \qquad (9\text{-}67)$$

where $\partial q_c/\partial t_e$ represents the dilution by entrainment, which has a rate

$$\mu = (1/m)\, dm/dz \qquad (9\text{-}68)$$

Replacing dz by $-RT\, dp/gp$ and integrating the last equation gives

$$m(p) = m_b(p/p_b)^{-R\overline{T}\mu/g}$$

where $m = -\omega_c\, a_c/g$ is the mass flux in the updraft at level p and $\overline{T}$ is the mean temperature between p and the cloud base pressure p_b. The total upward mass flux $M(p)$ is obtained by summing m over all clouds in the grid area $\Delta x \Delta y$, which for this case is $M(p) = -\Delta x \Delta y\; a\, \omega_c/g$. The value at the cloud base is $M_b = -\Delta x \Delta y\; a_b\, \omega_b/g$; thus

$$M(p)/M_b = a(p)\omega_c/a_b\omega_b = (p/p_b)^{-R\overline{T}\mu/g} \qquad (9\text{-}69)$$

From (9-61) and (9-67) the area-averaged condensation rate is

$$\overline{C}^* = aC_c^* = a(-\omega_c\, \partial q_c/\partial p + \partial q_c/\partial t_e) \qquad (9\text{-}70)$$

The change in cloud humidity by entrainment is

$$\partial q_c/\partial t_e = -(q_c - q_e)M^{-1}\, dM/dt \doteq -(q_c - q_e)\,\omega_c\, M^{-1}\, \partial M/\partial p \qquad (9\text{-}71)$$

Substituting from (9-69) and (9-71) into (9-70) leads to

$$\overline{C}^* = a_b\omega_b\, \{(M/M_b)\, [-\partial q_c/\partial p - (q_c - q_e)\, M^{-1}\, \partial M/\partial p]\} \equiv a_b\omega_b F \qquad (9\text{-}72)$$

where F defines the quantity in braces.

Next integrate (9-72) from p_t to p_b and use (9-65) to give

$$\int_{pt}^{pb} \overline{C}^*\, dp = (1 - d)\, g\, M_t = a_b\, \omega_b \int_{pt}^{pb} F\, dp \qquad (9\text{-}73)$$

Eliminating $a_b\, \omega_b$ from (9-72) and (9-73) yields

$$\overline{C}^* = (1 - d)\, g\, M_t F \Big/ \int_{pt}^{pb} F\, dp \qquad (9\text{-}74)$$

Thus the condensation rate $\overline{C}^*$ may be calculated at any level p provided q_e and M_t are available from the large-scale variables, q_c and M from the cloud model and d is known. Also note that $a_b\, \omega_b$ may be calculated subsequently from (9-73), and in turn, through (9-69) gives $a(p)\, \omega_c$. Then, given ω_c from the cloud model, $a(p)$ may be obtained, which is needed for the calculation of the eddy flux terms in (9-64).

Assuming a to be a constant in the vertical, Anthes shows that the calculation for a depends only on the mean cloud-scale condensation rate and therefore is rather insensitive to local fluctuations. This method produces reasonable values in a hurricane model, which, according to Anthes, were not attainable with Kuo's scheme.

It has been assumed that a fraction d, yet undetermined, of the total moisture convergence is used to increase the large-scale humidity at gridpoints where convection occurs. Thus

$$\partial\bar{q}/\partial t = \partial q^*/\partial t - \partial\overline{\omega' q'}/\partial p \tag{9-75}$$

where $\partial q^*/\partial t$ denotes the moistening due to uncondensed water vapor convergence or that which condenses and evaporates later. To obtain $\partial q^*/\partial t$, first integrate (9-75) using (9-65), to give the following integral constraint,

$$\int_0^{p_s} (\partial\bar{q}/\partial t)\, dp = \int_0^{p_s} (\partial q^*/\partial t)\, dp = dg\, M_t \tag{9-75}$$

Then, the vertical distribution of $\partial q^*/\partial t$ may be expressed as

$$\partial q^*/\partial t = dgM_t\, N'(p)/(p_b - p_t) \tag{9-76}$$

where $N'(p)$ is not yet specified, but $(p_b - p_t)^{-1} \int_{p_t}^{p_b} N'(p)\, dp = 1$. Anthes suggests the heurisitic form for $N'(p)$:

$$N'(p) = \frac{(1 - r)\, q_s(T)}{\langle(1 - r)\, q_s(T)\rangle} \tag{9-77}$$

where r is the relative humidity at pressure p and q_s is the saturation specific humidity at T, which is similar to Kuo's scheme. The fraction d is chosen empirically such that when the environment is saturated, that is, $\langle r\rangle = 1$, $d = 0$; and when the air is very dry, say, below some critical value, r_c, then $d = 1$. Thus d is defined as follows:

$$d = \begin{cases} [(1 - \langle r\rangle)/(1 - r_c)]^n & \text{when } \langle r\rangle \geq r_c \\ 1 & \text{when } \langle r\rangle \leq r_c \end{cases} \tag{9-78}$$

where n is a constant of the order 1 to be empirically determined. This scheme may be useful in mesoscale models where an entire grid square may be covered by a cloud cluster. Certain parameterization schemes without this feature tend to overpredict convective precipitation.

A summary of the steps required to apply Anthes' parameterization scheme is as follows:

1. Check large-scale variables at a gridpoint for the required conditional instability and moisture convergence.

2. Using (9-78) compute the fraction d of M_t that is not precipitated.
3. Use a cloud model to calculate the entrainment rate, cloud temperature, specific humidity as a function of pressure the vertical velocity ω_c (perhaps only ω_b). (The updraft mass flux is decreased linearly to zero by detrainment in the upper 10 percent of the cloud.)
4. Determine the vertical distribution of $\overline{C^*}$ from (9-74) using an entrainment rate such as (9-68).
5. Determine the cloud cover a as described after (9-74).
6. Compute the eddy flux by means of (9-64).
7. Compute $N'(p)$ by (9-77), $\partial q^*/\partial t$ by (9-76) and $\overline{\omega' q'}$ by (9-64).

The full details of the particular cloud model used in step 3 by Anthes in some experimental calculations will not be described; however, some general features will be mentioned. The equation for the vertical component of motion is

$$d\,(w_c^2/2)\,dz = g\,(T_{vc} - T_{ve})/T_{ve} - gM_\ell - \mu w^2 \tag{9-79}$$

where T_{vc} is the virtual temperature of the cloud and M_ℓ is the total liquid water content per unit mass of air that is a drag on the updraft. The entrainment rate μ is an empirical function of the radius R of the updraft

$$\mu = 0.183/R \tag{9-80}$$

First the updraft sounding is computed using saturated adiabatic equations modified by entrainment. Then the velocity is calculated by integration of (9-79). The liquid fallout is calculated because it produces the drag on the updraft. The calculations are quite sensitive to the cloud radius hence the determination of the spectrum of cloud radii as a function of large-scale parameters remains as an important problem.

9-6 ARAKAWA AND SCHUBERT MODEL

General Description. Based on earlier work of Arakawa, a theory of interaction between a cumulus ensemble and the large-scale environment has been developed by Arakawa and Schubert (1974). In brief, large-scale heat and moisture budget equations are developed for a subcloud layer of variable depth and separately for the region above in which there are terms for the effects of the cloud ensemble on the environment. As in other schemes the cumuli modify the large-scale temperature and humidity through detrainment of saturated air and condensation products and by the subsidence induced by the convection. One of the two important innovations is the partitioning of cumulus ensemble into subensembles, or cloud types, each characterized by a unique fractional entrainment rate λ. The vertical structure of the environment (referred to as *static control*) determines the cloud vertical mass flux normalized by its value at the cloud base, the cloud thermodynamic properties and the height of zero buoyancy for each subensemble. The distribution of the vertical mass flux at the cloud base into subensembles is determined by large-scale dynamical and physical processes together with a novel closure scheme devised by Arakawa and Schubert.

To relate the synoptic and cumulus scales the *cloud work function A* is defined, which represents the rate of kinetic energy generation by the buoyancy force and is determined by the vertical structure of the environment, the latter being affected by the cumulus ensemble as well as by large-scale processes. The character and general form of the cloud work function may be seen by considering a single cloud and writing (9-79) as

$$\frac{d\,(w^2/2)}{dz}\frac{dt}{dt} = \frac{1}{w}\frac{d\,(w^2/2)}{dt} = \frac{g\,(T_{vc} - \overline{T}_{ve})}{T_{ve}} - F_r \tag{9-81}$$

where F_r represents friction. Next replace $(T_{vc} - \overline{T}_{ve})$ by $(s_{vc} - \overline{s}_{ve})/c_p$, (9-15), (the subscript v denotes the vertical temperature, etc., and s_v i the dry static stability parameter corrected for water vapor). Then multiply by $\rho_c w$ and integrate through the depth of the cloud to give

$$\frac{d}{dt}\int_{pT}^{pB} g^{-1}\,(w^2/2)\,dp = \int_{zB}^{zT} (g/c_p\overline{T}_v)\,(s_{vc} - \overline{s}_{ve})\,\rho_c w\,dz - D$$

where D is the dissipation and $\rho_c dz \doteq -\,dp/g$. Denoting the mass flux $\rho_c w$ by m and normalizing it with the flux at the cloud base, $m/m_B = \eta$ leads to the general form

$$d\,(\overline{KE})\,/dt = A(\lambda)\,m_B\,(\lambda) - D\,(\lambda) \tag{9-82}$$

where λ, as defined earlier, denotes a particular cloud type and $A(\lambda)$ is the *cloud work function*

$$A(\lambda) = \int_{zB}^{zT} [gc_p/T_e\,(z)]\;\eta(z,\lambda)\;[s_{vc}\,(z,\lambda) - s_{ve}\,(z)]\;dz \tag{9-83}$$

Thus the cloud work function is an integral of the buoyancy force that governs the rate of kinetic energy generation in a subensemble. The buoyancy is affected by entrainment which, in turn, depends on the cloud type identified by λ.

In order to maintain a cumulus ensemble beyond the dissipative time scale of the clouds, the buoyancy force must be positive, which requires $A(\lambda)$ to be positive for a certain range of λ. The vertical transport of heat and moisture by the cumulus ensemble continuously tends to reduce the conditional instability in the environment, and therefore $A(\lambda)$. For discussion purposes the time change of the cloud work function will be divided into two parts, that due to the cumulus ensemble processes and that due to large-scale processes:

$$dA(\lambda)/dt \equiv [dA(\lambda)/dt]_c + [dA(\lambda)/dt]_{LS} \tag{9-84}$$

Next write $(dA/dt)_c$ in the symbolic form

$$[dA(\lambda)/dt]_c = \int_0^{\lambda_{max}} K(\lambda,\lambda')\, m_B(\lambda')\, d\lambda'$$

Here the *kernel* $K(\lambda,\lambda')$, which is typically negative, represents the rate of change of the cloud work function for type λ clouds through modification of the environment by type λ' clouds per unit vertical flux $m_B(\lambda')\, d\lambda'$. The kernel is ultimately determined entirely by the vertical structure of the environment; its specific form will be obtained later by differentiation of $A(\lambda)$ in (9-83). Arakawa and Schubert estimated that the time τ_{adj} for the environment to return from an unstable state to a neutral one to be about ¼ to 3 hours exclusive of large-scale forces.

If a cloud is to be maintained, $A(\lambda)$ must be increased by large-scale processes, say, $[dA(\lambda)/dt]_{LS} = F(\lambda)$, that tend to destabilize the environment, thereby countering the effect of the cumulus to stabilize the environment. Assuming the large-scale forcing has a synoptic time scale, then $\tau_{LS} >> \tau_{adj}$; and the adjustment is so efficient that $A(\lambda)$ tends to remain near zero as long as type λ clouds exist. As a consequence the cumulus ensemble will follow a sequence of near-equilibrium states with the large-scale forcing with $[dA(\lambda)/dt]_c + F(\lambda) \approx 0$, or

$$\int_0^{\lambda_{max}} K(\lambda,\lambda')\, m_B(\lambda')\, d\lambda' + F(\lambda) \approx 0, \quad m_B(\lambda) > 0 \tag{9-85}$$

This equation must hold for each existing cloud type, which requires that $m_B(\lambda) > 0$. When $A(\lambda)$ is negative or zero, that type of cloud is assumed not to exist. Even when $A(\lambda)$ is slightly positive, cloud type λ may still not exist if $dA(\lambda)/dt$ is negative due to combined large-scale forcing and the effects of other cloud types through the kernel, $K(\lambda,\lambda')$, that is, with

$$\int_0^{\lambda_{max}} K(\lambda,\lambda')\, m_B(\lambda)\, d\lambda' + F(\lambda) < 0 \qquad \text{and} \qquad m_B(\lambda) = 0 \tag{9-86}$$

It turns out that (9-85) permits the determination of $m_B(\lambda)$ provided the kernel $K(\lambda,\lambda')$ and large-scale forcing functions $F(\lambda)$ are known. Expressions for these functions may be obtained by differentiating $A(\lambda)$ in (9-83). Then dA/dt can be divided into two parts: first, $F(\lambda)$, corresponding to the large-scale processes both in the subcloud mixed layer and above in the cloud; and the second, the integral with the kernel function which involves the cloud mass flux, the detrainment and the mixed layer. Setting dA/dt to zero, corresponding to (9-85) provides a means of determining $m_B(\lambda)$, assuming that the cloud properties as well as large scale variables are known. A form of dA/dt is shown later, but the interested reader is referred to the original articles for the detailed development.

9-6-1 Large-Scale Budget Equations

In the preceding section the principal innovative features of the Arakawa-Schubert parameterization scheme were described. Next the incorporation of these features into a large-scale model will be discussed.

The governing equations for the large-scale variables, $\bar{s}$ and $\bar{q}$, above the mixed layer, have been expressed in a convenient form by Schubert (1974) as follows:

$$\frac{\partial \bar{s}}{\partial t} = -\bar{V} \cdot \nabla \bar{s} - \bar{\omega} \frac{\partial \bar{s}}{\partial p} + g \frac{\partial}{\partial p} F_{s-L\ell} + LR + Q_R \qquad (9\text{-}87)$$

$$\frac{\partial \bar{q}}{\partial t} = -\bar{\mathbf{V}} \cdot \nabla \bar{q} - \bar{\omega} \frac{\partial \bar{q}}{\partial p} + g \frac{\partial}{\partial p} F_{q+\ell} - R \qquad (9\text{-}88)$$

where the various flux terms are defined as follows:

$$F_s(p) \equiv \begin{cases} \displaystyle\int_0^{\lambda D(p)} \eta(p,\lambda)\, [s_c(p,\lambda) - \bar{s}(p)]\, m_B(\lambda)\, d\lambda, & p < p_B \\ (F_s)_0 + [(F_s)_B - (F_s)_0] \dfrac{p_0 - p}{p_0 - p_B}, & p_0 \ge p > p_B \end{cases} \qquad (9\text{-}89)$$

$$Fq(p) \equiv \begin{cases} \displaystyle\int_0^{\lambda D(p)} \eta(p,\lambda)\, [q_c(p,\lambda) - \bar{q}(p)]\, m_B(\lambda)\, d\lambda, & p < p_B \\ (Fq)_0 + [(F_q)_B - (F_q)_0] \dfrac{p_0 - p}{p_0 - p_B}, & p_0 \ge p > p_B \end{cases} \qquad (9\text{-}90)$$

$$Fd(p) \equiv \begin{cases} \displaystyle\int_0^{\lambda D} \eta(p,\lambda)\, \ell(p,\lambda)\, m_B(\lambda)\, d\lambda, & p < p_B \\ 0 & p_0 \ge p > p_B \end{cases} \qquad (9\text{-}91)$$

$$F_{q+\ell} = F_q + F_\ell;\ F_{s-L\ell} = F_s - LF_\ell;\ F_h = F_s + LF_q$$

$$R(p) \equiv \int_0^{\lambda D(p)} \eta(p,\lambda)\, r(p,\lambda)\, m_B(\lambda)\, d\lambda \qquad (9\text{-}92)$$

Most of the terms and notations appearing in the foregoing formulas have been used previously. As may be expected, the changes in $\bar{s}$ and $\bar{q}$ are due to large-scale advection, the radiation heating Q_R, the parameterized upward fluxes F_s, F_q, and F_ℓ due to the cumulus clouds and R, the sub-grid scale sink of liquid water, which is the integral of the subensemble sink, $\eta(p,\lambda)\ r(p,\lambda)\ m_B(\lambda)\ d\lambda$. The fluxes above the subcloud layer account for both the vapor and liquid water phases, including the effect of latent heat release on $\bar{s}$ by use of the flux term $F_{s-L\ell}$. The integrals with respect to λ provide for the entire ensemble by summing over subensembles. Also it is the differences between cloud and environment values in the integrands that produce changes in the environment because of the clouds. If there were no differences, the mixing would not change the environment. Note that, as defined earlier, $\eta(\lambda,p)\ m_B\ (\lambda) = m_c\ (\lambda,p)$ is the upward vertical mass flux in the cloud and the fractional entrainment is given by

$$\lambda = m_c^{-1}\ \partial m_c/\partial z = \eta^{-1}\ \partial\eta/\partial z$$

where λ is a constant for each cloud type λ. With a constant λ, integration of the foregoing equation gives

$$\eta(z,\lambda) = \begin{cases} \exp \lambda(z - z_B) & z_B > z > z_D(\lambda) \\ 0 & z > z_D \end{cases}$$

where z_D is the detrainment level, which is essentially the cloud top. With a discrete model, there are a finite number of detrainment levels (cloud types) and integrals with respect to λ become sums.

As an illustration of the physical interpretation of the terms in (9-87) and (9-88) consider the flux divergence of $F_{s-L\ell}$ (9-87), which is defined to be $\partial(F_{s-L\ell})/\partial p \equiv \partial F_s/\partial p - L\partial F_\ell/\partial p$. In Figure 9-2, note that there is flux convergence of s_c since $[F_s(p + \Delta p) - F_s(p)]/\Delta p > 0$, which tends to make $\bar{s}$ increase, assuming $s_c > \bar{s}$, that is, the cloud is buoyant. Similarly, $-L[F_\ell(p + \Delta p) - F_\ell(p)]\Delta p > 0$ in the illustration, implying that condensation has occurred with release of latent heat which tends to increase $\bar{s}$ also. A positive R, representing rainfall, implies additional condensation and concomitant latent heat release to increase $\bar{s}$.

The integrated equations for the mixed boundary layer are

$$\frac{\partial s_M}{\partial t} = -\mathbf{V}_M \cdot \nabla S_M + \frac{g}{p_0 - p_B}(F_{s0} - F_{sB}) + Q_{RM} \tag{9-93}$$

$$\frac{\partial q_M}{\partial t} = -\mathbf{V}_M \cdot \nabla q_M + \frac{g}{p_0 - p_B}(F_{q0} - F_{qB}) \tag{9-94}$$

where the subscript M refers to mean values for the mixed subcloud layer, the subscript 0 refers to the surface and B to the top of the mixed layer. Note that

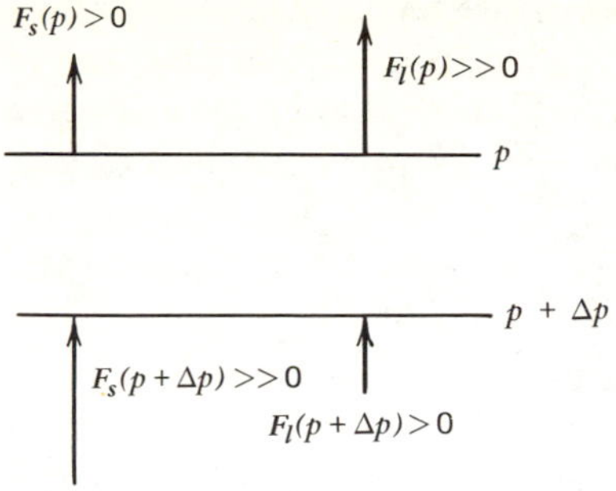

Figure 9-2 Illustrating flux divergence of s and ℓ.

the $(\mathbf{V} \cdot \boldsymbol{\nabla} q)_M$ approximation implies no correlation between the fluctuations of the horizontal wind and those of q_M or S_M.

Between the mixed boundary layer and the cloud base at z_B, there is assumed to be an infinitely thin transition layer across which there are discontinuities in temperature and moisture. The mean vertical mass flux per unit area at the top of the mixed layer, $\rho_B \overline{w}_B$, is the sum of the area weighted cloud flux M_B and clear air subsidence. Therefore the subsidence between clouds at the top of the mixed layer is given by $M_B - \rho_B \overline{w}_B$. Then the mass flux into the mixed layer, with a depth z_B changing with time, is given by $\rho_B(Dz_B/Dt - \overline{w}_B) + M_B$, where $D/Dt = \partial/\partial t + \mathbf{V}_B \cdot \boldsymbol{\nabla}$. The downward flux of s through the top of the thin transition layer at z_B+ and its bottom z_B are, respectively,

$$(s_M + \Delta s)\ [\rho_B(Dz_B/Dt - \overline{w}_B) + M_B]$$

and

$$s_M\ [\rho_B(Dz_B/Dt - \overline{w}_B) + M_B] - F_{sB}$$

where Δs is the change in s across the transition layer. Since the layer is infinitely thin, there is no accumulation and these two fluxes may be equated to give

$$\rho_B\, Dz_B/Dt = -(M_B - \rho_B \overline{w}_B) - F_{sB}/\Delta s \tag{9-95}$$

A similar equation applies to the moisture flux F_{qB}. Consistency between the two equations requires that

$$F_{qB}/\Delta q = F_{sB}/\Delta s \tag{9-96}$$

Next, as discussed in Chapter 8, the fluxes at the top of the mixed layer can be represented in terms of the surface flux of virtual s by

$$F_{svB} = -k\, F_{sv0} \tag{9-97}$$

where $F_{sv} = F_s + (c_p\, TR_d/R_v)F_q$ and k is one or two tenths (Lilly, 1968). Note that the flux at the top of the boundary layer is opposite to that at the surface. Replacing F_{svB} in (9-97) by the combination of F_s and F_q and using (9-96) gives $F_{sB} = -\, k\, (\Delta s/\Delta s_v)\, F_{sv0}$, where $\Delta s_v = \Delta s + c_p\, TR_d \Delta q/R_v$. Substituting the last result in (9-95) leads to

$$\rho_B\, Dz_B/Dt = -\, (M_B - \rho_B \overline{w}_B) + k\, F_{sv0}/\Delta s_v$$

When couched in terms of pressure coordinates this equation becomes

$$\frac{\partial p_B}{\partial t} = -\, \mathbf{V}_B \cdot \nabla p_B + \overline{\omega}_B + gM_B - gkF_{sv0}/\Delta s_v \tag{9-98}$$

The relationships (9-96) and (9-97) may be used to replace the fluxes F_{sB} and F_{qB} in (9-93) and (9-94). It should be mentioned that if Δs_v, Δs, or Δq become very small, a modification is necessary to avoid unrepresentative values.

The system of equations (9-87) and (9-88) can be solved for the large-scale variables provided $F_{s-L\ell}$, $F_{q+\ell}$, R and M_B can be determined, which, in turn, depend on $\eta(p,\lambda)$, $s_c(p,\lambda)$, $q_c(p,\lambda)$, $\ell(p,\lambda)$, $r(p,\lambda)$, $\lambda_D(p)$ and $m_B(\lambda)$. The last quantity is determined by large-scale dynamic control and the other by large-scale static control.

9-6-2 Cloud Budget Equations

The budget equations for a cloud subensemble mass, moist static energy and total water may be written

$$\partial\eta(p,\lambda)/\partial p = -\lambda H\, \eta(p,\lambda) \tag{9-99}$$

$$\partial(\eta h_c)/\partial p = -\lambda H \eta \overline{h} \tag{9-100}$$

$$\partial[\eta(q_c + \ell)]/\partial p = -H\eta\, (\lambda \overline{q} - r) \tag{9-101}$$

$$\partial(\eta q_c)/\partial p = -\lambda\, H\eta\overline{q},\ p_c < p < p_B \tag{9-102}$$

where $H = R\overline{T}\,(gp)^{-1}$, p_B and p_c are the pressures at the top of the mixed layer and the condensation level (see Figure 9-3 and explanation below). Since the cloud temperature above the condensation level differs only slightly from the environment temperature, a linear approximation suffices for q_c, that is,

$$\begin{aligned} q_c(p,\lambda) &\doteq \overline{q}^*\,(p) + [\gamma/(1+\gamma)L]\,(h_c - \overline{h}^*) \\ s_c &\doteq \overline{s} + (h_c - \overline{h}^*)/(1+\gamma) \end{aligned} \tag{9-103}$$

where $\gamma = (L/c_p)\,(\partial q^*/\partial T)_p$. To verify the last equation multiply it by $(1 + \gamma)$, replace h by $s + Lq$ and it reduces to: $(T_c - T)\,(\partial q^*/\partial T) \doteq q^*_c - q^*$, a linear approximation. Also the detrainment level is the level of zero buoyancy, thus,

$$s_{vc}(p,\lambda_D(p)) = \overline{s}_v(p) \tag{9-104}$$

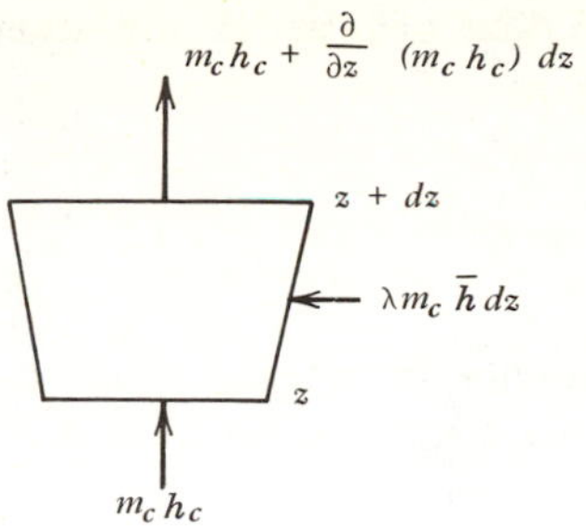

Figure 9-3 Illustrating flux of moist static energy.

The derivation of (9-99) to (9-102) may be illustrated with (9-100) by considering Figure 9-3, where the vertical flux of moist static energy h_c and level z in the cloud is $m_c h_c$, while at the top it is $m_c h_c + [\partial(m_c h_c)/\partial z]\, dz$. The lateral flux of environmental $\bar{h}$ per unit vertical distance is represented by $\lambda m_c \bar{h}$, since λ is defined to be the fractional entrainment rate, meaning that for m_c vertical flux there is λm_c entrainment. It follows that

$$\frac{\partial(m_c h_c)}{\partial z}\, dz = \lambda m_c \bar{h}\, dz \tag{9-105}$$

Canceling the dz, substituting $-dp/g\bar{\rho}$ for dz and dividing both sides of the foregoing equation by $m_B(\lambda)$ gives (9-100). A similar procedure obviously gives (9-102). It may also be noted that the mass flux alone may be considered by omitting $\bar{h}$ and h_c in the previous derivation, which gives (9-99) directly. The moisture relation (9-101) is somewhat more complicated since the cloud vertical flux of moisture includes liquid water ℓ as well as vapor q and also the allowance for a liquid water sink resulting from precipitation. If $r(p,\lambda)$ is regarded as a function of $\ell(p,\lambda)$, Equations 9-99 to 9-104 permit the determination of the cloud parameters, $\eta(p,\lambda)$, $s_c(p,\lambda)$, $q_c(p,\lambda)$, $\ell(p,\lambda)$, and $\lambda_D(p)$ for calculation of the vertical fluxes of heat and moisture due to convection, which modify the large-scale variable $\bar{s}$ and $\bar{q}$ in (9-87) and (9-88). The first four equations are integrated upward from p_B with boundary conditions at p_B as follows: $\eta(p_b,\lambda) = 1$, $h_c(p_B,\lambda) = h_M$, $q_c(p_B,\lambda) = q_M$ and $\ell(p_B,\lambda) = 0$.

The only remaining quantity needed for the calculation of the cumulus effects on the large-scale fields is $m_B(\lambda)$, which has been discussed earlier. The cloud work function (9-83) depends on the large-scale variables, hence its derivative can be written in terms of s_M, q_M, p_B, $\bar{s}$, and $\bar{q}$ as follows:

$$\frac{dA}{dt} = \frac{a_B}{\overline{H}_B}\frac{\partial s_{vM}}{\partial t} + \frac{b_B}{\overline{H}_B}\frac{\partial h_M}{\partial t} + \frac{1}{p_B}\frac{\partial p_B}{\partial t}[(\lambda a_B - 1)\Delta s_v + \lambda b_B\,\Delta H + \lambda\,\overline{H}_B A]$$

$$+ \int_{pD(\lambda)}^{pB} \eta\left[(\lambda a - 1)\frac{\partial \bar{s}_v}{\partial t} + \lambda b \frac{\partial \bar{h}}{\partial t}\right]\frac{dp}{p} \tag{9-106}$$

where $\overline{H}_B = R\overline{T}_B/g$, and a and b are known functions of p and λ. Equation 9-106 can be written in the form (9-85)

$$dA/dt = \int_0^{\lambda_{\max}} K(\lambda,\lambda')\, m_B(\lambda')\, d\lambda' + F(\lambda) = 0$$

as discussed earlier. The solution of the quasi-equilibrium integral equations (9-85) or (9-86) for $m_B(\lambda)$ is difficult because of the inequality; however Arakawa and Schubert have given an iterative method of solution.

For numerical modeling purposes it is not necessary to compute all of the terms that make up dA/dt, which are many. First a large-scale forecast is made without cloud effects, which will normally lead to a non-zero cloud work function at some gridpoint. Then the cumulus parameterization adjustment is made to the large-scale parameters, which returns the cloud work function to zero. Hence the value of A just prior to the adjustment approximates $(dA/dt)\Delta t$. Using this value for $F(\lambda)$, the integral equation (9-85) may be solved for $m_b(\lambda)\Delta t$. After that, the additional changes of $\overline{T}$ and $\overline{q}$ due to the cloud ensemble terms in (9-87) and (9-88) are calculated which bring the temporarily nonzero cloud work function $A(\lambda)$ back to zero. In actual practice, Arakawa and Schubert replace the spectral parameter λ by the detrainment height z_D. Since each subensemble is assumed to detrain at the same height, there is a one-to-one inverse relationships between λ representing a particular cloud type and the detrainment level, which is assumed to be the maximum height reached by that cloud type, that is, $z = z_D[\lambda_D(z)]$.

The parameterization schemes described here have been used in various NWP models and compared with observations. The convective adjustment scheme (Manabe et al., 1965) has been used extensively in the GFDL general circulation model for years. It is one of the simplest to apply but it tends to generate sizable gravity waves (4-mb amplitude) with the abrupt changes. When compared to the Kuo scheme, the latter gave more transient disturbances in the tropics and performed better in middle latitudes as well. The Kuo scheme is rather easy to apply and overall gives fairly satisfactory results; however, the vertical partitioning of the heating should be determined by the dynamics of systems and not by the imposition of an arbitrary distribution function applied everywhere. The Arakawa-Schubert scheme gives a better vertical distribution of condensational heating than the simpler convective adjustment, which gives most of the heating between 900 to 500 mb.

The tests of several PBL parameterizations in a GCM by Miyakoda and Sirutis (1974) (M-S), described in Chapter 8, also included comparisons of the dry convective adjustment (DCA) with a turbulent flux (TF) method and moist convective adjustment (MCA) with the Arakawa-Schubert cumulus parameterization (ASC). They found that DCA and TF gave similar temperature changes aloft; but DCA gave unrealistic negative changes at low levels while both the turbulent-flux and mixed-layer PBL parameterizations behaved satisfactorily there. Also DCA created more gravitational noise, or "shock," because of the abrupt changes in the temperature and mass distributions. MCA produced much more warming below 500 mb than did ASC, especially in the tropics, whereas ASC gave somewhat more heating above 500 mb than MCA. Heating due to large-scale condensation was large in the tropics with MCA but relatively small with ASC. In the waves in the tropical easterlies MCA gave maximum rainfall east of the trough, whereas ASC gave a more uniform distribution about the trough, which agrees better with observations [Reed and Recker (1971), Ogura and Cho (1974)]. This characteristic has an important influence on the dynamics of easterly waves since the covariance of heating and upward velocity is proportional to the conversion between potential and kinetic energy. In middle latitudes both MCA and ASC correctly give precipitation east of troughs. The ASC scheme gave a wider rainfall belt in the western Pacific but there was also rainfall in the doldrums. The inclusion of downdraft effects due to liquid water and falling rain inside cumulus clouds substantially affects the horizontal distribution of rainfall in the ASC parameterization and the ITCZ becomes narrower and doldrums drier [Lord, 1978].

As of this writing, the most comprehensive verification of the Arakawa-Schubert cumulus parameterization has been conducted by Lord (Ph.D. dissertation, 1978, UCLA). The scheme utilizes the fundamental assumption that the generation of moist convective instability by large-scale processes is in near equilibrium with the destruction of this instability by the vertical transport of heat and moisture within the clouds. Lord shows from GATE observational data that the work function $A(\lambda)$ is a quasi-universal function of cloud type (as defined by the cloud-top level). Variations in the mean cloud work function for each cloud type in varying synoptic conditions, both tropical and subtropical, were small when compared to changes due to large-scale processes only. This dictates a strong coupling between the temperature and moisture structure of the large-scale environment as affected by cumulus clouds. The predicted cumulus precipitation rates by the parameterization scheme agree well both in phase and magnitude with observed GATE[1] data and also neglect of dA/dt in the mass flux distribution equation generally changed precipitation rates negligibly, verifying the quasi-equilibrium assumption. The adiabatic cooling due to large-scale vertical motion dominates the forcing by horizontal advection of temperature and moisture and radiative cooling for deep and middle level clouds; however radiative cooling plays a major role in very shallow clouds and in decreasing calculated precipitation rates in regions of cirrus overcast.

Although the vertically integrated heating with the ASC scheme agreed well with observed data as represented by rainfall rates, the vertical distribution of temperature and moisture changes was not handled as well. In brief, the total eddy heat (sensible plus latent) flux convergence, is underestimated above 500 mb and below 800 mb, but overestimated between 800 and 550 mb. As a result

1. GATE: GARP Atlantic Tropical Experiment.

the warming of the large-scale environment is overestimated below 650 mb, and underestimated above with erroneous cooling above 300 mb. Drying is much overestimated below 700 mb and underestimated above 700 mb with erroneous moistening above 400 mb. Improvements in the cloud model can be expected to improve the vertical distributions. By allowing the precipitation produced at cloud top levels above the freezing level to evaporate into the environment below the freezing level, Lord reduced the overprediction of cooling and moistening in the uppermost layers and the warming and drying in the lower layers. It was also suggested that a better treatment of radiative cooling in forcing shallow clouds may help in this regard.

Downdrafts in cumulus clouds, which were neglected in the ASC scheme, may have important effects also. Overall, the results indicate that separating the cumulus and the synoptic time scales is valid for predicting the thermodynamic fields over a large-scale area in the tropics; but the cloud, meso, and synoptic scales may be more mutually interactive elsewhere. Lord (1978) found that the MCA and Kuo parameterization schemes were largely unsuccessful in predicting precipitation and the cumulus warming and drying effects over the GATE area.

The ASC scheme was not successful in generating a hurricane from a weak tropical vortex as has been achieved with the Kuo scheme and even simpler parameterizations. Rosenthal (1979) used the Ooyama (1971) cumulus parameterization scheme, which is somewhat similar to that of Arakawa and Schubert, in the simulation of an axisymmetrical hurricane from a weak, closed vortex. The resultant growth was strongly influenced by the number and character of the clouds making up the assumed ensemble and also by the manner in which resolvable supersaturation is treated. Rosenthal questioned the applicability of the Ooyama and Arakawa-Schubert schemes to hurricane simulation because (1) the schemes assume that cumulus cloud cover is a small fraction of the grid module, which is not true when the grid distance is a few tens of km or less and, (2) the further assumption that the periods of the larger-scale motions treated explicitly are much greater than the cumulus scale, which is true for synoptic scales but not necessarily for mesoscale phenomena such as hurricanes. Rosenthal (1978) and also Yamasaki (1975, 1977) successfully simulated the development of large-scale tropical cyclones in which the cumulus clouds were explicitly resolved. Yamasaki's model had a grid distance of only 400 m in the inner region. Rosenthal obtained a reasonable development and structure from latent heat release in convective elements resolved on a 20 km grid. Small-scale features predominate initially but are eventually organized by a developing larger-scale circulation in which boundary layer convergence (CISK type) exerts a strong control on the convection and growth of the tropical cyclone. After about 60 hr of simulated time, a hurricane-type circulation developed, including an eyewall.

In summary, parameterizing the effects of cumulus convection on large-scale disturbances is a complex and difficult problem. More observational verifications are needed with present schemes to eliminate their deficiencies, to delineate their applicability and to single out the best method, if possible. Among the existing schemes for synoptic-scale applications, the Arakawa-Schubert parameterization is the most elegant in terms of its physical basis and appears to have the greatest potential. But it is also the most complex short of using an explicit model to compute the vertical transports.

CHAPTER 10

Radiation Parameterization

10-1 TERRESTRIAL RADIATION

Ultimately, the primary factor driving the atmosphere is the differential solar (short-wave) radiation between the poles and the equator. But the actual radiational heating of the atmosphere depends on the difference between the incoming (solar) and the outgoing (terrestrial) radiations, which depend on many factors, such as temperature, clouds, water vapor, carbon dioxide, ozone, dust, etc. The processes involved are very complex and a detailed treatment for purposes of weather forecasting would require an enormous amount of computer time. Consequently, approximate solutions are sought that are realistic in terms of the design and objectives of a numerical prediction or simulation model including the period of the forecast, grid spacing, physical processes, the data base, etc. The treatment given here very closely follows the parameterization scheme for radiative transfer developed by Katayama (1974) for the UCLA general circulation model. While other parameterizations may differ in details, many basic concepts are illustrated by Katayama's treatment, which is the objective of the text, rather than presenting a catalogue of the various schemes in use.

The atmospheric long-wave radiation with wavelengths between 2.5 and 40 μ (microns) is primarily affected by absorption by water vapor, carbon dioxide, and ozone. In comparison to other atmosphere constituents absorption by ozone is neglected because of the primary emphasis on the troposphere. Although scattering of long-wave radiation by air molecules is negligible, scattering by large aerosols may be significant at times; nevertheless, the latter is also neglected in view of other simplifications and unavailability of observational data on aerosols.

A sufficiently dense cloud will act as a blackbody radiator at its top and bottom, while within the cloud the net flux of long-wave radiation is zero. Solar radiation is also strongly affected by cloud layers and will be discussed later.

According to Schwarzschild, the change in the intensity of monochromatic radiation at frequency υ entering at angle θ from the perpendicular across a plane sheet of absorbing matter of mass du (see Figure 10-1) is

$$dI_\upsilon = -k_\upsilon [I_\upsilon - B_\upsilon(T)] \sec\theta \, du \tag{10-1}$$

where $B_\upsilon(T)$ represents blackbody radiation at υ and T, k_υ is the absorption coefficient and $k_\upsilon B_\upsilon(T) \sec\theta\, du$ is the blackbody emission by the sheet. If there is no emission, integration of (10-1) gives the intensity after absorption, namely,

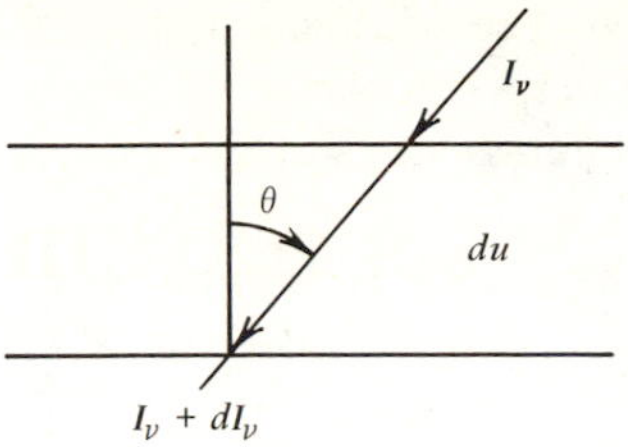

Figure 10-1

$$I_\upsilon = I_{\upsilon 0} \exp(-k_\upsilon \Delta u \sec\theta) \tag{10-2}$$

where $\Delta u > 0$ is the total mass of absorbing material.

Assume now the thin emitting slice is above an absorbing layer of thickness Δu as shown in Figure 10-2. The emission from the slice du in the direction of θ is, according to (10-1),

$$dI_\upsilon^i = k_\upsilon \sec\theta\, B_\upsilon(T)\, du \tag{10-3}$$

If for the present the emissions from the Δu are neglected, the intensity of the emission from the slice du after passing through the absorbing layer Δu may be obtained by substituting dI_υ^i of (10-3) into (10-2) in place of $I_{\upsilon 0}$, which yields

$$dI_{z\upsilon} = k_\upsilon \sec\theta\, B_\upsilon(T)\, du \exp(-k_\upsilon \Delta u \sec\theta) \tag{10-4}$$

Then the integration of this equation for all directions over a hemisphere gives the infinitesimal flux at frequency υ emerging at the bottom of the layer (at level z) from the slice du as follows:

$$dR_{z\upsilon}^{\downarrow} = \int_0^{2\pi} d\phi \int_0^{\pi/2} (dI_{z\upsilon} \cos\theta) \sin\theta\, d\theta\;\; 2\pi k_\upsilon B_\upsilon E_2(k_\upsilon \Delta u)\, du \tag{10-5}$$

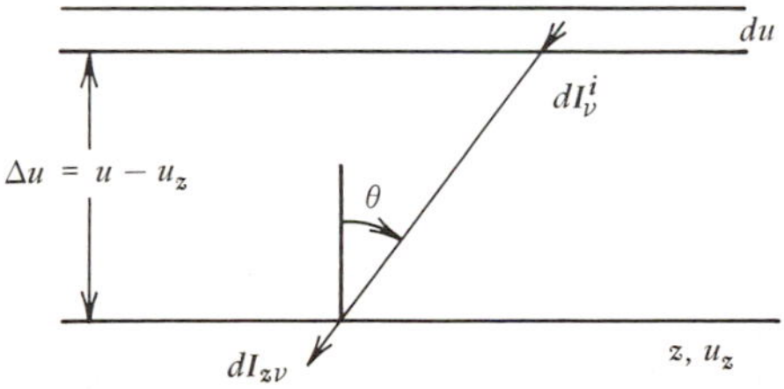

Figure 10-2 Illustrating emission dI^i from slice du at angle θ followed by absorption in finite layer Δu.

where $E_n(x) = \int_0^\infty \exp(-x\eta)\, d\eta/\eta^n$. The cos θ appears because a unit horizontal area at level z receives emission from an area cos θ perpendicular to the beam. The sin θ factor comes from the increasing area of circular rings of the slice as θ increases.

Next the *total downward flux* at level z and frequency υ from all slices above z is obtained by integrating (10-5) from u_z to u_∞ where $R_{z\upsilon}$ is assumed to vanish as z approaches ∞, giving

$$R_{z\upsilon}^{\downarrow} = 2\pi k_\upsilon \int_{u_z}^{u_\infty} B_\upsilon(T)\, E_2\,[k_\upsilon(u - u_z)]\, du \tag{10-6}$$

Since $dEi_n(x)/dx = Ei_{n-1}(x)$, (10-6) can be written as

$$R_{z\upsilon}^{\downarrow} = -\int_{u_z}^{u_\infty} \pi\, B_\upsilon(T) \frac{d}{du} \{2E_3\,[k_\upsilon(u - u_z)]\}\, du$$

Finally, the total downward flux is obtained by summing over all frequencies

$$R_z^{\downarrow} = -\int_0^\infty d\upsilon \int_{u_z}^\infty \pi\, B_\upsilon(T) \frac{d}{du} \{2E_3\,[k_\upsilon\,(u - u_z)]\}\, du \tag{10-7}$$

To simplify the evaluation of these integrals Elsasser (1942) smoothed the rapid variation of the absorption coefficient with frequency by using a running average of E_3 with respect to υ and introducing a transmission function, $\tau_f(\ell_\upsilon u)$:

$$\tau_f(\ell_\upsilon u) \equiv \frac{1}{\Delta\upsilon} \int_{\upsilon - \Delta\upsilon/2}^{\upsilon + \Delta\upsilon/2} 2E_3\,[k_\upsilon u]\, d\upsilon \tag{10-8}$$

Now treating τ_f as a continuous function of υ and introducing it into (10-7) gives

$$R_z^{\downarrow} = -\int_0^\infty d\upsilon \int_{u_z}^{u_\infty} \pi\, B_\upsilon(T) \frac{d}{du} \tau_f\,[\ell_\upsilon(u - u_z)]\, du \tag{10-9}$$

Integrating (10-9) by parts and introducing T as the integration variable yields

$$R_z^{\downarrow} = \int_0^\infty \pi\, B_\upsilon(T_z)\, d\upsilon + \int_0^\infty d\upsilon \int_{T_z}^{T_\infty} \frac{d}{dT} [\pi\, B_\upsilon(T)]\, \tau_f\,[\ell_\upsilon(u - u_z)]\, dT \tag{10-10}$$

Here $T(\infty) = 0$, while the transmission function is unity for $u = u_z$ and becomes zero as z goes to infinity. Above the level z_{ST}, u is assumed to be a constant u_{ST}; hence $u - u_z = u_{ST} - u_z =$ constant for $z \geq z_{ST}$. Next divide the integration with respect to T in (10-10) into two parts taking $B_\upsilon(0) = 0$ at $z = \infty$, with the result

$$R_z^{\downarrow} = \int_0^\infty \pi\, B_\upsilon(T_z)\, d\upsilon + \int_0^\infty \int_{T_z}^{TST} \pi \frac{dB_\upsilon(T)}{dT}\, \tau_f\,[\ell_\upsilon(u - u_z)]\, dT\, d\upsilon$$

$$- \int_0^\infty \pi B_\nu(T_{ST}) \tau_f [\ell_\nu(u_{ST} - u_z)] d\nu \tag{10-11}$$

In a similar manner Katayama obtains the upward flux $R_z^\uparrow$ at an arbitrary reference level z based on blackbody flux at the ground with temperature T_g,

$$R_z^\uparrow = \int_0^\infty \pi B_\nu(T_z) d\nu + \int_0^\infty d\nu \int_{T_z}^{T_g} \pi \frac{dB_\nu(T)}{dT} \tau_f [\ell_\nu(u_z - u)] dT \tag{10-12}$$

Subtracting (10-11) from (10-12) gives the net upward long-wave radiation flux R_z:

$$R_z = R_z^\uparrow - R_z^\downarrow \tag{10-13}$$

Moreover the heating rate is proportional to the flux divergence; thus

$$\frac{\partial T}{\partial t} = -\frac{1}{\rho c_p} \frac{\partial R_z}{\partial z} = \frac{g}{c_p} \frac{\partial R_z}{\partial p} \tag{10-14}$$

10-2 ABSORBING SUBSTANCES

Water vapor and carbon dioxide, denoted by W and C, are the principal absorbers of long-wave radiation in the troposphere, hence

$$\tau_f [\ell_\nu u] = \tau_f [(\ell_\nu u)_W + (\ell_\nu u)_C] \tag{10-15}$$

Also the broadening of the absorption lines by collisions makes ℓ_ν a function of pressure. This function can be approximated by applying a factor $(p/p_{00})^\alpha$ to the mass of absoring substance u and then using the absorption coefficient at standard pressure $\ell_{\nu 00}$. The resulting effective absorber amount u^* between an arbitrary level p and the surface p_s is

$$u_j^* = \frac{1}{g} \int_p^{p_s} q_j \left(\frac{p}{p_{00}}\right)^{\alpha_j} dp \tag{10-16}$$

where q_j is the mixing ratio of either H_2O or CO_2. The quantities u_j^* and $\ell_{\nu 00}$ may now be used in (10-15).

10-3 SIMPLIFIED TRANSMISSION FUNCTIONS

In order to adapt the flux equations (10-11) and (10-12) to a general circulation model, Katayama defines two weighted-mean transmission functions as follows:

$$\tau(u^*, T) \equiv \left[\pi \frac{dB\,(T)}{dT}\right]^{-1} \int_0^\infty \pi \frac{dB_\upsilon(T)}{dT} \tau_f\,(\ell_{\upsilon 00}\, u^*)\, d\upsilon \tag{10-17}$$

and

$$\bar{\tau}\,(u^*, T) \equiv [\pi\, B\,(T)]^{-1} \int_0^\infty \pi\, B_\upsilon(T)\, \tau_f\,(\ell_{\upsilon 00}\, u^*)\, d\upsilon \tag{10-18}$$

where

$$\pi\, B\,(T) = \int_0^\infty \pi\, B_\upsilon(T)\, d\upsilon = \sigma T^4 \tag{10-19}$$

Substituting the foregoing quantities into (10-11) and (10-12) leads to

$$R_z^\downarrow = \pi\, B\,(T_z) + \int_{T_z}^{T_{ST}} \pi \frac{dB\,(T)}{dT} \tau(u^* - u_z^*, T)\, dT$$

$$- \pi\, B\,(T_{ST})\, \bar{\tau}(u_{ST}^* - u_z^*, T_{ST}) \tag{10-20}$$

$$R_z^\uparrow = \pi\, B\,(T_z) + \int_{T_z}^{T_g} \pi \frac{dB\,(T)}{dT} \tau(u_z^* - u^*, T)\, dT \tag{10-21}$$

In 1952 Yamamoto showed that for a given u^*, the variation of τ with temperature is small in the range 210 K to 320 K, whereas below 210 K decreases rapidly with T; hence

$$\tau(u^*, T) \doteq \tau(u^*, \bar{T}) \text{ for } T > T_c = 210\text{ K} \quad \bar{T} = 260\text{ K} \tag{10-22}$$

With these approximations and (10-18), the last term in (10-20) becomes

$$\pi\, B\,(T_{ST})\, \bar{\tau}\,(u_{ST}^* - u_z^*, T_{ST}) \equiv \int_0^\infty \pi\, B_\upsilon(T_{ST})\, \tau_f\,[\ell_{\upsilon\,00}\,(u_{ST}^* - u_z^*)]\, d\upsilon$$

$$= \int_0^\infty \pi\, B_\upsilon(T_c)\, \tau_f\,[\ell_{\upsilon\,00}\,(u_{ST}^* - u_z^*)]\, d\upsilon$$

$$+ \int_0^\infty \int_{T_c}^{T_{ST}} \pi \frac{dB_\upsilon(T)}{dT} \tau_f\,[\ell_{\upsilon\,00}\,(u_{ST}^* - u_z^*)]\, dT d\upsilon$$

$$= \pi\, B\,(T_c)\, \bar{\tau}\,(u_{ST}^* - u_z^*, T_c)$$

$$+ \int_{T_c}^{T_{ST}} \pi \frac{dB\,(T)}{dT} \tau\,(u_{ST}^* - u_z, \bar{T})\, dT = \pi\, B\,(T_c)\, \bar{\tau}\,(u_{ST}^* - u_z^*, T_c)$$

$$+ \pi\,[B\,(T_{ST}) - B\,(T_c)]\, \tau\,(u_{ST}^* - u_z^*, \bar{T}) \tag{10-23}$$

To arrive at the last result both (10-17) and (10-18) have been used, the temperature dependence of τ_f in the range, $T_{ST} \leq T \leq T_c$, has been ignored and $\bar{T}$ is used in τ. Substituting this result into (10-20) leads to

$$R_z^{\downarrow} = \pi B_z - \pi B_c \tilde{\tau} (u_{ST}^* - u_z^*, T_c) - (\pi B_{ST} - \pi B_c) \tau (u_{ST}^* - u_z^*, \bar{T})$$

$$+ \int_{\pi B_z}^{\pi B_{ST}} \tau (u^* - u_z^*, \bar{T}) \, d(\pi B) \qquad (10\text{-}24)$$

where $\pi B_i = \pi B(T_i) = \pi \sigma T_i^4$. Also using (10-23) in (10-21) gives

$$R_z^{\uparrow} = \pi B_z + \int_{\pi B_z}^{\pi B_g} \tau (u_z^* - u^*, \bar{T}) \, d(\pi B) \qquad (10\text{-}25)$$

10-4 DISCRETIZATION, LONG-WAVE RADIATION

10-4-1 Clear Sky

To apply the continuous form of the radiative fluxes (10-24) and (10-25) to a numerical model, the atmosphere is discretized as shown in Figure 10-3, where ℓ represents a reference layer with top at z. The absorber amount u_ℓ^* from the ground level (upper level of layer $LM + 1$) to the level z at the top of layer ℓ corresponds to the u_z^* used earlier. With the definitions

$$\tilde{\tau}_\ell \equiv \tilde{\tau} (u_{ST}^* - u_\ell^*, T_c) \qquad (\tau_{ST,\ell} \equiv \tau (u_{ST}^*, - u_\ell^*, \bar{T}) \qquad (10\text{-}26)$$

the semidiscrete forms of (10-24) and (10-25) are

$$R_\ell^{\downarrow} = \pi B_\ell - \pi B_c \tilde{\tau}_\ell - (\pi B_{ST} - \pi B_C) \tau_{ST,\ell}$$

$$+ \int_{\pi B_C}^{\pi B_{ST}} \tau (u^* - u_\ell^*, \bar{T}) \, d(\pi B) \qquad (10\text{-}27a)$$

$$R_\ell^{\uparrow} = \pi B_\ell + \int_{\pi B_\ell}^{\pi B_g} \tau (u_\ell^* - u^*, \bar{T}) \, d(\pi B)$$

$$= \pi B_\ell + \int_{\pi B_\ell}^{\pi B_{LM+1}} \tau (u_\ell^* - u^*, \bar{T}) \, d(\pi B)$$

$$+ (\pi B_g - \pi B_{LM+1}) \tau_{\ell LM+1} \qquad (10\text{-}27b)$$

Here ℓ ranges from $LTRP$ to $LM + 1$ and πB_g refers to ground temperature, while πB_{LM+1} refers to surface air temperature.

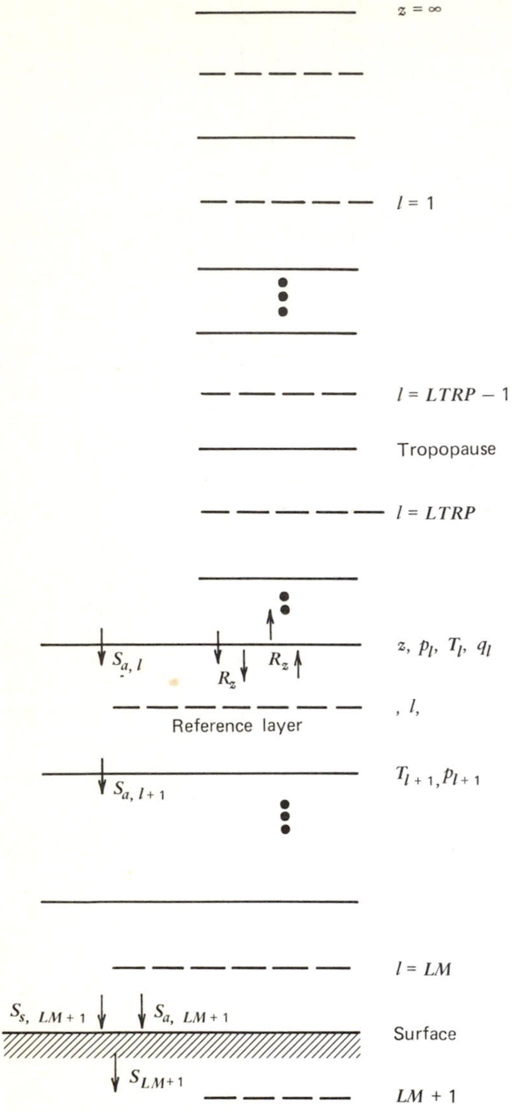

Figure 10-3 Vertical indexing and schematic fluxes. Solar fluxes denoted by S's will be described later.

The contribution to the flux at the upper level of layer ℓ from an arbitrary layer ℓ' is denoted by

$$C_{\ell',\ell} \equiv \int_{\pi B_{\ell'}}^{\pi B_{\ell'+1}} \tau\,(|u^* - u_\ell^*|, \overline{T})\, d\,(\pi B) \tag{10-28}$$

Dividing the integral in (10-27a) into integrals from πB_ℓ to πB_{LTRP} and from πB_{LTRP} to πB_{ST}, approximating the latter by $(\pi B_{ST} - \pi B_{LTRP})\,\tau_{LTRP,\ell}$, and using a finite sum gives (see Figure 10-4)

$$R_\ell^{\downarrow} = \pi B_\ell - \sum_{\ell'=\ell-1}^{LTRP} C_{\ell',\ell} - (\pi B_{LTRP} - \pi B_{ST})\,\tau_{LTRP,\ell} - (\pi B_{ST} - \pi B_C)\,\tau_{ST,\ell} - \pi B_C\,\tilde{\tau}_\ell \tag{10-29}$$

Also

$$R_\ell^{\uparrow} = \pi B_\ell + \sum_{\ell'=\ell}^{LM} C_{\ell',\ell} + (\pi B_g - \pi B_{LM+1})\,\tau_{\ell,LM+1} \tag{10-30}$$

Assuming τ varies nearly linearly within layer ℓ', then $C_{\ell',\ell}$ may be approximated with

$$C_{\ell',\ell} = \tfrac{1}{2}(\tau_{\ell'+1,\ell} + \tau_{\ell',\ell})\,(\pi B_{\ell'+1} - \pi B_{\ell'}) \tag{10-31}$$

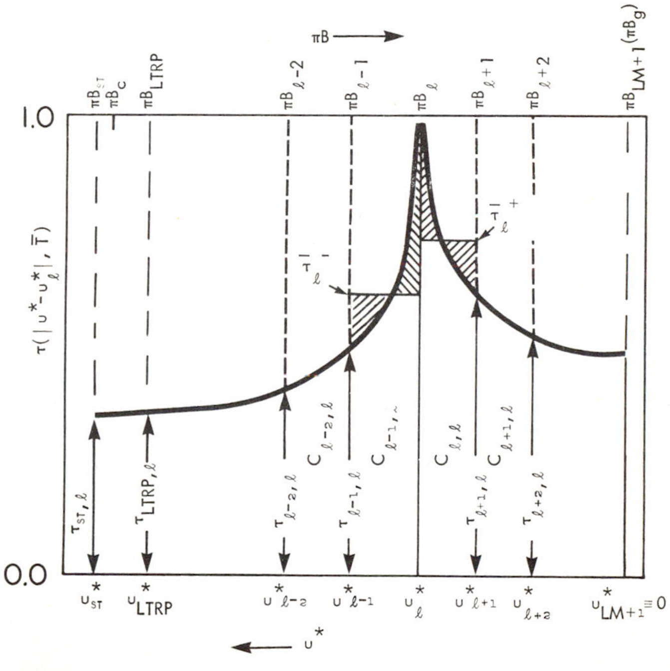

Figure 10-4 Schematic representation of $\tau(|u^* - u_\ell^*|, T)$ employed in the net flux of long wave radiation at layer ℓ after Katayama. (*See Arakawa et al. 1974.*)

This form is valid except for $\ell' = \ell + 1$ and $\ell' = \ell$ where τ varies rapidly with πB. Therefore two bulk transmission functions $\bar{\tau}^{\pm}$ (see Figure 10-4) introduced as follows:

$$C_{\ell-1,\ell} = \bar{\tau}_\ell^- (\pi B_\ell - \pi B_{\ell-1})$$
$$C_{\ell',\ell} = \bar{\tau}_\ell^+ (\pi B_{\ell+1} - \pi B_\ell) \tag{10-32}$$

where the $\bar{\tau}^{\pm}$ are given later. Substitution of (10-32) and (10-31) into (10-29) and (10-30) gives

$$R_\ell^\downarrow = \pi B_\ell - (\pi B_\ell - B_{\ell-1})\bar{\tau}_\ell^- - ½ \sum_{\ell'=\ell-2}^{LTRP} (\tau_{\ell'+1,\ell} + \tau_{\ell',\ell})(\pi B_{\ell'+1} - \pi B_{\ell'})$$
$$- (\pi B_{LTRP} - \pi B_{ST})\tau_{LTRP,\ell} - (\pi B_{ST} - \pi B_c)\tau_{ST,\ell} - \pi B_C \bar{\tau}_\ell \tag{10-33}$$

$$R_\ell^\uparrow = \pi B_\ell + (\pi B_{\ell+1} - \pi B_\ell)\bar{\tau}_\ell^+ + ½ \sum_{\ell'=\ell+1}^{LM}$$
$$(\tau_{\ell'+1,\ell} + \tau_{\ell',\ell})(\pi B_{\ell'+1} - \pi B_{\ell'}) + (\pi B_g - \pi B_{LM+1})\tau_{\ell,LM+1} \tag{10-34}$$

10-4-2 Cloudy Sky

The UCLA model has three types of clouds: (1) clouds associated with grid-scale supersaturation, (2) the subgrid scale convection discussed in Chapter 9 and (3) boundary-layer stratus associated with supersaturation, of which the first two are considered here. Clouds may occur in any of the model layers and are assumed to fill an entire layer with overcast conditions ($CL_\ell = 1$). A tropospheric layer is assumed to be a cloud layer if the mixing ratio exceeds the saturation value or if there is mass flux into the layer by convection. For cumulus, only the detrainment layer of the penetrating type is permitted to be a cloud layer, which restricts the latter to layers above 400 mb. Cloud layers for which the midlevel temperature is greater than $-40°$C are assumed to consist of water droplets, and are treated as blackbody radiators. Below that temperature, cirrus clouds consisting of ice crystals are assumed to exist and are treated as blackbody radiators, but with a fractional cloudiness of only one-half ($CL_\ell = 0.5$). When cloud layers exist the flux equations (10-33) and (10-34) are modified as follows:

$$R_\ell^\downarrow = \pi B_\ell - (\pi B_\ell - \pi B_{\ell-1})\bar{\tau}_\ell^- (1 - CL_{\ell-1})$$
$$- ½ \sum_{\ell'=\ell-2}^{LTRP} (\tau_{\ell'+1,\ell} + \tau_{\ell',\ell})(\pi B'_{\ell+1} - \pi B_{\ell'}) \prod_{k=\ell-1}^{\ell'} (1 - CL_k)$$
$$- (\pi B_{LTRP} - \pi B_{ST})\tau_{LTRP,\ell}$$

$$+ (\pi B_{ST} - \pi B_c)\, \tau_{ST,\ell} + \pi B_c\, \tilde{\tau}_\ell] \prod_{k=\ell-1}^{LTRP} (1 - CL_k)$$

$$R_\ell^\uparrow = \pi B_\ell + (\pi B_{\ell+1} - \pi B_\ell)\, \bar{\tau}_\ell^+ (1 - CL_\ell)$$

$$+ \tfrac{1}{2} \sum_{\ell'=\ell+1}^{LM} (\tau_{\ell'+1,\ell} + \tau_{\ell',\ell})\, (\pi B_{\ell'+1} - \pi B_{\ell'}) \prod_{k=\ell}^{\ell'} (1 - CL_k)$$

$$+ (\pi B_g - \pi B_{LM+1})\, \tau_{\ell,LM+1} \prod_{k=\ell}^{LM} (1 - CL_k) \tag{10-36}$$

The transmission functions, which result from the combined effects of the absorbers, H_2O and CO_2, are assumed to be the products of the individual functions, $\tau(u^*, T) = \tau(u^*_{H_2O}, T)\, \tau(u^*_{CO_2})$, where the temperature dependence is neglected in the case of CO_2, and similarly for $\tilde{\tau}$. Empirical functions for τ and $\tilde{\tau}$ for water vapor and CO_2 have been determined by Katayama from Yamamoto's 1952 data and may be found in the detailed description of the UCLA GCM (1974).

The bulk transmission functions $\tau_\ell^\pm$ are evaluated by linear interpolation between $\tau^\pm = 1$ for $|u^* - u_\ell^*| = 0$, and $\tau_\ell^\pm = \tau_{\ell+1,\ell}$. Thus

$$\bar{\tau}_\ell^\pm \equiv (1 + m_\ell^\pm\, \tau_{\ell\pm1,\ell})/(1 \pm m_\ell^\pm)$$

where the factors $m_\ell^\pm$ are functions of pressure, temperature, water vapor, mixing ratio, its lapse rate at the upper level of layer ℓ, and the pressure thickness.

In addition some further simplifications are made regarding the vertical distribution of CO_2 and water vapor for the purpose of computing the radiative fluxes, but these details are not included here.

10-5 SOLAR RADIATION

As in the case of terrestrial radiation, an exact treatment of solar radiation would be very complex and too time consuming to compute for numerical prediction purposes. Hence simplified versions are used, such as the treatment of Katayama for the UCLA GCM, which is followed here.

To begin with, the insolation incident at the outer limits of the atmosphere, $\bar{S}_0 \cos\alpha$, is a function of the mean solar constant $\bar{S}_0$, the ratio of the earth-sun distance r_E to the mean distance $\bar{r}_E$ and the zenith angle α, which, in turn, depends on latitude φ, the hour angle h and the declination angle δ.

$$\begin{aligned} S_0 \cos\alpha &= \bar{S}_0\, (\bar{r}_E/r_E)^2 \cos\alpha \\ \cos\alpha &= \sin\varphi \sin\delta + \cos\varphi \cos\delta \cos h \end{aligned} \tag{10-37}$$

The principal absorption of solar radiation by water vapor occurs in wavelengths λ greater than 0.9 μ (microns), the weak absorption bands $\lambda < 0.9\ \mu$ are therefore neglected. On the other hand, the Rayleigh scattering is inversely proportional to the fourth power of the wavelength and only a small portion is scattered for $\lambda > 0.9\ \mu$. On this basis the incident solar radiation at the top of the atmosphere is divided into two parts, a scattered part S_0^s and an absorbed part, S_0^a:

$$\begin{aligned} S_0^s &= 0.651\ S_0 \cos\alpha, \text{ scattered part} \\ S_0^a &= 0.349\ S_0 \cos\alpha, \text{ absorbed part} \end{aligned} \tag{10-38}$$

Manabe and Möller (1961) found the absorption by water vapor to be $0.189\ (u^* \sec\alpha)^{0.303}$ ly/min. The absorptivity of the absorbed part is found by dividing by $0.349\ \overline{S}_0$ with the final result

$$A\ (x) = 0.279\ x^{0.303} \tag{10-39}$$

where

$$x = u^*M = u^*\ 35 \sec\alpha/(1224 + \sec^2\alpha)^{1/2} \tag{10-40}$$

M is a magnification factor after Rodgers (1967) and u^* is the effective water vapor mass.

The *albedo* of a cloudless atmosphere due to Rayleigh scattering is

$$a_0 = 0.085 - 0.247 \log_{10}\left(\frac{p_S}{1000}\cos\alpha\right);\ \text{clear skies} \tag{10-41}$$

where p_S is the surface pressure

10-5-1 Clear Sky

Neglecting absorption of ground reflected radiation, the net downward flux of the absorbed part at the top of layer ℓ, $S_{a,\ell}$, is

$$S_{a,\ell} = S_0^a\{1 - A\ [(u_\infty^* - u_\ell^*)\ M]\} \qquad \ell = LTRP \text{ to } LM + 1 \tag{10-42}$$

where $u_\infty^* = u^*\ (p = 0)$. The resulting absorption of solar radiation in layer ℓ is

$$AS_\ell = S_{a,\ell} - S_{a,\ell+1} \qquad \ell = (LTRP,\ LM) \tag{10-43}$$

The solar radiations reaching the earth's surface in the "absorbed" and "scattered" parts are, respectively,

$$S_{a,LM+1} = S_0^a\ [1 - A\ (u_\infty^*\ M)] \tag{10-44a}$$

$$S_{s,LM+1} = S_0^s\ (1 - a_0)/(1 - a_0\ a_s) \tag{10-44b}$$

where a_s is the surface albedo and $u^*_\infty = u^*$ $(p = 0)$. The denominator $(1 - a_0\, a_s)$ in (10-44b) is due to multiple reflections between the atmosphere and the earth's surface. The amount initially reaching the surface is $(1 - a_0)\, S^s_0$. For each unit of the latter, the fractional surface reflection upward is a_s, of which a fraction a_0 is reflected back again toward the earth, giving $a_0{}'a_s$. Of the $a_0 a_s$, $(a_s a_0)\, a_s$ is reflected upward again and of this $(a^2_s\, a_0)\, a_0$ is reflected downward. Then $a^2_s\, a^2_0\, a_s$ is reflected upward, and so forth. Summing the series of scattered fractions reaching the earth, that is, $1 + a_0\, a_s + a^2_0\, a^2_s + \cdots = 1/(1 - a_0\, a_s)$, gives the denominator in (10-44b). Finally, the total absorption at the surface is the sum of (10-44a) and (10-44b) multiplied by $(1 - a_s)$. Thus

$$S_{LM+1} = (1 - a_s)\,(S_{a,LM+1} + S_{s,LM+1});\ \text{clear sky} \qquad (10\text{-}45)$$

10-5-2 Cloudy Sky, One Cloud Layer

Consider a cloud in layer ℓ as shown in Figure 10-3. Let $S_{a,\ell}$ be the flux at level ℓ, which is

$$S_{a,\ell} = S^a_0\,\{1 - A\,[(u^*_\infty - u^*_\ell)\,M]\} \qquad (10\text{-}46)$$

After passing through the cloud, the flux at level $\ell + 1$ is

$$S_{a,\ell+1} = [1 - R_{c,\ell} - A_{c,\ell}(p_{\ell+1} - p_\ell)]\,S_{a,\ell} \qquad (10\text{-}47)$$

where $A_{c,\ell}$ and $R_{c,\ell}$ denote, respectively, the absorptivity per unit pressure thickness and the reflectivity of cloud layer ℓ, which together determine the transmissivity of the layer.

To evaluate the flux at the top of a layer below the cloud, Katayama introduces an *equivalent total optical thickness* of water vapor from $z = \infty$ to the base of the cloud layer, $\delta_{\ell+1}$, as follows:

$$S_{a,\ell+1} = S^a_0\,[1 - A\,(\delta_{a,\ell+1})] \qquad (10\text{-}48)$$

By solving for (u^*M) in (10-39), it may be seen that

$$\delta_{\ell+1} = [(1 - S_{a,\ell+1}/S^a_0)/0.279]^{1/0.303} \qquad (10\text{-}49)$$

Then the flux across the top of any layer ℓ' below the cloud base may be expressed as

$$S_{a,\ell'} = S^a_0\,\{1 - A\,[\delta_{\ell+1} + 1.66\,(u^*_{\ell+1} - u^*_{\ell'})]\} \qquad \ell' > \ell + 1 \qquad (10\text{-}50)$$

where the 1.66 is an augmentation factor for diffuse radiation below the cloud. Moreover the absorption in any layer is given by

$$AS_{\ell'} = S_{a,\ell'} - S_{a,\ell'+1} \qquad \ell' \neq \ell \qquad (10\text{-}51)$$

while the absorption in cloudy layer ℓ (analogous to 10-43) for the clear case) is

$$AS_\ell = (1 - R_{c,\ell})\, S_{a,\ell} - S_{a,\ell+1} \qquad (10\text{-}52)$$

$R_{c,\ell}$ is the reflectivity of the cloud layer ℓ.

With the single cloud the solar radiation reaching the earth's surface is

$$S_{a,LM+1} = S_0^a\,[1 - A\,(\delta_{\ell+1} + 1.66\, u^*_{\ell+1})] \qquad (10\text{-}53)$$

Absorbed part
SINGLE CLOUD

$$S_{s,LM+1} = S_0^s\,(1 - a_c)/(1 - a_c a_s) \qquad (10\text{-}54)$$

Scattered part

where $$a_c = 1 - (1 - R'_{c,\ell})\,(1 - a_0) \qquad (10\text{-}55)$$

Here a_c is the albedo for the cloudy atmosphere and $R'_{c,\ell}$ is the reflectivity of the cloud layer ℓ for the scattered part of the radiation. The *total absorption* at the earth's surface for the cloudy case is *similar to (10-45)* except that (10-53) and (10-54) are used.

10-5-3 Two Contiguous Cloud Layers

When two contiguous cloud layers exist, ℓ and $\ell + 1$, the flux at the top of layer ℓ is identical to (10-46). Similarly the flux at level $\ell + 1$ is similar to (10-47) except that $\overline{R}_c$ is used, where

$$\overline{R}_c = (p_{\ell+2} - p_\ell)^{-1} \sum_{\ell'=\ell}^{\ell+1} R_{c,\ell'}\,(p_{\ell'+1} - p_{\ell'}) \qquad (10\text{-}56)$$

The flux at the top of layer $\ell + 2$ is

$$S_{a,\ell+2} = [1 - \overline{R}_c - A_{c,\ell}(p_{\ell+1} - p_\ell)\, A_{c,\ell+1}\,(p_{\ell+2} - p_{\ell+1})]\, S_{c,\ell} \qquad (10\text{-}57)$$

The flux across the top of the layer beneath the cloud base is

$$S_{a,\ell'} = S_0^a\,\{1 - A\,[\delta_{\ell+2} + 1.66\,(u^*_{\ell+2} - u^*_{\ell'})]\} \qquad \ell' > \ell + 2 \qquad (10\text{-}58)$$

The absorption of solar radiation in layer ℓ is similar to (10-52), but with $\overline{R}_c$ instead of R_c. Finally, the solar radiation reaching the ground in the two-contiguous cloud case is analogous to (10-53) to (10-54) with $\ell + 1$ replaced by $\ell + 2$ and $\overline{R}_c$ replaced by $\overline{R}'_c$, which, in turn, is similar to $\overline{R}_c$ with $R_{c,\ell'}$ replaced by $R'_{c,\ell'}$.

10-5-4 Two Separated Cloud Layers

For two separated cloud layers, ℓ_1 and another below, ℓ_2, with clear layers between, the flux for levels $\ell \leq \ell_1$ is given by (10-42). For level $\ell_1 + 1$ the flux is similar to (10-47) except that ℓ is replaced by ℓ_1 and $R_{c,\ell}$ is replaced by $\overline{R}_{c,1}$, the mean cloud albedo for the absorbed part of the radiation. The total equivalent optical thickness from the top of the atmosphere to the base of cloud 1 is analogous to (10-49) with ℓ replaced by ℓ_1. The flux across the top of the layers, $\ell_1 + 2 \leq \ell \leq \ell_2$ is

$$S_{a,\ell} = S_0^a \{1 - A [\delta_1 + 1.66 (u^*_{\ell_1+2} - u^*_\ell)]\} \qquad \ell_1 + 2 \leq \ell \leq \ell_2 \qquad (10\text{-}59)$$

and analogous to (10-47)

$$S_{a,\ell_2+1} = [1 - \overline{R}_{c,2} - A_{c,\ell_2} (p_{\ell_2+1} - p_{\ell_2})] \, S_{a,\ell_2} \qquad (10\text{-}60)$$

where the total optical thickness is a function of the overlying cloud

$$\delta_2 = [(1 - S_{a,\ell_2+1}/S_0^a)/0.279]^{1/0.303}$$

The flux across the upper level of layers, $\ell \geq \ell_2 + 2$, is

$$S_{a,\ell} = S_0^a \{1 - A [\delta_2 + 1.66 (u^*_{\ell_2+2} - u^*_\ell)]\} \qquad \ell \geq \ell_2 + 2 \qquad (10\text{-}61)$$

The absorption of solar radiation, AS_ℓ is

$$AS_\ell = \begin{cases} S_{a,\ell} - S_{a,\ell+1} & , \ell \neq \ell_1 \text{ or } \ell_2 \\ (1 - \overline{R}_{c,i}) \, S_{a,\ell_i} - S_{a,\ell_i+1} & , \ell_1 = \ell_1 \text{ or } \ell_2 \end{cases} \qquad (10\text{-}62)$$

The *direct* solar radiation in the absorbed part that reaches the earth's surface is

$$S^d_{a,LM+1} = S_0^a [1 - A (\delta_2 + 1.66 \, u^*_{\ell_2+2})] \qquad (10\text{-}63)$$

The *indirect* radiation in the absorbed part that reaches the earth's surface after multiple reflections between the two clouds is

$$S^i_{a,LM+1} = (\overline{R}_{c,2} \, S_{a,\ell_2}) \left(\frac{\overline{R}_{c,1}}{1 - \overline{R}_{c,1} \, \overline{R}_{c,2}} \right) (1 - \overline{R}_{c,2}) \left(\frac{1}{1 - \overline{R}_{c,12} \, a_s} \right) \qquad (10\text{-}64)$$

where

$$\overline{R}_{c,12} = 1 - \frac{(1 - \overline{R}_{c,1})(1 - \overline{R}_{c,2})}{1 - \overline{R}_{c,1}\overline{R}_{c,2}} \tag{10-65}$$

is the albedo of the two clouds (neglecting atmospheric absorption of reflected radiation). In (10-64) $\overline{R}_{c,2} S_{a,\ell_2}$ is the absorbed part of the solar radiation reflected from cloud 2. After multiple reflections, the fraction $\overline{R}_{c,1}/(1 - \overline{R}_{c,1}\overline{R}_{c,2})$ has been scattered downward toward cloud 2. The fraction of this, $(1 - \overline{R}_{c,2})$ is transmitted to reach the earth's surface. Here it experiences multiple reflections between the earth's surface and the clouds, as represented by $1/(1 - \overline{R}_{c,12}\, a_s)$.

The *total solar* radiation in the *absorbed part* reaching the ground is

$$S_{a,LM+1} = S^d_{a,LM+1} + S^i_{a,LM+1} \tag{10-66}$$

Finally, the scattered part of the solar radiation that reaches the ground is

$$S_{s,LM+1} = S^s_0\,(1 - a_c)/(1 - a_c a_s) \tag{10-67}$$

where

$$a_c = 1 - (1 - \overline{R'_{c,12}})/(1 - a_0) \tag{10-68}$$

and $\overline{R'_{c,12}}$ is given by (10-65) with $\overline{R}$ replaced by $\overline{R'}$ (the prime referring to the scattered part of the radiation). As in (10-45) the total radiation absorbed at the earth's surface is the sum of (10-66) and (10-67). The two-cloud cases may be generalized to more cloud layers.

The reflectivity and absorptivity of the clouds are functions of vapor, liquid, and solid water content and the zenith angle of the sun.

To give the reader a general idea of the magnitude of some of the parameters involved, some values that Katayama (1974) adapted from Rodgers (1967) for a three-layer version of the radiative transfer are given in Table 10-1.

10-6 MISCELLANY

When the stratosphere is important, the thermodynamic equation should contain a source term for the absorption of solar radiation, principally by ozone, and a sink due to long-wave cooling mainly due to the 15-μ band of CO_2. The complicated ozone photochemistry and stratosphere dynamics are less well known, but recent versions of general circulation models at various laboratories (GFDL, UCLA, and NCAR) include representations of these phenomena with varying degrees of complexity. In simple models with primary emphasis on the troposphere, Newtonian cooling of the form, $\partial T/\partial t = -a(T - T_E)$, is often used, where T_E is a radiative equilibrium temperature.

Table 10-1 Properties of a Cloud Layer ℓ, Lying in One of Three Layers

$A_{c,\ell}$	$R_{c,\ell}$	$R'_{c,\ell}$	
0.05/300 mb	0.19	(0.21)	$100 \le p_\ell \le 400$ mb; or for cirrus clouds
0.20/400 mb	0.46	(0.54)	for $400 \le p_\ell \le 800$ mb; cloud not cirrus
0.30/200 mb	0.50	(0.66)	$p_\ell > 800$ mb; cloud not cirrus

Surface Albedoes	α_s
Snow-free land	0.14
Sea	0.07
Sea ice	0.4
Temporary snow	0.7
Permanent land ice and snow. Minimum of:	$(0.85 \text{ or } 0.7 + 0.00015\, z_s)$,

where z_s = surface elevation in meters

CHAPTER 11

Objective Analysis and Initialization

11-1 INTRODUCTION

To carry out a numerical forecast it is necessary to specify the meteorological variables at the beginning of the forecast period, that is, to provide the initial state from which the system of differential equations is integrated forward in time.

Some of the first efforts at objective analysis (e.g., Panofsky, 1949) involved the fitting of polynomial surfaces to approximate the distribution of a meteorological variable in piecemeal fashion over a section of the region being analyzed. However, this leads to difficulties, particularly in sparse data areas; and, following the practice of synoptic analysts, a procedure was soon instituted that begins with a first ''guess'' field, such as the forecast from a previous analysis, or climatology, and follows with a modification of the guess field to fit observed data.

To illustrate the procedure, let $z_G^{(0)}$ represent the first estimate of the pressure height at a gridpoint and z_0 the observed value at some point 0 in the neighborhood of the gridpoint. Then a new estimate $z_G^{(1)}$ of the height at the gridpoint G can be obtained from the relationship

$$z_G^{(1)} - z_G^{(0)} = z_0 - z_0^{(0)} \tag{11-1}$$

where $z_0^{(0)}$ is obtained by interpolating between gridpoints to the observation point 0. Equation 11-1 simply estimates that the error in the first guess at the gridpoint equals the error at the observation point. Figure 11-1 illustrates a second method of adjusting the first guess as follows:

$$z_G^{(1)} = z_0 + \mathbf{r} \cdot \nabla z_0 \tag{11-2}$$

where $\mathbf{r}$ is the vector between 0 and G and ∇z_0 is an estimate of the gradient of height at 0. The gradient can be estimated (1) from the first guess field at G or 0, or (2) from a wind observation at 0 using the geostrophic relation, that is,

$$(1)\ \nabla z_0 \doteq \nabla z_0^{(0)} \quad \text{or} \quad \nabla z_G^{(0)} \quad \text{or} \quad (2)\ \nabla z_0 \doteq \mathbf{V}_0 \times \frac{f}{g}\mathbf{k}$$

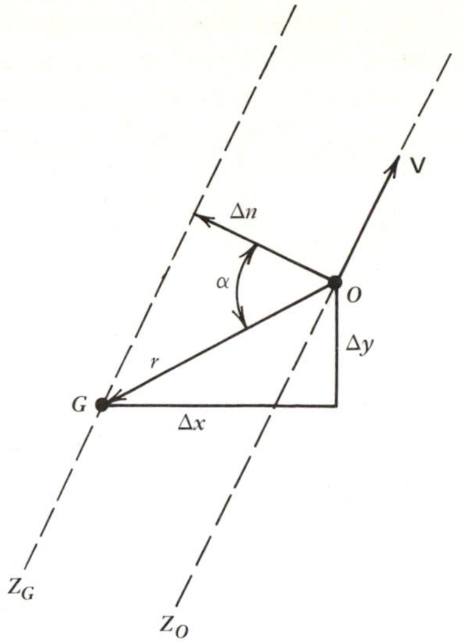

Figure 11-1 Estimation of the pressure height at a gridpoint G from the observed wind vector at point 0.

Since various methods of adjusting the first guess field are available and some may be more reliable than others, the best approximation z_G may in the long run be a weighted average of various estimates,

$$z_G = \Sigma W_{Gi} \, z_{Gi} / \Sigma W_{Gi} \tag{11-3}$$

where W_{Gi} are weight factors that may be determined through a statistical analysis. Cressman (1959) introduced a weighting which was inversely proportional to the distance r between the observation point and the gridpoint as follows:

$$W = \begin{cases} \dfrac{n^2 - r^2}{n^2 + r^2}, & r < n \\ 0 & , r \geq n \end{cases} \tag{11-4}$$

where n is a multiple of the gridlength. Thus observations n gridlengths distant or farther from a gridpoint will not be counted. The procedure may be iterated with decreasing values of n to analyze ever smaller features. Another possibility is to have the weight decrease exponentially with distance [e.g., $W = a \exp(-br^2)$, where a and b are empirical constants].

Prior to an objective analysis procedure, such as described previously, the observational data first undergo a detailed preanalysis processing, which involves checking location of observations, gross-error checks, recalculation of upper air soundings for hydrostatic consistency, etc. The various error tolerances depend on the variability of the field as determined from climatology and subsequently based on real data usage. After the preliminary error checks, the fields can be analyzed level by level or three dimensionally, as described in Section 11-3.

11-2 A THREE-DIMENSIONAL ANLAYSIS

Holl (1963) has developed a three-dimensional objective scheme that begins with an analysis of the static stability. The latter is constrained to be statically stable everywhere, which is certainly desirable since superadiabatic lapse rates can cause difficulties in NWP models not geared to cope with them. Moreover, superadiabatic lapse rates are relatively rare in the atmosphere, except very near the ground. Holl's procedure begins with an analysis of a static stability parameter

$$\sigma = -Rp_0^{-\kappa}\, p^{1+\kappa}\, \partial\theta_v/\partial p \qquad \kappa = R/c_p \tag{11-5}$$

for each of eight layers (defined by the levels p_0 = 1000, 775, 600, 450, 350, 275, 225, and 175 mb) based on observed pressure-height data at the 10 mandatory levels. The end product is a relationship between the 10 mandatory levels on one hand, and on the other, the eight static stabilities, the 1000-mb height and a virtual temperature parameter, the last being either the 100-500 mb or 1000-300-mb thickness.

If (11-5) is integrated through a layer of constant σ, the result is

$$T_v = \sigma(R\kappa)^{-1} - Mg\, c_p^{-1}\, p^{\kappa} \tag{11-6}$$

where σ and M are constants for the layer. A second relationship is obtainable by integrating the hydrostatic equations with the foregoing value of T_v which gives

$$z = N + Mp^{\kappa} - \sigma(g\kappa)^{-1}\, \ell n p \tag{11-7}$$

Continuity of z and T_v is required at the interfaces although σ is discontinuous. In terms of (11-5) and (11-7) there are three constants N, M, and σ for each of eight layers, totaling 24 parameters. These are determinable from the 10 mandatory heights and two continuity conditions at each of seven interfaces. The resulting relationship may be expressed in matrix form as

$$\boldsymbol{\sigma} = D\mathbf{Z} \tag{11-8}$$

where $\boldsymbol{\sigma}$ is a column vector consisting of the eight static stabilities, the 1000-mb height and the 1000 to 300-mb thickness, $\mathbf{Z}$ consists of the ten mandatory height levels, and D is a matrix of constants. The virtual temperatures at the ten mandatory levels are specified by a similar relation

$$\mathbf{T} = Q\mathbf{Z} \tag{11-9}$$

The σ's generated from the upper-air sounding are used to carry out two-dimensional objective analyses of the σ-fields using the previous σ-analysis as a first guess, and similarly for the 1000- and 300-mb fields. The two height analyses also use wind data to estimate height gradients. Then Equations 11-8 and 11-9 are used to obtain the heights and temperatures at the mass-structure model level. The analyzed fields are then further modified to fit observations more closely. Several iterations of the entire procedure insure a close fit to the observed data while retaining statically stable temperature fields. A weakness of this method is that a single observation of static stability may not be representative of a grid square and temperature inversions cannot be handled well, but the latter is true of other schemes as well.

11-3 STATISTICAL METHODS, MULTIVARIATE ANALYSIS

Eliassen (1954) and Gandin (1959, 1963, 1964) proposed methods for producing an objective analysis that statistically extract the maximum information from data sources including the observations, climatological records, space correlations between the meteorological variables, etc. This approach, referred to as *optimum interpolation,* requires a knowledge of the statistical structure of the fields of the variables. The variables may be analyzed separately, referred to as *univariate* analysis, or when several variables are analyzed simultaneously, as *multivariate* objective analysis. At the time of Gandin's proposal the necessary cross correlations were not available nor was computer power adequate for operational application of the multivariate scheme. Since then Kluge (1970), Rutherford (1973), and Schlatter (1975) have used this objective analysis technique. The description here follows Schlatter.

Let h, u, and v be the desired gridpoint values of pressure height and wind components that are assumed to be related to the observations in the near vicinity of the gridpoint by the matrix relationship

$$\begin{pmatrix} h \\ u \\ v \end{pmatrix} \equiv \mathbf{Z} = \mathbf{Z}_f + \sum_{i=1}^{I} [A^i] (\mathbf{Z}_i - \mathbf{Z}_{fi}) \tag{11-10}$$

where the subscript f denotes a first-guess field; the unsubscripted variables denote the analyzed gridpoint values; the $[A^i]$ are 3×3 matrices; each consisting of nine weights, A^i_{kj}; and the superscript i denotes an observation point.

The $\mathbf{Z}_{fi}$ represent interpolations from gridpoint values of the first-guess fields to the I observation points.

The weighting coefficients A_{ij}^{k} are determined by requiring, in a least-squares sense, that the diagonal elements of the following matrix, which are the mean-square errors of h, u, and v, are minimized:

$$<(\mathbf{Z}_t - \mathbf{Z})(\mathbf{Z}_t - \mathbf{Z})^T> \tag{11-11}$$

In the foregoing 3×3 matrix T represents the transpose of a vector; the subscript, t, the true values of h, u, and v; and the symbol, $<>$, an average over many analyses. Schlatter takes only the five observations nearest any gridpoint, so $I = 5$ in (11-10). Thus there will be $5 \times 3 \times 3 = 45$ weight factors associated with each gridpoint. The usual least-squares procedure of substituting the $\mathbf{Z}$ from (11-10) into (11-11), followed by setting the derivatives with respect to the A_{kj}^{i} to zero as required to give a minimum, leads to a system of equations for the A_{kj}^{i}.

Some insight into this procedure may be gained by expanding (11-10) as follows. Let S_k with $k = 1, 2$ and 3 denote h, u, and v, respectively. Then the matrix equations (11-10) and (11-11) for $I = 5$ may be expressed in scalar form as

$$S_k = S_{fk} + \sum_{i=1}^{5} \sum_{j=1}^{3} A_{kj}^{i} (S_j^i - S_{fj}^i) \qquad k = 1, 2, 3 \tag{11-12}$$

$$< \left[S_{tk} - S_{fk} - \sum_{i=1}^{5} \sum_{j=1}^{3} A_{kj}^{i} (S_j^i - S_{fj}^i) \right]^2 > = M_k \tag{11-13}$$

Equation 11-12 shows that there are 15 A's for each k and hence a total of 45 A_{kj}^{i} to be determined by minimization of (11-13) for each k. Setting the derivatives of the M_k with respect to the A_{kj}^{i} to zero as required for a minimum, leads to the following system of 15 equations and 15 unknown A's for each k

$$\frac{\partial M_k}{\partial A_{kj}^{i}} = - <[S_{tk} - S_{fk} - \sum_{n=1}^{5} \sum_{m=1}^{3} A_{km}^{n} (S_m^n - S_{fm}^n)] (S_j^i - S_{fj}^i)> = 0 \tag{11-14}$$

$$i = 1, 2, \ldots 5 \qquad j = 1, 2, 3$$

Solving these equations requires the inversion of three 15×15 matrices, one for each of the three k's. This must be repeated for each gridpoint of the two-dimensional array and for many levels in a multilevel model, which consumes much time on a computer.

The solution for the weighting coefficient A_{kj}^{i} may be put in the following matrix form in order to bring into focus the relevant covariances:

$$\begin{bmatrix} A_{11}^1\, A_{12}^1\, A_{13}^1\, A_{11}^2 \cdots A_{13}^5 \\ A_{21}^1 \cdots & \\ A_{31}^1 \cdots \qquad A_{33}^5 \end{bmatrix} = \begin{bmatrix} [C_{g1}] \cdots [C_{g5}] \end{bmatrix} \begin{bmatrix} [C_{11}] \cdots [C_{15}] \\ [C_{12}] \cdots \\ \cdots \\ [C_{15}] \cdots [C_{55}] \end{bmatrix}^{-1} \tag{11-15}$$

The elements of the five 3 × 3 matrices $[C_{gi}]$ are the covariances of the differences between the true and first-guess values of the meteorological variables u, v, and h at the gridpoint and at the observation point i, that is,

$$[C_{gi}] = \begin{bmatrix} <(h_t - h_f)(h_i - h_{fi})> & <(h_t - h_f)(u_i - u_{fi})> & <(h_t - h_f)(v_i - v_{fi})> \\ <(u_t - u_f)(h_i - h_{fi})> & <(u_t - u_f)(u_i - u_{fi})> & <(u_t - u_f)(v_i - v_{fi})> \\ <(v_t - v_f)(h_i - h_{fi})> & <(v_t - v_f)(u_i - u_{fi})> & <(v_t - v_f)(v_i - v_{fi})> \end{bmatrix}$$
$$i = 1, 2, \ldots 5 \tag{11-16}$$

On the other hand, the elements of the 3 × 3 matrix (C_{ij}) are the covariances of the difference between the observed and interpolated first-guess values of u, v, or h at an observation point i and a similar difference of each one of these variables at observation point j, that is,

$$[C_{ij}] = \begin{bmatrix} <(h_i - h_{fi})(h_j - h_{fj})> & <(h_i - h_{fi})(u_j - u_{fj})> & <(h_i - h_{fi})(v_j - v_{fj})> \\ <(u_i - u_{fi})(h_j - h_{fj})> & <(u_i - u_{fi})(u_j - u_{fj})> & <(u_i - u_{fi})(v_j - v_{fj})> \\ <(v_i - v_{fi})(h_j - h_{fj})> & <(v_i - v_{fi})(u_j - u_{fj})> & <(v_i - v_{fi})(v_j - v_{fj})> \end{bmatrix} \tag{11-17}$$

Since i and j can range from 1 to 5, there are 25 matrices of the type $[C_{ij}]$; hence the last matrix in (11-15) is 15 × 15 and consists of 225 covariances. Presumably the covariances are to be obtained from data records sufficiently long to provide stable values, both for observation and first-guess fields. However it is difficult to compute the $[C_{ij}]$ from data, and the true fields needed in $[C_{gi}]$ are never known exactly at gridpoints. Also the $[C_{ij}]$ is not strictly a covariance matrix unless $<h_i - h_{fi}> = <u_i - u_{fi}> = <v_i - v_{fi}> = 0$, which will be assumed. To avoid these difficulties both $[C_{ij}]$ and $[C_{gi}]$ were estimated using a statistical "model."

With respect to the first-guess fields, the 12-hr forecasts from the previous analyses are usually used in most operational prediction models. But due to frequent model changes and various other factors, long records of model performance are difficult to obtain.

Hence to test the multivariate scheme, Schlatter used a damped persistence forecast and climatology as first-guess fields in order to determine the covariances. The former is given by

$$\mathbf{Z}_j = \mathbf{Z}_0 + e^{-at} (\mathbf{Z}_0 - \mathbf{Z}_c) \tag{11-18}$$

where $\mathbf{Z}_0$ represents initial values of u, v, and h; $\mathbf{Z}_c$, corresponding climatological values; t is the length of the forecast and α is a damping coefficient. As limiting cases, the choice, $\alpha = 0$, makes persistence the first guess; while for $\alpha \rightarrow \infty$, climatology becomes the first guess. He assumes that differences of the variables are a function only of distance between points not direction. Data from over 50 upper-air sounding stations determined the 500-mb height fields, which, together with a damped persistence forecast with $t = 1$ day for the first guess, were used to calculate the autocovariances, $\langle (h_i - h_{fi})(h_j - h_{fj}) \rangle$. The dots in Figures 11-2 and 11-3 correspond to a value of $\alpha = 0.23$ day^{-1}, and in addition, climatology curves are also shown in Figure 11-3. The ordinate gives the correlations as a function of distance (abscissa) between observing stations, with the expected result that correlation decreases with increasing distance between observation points then becomes negative and eventually goes to zero again. For modeling purposes the correlations were averaged over 50-mile intervals and fitted with Gaussian curves, which are shown in Figure 11-3 and given by

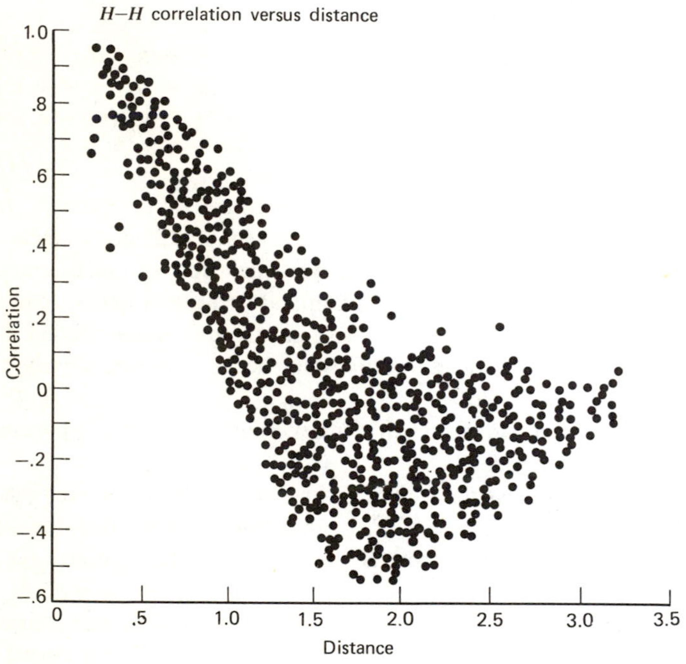

Figure 11-2 Forecast-error correlation for the height field as a function of separation distance (10^3 km) between every pair of points for 50 U. S. radiosonde stations. The damped persistence forecast was used as a first guess. (*After Schlatter, 1975.*) (From T. Schlatter, "Some Experiments with a Multivariate Statistical Objective Analysis Scheme." *American Meteorological Society,* 1975.)

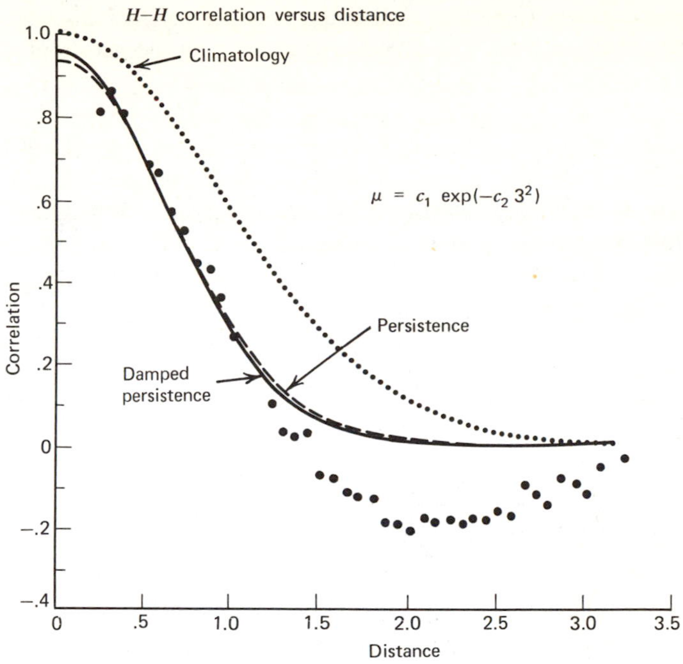

Figure 11-3 Gaussian autocorrelation curve fit to data of Figure 11-1 after averaging of points with adjacent distance intervals. Points corresponding to negative correlations were not considered. Distance are in units of 10^3 km. Dashed curve is for first guess of persistence; dotted curve is for first guess of climatology. (*After Schlatter, 1975*.) (From T. Schlatter, "Some Experiments with a Multivariate Statistical Objective Analysis Scheme." *American Meteorological Society*, 1975.)

$$<(h_i - h_{fi})(h_j - h_{fj})> = C_1 \exp(-C_2 r_{ij}^2) \qquad C_1 = 0.96 \qquad C_2 = 1.24$$

Points corresponding to negative correlations were not included since only the nearest five observations to any gridpoint were to be used in applying the statistical technique. A damped cosine curve can include negative correlations; however there was no improvement in the forecasts when the cosine curve was used instead of the Gaussian curve for the analysis.

The $(h - h)$ autocovariances are related to the autocorrelations by the equation

$$<(h_i - h_{fi})(h_j - h_{fj})> = \sigma_i \mu_{ij} \sigma_j \qquad (11\text{-}19)$$

where $\sigma_i = <(h_i - h_{fi})^2>$ is the standard deviation at point i and μ_{ij} is the correlation coefficient.

The cross covariances between the wind component-pressure heights were modeled by relating them to the $(h - h)$ covariance through the geostrophic wind relations.

$$u_i = -\frac{g}{f}\frac{1}{a}\frac{\partial h_i}{\partial \varphi} \qquad v_i = \frac{g}{f}\frac{1}{a\cos\varphi}\frac{\partial h_i}{\partial \lambda} \tag{11-20}$$

If these relations are assumed equally applicable to the observed and first-guess fields, then the cross covariances become, for example,

$$<h_i' \, u_j'> = -\frac{g}{af_i}\frac{\partial}{\partial \varphi_j} <h_i' \, h_j'>$$

$$<h_i' \, v_j'> = \frac{g}{af_j \cos\varphi_j}\frac{\partial}{\partial \lambda_j} <h_i' \, h_j'> \tag{11-21}$$

$$<u_i' \, v_j'> = \frac{-g^2}{a^2 f_i f_j \cos\varphi_i}\frac{\partial^2}{\partial \varphi_i \, \partial \lambda_j} <h_i' \, h_j'>$$

and so forth, where $h_i' = (h_i - h_{fi})$, etc. and the subscripts on φ_j and λ_j denote the variable being differentiated. The geostrophic assumption is not valid near the equator so a stream function is introduced there. Also in spherical polar coordinates, the singular point at the poles must be avoided, which can be accomplished by using polar stereographic coordinates near a pole.

The cross-correlations computed from (11-21) show considerable asymmetry, but do correspond reasonably well to some cross-correlations computed from actual wind and height data. In general, modeling the covariances using (11-21) produces satisfactory results, thus reducing the need for long records of observational data, model performance, etc.

The covariance matrix relating observed-minus-forecast values of h, u, and v may be expressed in terms of observation errors and forecast errors by adding and subtracting the true value of the variable, for example,

$$<(-h_{ti} + h_i + h_{ti} - h_{fi})\,(-h_{tj} + h_j + h_{tj} - h_{fj})> \equiv$$
$$<(\varepsilon_{fi} - \varepsilon_i)\,(\varepsilon_{fj} - \varepsilon_j)> \tag{11-22}$$

where $h_{ti} - h_i = \varepsilon_i$, etc. Of the various products in (11-22), $\varepsilon_{fi}\,\varepsilon_{fj}$ is difficult to obtain because of model changes, etc.; $<\varepsilon_i\,\varepsilon_j> = 0$, $i \neq j$, if the errors are truly random (but the errors may be correlated, for example, from satellite observations); $<\varepsilon_i\,\varepsilon_{fj}>$ has been neglected assuming ε_i and ε_{fj} are uncorrelated. When $i = j$, random errors in the data will lead to systematic errors in the characteristics of the statistical structure. If x is a variable with a random error ε it can be written in terms of the true value as $x = x_t + \varepsilon_x$. Then the cross-covariance between x and y becomes

$$<x\,y> = <(x_t + \varepsilon_x)(y_t + \varepsilon_y)> =$$

$$<x_t\, y_t> + <\varepsilon_x\, \varepsilon_y> + <\varepsilon_x\, y_t> + <x_t\, \varepsilon_y> \qquad (11\text{-}23)$$

If the errors are uncorrelated with each other and with x_t and y_t, the result is

$$<x\,y> = <x_t\, y_t> \qquad (11\text{-}24)$$

so the random errors do not contaminate the result. However for the variances contamination does occur as follows

$$<xx> = <x_t\, x_t> + <\varepsilon_x\, \varepsilon_x> \qquad (11\text{-}25)$$

11-4 INITIALIZATION

11-4-1 Introduction

The objective analysis procedures described in the foregoing sections generally do not provide fields of mass and motion that are in optimal form to initiate a forecast, particularly if the momentum (primitive) equations are used in the prediction model. Observations show that in the atmosphere, the wind and pressure fields are in a quasi-geostrophic, quasi-nondivergent state and the energy associated with the ageostrophic motions is relatively small. As described in Chapter 4, this partitioning of energy is a consequence of the natural forcing and dissipative mechanisms, dynamic instabilities, nonlinear energy transfers, energy dispersion, etc. Although the high-frequency inertial-gravity modes may be significant near mountains, local heat sources, etc., overall they have small energy compared to the low-frequency Rossby modes constituting the quasi-balanced systems.

Upon completion of one of the objective analysis schemes described earlier, the mass and motion fields are neither in the rather delicate state of balance, or more accurately, state of imbalance, that exists in the atmosphere nor in a typical PE model that has been running for several days of simulated time. Consequently, the use of such objectively analyzed data to initialize an NWP model may generate large, spurious inertial-gravity modes, provided, of course, that the model permits such modes. As described earlier in the discussion on geostophic adjustment in a continuous system, such imbalances are gradually removed by redistribution of the mass and wind fields through the dispersion and dissipation of the inertial-gravity waves generated by the imbalances. Thus the atmosphere tends toward a quasi-geostrophic balanced state. Unlike the real atmosphere a numerical model has a finite number of degrees of freedom and hence is limited in the scales of motion that can be resolved and represented. Consequently the model does not behave exactly like the atmosphere nor even a simple continuous model, nevertheless, spurious inertial-gravity waves or "noise" generated by defects in the initial data will eventually be dispersed and dissipated. The noise cannot be dissipated locally because of the relatively low resolution in NWP models, which tends to prolong the life of the gravity waves. If there were no mechanisms in a numerical model for dissipating the noise, significant noise could reappear elsewhere after dispersion from the source region; however explicit dissipation terms, nonlinear interactions, vertical energy flux, etc., eventually dissipate the noise. The dispersive properties of a model through the phase and group velocities may vary considerably depending on the arrangement of the variables at the gridpoints and the differencing scheme.

The objective of an initialization procedure is to prepare gridpoint data with which the model can integrate forward in time with a minimum of noise and maximum accuracy of the forecasts of the meteorological scales that the model is designed to simulate. If the data prepared by a typical objective analysis scheme is inserted directly into a PE model considerable noise is generated while the mass and motion fields adjust to one another; however the noise declines more or less steadily as adjustment occurs so that in one or two days the noise is usually reduced to an acceptable level. A reasonable question then is why not ignore it, and, in fact, that is sometimes what is done. However it would be very desirable if the adjustment could be effected prior to the beginning of the forecast for several reasons. One hopes that the forecasts at the end of 24, 48 hr, etc. will be better if the model is given well-adjusted data to begin the forecast, although quite a few attempts with sophisticated initialization procedures have produced little improvement, if any, in the 24- and 48-hr forecasts, at least, by conventional verification schemes. Equally important, values of vertical velocity, precipitation, surface wind, pressure, etc., in the early stages of a forecast may be strongly affected by the spurious gravity waves. Also, as indicated in Chapter 4, it takes longer for the model processes of momentum, heat, and moisture transport to become established in the tropics and perhaps in regions of low barotropic and baroclinic activity.

Still another reason for trying to reduce the time for adjustment relates to the incorporation of observations between the regular 12-hr intervals of upper-air soundings, a process known as *four-dimensional data assimilation*. When off-time data was limited and perhaps less accurate, such as aircraft winds, it could be simply grouped with the nearest synoptic observation time and the time difference ignored or some kind of advection scheme used to adjust it in some fashion to the synoptic time. However the advent of satellite infrared spectrometers, which can sound the atmosphere from space has provided a wealth of continuous data that is especially useful over otherwise sparse-data areas. In order to utilize this data most effectively it is desirable to incorporate it into the model at the time of observation. Therefore it becomes increasingly important to reduce the "shock" of data insertion; otherwise the model will be in a state of continuous imbalance during such *updating*. An update might be performed as follows. Suppose forecasts are prepared from 0000 GMT initial fields. At the next analysis time, say, 1200 GMT, the first-guess fields may be the 12-hr forecast from 0000 GMT to which the 1200 GMT data is added. To improve the 12-hr forecast from 0000 GMT, off-time data between 0000 and 1200 could be inserted into the model, perhaps at 0300, 0600, and 0900, treating the data 1½ hr on either side of these times as occurring at the 3-hr interval.

Presumably, the consequence would be a better first guess at 1200 GMT, hence a better objective analysis and thus better forecasts from the 1200 data. Such a scenario is plausible only if the 3-hourly insertion of data, which may be in large quantity from satellites, doesn't unduly shock the system. Considering the errors in the data, it is unlikely that insertion of new data at intervals more frequent than 3 hr will be fruitful, in fact, perhaps a single insertion at 0600 may be adequate considering all factors including data accuracy, computer time for processing, etc. Some further comments on this subject will appear later.

11-4-2 Damping Techniques

An obvious approach to reducing gravitational "noise" would be a direct effort to dampen or filter the noise hopefully without adversely affecting the meteorological modes. One such method is the use of an integration method which would selectively dampen high-frequency modes. The Euler backward [or Matsuno, (1966b)] scheme (5-67) is an effective dampener for high-frequency gravity modes. However, as shown by Okland (1972), this scheme is not effective for the higher internal modes, waves of large horizontal extent nor gravity waves in the tropics. Another drawback of the Euler backward scheme is that it requires double the computer time than the leapfrog scheme. It might be used for only the first 6 to 12 hr of a 72-hr forecast, which would be less time consuming; but operational units have not followed this practice, apparently for lack of enough improvement to warrant the extra computer time.

Gravity waves are associated with high-frequency fluctuations in velocity divergence which, in turn, is reflected in the vertical velocity. Talagrand (1972) suggested the addition of a divergence damping term in the momentum equation as follows:

$$\frac{\partial \mathbf{V}}{\partial t} + \cdots = -\nabla\phi \cdots + \upsilon\nabla D \tag{11-26}$$

where $D = \nabla \cdot \mathbf{V}$ and υ is a diffusion coefficient. Taking the divergence of (11-26) gives

$$\frac{\partial D}{\partial t} = -\nabla^2\phi + \upsilon\nabla^2 D + \cdots \tag{11-27}$$

which shows that D will be diffused, thus decreasing the amplitude of the fluctuations of D, especially those of high frequency. Experiments at NMC with $\upsilon = 2.5 \times 10^8$ m^2/sec verified expectations; however there were some unfortunate side effects. Abnormally high pressure occurred in the vicinity of mountains and values of $\upsilon > 10^7$ m^2/sec eliminated precipitation in their 8-layer σ-coordinate PE model.

11-4-3 Static Initialization

Balance Equation. The term, *static initialization,* refers to any procedure which adjusts the data at a single time level, usually to conform to some dynamical constraint(s) in order to reduce or eliminate the generation of inertial-gravity noise. In the early PE models, and even to date, a standard practice is first to analyze the geopotential field ϕ using all pressure-height data and also wind observations to estimate the gradient of ϕ using a simple wind law, usually the geostrophic relation. Then the analyzed geopotential fields on the p-surfaces are used in the balance equation (7-28) to obtain the streamfunction ψ, from which, in turn, the rotational wind component $\mathbf{V}_\psi = \mathbf{k} \times \nabla\psi$ can be computed. There are several difficulties associated with this procedure. First, (7-28) is a Monge-Ampere type equation, which is elliptic over most of the geopotential field; however it may become hyperbolic in some areas, particularly where the absolute vorticity tends toward negative values, for example, in sharply anticyclonically curved jets or on the anticyclonic side of a low latitude jet. In order to insure ellipticity in those areas so that the numerical methods for the solution of elliptic equations will apply, the geopotential fields must be altered somewhat. Arnason (1957) found that the ellipticity criterion for the balance equation can be written

$$(\tfrac{1}{2} f + \psi_{xx})(\tfrac{1}{2} f + \psi_{yy}) - \psi_{xy}^2 > 0$$

or using (7-28),

$$\nabla^2\phi + \tfrac{1}{2} f^2 - \nabla f \cdot \nabla\psi = 0 \qquad (11\text{-}28)$$

The last term is small and can be approximated geostrophically. At a gridpoint where the condition is not fulfilled, the negative residual is spread over the four surrounding points until the ellipticity condition is satisfied. In practice convergence is achieved by applying the criterion

$$\psi_{xx}^{(n)} + \psi_{yy}^{(n)} + f > \varepsilon \qquad (11\text{-}29)$$

to successive estimates of ψ denoted by the superscript n. Thus a solution can be obtained, though at the expense of having to alter the geopotential field in some areas which, although percentagewise are small, is undesirable. The balanced winds reduce the noise considerably at the beginning of a PE forecast when compared to direct initialization with objectively analyzed winds. At the National Meteorological Center (NMC), initialization with balanced winds was abandoned in favor of extracting the rotational component from objectively analyzed winds $\mathbf{V}_0$. The stream function ψ was obtained from $\nabla^2\psi = \mathbf{k} \cdot \nabla$

$\times$ $\mathbf{V}_0$. It was reported that better delineation of jet streams was obtained with about the same noise as with the balance equation ψ.

A second, and perhaps more important, limitation of using the balance equation to determine a rotational wind for initializing a PE model is that the lack of a divergent wind component guarantees the presence of gravitational modes. Hinkelmann (1951) and Phillips (1960b) showed, by means of a simple linear barotropic PE model, that the gravity modes could be completely eliminated at the onset of integration only by including the quasi-geostrophic divergent wind component in addition to the rotational wind in the initial wind field (Section 2-7). In more sophisticated baroclinic filtered models, an approximate divergent component can be obtained by first solving a quasi-geostrophic or an approximate balanced ω-equation for ω, then solving for the divergent velocity potential χ from the continuity equation (7-22), $\nabla^2\chi = -\partial\omega/\partial p$, and, finally computing the divergent component, $\mathbf{V}_\chi = \nabla\chi$. Success, if any, can be expected only where the Rossby number is less than 1. Some experiments with this approach indicated neither sufficient noise reduction nor improvement in forecasts to warrant the effort. Similarly 12-hr forecast divergent wind components generated from the previous analysis gave neither significant improvement in noise reduction nor forecast accuracy over initialization with rotational winds only. The ω-equation energetically consistent with the nonlinear balance equation is much more complicated than the quasi-geostrophic form and can be obtained only by an involved iterative procedure (Section 7-1-4); however, some approximations can be made to speed the solution with a resulting ω-field, which is probably more accurate than the geostrophic form, although not strictly consistent with the balanced system. Dickinson and Williamson (1972, 1976) used a linearized version of the NCAR GCM to determine the eigenfunctions of this model from which the Rossby and gravity modes could be identified and selective filtering applied to the initial data.

When a σ-coordinate model is used for prediction, the rotational winds and other variables obtained by analyses on p-surfaces are interpolated to the σ-surfaces, which certainly destroys the balance somewhat. Sundquist (1975) showed that some reduction in noise was feasible by solving a balance equation on σ-surfaces for a stream function such that $p_s\mathbf{V}_\psi = \mathbf{k} \times \nabla\psi$. The continuity equation in σ-coordinates (1-69) shows that the surface pressure tendency would vanish for such a wind field since $\nabla \cdot p_s\mathbf{V}_\psi \equiv 0$, also damping the vertical velocity.

11-4-4 Variational Method

Sasaki (1958, 1969) has developed an initialization method based on the calculus of variations in which differences between the objectively analyzed values and the newly adjusted values are minimized in a least-squares sense subject to one or more dynamical constraints. The latter may include, for example, the balance equation, hydrostatic relation, steady-state momentum equations, integral relations conserving energy and mass, zeroing integrated mass divergence, etc.

First it is desirable to review some aspects of the calculus of variations. Let $F(x,y,y')$ be a twice differentiable function of the three designated variables and suppose it is desired to determine a function $y = f(x)$ such that the following integral is a maximum or minimum:

$$I = \int_a^b F(x,y,y')\, dx \tag{11-30}$$

Here the end points a and b are considered fixed as well as $f(a) = A$ and $f(b) = B$. Now suppose there is a small change from $y = f(x)$ to $y + \delta y = f(x) + \varepsilon\, g(x)$, where ε is a parameter and $g(x)$ is arbitrary except that $g(a) = g(b) = 0$.

Then the integral (11-30) will be modified to

$$I + \delta I = \int_a^b (F + \delta F)\, dx \tag{11-31}$$

where δF represents the change in the integrand due to the modification in y and y'. Subtracting (11-30) from (11-31) gives

$$\delta I = \int_a^b \delta F\, dx \tag{11-32}$$

where

$$\delta F = F_y\, \delta y + F_{y'}\, \delta y' \tag{11-33}$$

and the subscripts denote partial derivatives. It is easily seen from Figure 11-4 that

$$\delta y' = \delta(dy/dx) = d(\delta y)/dx$$

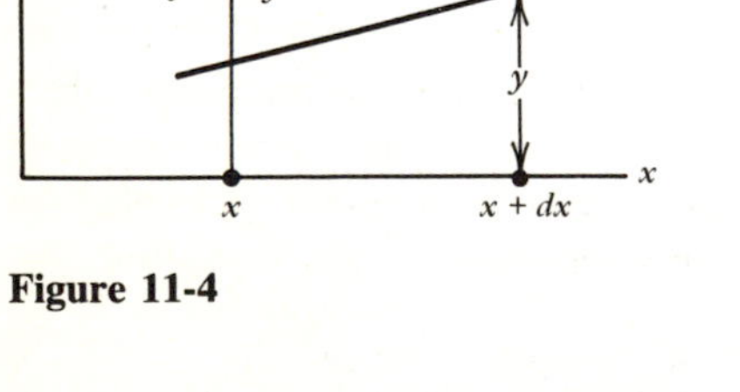

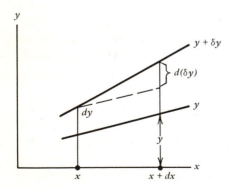

Figure 11-4

since the difference in slope between the points x and $x + dx$ is due to the change in δy between x and $x + dx$, that is, $d(\delta y)$. Thus

$$F_{y'}\,\delta y' = F_{y'}\frac{d(\delta y)}{dx} = \frac{d}{dx}(F_{y'}\,\delta y) - \delta y\frac{d}{dx}(F_{y'}) \tag{11-34}$$

Substituting (11-34) into (11-33) and the resulting expression for δF into (11-32) and then integrating from a to b gives

$$\delta I = \int_a^b \left(F_y - \frac{d}{dx}F_{y'}\right)\delta y\,dx \tag{11-35}$$

The exact differential $d(F_{y'}\,\delta y)$ vanished when integrated because $\delta y = 0$ at a and b. Now if $f(x)$ gives a maximum or minimum for the integral I in (11-30), then the variation δI must be zero when $y = f(x)$ in the same fashion as the ordinary derivative is zero at a maximum or minimum. Moreover, since $\delta y = \varepsilon\, g(x)$ is arbitrary and δI is zero, the integrand of (11-35) must vanish. For if it is not zero and of the same sign in small neighborhood, δy could be chosen to be zero everywhere but in that small neighborhood in which case δI would not vanish.

Thus a necessary condition for a minimum is

$$F_y - \frac{d}{dx}F_{y'} = 0 \tag{11-36}$$

which is referred to as the Euler or Euler-Lagrange equation. (This result also may be obtained by setting $dI/d\varepsilon = 0$ at $\varepsilon = 0$.) Expanding (11-36) gives the following second-order differential equation for y:

$$F_y - F_{xy'} - F_{yy'}y' - F_{y'y'}y'' = 0 \tag{11-37}$$

If the function F contains higher-order derivatives, say y'', the Euler equation includes the term $d^2F_{y''}/dx^2$. On the other hand, if F contains two functions, $y(x)$ and $z(x)$, that is, $F = F(x,y,z,y',z')$, then there are two Euler equations to be satisfied, (11-37) and a similar one with z and z' in place of y and y'.

Another possibility is when the integral (11-30) is to be minimized subject to a constraint that may be another integral; or in the case of two functions, the constraint may be another equation, say, $G(x,y,z) = 0$. In the latter case a Lagrange multiplier may be introduced and the resulting Euler-Lagrange equations are

$$F_y - \frac{d}{dx}(F_{y'}) - \lambda G_y = 0 \qquad F_z - \frac{d}{dx}(F_{z'}) - \lambda G_z = 0 \tag{11-38}$$

Hydrostatic Balance. As a simple illustration of the variational method applied to a meteorological problem, assume that the geopotential and temperature are more or less independently observed functions of a pressure parameter, $P =$

$-R\ell n\, p/p_0$, and it is desired to adjust them so that they satisfy the hydrostatic equation $d\phi/dP = T$. Then an appropriate integral to be minimized might be

$$I = \int_{P_1}^{P_2} [\alpha(\phi - \phi_0)^2 + \beta(T - T_0)^2]\, dP \tag{11-39}$$

where α and β are weight factors assigned to each variable governing their relative adjustments in a least-squares sense. If T is replaced by $d\phi/dP$, the integrand is of the form, $F(P,\phi,\phi')$, where $\phi' = d\phi/dP$. The Euler-Lagrange equation which must be satisfied for a minimum I is

$$\frac{d^2\phi}{dP^2} - \frac{\alpha}{\beta}\phi = -\frac{\alpha}{\beta}\phi_0 + \frac{dT_0}{dP} \tag{11-40}$$

Solution of this equation for ϕ with appropriate boundary conditions, followed by calculation of $T = d\phi/dP$, would complete the solution.

Since numerical modeling of meteorological parameters is done at discrete intervals, the foregoing problem can be couched in finite differenced from as follows:

$$I = \sum_k \alpha(\phi_k - \phi_{k0})^2 + \beta(T_k - T_{k0})^2 \tag{11-41}$$

$$\delta I = \sum_k 2\alpha(\phi_k - \phi_{k0})\, \delta\phi_k + 2\beta(T_k - T_{k0})\, \delta T_k \tag{11-42}$$

Now suppose that the hydrostatic equation is approximated by the central difference approximation $\nabla_P\phi_k = (\phi_{k+1} - \phi_{k-1})/2\Delta P = T_k$, then the variation becomes

$$\delta I = 2\Sigma[\alpha(\phi_k - \phi_{k0})\, \delta\phi_k + \beta(\nabla_P\phi_k - T_{k0})\nabla_P\delta\phi_k] \tag{11-43}$$

Next the equivalent of integration by parts is carried out by writing the identities

$$\begin{aligned}(\nabla_P\phi)_k\,(\nabla_P\delta\phi)_k &= -\,\delta\phi_k[\nabla_P(\nabla_P\phi)] + (D_k - D_{k-1})\\ T_{0k}(\nabla_P\delta\phi)_k &= -\,\delta\phi_k(\nabla_P T)_k + (E_k - E_{k-1})\end{aligned} \tag{11-44}$$

where

$$D_k = (\nabla_P\phi)_{k+1}\,(\nabla_P\delta\phi)_k + (\nabla_P\phi)_k\,(\nabla_P\delta\phi)_{k+1}$$

$$E_k = T_{0k+1}\,\delta\phi_k + T_{0k}\,\delta\phi_{k+1}$$

When summed in the vertical the last terms of each equation of (11-44) vanish identically at the interior points and at the end points with appropriate conditions on $\delta\phi$ at the boundaries ($\delta\phi = 0$ in this case). Hence substitution of (11-44) into (11-43) and setting the coefficient of $\delta\phi_k$ to zero as required for a minimum leads to the Euler-Lagrange (E-L) equation

$$\nabla_P \nabla_P \phi_k - \frac{\alpha}{\beta}\phi_k = -\frac{\alpha}{\beta}\phi_{0k} + \nabla_P T_{0k} \qquad (11\text{-}45)$$

This finite difference equation, which is an approximation to (11-40), is a one-dimensional elliptic equation of the Helmholtz type and can be solved by relaxation or direct methods given the upper and lower boundary conditions.

Geostrophic Balance. For the case of horizontal analyses of the wind and geopotential fields an integral (or sum) of the following form can be minimized

$$\int \left[\alpha(\phi - \phi_0)^2 + \beta(u - u_0)^2 + \beta(v - v_0)^2 + \gamma\left(fu + \frac{\partial\phi}{\partial y}\right)^2 + \gamma\left(fv - \frac{\partial\phi}{\partial x}\right)^2\right] dxdy \qquad (11\text{-}46)$$

Here the last two terms represent geostrophic relations that are treated as *weak constraints* in the variational sense. How closely these constraints are imposed depends directly on the magnitude of the weight factor γ. Another weak constraint that may be added is of the form $\varepsilon[(\partial u/\partial t)^2 + (\partial v/\partial t)^2]$ with the objective of reducing high-frequency oscillations of the inertial-gravity type. In the variational manipulations, the local time derivatives are replaced by their equivalents from the equations of motion.

Balance Equation Constraint. Barker, Haltiner, and Sasaki (1975, 1976, 1977) have obtained balanced global winds by a variational technique with the principal objectives of (1) making use of both wind and geopotential information in all latitudes when achieving the balance and (2) reducing the noise at the beginning of a forecast. The first step in the procedure involves minimizing the integral

$$I = \int [\alpha(\phi - \tilde{\phi})^2 + \beta(\nabla\psi + \mathbf{k} \times \tilde{\mathbf{V}})^2 + 2\lambda M]\, dS \qquad (11\text{-}47)$$

where ψ is a streamfunction to be determined; the tilde denotes objectively-analyzed fields; λ is a Lagrange multiplier that establishes $M = 0$ as a *strong constraint; S*, an area element on a sphere; and $M = 0$ represents the balance equation, (or in a more general case the divergence of the steady-state motion equation, that is, $\partial\nabla \cdot \mathbf{V}/\partial t = 0 = -\nabla \cdot (\mathbf{V} \cdot \nabla\mathbf{V}) - \nabla \cdot (f\mathbf{k} \times \mathbf{V}) - \nabla^2\phi + \cdots$)

$$M(\phi,\psi) = f\nabla^2\psi + \nabla f \cdot \nabla\psi + 2J(u_\psi, v_\psi) - \nabla^2\phi \qquad (11\text{-}48)$$

Here J is the Jacobian. Taking the variation of I gives

$$\delta I = \int [\alpha(\phi - \tilde{\phi})\delta\phi + \beta(\nabla\psi + \mathbf{k} \times \tilde{\mathbf{V}}) \cdot \nabla\delta\psi + M\delta\lambda + \lambda[\nabla \cdot (f\nabla\delta\psi) + \delta A - \nabla \cdot (\nabla\delta\phi)]\, dS \qquad (11\text{-}49)$$

The variation of the nonlinear terms δA will be neglected. Next various mathematical manipulations are performed to extract $\delta\psi$ and $\delta\phi$ from within differential operators using exact differential forms for the purpose of integration by parts, for example,

$$\begin{aligned}&\beta(\nabla\psi + \mathbf{k} \times \tilde{\mathbf{V}}) \cdot \nabla\delta\psi \\ &\qquad = \nabla \cdot [\beta(\nabla\psi + \mathbf{k} \times \tilde{\mathbf{V}})\delta\psi] - \delta\psi\nabla \cdot [\beta(\nabla\psi + \mathbf{k} \times \tilde{\mathbf{V}})]\end{aligned} \quad (11\text{-}50)$$

When the variation of M is performed, the variation of the nonlinear term is neglected; however this term is retained in developing a final equation for the Lagrange multiplier. After all of the terms of δI have been put in a form containing only terms that are either exact differentials or where $\delta\psi$, $\delta\phi$, and $\delta\lambda$ appear explicitly with coefficients that do not contain them, then the coefficients of these differentials are set to zero. The resulting E-L equations are

$$\nabla^2\psi = \tilde{\zeta} - \frac{\nabla\beta}{\beta} \cdot (\nabla\psi + \mathbf{k} \times \mathbf{V}) + \frac{1}{\beta}\nabla \cdot (f\nabla\lambda)$$

$$\phi = \tilde{\phi} + \frac{1}{\alpha}\nabla^2\lambda$$

$$f\nabla^2\psi + \nabla f \cdot \nabla\psi = \nabla^2\phi - 2J(u_\psi, v_\psi) \quad (11\text{-}51)$$

Only the variation of α and β with latitude was considered with the assumption that β would have relatively greater weight than α in low latitudes where the wind is a more reliable parameter for analysis and prediction than the geopotential field because of the latter's weak gradients in the tropics. In higher latitudes geopotential should have equal or greater weight than the objectively analyzed wind data. Also this is consistent with geostrophic adjustment theory (Section 2-8).

The first equation of (11-51) shows that vorticity of the adjusted wind field equals the objectively analyzed vorticity modified by two terms, one involving the gradient of the weight factor on the wind and the other, the Lagrange multiplier of the dynamical constraint. It is apparent that if β is relatively large, the vorticity of the adjusted wind field will nearly equal that of the objective analysis and the resulting adjusted wind will be merely the rotational component of the objectively analyzed winds. The second equation shows that if α is relatively large, the ϕ field will change little. In addition to satisfying (11-51), certain integrals must be zero for the integral (11-47) to vanish; however for global integration with no lateral boundaries, this turns out to be trivial.

In order to determine the adjusted geopotential and rotational wind fields, it is necessary to determine the Lagrange multiplier λ. An equation for λ is obtained by substituting from the first two equations of (11-51) for $\nabla^2\psi$ and $\nabla^2\phi$ into the third equation. The result is a fourth-order equation

$$\nabla^2\lambda^* - \frac{\alpha f^2}{\beta}\lambda^* = F \quad (11\text{-}52)$$

where $\lambda^* = \nabla^2\lambda$ and F is a rather involved function of the objectively analyzed fields, the weighting coefficients and also lower-order terms in λ. As a consequence of the last feature, the solution for λ^* is obtained by iteration which updates the right side of (11-52) with new values of λ as determined by solution of the Poisson equation $\nabla^2\lambda = \lambda^*$. Finally, the value of ψ and ϕ are obtained by utilization of the λ field in the first two equations of (11-51). The entire procedure is very fast on a computer, equivalent to no more than a few time steps of the prediction phase.

The foregoing procedure improves the analyses of the velocity and geopotential fields and reduces noise considerably in numerical forecasts, even though only a rotational wind field is used. In a σ-coordinate PE model, it is necessary to interpolate the wind and ϕ to the σ-levels. As a result of the interpolation some of the dynamic balance is lost and some of the noise reappears; hence some further processing is desirable.

Removal of the Integrated Mass Divergence. High-frequency fluctuations in the surface-pressure tendency reflect the presence of external gravity waves. In terms of the σ-coordinate system the surface pressure tendency is given by [see (1-69)]

$$\partial p_s/\partial t = -\sum_{k=1}^{K} \nabla \cdot (p_s \mathbf{V}_k)\Delta\sigma_k \equiv F(\mathbf{V}_k) \tag{11-53}$$

where k is a vertical index for σ. Thus external gravity waves may be suppressed by adjusting the wind field with the strong dynamical constraint that the integral of $\nabla \cdot (p_s\mathbf{V})$ vanish so that

$$I = \int_S \sum_{k=1}^{K} [(\mathbf{V}_k - \tilde{\mathbf{V}}_k)^2 + 2\lambda\nabla \cdot (p_s\mathbf{V}_k)]\, \Delta\sigma dS \tag{11-54}$$

Posed in this fashion the Lagrange multiplier varies only in the horizontal direction. Taking the variation of (11-54), but retaining the field of p_s, and setting the coefficients of $\delta\mathbf{V}_k$ and $\delta\lambda$ to zero leads to the E-L equations

$$\begin{aligned} \mathbf{V}_k &= \tilde{\mathbf{V}}_k + p_s \nabla\lambda \\ F(\mathbf{V}_k) &\equiv -\sum_{k=1} \nabla \cdot (p_s\mathbf{V}_k)\Delta\sigma = 0 \end{aligned} \tag{11-55}$$

Substituting the first equation into the second gives the equation for the Lagrange multiplier

$$\sum_{k=1}^{K} \nabla \cdot (p_s\tilde{\mathbf{V}}_k + p_s^2\nabla\lambda)\Delta\sigma_k = 0 \qquad \sum_{k=1}^{K} \Delta\sigma_k = 1$$

$$\text{or} \quad p_s^2\nabla^2\lambda = F(\tilde{\mathbf{V}}_k) - \nabla p_s^2 \cdot \nabla\lambda \tag{11-56}$$

Since the right side of (11-56) involves λ, it is solved iteratively as follows:

$$p_s^2 \nabla^2 \lambda^{(n)} = F(\tilde{\mathbf{V}}_k) - \nabla p_s^2 \cdot \nabla \lambda^{(n-1)}$$

where n represents the iteration step. The term $F(\tilde{\mathbf{V}}_k)$ is computed but once during the iteration procedure. Moreover, a PE prediction model includes a program for computing $F(\mathbf{V}_k)$ for the purpose of calculating the surface pressure tendency.

In the vicinity of mountains particularly and also where local heat sources exist, gravity waves are frequently generated by PE models. As a means of further suppressing noise a second constraint may be imposed requiring the adjusted wind field to satisfy the condition

$$\frac{\partial^2 p_s}{\partial t^2} = -\int_0^1 \nabla \cdot \left(\frac{\partial}{\partial t} (p_s \mathbf{V}) \right) d\sigma = 0 \qquad (11\text{-}57)$$

This adjustment may be achieved by the variational method by minimizing the integral

$$I = \int_S \left\{ \sum_{k=1}^{K} \left[\beta(\mathbf{V}_h - \tilde{\mathbf{V}}_k)^2 + (T_k - \tilde{T}_h)^2 + 2\lambda \nabla \cdot \frac{\partial (p_s \mathbf{V})}{\partial t} \right] \Delta\sigma_k \right\} dS \qquad (11\text{-}58)$$

The constraint term is evaluated from the divergence of the model prediction equation

$$\frac{\partial (p_s \mathbf{V}_k)}{\partial t} = -p_s \nabla_\sigma \phi_k - RT_k \nabla p_s - f p_s \mathbf{k} \times \mathbf{V}_k + \mathbf{N} \qquad (11\text{-}59)$$

where $\mathbf{N}$ represents the nonlinear terms. When δI is formed the variations of $\mathbf{N}$ and p_s, that is, $\delta\mathbf{N}$ and δp_s are neglected. The geopotential in (11-58) is replaced by the temperature through the use of the model hydrostatic equation, so that the only two quantities that are adjusted are wind and temperature, as suggested by the form of I in (11-58). After the adjustment of T has been made, ϕ is calculated using the model hydrostatic equation, which is usually incorporated into the prediction programs. As shown in some tests with a multilevel PE model this second constraint does indeed further reduce gravitational noise at the beginning of a forecast; however, this further refinement may not be needed (Barker et al., 1977).

Several types of constraints have been described for use with the variational method of adjusting objective analyses to bring the wind and mass fields into better dynamical consistency for the purpose of beginning a forecast. While it would be desirable to apply these constraints simultaneously, the variational equations can become very complicated. As an alternative, variational procedures containing a single constraint can be applied sequentially, and, if need be, cycled through two or three times with very satisfactory results.

11-4-5 Normal Mode Expansions

The foregoing methods of static initialization are based on the distinction between gravity modes with relatively high divergence and the meteorological Rossby modes of the quasi-geostrophic type with small divergence and relatively large vorticity. In the tropics the separation is far less clear cut. Observations indicate highly divergent modes detectable in the network, high-speed, nearly nondivergent Rossby modes, etc.; and in general some blurring between the meteorologically significant modes and gravity waves that are usually considered noise (Sections 4-12 and 4-13). Dickinson and Williamson (1972) noted these difficulties, and also that the degrees of freedom in NWP models with spherical geometry may differ considerably from plane geometry and, of course, from the infinite degrees of freedom in the real atmosphere. Therefore they proposed that the relative importance of the various modes representable by a model be determined from long-term integrations. Similarly the observational data can be expanded in the modes of the model and comparisons made. Then those components in data to be used for initializing an NWP model that are not of significant amplitude in the long-term data can be discarded as noise. The modes that are retained would include both rotational and divergent wind components.

To test this concept, Williamson and Dickinson (1976) established the normal modes of a simplified version of the NCAR GCM by means of small amplitude perturbations about a state of rest on a smooth spherical earth. Neglect of mean winds, orographic effects, and dissipative and diabatic heating terms ensures real frequencies for the calculated modes and precludes damped and amplifying modes. The primary purpose was to establish the relative importance of various gravity modes in the GCM and also the amplitudes of the computational modes, the latter establishing a noise level that must be exceeded in terms of amplitude by other modes if they are to be considered significant. Computations showed that the computational modes were at least an order of magnitude less than the dominant Rossby modes in amplitude. Williamson and Dickinson also found that the model gravity waves generally had magnitudes no larger than the noise level, except for Kelvin waves that may be important in tropical climatology.

Flattery (1970) developed a spectral method of objective analysis that fits the eigenfunctions of Laplace's tidal equations to the observed data by a least squares method. The objective analysis scheme has been used operationally at NMC.

11-4-6 Variational Normal Mode Initialization

Daley (1978) applied a variational procedure to the normal mode initialization procedure for the shallow water equations. Unlike the balance equation constraint (Barker, Haltiner, and Sasaki, 1975, 1976) and (Barker, et al., 1977), which yields only a nondivergent wind component, the normal mode procedure produces a divergent component as well. Although winds derived from the balance equation reduce the gravity-wave noise, a divergent component is necessary to remove inertial gravity waves (Section 2-7). The variational approach makes an optimal use of the observed data by adjusting both mass and motion fields while achieving dynamical consistency through appropriate constraints.

In the linear normal mode initialization the original (objectively analyzed fields) are adjusted to orthogonalize them to undesirable gravity and computational modes based on linearized versions of the model equation. However the nonlinear terms tend to regenerate the high-frequency modes, and also curvature in the flow is neglected so that the fit with the original data may suffer.

The nonlinear normal mode initialization techniques of Machenhauer (1977) and Baer (1977) overcome these difficulties. Daley's variational version of nonlinear normal mode initialization is also very successful in eliminating gravity noise. All three have been applied to the "shallow-water" (barotropic) equations which may be expressed as follows (Section 6-7):

$$\begin{aligned}
&\frac{\partial}{\partial t}\nabla^2\psi + 2\Omega\mu\nabla^2\chi + \frac{2\Omega}{a^2}\left[\frac{\partial\psi}{\partial\lambda} + (1-\mu^2)\frac{\partial\chi}{\partial\mu}\right] = R_\psi \\
&\frac{\partial}{\partial t}\nabla^2\chi - 2\Omega\mu\nabla^2\psi + \frac{2\Omega}{a^2}\left[\frac{\partial\chi}{\partial\lambda} - (1-\mu^2)\frac{\partial\psi}{\partial\mu}\right] + \nabla^2\phi = R_\chi \qquad (11\text{-}60) \\
&\frac{\partial\phi}{\partial t} + \bar{\phi}\nabla^2\chi = R_\phi
\end{aligned}$$

where

$$\begin{aligned}
R_\psi &= -\frac{1}{a}\left[\frac{1}{1-\mu^2}\frac{\partial}{\partial\lambda}(U\nabla^2\psi) + \frac{\partial}{\partial\mu}(V\nabla^2\psi)\right] \\
R_\chi &= \frac{1}{a}\left[\frac{1}{1-\mu^2}\frac{\partial}{\partial\lambda}(V\nabla^2\psi) - \frac{\partial}{\partial\mu}(U\nabla^2\psi)\right] - \tfrac{1}{2}\nabla^2\left(\frac{U^2+V^2}{1-\mu^2}\right) \\
R_\phi &= -\frac{1}{a}\left[\frac{1}{1-\mu^2}\frac{\partial}{\partial\lambda}(U\phi) + \frac{\partial}{\partial\mu}(V\phi)\right] \qquad (11\text{-}61)
\end{aligned}$$

$\mu = \sin\varphi$, $\bar{\phi}$ is the horizontal mean, ∇^2 is the spherical Laplacian, and

$$U = -\frac{(1-\mu^2)}{a}\frac{\partial\psi}{\partial\mu} + \frac{1}{a}\frac{\partial\chi}{\partial\lambda} \qquad V = \frac{1}{a}\frac{\partial\psi}{\partial\lambda} + \frac{1-\mu^2}{a}\frac{\partial\chi}{\partial\mu} \qquad (11\text{-}62)$$

The free normal modes of the linearized version of (11-60) about a state of rest with an equivalent depth of $\bar{\phi}/g$ are found by neglecting the R's and assuming solutions of the form,

$$\mathbf{Y} = \begin{bmatrix}\psi \\ \chi \\ \phi\end{bmatrix} = \sum_{n=s}^{\infty}\begin{bmatrix}A_n^s \\ i\,B_n^s \\ 2\Omega C_n^s\end{bmatrix} P_n^s(\mu)\exp(is\lambda - 2\Omega i\sigma t) \qquad (11\text{-}63)$$

Here s is the zonal wave number, $P_n^s\ (\mu)$ is the associated Legendre function of the first kind of degree s and order n (see 6-42), σ is the normalized frequency, and the A, B, and C's are real expansion coefficients of the Legendre functions. Also,

$$\int_{-1}^{1} P_n^s\ (\mu)\ P_m^s\ (\mu)\ d\mu\ =\ \delta_m^n \tag{11-64}$$

Then substituting the assumed solutions (11-63) into (11-60), multiplying by $P_m^n\ (\mu)\ \exp\ (-ir\lambda)$, and integrating over the sphere leads to the relations

$$\begin{aligned} &-\frac{s}{n\ (n\ +\ 1)} A_n^s + \frac{n-1}{n}\varepsilon_n^s B_{n-1}^s + \frac{n+2}{n+1}\varepsilon_{n+1} B_{n+1}^s = \sigma A_n^s \\ &\frac{n-1}{n}\varepsilon_n^s A_{n-1}^s + \frac{n+2}{n+1}\varepsilon_{n+1}^s A_{n+1}^s - \frac{s}{n\ (n\ +\ 1)} B_n^s - C_n^s = \sigma B_n^s \\ &-n\ (n\ +\ 1)\ kB_n^s = \sigma C_n^s \end{aligned} \tag{11-65}$$

where

$$\varepsilon_n^s = [(n^2 - s^2)/(4_n^2 - 1)]^{½} \qquad k = \bar{\phi}/4\Omega^2 a^2$$

Globally, the foregoing system constitutes two matrix problems: the *symmetric* one, for which χ and ϕ are symmetric and ψ is antisymmetric with respect to the equator; and the *antisymmetric* second, for which χ and ϕ are antisymmetric and ψ symmetric. For a hemisphere only the first one is required.

For numerical purposes, a finite number of terms in (11-63) is considered, say $n = s + N$. Then for each zonal wave number s and a given even N, there are the symmetric and antisymmetric matrices of order $3N/2$ and $3N$ eigenvalues and eigenvectors. The latter include N low-frequency westward moving Rossby modes and $2N$ gravity modes. For large $\bar{\phi}$, the separation between the two types is large, but the separation diminishes with decreasing $\bar{\phi}$. The meridional structure functions are the tidal (Hough) functions used by Flattery. When $s = 0$, there is a degeneracy and some of the modes, usually Rossby type, are stationary ($\sigma = 0$), which for the symmetric case are $(N/2) + 2$ in number. The remaining $N - 2$ gravity modes have nonzero frequency and their structure can be determined.

The horizontal structure of a specific free mode $\mathbf{Y}_j^s\ (\mu,\lambda)$ with eigenfrequency σ_j^s is given by

$$\hat{\mathbf{Y}}_j^s = \begin{bmatrix} \hat{\psi}_j^s \\ \hat{\chi}_j^s \\ \hat{\phi}_j^s \end{bmatrix} = \sum_{n=s}^{s+N} \begin{bmatrix} A_n^s\ (j) \\ iB_n^s\ (j) \\ 2\Omega C_n^s\ (j) \end{bmatrix} P_n^s\ (\mu)\ \exp\ (is\lambda) \tag{11-66}$$

where $\hat{\psi}_j^s$, $\hat{\chi}_j^s$, and $\hat{\phi}_j^s$ are known complex functions of latitude and longitude and j denotes an ordering of the eigenmodes according to frequency, $j = 0$ to $3N$. The total energy, kinetic plus potential, is given by the product

$$<\mathbf{Y} \cdot \mathbf{Y}^*> = \frac{1}{4\pi} \int_{-1}^{1} \int_{0}^{2\pi} [\phi\phi_j^{*s} - \bar{\phi}(\hat{\psi}_j^{*s} \nabla^2\psi - \hat{\chi}_j^{*s} \nabla^2\chi)] d\mu d\lambda \tag{11-67}$$

where the * denotes complex conjugate and **Y** represents arbitrary fields of ψ, χ, and ϕ. **Y** can be expanded in spherical harmonics

$$\mathbf{Y} = \sum_{s=-M}^{M} \sum_{n=s}^{s+N} \begin{bmatrix} \psi_n^s \\ i\chi_n^s \\ 2\Omega\phi_n^s \end{bmatrix} P_n^s(\mu) \exp(is\lambda) \tag{11-68}$$

where ψ_n^s, χ_n^s, and ϕ_n^s are the complex expansion coefficients. Moreover,

$$<\mathbf{Y} \cdot \mathbf{Y}_j^{*s}> = 4\Omega^2 \sum_{n=s}^{s+N} \phi_n^s C_n^s(j) + n(n+1)k[\psi_n^s A_n^s(j) + \chi_n^s B_n^s(j)]$$

$$-M \le j < M \tag{11-70}$$

The normal mode magnitudes, determined from the homogeneous system (11-65), have a degree of freedom that may be specified by normalizing the orthogonal solutions; thus

$$<\hat{\mathbf{Y}}_\ell^r \cdot \hat{\mathbf{Y}}_j^{*s}> = 4\Omega^2 \delta_r^s \delta_j^\ell \tag{11-70}$$

The arbitrary field **Y** may also be expanded in terms of the normal modes, that is,

$$\mathbf{Y} = \sum_{s=-M}^{M} \sum_{j=1}^{3N} \gamma_j^s \hat{\mathbf{Y}}_j^s \tag{11-71}$$

where according to (11-69) and (11-70) the expansion coefficients are given by

$$\gamma_j^s = \frac{1}{4\Omega^2} <\mathbf{Y} \cdot \mathbf{Y}_j^{*s}> \tag{11-72}$$

When the normal modes of the linearized version of (11-60) have been determined, they may be used to adjust objectively analyzed fields of ψ, χ, and ϕ, say **Y**(0), for subsequent numerical integration. To effect the linear initialization procedure the amplitudes of the gravity modes in **Y**(0) may be calculated as follows:

$$\gamma_j^s(0) = (1/4\Omega^2) <\mathbf{Y}(0) \cdot \hat{\mathbf{Y}}_j^{*s}> \qquad -M \le S \le M \qquad j\varepsilon[j_G] \tag{11-73}$$

where $[j_G]$ represents the modes that are to be suppressed. These modes are then removed from **Y**(0),

$$\mathbf{Y}(1) = \mathbf{Y}(0) - \sum_{s}^{M} \sum_{j}^{G} \gamma_j^s(0) \hat{\mathbf{Y}}_j^s \tag{11-74}$$

However the filtered high-frequency modes are not removed for all times. When the nonlinear system is integrated, these oscillations reappear, although with lesser amplitudes than without any initialization, because the $\hat{\mathbf{Y}}_j^s$ are the only eigenmodes of the linearized version of (11-60). While it is not possible to obtain the normal modes of the nonlinear system, Baer's and Machenhauer's methods can approach this ideal by an iterative procedure, which requires that the time tendencies of amplitudes of the filtered high-frequency modes are initially zero. Although the initial amplitudes of the high-frequency modes are not zero, the time tendencies of the initialized fields would be orthogonal to the time tendencies of the high-frequency linear modes.

In this case, the normal mode expansions (11-71) are substituted into the nonlinear equations (11-60). Then multiplication by $\hat{\psi}_j^{*s}$, $\hat{\chi}_j^{*s}$, and $\hat{\phi}_j^{*s}$, respectively, addition and integration over the sphere leads to an equation for the time tendency of γ_j^s

$$\dot{\gamma}_j^s = -2\Omega i\sigma_j^s \gamma_j^s + (\tfrac{1}{4}\Omega^2)\, F(R_\psi, R_\chi, R_\phi) \tag{11-75}$$

where

$$F = \frac{1}{4\pi}\int_{-1}^{1}\int_{0}^{2\pi} [R_\phi\, \hat{\phi}_j^{*s} - \overline{\phi}(R_\psi\, \hat{\psi}_j^{*s} + R_\chi\, \hat{\chi}_j^{*s})]\, d\lambda\, d\mu$$

When $\dot{\gamma}_j^{s}$ for a specific mode is set to zero, (11-75) gives

$$\gamma_j^s(1) = (1/8\Omega^3 i\sigma_j^s)\, F \tag{11-76}$$

The adjusted fields are then obtained by replacing the amplitudes, $\gamma_j^s\,(0)$ by $\gamma_j^s(1)$ and

$$\mathbf{Y}(1) = \mathbf{Y}(0) + \sum_{-M}^{M}\sum^{G} (\gamma_j^s(1) - \gamma_j^s(0)]\, \hat{\mathbf{Y}}_j^s \tag{11-77}$$

The R's used in the foregoing were calculated from $\mathbf{Y}(0)$ hence the procedure can be repeated with $\mathbf{Y}(1)$ used in calculating the R's. Then (11-76) will give a new set of coefficients $\gamma_j^s\,(2)$ for use in (11-77), and so forth. This procedure is highly effective in removing spurious high-frequency oscillations during integration of the shallow-water equations. Baer (1977) used a Rossby number expansion to accomplish a similar result.

Daley points out that for each zonal wave number s there are $2N$ gravity modes but $3N$ degrees of freedom for ψ, χ, and ϕ, hence the latter can be adjusted in many ways to satisfy (11-76) and (11-77) for the $2N$ gravity modes. Thus a variational procedure may be used to minimize adjustments to ψ, χ, and ϕ subject to the constraint (11-76) and (11-77) on the high-frequency modes. The selection of preassigned weight factors W is based on the confidence in the original fields. The variational integral to be minimized is

$$I(\Delta \mathbf{Y}, \mathbf{W}_y) = (a^2/4\pi) \int_{-1}^{1} \int_{0}^{2\pi} [W_\psi(\nabla \Delta\psi)^2 + W_\chi(\nabla \Delta\chi)^2 + (W_\phi/4\Omega^2)(\nabla \Delta\phi)^2] \, d\lambda d\mu \quad (11\text{-}78)$$

where $\Delta \mathbf{Y} = \mathbf{Y}(1) - \mathbf{Y}(0)$ and $\mathbf{W}_y = [W_\psi(\mu,\lambda), W_\chi(\mu,\lambda), W_\phi(\mu,\lambda)]^T$

(T denotes transpose). Note that the gradients of the adjustments to ψ, χ, and ϕ are minimized, which is geostrophically consistent with respect to ϕ and ψ. Next, constraints will be imposed so that (11-73) holds, which implies that the adjustment $\Delta \mathbf{Y}$ must alter the original amplitudes $\gamma_j^s(0)$ of the undesirable mode to $\gamma_j^s(1)$. For this purpose $< \mathbf{Y} \cdot \mathbf{Y}_j^{*s} >$ is eliminated from (11-69) and (11-72) and the variation taken, which relates the adjustments in ψ, χ, ϕ to $\gamma_j^s(1)$, and $\gamma_j^s(0)$.

$$(1/4\pi) \int_{-1}^{1} \int_{0}^{2\pi} [\Delta\phi\hat{\phi}_j^{*s} + \bar{\phi}(\Delta\psi\nabla^2\hat{\psi}_j^{*s} + \Delta\chi\nabla^2\hat{\chi}_j^{*s})] \, d\lambda d\mu = 4\Omega^2[\gamma_j^s(1) - \gamma_j^s(0)] \quad (11\text{-}79)$$

The foregoing relationship is applied only to those modes that are to be suppressed. The horizontal eigenfunctions $\hat{\psi}_j^{*s}$, $\hat{\chi}_j^{*s}$, $\hat{\phi}_j^{*s}$ in (11-79) are known from (11-63); $\gamma_j^s(0)$, a function of $\mathbf{Y}(0)$, is determinable from (11-73); and $\gamma_j^s(1)$ is obtainable by calculating R_ψ, R_χ, R_ϕ from $\mathbf{Y}(0)$ using (11-61) and (11-73), (11-74). Applying (11-79) as strong constraints requires the introduction of Lagrange multipliers and is accomplished by the following variational integral, $J(\Delta \mathbf{Y}, \mathbf{W}_y)$,

$$J(\Delta \mathbf{Y}, \mathbf{W}_y) = I(\Delta \mathbf{Y}, \mathbf{W}_y) + \sum_s \sum_j^G a_j^s[\gamma_j^s(1) - \gamma_j^s(0)]^2 \quad (11\text{-}80)$$

With an integral constraint the complex multipliers a_j^s, which are independent of latitude and longitude, must be determined. The variational procedure leads to a system of Euler-Lagrange differential equations, which must be solved for the Lagrange multipliers a_j^s, and for $\Delta\psi$, $\Delta\chi$, and $\Delta\phi$. To solve the differential system, $\Delta \mathbf{Y}$ is expressed as a finite series of spherical harmonics, as in (11-66), which is substituted into the Euler-Lagrange equations and the constraint equations (11-79). This leads to a set of linear algebraic equations in the coefficients $\Delta\psi_m^s$, $\Delta\chi_m^s$, $\Delta\phi_m^s$, and a_j^s, the solution of which provides the necessary adjustments in ψ, χ, and ϕ to suppress the gravity modes. Daley demonstrates that a particular choice of the variational integral is equivalent to the normal mode technique of Machenhauer. It is also shown the latter scheme is energetically consistent and gives a lesser weight to small horizontal scales of ϕ and forces heights to the winds more strongly than (11-78).

In summary, gravity noise suppression with ''shallow-water models'' can be achieved by either the method of Machenhauer (1977), Baer (1977), or the variational procedure of Daley; however, the last gives greater control of the adjustment process and permits an optimal use of the data.

Andersen (1977) and Daley (1979) have extended Machenhauer's nonlinear initialization scheme to baroclinic models with a spectral representation in the horizontal and σ-coordinates in the vertical, Andersen by vertical finite differences and Daley by vertical finite elements. Temperton and Williamson (1979) developed a normal mode initialization procedure for the ECMRWF global gridpoint model, which gives excellent results. The linear version had some problems that were alleviated by applying Machenhauer's 1977 iterative nonlinear procedure. In this initialization scheme the initial Rossby-mode coefficients are left unchanged but the initial gravity mode coefficients are altered in such a way that the linear contribution to the time derivative of each coefficient, which depends on the coefficient, exactly balances the contribution from the nonlinear interactions between all modes. The linear modes were expanded about a state of rest because Machenhauer had found that inclusion of a zonal wind did not improve results, nor was the choice of the basic vertical temperature structure important. Such changes in the basic state are compensated by changes in the nonlinear forcing; however, this makes the splitting into linear and nonlinear forcing somewhat arbitrary. The normal mode initialization requires the separability of the model's linearized equations in the vertical and horizontal directions (see Section 7-8). The nonlinear iterative procedure appears to converge to good initial conditions when up to five vertical modes are initialized in a nine-level adiabatic, frictionless model. Use of all nine vertical modes leads to divergence of the iterative scheme. Two iterations with five vertical modes appears to give very satisfactory results and does not require excessive computer time (Figure 11-5). Initialization of *only the external mode* eliminates the highest frequencies and reduces the amplitude of the excessive noise (with amplitudes to 8 mb) present with unintialized data, but considerable noise remains. The inclusion of mountains in the forecast model had no adverse effect on the nonlinear scheme. Comparison with a dynamic initialization scheme (see Section 11-5) due to Okamura (Nitta 1969) showed the nonlinear normal mode initialization to be clearly superior and to take far less computer time (Figure 11-6). Forecasts made with and without initialization showed very similar results poleward of 30*N*, but equatorward the forecasts were quite different with unrealistic geopotential variations due to gravity waves in the uninitialized case. However the forecasts turned out to be very similar whether the ''initialization'' (filtering) was done at the beginning or end of the forecast period, which suggests little interaction between the gravity and Rossby modes. Different results may be expected if physical processes involving vertical motions and the release of latent heat are present. The inclusion of a simple surface drag type of friction in the forecast *after* frictionless initialization does not regenerate significant gravity-wave noise. To include it in the initialization pro-

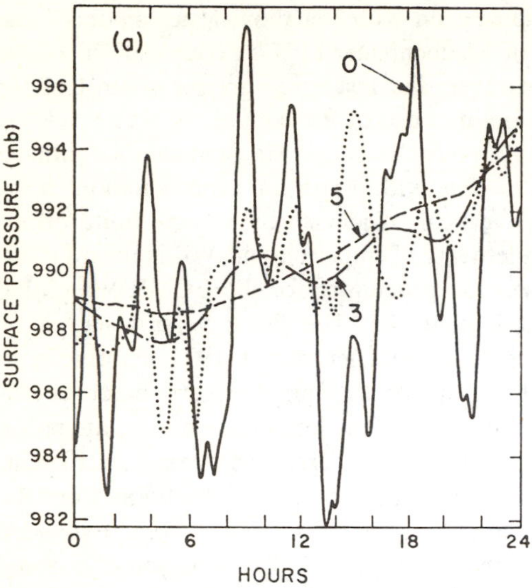

Figure 11-5 Surface pressure versus time (*a*) at 40°N, 90°W after two nonlinear iterations with the first three (3) and five (5) vertical modes and with no initialization (0), and after linear normal mode initialization (dotted). (*After Temperton and Williamson, 1979.*)

cedure in order to produce cross-isobar flow in the PBL would require all nine vertical modes, which resulted in problems in the iteration procedure.

Experimental forecasts with a 15-level model including the usual physics (except radiation for economy of computer time) showed that *adiabatic nonlinear initialization* with five vertical modes is quite adequate for removing high-frequency oscillations, even with only two iterations, although four iterations gave further improvement. Boundary layer effects present in the original data are not removed by this initialization procedure, nor are they introduced with only five modes if not there originally. Inclusion of the physics in the initialization procedures leads to computational divergence, after two iterations for the fifth vertical mode and all modes by the third iteration. Further experiments led to the conclusion that Machenhauer's iteration procedure will not work for the higher internal vertical modes in a multilevel gridpoint model, and particularly when diabatic terms are included in the nonlinear forcing.

The average change in the wind and mass fields from analysis to initialization is within observational error; however, changes at individual gridpoints may be quite large. This could be alleviated by the variational approach but more complexity would be involved as well as more computer time for the initialization phase. Daley's (1979) application of the nonlinear normal mode

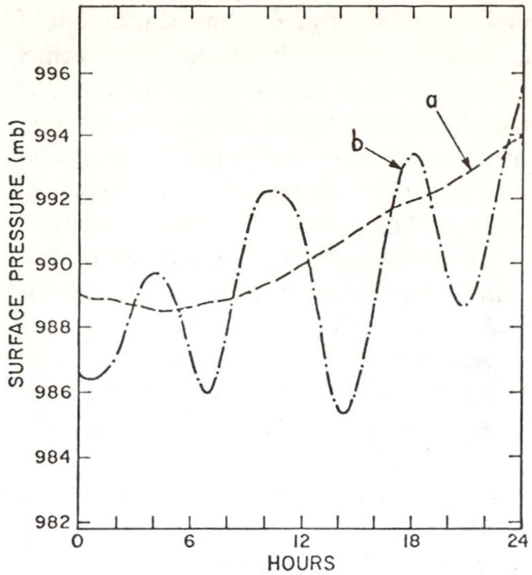

Figure 11-6 Surface pressure versus time at 40°N, 90°W after (*a*) linear initialization followed by two nonlinear iterations (*b*) 6 h of dynamic initialization. (*After Temperton and Williamson, 1979.*)

to a spectral model gave very good results similar to those of Temperton and Williamson. In conclusion, the adiabatic nonlinear normal mode method of initialization appears to be the most promising at present when compared to other methods of initialization in terms of noise removal and improvement of forecasts, particularly in the early stages of a forecast when the vertical motion field is developing. Some further refinements may be needed along with more testing with a variety of real data sets.

In an interesting paper Leith (1979) has shown that the first iteration of the nonlinear procedure leads to quasi-rotational dynamical and diagnostic equations consistent with classical quasi-geostrophic theory. The resulting balance equation is similar to (7-28) (Charney, 1955a), but is three dimensional.

11-5 DYNAMIC BALANCING

As discussed in Section 2-8, NWP primitive equation models inherently possess the mechanism for the geostrophic adjustment process. Then why not let the model do the job? Indeed, the mass and velocity fields do mutually adjust to one another and tend toward a quasi-geostrophic state, which is characteristic of the atmosphere. This does not imply that the mean spectral distribution of energy in numerical forecasts is the same as in the atmosphere. The former soon show more KE in the zonal flow and less disturbance KE than in the atmosphere. The adjustment is effected by inertial gravity waves that disperse outward from an area of imbalance and alter the mass and motion fields. However the amplitude of these gravity waves may be erroneously large compared to the real atmosphere, especially during the first 12 to 24 hr of the simulation, and they produce spurious pressure fluctuations, vertical velocities and precipitation, mechanisms that apparently take longer to establish properly from the initial conditions provided by typical objective analyses.

The purpose of an initialization procedure is to speed up the process of adjustment, reduce the gravity noise, and improve the quality of the forecast. Clearly it would be desirable to accomplish this prior to beginning the forecast, rather than during it.

Conceptually, the simplest approach is to integrate the model forward and backward about the initial time and let the model adjust itself before starting the forecast. During this process it may be desirable to use an integration scheme with selective damping characteristics, such as the Lax-Wendroff or the Euler-backward scheme, despite its limitations. One precaution that should be taken during this ''running in place'' is to remove terms from the prediction equations that are irreversible, except for those specifically included to dampen the gravity noise.

Miyakoda and Moyer (1968) and Nitta and Hovermale (1969) carried out some early experiments that accomplished the initialization adjustment by integrating back and forth in time about the initial state, say, time zero. Since then there have been many variations of this basic concept. Either the mass or the wind field may be partially or wholly restored on passing through zero time, after integrating n steps forward, then backward, and then vice versa. Temperton (1973) integrated the nonlinear shallow-water equations in flux form with spherical coordinates forward and backward in a variety of experiments. By integrating for a sufficiently long period to eliminate the noise and bring about full adjustment, then for two more days as a control run and finally repeating those last two days starting with the rotational wind only, he verified that gravity noise returned. Indeed a divergent wind component is needed to minimize gravity noise, as predicted with a simple linear model (Section 2-7). Temperton's other experiments showed success in damping the noise by repeated cycles of integrating one hour forward, then one hour backward from the initial time and averaging the end results of wind. Twenty such cycles with mass restored after each cycle gave a considerable reduction in noise, but another 20 such cycles with the wind and mass roles reversed were necessary to reduce gravity noise approximately to that of the control run. The total processing of 40 cycles is roughly equivalent to a 80-hr forecast in computer time—much too long for operational use. The Euler backward scheme gave no better results than the leapfrog method.

Haltiner and McCullough (1975) combined the Temperton averaging method with a Robert (1966) time filter in a five-level global baroclinic PE model and reduced gravity noise substantially in the equivalent of about 12 hr of integration time, a figure somewhat more acceptable for operational use. However, the model had no mountains and contained no heat sources, both of which are primary sources for inertial gravity noise.

The following iterative scheme by Okamura (Nitta, 1969) has been shown by Temperton (1976) to be quite effective in damping external waves in a barotropic shallow-water model. Each iteration consists of a forward step, then a backward step and finally an averaging.

$$\begin{aligned} u^*_{n+1} &= u_n + \Delta t\,(\partial u/\partial t)_n \\ u^{**}_n &= u^*_{n+1} - \Delta t\,(\partial u^*/\partial t)_{n+1} \\ \overline{u}_n &= 3u_n - 2u^{**}_n \end{aligned} \tag{11-81}$$

A similar iterative procedure is applied to the geopotential field. If a harmonic solution $u_n = u_0 \exp\,[i\mu(x - ct)]$ is substituted into (11-81), the result is $\overline{u}_n = u_n(1 - 2c^2\,\mu^2\,\Delta t^2)$, which shows that the dynamic smoothing damps short wavelengths and high-frequency waves. The mass field can be restored after each iteration while the wind is forced to adjust, or the roles of the wind and geopotential fields can be reversed, or both fields can be allowed to adjust freely. An obvious drawback to the foregoing scheme is that each iteration requires the equivalent of two prognostic steps. To dampen the gravitational noise sufficiently would require many iterations that would take considerable computer time. Also such dynamic initialization is unable to distinguish between large-scale gravity modes and small-scale Rossby modes. The shorter the time between observation and the release of the forecast, the more effective the latter is, with due concern for accuracy, of course.

11-6 FOUR-DIMENSIONAL DATA ASSIMILATION

In addition to the regular upper-air observations at 12-hr intervals, 0000Z and 1200Z, there is considerable asynoptic data available between these times, especially from satellites, but also from aircraft and other occasional sources. Certainly an important part of striving for maximum accuracy of meteorological forecasts is the optimal use of observational data. As mentioned earlier, past techniques for utilizing off-time upper air data have been simply to treat it as if it were synoptic with the nearest regular upper air observation time or advect it to a new position in some rudimentary fashion. The basic concept of *four-dimensional data assimilation* is to incorporate data into a prediction model at the time of observation. However, several factors must be taken into consideration, for example, introduction of new data shocks the model and creates spurious inertial gravity noise, also observational errors may be greater than changes in the meteorological variables during a period of one to several hours, and the additional computer time needed to process the asynoptic data must be considered. As a practical matter, therefore, data should probably be incorporated at intervals of no less than several hours, perhaps three.

The typical analysis-forecast cycle for many years has consisted of analyses at 12-hr intervals followed by forecasts to 72 hr or more. The 12-hr forecast, say from 0000Z, is normally used as a first-guess field for the next objective analysis at 1200Z. However, between 0000Z and 1200Z considerable asynoptic data is available that could be used to obtain a better first-guess field for the 1200Z analysis than the original 12-hr forecast from 0000Z. To assimilate the asynoptic data, new data between say 2100Z and 0300Z, could be considered to be synoptic with 0000Z data for an updated analysis; and data between 0300 and 0900 synoptic at 0600Z, at which time an objective analysis and initialization procedure could be applied using a forecast from reanalyzed 0000Z data as a first guess. After the initialization at 0600Z is completed a prediction would be carried out to 1200Z. Then data observed between 0900Z and 1200Z would be assimilated with the regular synoptic 1200Z data. The cycle would be repeated to reach the next regular observation time at 0000Z, and so forth.

The choice of one asynoptic assimilation at 0600Z is arbitrary and only used for illustration purposes, *two* or *three* assimilations between synoptic times may be preferable. In any event, the entire asynoptic assimilation procedure need not be applied over the entire forecast region, but perhaps confined to areas where asynoptic data is available; elsewhere the forecast may be accepted without alteration. Note however that new information may be advected into sparse-data areas improving the analysis and forecast there.

The success of the foregoing suggested four-dimensional assimilation scheme is dependent on the ability of the assimilation scheme to control the spurious inertial gravity noise produced by data ingestion. Several possibilities described earlier are the following: a multivariate analysis scheme including hydrostatic and balanced constraints or a static initialization procedure, perhaps followed by some dynamical filtering using a differencing scheme with selective scale and frequency damping. As another alternative, Bengtsson (1976) has suggested the use of a filtered model to assimilate observations during a 12-hr interval, thus generating no noise. A spectral model with stream function ψ and velocity potential χ could also be used to suppress nonmeteorological modes. And the normal mode initialization procedure could be used either with a spectral or gridpoint model, but this would be at least on a hemisphere basis and therefore probably best confined to the standard upper-air observation times. Sasaki (1975) has suggested a "noise freezing" technique whereby the gravity waves are caused to remain nearly stationary while assimilation of asynoptic data is effected between regular synoptic times. Bengtsson (1976) has given a detailed summary of data processing, objective analysis, and initialization schemes in use as of that date.

11-7 NEWTONIAN RELAXATION OR "NUDGING"

Another technique of dynamic initialization and four-dimensional assimilation is known as Newtonian relaxation or more simply as "nudging" [Kistler (1974), Anthes et al., (1974), and Hoke and Anthes (1976)]. In this method there is preforecast integration period during which the model variables are driven toward the observations by extra forcing terms in the equations. When the actual initial time is reached, the extra terms are dropped from the model equations and the forecast proceeds minus any forcing. A principal objective is to bring the data and model in harmony and provide a relatively noise-free start. The steps may be summarized as follows:

1. Specify the initial condition for the preforecast period T at say, $(t_0 - T)$, where t_0 is the initial time for a new forecast, presumably a standard analysis time.
2. Carry out the preforecast or assimilation integration from $(t_0 - T)$ to t_0 by including extra terms in the model equations to force the variables during the preforecast toward gridpoint values determined by observations.
3. Carry out the actual forecast from t_0 after dropping the forcing or nudging terms.

The equations for a particular gridpoint variable α may be expressed in the form

$$\frac{\partial \alpha}{\partial t} = F + N(\alpha,t)\,\varepsilon[\alpha^{(0)} - \alpha] \qquad (11\text{-}82)$$

where F represents the usual terms in the model equations; $N(\alpha,t)$ is a non-negative nudging coefficient; and ε, a positive weight factor ≤ 1, is a confidence factor with respect to the accuracy of the gridpoint value $\alpha^{(0)}(t)$ which is a best estimate based upon observations. If $\alpha^{(0)}(t)$ is assumed to be the true value, ε would be 1.

In order to get a feeling for the effects of nudging, consider a few very simple cases. First assume that the physical forcing F is zero, and further that N is constant and $\varepsilon = 1$. (Then 11-82) reduces to

$$\frac{\partial \alpha}{\partial t} = N[\alpha^{(0)} - \alpha], \text{ or } \alpha = \alpha_0 e^{-Nt} + Ne^{-Nt}\int_0^t e^{Nt}\alpha^{(0)}\,dt \qquad (11\text{-}83)$$

where $t = 0$ represents the beginning of the preforecast period and α_0 is the value of α at $t = 0$. If $\alpha^{(0)}(t)$ is assumed to be constant in time toward which α is nudged, the solution of (11-83) is

$$\alpha = \alpha^{(0)} + (\alpha_0 - \alpha^{(0)})\, e^{-Nt}$$

Thus α approaches the observed value $\alpha^{(0)}$ as time passes, though of course never reaching it in a finite time T.

As a second case assume the atmosphere and also the observations are changing linearly with time [i.e., $\alpha^{(0)} = \alpha_0^{(0)} + at$]. The solution for this case is

$$\alpha = \alpha^{(0)}(t) + [\alpha_0 - \alpha_0^{(0)}]\, e^{-Nt} - (a/N)\,(1 - e^{-Nt})$$

In this instance it is seen that the initial error, if such exists, is damped toward zero with increasing time (second term on right-hand side) but the third term approaches $(-a/N)$. Thus at best α approaches the observationally determined value $\alpha^{(0)}$ only to within the constant a/N, which is the ratio of the rate of change of $\alpha^{(0)}$ to the nudging constant. Also for a large N, the last term will be small.

The nudging method can be used to drive the model vorticity toward an "observed" value by including the terms of the form, $-N\, \partial[\zeta - \zeta^{(0)}]/\partial y$ and $N\, \partial[\zeta - \zeta^{(0)}]/\partial x$ in the right side of the x- and y-momentum equations. Or again, divergence may be damped by a "nudging" term as discussed in Section 11-4-2. The latter would tend to reduce the magnitude of divergent wind components while the former drives the wind velocity toward the "observed" rotational wind component. Note also that because of the nature of the nudging terms, that is, damping or diffusion, the terms must be evaluated at $(t - \Delta t)$, (time step $n - 1$), when central time differencing (leapfrog) is applied to the numerical integration of the preforecast period in order to maintain computational stability (see Section 5-9).

The preceding simple cases have been mainly concerned only with a single variable rather than a complete system of equations and the physical forcing has been omitted. In order to treat a more complete system analytically, the shallow water equations with nudging terms added are linearized about a state of rest with constant coriolis parameter f and no variation in the y-direction [Hoke and Anthes (1976)]. Assuming periodic disturbances of the form

$$\overline{\mathbf{X}}' = \sum_m \hat{X}_m \exp(ik_m x)$$

where $\overline{\mathbf{X}}'$ is a column vector of the perturbation quantities u', v', and h', $k_m = 2\pi/L_m$, is the mth wavenumber and the $\hat{X}_m$ are the corresponding amplitudes, the equations for the amplitudes take the form

$$\frac{\partial}{\partial t}\begin{pmatrix} \hat{u}_m \\ \hat{v}_m \\ \hat{h}_m \end{pmatrix} + \begin{pmatrix} N_u & -f & ik_m g \\ f & N_v & 0 \\ ik_m H & 0 & N_h \end{pmatrix}\begin{pmatrix} \hat{u}_m \\ \hat{v}_m \\ \hat{h}_m \end{pmatrix} = \begin{pmatrix} N_u\, \hat{u}_m^{(0)} \\ N_v\, \hat{v}_m^{(0)} \\ N_h\, \hat{h}_m^{(0)} \end{pmatrix}$$

or

$$\partial \mathbf{X}/\partial t + A\mathbf{X} = \mathbf{B}$$

Assuming the nudging coefficients and "observations" do not vary in time, the matrix A and vector $\mathbf{B}$ are constants, and the solution is given by a constant vector, $A^{-1}\mathbf{B}$, and a time-varying part:

$$\mathbf{X} = A^{-1}\mathbf{B} + \sum_{j=1}^{3} \mathbf{C}_j e^{-\sigma_j t} \tag{11-84a}$$

where the σ_j are the eigenvalues of A and the $\mathbf{C}_j$ are constant vectors that depend on the initial conditions $\mathbf{X}(0)$ and $A^{-1}\mathbf{B}$. The $\mathbf{C}_j$ can be determined given $\mathbf{X}(0)$ and $\mathbf{X}^{(0)}$ by placing $t = 0$ in (11-84a). In the case where the constant "observations" are in geostrophic balance, that is, $\hat{u}_m^{(0)} = 0$ and $\hat{v}_m^{(0)} = (igk_m/f)\hat{h}^{(0)}$, then $\mathbf{X}^{(0)} = A^{-1}\mathbf{B}$; hence

$$\mathbf{X} - \mathbf{X}^{(0)} = \mathbf{C}_1 e^{-\sigma_1 t} + \mathbf{C}_2 e^{-\sigma_2 t} + \mathbf{C}_3 e^{-\sigma_3 t} \tag{11-84b}$$

Assuming further that the nudging coefficients are all equal to N leads to a stationary mode $\sigma_1 = N$, and $\sigma_{2,3} = N \pm i\upsilon$, where $\upsilon^2 = \omega^2 + f^2$. Here υ is the frequency of inertial gravity waves and $\omega^2 = k_m^2\, gH$. Thus there is a stationary mode damped by the nudging coefficient and two damped inertial gravity modes with a resulting approach toward the observational values $\mathbf{X}^{(0)}$.

Hoke and Anthes (1976) consider some more general cases where all of the variables are not known and the geostrophic balance is not imposed. Using a typical midlatitude value of f and $H = 10^3$m corresponding more to an internal gravity mode the following results were obtained for strong and moderate nudging of either winds or geopotential. With *strong* nudging ($N = 10^{-3}$ sec^{-1}) of the total wind, long stationary waves are damped very slowly; however, the oscillating modes are rapidly damped. Strong nudging of the *rotational* wind component damps only the stationary mode well, but not the oscillating modes. Finally, strong nudging of the geopotential only gives poor damping of both the stationary short waves and the long oscillating waves. With open boundary conditions for a limited area, intialization with the rotational wind only is better than with the total wind because by not interfering with the divergent wind component the geostrophic adjustment process can take place and the oscillating waves can leave the region.

With *moderate* nudging (10^{-4} sec^{-1}) the damping is reduced and a more natural inertial gravity-wave response is permitted, nevertheless the damping is satisfactory for preinitialization periods of 1 day. Nudging the *geopotential* only damps the long stationary wave quite rapidly but not short waves; the opposite is true of the oscillating waves. Nudging *both wind* components damps only the short stationary wave but damps all oscillating modes. Nudging only the divergent component damps only the short stationary waves and the long oscillating mode. Overall, then, *moderate* nudging of the total wind is best compromise, although not ideal.

The previous analytical results, obtained from the linearized shallow-water equations, were borne out with a numerically integrated nonlinear version that included some simple diffusion terms. Some further results were that dynamic initialization by nudging should be avoided at isolated points near boundaries to avoid increasing noise that tends to develop. The latter can be controlled by diffusion terms and, if feasible, the use of sponge boundary conditions that absorb perturbations. Also when nudging is performed to observations that are locally concentrated or isolated, local adjustments take place that lead to small-scale fluctuations. This problem can be reduced by carrying out a careful static initialization prior to the dynamic part over a sizable area, or the entire region, in order to extend the influence of the observations in a consistent dynamical way.

If this technique is applied to assimilate asynoptic data during the preforecast integration period, say from 0000 to 1200, the procedure would begin with the usual analysis of the 1200 data by optimal interpolation or another method, based upon an already completed forecast from 0000 as a first guess. Also analyses could be prepared over limited areas where asynoptic data were adequate, perhaps at 0300, 0600, and 0900 between the complete analyses at 0000 and 1200. By interpolation between these times observational fields $\alpha^{(0)}(n\Delta t)$ could be generated, toward which the variables could be nudged for each time step. The procedure would be rather complex and problems can arise at the edges of analyses of asynoptic data (e.g., satellite swaths). In conclusion, the method appears to have promise but more experimentation is needed.

11-8 SMOOTHING AND FILTERING

In various places in the text it has been mentioned that because of numerical errors, computational instabilities, etc., there may be a spurious growth of short waves, which if left unchecked could blow up and obscure a meteorological forecast. Even if a catastrophic instability does not arise it is usually desirable to eliminate very high wave number components for aesthetic reasons. In spectral models short waves can be automatically removed by systematically omitting wave numbers larger than some arbitrarily chosen value. In the finite-difference integration schemes, explicit or implicit diffusion can be included in the difference equations to suppress the high wave numbers. Nevertheless, systematic explicit smoothing is very often included in operational prediction schemes, at least for the final products.

In order to gain some insight about smoothing techniques, consider the simple one-dimensional three-point operator (Shapiro, 1970, 1975)

$$\overline{f}_j = (1 - S)f_j + \frac{S}{2}(f_{j+1} + f_{j-1}) \qquad (11\text{-}85)$$

where $x = j\Delta x$ and S is a constant which may be negative. If the operator is applied to the harmonic form

$$f = Ae^{ikx}$$

where the wave number $k = 2\pi/L$ and A is a constant which may be complex, the result is

$$\bar{f} = Rf \tag{11-86a}$$

Here R, referred to as the *response* function, is given by

$$R = 1 - S(1 - \cos k\Delta x) = 1 - 2S \sin^2 \pi\Delta x/L \tag{11-86b}$$

It is evident that this particular smoothing operator does not affect the wave number nor the phase (provided $R \geq 0$) of the original wave but only its amplitude. If $|R| > 1$, the wave is *amplified* by the operation, while $|R| < 1$ results in *damping*. Note that a negative R would be undesirable here since the operation would then produce a 180° phase shift from the original wave.

It may also be shown that the average value of the smoothed function approaches that of the original function as the domain increases. From (11-85) it follows that

$$\frac{1}{2J+1}\sum_{j=-J}^{J} \bar{f}_j = \frac{1}{2J+1}\sum_{j=-J}^{J} f_j + \frac{S}{2(2J+1)}\sum_{j=-J}^{J} (f_{j+1} - 2f_j + f_{j-1})$$

$$= \frac{1}{2J+1}\sum f_j + \frac{S}{4J+2}(f_{J+1} - f_J - f_{-J} + f_{-J-1})$$

It may now be seen that the last term will approach zero as J approaches infinity, which establishes the desired result.

Consider next some special cases. With $S = \frac{1}{2}$ (11-85) becomes

$$\bar{f}_j = f_j + \tfrac{1}{4}(f_{j+1} - 2f_j + f_{j-1}) = \tfrac{1}{4}(f_{j+1} + 2f_j + f_{j-1})$$

or

$$\bar{f}_j = f_j + \tfrac{1}{4}\nabla_x^2 f_j \tag{11-87}$$

where

$$\nabla_x^2 f_j = f_{j+1} - 2f_j + f_{j-1}$$

From (11-86) the response function with $S = \frac{1}{2}$ is

$$R(\tfrac{1}{2}) = 1 - \tfrac{1}{2}(1 - \cos k\,\Delta x) = 1 - \sin^2 \pi\Delta x/L = \cos^2 \pi\Delta x/L \tag{11-88}$$

Now for $L = 2\Delta x$, $R = 0$, hence *two-gridlength waves will be removed* by the smoother (11-87). As pointed out in Chapter 5, wavelengths less than $2\Delta x$

cannot be resolved on a grid with a spacing of Δx, hence any such harmonics will appear in longer wavelengths through aliasing. Moreover according to (11-88), wavelengths larger than $2\Delta x$ will be damped by the smoother. For example, with $L = 10\Delta x$,

$$R(\tfrac{1}{2}) = \cos^2 \pi/10 = 0.905$$

which is less than 10 percent reduction in amplitude. However if this smoothing operator is applied 10 times the amplitude is reduced to 0.37 of the original value, and after 100 applications a wavelength of $10\Delta x$ will have essentially vanished. For such repetitions of the simple operator (11-87) the response function is obviously

$$R^m(\tfrac{1}{2}) = \cos^{2m} \pi \Delta x/L \tag{11-89}$$

Consider next the case $S = 1$, for which $\bar{f}_j = (f_{j+1} + f_{j-1})/2$. Then the response function turns out to be

$$R(1) = \cos 2\pi \, \Delta x/L \tag{11-90}$$

which results in a 180° phase change for wavelengths between $4\Delta x/3$ and $4\Delta x$. With two applications of this operator the phase change is prevented since $R^2(1) = \cos^2 2\pi \, \Delta x/L$. This result is similar to (11-89) except that it applies to twice the grid distance.

It is apparent that repeated applications of the simple smoother (11-87) would be undesirable because of excessive damping of even medium and long waves. In fact, it would be desirable to leave waves longer than several grid-lengths relatively unaffected. It is possible to accomplish this objective by a judicious combination of several smoothers, which results in an effective filter for a specified wave band.

According to (11-86) the response function corresponding to a series of smoothers of the form (11-85) with coefficients $S_1, S_2, \ldots, S_n$ would be

$$R_n(S, k) = R_1 R_2 \ldots R_n = \prod_{i=1}^{n} (1 - 2S_i \sin^2 k \, \Delta x/2) \tag{11-91}$$

Consider the case with just two smoothing operators. Since it is generally desirable to remove two-gridlength noise, one of the two operators will be (11-90), hence $S_1 = \tfrac{1}{2}$. The second constant S_2 is undetermined as yet. Thus the response function may be written

$$R_2(S_2, k) = (1 - \sin^2 k \, \Delta x/2)(1 - 2S_2 \sin^2 k \, \Delta x/2) \tag{11-92}$$

It follows that $R_2 = 0$ for $k = \pi/\Delta x$, i.e., $L = 2\Delta x$. Moreover R approaches 1 as k approaches 0, i.e., as $L \to \infty$; so that infinitely long waves remain unaffected. In order to specify other properties of the response function (11-

92), the first and second derivatives of R_2 with respect to k may be calculated with the results

$$\frac{dR_2}{dk} = -\Delta x \sin\frac{k\,\Delta x}{2}\cos\frac{k\,\Delta x}{2}(1 + 2S_2\cos k\,\Delta x) \tag{11-93}$$

$$\frac{d^2R_2}{dk^2} = (\Delta x)^2[S_2\sin^2 k\,\Delta x - \tfrac{1}{2}\cos k\,\Delta x(1 + 2S_2\cos k\,\Delta x)] \tag{11-94}$$

It is evident from (11-93) that the extrema, for which $dR_2/dk = 0$, occur at the following values of k:

$$k\,\Delta x/2 = 0, \pi/2, \pi, 3\pi/2, 2\pi, \ldots \tag{11-95}$$

and also at the particular wave number k^* for which

$$\cos k^*\,\Delta x = -1/2S_2 \tag{11-96}$$

The values of k in (11-95) correspond to the wavelengths $L = \infty, 2\Delta x, \Delta x, 2\Delta x/3, \Delta x/2$, etc., and the corresponding values of R_2 are either 1 or 0. When the relation (11-96) is substituted into (11-74) it may be seen that R_2 is a maximum or a minimum according to whether S_2 is negative or positive, respectively. The corresponding value of R_2 at k^* is found to be

$$R_2 = -\frac{1}{8S_2}(2S_2 - 1)^2 \tag{11-97}$$

If there is to be no amplification of any wave, then R_2 cannot exceed 1. Substituting the maximum value $R_2 = 1$ into (11-97) gives the value $S_2 = -\tfrac{1}{2}$. On the other hand, if phase changes are to be avoided, the minimum value of the response function R_2 at k^* must be zero. Now for $R_2 = 0$, (11-97) gives $S = \tfrac{1}{2}$. However, the use of this value in (11-92) merely corresponds to $m = 2$ in (11-89) and produces further damping of all wavelengths larger than $2\Delta x$. Since the objective is to restore the amplitudes of wavelengths larger than $2\Delta x$, the value $S_2 = -\tfrac{1}{2}$ is chosen with the resulting response

$$\begin{aligned} R_2(k) &= (1 - \sin^2 k\,\Delta x/2)(1 + \sin^2 k\,\Delta x/2) \\ &= (1 - \sin^4 k\,\Delta x/2) \end{aligned} \tag{11-98}$$

For values of $S_2 < -\tfrac{1}{2}$, there will be amplification of some wavelengths. If $2S_2 = -(1 + \varepsilon)$, where $\varepsilon > 0$, then

$$R_2(L) > 1 \qquad \text{when} \qquad \sin^2 \pi\,\Delta x/L < \varepsilon/(1 + \varepsilon)$$

This results in amplification of waves longer than a certain critical value and also certain short waves that are not resolvable on the grid system, but by aliasing can feed energy into longer waves. In general this is undesirable but may be acceptable under some circumstances.

If it is desired to restore the amplitude of a particular wavelength L' to the original value, the value of $k' = 2\pi/L'$ can be substituted into (11-92) with $R_2(S_2, k') = 1$. The appropriate value of S_2 is then found to be

$$S_2 = -\tfrac{1}{2} \sec^2 \pi \, \Delta x/L' \tag{11-99}$$

The procedure described here for restoring the amplitude of wavelengths larger than $2\Delta x$ with the resulting response function (11-92) can be extended to more operators. A logical extension might be to find a constant S_3 corresponding to the response function

$$R_3 = (1 - \sin^4 k \, \Delta x/2)(1 - 2S_3 \sin^2 k \, \Delta x/2) \tag{11-100}$$

Proceeding as before, it is found that $S_2 = \pm i/4$. As a consequence, these values must be used as a complex conjugate pair in order for the smoothed result to remain real. Thus (11-100) should have had the form

$$R_4 = (1 - \sin^4 k \, \Delta x/2)(1 - 2S_3 \sin^2 k \, \Delta x/2)(1 + 2S_3 \sin^2 k \, \Delta x/2)$$

and the procedure now leads to $S_3 = \pm i/2$. The resulting response function is

$$R_4 = (1 - \sin^4 k \, \Delta x/2)(1 - i \sin^2 k \, \Delta x/2)(1 + i \sin^2 k \, \Delta x/2)$$

$$= (1 - \sin^8 k \, \Delta x/2) \tag{11-101}$$

This procedure can be generalized to yield an operator which will filter two-gridlength "noise"; and, with neither amplification nor phase change of any wave, result in arbitrarily small damping of longer wavelengths. An operator with such a response function is referred to as a *low-pass filter*. For an n'th order operator consisting of constants $S_1 = \tfrac{1}{2}, S_2, S_3, \ldots, S_n$, there are two real smoothing elements and $(n - 2)$ elements comprised of complex conjugate pairs with n restricted to the values

$$n = 2^j \qquad j = 0, 1, 2, \ldots \tag{11-102}$$

For $j \geq 1$, there are $(j - 1)$ conjugate pairs. For example, where $n = 8$, $j = 3$, and there are two conjugate pairs $\pm \tfrac{1}{2}i^{1/2}$, $\pm \tfrac{1}{2}ii^{1/2}$, in addition to the previous set corresponding to (11-101), namely, $S_1 = \tfrac{1}{2}$, $S_2 = -\tfrac{1}{2}$, $S_3 = \pm i/2$. The resulting response function is easily found to be

$$R_8 = (1 - \sin^{16} k \, \Delta x/2) \tag{11-103}$$

For a wavelength of $4\Delta x$, the response function is $R_4 = 0.93750$ and $R_8 = 0.99609$; while for $L = 3\Delta x$, $R_8 = 0.89989$.

In progressively obtaining the smoothing coefficients corresponding to the general response function $(1 - \sin^{2n} k \, \Delta x/2)$, the coefficients corresponding to the factor $(1 - \sin^n k \, \Delta x/2)$ would have already been determined; hence only those associated with the factor $(1 + \sin^n k\, \Delta x/2)$ would have to be found. These may be constructed for any value of n from the roots of the equation

$$(2S)^{n/2} = -1 \tag{11-104}$$

For example, with $n = 1$, $S = ½$, with $n = 2$, $S = -½$, and with $n = 4$, $S = \pm i/2$, and so forth.

11-8-1 Two-Dimensional Smoothers

The smoothing procedures described previously for one dimension can be easily extended to two dimensions. For example, the simple smoother (11-85) can be applied sequentially to the two directions or simultaneously, namely,

$$\overline{f}_{i\,j}^{i,\,j} = \overline{f}_{i\,j}^{i\;\;i} = \overline{f}_{i\,j}^{j\;\;i} \tag{11-105}$$

$$\overline{f}_{i\,j}^{i\,j} = ½(\overline{f}_{i\,j}^{i} + \overline{f}_{i\,j}^{j}) \tag{11-106}$$

The sequential application (11-105) clearly represents a nine-point operator, while (11-106) is a five-point operator. Note that the order of applying the operators is immaterial. Expanding (11-105) and (11-106) gives

$$\begin{aligned}\overline{f}_{i\,j}^{i,\,j} = (1 - S)^2 f_{i\,j} + S(S - 1)\,(f_{i+1j} + f_{i-1j} + f_{ij+1} + f_{ij-1})/2 \\ + S^2\,(f_{i-1j-1} + f_{i-1j+1} + f_{i+1j} + f_{i-1j-1})/4\end{aligned} \tag{11-107}$$

$$\overline{f}_{i\,j}^{i\,j} = (1 - S)\,f_{i\,j} + S(f_{i-1j} + f_{i+1j} + f_{ij-1} + f_{ij+1})/4 \tag{11-108}$$

If the simple harmonic function $Ae^{i(kx+ly)}$ is substituted into (11-107) and (11-108), it is easily found that the corresponding response functions are, respectively,

$$R(k,\, 1) = (1 - 2S \sin^2 k\, \Delta x/2)(1 - 2S \sin^2 l\, \Delta y/2) \tag{11-109}$$

$$R(k1) = i - S(\sin^2 k\, \Delta x/2 + \sin^2 l\, \Delta y/2) \tag{11-110}$$

The response function (11-109) corresponding to the nine-point operator (11-107) has the same form as (11-85) and hence has the advantage that the technique used earlier to generalize the one-dimensional operators is applicable.

11-8-2 Bandpass Filters

The emphasis in the discussion thus far has been on low-pass filters, which remove the undesirable short wavelength components. However, this filter may be utilized to isolate and retain the short wavelengths. This is easily accomplished by subtracting the filtered field from the original function, which is equivalent to a *high-bandpass* filter with the response function $(1 - R_n)$.

Linear combinations of operators may also be used to dampen or isolate a particular band of wavelengths, the result being a *bandpass filter*. Thus the response function of a bandpass filter would be $R_a(f) - R_b(f)$, provided $a < b$. Particular bands can be isolated by appropriate choices of a and b.

11-8-3 Boundary Effects

No mention has been made thus far about the effects of boundaries on the smoothed functions. However, it is evident from the simple smoothing operator (11-85) that a boundary value will influence the smoothed value at the first interior point after one application. With repeated applications of the smoothing operator the influence of the boundary value will propagate inward one gridpoint per application. The final result after a large number of applications depends on the form of the smoothing operator and the type of boundary conditions.

When zero boundary conditions are imposed, a non-zero mean value of the function may be decreased and spurious growth may occur for certain long-wave components if the coefficient $S_2 < -\frac{1}{2}$. This problem can sometimes be avoided by insuring that the function has a zero mean value over the domain. Of course, another way of avoiding this problem is to use an operator that does not amplify any wave.

In general, when dealing with finite domains, periodic boundary conditions are ideal, according to Shapiro. However, if the imposition of such periodicity is not feasible, a nonamplifying smoothing operator is probably best.

CHAPTER 12

Ocean Dynamics and Modeling

12-1 INTRODUCTION

The large-scale ocean circulation is primarily driven by atmospheric wind stress and the exchange of heat with the atmosphere including solar insolation. Processes that affect the salinity such as evaporation, precipitation, and river runoff may also play a role. Numerical weather prediction techniques have been successfully applied to the simulation of large-scale ocean circulations. These modeling efforts are similar to the general circulation models of the atmosphere, but they must also treat the different time and space scales in the ocean.

This chapter treats the construction of various ocean models and it provides some supporting dyamical theory. The synoptic scale eddies, which have a large amplitude in many parts of the ocean, are discussed because they can affect the large-scale ocean circulations. Finally, models of the surface or mixed layer of the ocean are also described because of their importance in the interaction between the atmosphere and the ocean. In addition to a direct importance with respect to the ocean, a capability of predicting the sea surface temperatures is an obvious benefit to forecasting weather elements such as fog, visibility, wind, turbulence, etc. over local areas and through heat and moisture fluxes over large regions for their effect on the synoptic and planetary scales for both short and long range. Recent studies by Namias (1978) have indicated a possible relationship between sea surface temperature anomalies in the Pacific Ocean and West Coast weather over periods of several months.

12-2 WIND-DRIVEN BAROTROPIC MODELS

This section treats a barotropic ocean that is forced by a simple time-invariant wind stress field. The ocean is confined in a rectangular basin and the depth is uniform. The equation of motion for a fluid of constant density with horizontal and vertical friction is:

$$\frac{\partial \mathbf{V}}{\partial t} + \mathbf{V} \cdot \nabla \mathbf{V} + w \frac{\partial \mathbf{V}}{\partial z} = -\frac{1}{\rho_0} \nabla p - f\mathbf{k} \times \mathbf{V} + \frac{1}{\rho_0} \frac{\partial \boldsymbol{\tau}}{\partial z} + A \nabla^2 \mathbf{V} \quad (12\text{-}1)$$

where $\boldsymbol{\tau}$ is the Reynolds stress that involves the turbulent vertical motion and A is the horizontal eddy diffusion coefficient. The hydrostatic equation is written

$$\frac{\partial p}{\partial z} = - \rho_0 g \tag{12-2}$$

This equation shows that the horizontal pressure gradient force is independent of z (take del of (12-2)), so that it is appropriate to take $\mathbf{V}$ independent of z except in the boundary layers at the top and bottom of the ocean. A vorticity equation can be formed by applying $\mathbf{k} \cdot \nabla \times$ to (12-1), which gives

$$\frac{\partial \zeta}{\partial t} + \mathbf{V} \cdot \nabla \zeta + v\beta + (\zeta + f)\, \nabla \cdot \mathbf{V} = \frac{1}{\rho_0} \mathbf{k} \cdot \nabla \times \frac{\partial \boldsymbol{\tau}}{\partial z} + A\nabla^2 \zeta \tag{12-3}$$

The Rossby number ($Ro = V/fL$) is quite small in the ocean and it reaches 0.1 only in the boundary currents where the velocity is large ($V \sim 1$ m sec^{-1}) and the scale is small ($L \sim 10^5$ m). Thus the currents are highly geostrophic and also $f >> \zeta$ as was shown in Chapter 3. The continuity equation for incompressible flow is

$$\nabla \cdot \mathbf{V} = - \frac{\partial w}{\partial z} \tag{12-4}$$

which can be used to replace the divergence term in (12-3) with $- f\partial w/\partial z$.

The upper free surface is replaced by a rigid boundary at $z = 0$ and the lower boundary, which is flat, is placed at $z = -H$. The former condition excludes external gravity waves. Now, integrate the modified form of (12-3) from $z = -H$ to $z = 0$ and use $\partial \mathbf{V}/\partial z = 0$ (excluding boundary layers), which yields:

$$\frac{\partial \zeta}{\partial t} + \mathbf{V} \cdot \nabla \zeta + v\beta - \frac{f}{H}[w(0) - w(-H)]$$

$$= \frac{1}{H\rho_0} \mathbf{k} \cdot \nabla \times [\boldsymbol{\tau}(0) - \boldsymbol{\tau}(-H)] + A\nabla^2 \zeta$$

The vertical boundary conditions are:

$$w(-H) = w(0) = 0 \tag{12-5}$$

$$\boldsymbol{\tau}(-H) = c\mathbf{V}, \qquad \boldsymbol{\tau}(0) = \boldsymbol{\tau}_0 \tag{12-6}$$

where $\boldsymbol{\tau}_0$ is the surface wind stress. When these boundary conditions are used the vorticity equation reduces to the form:

$$\frac{\partial \zeta}{\partial t} + \mathbf{V} \cdot \nabla \zeta + v\beta = \mathbf{k} \cdot \nabla \times (\boldsymbol{\tau}_0/H\rho_0) - K\zeta + A\nabla^2 \zeta \tag{12-7}$$

An equation with the same form as (12-7) can be obtained by integrating from the top of the lower boundary layer to the bottom of the upper boundary layer.

The vertical velocities are no longer zero, but they are obtained by integrating the Ekman layer solutions (see Section 8-3). The form is exactly the same as (12-7), but $K = (c_v/f)^{1/2}$ where c_v is the vertical eddy diffusion coefficient.

The first term on the right of (12-7) provides the forcing and the other terms on the right lead to damping. The beta term is the largest term on the left throughout most of the ocean.

Stommel (1948) solved (12-3) by assuming a steady state, and neglecting the vorticity advection and diffusion ($A = 0$). He used the following wind stress field:

$$\boldsymbol{\tau}_0 = \tau_0 \cos(\pi y/W)\mathbf{i} \tag{12-8}$$

where τ_0 is a constant. The ocean is confined in the region that is defined by $0 \leq x \leq W$, $0 \leq y \leq W$. This stress profile roughly approximates the mean surface zonal wind, which varies from easterly at low latitudes to westerly at higher latitudes. With these simplifications the vorticity equation (12-7) becomes

$$\beta \frac{\partial \psi}{\partial x} + K\nabla^2\psi = -\frac{\tau_0 \pi}{\rho_0 H W} \sin \pi y/W \tag{12-9}$$

where the stream function is introduced through $\mathbf{V} = \mathbf{k} \times \nabla\psi$, which is a good approximation since the Rossby number is small (see Chapter 3). The boundary conditions on ψ are:

$$\psi = 0 \begin{cases} x = 0, W; & 0 \leq y \leq W \\ y = 0, W; & 0 \leq x \leq W \end{cases} \tag{12-10}$$

Equation 12-9 may be solved by writing

$$\psi = F(x) \sin \pi y/W$$

When this expression is introduced into (12-9), the resulting equation for F can be solved so that $F = 0$ for $x = 0, W$. This solution is given by

$$\psi = \frac{\tau_0 W}{\rho_0 \pi K H}$$

$$\left\{1 - e^{-\alpha x} \frac{[(e^{-2rW} - e^{(\alpha - r)W})\, e^{rx} + (e^{(\alpha - r)W} - 1)\, e^{-rx}]}{e^{-2rW} - 1}\right\} \sin \pi y/W \tag{12-11}$$

where $\alpha \equiv \beta/(2K)$, $r \equiv (\alpha^2 + (\pi/W)^2)^{1/2}$. Figure 12-1 shows the circulation pattern for this solution. This circulation is strongly asymmetric, with a strong jet from south to north along the western boundary and a weak flow toward the south throughout the rest of the ocean.

The general behavior of this solution can be explained by performing a scale analysis (see Chapter 3) on the left-hand side of (12-9). If L is the horizontal length scale, the ratio of the terms is given by

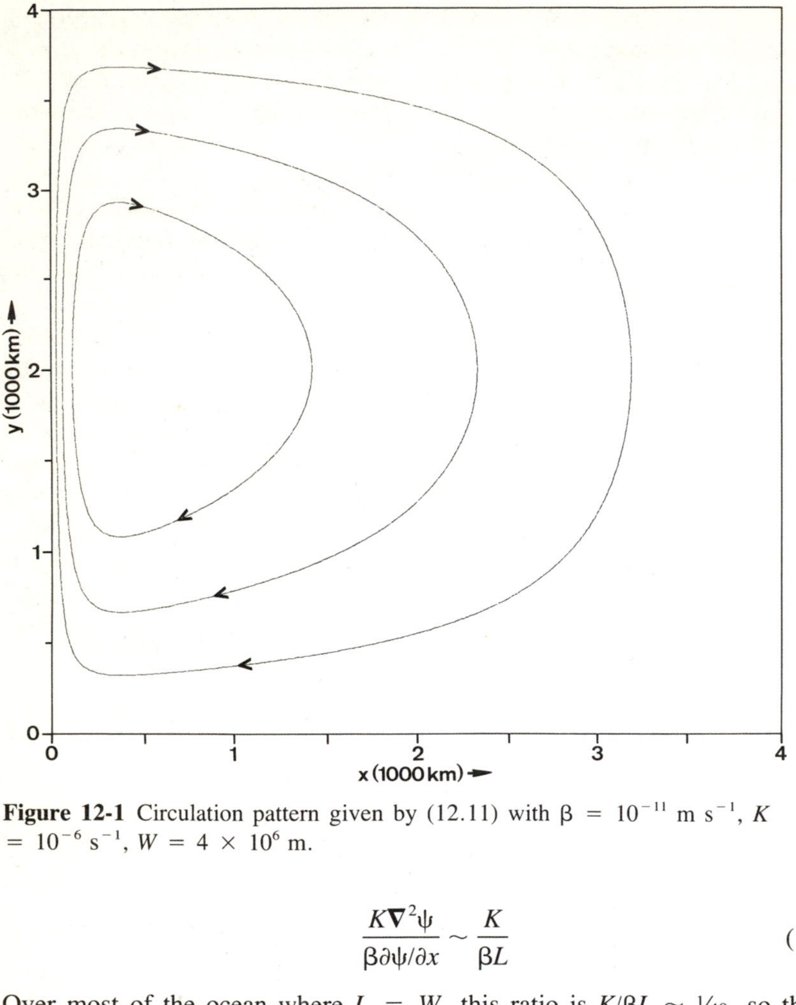

Figure 12-1 Circulation pattern given by (12.11) with $\beta = 10^{-11}$ m s^{-1}, $K = 10^{-6}$ s^{-1}, $W = 4 \times 10^6$ m.

$$\frac{K\nabla^2\psi}{\beta\partial\psi/\partial x} \sim \frac{K}{\beta L} \tag{12-12}$$

Over most of the ocean where $L = W$, this ratio is $K/\beta L \sim$ 1/40, so that the friction term can be dropped. Equation 12-9 then reduces to

$$\beta\frac{\partial\psi}{\partial x} = \beta v = -\frac{\tau_0\pi}{\rho_0 HW}\sin(\pi y/W) \tag{12-13}$$

which is called the *Sverdrup balance*. Note that this current is everywhere southward (because of the form of Stommel's wind field), so that a strong northward boundary current is required for mass balance. In the western boundary region the beta term must be large and it can no longer be balanced by the wind stress term, but it can be balanced by the friction term if the ratio in (12-12) is of order 1, which gives the length scale

$$L_B \sim \frac{K}{\beta} \tag{12-14}$$

With the numbers used above (which are somewhat arbitrary), this gives a boundary layer thickness of 100 km. Ocean problems where most of the region has a simple balance such as (12-13) but where boundary layers are required, are ideally suited to boundary layer techniques (Veronis, 1965; Greenspan, 1968).

The circulation shown in Figure 12-1 is generally similar to that observed in the North Atlantic. The boundary current corresponds to the Gulf Stream and its scale of about 100 km is reasonable. Velocities of 1 m $\sec^{-1}$ in the boundary current and a few cm $\sec^{-1}$ in the Sverdrup region can be computed from (12-13) by setting $\tau_0 = 1$ dyne cm^{-2}, $H = 200$ m. This value of H, which is small in comparison with the average ocean depth (4 km), is chosen because the strongest currents are mainly near the surface. The computed typical velocities are again reasonable for the North Atlantic and other ocean basins.

Other barotropic ocean circulation models are obtained by dropping or retaining different terms in (12-7). In most models the balance in the ocean interior is between the beta term and the curl of the wind stress, which gives the Sverdrup transport. In the boundary layer the beta term is balanced by one of the friction terms or by vorticity advection. Each model gives an anticyclonic gyre with the main differences being near the boundaries.

Munk (1950) included the horizontal diffusion term, but he neglected bottom friction, which reduces (12-7) to:

$$\beta \frac{\partial \psi}{\partial x} - A\nabla^4\psi = \frac{1}{\rho_0 H} \mathbf{k} \cdot \nabla \times \boldsymbol{\tau}_0 \qquad (12\text{-}15)$$

With this form of friction both the normal and the tangential components of the velocity must vanish on lateral boundaries, that is

$$\psi = 0, \text{ on boundaries} \qquad (12\text{-}16)$$

$$\partial\psi/\partial n = 0, \text{ on boundaries} \qquad (12\text{-}17)$$

Here n represents the distance normal to the boundary. Munk solved (12-15) analytically in the same manner as Stommel, but since (12-15) is of higher order than (12-9), Munk used (12-17) in addition to the (12-16) condition which was used by Stommel.

When (12-15) is solved with the wind stress (12-8) in the square domain, the solution is very similar to that given in Figure 12-1. The Sverdrup balance is found outside of the western boundary region. In the boundary current the balance is between the beta term and the horizontal diffusion term. Scale analysis of this balance leads to the following scale for the boundary current:

$$L_B \sim (A/\beta)^{1/3} \qquad (12\text{-}18)$$

This gives a reasonable boundary current width when $A \sim 10^4 \text{ m}^2 \sec^{-1}$. In Stommel's model the current speed is maximum at the coast, while Munk's model gives the maximum some distance offshore as a result of the no-slip condition (12-17). It will be seen later that this difference is important when vorticity advection is added.

12-3 NONLINEAR EFFECTS

The models of Stommel and Munk, which were presented in the last section, are linear and they give solutions that are symmetric about $y = W/2$ for wind fields with proper symmetry. When the vorticity advection term, $\mathbf{V} \cdot \nabla\zeta$ is added to either model this symmetry is lost. In particular, Veronis (1966a) used a perturbation method with Stommel's model to show that the maximum velocity shifts to the north as the importance of this term increases.

In the boundary layer, the scale of the vorticity advection becomes

$$\mathbf{k} \times \nabla\psi \cdot \nabla\nabla^2\psi \simeq \frac{\partial\psi}{\partial x}\frac{\partial^3\psi}{\partial y\partial x^2} - \frac{\partial\psi}{\partial y}\frac{\partial^3\psi}{\partial x^3} \sim \frac{\Psi^2}{WL^3} \tag{12-19}$$

where Ψ is that scale of the ψ field. If it is assumed that the Sverdrup balance (12-13) is valid in the interior, then $\Psi \sim \tau_0/\rho_0 H\beta$. The beta term can now be balanced by vorticity advection (12-19) if the boundary layer scale is

$$L_B \sim \left(\frac{\tau_0}{W\rho_0 H}\right)^{1/2} \frac{1}{\beta} \tag{12-20}$$

If the typical values used above are inserted, $L_B \sim 50$ km which is close enough to the observed Gulf Stream scale to indicate that this nonlinear effect is important.

However, it is not possible to have wind-stress forcing balanced only by the beta term and vorticity advection. Friction must be important in some portion of the ocean so that the vorticity introduced by the wind stress can be removed. Charney (1955b) and Morgan (1956) formulated nonlinear or "inertial" theories of the Gulf Stream, which neglect friction in the inflow region. Their theories do not treat the northern portion of the Gulf Stream where both friction and nonlinear effects are important. Numerical solutions are required in these regions.

12-4 BAROTROPIC NUMERICAL MODELS

Bryan (1963) and Veronis (1966b) studied the ocean circulation by integrating (12-7) in time with a constant forcing. In these models it is necessary to use a small enough grid size to resolve the boundary currents. Estimates of the boundary layer width are given by bottom friction (12-14), diffusion (12-18), and advection (12-20), depending on which term balances the beta term (i.e., which boundary layer is wider). Bryan (1963) excluded bottom friction by setting $K = 0$, while Veronis (1966b) excluded horizontal friction with $A = 0$. The vorticity equation (12-7) was integrated using the finite difference methods described in Chapter 5. Starting from a state of rest the ocean circulation spins up in a time of order $(\beta L_B)^{-1}$ where L_B is the appropriate boundary layer scale. Veronis achieved a steady solution in all experiments by continuing the time integration, but Bryan's solutions only become steady when the nonlinear effects were weak. In experiments of this type, the nonlinearity can be changed by increasing τ_0 or by decreasing H. As the nonlinearity was increased, Veronis found that his solutions became very similar to the inertial solutions derived by Fofonoff (1954). These solutions were symmetric about $x = W/2$ and had a strong jet along the northern boundary. Fofonoff neglected both wind stress and friction in order to obtain analytic nonlinear solutions. As the nonlinearity in his model was increased, Bryan found oscillations in the northern portion of the boundary current that he identified as Rossby waves. Bryan suggested that these disturbances were the result of barotropic instability in the strong jet along the coast.

The large difference between the solutions obtained by Veronis and Bryan is surprising since they only differ in the form of friction which was used. However, Blandford (1971) demonstrated that this difference was caused by the boundary conditions rather than the actual form of the friction. Figure 12-2 contains sketches of the boundary current for the Veronis model (*a*) and for the Bryan model (*b*). The free-slip condition used by Veronis gives a maximum speed at the coastline while the no-slip condition used by Bryan gives a maximum offshore. Barotropic instability can occur if the profile curvature changes sign in the region (see Section 4-3). Clearly profile (*b*) satisfies the condition while profile (*a*) does not. Bryan actually obtained barotropic instability that prevented steady solutions and also prevented the formation of the east-west jet found by Veronis.

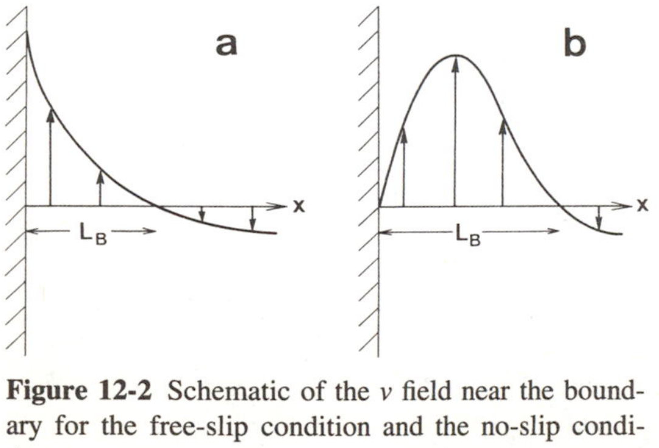

Figure 12-2 Schematic of the v field near the boundary for the free-slip condition and the no-slip condition.

12-5 SIMPLE THERMOHALINE MODELS

In addition to wind stress, the ocean circulation is forced by processes that affect the density field. Since the density is a function of temperature and salinity, there is a "thermohaline" circulation driven by heating, cooling, precipitation minus evaporation, and by the inflow of rivers. Consider an idealized, zonally symmetric, rotating ocean that is driven by heating at low latitudes and cooling at high latitudes. The wind stress has been neglected. Figure 12-3 indicates the type of circulation that might be expected. The response to surface heating indicated in the figure has been verified with laboratory experiments and numerical simulations. It is also similar to the real ocean circulation inferred from water mass characteristics. The heating in the tropics forms a layer of warm water that surmounts a stable region of rapid temperature increase called the *thermocline*. In the north the cooling produces a region of almost neutral stratification where there is strong sinking motion. Vertical diffusion of heat is important in maintaining equilibrium in the thermocline where there is weak upwelling. This is a thermally direct circulation since the warm water is rising and the cool water is sinking.

When north-south coastlines are introduced into the model shown in Figure 12-3, the temperature field is not greatly affected, but the velocities are changed. In the symmetric model there is no geostrophic v component since the pressure is independent of longitude. When coastlines are present, it is possible to build up a pressure gradient across an ocean basin that will support a geostrophic v field.

In the simplest thermocline model the density is assumed to depend only on temperature as follows:

$$\rho = \rho_0(1 - \alpha T) \tag{12-21}$$

where α is the thermal expansion coefficient, ρ_0 is a constant reference density

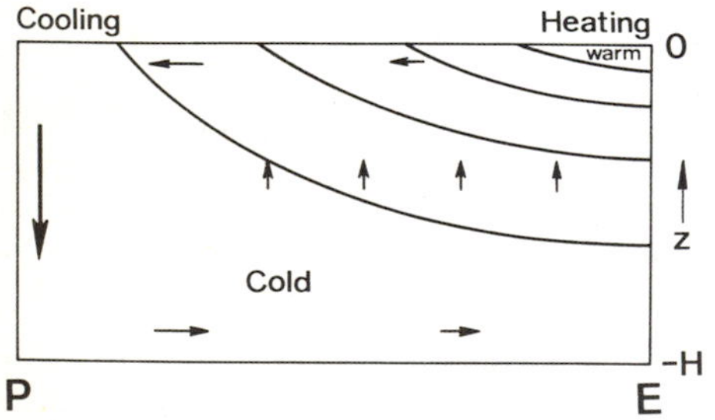

Figure 12-3 Cross section of temperature (isolines) and vertical velocity (arrows) from equator to pole for zonally symmetric ocean driven by surface heating.

and T is the departure from a reference temperature. In the interior of the ocean away from boundary layers, the basic equations can be written:

$$\frac{d\mathbf{V}}{dt} = -\frac{1}{\rho_0}\nabla p - f\mathbf{k} \times \mathbf{V}$$

$$0 = \alpha g T - \frac{1}{\rho_0}\frac{\partial p}{\partial z}$$

$$\nabla \cdot \mathbf{V} + \partial w/\partial z = 0 \tag{12-22}$$

$$\frac{dT}{dt} = k\, \partial^2 T/\partial z^2$$

$$\frac{d}{dt} = \frac{\partial}{\partial t} + \mathbf{V} \cdot \nabla + w\frac{\partial}{\partial z}$$

where p is the departure from $g\rho_0 z$ and k is the vertical diffusion coefficient. These equations employ the Boussinesq approximation wherein ρ is replaced by ρ_0 except in the buoyancy term, which occurs in the hydrostatic equation [see Stern (1975)].

The equation set (12-22) has essentially the same form as the equations which were scale analyzed in Section 3-3. In fact, (12-22) is slightly simpler since the compressibility has been neglected in the continuity equation. The nondimensional parameters are $Ro = V/fL$, L/a and $\varepsilon = L^2/L_R^2$, where the baroclinic Rossby radius of deformation is given by:

$$L_R = H\,(g\alpha\partial\overline{T}/\partial z)^{1/2}/f \tag{12-23}$$

In this definition H is the vertical scale and $\overline{T}(z)$ is an appropriate average temperature. For the open ocean the following scales are reasonable: $V \sim 0.1$ m sec^{-1}, $L \sim 10^7$ m, $f \sim 10^{-4}$sec^{-1}, $L_R \sim 10^5$ m. The nondimensional parameters then become:

$$Ro \sim 10^{-4} \qquad L/a \sim 1 \qquad \varepsilon \sim 10^4 \qquad \beta a/f \sim 1$$

This combination gives the same scale analysis as for the atmospheric planetary scale (Section 3-6), since $Ro\ \varepsilon \sim 1$ and the other parameters are the same. Using the results from Section 3-6, the basic equation set becomes:

$$\mathbf{V} = f^{-1}\rho_0^{-1}\mathbf{k} \times \nabla p$$

$$\nabla \cdot \mathbf{V} + \partial w/\partial z = 0 \qquad \partial p/\partial z = \alpha\rho_0 g T \tag{12-24}$$

$$\frac{\partial T}{\partial t} + \mathbf{V} \cdot \nabla T + w\frac{\partial T}{\partial z} = k\frac{\partial^2 T}{\partial z^2}$$

The diffusion term is retained because it should be important in the thermocline region.

This equation set is difficult to solve analytically because of the nonlinear advection terms in the temperature equation. Similarity solutions have been obtained [Robinson and Stommel (1959)], but it is not easy to satisfy the boundary conditions with them. However, it is possible to obtain an estimate of the circulation by assuming that the temperature and vertical motion pattern in Figure 12-3 is not greatly affected by the presence of coastlines. This is not unreasonable from geostrophic adjustment theory since the $L >> L_R$ (see Section 2-7). Substituting the geostrophic velocity into the continuity equation gives:

$$v\beta = f\partial w/\partial z \tag{12-25}$$

This equation can also be derived by retaining only the beta term and $f\mathbf{\nabla} \cdot \mathbf{V}$ in the vorticity equation (12-3). Assuming for the present that w is a maximum within the thermocline, then below this maximum $\partial w/\partial z > 0$ so that (12-25) gives a component of flow toward the north throughout the region. Since there is sinking from above in the north, a boundary current is required for mass continuity. This boundary current also occurs on the west side of the ocean, so that in the North Atlantic it flows opposite to the Gulf Stream, which is above it. This flow pattern is known as the abyssal circulation. Above the level of maximum vertical motion, $\partial w/\partial z < 0$ so that (12-25) gives a drift to the south. Again since there is rising motion in the south, a boundary current must occur for mass continuity. It turns out that this boundary current is also on the west side of the ocean so that the thermohaline forced circulation in the upper ocean greatly resembles the wind-driven circulation presented earlier in the chapter.

Further information can be obtained from (12-24) by differentiating the velocity with respect to z, substituting from the hydrostatic equation, and taking the **i** component:

$$\frac{\partial u}{\partial z} = -\alpha g f^{-1}\frac{\partial T}{\partial y} \tag{12-26}$$

In midlatitudes where $-\partial T/\partial y$ is large, the vertical shear of the east-west component will be large so that near the surface there will be a geostrophic component toward the east. This will cause rising or upwelling along the west side of the ocean and sinking along the east side.

Figure 12-4 is a schematic drawing of the thermohaline circulation found in numerical models by Bryan (1975). Note the clockwise gyre near the surface and the counterclockwise gyre in the deep water. There is weak upwelling in the interior and strong upwelling in the western boundary current. The sinking is concentrated in the northeastern corner. These features are consistent with the earlier discussion. More detail on thermohaline circulation models can be found in Stern (1975).

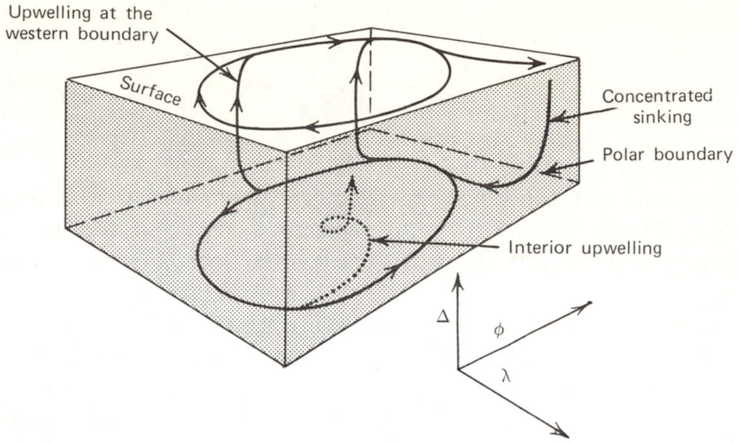

Figure 12-4. Schematic drawing of the thermohaline circulation found in numerical models (Bryan, 1975). (From K. Bryan, "Numerical Model Ocean Circulation." *National Academy of Sciences,* 1975: Reproduced from Numerical Models of Ocean Circulation (1975), page 98, with permission of the National Academy of Sciences, Washington, D.C.)

12-6 BAROCLINIC NUMERICAL MODELS

A baroclinic ocean model that treats both wind stress and thermohaline effects must include the dynamical terms required in each region and must have appropriate resolution for each boundary layer. The basic equations can be written as follows:

$$\frac{d\mathbf{V}}{dt} = -\frac{1}{\rho_0}\nabla p - f\mathbf{k} \times \mathbf{V} + \mathbf{F} \tag{12-27}$$

$$\frac{\partial p}{\partial z} = -\rho g \tag{12-28}$$

$$\rho = \rho(p,T,S) \tag{12-29}$$

$$\frac{\partial w}{\partial z} + \nabla \cdot \mathbf{V} = 0 \tag{12-30}$$

$$\frac{dT}{dt} = A_T \nabla^2 T + k_T \frac{\partial^2 T}{\partial z^2} + \delta_c(\rho) \tag{12-31}$$

$$\frac{dS}{dt} = A_S \nabla^2 S + k_S \frac{\partial^2 S}{\partial z^2} + \gamma_c(\rho) \tag{12-32}$$

where

$$\frac{d}{dt} = \frac{\partial}{\partial t} + \mathbf{V} \cdot \nabla + w\frac{\partial}{\partial z} \qquad \text{and} \qquad \mathbf{F} = A_m \nabla^2 \mathbf{V} + k_m \frac{\partial^2 \mathbf{V}}{\partial z^2}$$

and S is the salinity.

The various turbulent diffusion terms have been approximated with constant coefficients. The functions $\delta_c(\rho)$, $\gamma_c(\rho)$ represent a convective adjustment to keep the density field convectively stable. The boundary conditions must also be specified.

Most numerical baroclinic ocean models use a modified form of the primitive equation system, (12-27) to (12-32), as opposed to the quasi-geostrophic equations (Section 3-4). The latter equations are inappropriate for the thermohaline circulation in the same way that they fail for the planetary scale motions in the atmosphere. Note that the temperature and salinity equations have the same form except for the eddy diffusion coefficients. The equation of state (12-29) is often simplified as follows:

$$\rho = \rho_0[1 - \alpha(T - T_0) + \sigma(S - S_0)] \qquad (12\text{-}33)$$

where α and σ are expansion coefficients, and T_0 and S_0 are reference values. Next an apparent temperature

$$\theta = T - T_0 - \frac{\sigma}{\alpha}(S - S_0) \qquad (12\text{-}34)$$

is defined. Substituting (12-34) into (12-33) gives

$$\rho = \rho_0[1 - \alpha\theta] \qquad (12\text{-}35)$$

If the diffusion coefficients in the temperature and salinity equations are assumed to be equal (12-31) and (12-32) can be combined to give:

$$\frac{d\theta}{dt} = A_\theta \nabla^2 \theta + k_\theta \frac{\partial^2 \theta}{\partial z^2} + \gamma_c(\theta) \qquad (12\text{-}36)$$

The boundary conditions for θ are obtained from the boundary conditions for T and S with the use of (12-34).

If the system (12-27) to (12-32) is integrated with the usual explicit time differencing, the time step must satisfy $\Delta t < \Delta x/(\sqrt{2}\, c_{max})$, where c_{max} is the maximum phase speed that can occur in the system. If the diffusion is large Δt will be further restricted. These equations permit external and internal gravity waves, inertial oscillations and Rossby waves (see Chapter 2). The external gravity waves have the speed $c \sim \sqrt{gH}$, which gives $c \sim 200$ m sec^{-1} for $H \sim 4$ km. This requires a very small Δt in comparison to the typical time scale of oceanic motions. The external gravity waves can be excluded by placing a lid on the surface, that is, by setting $w = 0$ at the upper boundary ($z = 0$). This approximation affects the phase speed of transient Rossby waves, but it will have no effect when only the final steady state is required. Without the external waves, a much larger time step can be taken since the internal waves have $c \lesssim 10$ m sec^{-1} and the current speeds are also small. The inertial oscillations can be handled easily by treating the coriolis terms implicitly.

The equations have to be reformulated when the external gravity waves are excluded because the pressure cannot be obtained by integrating the hydrostatic equation from the free surface. If the bottom is flat the vertical boundary conditions become

$$w(0) = w(-H) = 0 \tag{12-37}$$

Now, integrate the continuity equation in (12-30) from $z = -H$ to $z = 0$, and use (12-37) which leads to:

$$\nabla \cdot \langle \mathbf{V} \rangle = 0 \tag{12-38}$$

where $\langle(\ \ )\rangle = H^{-1} \int_{-H}^{0} (\ \ )\, dz$

Equation 12-38 shows that the vertically averaged current is nondivergent so that a streamfunction can be introduced as follows:

$$\langle \mathbf{V} \rangle = \mathbf{k} \times \nabla \psi \tag{12-39}$$

Next take the vertical average of the equation of motion (12-27), which gives

$$\frac{\partial}{\partial t} \langle \mathbf{V} \rangle = -\left\langle \mathbf{V} \cdot \nabla \mathbf{V} + w \frac{\partial \mathbf{V}}{\partial z} \right\rangle - f\mathbf{k} \times \langle \mathbf{V} \rangle - \frac{1}{\rho_0} \nabla \langle p \rangle + \langle \mathbf{F} \rangle \tag{12-40}$$

A vorticity equation can be formed by applying $\mathbf{k} \cdot \nabla \times$ to (12-40), which yields:

$$\frac{\partial}{\partial t} \nabla^2 \psi = -\mathbf{k} \cdot \nabla \times \left\langle \mathbf{V} \cdot \nabla \mathbf{V} + w \frac{\partial \mathbf{V}}{\partial z} + \mathbf{F} \right\rangle - \langle \mathbf{V} \rangle \cdot \nabla f \tag{12-41}$$

where the streamfunction is introduced through (12-39). This equation is used to predict the vertical mean current. The departure from the mean is defined as follows:

$$\mathbf{V} = \langle \mathbf{V} \rangle + \mathbf{V}' \tag{12-42}$$

Now substitute (12-42) into (12-27) and subtract (12-40) from the resulting equation which yields:

$$\frac{\partial \mathbf{V}'}{\partial t} = -\left(\mathbf{V} \cdot \nabla \mathbf{V} + w\frac{\partial \mathbf{V}}{\partial z}\right) + \left\langle \mathbf{V} \cdot \nabla \mathbf{V} + w\frac{\partial \mathbf{V}}{\partial z}\right\rangle$$
$$- f\mathbf{k} \times \mathbf{V}' - \frac{1}{\rho_0}\nabla p' + \mathbf{F} - \langle \mathbf{F} \rangle \tag{12-43}$$

where $p' = p - \langle p \rangle$. If $p = \langle p \rangle + p'$ is introduced into the hydrostatic equation (12-28) it becomes:

$$\frac{\partial p'}{\partial z} = -g\rho \tag{12-44}$$

This equation can be integrated from $-H$ to z, which gives

$$p' = p'(-H) - g\int_{-H}^{z} \rho \, dz \tag{12-45}$$

When the condition $\langle p' \rangle = 0$ is applied to (12-45), it can be written

$$p' = -g\int_{-H}^{z} \rho \, dz + g\left\langle \int_{-H}^{z} \rho \, dz \right\rangle \tag{12-46}$$

The first step in the forecast is to solve (12-41) for ψ, which can be used to compute $\langle \mathbf{V} \rangle$. Note that $\mathbf{V}'$ is involved on the right side of (12-41). Then (12-43) and (12-36) are solved for $\mathbf{V}$ and θ, respectively. The new ρ field is obtained from (12-35), and p' is then computed from (12-46). Integration of the continuity equation (12-30) gives the vertical velocity.

This system of equations can be integrated rapidly even though a Poisson equation (12-41) must be solved at each step, since a large time step can be used. This general formulation was used by Smagorinsky (1958) in an atmospheric prediction model. Gates (1968) and Alexander (1973) developed ocean prediction models with free upper surfaces but they used a shallow ocean to slow the external gravity waves. Another approach for large-scale ocean modeling is the use of semi-implicit time differencing (Section 5-7-4), as was done by Madala and Piacsek (1977). This requires about the same computer time as the rigid lid models, but it should treat traveling Rossby waves more correctly.

Bryan and Cox (1967) formulated a baroclinic model to compare the effects of wind stress and thermohaline forcing. They used the rigid lid procedure that was described earlier in the section. A nonuniform grid spacing was used that provided higher resolution near the western boundary area and near the surface. This provided a more accurate treatment of the western boundary currents and the thermocline region. The motion was forced with the following boundary conditions:

$$\theta(x,y,0,t) = \theta^*(y) \tag{12-47}$$

$$k_m \frac{\partial u}{\partial z}(x,y,0,t) = \tau^*(y) \tag{12-48}$$

The bottom stress was neglected.

The equations were integrated until the solutions were approximately steady. The upper ocean and the boundary currents spun up in a time comparable to the time for a barotropic ocean. However, the deep ocean took a very long time to reach a steady state. Bryan (1975) estimates the adjustment time for the deep ocean to be of order H^2/k_θ. Thus if $H \sim 4$ km and $k_\theta = 1\ \text{cm}^2\ \text{sec}^{-1}$, then $H^2/k_\theta \sim 4000$ years whereas the barotropic models adjust in about 50 days!

Bryan and Cox (1967) obtained a thermohaline circulation that was consistent with other studies. When surface wind stress was added, the solutions become more similar to observed data. In particular, the presence of wind stress caused the thermocline to tilt downward toward the west.

Bryan and Cox (1968a, b) continued their study of the baroclinic ocean circulation with essentially the same model. In order to reach adjustment with less computer time, the integration was carried out in two stages. In the first stage the grid size was uniform except near the western boundary where it was about half of the interior value. After about 180 years of forecast time the fields were interpolated to a small grid and the forecast was continued another 7 years. The new grid had higher resolution everywhere, with extra high resolution along all four boundaries of the rectangular ocean. This numerical experiment provided an improved simulation of the ocean circulation that included an approximation to the Cromwell current, which is a strong "counter" current that flows eastward along the equator just below the surface.

Ocean general circulation models have a variety of uses. Haney, Shiver, and Hunt (1978) used the ocean circulation model developed by Haney (1974) to simulate the evolution of temperature anomalies in the ocean. The results of these simulations were very encouraging. This type of model will be very useful in understanding the role of air-sea interaction in seasonal and climatic variations. Ocean circulation models have also been used in a diagnostic mode to determine currents from observed density data [Holland and Hirschman (1972) and Sarkisyan (1977)].

12-7 BOTTOM TOPOGRAPHY EFFECTS

The models discussed thus far have flat bottoms while the actual oceans have considerable variation in the depth, especially near the coastlines. Holland (1967) added bottom topography to the model that was developed by Bryan (1963), and he also assumed a steady state. Holland solved the following equation:

$$H\mathbf{V} \cdot \nabla \left(\frac{\zeta + f}{H}\right) = \frac{1}{H\rho_0}\mathbf{k} \cdot \nabla \times \frac{\boldsymbol{\tau}_0}{H} + A\nabla^2\zeta \qquad (12\text{-}49)$$

where H is the variable depth. Note that when $\boldsymbol{\tau}_0 = 0$ and $A = 0$, (12-49) reduces to the steady-state potential vorticity equation (2-39b). A stream function for the transport $H\mathbf{V}$ can be introduced so that

$$H\mathbf{V} = \mathbf{k} \times \nabla\psi \qquad \zeta = \nabla \cdot (\nabla\psi/H) \qquad (12\text{-}50)$$

Holland substituted (12-50) into (12-49), introduced finite differences and solved the resulting equation for ψ by relaxation. He found that the motion tends to follow lines of constant f/H. Warren (1963) proposed that the separation of the Gulf Stream from the coast could be explained by the bottom topography which does not follow the coast in that region. Holland examined a case where the H field had a 45° angle to the coast and he found that the boundary current meandered along the lines of constant H.

It is more difficult to estimate topographic effects in a baroclinic model where the currents may be in opposite directions at the top and bottom of the ocean. Holland (1973) developed a baroclinic prediction model with bottom topography. He obtained solutions for the following three cases: (1) a constant-depth, baroclinic ocean, (2) a variable-depth, homogeneous ocean and (3) a variable-depth, baroclinic ocean. The results were quite different among the three cases and case (3) had the largest mass transport. Holland found that the effect of pressure forces acting against bottom relief was especially important in case (3).

Baroclinic ocean models with variable depth have thus far used z-coordinates with the forced vertical motion inserted at the appropriate level. It appears that a coordinate system similar to the sigma system (see Section 1-9-1) would be very useful in these experiments. Vertical walls might still be required near the coastlines to keep H from being zero except where the normal velocity vanishes.

12-8 SYNOPTIC SCALE EDDIES

The previous sections of this chapter have treated the large-scale features of the general ocean circulation including the smaller-scale boundary layers required for mass continuity. It is now clear that the oceans contain smaller-scale circulations that are time dependent and in some areas contain velocities much larger than the time-averaged local currents. These "eddies" have a spatial scale of the order of the Rossby radius of deformation L_R, which is about 50 km, and a period of the order of 50 days. They are called synoptic scale eddies since they are dynamically similar to the synoptic eddies in the atmosphere even though they are of different scale. The presence of these eddies is important even for the prediction of the large-scale circulation, since the eddy transports of heat and momentum may not be properly represented by the diffusion terms given in (12-27) and (12-36).

Koshlyakov and Monin (1978) have reviewed the observational data on the synoptic eddies. Special observational studies include the Soviet POLYGON-70 experiment [Brekhovskikh et al. (1971)] and the American-British Mid-Ocean Dynamics Experiment [U.S. POLYMODE Organizing Committee (1976)]. Their field studies showed that the eddies have a very coherent vertical structure and they propagate westward relative to the mean flow as Rossby waves do. In fact in MODE the observed phase speeds were given accurately by the first internal Rossby wave (see 4-81). Other observations show that the eddies are quite widespread with the largest amplitudes occurring near the major currents. Except in these regions the eddies often have much larger current speeds than the local mean flow.

Since the scale of the synoptic eddies is near L_R, it seems likely that baroclinic instability must play a role in their formation. The development of these eddies has been studied by reducing the grid size and the lateral diffusion coefficent in large-scale ocean models [Holland and Lin (1975), Robinson et al. (1977) and Semtner and Mintz (1977)]. Semtner and Mintz treated a rectangular region of the North Atlantic and they included bottom topography. They found that eddy kinetic energy was produced in the Gulf Stream region over the continental slope by a baroclinic-barotropic instability. Baroclinic instability was also found in the North Equatorial Current. These results suggest that the eddies are formed in regions of unstable mean currents and that they propagate into quieter regions of the oceans as Rossby waves. The numerical models show that the eddies play an important role in heat and momentum transports and these subgrid scale effects are poorly approximated by the terms such as $A\,\nabla^2\theta$. It appears that evolution of the eddies could be predicted for over a long time interval if the initial data were adequate.

12-9 MIXED LAYER MODELS

The upper layer of the ocean where turbulent mixing is dominant is called the mixed layer. In this layer as is shown in Figure 12-5, temperature, salinity, and the mean horizontal velocity are nearly uniform, while the quantities change rapidly in the thermocline below. The average properties in the mixed layer and its depth are strongly influenced by the atmospheric conditions above. The mixed layer has time variations from the diurnal scale to climatic scales. Since the atmosphere is very sensitive to the ocean surface temperature, changes in the mixed layer will have more influence on atmospheric phenomena than changes in other regions of the ocean. An example of an important interaction between the atmosphere and the mixed layer involves the ocean temperature changes caused by a mature hurricane (O'Brien and Reid, 1967; Elsberry et al.,

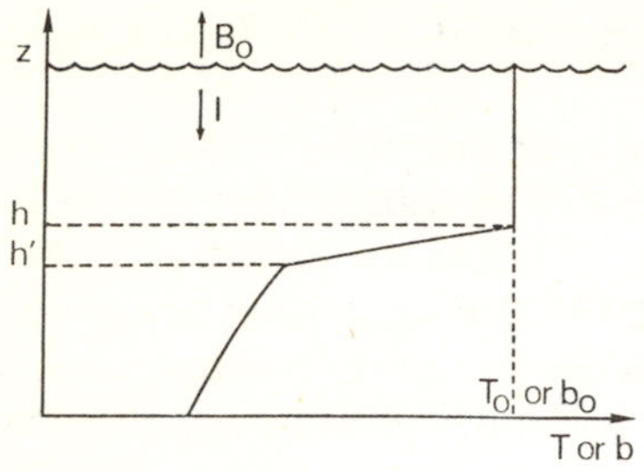

Figure 12-5 Schematic of mixed layer model. (*From Niiler and Kraus, 1977.*) (From Niiler and E. Kraus, "One-dimensional of the Upper Layers of the Ocean." Pergamon Press Ltd. from *Modeling and Prediction of the Upper Layers of the Ocean,* 1977.)

1976). Any longer range atmospheric prediction model must contain a proper description of the interaction between the atmosphere and the mixed layer.

The ocean circulation models that have been described in this chapter do not give an accurate treatment of the mixed layer since they employ constant vertical diffusion coefficients. Recently one-dimensional mixed layer models have been developed that have been successfully used to predict changes in mixed layer properties. Niiler and Kraus (1977) provide an excellent review of these models that will be followed in this section.

In one-dimensional models the horizontal variations are neglected in comparison with the vertical changes. Each variable such as, the temperature for example, is written

$$T = \overline{T} + T' \tag{12-51}$$

where $\overline{T}$ is the time average and T' is the departure, and it is further assumed that $T' = 0$. When the continuity equation (12-30) is time averaged it follows that $\overline{w} = 0$. The time-averaged equation of motion (12-27) can be written:

$$\frac{\partial \overline{\mathbf{V}}}{\partial t} + f\mathbf{k} \times \overline{\mathbf{V}} + \frac{\partial}{\partial z}\overline{w'\mathbf{V}'} = 0 \tag{12-52}$$

where the friction now appears in the Reynolds stress term. The temperature equation (12-31) and the salinity equation (12-32) become:

$$\frac{\partial \overline{T}}{\partial t} + \frac{\partial}{\partial z}\overline{w'T'} = -\frac{1}{\rho c}\frac{\partial I}{\partial z} \tag{12-53}$$

$$\frac{\partial \overline{S}}{\partial t} + \frac{\partial}{\partial z}\overline{S'T'} = 0 \tag{12-54}$$

where I is the penetrating component of the solar radiation and c is the specific heat.

Since the buoyancy depends on both T and S it is useful to introduce the following expression for the buoyancy:

$$b = -g\frac{(\rho - \rho_0)}{\rho_0} = g[\alpha(T - T_0) - \sigma(S - S_0)] \tag{12-55}$$

which uses the simplified equation of state (12-33). This equation along with (12-53) and (12-54) can be combined to yield

$$\frac{\partial \bar{b}}{\partial t} + \frac{\partial \overline{w'b'}}{\partial z} = -\frac{g\alpha}{\rho c}\frac{\partial I}{\partial z} \tag{12-56}$$

which is a conservation equation for buoyancy.

The mixed layer formulation assumes that $\overline{T}$, $\overline{S}$, and $\overline{\mathbf{V}}$ have constant values T_0, S_0, and $\mathbf{V}_0$ throughout the mixed layer. At the bottom of the mixed layer ($z = -h$), there will usually be large changes in the variables as can be seen in Figure 12-5. Equation 12-53 can now be integrated from $z = -h$ to $z = 0$, which gives

$$\frac{dT_0}{dt} = -\frac{1}{h}[(\overline{w'T'})_0 - (\overline{w'T'})_{-h}] - \frac{1}{\rho c\, h}[I_0 - I_{-h}] \tag{12-57}$$

and (12-52), (12-54), and (12-56) can be integrated in the same manner. The system will be closed when the boundary fluxes have been specified and an expression is found for dh/dt.

The surface fluxes of sensible heat, salinity, and buoyancy can be specified by the bulk aerodynamic formulas (see Section 8-3):

$$\begin{aligned}\rho c(\overline{w'T'})_0 &= R_0 - I_0 + H_0 + L\,Q_0 \\ &= R_0 - I_0 + \rho_a\,C_a\,u_a\,\{c_p(T_0 - T_a) + L\,[q_*\,(T_0) - q_a\},\end{aligned} \tag{12-58}$$

$$\rho(\overline{w'S'})_0 = (P_0 - Q_0)\,S_0 \tag{12-59}$$

$$(\overline{w'b'})_0 = g[\alpha(\overline{w'T'})_0 - \beta(\overline{w'S'})_0] \equiv B_0 \tag{12-60}$$

Th subscript 0 refers to conditions at the water surface and the subscript a refers to conditions in the atmosphere at reference level $z = a$. The various symbols used in (12-58) to (12-60) have the following meanings:

R_0 = surface flux of solar and terrestrial radiant energy per unit area
I_0 = surface flux of penetrating solar radiation
H_0 = surface flux of sensible heat
Q_0 = surface flux of water vapor (evaporation)
L = latent heat of evaporation
C_a = surface drag coefficient
u_a = wind speed

P_0 = precipitation rate
q = specific humidity
q_* = saturation specific humidity
Note that all fluxes are positive when directed upward.

The surface flux B_0 specifies the rate at which buoyancy is removed from the water column by surface cooling and salinity changes:

$$B_0 \equiv \frac{g}{\rho}\left[\frac{\alpha}{c}(R_0 - I_0 + H_0) - \beta P_0 S + \left(\frac{\alpha L}{c} + \beta S_0\right) Q_0\right] \quad (12\text{-}61)$$

The Reynolds stress is related to the wind stress as follows:

$$|\overline{w'\mathbf{V}'}| = \boldsymbol{\tau}_0/\rho \quad (12\text{-}62)$$

where $\tau_0 = \rho_a C_a u_a^2$ and where $\boldsymbol{\tau}_0$ has the same direction as $\mathbf{V}_a$.

At the bottom of the mixed layer it is assumed that entrainment operates to add water to the mixed layer from below while none of the mixed layer water is lost into the quiet water below. Thus if $\overline{w} = 0$, any deepening of the layer must be equal to the rate w_e with which water is entrained from the interior below. When the layer becomes shallower the entrainment must cease so that:

$$\begin{aligned} w_e &= dh/dt \qquad \text{for } dh/dt > 0 \\ w_e &= 0 \qquad \text{for } dh/dt \leq 0 \end{aligned} \quad (12\text{-}63)$$

Now the fluxes at the bottom of the mixed layer can be written:

$$\begin{aligned} (\overline{w'T'})_{-h} + w_e\,\Delta T &= 0 \\ (\overline{w'S'})_{-h} + w_e\,\Delta S &= 0 \\ (\overline{w'b'})_{-h} + w_e\,\Delta b &= 0 \end{aligned} \quad (12\text{-}64)$$

where ΔT, ΔS, and Δb represent the quasi-discontinuous changes of the quantity across the base of the mixed layer (see Figure 12-5).

The boundary condition for the Reynolds stress at the bottom is not so simple because Pollard and Millard (1970) have pointed out that internal gravity waves can radiate momentum into the stable layers below. This gives a drag that is approximated as follows:

$$(\overline{w'\mathbf{V}})_{-h} + w_e\,\overline{\mathbf{V}} = C\,\overline{V}\,\overline{\mathbf{V}} \quad (12\text{-}65)$$

where C is an appropriate drag coefficient, and it is assumed that the mean velocity is zero below the mixed layer.

The turbulent kinetic energy equation (Kraus, 1972), which can be written

$$\frac{1}{2}\frac{\partial}{\partial t}q^2 = -\overline{w'\mathbf{V}'}\cdot\frac{\partial\overline{\mathbf{V}}}{\partial z} + \overline{w'b'} - \frac{\partial}{\partial z}\left[\frac{\overline{w'(w'^2+\mathbf{V}'^2)}}{2} + \rho^{-1}\overline{w'p'}\right] - \varepsilon \qquad (12\text{-}66)$$

will be used to obtain an expression for w_e. Here $q^2 \equiv \overline{w'^2} + \overline{\mathbf{V}'^2}$ is the turbulent kinetic energy. The terms on the right represent, respectively, the conversion of mean shear energy into q^2, the work by the buoyancy force, the vertical convergence of the turbulent energy flux, the work by the pressure fluctuations, and the dissipation rate ε. The next step is to neglect the time derivative in (12-66) and integrate from $z = -h$ to $z = 0$, which gives

$$0 = -\int_{-h}^{0}\overline{w'\mathbf{V}'}\cdot\frac{\partial\overline{\mathbf{V}}}{\partial z}\,dz + \int_{-h}^{0}\overline{w'b'}\,dz - \overline{[\tfrac{1}{2}\,w'\,(w'^2 + \mathbf{V}'^2) + \rho^{-1}\,w'p']_0}$$

$$+ \overline{[\tfrac{1}{2}\,w'\,(w'^2 + \mathbf{V}'^2) + \rho^{-1}\,w'p']_{-h}} - \int_{-h}^{0}\varepsilon\,dz \qquad (12\text{-}67)$$

The first square-bracket term in (12-67) represents the eddy flux of the turbulent kinetic energy and pressure fluctuations at the surface, which must be proportional to the rate of work done by the wind. This expression is approximated as follows:

$$-\overline{[w'(w'^2 + \mathbf{V}'^2)/2} + \rho^{-1}\overline{w'p']_0} = m_1\,(\tau/\rho)^{\frac{3}{2}} \qquad (12\text{-}68)$$

where m_1 is a proportionality factor. At the bottom of the layer the flux is given by

$$\overline{[\tfrac{1}{2}\,w'(w'^2 + \mathbf{V}'^2) + \rho^{-1}\,w'p']_{-h}} + \tfrac{1}{2}\,w_e\,q^2 = 0 \qquad (12\text{-}69)$$

An expression for the buoyancy flux $\overline{w'b'}$ in (12-67) is obtained by integrating (12-56) from z to 0 and again from $-h$ to 0. The time derivative db_0/dt can then be eliminated, which gives:

$$\overline{w'b'} = B_0 + \frac{z}{h}\,[B_0 + w_e\,\Delta b - (J_0 - J_{-h})] - (J_0 - J) \qquad (12\text{-}70)$$

where for convenience $J = g\alpha I/\rho c$. Now integrate (12-70) from $z = -h$ to $z = 0$, giving

$$\int_{-h}^{0} \overline{w'b'}\, dz = \tfrac{1}{2} hB_0 - \tfrac{1}{2} w_e \Delta bh + h\left[\tfrac{1}{2}(J_0 + J_{-h}) - \frac{1}{h}\int_{-h}^{0} Jdz\right] \quad (12\text{-}71)$$

The first term in (12-67) is not straightforward because $\partial \mathbf{V}/\partial z$ is 0 within the layer but it is infinite at the bottom. The contribution from the thin transition layer between $-h'$ and $-h$ (see Figure 12-5) can be estimated as follows:

$$\int_{-h'}^{-h} -\overline{w'\mathbf{V}'} \cdot \frac{\partial \overline{\mathbf{V}}}{\partial z}\, dz = \int_{-h'}^{-h} (w_e \overline{\mathbf{V}} - C\overline{V}\,\overline{\mathbf{V}}) \cdot \frac{\partial \overline{\mathbf{V}}}{\partial z}\, dz \simeq \tfrac{1}{2} w_e \overline{V}^2 - \tfrac{1}{3} C|'\overline{V}|^3 \quad (12\text{-}72)$$

where $\overline{w'\mathbf{V}'}$ has been evaluated from (12-65).

Equation 12-67 can be evaluated by substitution from (12-68), (12-69), (12-71), and (12-72) and then it can be rewritten in the following form:

$$\tfrac{1}{2} w_e(q^2 + c_i^2 - \overline{V}^2) = m_1 (\tau/\rho)^{3/2} + \tfrac{1}{2} hB_0 + h\left[\tfrac{1}{2}(J_0 + J_{-h}) - \frac{1}{h}\int_{-h}^{0} Jdz\right] - \frac{C}{3}|V|^3 - \int_{-h}^{0} \varepsilon dz \quad (12\text{-}73)$$

where $c_i = (\Delta bh)^{1/2}$ is the speed of the long internal waves. The left-hand side of the equation represents, respectively, the rate of work needed to agitate and lift the entrained water and the rate at which energy of the mean velocity is decreased by mixing with the motionless water beneath the interface. The right-hand side of the equation contains, respectively, the rate of working by the wind, the rate of potential energy change produced by fluxes across the sea surface and by penetrating solar radiation, and the rate of energy loss by internal waves from the bottom of the layer and the dissipation.

The most arbitrary link in mixed layer models is the formulation of the dissipation. In this model the dissipation is related to the source terms for turbulent energy as follows:

$$\int_{-h}^{0} \varepsilon dz = (m_1 - m)u_*^3 + (1 - S)\,\tfrac{1}{2} w_e \overline{\mathbf{V}}^2 + (1 - n)\,\tfrac{1}{2}h \frac{B_0 + |B_0'|}{2} \quad (12\text{-}74)$$

The proportionality factors $(m_1 - m)$, $(1 - S)$, and $(1 - n)$ are written in this form for convenience and the B_0 term is written so that it will be nonzero only when there is surface cooling ($B_0 > 0$). It can be shown that $c_i^2 >> q^2$ so that the first term on the left in (12-73) may be neglected. Also the next to last term on the right is considered to be small in comparison with the wind stress term.

With these simplifications and with the use of (12-74), Equation 12-73 becomes:

$$w_e = \frac{2m\, u_*^3 + \frac{h}{2}[(1 + n)B_0 - (1 - n)\,|B_0|] + h(J_0 + J_{-h} - \frac{2}{h}\int_{-h}^{0} Jdz)}{c_i^2 - SV^2} \tag{12-75}$$

This equation can now be used to determine the mixed layer depth. If (12-75) gives $w_e > 0$, then the equation $dh/dt = w_e$ is integrated numerically. However, if $w_e < 0$, it is necessary to set $w_e = 0$ in (12-75). The resulting diagnostic equation can then be solved for h, but if it turns out that $h < 0$ then there is no mixed layer. The mean equations (12-52) and (12-56) can be written in the same form as (12-57) with the use of the fluxes (12-60), (12-62), and (12-65). The resulting system and (12-75) can be integrated in time to give the time evolution of the mixed layer. Other investigators have used different formulations to obtain w_e. The approach by Garwood (1977) is notably different from that presented in this section in that it uses second order closure to predict the turbulent transports. De Szoeke and Rhines (1976) retained the time-derivative term in the turbulent kinetic energy equation (12-66) in their formulation.

12-10 PROBLEMS IN OCEAN MODELING

A major problem in numerical modeling of the large-scale ocean circulation is the resolution of the boundary currents along coastlines and along the equator. As pointed out earlier the grid size must be small enough to resolve the boundary current scale, which depends on the local balance. Haney and Wright (1975), following Smagorinsky, have formulated a nonlinear horizontal viscosity that is large in the boundary current, but small in the rest of the ocean. This allows the whole ocean to be treated with a larger grid size. However, Veronis (1975) has pointed out that the use of large viscosity in baroclinic models may give unrealistic vertical motion fields. A better approach would be to use a nested grid as discussed in Section 7-7. Bryan and Cox have used a smaller grid size in the boundary current regions. Another possibility would be to formulate a finite element model as discussed in Chapter 6. This would allow variable mesh size and also irregular coastlines. In fact Gallagher and Chan (1973) have formulated a steady-state lake model with finite elements and Galt (1975) has developed a finite element diagnostic model for ocean data.

Most of the models that have been discussed have been used mainly to improve understanding of the observed ocean circulation. A coupled atmosphere-ocean model could be used for longer-range forecasts, but the model should include an appropriate mixed-layer formulation. An ocean circulation model could also be used diagnostically if data and atmospheric forcing were fed into the model continuously in those areas where it was available. This would provide reasonable data in regions where oceanographic observations are made infrequently. This would resemble the data-assimilation methods discussed in Section 11-6.

CHAPTER 13

Weather and Climate Prediction

13-1 INTRODUCTION

In this chapter some data are presented that indicate current accuracy of weather forecasting, the upward trend in skill during the past quarter century, and the future prospects. The last is related to inherent limits on the predictability of the atmosphere, a subject that has been explored on purely theoretical grounds as well as on indications from observational data. This is followed by a brief discussion on the application of statistical methods for the purpose of either improving the dynamical-numerical predictions or forecasting those parameters or phenomena not predicted by, or derived directly from, NWP models.

The last section introduces the subject of climate prediction, which is in its infancy. However, because of the enormous economic benefits that could accrue from even a modest skill in seasonal forecasts, considerable research backed by substantial financial support will be directed toward long-range forecasts during the next decade or so.

13-2 CURRENT FORECASTING SKILL

Recently George P. Cressman (1978), President of the American Meteorological Society and Head of the National Weather Service described the forecasts of two record-breaking storms in the winter of 1978 as ''outstanding in practically every respect. The ability to accomplish this feat is new. Fifteen years ago such successful forecasts of these extremely rapid developments would have been almost inconceivable. I am pleased to congratulate the National Meteorological Center for the outstanding work they did with their new models. The numerical predictions they furnished were without any doubt the basis for both of these successes.'' Although there are a few dissenters the vast majority of meteorologists and the general public recognize the continued improvement in weather forecasting.

13-2-1 Short Range

More specific evidence of the quality of forecasts is presented by Shuman (1978) describing the accuracy of forecasts by the NWS, which is probably typical of other public services. A wide variety of forecasts are issued by NWS for periods ranging from a matter of minutes for tornado warnings to outlooks for several months. The National Meteorological Center (NMC) issues a wealth of information in the form of about 500 maps daily, containing weather information—analyses and/or prognoses of pressure, temperature, wind velocity, clouds, precipitation, severe weather, etc., plus teletype messages. These data are mainly used as guidance by some 300 regional and local NWS offices throughout the nation. The longer the forecast period the less detail. One thing is certain, dynamical predictions by numerical methods using high-speed electronic computers form the basis of modern weather forecasting and has led to more accurate forecasts and more diverse applications. Other factors have also contributed to the increased skill, particularly satellite observations.

As a measure of skill Figure 13-1 shows a dramatic improvement of the NMC 500-mb prognoses for North America. Here skill is measured in terms of the normalized error in horizontal pressure gradients as represented by the S_1 score of Teweles and Wobus (1954). A score of 20 is considered near perfect while 70 shows little or no skill. The ordinate is given in a percent, $2 \times (70 - S_1)$, which gives zero for $S_1 = 70$ and 100 for $S_1 = 20$. The chart indicates the model used for prognosis, as well as the type of computer, as a function of time. The dot representing forecasts made with a regional model out to 48 hr, shows promise of an even higher level of skill. Predicted circulation at other levels in the atmosphere has shown a similar increase in skill. Moreover, the length of the forecast period showing skill over climatology or persistence (forecast for tomorrow same as today) has doubled from 3 to 6 days during the two decades. Figure 13-2 is a similar chart for the surface and Figures 13-3 and 13-4 provide some statistics on temperature and weather that also show steady improvement in forecast accuracy.

Precipitation forecasts are more difficult but have shown a modest improvement from about 80 to 85 percent on whether or not precipitation will occur in the period (0-12 hr). The accuracy of quantitative forecasts of precipitation exceeding 25 mm in the period (0-24 hr) rose sharply from 1958 to 1961, but then remained more or less constant through 1976. However, recent experiments with fine-mesh models have shown increasing skill in forecasts of precipitation and the pressure field with increasing resolution. A 60-km grid has been used by NMC when a hurricane threatens the United States, and the U.S. Navy (FNWC) uses a fine-mesh model to forecast movement of tropical storms in the western Pacific. Hydrologists have found such forecasts to be valuable when there is a threat of flash floods because of heavy rains. A more advanced computer system will be placed into operation at NMC and FNWC in the early 1980s that will permit fine resolution models to be run with more sophisticated physics than in existing models, giving more realistic simulations of the pro-

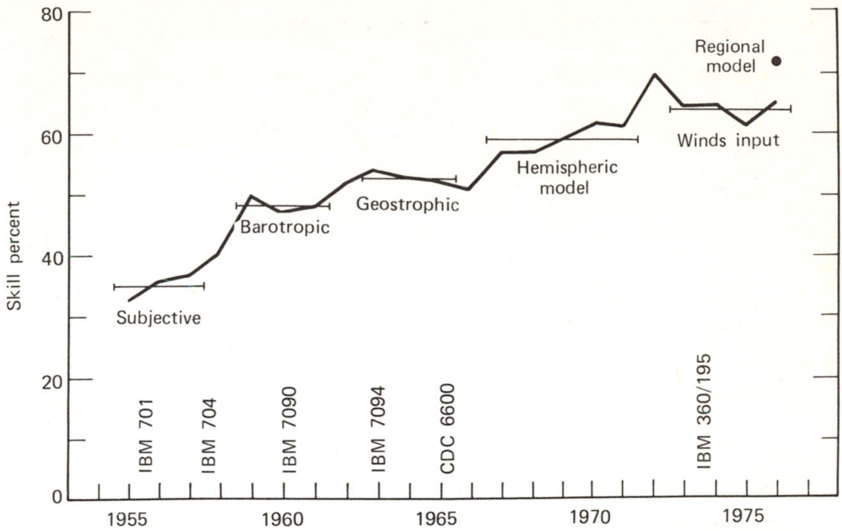

Figure 13-1 Record of skill, averaged annually, of the NMC 36-h, 500-mb (5.6 km high) circulation predictions over North America. The horizontal bars show averages for the years during which no major changes in models occurred. Years of transition are not included in the averages. The geostrophic model is a generalization of the barotropic model, to account for baroclinic effects. The last bar shows the effect on skill of a change in input wind. Prior to 1972 a quasi-geostrophic wind field, derived from the pressure field, was used for initial winds. During 1972, analyses of observed winds were used instead. The measure of skill is based on the so-called S_1 score (Teweles and Wobus, 1954), which is a measure of normalized error in horizontal pressure gradients. A chart with an S_1 score of 20 is virtually perfect, and one with 70 is worthless. As shown, skill (percent) is $2 \times (70 - S_1)$, which yields 0 for a worthless chart, and 100 for a virtually perfect one (Shuman 1978).

cesses involved with clouds and precipitation, radiative transfer, boundary layer fluxes, etc.

Clearly there are practical limits here since merely halving the grid size in three dimensions increases the computing time by a factor of 16. In addition to computer limitations, there may be insufficient data to establish an accurate initial state and increasing the data base is very expensive. Note, however, that a smaller grid size than warranted merely by the data base can still improve forecasts by reducing truncation errors in the numerical approximations (more accurate phase velocities), better representation of the conversion of potential to kinetic energy and better simulation of nonlinear transfer processes.

The Navy Fleet Numerical Weather Central (FNWC)[1] and the Air Force

[1] FNWC recently renamed the FLEET NUMERICAL OCEANOGRAPHY CENTER to reflect the greater emphasis on oceanography.

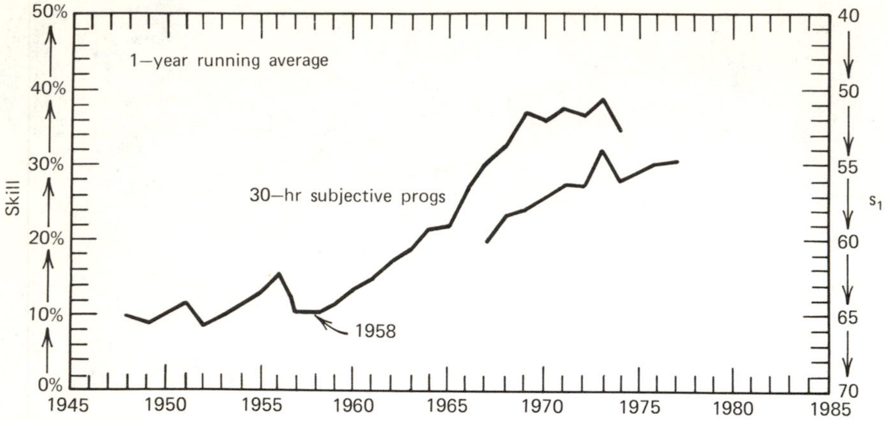

Figure 13-2 NMC 30-h surface prognostic charts, 1948–1974; NMC 36-hour PE surface prognostic charts, 1967–1977 (Shuman, 1978).

Global Weather Central provide weather predictions for military applications. FNWC makes global forecasts daily to meet Fleet commitments the world over from pole to pole. Besides the marine weather, FNWC provides oceanographic forecasts of wave and surf conditions, the ocean thermal structure from the surface to the bottom and ocean currents. This environmental information is used to support all types of naval operations including weather and sea conditions for ships, ship routing, aircraft flight conditions, optimum-path aircraft routing, radar, optical and sonar propagation characteristics, ballistic winds and densities, radiological fallout predictions, search and rescue missions, and more. Similarly, the USAF AWS provides weather information for a wide variety of air operations and for the U. S. Army as well.

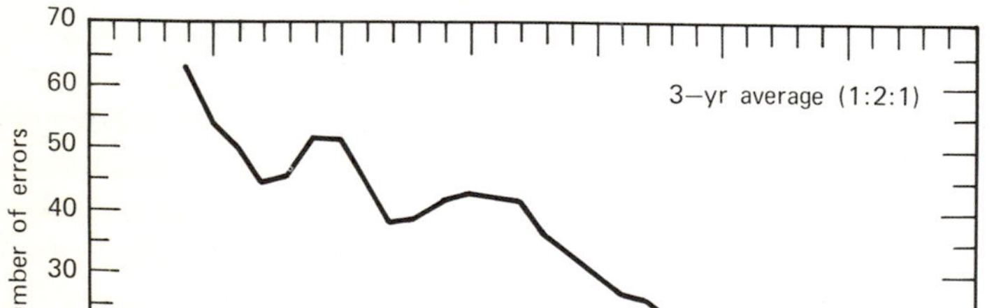

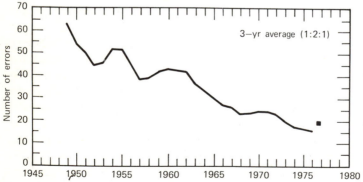

Figure 13-3 Temperature forecast errors ≥ 10°, Salt Lake City, Utah, 1948–1977 (Shuman, 1978).

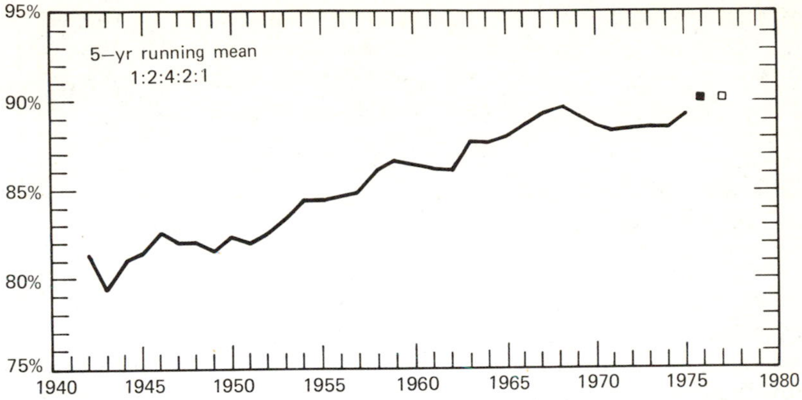

Figure 13-4 Percentage of correct weather and temperature forecasts, Chicago, Illinois, 1942–1977 (Shuman, 1978).

13-2-2 Medium and Longer Ranges

For predictions of *3, 4, and 5 days,* NMC issues one set of prognostic charts daily. For *days 6-10* three charts giving the 5-day average circulation, *temperature,* and *precipitation* are issued three times a week. The *temperature* forecasts are given in five categories: *normal, above or below normal,* and *much above or much below normal;* while *precipitation* is categorized as: *heavy, light* and *moderate,* relative to normal.

A *30-day outlook* is issued twice monthly in the form of three charts each for North America, Europe, and Asia, which give three categories of *mean temperature—above, below,* and *near normal,* and similarly for *precipitation.* Skill over climatology at present is very modest, but recipients find the information useful and there is likely to be significant improvements during the next decade.

Seasonal outlooks for *90 days* are issued four times annually for temperature in two categories, *above* and *below normal,* plus a *no-forecast* for areas in doubt. Ninety-day experimental precipitation forecasts show no skill at present. The length of a season is a natural period and successful forecasts could have significant benefits, especially in agriculture and perhaps energy consumption. There is promising current research attempting to relate ocean surface temperature anomalies to long-range weather anomalies [Namias (1977)].

The new Climate Analysis Center (CAC) of NWS produces information on climate fluctuations which is used by NOAA's Center for Climatic and Environmental Assessment to interpret these fluctuations in terms of agriculture, water supply and energy requirements. A goal is to increase the accuracy of *above* and *below normal* forecasts to 75 percent and increase the lead time three to nine months. Empirical methods will predominate for the present and near future, but statistical dynamical, interacting atmosphere-ocean models are likely to be a primary method eventually. Research on climate is being conducted in a number of universities in and outside of the United States. The World Meteorological Organization (WMO) has organized a World Climate Program that will play an important role in climate research and its applications.

13-2-3 Additional Comments on Forecasting

The accuracy of weather forecasts is a function of the initial state as determined from the observational base, the correctness of the representation and simulation of the physical processes of the atmosphere, and numerical errors. The last item was discussed in considerable detail in Chapters 5 and 6. It is quite obvious that if the initial state is erroneous, the forecast will be in error also, except in the unusual situation where errors fortuitously cancel. The initial state will always be in error to some degree and perhaps seriously so in areas where data are absent or sparse. Moreover these errors will tend to contaminate forecasts in adjacent areas, especially downwind, but the reverse can also be true where forecasts from good data areas propagate disturbances into sparse data areas and improve the analyses by a better first guess. Understanding of atmospheric physical processes grows steadily, although many phenomena are still not well understood and some hardly at all. Even when understood moderately well a simulation may be rather poor because the small scales require parameterization in models with too large a grid distance to treat them explicitly, or because initial data may be lacking for small scales even if the gridlength is adequate. Despite the remarkable advances in computer technology, modelers have an insatiable appetite for faster computation and larger rapid-access storage. To be useful a forecast must be in the hands of the customer sufficiently far in advance to take advantage of the information. A perfect 24-hr "forecast" is of little value to the customer if it takes a day to prepare and deliver it to him.

A fundamental question related to accuracy is whether there exists an inherent limit to the range over which weather phenomena can be forecast with skill (measured against some kind of persistence and/or climatology). To put it another way, given unlimited computing power, correct representation of all the physical processes involved and accurate initial conditions, will it be possible to forecast with precision indefinitely into the future, or is there a fundamental limit to the predictability of the atmosphere? According to the present view the answer is that there are inherent limits, as discussed in the next section.

13-3 PREDICTABILITY OF THE ATMOSPHERE

Much has already been said or implied about the complexity of processes influencing the behavior of the atmosphere in which phenomena occur with scales ranging from the molecular to planetary and from microseconds to years, even millenia. Superficially at least, there appears to be a randomness in weather phenomena, except for a few obvious periodicities, such as the diurnal and annual cycles due to the daily rotation of the earth and to its revolution about the sun. Somewhat less regular, but also apparent, are related land-sea breeze, mountain-valley circulations, and other orographic forcing. Beyond these and perhaps a few others the weather varies in response to a myriad of atmospheric perturbations in the form of waves, vortices, circulations, etc., having life cycles ranging from minutes or less to days, weeks, months, and longer.

Intuitively we might expect that by and large the behavior of small size, short-lived perturbations would be predictable at most for only short periods of time, while the larger scales in space and time could be extrapolated forward in time for longer periods, assuming of course, that there is any predictable future behavior of a phenomenon beyond mere recognition of its existence at some given time. Practicing meteorologists are well aware of limitations to forecasting, such as insufficient data, incomplete understanding of various physical processes, etc. An important question however, perhaps philosophical at present but of eventual practical importance, is whether there is an *inherent limit* to the predictability of the atmosphere. To put it another way, if the physical processes were thoroughly understood, if the initial data were complete, and if there were unlimited computing power, would it be possible to make perfect forecasts indefinitely into the future? As might be anticipated the answer is *no,* as first discussed by Lorenz (1963a). He noted (1965) that the governing laws of motion are only approximations, the system of equations is not strictly deterministic and, finally, the initial state can never be perfectly known. Even if the system were strictly determined, two initial states, only very slightly different, depart from one another as time progresses and eventually become as different as two solutions chosen randomly from similar dates in past years. Since there will always be errors in the initial state and there is a natural tendency for errors to grow because of the nonlinearity of the equations and the instabilities in the atmosphere (barotropic, baroclinic, etc.), there is a fundamental time limit to atmospheric prediction.

Lorenz (1969a) suggested three approaches to estimating the error-growth rate and thus to the predictability of the atmosphere: (1) the dynamical method where a system of equations resembling the true system for the atmosphere is integrated forward in time from two slightly different initial states and the rate of amplification of their difference is determined; (2) a strictly empirical approach where historical data is examined to find pairs of initial states resembling one another as closely as possible and then the divergence of the pair of ''analogues'' with time is determined; and (3) the third method utilizes statistical theories of turbulence to study the nonlinear transfer of error between scales of motion and the error growth. Method 1 has been applied to the general circulation models by first integrating them forward in time from some arbitrary initial state until the fields are in approximate balance at, say t_0. Then the integration is continued as a *control run* for perhaps several weeks of simulated time after which a new run is begun again from t_0 with slight changes in one or more of the variables. For example, Smagorinsky (1969) at GFDL using their 10-level GCM imposed a random temperature disturbance with a standard deviation of 0.5°C at all levels. The vertical average of the standard deviation dropped from 0.5 to 0.2°C after 1 day reflecting a ''geostrophic-adjustment'' between the disturbance and the undisturbed fields. Thereafter the error growth was exponential for the next 7 days with a doubling time of about 2.5 days. Smagorinsky concluded that the deterministic limit of predictability for synoptic scale disturbances to be about three weeks, although at present skill runs out in less than a week. As expected, short-wave predictability decays most rapidly. When the same random errors were confined to an area in the southeast North Pacific they soon propagated outward and in about two weeks there were significant differences from the control run halfway around the globe in middle latitudes. Since it cannot be hoped to determine the initial state with such accuracy due to instrument errors, data gaps, etc., there is an obvious limit to forecasting. Smagorinsky concluded that the error growth was principally due to baroclinic stability, although Lorenz (1972) suggested barotropic instability as a possible secondary cause. If the grid is too coarse (mesh $> 5°$), energy conversion processes are impeded producing too-low energy levels. This slows error growth mechanisms and may lead to overoptimistic estimates of predictability.

Somerville (1979) pointed out that theory not only prescribes an inherent limit to the predictability of the atmosphere but indicates how forecasting skill decays with increasing time. Observational errors, usually in the smaller scales, amplify and through nonlinear interactions gradually spread to the longer scales eventually destroying all skill. As mentioned earlier this would occur no matter how perfect a prediction model beginning with nearly perfect data. The skill of actual forecasts done with imperfect models and initial data naturally falls considerably short of any inherent limits. Nevertheless the ultra-long waves ought to be forecast better than short waves since they are affected last by errors in the high wave numbers, but this is not the case with most NWP models. Somerville made intercomparisons of 5-day forecasts with several NWP models, including spectral types. He found that deficiencies in tropical data and limitation to a hemispheric domain accounted for significant errors in the ultra-long waves. A hemispheric model including tropical data fell between the best results with a global model with tropical data and the worst with a hemispheric model with data absent or severely constrained equatorward of 20 degrees latitude. The errors due to restricting domain to a hemisphere apparently produced significant errors late in the 5-day period; while eliminating data south of 20N appeared to cause significant errors in the ultra-long wave prediction very quickly in midlatitudes. Moreover the forecasts with a 2.5 degree grid produced substantially better results than a 4 by 5 degree grid but an even finer resolution did not yield much further improvement.

For method 2 Lorenz (1969c) utilized five years of twice daily heights of the 200-, 500-, and 850-mb pressure levels to find "analogues." Numerous mediocre analogues were found but no really good ones, as measured by RMS differences. He then observed the growth of error and concluded that very small errors double in about 2.5 days, which compares well with Smagorinsky's estimate. Lorenz also found that atmospheric states separated by 12 days resembled one another more than randomly chosen states even after an adjustment for seasonal trend. Higher correlations were obtained with a form of damped persistence. His results demonstrate the existence of partial predictability of weather patterns to at least 12 days.

Lorenz (1969b) also applied statistical theory to the spectral form of the two-dimensional vorticity equation to estimate predictability by method 3. Similar to Thompson (1957), he derived an equation for the error energy. To close the system Lorenz assumed a $-5/3$ law for the smaller scales in the mean kinetic energy spectrum. Numerical solutions gave rapid growth of error for the very small scales and very slow error growth for the large scales which led to a predictability time of about one hour for cumulus scales, a few days for synoptic disturbances and about 2½ weeks for the largest scales. If the initial error is confined to the smallest scales, the error in those scales quickly reaches the maximum error. Then error growth occurs in the next larger scales and so on until the error reaches the largest scales. Lorenz points out that if the error in the smallest scales is reduced, the range of predictability of the large scale features is only increased by a time interval something less than the limit of predictability of the small scales where the error was reduced. The foregoing results are critically dependent on the $-5/3$ *power law*.

This law led Robinson (1971) to conclude that the atmosphere was predictable for only a day or two. But Wiin-Nielsen et al. (1964) and Wiin-Nielsen (1967) showed from observations that a -3 *power law* fits the observational data better. Using this value Leith and Kraichman (1972) made predictability calculations with a two-dimensional turbulence model and gave a RMS error doubling time of two days, which is very close to previous results considering the simplicity of their model. They concluded that an initial state determined by a horizontal resolution feasible with a satellite-based observing system would result in a significant predictability of large-scale motion for more than a week.

In summary, predictability studies suggest that specific synoptic-scale weather patterns and events are predictable with skill for periods of roughly one to a couple weeks. Furthermore, the possibility exists that predicting trends of temperature and precipitation above or below normal for longer periods may be possible, and as discussed in Section 13-2-2, there already appears to be slight skill.

The foregoing discussion considered the predictability of dynamical models limited only by uncertainty in the initial state. For example, since the GCM integrations from slightly perturbed initial states were compared to the control runs to determine error growth, imperfections in the model physics, numerical errors, etc., were ignored. Real models are not perfect, and to understand actual predictive skill, it is desirable to sort out the influences of observation errors, analysis errors, model imperfections and inherent errors. Although RMS errors are often used as a measure of skill, error variance is more natural because it is additive for independent error sources.

Leith (1978) considers a simple error growth equation

$$\dot{E} = \alpha E + S \tag{13-1}$$

where the coefficient α gives the inherent error-growth rate and S accounts for model deficiencies. For an RMS doubling rate of 2.5 days, corresponding to a quadrupling of the error variance, $\alpha = 0.55$/day. Analysis and observational error variance are represented by E_0, which provides an initial value for E at $t = 0$. Integration (13-1) then gives

$$E_p(t) = 2E_0 + (E_0 + S/\alpha)\,[\exp(\alpha t) - 1] \tag{13-2}$$

where $E_p = E + E_0$, with the added E_0 accounting for the further error resulting from verification against a later analysis.

Data from the Goddard Institute (GISS) model used by Leith in connection with (13-2) gives $S/\alpha = 1650\ \text{m}^2$ and $E_0 = 200\ \text{m}^2$. Persistence forecasts correspond to $S_0/\alpha = 5280\ \text{m}^2$. Although these are only rough estimates, some interesting conclusions may be drawn. A natural measure of the relative importance of analysis errors versus model deficiencies is given by the ratio $E_0/(S/\alpha) = 0.12$, while the ratio of $1650\ \text{m}^2/5280\ \text{m}^2 = 0.31$ gives a measure of the GISS model-error-growth compared to persistence error growth. It is clear from these figures that the error growth for the model is much less than persistence and that for forecasting the 500-mb geopotential field, more skill is to be gained at present by improving the model than the analysis. Note, however, that if the value of E_0 is much larger, which could be true in sparse data areas, the analysis and model errors would be more similar. Somewhat different results are obtained for wind velocity errors by taking $E_0 = 15\ \text{m}^2/\text{sec}^2$ and $S/\alpha = 31.3\ \text{m}^2/\text{sec}^2$, which gives a ratio, $E_0/(S/\alpha) = 0.48$. Here the influence of analysis errors is closer to model imperfections; the reason is that the winds are related to geopotential gradients and therefore determined by smaller scales, which are analyzed less accurately.

The general conclusion from predictability studies is that the accuracy of NWP methods of forecasting has not yet reached the theoretical limits of skill and much can yet be done in modeling and also analysis to obtain more accuracy. Robert (1974) made some sensitivity experiments to determine the most important sources of possible improvements by running parallel experiments and suggested, in decreasing order of importance: horizontal resolution, mountain effects, precipitation, vertical resolution, initial data, horizontal eddy viscosity, and surface drag. Improving horizontal resolution, which has been studied most, not only improves phase propagation by reducing truncation errors, but also improves the nonlinear transfers of energy, vorticity, etc. between scales and the conversion of potential to kinetic energy, as mentioned earlier. Kraichman (1976) has shown that for an enstrophy-cascading (-3)-power energy spectrum in two-dimensional turbulence, which corresponds to the atmosphere, the error variance with truncation at wave number N would be fed into lower wave numbers at a rate proportional to N^{-2}.

13-4 STATISTICAL-DYNAMICAL PREDICTION

13-4-1 Simple Empirical Corrections

The models used for numerical prediction involve approximations of various sorts. Some of the meteorological quantities of interest, such as visibility, ceiling, maximum or minimum temperature, precipitation, etc. may not even be directly predicted. The use of statistical methods may be attempted either to improve the forecast of the dynamically predicted variables themselves or to use the predicted variables in multiple regression forecasts of variables that are not explicitly predicted. Early statistical attempts used the "*perfect prog*" method, that is, using as predictors observed data that are valid at the same time as the predictand. The regression equations so derived were then applied using the dynamically predicted variables as predictors in the regression equations. This technique was not very successful because whatever skill the regression equations possessed was largely lost due to errors in the dynamical forecast, that is, the "progs" are not perfect. However, since a dynamical model may have certain more or less characteristic errors, it was logical to consider developing the regression coefficients using the dynamically predicted variables as predictors, a method that is commonly referred to as "model output statistics" (MOS), [e.g., see Klein and Glahn (1974)]. The MOS procedure is widely used by the National Weather Service to provide probability forecasts of precipitation amount, maximum and minimum temperature, etc.

Leith (1978) discusses the statistical method of finding empirical corrections to variables explicitly predicted by dynamical methods as follows. Assume a dynamical system of the form

$$\dot{x} = q(x) + q' \tag{13-3}$$

where $q(x)$ represents the dynamical model and q' the rate of change of x from unknown processes. Next is is assumed that the dynamical system has a stationary ensemble or *climate* for which there is a known mean of x, $\langle x(t) \rangle = \mu$, and time-lagged covariance,

$$\langle [x(t + \tau) - \mu]^2 \rangle = \chi(\tau)$$

In addition, it is assumed that the model may be used to compute $<q[x(t)]> = \upsilon$ and the cross covariance,

$$<\{q[x(t) + \tau)] - \upsilon\} \quad \{x(t) - \mu\}> = T(\tau)$$

What is needed is an estimate of q' in terms of the known variable x. The linear regression estimate may be expressed as

$$\hat{q}' = <\dot{x} - q(x)> + (x - \mu)R$$

where R is the regression coefficient

$$R = <[\dot{x} - q(x) + \upsilon]\ [x - \mu]> x^{-1}(0)$$

Then the modified prediction equation (13-3) becomes

$$\dot{x} = q(x) - \upsilon + (x - \mu)R \tag{13-4}$$

From (13-4) it follows that $<\dot{x}>$ is zero, so the mean is preserved; and also the initial rate of change of the time-lagged second moment may be shown to be correct. Thus the modified model preserves the single-time second moments of the original dynamical ensemble, as well as yielding the best forecast in a least-squares sense. Leith generalized this scheme to an arbitrary number of variables. He points out that the regression matrix is subject to sampling-error limitations and also there is the problem of finding a few significant predictors for each component of $\mathbf{q}'$. He suggests that since correlations are local in space, the choice of predictors may be more effective in a gridpoint model than a spectral model.

13-4-2 Stochastic-Dynamical Prediction

Epstein (1969) introduced a more general statistical-dynamical approach that takes into account random errors in the observations and analysis that gives rise to uncertainties in the initial state. An ensemble of equally likely states leads to a series of forecasts whose mean gives the best forecasts. The spectral forms of the prediction equations are averaged over the ensemble which leads to an equation for *ensemble average* or *expected value* for each variable. These equations contain second moments in the form of variances and covariances between the dependent variables. Equations for the time change of the second moments are obtained by multiplying each equation by each of the variables and again forming an ensemble average. These equations contain third moments, and so forth, giving rise to the closure problem of classical turbulence theory. Epstein closed his system by neglecting the third moments about the instantaneous mean. He specified the initial expected value and its variance; initial covariances were set to zero. Integrations showed that the deterministic solution eventually diverges from the stochastic prediction of the expected value while the latter should be a better result. The predicted variances grow in time, which shows the influence of initial errors.

Also a large number of deterministic forecasts were made with slightly different initial conditions. The difference between a Monte Carlo average and the stochastic solution is a measure of the error caused by the closure assumption. In some of the solutions these quantities remained close, while in others they began to diverge.

Fleming (1971a) extended Epstein's model by including third-order moments, the equations for which involve quasi-normal approximations for the fourth-order moments in terms of second-order moments, and also included a linear damping term to avoid instability. Very good results were obtained; however, such stochastic-dynamic models use excessive computer time. As pointed out by Leith (1978), for a dynamical model with N degrees of freedom, there are N equations for developing first moments and $N(N + 1)/2$ for second moments, which already represents an increase of order N in arithmetic over the ordinary single model.

Leith (1974) concluded that such stochastic models cannot be used for large numerical models and suggested the Monte Carlo procedure of using a sample of m deterministic forecasts from different m initial states, which obviously increases the arithmetic by only a factor of m over an integration from a single initial state. Leith found sampling errors for $m = 8$ are relatively small for the determination of the ensemble mean, although not necessarily so for second moments. He also points out that statistical-dynamical methods based on the perfect-model assumption provide unrealistically low estimates of the growth of uncertainty as indicated by second-moment terms. As a result the benefits of such methods must await improvements in present dynamical models and there are plenty of opportunities for the latter. Forecasting accuracy is still considerably short of any estimated inherent limits. More research is needed in parameterization of sub-grid-scale process, treatment of moisture, mountains, etc.

13-5 CLIMATE AND CLIMATE PREDICTION

Climate and climate change have always interested humans and there are even more compelling reasons now because climate affects economic and social stability more than ever before. Global patterns of food production and population are closely dependent on climate, and human activities may cause undesirable changes in climate. While ice ages are only a remote possibility, they are not considered to be a real threat. Instead it is the irregular fluctuations in rainfall, temperature, and frost in agricultural areas, particularly in the marginal areas, such as the dry subtropics and colder places like Canada, Siberia, etc., where small changes in rainfall or temperature can be disastrous to the population.

Food production is highly dependent on favorable weather conditions during the growing season. Since the world's grain reserves are only a few percent of annual consumption, an unfavorable year with drought or cold temperatures has immediate consequences. As the world population increases the situation will become even more critical. Land suitable for agriculture and grazing is approaching full use, placing even greater dependence on climate. Any hope to reduce the impact of climate depends on a more thorough understanding of climate and climate change, including an assessment of artificial influences. Considerable knowledge has been accumulated about climate but little is understood about climate variability, which is essentially unpredictable at present. For example, there are divergent views about the cause of recent droughts and cold winters except for superficialities, and widely different predictions about coming seasons.

The World Meteorological Organization (WMO) and the International Council of Scientific Unions (ICSU) created a Joint Organizing Committee with the responsibility for planning a program for increased understanding of those large-scale fluctuations of the atmosphere that control weather with the aim of improving forecasting for periods of one day to several weeks and for predicting climate changes if possible. Toward the latter objective numerical models are to be developed to reconstruct the present and past climates including nearly equilibrium states. Climate research is to receive the primary research support during the 1980s.

The climate system, which is extremely complex, may be subdivided into the following components (τ gives approximate response time):

1. Atmosphere: the highly variable gaseous envelope encircling the earth, $\tau \sim$ 1 mo.
2. Oceans: the saline water of the oceans and the adjacent seas, for the upper layers, $\tau \sim$ 1 mo. to years: deep layers, $\tau \sim$ centuries.
3. Cryosphere: total snow deposits and ice masses of all kinds; $\tau \sim$ days to centuries.
4. Land: land, lakes, rivers, and ground water (part of hydrological cycle).
5. Biomass: humans, animals, plants, etc., which are important in the CO_2 budget, the vegetation cover and therefore the hydrological cycle.

The various influences on climate (which may be part of it) include variations in the rotation of the earth, the (related) amount of solar radiation, earth albedo, cloud cover, winds, water vapor, carbon dioxide and ozone content, ocean currents, and snow cover and ice, etc.

The largest single direct heat source for the atmosphere is the latent heat involved in the heat balance at the surface, especially over water and moist land, and aloft through condensation.

Because of the complexity of the climate system, even qualitative inferences are very difficult to make regarding the courses of climate change or the effects of a variation in some feature of one of the components of the system.

Consequently, physical mathematical models are expected to play an important role. The present GCM's (GFDL, UCLA, NCAR, GISS) have already provided valuable insights into the general circulation of the atmosphere, but they are not without shortcomings. Some common deficiencies are unrealistically cold polar regions, excessive vertical wind shear of the mean zonal winds, and too-weak transient planetary and cyclone scale eddies. Circulation differences between the two hemispheres are not fully understood, although differences in the land-sea masses are obviously important. Also the role of snow cover in forcing the large-scale circulation must be studied.

As described in earlier chapters good numerical models must not only properly simulate the scales of motion explicitly resolved but also correctly represent statistically the interactions between the resolvable scales and the sub-grid-scale phenomena that are parameterized. Among the latter are cumulus convection, the boundary layer, topographic affects, and radiative heating. Models conceived with climate and climate change in mind will have to parameterize many other processes in addition.

The use of the present GCM's in climate studies is limited by computing capability and is expected to remain so for the foreseeable future because of the short time step necessary to maintain computational stability and the long time scale of climate changes that may be measured in terms of millenia. It follows that highly parameterized models permitting large time steps must be used in attempting to simulate long-term climate changes such as glacial cycles and even much shorter ones as well.

Sources of data related to climate modeling include: (1) about 100 years of surface synoptic data, (2) about 40 years of upper-air synoptic data, (3) geological cores and (4) tree ring data. This is far from an adequate data base and coordinated efforts on a global scale are needed to augment present data. Planktonic records from ocean sediments and pollen records from bog and lake sediments are valuable for studying the long-term climatic changes. In general, the existing data monitoring should continue and be augmented by newer sources of data (e.g., from satellites). Very importantly the data must be put in convenient form (e.g., magnetic tapes) and made available to scientists.

Some interesting items from existing data and other sources are:

1. The Northern Hemisphere mean temperature increased from 1880 to 1940, which was as warm or warmer than any period in the last 500 years, but T has decreased since then (e.g., from 1958 to 1963, a decrease of 0.6°C).
2. CO_2 increased by 4 percent from 1958 to 1972 and about 13 percent from 1950 to 1977. The present prediction is for a continued increase of 32 percent by the year 2000 with an accompanying increase of 0.6°C in temperature.
3. Heat from thermal nuclear reactors might become a significant heat source.
4. Major glacial cycles are believed to be caused by changes in the distribution of solar radiation.
5. Variations in the orbital characteristics of the earth are considered to be the cause of major changes in climate about a half billion years ago.

6. The U. S. drought of the 1930s created a dust bowl that was followed by a low grain yield for years.

Dry years in developing countries can cause starvation and large-scale human migration. Indian agriculture is extremely dependent on the southwest-monsoon and disaster often follows a weak monsoon. The West Coast drought of 1976 and 1977 and the cold winters in the eastern half of the country caused considerable hardship even in our technologically advanced country.

As mentioned previously, the oceans and even large inland seas and lakes are a major influence on weather and climate. Because of their large heat-storage capacity, the major ocean currents may persistently warm or cool a region. Also as a result of the associated strong temperature gradients a displacement of a major current and/or the development of large eddies can result in ocean temperature anomalies that extend well into the thermocline and are reflected in SST differences of several degrees over thousands of kilometers. These anomalies may persist for periods of weeks to years and influence weather systems over a wide range of scales, not just for a matter of days, but over broad regions for months, even years. In the Northern Hemisphere the maximum heat flux from the ocean to the atmosphere takes place at about 40N off the east coasts of North America and Asia in winter where it has a strong influence on weather systems. Various experiments have been undertaken to study air-sea interactions [e.g., Barbados Oceanographic and Meteorological Experiment (BOMEX), the International Field Year of the Great Lakes (IFYGL), Garp Atlantic Tropical Experiment (GATE), Air-Mass Transformation Experiment (AMTEX), Mixed Layer Experiment (MILE), Joint Air-Sea Interaction Experiment (JASIN), and the Northern Pacific Experiment (NORPAX)].

Some data suggest that the meridional heat transports in the ocean are of the same order of magnitude though smaller than in the atmosphere. If so, it would be especially important to treat the ocean as an integral component of the climate system with coupled ocean-atmosphere models. In any case a better understanding of heat transport in the ocean by the mean vertical-meridional cells, mean large horizontal gyres, and also by eddies and surface transport is needed.

Even a modest skill in seasonal prediction would be very valuable. There are some claims that such skill already exists, but the more widely accepted view is that our understanding of climate and its variability is too meager to warrant predictions of this sort. It is also not possible to predict with confidence what the eventual effects of any large-scale efforts to modify climate might be except possibly in general terms, nor is it clear to what extent our activities have already inadvertently contributed to large-scale variations in climate as contrasted to the obvious small-scale effects of urbanization, such as pollution. On the other hand, with the present rate of energy consumption with its annual 5 percent increase there may be an eventual global impact. The resulting CO_2 increase and thermal pollution tend to produce a warming effect, while the aerosols may tend to produce net cooling. Considerably more effort can be made to refine the quantitative knowledge of past climatic variations and to establish causal factors. A hierarchy of climatic systems may be developed by shifting one of the components to an external role, for example, the ice or the ocean, to study the interactions or feedbacks between the diverse variables. The latter may, as internal controls with time scales of fractions of a year to thousands of years, amplify or dampen anomalies. Climate is very complex and an anomaly may trigger unforeseen events, hence varying internal and external parameters to test the effects of such perturbations are important *sensitivity* tests to be made.

Climate models will require conservation equations for atmospheric CO_2 and ozone, oceanic salt, and other important trace substances. In addition to previously discussed parameterizations, the formation of sea ice, hydrological processes, and aerosols must be included. In general, the longer the simulation period the more internal components to the system and parameterizations are required and the more statistical is the approach (versus dynamical). For example, in climate models the meridional transports of heat, moisture, momentum, and energy by synoptic-scale disturbances may be parameterized in terms of zonal values. Statistical properties determined by short runs with high-resolution models together with real data will be used to fix the parameterized processes in the low-resolution climate models.

In summary, the processes that determine climate are extremely complex and not well understood. The ability to predict climate change does not exist at present. But the disastrous effects of severe droughts and very cold temperatures are so great that even a very modest skill in forecasting temperatures and precipitation to be above, below, or near normal for coming seasons would be of great benefit. Consequently a substantial effort is being launched to study seasonal and longer-term climate variations and to develop methods of prediction if possible.

APPENDIX

Mathematical Relations

0.1 VECTOR OPERATIONS
0.2 INTEGRAL THEOREMS
0.3 GENERAL ORTHOGONAL COORDINATES
0.4 FOURIER SERIES
0.5 PARTIAL DIFFERENTIAL EQUATIONS

A-1 VECTOR OPERATIONS

$$\mathbf{A} \cdot (\mathbf{B} \times \mathbf{C}) = (\mathbf{A} \times \mathbf{B}) \cdot \mathbf{C} = (\mathbf{C} \times \mathbf{A}) \cdot \mathbf{B}$$

$$\mathbf{A} \times (\mathbf{B} \times \mathbf{C}) = (\mathbf{A} \cdot \mathbf{C})\mathbf{B} - (\mathbf{A} \cdot \mathbf{B})\mathbf{C} \tag{A-1}$$

$$\nabla \times \nabla \mathrm{a} = 0 \qquad \nabla \cdot \nabla \times \mathbf{A} = 0 \tag{A-2}$$

$$\nabla \cdot (\mathbf{aA}) = a\nabla \cdot \mathbf{A} + \mathbf{A} \cdot \nabla a \tag{A-3}$$

$$\nabla \times (a\mathbf{A}) = a\nabla \times \mathbf{A} - \mathbf{A} \times \nabla a \tag{A-4}$$

$$\nabla(\mathbf{A} \cdot \mathbf{B}) = (\mathbf{A} \cdot \nabla)\mathbf{B} + (\mathbf{B} \cdot \nabla)\mathbf{A} + \mathbf{A} \times (\nabla \times \mathbf{B}) + \mathbf{B} \times (\nabla \times \mathbf{A}) \tag{A-5}$$

$$\nabla \cdot (\mathbf{A} \times \mathbf{B}) = \mathbf{B} \cdot \nabla \times \mathbf{A} - \mathbf{A} \cdot \nabla \times \mathbf{B} \tag{A-6}$$

$$\nabla \times (\mathbf{A} \times \mathbf{B}) = \mathbf{A}\, \nabla \cdot \mathbf{B} - \mathbf{B}\, \nabla \cdot \mathbf{A} + (\mathbf{B} \cdot \nabla)\mathbf{A} - (\mathbf{A} \cdot \nabla)\mathbf{B} \tag{A-7}$$

$$(\mathbf{V} \cdot \nabla)\mathbf{V} = \nabla(\mathbf{V}^2/2) + (\nabla \times \mathbf{V}) \times \mathbf{V}, \text{ three dimensional} \tag{A-8}$$

$$(\mathbf{V}_H \cdot \nabla)\mathbf{V}_H = \nabla(\mathbf{V}_H^2/2) + \zeta\mathbf{k} \times \mathbf{V}_H;\ \zeta = \mathbf{k} \cdot \nabla \times \mathbf{V}_H, \text{ two dimensional} \tag{A-9}$$

$$\nabla \times (\nabla \times \mathbf{A}) = \nabla(\nabla \cdot \mathbf{A}) - \nabla^2\mathbf{A} \tag{A-10}$$

Let $\mathbf{V} = \mathbf{V}_\chi + \mathbf{V}_\psi$ where $\nabla \times \mathbf{V}_\chi = 0$ and $\nabla \cdot \mathbf{V}_\psi = 0$, (A-11)

then $\mathbf{V}_\chi = \nabla\chi$, $\mathbf{V}_\psi = -\nabla \times \boldsymbol{\Psi}$, where $\nabla^2\chi = \nabla \cdot \mathbf{V}_\chi = \nabla \cdot \mathbf{V}$

$$\nabla^2\boldsymbol{\Psi} = \nabla \times \mathbf{V}_\psi = \nabla \times \mathbf{V}$$

A-2 INTEGRAL THEOREMS

Definitions

dv: volume element
V: volume
$d\sigma$: surface element
Σ: surface enclosing V
S: plane surface
C: curve enclosing S
ds distance element along C
n: unit vector normal outward from Σ or C
t: unit tangent to C, S on left

Gauss Divergence Theorem

Three dimensional: (A-12)

$$\int_V \nabla \cdot \mathbf{A}\, dv = \int_\Sigma \mathbf{A} \cdot \mathbf{n}\, d\sigma$$

Two dimensional: (A-13)

$$\int_S \nabla \cdot \mathbf{A}\, d\sigma = \oint_C \mathbf{A} \cdot \mathbf{n}\, ds$$

Stokes Theorem (A-14)

$$\int_V \nabla \times \mathbf{A}\, dv = \int_\Sigma \mathbf{n} \times \mathbf{A}\, d\sigma$$

$$\int_S \mathbf{n} \cdot \nabla \times \mathbf{A}\, d\sigma = \oint_C \mathbf{A} \cdot \mathbf{t}\, ds \tag{A-15}$$

$$\int_V \nabla a\, dv = \int_\Sigma a\mathbf{n}\, d\sigma \tag{A-16}$$

A-3 GENERAL ORTHOGONAL COORDINATES

Let s_1, s_2, s_3 be scalar curvilinear distances; $\mathbf{a}_1$, $\mathbf{a}_2$, $\mathbf{a}_3$, local unit vectors in the direction of the coordinates, x_1, x_2, x_3; and define metric coefficients h_j such that $ds_j = h_j\, dx_j$. Then

$$\text{grad}\, A = \nabla A = \frac{\mathbf{a}_1}{h_1}\frac{\partial A}{\partial x_1} + \frac{\mathbf{a}_2}{h_2}\frac{\partial A}{\partial x_2} + \frac{\mathbf{a}_3}{h_3}\frac{\partial A}{\partial x_3} \tag{A-17}$$

$$\begin{aligned}\text{div}\,\mathbf{F} &= \nabla \cdot \mathbf{F} \\ &= \frac{1}{h_1 h_2 h_3}\left[\frac{\partial}{\partial x_1}(h_2 h_3 F_1) + \frac{\partial}{\partial x_2}(h_1 h_3 F_2) + \frac{\partial}{\partial x_3}(h_1 h_2 F_3)\right]\end{aligned} \tag{A-18}$$

$$\nabla^2 A = \frac{1}{h_1 h_2 h_3}\left[\frac{\partial}{\partial x_1}\left(\frac{h_2 h_3}{h_1}\frac{\partial A}{\partial x_1}\right) + \frac{\partial}{\partial x_2}\left(\frac{h_1 h_3}{h_2}\frac{\partial A}{\partial x_2}\right) + \frac{\partial}{\partial x_3}\left(\frac{h_1 h_2}{h_3}\frac{\partial A}{\partial x_3}\right)\right] \tag{A-19}$$

$$\begin{aligned}\text{curl}\,\mathbf{F} = {}& \frac{\mathbf{a}_1}{h_2 h_3}\left[\frac{\partial}{\partial x_2}(h_3 F_3) - \frac{\partial}{\partial x_3}(h_2 F_2)\right] + \frac{\mathbf{a}_2}{h_3 h_1}\left[\frac{\partial}{\partial x_3}(h_1 F_1) - \frac{\partial}{\partial x_1}(h_3 F_3)\right] \\ & + \frac{\mathbf{a}_3}{h_1 h_2}\left[\frac{\partial}{\partial x_1}(h_2 F_2) - \frac{\partial}{\partial x_2}(h_1 F_1)\right]\end{aligned} \tag{A-20}$$

$$\begin{aligned}\frac{dA}{dt} &= \frac{\partial A}{\partial t} + \frac{dx_1}{dt}\frac{\partial A}{\partial x_1} + \frac{dx_2}{dt}\frac{\partial A}{\partial x_2} + \frac{dx_3}{dt}\frac{\partial A}{\partial x_3} \\ &= \frac{\partial A}{\partial t} + \frac{v_1}{h_1}\frac{\partial A}{\partial x_1} + \frac{v_2}{h_2}\frac{\partial A}{\partial x_2} + \frac{v_3}{h_3}\frac{\partial A}{\partial x_3}, = \frac{\partial A}{\partial t} + (\mathbf{V} \cdot \nabla)A\end{aligned} \tag{A-21}$$

where $v_1 = ds_1/dt = h_1\, dx_1/dt$, etc., and $\mathbf{V} = v_1\mathbf{a}_1 + v_2\mathbf{a}_2 + v_3\mathbf{a}_3$

$$\frac{d\mathbf{F}}{dt} = \frac{dF_1}{dt}\mathbf{a}_1 + \frac{dF_2}{dt}\mathbf{a}_2 + \frac{dF_3}{dt}\mathbf{a}_3 + F_1\frac{d\mathbf{a}_1}{dt} + F_2\frac{d\mathbf{a}_2}{dt} + F_3\frac{d\mathbf{a}_3}{dt} \tag{A-22}$$

$$= \sum_{j=1}^{3}\left[\left(\frac{\partial F_j}{\partial t} + \mathbf{V}\cdot\nabla F_j\right)\mathbf{a}_j + F_j\sum_{i=1}^{3}\left(\frac{v_i}{h_i}\frac{\partial \mathbf{a}_j}{\partial x_i}\right)\right]$$

For $\mathbf{F} = \mathbf{V}$ (A-23)

$$\frac{d\mathbf{V}}{dt} = \sum_{j=1}^{3}\left[\left(\frac{\partial v_j}{\partial t} + \mathbf{V}\cdot\nabla v_j\right) + \sum_{\substack{i=1\\ i=j}}^{3}\left(\frac{v_j}{h_j}\frac{v_i}{h_i}\frac{\partial h_j}{\partial x_i} - \frac{v_i v_i}{h_i h_j}\frac{\partial h_i}{\partial x_j}\right)\right]\mathbf{a}_j$$

Examples:

Cartesian coordinates: x,y,z; $h_1 = h_2 = h_3 = 1$; $\mathbf{a}_1 = \mathbf{i}$, $\mathbf{a}_2 = \mathbf{j}$, $\mathbf{a}_3 = \mathbf{k}$
Spherical coordinates: λ, longitude; φ, latitude; radius r; metric coefficients: $h_\lambda = r\cos\varphi$, $h_\varphi = r$, $h_r = 1$.
Cylindrical coordinates: λ, r, z; $h_\lambda = r$, $h_r = h_z = 1$ (A-24)

A-4 FOURIER SERIES

If $f(x)$ is a continuously differentiable periodic function of period 2π, then

$$f(x) \sim \tfrac{1}{2}a_0 + \sum_{j=1}^{\infty}(a_j \cos jx + b_j \sin jx) \tag{A-25}$$

where

$$a_k = \frac{1}{\pi}\int_{-\pi}^{\pi} f(x)\cos kx\, dx,\quad b_k = \frac{1}{\pi}\int_{-\pi}^{\pi} f(x)\sin kx\, dx \tag{A-26}$$

FOURIER INTEGRAL

If $f(x)$ is sectionally continuous on every finite interval and $\int_{-\infty}^{\infty} f(x)\, dx$ converges, then

$$\tfrac{1}{2}[f(x+0) + f(x-0)] = \frac{1}{2\pi}\int_{-\infty}^{\infty} F(k)\, e^{-ixk}\, dk \tag{A-27}$$

$$F(k) = \int_{-\infty}^{\infty} e^{-ikx} f(x)\, dx \tag{A-28}$$

A-5 PARTIAL DIFFERENTIAL EQUATIONS

(a) Linear System

$$a_1u_x + b_1u_y + c_1v_x + d_1v_y = f_1 \tag{A-29}$$

$$a_2u_x + b_2u_y + c_2v_x + d_2v_y = f_2$$

The system A-29 is *hyperbolic, parabolic* or *elliptic* according to whether the *discriminant*

$$(a_1d_2 - a_2d_1 + b_1c_2 - b_2c_1)^2 - 4(a_1c_2 - a_2c_1)(b_1d_2 - b_2d_1) \gtreqless 0 \tag{A-30}$$

(b) Second-Order Equation

$$au_{xx} + bu_{xy} + cu_{yy} = f \tag{A-31}$$

Equation A-31 is hyperbolic, parabolic, or elliptic according to whether

$$b^2 - 4ac \begin{array}{lll} > 0 & \text{hyperbolic,} & \text{(two real characteristics)} \\ = 0 & \text{parabolic,} & \text{(two real identical characteristics)} \\ < 0 & \text{elliptic,} & \text{(two complex characteristics)} \end{array} \tag{A-32}$$

Characteristics are curves along which the second derivatives are indeterminate and thus provide paths along which discontinuities propagate. Hyperbolic and parabolic equations may be integrated along the characteristics to give future values of a dependent variable, whereas this is not possible with elliptic equations that do not have real characteristics. Hyperbolic and parabolic equations occur with initial value problems, while elliptic equations result from boundary value problems.

REFERENCES

Adams, J., P. Swarztrauber and R. Sweet, 1978: Efficient fortran subprograms for the solution of separable elliptic partial differential equations. Version 3. NCAR, Box 3000, Boulder, Colorado 80307.

Alexander, R. C., 1973: Ocean circulation and temperature prediction models: I, the Pacific. *The Rand Corporation, R-1296-ARPA,* 61 pp.

Andersen, J. H., 1977: A routine for normal mode initialization with nonlinear correction for a multilevel spectral model with triangular truncation. ECMWF Internal Report No. 15, 41 pp.

Anthes, R. A., N. Seaman, J. Sobel, and T. Warner, 1974: The development of mesoscale models suitable for air pollution studies. *Select Group in Air Pollution Meterorology, Second Annual Progress Report. Vol. 1.* Environmental Protection Agency, Research Triangle Park, N.C. 27711, 271 pp.

Anthes, R. A., 1976: Data assimilation and initialization of hurricane prediction models. *J. Atmos. Sci., 31,* 702-719.

Anthes, R. A., 1977a: Meteorological aspects of regional-scale air-quality modeling. *Adv. Envir. Sci. Eng., 1.*

Anthes, R. A., 1977b: A cumulus parameterization scheme utilizing a one-dimensional cloud model. *Mon. Wea. Rev., 105,* 270-286.

Anthes, R. A., 1977c: Hurricane model experiments with a new cumulus parameterization scheme. *Mon. Wea. Rev., 105,* 287-300.

Anthes, R. A., 1978: *The Thunderstorm: A Social, Scientific, Documentary.* Editor, Edwin Kessler, Oklahoma University Press.

Arakawa, A., 1960: Nongeostrophic effects in baroclinic prognostic equations. *Proc. Intern. Symp. Numerical Weather Prediction,* Tokyo.

Arakawa, A., 1962: The life cycle of large-scale disturbances. Paper delivered at the Fourth Numerical Prediction Conference, Los Angeles.

Arakawa, A., 1966: Computational design for long-term numerical integrations of the equations of atmospheric motion. *J. Comput. Phys., 1,* 119-143.

Arakawa, A., 1968: Numerical simulation of large-scale atmospheric motions. Numerical solution of field problems in continuum physics. *Proc. Symp. Appl. Math.,* Durham, N.C., 1968. *SIAM-AMS Proc., 2,* 24-40.

Arakawa, A., A. Katayama, and Y. Mintz, 1968: Numerical simulation of the general circulation of the atmosphere. *Proc. WMO/IUGG Symp. Numerical Weather Prediction,* Tokyo.

Arakawa, A., 1969: Parameterization of cumulus convection. *Proc. WMO/IUGG Symp. Numerical Weather Prediction,* Tokyo.

Arakawa, A., 1972: Design of the UCLA general circulation model. Numerical Simulation of Weather and Climate, Dept. of Meteorology, University of California, Los Angeles, *Tech. Rept. 7,* 116 pp.

Arakawa, A., and W. H. Schubert, 1974: Interaction of cumulus cloud ensemble with the large-scale environment, part I. *J. Atmos. Sci., 31,* 674-701.

Arakawa, A., Y. Mintz, A. Katayama, J.-W. Kim, W. Schubert, T. Tokioka, M. Schlesinger, W. Chao, D. Randall, and S. Lord, 1974: The UCLA atmospheric general circulation model. Notes distributed at workshop 26 March-April, University of California, Los Angeles.

Arakawa, A., and V. R. Lamb, 1977: Computational design of the basic dynamical processes of the UCLA general circulation model. *Methods in Computational Physics, Vol. 17,* Academic Press, 174-265, 337 pp.

Arakawa, A., and V. R. Lamb, 1978: Finite difference scheme for the nonlinear shallow-water equations. Unpublished Manuscript (replaces section IV-C in Arakawa and Lamb (1977).)

Arakawa, A., 1978: Numerical simulation of flow with a potential enstrophy conserving scheme for the shallow water equations. *NSA Simulation Seminar, Paper #20,* 111-115.

Arnason, G., 1957: A convergent method for solving the balance equation. *Joint NWP Unit Tech. Note,* Suitland, Md.

Asselin, R. A., 1972: Frequency filter for time integrations. *Mon. Wea. Rev., 100,* 487-490.

Baer, F., and G. W. Platzman, 1961: A procedure for numerical integration of the spectral vorticity equation. *J. Meteor., 18,* 393-401.

Baer, F., 1964: Integration of the spectral vorticity equation. *J. Atmos. Sci., 21,* 260-276.

Baer, F., 1968: Studies in low-order spectral systems. *Atmos. Sci. Paper No. 129,* Dept. of Atmos. Sci., Colorado State University.

Baer, F., 1977: Adjustment of initial conditions required to suppress gravity oscillations in nonlinear flows. *Contrib. Atmos. Phys., 50,* 350-366.

Baer, F., and J. Tribbia, 1977: On complete filtering of gravity modes through nonlinear initialization. *Mon. Wea. Rev., 105,* 1536-1539.

Barker, E., G. Haltiner, and Y. Sasaki, 1977: Three-dimensional initialization using variational analysis. *Proceedings of the Third Conference on Numerical Weather Prediction of the American Meteorological Society,* Omaha.

Bengtsson, L., 1975: 4-dimensional assimilation of meteorological observations. WMO/ICSU Joint Organizing Committee, *GARP Publications Series No. 15,* 76 pp.

Bengtsson, L., 1976: Initial data and some practical aspects of weather forecasting. *Weather Forecasting and Weather Forecasts: Models, Systems and Users, Vol. 1,* NCAR/CQ-5 + 1976 ASP.

Bjerknes, V., 1904: Das problem von der wettervorhersage, betrachtet vom standpunkt der mechanik und der physik. *Meteor. Z., 21,* 1-7.

Blackadar, A. K., 1962: The vertical distribution of wind and turbulent exchange in a neutral atmosphere. *J. Geophys. Res., 67,* 3095-3102.

Blackadar, A. K., and H. Tennekes, 1968: Asymptotic similarity in neutral barotropic planetary boundary layers. *J. Atmos. Sci., 25*(6), 1015-1020.

Blackadar, A. K. 1974: Experiments with simplified second-moment approximations for use in regional scale models. *Select Research Group in Air Pollution Meteorology, Second Annual Progress Report,* EPA-650/4-74-045, 676 pp.

Blackadar, A. K., 1977: High resolution models of the planetary boundary layer. *Advances Environmental Science and Engineering, Vol. 1.,* Editors: Pfafflin & Ziegler, Gordon & Breach, Scientific Publishers.

Blandford, R., 1971: Boundary conditions in homogeneous ocean models. *Deep-Sea Res., 18,* 739-751.

Bleck, R., 1973: Numerical forecasting experiments based on the conservation of potential vorticity on isentropic surfaces. *Journal of Applied Meteorology, 12*, 737-752.

Bleck, R., 1974: Short-range prediction in isentropic coordinates with filtered and unfiltered numerical models. *Mon. Wea. Rev., 102,* 813-829.

Bleck, R., 1977: Numerical simulation of lee cyclogenesis in the Gulf of Genoa. *Mon. Wea. Rev., 105,* 428-445.

Bleck, R., 1978: On the use of hybrid vertical coordinates in numerical weather prediction models. *Mon. Wea. Rev., 106,* 1233-1244.

Bourke, W., 1972: An efficient, one-level, primitive-equation spectral model. *Mon. Wea. Rev., 100,* 683-689.

Bourke, W., B. McAvaney, K. Puri, and R. Thurling, 1977: Global modeling of atmospheric flow by spectral methods. *Methods in Computational Physics, Vol. 17,* Academic Press, 267-324, 337 pp.

Brekhovskikh, L. M., K. N. Fedorov, L. M. Fomin, M. Koshlyakov, and A. D. Yampolsky, 1971: Large-scale multibuoy experiment in the Tropical Atlantic. *Deep-Sea Res., 18,* 1189-1206.

Brown, H. A., and K. A. Campana, 1978: An economical time-differencing system for numerical weather prediction. *Mon. Wea. Rev., 106,* 1025-1036.

Bryan, K., 1963: A numerical investigation of a nonlinear model of a wind-driven ocean. *J. Atmos. Sci., 20,* 594-606.

Bryan, K., and M. D. Cox, 1967: A numerical investigation of the oceanic general circulation. *Tellus, 19,* 54-80.

Bryan, K., and M. D. Cox, 1968a: A nonlinear model of an ocean driven by wind and differential heating: Part I. Description of the three-dimensional velocity and density fields. *J. Atmos. Sci., 25,* 945-967.

Bryan, K., and M. D. Cox, 1968b: A nonlinear model of an ocean driven by wind and differential heating: Part II. An analysis of the heat, vorticity and energy balance. *J. Atmos. Sci., 25,* 968-978.

Bryan, K., 1975: Three-dimensional numerical models of the ocean circulation. *Proc. Symp. on Numerical Models of Ocean Circulation,* Durham, N.H. National Academy of Sciences, Washington, D. C., 94-106.

Buneman, O., 1969: A compact non-iterative Poisson solver. *SUIPR Rep. No. 294,* Inst. for Plasma Research, Stanford University.

Burger, A., 1958: Scale considerations of planetary motions of the atmosphere. *Tellus, 10,* 195-205.

Burger, A., 1962: On the non-existence of critical wavelengths in a continuous baroclinic stability problem. *J. Atmos. Sci., 19,* 30-38.

Burridge, D. M., and F. R. Hayes, 1974: Development of the British operational model. *The GARP Programme on Numerical Experimentation, Rept. 4,* 102-104.

Burridge, D. M., and J. Haseler, 1977: A model for medium range weather forecasting. *European Centre for Medium Range Weather Forecasting, Tech Rept. No. 4,* Bracknell, Berks, U.K.

Busch, N. E., S. W. Chang, and R. A. Anthes, 1976: A multi-level model of the planetary boundary layer suitable for use with mesoscale dynamic models. *J. Appl. Meteor., 15,* 909-919.

Businger, J. A., J. C. Wyngaard, Y. Izumi, and E. F. Bradley, 1971: Flux profile relationships in the atmospheric surface layer. *J. Atmos. Sci., 28,* 181-189.

Businger, J. A., and S. P. S. Arya, 1974: Height of the mixed layer in the stably stratified planetary boundary layer. *Advances in Geophysics, Vol. 18A,* Academic Press, 73-92.

Buzbee, B. L., G. H. Golub and C. W. Nielson, 1970: On direct methods for solving Poisson's equations. S.I.A.M., *J. of Numerical Analysis, 7,* 627-655.

Cahn, A., 1945: An investigation of the free oscillations of a simple current system. *J. Meteor., 2,* 113-119.

Camerlengo, A., and J. J. O'Brien, 1979: Open boundary conditions in rotating fluids. To be published, *J. Comp. Phys.*

Case, K. M., 1960: Stability of plane couette flow. *Phys. Fluids, 3,* 143-148.

Chang, C.-P., 1976: Forcing of stratospheric Kelvin waves by tropospheric heat sources. *J. Atmos. Sci., 33,* 740-744.

Chang, C.-P., 1977: Viscous internal gravity waves and low-frequency oscillation in the tropics. *J. Atmos. Sci., 34,* 901-910.

Charney, J. G., R. Fjørtoft, and J. von Neumann, 1950: Numerical integration of the barotropic vorticity equation. *Tellus, 2,* 237-254.

Charney, J. G., 1947: The dynamics of long waves in a baroclinic westerly current. *J. Meteor., 4,* 135-162.

Charney, J. G., 1948: On the scale of atmospheric motions. *Geofys. publik., 17,* 17 pp.

Charney, J. G., 1949: On a physical basis for numerical prediction of large-scale motions in the atmosphere. *J. Meteor., 6,* 371-385.

Charney, J. G., and A. Eliassen, 1949: A numerical method for predicting the perturbations on the middle-latitude westerlies. *Tellus, 1,* 38-54.

Charney, J. G., and N. A. Phillips, 1953: Numerical integration of the quasi-geostrophic equations for barotropic and simple baroclinic flows. *J. Meteor., 10,* 71-99.

Charney, J. G., 1954: Numerical prediction of cyclogenesis. *Proc. Natl. Acad. Sci. U.S., 40,* no. 2, 99-110.

Charney, J. G., 1955a: The use of the primitive equations of motion in numerical prediction. *Tellus, 7,* 22-26.

Charney, J. G., 1955b: The Gulf Stream as an inertial boundary layer, *Proc. Natl. Acad. Sci. U.S., 41,* no. 10, 731-740.

Charney, J. G., B. Gilchrist, and F. Shuman, 1956: The prediction of general quasi-geostrophic motions. *J. Meteor., 13,* 489-499.

Charney, J. G., and P. G. Drazin, 1961: Propagation of planetary-scale disturbances from the lower into the upper atmosphere. *J. Geophys. Res., 66,* 83-109.

Charney, J. G., 1962: Integration of the primitive and balance equations. *Proc. Intern. Symp. Numerical Weather Prediction,* Tokyo.

Charney, J. G., and M. Stern, 1962: On the stability of internal baroclinic jets in rotating atmosphere. *J. Atmos. Sci., 19,* 159-172.

Charney, J. G., and J. Pedlosky, 1963: On the trapping of unstable planetary waves in the atmosphere. *J. Geophys. Res., 68,* 6441-6442.

Charney, J. G., 1963: A note on large-scale motions in the tropics. *J. Atmos. Sci., 20,* 607-609.

Charney, J. G., 1966: Some remaining problems in numerical weather prediction. *Advances in Numerical Weather Prediction,* Hartford, Conn., Travelers Research Center, Inc., 61-70.

Charnock, H., 1955: Wind stress on the water surface. *Quart. J. Roy. Meteor. Soc., 81,* 639-640.

Clarke, R. H., 1970: Recommended methods for the treatment of the boundary layer in numerical models. *Austral. Meteor. Mag., 18,* 51-73.

Cooley, J. W., and J. W. Tukey, 1965: An algorithm for the machine computation of complex Fourier series. *Math. Comp., 19,* 297-301.

Corby, G. A., A. Gilchrist, and R. L. Newson, 1972: A general circulation model of the atmosphere suitable for long period integrations. *Quart J. Roy. Meteor. Soc., 98,* 809-832.

Coulson, L. L., 1959: Radiative flux from the top of a Rayleigh atmosphere. Ph.D. Thesis, Dept. Met., UCLA, 176 pp.

Courant, R., K. O. Friedrichs, and H. Lewy, 1928: Uber die partiellen differenzengleichungen der mathematischen physik. *Math. Annalen, 100,* 32-74.

Cressman, G. P., 1958: Barotropic divergence and very long atmospheric waves. *Mon. Wea. Rev., 86,* 293-297.

Cressman, G. P., 1959: An operative objective analysis scheme. *Mon. Wea. Rev., 87,* 367-374.

Cressman, G. P., 1960: Improved terrain effects in barotropic forecasts. *Mon. Wea. Rev., 88,* 327-342.

Cressman, G. P., 1963: A three-level model suitable for daily numerical forecasting. *Natl. Meteor. Center, U.S. Weather Bureau, Tech. Memo.*

Cressman, G. P., 1978: A notable forecasting achievement. *Bull. Am. Met. Soc., 59,* 370.

Cullen, M. J. P., 1973: A simple finite element method for meteorological problems. *J. Inst. Math. Applics., 11,* 15-31.

Cullen, M. J. P., 1974: Integration of the primitive equations on a sphere using the finite element method. *Quart. J. Roy. Meteor. Soc., 100,* 555-562.

Cullen, M. J. P., 1976: On the use of artificial smoothing in Galerkin and finite difference solutions of the primitive equations. *Quart. J. Roy. Meteor. Soc., 102,* 77-93.

Daley, R., C. Girard, J. Henderson, and I. Simmonds, 1976: Short-term forecasting with a multi-level spectral primitive equation model. *Atmos., 14,* 98-116.

Daley, R., 1978: Variational nonlinear normal mode initialization. *Tellus, 30,* 201-218.

Daley, R., 1979: The application of nonlinear normal mode initialization to an operational forecast model. *Atmos.-Ocean, 17,* 98-123.

Deardorff, J. W., 1972: Parameterization of the planetary boundary layer for use in general circulation models. *Mon. Wea. Rev., 100,* 93-106.

Deardorff, J. W., 1974: Three-dimensional numerical study of turbulence in an entraining mixed layer. *Bound. Layer Meteor., 7,* 199-226.

Deardorff, J. W., 1976: On the entrainment rate of a stratocumulus-topped mixed layer. *Quart. J. Roy. Meteor. Soc., 102,* 563-582.

Delsol, F., K. Miyakoda, and R. H. Clarke, 1971: Parameterized processes in the surface boundary layer of an atmospheric circulation model. *Quart. J. Roy. Meteor. Soc., 97,* 181-208.

Desai, C. S., and J. Abel, 1972: *Introduction to the Finite Element Method.* Van Nostrand Reinhold, 477 pp.

DeSzoeke, R. A., and P. B. Rhines, 1976: Asymptotic regimes in mixed layer deepening. *J. Mar. Res., 34,* 111-116.

Dickinson, R. E., 1969: Vertical propagation of planetary Rossby waves through an atmosphere with Newtonian cooling. *J. Geophys. Res., 74,* 929-938.

Dickinson, R. E., and D. L. Williamson, 1972: Free oscillations of a discrete stratified fluid with application to numerical weather prediction. *J. Atmos. Sci., 29,* 623-640.

Dickinson, R. E., 1973: Method of parameterization for infrared cooling between the altitudes of 30 and 70 kilometers. *J. Geophys. Res., 78,* 4451-4457.

Doron, E., A. Hollingsworth, B. J. Hoskins, and A. Simmons, 1974: A comparison of grid-point and spectral methods in a meteorological problem. *Quart. J. Roy. Meteor. Soc., 100,* 371-383.

Dyer, A. J., 1974: A review of flux-profile relationships. *Bound. Layer Meteor., 7,* 363-372.

Eady, E. T., 1949: Long waves and cyclone waves. *Tellus, 1,* no. 3, 33-52.

Ekman, V. W., 1902: *Myt. Mag. Naturo., 40.*

Eliassen, A., 1949: The quasi-static equations of motion with pressure as independent variable. *Geofys. Publik., 17,* no. 3, 44 pp.

Eliassen, A., 1954: Provisional report on calculation of spatial covariance and autocorrelation of the pressure field. *Inst. Weather and Climate Res. Academy Science,* Oslo, Rep. No. 5, 11 pp.

Eliassen, A., 1956: A procedure for numerical integration of the primitive equations of the two-parameter model of the atmosphere. *Sci. Rept. no. 4,* Dept. of Meteorology, UCLA.

Eliassen, A., and E. Palm, 1960: On the transfer of energy in stationary mountain waves. *Geofys. Publ. 22,* no. 3, 22 pp.

Eliassen, A., and E. Raustein, 1968: A numerical integration experiment with a model atmosphere based on isentropic coordinates. *Meteor. Ann., 5,* 45-63.

Eliassen, A., and E. Raustein, 1970: A numerical integration experiment with a six-level atmospheric model with isentropic information surface. *Meteor. Ann., 5,* 429-449.

Eliasen, E., B. Machenhauer, and E. Rasmussen, 1970: On a numerical method for integration of the hydrodynamical equations with a spectral representation of the horizontal fields, *Rept. No. 2,* Institut for Teoretisk Meteorologi, Kobenhavns Universitet, Denmark, 35 pp.

Elsasser, W. M., 1942: Heat transfer by infrared radiation in the atmosphere. *Harvard Meteorological Studies,* no. 6, 107 pp.

Elsberry, R. L., T. S. Fraim, and R. N. Trapnell, Jr., 1976: A mixed-layer model of the oceanic thermal response to hurricanes. *J. Geophys. Res., 81,* 1153-1162.

Elvius, T., and A. Sundström, 1973: Computationally efficient schemes and boundary conditions for a fine mesh barotropic model based on the shallow water equations. *Tellus, 25,* 132-156.

Epstein, E. S., 1969: Stochastic dynamic prediction. *Tellus, 21,* 739-757.

Ertel, H., 1942: Ein neuer hydrodynamis cher Wirbelsatz, *Meteorol. Z., 59,* 277-281.

Estoque, M. A., and C. M. Bhumralkar, 1970: A method for solving the planetary boundary layer equations. *Bound. Layer Meteor., 1,* 169-194.

Faulkner, F. D., 1976: The numerical solution of the Helmholtz equation on a sphere. NPS-53Fa76025, Naval Postgraduate School, Monterey, Calif.

Faulkner, F. D., and T. E. Rosmond, 1976: Direct solution of elliptic equations by block cyclic reduction and factorization. *Mon. Wea. Rev., 104,* 641-649.

Fix, G., 1975: Finite element models for ocean circulation problems. *SIAM J. Appl. Math., 29,* 371-387.

Fjørtoft, R., 1953. On the changes in the spectral distribution of kinetic energy for two-dimensional, nondivergent flow. *Tellus, 5,* 225-230.

Flattery, T. W., 1967: Hough functions. *Tech. Rept. 21,* Dept. Geophys. Sci., The University of Chicago.

Flattery, T. W., 1971: Spectral models for global analysis and forecasting. *Proc. AWS Tech. Exch. Conf. U.S. Naval Academy,* September 1970, 42-54.

Fleming, R. J., 1971a: On stochastic dynamic prediction: I. The energetics of uncertainty and the question of closure. *Mon. Wea. Rev., 99,* 851-872.

Fleming, R. J., 1971b: On stochastic dynamic prediction: II. Predictability and utility. *Mon. Wea. Rev., 99,* 927-938.

Fleming, R. J., 1972: Predictability with and without the influence of random external forces. *J. Appl. Meteor., 11,* 1155-1163.

Fofonoff, N. P., 1954: Steady flow in a frictionless homogeneous ocean. *J. Mar. Res., 13,* 254-262.

Gadd, A. J., and Keers, J. F., 1970: Surface exchanges of sensible and latent heat in a 10-level model atmosphere: *Quart. J. Roy. Meteor. Soc., 96,* 297-308.

Gadd, A. J., 1974a: An economical explicit integration scheme. *Meteor. Office Tech. Note 44,* 7 pp.

Gadd, A. J., 1974b: Fourth-order advection schemes for the 10 level model. *Meteor. Office Tech. Note 45,* 8 pp.

Gadd, A. J., 1978: A split explicit integration scheme for numerical weather prediction. *Quart. J. Roy. Meteor. Soc., 104,* 569-582.

Gall, R. L., 1972: Prediction of a quasi-steady propagating jet core with an isentropic numerical model. Ph.D. thesis, University of Wisconsin, 121 pp.

Gall, R. L., 1976: A comparison of linear baroclinic theory with the eddy statistics of a general circulation model. *J. Atmos. Sci., 33,* 349-373.

Gall, R. L., R. Blakeslee, and R. C. J. Somerville, 1979: Baroclinic instability and the selection of the zonal scale of the transient eddies of middle latitudes. *J. Atmos. Sci., 37,* 767-784.

Gallagher, R., and S. Chan, 1973: Higher order finite element analysis of lake circulation. *Computers and Fluids, 1,* 119-132.

Galt, J. A., 1975: Development of a simplified diagnostic model for interpretation of oceanographic data. *NOAA Technical Report ERL339-PMEL25,* 46 pp.

Gambo, K., 1950: The criteria for stability of the westerlies. *Geophys. Notes, Japan, 3,* 1-13.

Gambo, K., 1957: The scale of atmospheric motions and the effect of topography on numerical weather prediction in the lower atmosphere. *Papers in Meteorology and Geophys., 8, no. 1,* 1-24.

GARP Working Group on Numerical Experimentation, 1974: Report of the International Symposium on spectral methods in numerical weather prediction. *Report No. 7,* 503 pp.

Gandin, L. S., 1959: A problem of optimum interpolation. Proc. Main Geophys., Obs. 99.

Gandin, L. S., 1963: Objective analysis of meteorological fields. Guidrometeorizdat. Izdaf., Leningrad.

Gandin, L. S., 1964: On optimal interpolation of vector fields. Trudy GGO, No. 165, 47-69.

Garret, J. R., 1977: Review of drag coefficients over oceans and continents. *Mon. Wea. Rev., 105,* 915-929.

Garwood, R. W., Jr., 1977: An oceanic mixed layer model capable of simulating cyclic states. *J. Phys. Oceanogr., 7,* 455-468.

Gates, W. L., 1959: On the truncation error, stability and convergence of difference solutions of the barotropic vorticity equation. *J. Meteor., 16,* 556-568.

Gates, W. L., 1961: The stability properties and energy transformations of the two-layer model of variable static stability. *Tellus, 13,* 460-471.

Gates, W. L., and C. A. Riegel, 1962: A study of numerical errors in the integration of barotropic flow on a spherical grid. *J. Geoph. Res., 67,* 773-784.

Gates, W. L., 1968: A numerical study of transient Rossby waves in a wind-driven homogeneous ocean. *J. Atmos. Sci., 25,* 3-22.

Gerald, C. F., 1978: *Applied Numerical Analysis.* Addison-Wesley Publishing Co., 577 pp.

Gerrity, J. P., Jr., and McPherson, R. D., 1971: On an efficient scheme for the numerical integration of a primitive-equation barotropic model. *J. Appl. Meteor., 10,* 353-363.

Gerrity, J. P., 1973: On map projections for numerical weather predictions. *NOAA, NWS, NMC Office Note 87.*

Gerrity, J. P., 1978: Global weather experiment—perspectives on its implementation and exploitation. Report of FGGE Advisory Panel, National Academy of Science.

Gordon, T., and W. Stern, 1974: *Spectral Modeling at GFDL.* GARP Working Group on Numerical Experimental, no. 7, 46-82.

Green, J. S. A., 1960: A problem in baroclinic stability, *Quart J. Roy. Meteor. Soc., 86,* 237-251.

Greenspan, H. P., 1968: *The Theory of Rotating Fluids.* Cambridge University Press, 327 pp.

Gustafson, T., and B. Kullenberg, 1936: Untersuchungen von Trägheits-Stromungen in der Ostsee. *Svenska Hydrogr.-Biol. Komm. Skr.,* Ny, Hydro 13, 28 pp.

Haltiner, G. J., and F. L. Martin, 1957: *Dynamical and Physical Meteorology.* McGraw-Hill Book Co., 470 pp.

Haltiner, G. J., 1959: On the theory of convective currents. *Tellus, 11,* 4-15.

Haltiner, G. J., 1960: Some further results on convective currents. *Tellus, 12,* 393-398.

Haltiner, G. J., G. Arnason, and J. Frawley, 1962; Higher order geostrophic wind approximations. *Mon. Wea. Rev., 90,* 175-185.

Haltiner, G. J., and D. E. Caverly, 1965: The effect of friction on the growth and structure of baroclinic waves. *Quart. J. Roy. Meteor. Soc., 91,* 209-214.

Haltiner, G. J., 1967: The effects of sensible heat exchange on the dynamics of baroclinic waves. *Tellus, 19,* 183-198.

Haltiner, G. J., 1971: *Numerical Weather Prediction.* John Wiley and Sons, Inc., 317 pp.

Haltiner, G. J., and J. M. McCollough, 1975: Experiments in initialization. *J. Appl. Meteor., 14,* 281-288.

Haltiner, G. J., Y. K. Sasaki, and E. H. Barker, 1975: A variational procedure for obtaining global balanced winds. *Proceedings of the JOC Study Group Conference on Four-Dimensional Data Assimilation.* Paris, 17-21 November, *11,* 198-223.

Haltiner, G. J., and E. H. Barker, 1976: Initial balancing with a variational method. *Analen Der Meteorologie. Neue Folge Nr. 11,* 119-121.

Haney, R. L., 1974: A numerical study of the response of an idealized ocean to large-scale surface heat and momentum flux. *J. Phys. Oceanogr., 2,* 145-167.

Haney, R. L., and J. M. Wright Jr., 1975: The relationship between the grid size and the coefficient of nonlinear lateral eddy viscosity in numerical ocean circulation models. *J. Comp. Phys., 19,* 257-266.

Haney, R. L., W. S. Shiver, and K. H. Hunt, 1978: A dynamical-numerical study of the formation and evolution of large-scale ocean anomalies, *J. Phys. Oceanogr., 8,* 952-969.

Haque, S. M. A., 1952: The initiation of cyclonic circulation in a vertically unstable stagnant air mass. *Quart. J. Roy. Meteor. Soc., 78,* 394-406.

Harrison, E. J., Jr., and R. L. Elsberry, 1972: A method for incorporating nested finite grids in the solution of systems of geophysical equations. *J. Atmos. Sci., 29,* 1235-1245.

Harrison, E. J., Jr., 1973: Three-dimensional numerical simulations of tropical systems utilizing nested finite grids. *J. Atmos. Sci., 30,* 1528-1543.

Haurwitz, B., 1940: The motion of atmospheric disturbances on the spherical earth. *J. Marine Res., 3,* 254-267.

Hayashi, Y., 1976: Non-singular resonance of equatorial waves under the radiation condition. *J. Atmos. Sci., 33,* 183-201.

Hinkelmann, K., 1951: Der mechanismus des meteorologischen Larmes. *Tellus, 3,* 285-296.

Hinkelmann, K., 1959: Ein numerisches experiment mit den primitiven gleichungen. *The Atmosphere and the Sea in Motion,* Rossby Memorial Volume, Rockefeller Institute Press, 486-500, 509 pp.

Hinsman, D. E., 1975: Application of a finite element method to the barotropic primitive equations. M.S. thesis, Naval Postgraduate School, Monterey, Calif., 116 pp.

Hoke, J. E., and R. A. Anthes, 1976: The initialization of numerical models by a dynamic initialization technique. *Mon. Wea. Rev., 104,* 1551-1556.

Holland, W. R., 1967: On the wind-driven circulation in an ocean with bottom topography. *Tellus, 19,* 582-600.

Holland, W. R., and A. D. Hirschman, 1972: A numerical calculation of the circulation in the North Atlantic Ocean. *J. Phys. Oceanogr., 2,* 336-354.

Holland, W. R., 1973: Baroclinic and topographic influences on the transport in western boundary currents. *Geophys. Fluid Dyn., 4,* 187-210.

Holland, W. R., and L. B. Lin, 1975: On the generation of mesoscale eddies and their contribution to the oceanic general circulation. I. A preliminary numerical experiment. *J. Phys. Oceanogr., 5,* 642-657.

Holton, J. R., 1970: A note on forced equatorial waves. *Mon. Wea. Rev., 98,* 614-615.

Holton, J. R., 1972a: *An Introduction to Dynamic Meteorology.* Academic Press, 319 pp.

Holton, J. R., 1972b: Waves in the equatorial stratosphere generated by tropospheric heat sources. *J. Atmos. Sci., 29,* 368-375.

Holton, J. R., and R. Lindzen, 1972: An updated theory for the quasi-biennial cycle of the tropical stratosphere. *J. Atmos. Sci., 29,* 1076-1080.

Holton, J. R., 1975: *The Dynamic Meteorology of the Stratosphere and Mesosphere.* American Meteorological Society, 218 pp.

Hoskins, B. J., and A. J. Simmons, 1975: A multi-layer spectral model and the semi-implicit method. *Quart. J. Roy. Meteor. Soc., 101,* 637-655.

Hough, S. S., 1898: On the application of harmonic analysis to the dynamical theory of tides, 2, On the general integration of Laplace's dynamical equations, *Phil. Trans. Roy. Soc. London,* A, *191,* 139-185.

Joint Organizing Committee, 1974: Modeling for the first GARP global experiment. *GARP Publication Series No. 14,* WMO/ICSU Joint Organizing Committee, 260 pp.

Jones, R. W., 1977: A nested grid for a three-dimensional model of a cyclone. *J. Atmos. Sci., 34,* 1528-1553.

Joseph, J. H., 1966: Calculation of radiative heating in numerical general circulation models, *Numerical Simulation of Weather And Climate, Tech. Rept. No. 1,* Dept. Met., UCLA, 60 pp.

Joseph, J. H., 1970: On the calculation of solar radiation fluxes in the troposphere. *Solar Energy, 13,* 251-261.

Kasahara, A., 1965: On certain finite-difference methods for fluid dynamics. *Mon. Wea. Rev., 93,* 27-31.

Kasahara, A., and T. Asai, 1967: Effects of an ensemble of convective elements on the large-scale motions of the atmosphere. *J. Meteor. Soc. Japan,* Ser. II, *45,* No. 4, 280-291.

Kasahara, A., and W. M. Washington, 1967: NCAR global general circulation model of the atmosphere. *Mon. Wea. Rev., 95,* 389-402.

Kasahara, A., 1969: Simulation of the earth's atmosphere. National Center for Atmospheric Research, Boulder, Colo., NCAR Manuscript, 69-27, 42 pp.

Kasahara, A., 1974: Various vertical coordinate systems used for numerical weather prediction. *Mon. Wea. Rev., 102,* 504-522.

Kasahara, A., 1976: Normal modes of ultra-long waves in the atmosphere. *Mon. Wea. Rev., 104,* 669-690.

Kasahara, A., 1977: Computational aspects of numerical models for weather prediction and climate simulation. *Methods in Computational Physics, 17,* Academic Press, 2-66, 337 pp.

Katayama, A., 1966: On the radiation budget of the troposphere over the northern hemisphere. (1). *J. Meteor. Soc. Japan,* SII, *44,* 381-401.

Katayama, A., 1974: A simplified scheme for computing radiative transfer in the troposphere, *Tech. Rep. No. 6,* Dept. Met., UCLA, 77 pp.

Kessler, E., 1969: On the distribution and continuity of water substance in atmospheric circulation. *Meteorological Monographs, 10,* no. 32, AMS.

Kirkwood, E., and J. Derome, 1977: Some effects of the upper boundary condition and vertical resolution and modeling forced stationary planetary waves. *Mon. Wea. Rev., 105,* 1239-1251.

Kistler, R. E., 1974: A study of data assimilation techniques in an autobarotropic, primitive equation, channel model. M.S. thesis, Penn. State Univ., 84B.

Klein, W. H. and H. R. Glahn, 1974: Forecasting local weather by means of model output statistics. *Bull. Amer. Met. Soc.*, *55*, 1217-1227.

Kluge, J., 1970: Ausnutzung der winddaten bei der numerischen analyze des geopotentials der AT der mittleren trophosphäre mittels optimaler interpolaten. Z. Meteor., 21, 286-292.

Kolmogoroff, A. N., 1942: The equations of turbulent motion in an incompressible fluid. *Isv. Akad. Nauk SSSR, Ser. Fiz.*, *6*, no. 1, 2, 56, 58.

Koshlyakov, M. N., and A. S. Monin, 1978: Synoptic eddies in the ocean, *Ann. Rev. of Earth and Plan. Sci.*, 495-523.

Kraichman, R. H., 1971: An almost-Markovian Gallilian invariant turbulence model. *J. Fluid Mech.*, *47*, 513-524.

Kraichman, R. H., 1976: Eddy viscosity in two and three dimensions. *J. Atmos. Sci.*, *33*, 1521-1536.

Kraus, E. N., 1972: *Atmosphere-Ocean Interaction*. Clarendon Press, 275 pp.

Kreiss, H.-O., 1970: Initial boundary value problems for hyperbolic systems. *Comm. Pure and Appl. Math.*, *23*, 277-298.

Kreiss, H.-O., 1971: Difference approximations for mixed initial boundary value problems, *Proc. Roy. Soc. London*, Ser A., *323*, 255-261.

Kreiss, H.-O., B. Gustafsson, and A. Sundstrom, 1972: Stability theory of difference approximations for mixed initial boundary value problems, II. *Math. Comp.*, *26*, 649-686.

Kreiss, H.-O., and J. Oliger, 1973: Methods for the approximate solution of time dependent problems. *GARP Publications Series No. 10*, WMO/ICSU Joint Organizing Committee, 107 pp.

Kuo, H. L., 1949: Dynamical instability of two-dimensional nondivergent flow in a barotropic atmosphere. *J. Meteor.*, *6*, 105-122.

Kuo, J. L., 1951: Dynamical aspects of the general circulation and the stability of zonal flow. *Tellus*, *3*, 268-284.

Kuo, H. L., 1952: Three-dimensional disturbances in a baroclinic zonal current. *J. Meteor.*, *9*, 260-278.

Kuo, H. L., 1953: The stability properties and structure of disturbances in a baroclinic atmosphere. *J. Meteor.*, *10*, 235-243.

Kuo, H. L., and J. Nordo, 1959: Integration of four-level prognostic equations over the hemisphere. *Tellus*, *11*, 412-424.

Kuo, H. L., 1965: On formation and intensification of tropical cyclones through latent heat release by cumulus convection. *J. Atmos. Sci.*, *22*, 40-63.

Kuo, H. L., 1971: A theory of parameterization of cumulus convection. *J. Meteor. Soc. Japan*, *49*, 744-756.

Kuo, H. L., 1973: Dynamics of quasi-geostrophic flows and instability theory. *Advances in Applied Mechanics, vol. 13*, Academic Press, 247-330.

Kuo, J. L., 1974: Further studies of the parameterization of the influence of cumulus convection on large-scale flow. *J. Atmos. Sci., 31,* 1232-1240.

Kurihara, Y., 1965: On the use of implicit and iterative methods for the time integration of the wave equation. *Mon. Wea. Rev., 93,* 33-46.

Kurihara, Y., and J. L. Holloway, Jr., 1967: Numerical integrations of a nine-level global primitive equations model formulated by the box method. *Mon. Wea. Rev., 95,* 509-530.

Kurihara, Y., 1968: Note on finite difference expressions for the hydrostatic relation and pressure gradient force. *Mon. Wea. Rev., 96,* 654-656.

Kwizak, M., and A. J. Robert, 1971: A semi-implicit scheme for grid point atmospheric models of the primitive equations. *Mon. Wea. Rev., 99,* 32-36.

Lax, P., and R. Richtmyer, 1956: Survey of the stability of linear finite difference equations. *Comm. Pure and Appl. Math, 9,* 267-293.

Lax, P., and B. Wendroff, 1960: Systems of conservation laws. *Comm. Pure and Appl. Math.,* 13, 217-237.

Leipper, D. F., 1967: Observed ocean conditions and hurricane Hilda 1964. *J. Atmos. Sci., 24,* 182-186.

Leith, C. E., 1964: Numerical simulation of the earth's atmosphere. *Rept. UCRL 7986-T,* 40 pp.

Leith, C. E., 1965: Lagrangian advection in an atmospheric model. WMO-IUGG sympoisum on research and development aspects of long range forecasting, Boulder, Colo., *WMO Tech. Note 66,* 168-176.

Leith, C. E., 1971: Atmospheric predictability and two-dimensional turbulence. *J. Atmos. Sci., 28,* 145-161.

Leith, C. E., and R. H. Kraichman, 1972: Predictability of turbulent flows. *J. Atmos. Sci., 29,* 1041-1058.

Leith, C. E., 1974: Theoretical skill of Monte Carlo forecasts. *Mon. Wea. Rev., 102,* 409-418.

Leith, C. E., 1978: Objective methods for weather prediction. *Ann. Rev. of Fluid Mechanics, 10,* 107-128.

Leith, C. E., 1979: Nonlinear normal mode initialization and quasi-geostrophic theory. NCAR MS 0901-79-01.

Leslie, L. M., and B. J. McAvaney, 1973: Comparative test of direct and iterative methods for solving Helmholtz type equations. *Mon. Wea. Rev., 101,* 235-239.

Lewis, J. M., 1972: An operational upper air analysis using the variational method. *Tellus, 24,* 514-530.

Lilly, D. K., 1960: On the theory of disturbances in a conditionally unstable atmosphere. *Mon. Wea. Rev., 88,* No. 1.

Lilly, D. K., 1965: On the computational stability of numerical solutions of time-dependent non-linear geophysical fluid dynamics problems. *Mon. Wea. Rev., 93,* 11-26.

Lilly, D. K., 1968: Models of cloud-topped mixed layers under a strong inversion. *Quart. J. Roy. Meteor. Soc., 94,* 292-309.

Lilly, D. K., 1973: A note on barotropic instability and predictability. *J. Atmos. Sci., 30,* 145-147.

Lin, C. C., 1955: *The Theory of Hydrodynamic Stability*, Cambridge U. Press, 155 pp.

Lindzen, R. S., 1966: On the relation of wave behavior to source strength and distribution in a propagating medium. *J. Atmos. Sci., 23,* 630-632.

Lindzen, R. S., 1967: Planetary waves on beta-planes. *Mon. Wea. Rev., 95,* 441-451.

Lindzen, R. S., E. S. Batten, and J. W. Kim, 1968: Oscillations in atmospheres with tops. *Mon. Wea. Rev., 96,* 133-140.

Lord, S. J., 1978: Development and observational verification of a cumulus cloud parameterization. Ph.D. thesis, UCLA.

Lorenz, E. N., 1955: Available potential energy and the maintenance of the general circulation. *Tellus, 7,* 157-167.

Lorenz, E. N., 1960a: Maximum simplification of the dynamic equations. *Tellus, 12,* 243-254.

Lorenz, E. N., 1960b: Energy and numerical weather prediction. *Tellus, 12,* 364-373.

Lorenz, E. N., 1963a: The predictability of hydrodynamic flow. *Trans. N.Y. Acad. Sci.*, ser. II, *25,* 409-432.

Lorenz, E. N., 1963b: Deterministic nonperiodic flow. *J. Atmos. Sci., 20,* 130-141.

Lorenz, E. N., 1965: A study of the predictability of a 28-variable atmospheric model. *Tellus, 17,* 321-333.

Lorenz, E. N., 1969a: Three approaches to atmospheric predictability. *Bull. Amer. Soc., 50,* 345-349.

Lorenz, E. N., 1969b: The predictability of a flow which possesses many scales of motion. *Tellus, 21,* 289-307.

Lorenz, E. N., 1969c: Atmospheric predictability as revealed by naturally occurring analogues. *J. Atmos. Sci., 25,* 636-646.

Lorenz, E. N., 1972: Barotropic instability of Rossby wave motion. *J. Atmos. Sci., 29,* 258-264.

Lorenz, E. N., 1973: On the existence of extended range predictability. *J. Appl. Meteor., 12,* 543-546.

Lubeck, O. M., T. Rosmond, and R. T. Williams, 1977: Divergent initialization experiments using a spectral model. *Naval Postgraduate School Report,* NPS-63Wu7791, 81 pp.

Lumley, J. L., and H. A. Panofsky, 1964: *The Structure of Atmospheric Turbulence.* Interscience, 239 pp.

Machenhauer, B., and R. Daley, 1972: A baroclinic primitive equation model with a spectral representation in three dimensions. *Rep. No. 4,* Institut for Teoretisk Meteorologi, Kobenhavns Universitet, Denmark.

Machenhauer, B., and E. Rasmussen, 1972: On the integration of the spectral hydrodynamical equation by a transform method. *Rep. No. 3,* Institut for Teoretisk Meteorologi, Kobenhavns Universitet, Denmark, 44 pp.

Machenhauer, B., 1977: On the dynamics of gravity oscillations in a shallow water model, with application to normal mode initialization. *Contrib. Atmos. Phys., 50,* 253-271.

Madala, R. V., and S. A. Piacsek, 1977: A semi-implicit numerical model for baroclinic oceans. *J. Comp. Phys., 23,* 167-178.

Madala, R. V., 1978: An efficient direct solver for separable and non-separable elliptic equations. *Mon. Wea. Rev., 106,* 1735-1741.

Madden, R. A., and P. R. Julian, 1971: Detection of a 40-50 day oscillation in the zonal wind in the tropical Pacific. *J. Atmos. Sci., 28,* 702-708.

Madden, R. A., and P. R. Julian, 1972: Description of a global scale circulation cells in the tropics with a 40-50 day period. *J. Atmos. Sci., 29,* 1109-1123.

Manabe, S., and F. Möller, 1961: On the radiative equilibrium and heat balance of the atmosphere. *Mon. Wea. Rev., 89,* 503-532.

Manabe, S., and R. F. Strickler, 1964: On the thermal equilibrium of the atmosphere with a convective adjustment. *J. Atmos. Sci., 21,* no. 4, 361-385.

Manabe, S., J. Smagorinsky, and R. F. Strickler, 1965: Simulated climatology of a general circulation model with a hydrologic cycle. *Mon. Wea. Rev., 93,* 769-798.

Marchuk, G. I., 1974: *Numerical Methods in Weather Prediction,* Academic Press, 277 pp.

Matsuno, T., 1966a: Quasi-geostrophic motions in the equatorial area. *J. Meteor. Soc. Japan, 44,* 25-43.

Matsuno, T., 1966b: Numerical integrations of the primitive equations by a simulated backward difference method. *J. Meteor. Soc. Japan,* Ser. 2, *44,* 76-84.

Matsuno, T., 1966c: A finite difference scheme for time integrations of oscillatory equations with second order accuracy and sharp cut-off for high frequencies. *J. Meteor. Soc. Japan,* Ser. 2, *44,* 85-88.

Matsuno, T., 1966d: False reflection of waves at the boundary due to the use of finite differences. *J. Meteor. Soc. Japan,* Ser. 2, *44,* 145-157.

Matsuno, T., 1970: Vertical propagation of stationary planetary waves in the winter Northern Hemisphere. *J. Atmos. Sci., 27,* 871-883.

Melgarejo, J. W., and J. W. Deardorff, 1974: Revision to stability functions for the boundary-layer resistance laws based upon observed boundary-layer height. *J. Atmos. Sci., 32,* 837-839.

Mellor, G. L., 1973: Analytic prediction of properties of stratified boundary layers. *J. Atmos. Sci., 30,* 1061-1069.

Mellor, G. L., and T. Yamada, 1974: A hierarchy of turbulence closure models for planetary boundary layers. *J. Atmos. Sci., 31,* 1791-1806.

Mesinger, F., 1971: Numerical integration of the primitive equations with a floating set of computation points: Experiments with a barotropic global model. *Mon. Wea. Rev., 99,* 15-29.

Mesinger, F., 1973: A method for construction of second-order accuracy difference schemes permitting no false two-grid-interval wave in the height field. *Tellus, 25,* 444-458.

Mesinger, F., 1974: An economical explicit scheme which inherently prevents the false two-grid-interval wave in the forecast fields. Difference and spectral methods for atmosphere and ocean dynamics problems, *Proc. Symp.*, Novosibirsk, 1973, Part II, 18-34.

Mesinger, F., and Z. I. Janjic, 1974: Noise due to time-dependent boundary conditions in limited area models. *The GARP Programme on Numerical Experimentation, Rept. 4,* 31-32.

Mesinger, F., and A. Arakawa, 1976: Numerical methods used in atmospheric models. *GARP Publication Series No. 14,* WMO/ICSU Joint Organizing Committee, 64 pp.

Miyakoda, K., and R. W. Moyer, 1968: A method of initialization for dynamic weather forecasting. *Tellus, 20,* 115-128.

Miyakoda, K., J. Smagorinsky, R. F. Strickler, and G. D. Hembree, 1969: Experimental extended predictions with a nine-level hemispheric model. *Mon. Wea. Rev., 97,* No. 1, 1-76.

Miyakoda, K., and A. Rosati, 1977: One-way nested grid models: The interface conditions and the numerical accuracy. *Mon. Wea. Rev., 105,* 1092-1107.

Miyakoda, K., and J. Sirutis, 1977: Comparative integrations of global models with various parameterized processes of sub-grid-scale vertical transports: Description of the parameterizations and preliminary results. *Beitr. Phys. Atmos., 50,* 445-487.

Monaco, A. V., and R. T. Williams, 1975: An atmospheric global prediction model using a modified Arakawa differencing scheme. *Naval Postgraduate School Report,* NPS-51WU 75041, 86 pp.

Monin, A. S., and A. M. Obukhov, 1954: Basic laws of turbulent mixing in the ground layer of the atmosphere. *Akad. Nauk SSSR Geofiz. Inst. Tr. 151,* 163-187.

Morgan, G. W., 1956: On the wind-driven ocean circulation, *Tellus, 8,* 301-320.

Mügge, R., and F. Möller, 1932: Zun berechnung von strahlungsströmen und temperäturäderungen in atmospharen von beliebigen aufbau. *Z. fur Geophys. 8,* 53-64.

Munk, W. H., 1950: On the wind-driven ocean circulation. *J. Meteor., 7,* 79-93.

Namias, J., 1978: Multiple causes of the North American abnormal winter 1976-77, *Mon. Wea. Rev., 106,* 279-295.

NAS, 1978: Elements of the Research Strategy for the United States Climate Program. National Academy of Sciences Report by Climate Dynamics Panel.

Navon, I. M. and H. A. Riphagen, 1979: An implicit compact fourth-order algorithm for solving the shallow-water equations in conservation-law form. *Mon. Wea. Rev., 107,* 1107-1127.

Newton, C. N., 1966: Dynamics of severe convective storms. *Meteorological Monographs, 5,* no. 27, pp. 33-58.

Niiler, P. P., and E. B. Kraus, 1977: *One Dimensional Models of the Upper Ocean, Modeling and Prediction of the Upper Layers of the Ocean.* Editor E. B. Kraus, Pergamon Press, 143-172, 325 pp.

Nitta, T., and M. Yanai, 1968: A note on the barotropic instability of the tropical easterly current. *J. Meteor. Soc. Japan, 47,* no. 2.

Nitta, T., 1969: Initialization and analysis for the primitive equation model. *Proc. WMO/IUGG Symp. on Numerical Weather Prediction*. Tokyo.

Nitta, T., and J. B. Hovermale, 1969: A technique of objective analysis and initialization for the primitive forecast equations. *Mon. Wea. Rev., 97,* 652-658.

O'Brien, J. J., and R. V. Reid, 1967: The non-linear response of a two-layer baroclinic ocean to a stationary axially-symmetric hurricane. Part I, *J. Atmos. Sci., 24,* 197-207.

O'Brien, J. J., 1970: A note on the vertical structure of the eddy exchange coefficient in the planetary boundary layer. *J. Atmos. Sci., 27,* 1213-1215.

O'Brien, J. J., and R. Grotjahn, 1976: Some inaccuracies in finite differencing hyperbolic equations. *Mon. Wea. Rev., 104,* 180-194.

Obukhov, A. M., 1949: *Bul. Acad. Sci. USSR, Geograph., Geophys. Series 4,* 627.

Obukhov, A. M., 1949: K. Voprosu O Geostrofichesko Vetra. *Izv. Akad. Nauk SSSR Ser Geograf. Geofiz, 13,* 281-306.

Ogura, Y., and T. Takahashi, 1971: Numerical simulation of the life cycle of a thunderstorm cell. *Mon. Wea. Rev., 99,* 895-911.

Ogura, Y., and H. R. Cho, 1974: On the interaction between the subcloud and cloud layers in tropical regions. *J. Atmos. Sci., 31,* 1850-1859.

Okland, H., 1970: Adjustment toward balance in primitive equation numerical models. *Mon. Wea. Rev., 98,* 271-279.

Okland, H., 1972: On the balance, initialization and data assimilation in primitive equation models. *J. Atmos. Sci., 29,* 641-648.

Oliger, J., and A. Sundström, 1976: Theoretical and practical aspects of some initial boundary value problems in fluid dynamics. Stanford University Computer Science Dept. Rept. Stan-CS-76-578, 61 pp.

Ookochi, Y., 1972: A computational scheme for the nesting mesh in the primitive equation model. *J. Meteor. Soc. Japan, 50,* 37-48.

Oort, A. H., 1964: On estimates of the atmospheric energy cycle. *Mon. Wea. Rev., 92,* 483-493.

Ooyama, K., 1964: A dynamical model for the study of tropical cyclone development. *Geofis, Int., 4,* 187-198.

Ooyama, K., 1971: A theory on parameterization of cumulus convection. *J. Meteor. Soc. Japan, 49,* Special Issue, 744-756.

Ooyama, K., 1969: Numerical simulation of the life cycle of tropical cyclones. *J. Atmos. Sci., 26,* 3-40.

Orlanski, I., 1976: A simple boundary condition for unbounded hyperbolic flows. *J. Comp. Phys., 21,* 251-269.

Orszag, S. A., 1969: Numerical methods for the simulation of turbulence. *Phys. Fluids, Suppl. 11, 12,* 250-257.

Orszag, S. A., 1970: Transform method for the calculation of vector-coupled sums: Application to the spectral form of the vorticity equation. *J. Atmos. Sci., 27,* 890-895.

Orszag, S. A., 1971a: Numerical simulation of incompressible flows within simple boundaries: Galerkin, spectral representation. *Studies in Appl. math., 50,* 293-327.

Orszag, S. A., 1971b: On the elimination of aliasing in finite-difference schemes by filtering high-wavenumber components. *J. Atmos. Sci., 28,* 1074.

Panofsky, H., 1949: Objective weather map analysis. *J. Meteor., 5,* 386-392.

Panofsky, H., A. K. Blackadar, and G. E. McVehil, 1960: The diabatic wind profile. *Quart. J. Roy. Meteor. Soc., 86,* 390-398.

Paulson, C. A., 1970: The mathematical representation of wind speed and temperature profiles in the unstable atmospheric surface layer. *J. Appl. Meteor., 9,* 857-861.

Pearson, R. A., 1974: Consistent boundary conditions for numerical models of systems that admit dispersive waves. *J. Atmos. Sci., 31,* 1481-1489.

Pedlosky, J., 1964a: The stability of currents in the atmosphere and the ocean, Part I. *J. Atmos. Sci., 21,* 201-219.

Pedlosky, J., 1964b: An initial value problem in the theory of baroclinic instability. *Tellus, 16,* 12-17.

Perkey, D. J., and C. W. Kreitzberg, 1976: Release of potential instability, Part I. *J. Atmos. Sci., 33,* 456-475.

Perkey, D. J., and C. W. Kreitzberg, 1976: A time-dependent lateral boundary scheme for limited-area primitive equation models. *Mon. Wea. Rev., 104,* 744-755.

Phillips, N. A., 1951: A simple three-dimensional model for the study of large-scale extratropical flow patterns, *J. Meteor., 8,* 381-394.

Phillips, N. A., 1956: The general circulation of the atmosphere: A numerical experiment. *Quart. J. Roy. Meteor. Soc., 82,* 123-164.

Phillips, N. A., 1957: A coordinate system having some special advantages for numerical forecasting. *J. Meteor., 14,* 184-185.

Phillips, N. A., 1959: An example of non-linear computational instability. *The Atmosphere and the Sea in Motion,* Rossby Memorial Volume, Rockefeller Institute Press, 501-504, 509 pp.

Phillips, N. A., 1960a: Numerical weather prediction. *Advances in Computers, Vol. 1,* Academic Press, 43-90.

Phillips, N. A., 1960b: On the problem of initial data for the primitive equations. *Tellus, 12,* 121-126.

Phillips, N. A., 1962: Numerical integration of the hydrostatic system of equations with a modified version of the Eliassen finite-difference grid. *Proc. Intern. Symp. Numerical Weather Prediction,* Tokyo.

Phillips, N. A., 1963: Geostrophic motion. *Rev. Geophys., 1,* 123-176.

Phillips, N. A., 1966: The equations of motion for a shallow rotating atmosphere and the traditional approximation. *J. Atmos. Sci., 23,* p. 626.

Phillips, N. A., 1973: Principles of large scale numerical weather prediction. *Dynamic Meterology,* Editor, P. Morel, Reidel Publishing Co., 1-96, 622 pp.

Phillips, N. A., and J. Shukla, 1973: On the strategy of combining coarse and fine grid meshes in numerical weather prediction. *J. Appl. Meteor., 12,* 763-770.

Phillips, N. A., 1974: Natl. Meteor. Cent. Off.: Note 104. Natl. Weather Service, Washington, D.C.

Phillips, N. A., 1979: The nested grid model. *NOAA Tech. Rept. NWS 22,* 80 pp.

Pinder, G. F., and W. G. Gray, 1977: *Finite Element Simulation in Surface and Subsurface Hydrology*. Academic Press, 295 pp.

Platzman, G. W., 1954: The computational stability of boundary conditions in numerical integration of the vorticity equation. *Arch. Meteor. Geophys. u. Bioklimatol, Ser. A7,* 29-40.

Platzman, G. W., 1958: The lattice structure of the finite-difference primitive and vorticity equations. *Mon. Wea. Rev., 86,* 285-292.

Platzman, G. W., 1960: The spectral form of the vorticity equation. *J. Meteor., 17,* 635-644.

Pollard, R. T., and R. C. Millard, Jr., 1970: Comparison between observed and simulated wind-generated inertial oscillations. *Deep-Sea Res., 17,* 813-821.

Randall, D. A., 1976: The interaction of the planetary boundary layer with large-scale circulations, Ph.D. Thesis, UCLA.

Randall, D. A., and Arakawa, 1974: A parameterization of the planetary boundary layer for numerical models for the atmosphere. UCLA Atmospheric General Circulation Model.

Rayleigh, Lord, 1880: On the stability or instability, of certain fluid motions. *Scientific Papers, Vol. 3,* Cambridge University Press, 594-596.

Reed, R. J., 1963: Experiments in 1000-mb prognosis. *Natl. Meteor. Cen., Wea. Bur.,* ESSA, Tech. Memo., *26,* U.S. Department of Commerce.

Reed, R. J., and E. E. Recker, 1971: Structure and properties of synoptic-scale wave disturbances in the equatorial western Pacific. *J. Atmos. Sci., 28,* 1117-1133.

Reed, R. J., 1977: The development and status of modern weather prediction. *Bull. Amer. Met. Soc., 58,* 390-400.

Renard, R. J., and L. C. Clarke, 1965: Experiments in numerical objective frontal analysis. Paper presented at the 45th annual American Meteorology Society Meeting in New York City.

Richardson, L. F., 1922: *Weather Prediction by Numerical Process.* Cambridge University Press, reprinted Dover, 1965, 236 pp.

Richtmyer, R. D., 1963: *A Survey of Difference Methods for Non-steady Fluid Dynamics.* Natl. Cen. for Atmospheric Research, Boulder, Colo., *NCAR Tech. Notes,* 63-62, 25 pp.

Richtmyer, R. D., and Morton, K. W., 1967: *Difference Methods* for *Initial Value Problems. Interscience,* 406 pp.

Riehl, H., and R. P. Pearce, 1968: Studies on interaction between synoptic and mesoscale weather elements in the tropics. *Atmos. Sci. Paper No. 126,* Colorado State University, 64 pp.

Robert, A. J., 1966: The integration of a low order spectral form of the primitive meteorological equations. *J. Meteor. Soc. Japan,* Ser. 2, *44,* 237-245.

Robert, A. J., 1969: The integration of a spectral model of the atmosphere by the implicit method. *Proc. WMO/IUGG Symp. on Numerical Weather Prediction Tokyo. Meteor. Soc. Japan. VII-19-VII-24.*

Robert, A. J., H. Henderson, and C. Turnbull, 1972: An implicit time integration scheme for baroclinic models of the atmosphere. *Mon. Wea. Rev., 100,* 329-335.

Robert, A. J., 1974: GARP activities related to computational considerations. The *GARP Programme on Numerical Computation,* Report No. 4, 2-23, 113 p.

Robert, A. J., 1974: Computational resolution requirements for accurate medium range numerical predictions. Difference and spectral methods for atmosphere and ocean dynamics problems, *Proc. Symp.,* Novosibirsk, 1973, Part I, 82-102.

Robinson, A., and H. Stommel, 1959: The oceanic thermocline and the associated thermohaline circulation. *Tellus, 11,* 295-308.

Robinson, A., D. E. Harrison, Y. Mintz, and A. J. Semtner, 1977: Eddies and the general circulation of an idealized oceanic gyre: A wind and thermally driven primitive equation numerical experiment. *J. Phys. Oceanogr., 7,* 182-207.

Robinson, G. D., 1967: Some current projects for global meteorological observation and experiment. *Quart. J. Roy. Meteor. Soc., 93,* 409-418.

Robinson, G. D., 1971: The predictability of a dissipative flow. *Quart. J. Roy. Meteor. Soc., 97,* 300-312.

Rodgers, D. C., 1967: The radiative heat budget of the troposphere and lower stratosphere. Planetary Circulation Project, Dept. Met., MIT, *Rept. No. 2,* 99 pp.

Rosenthal, S. L., 1979: The sensitivity of simulated hurricane development to cumulus parameterization details. *Mon. Wea. Rev., 107,* 193-197.

Rosmond, T. E., 1975: Subroutines for direct solution of two-dimensional elliptic equations. Navy Envir. Pred. Res. Facility, NPS, *Rept. No. 23.*

Rosmond, T. E., and F. D. Faulkner, 1976: Direct solution of elliptic equations by block cyclic reduction and factorization. *Mon. Wea. Rev., 104,* 641-649.

Rosmond, T. E., 1977: Subroutines for direct solution of three-dimensional elliptic equations. Naval Envir. Pred. Res. Facility, *Note No. 22.*

Rossby, C. G., 1938: On the mutual adjustment of pressure and velocity distribution in certain simple current systems, II. *J. Marine Res.* (Sears Foundation), 239-263.

Rossby, C. G., 1939: Relation between variations in the intensity of the zonal circulation of the atmosphere and the displacements of the semi-permanent centers of action. *J. Marine Res., 2,* 38-55.

Rossby, C. G., 1940: Planetary flow patterns in the atmosphere. *Quart. J. Roy. Meteor. Soc., 66,* 68-87.

Rossby, C. G., 1945: On the propagation of frequencies and energies in certain types of oceanic and atmospheric waves. *J. Meteor., 2,* 187-204.

Rossby, C. G., 1949: On the dispersion of planetary waves in a barotropic atmosphere. *Tellus, 1,* 54-58.

Rotta, J. C., 1951: Statistische theorie nichthomogener turbulenz. *Z. Phys., 129,* 547-572; *131,* 51-77.

Rotta, J. C., 1962: Turbulent boundary layers in incompressible flow. *Progress in Aeronautical Sciences, Vol. 2,* Pergamon Press, The MacMillan Co., 1-219.

Rutherford, I. D., 1972: Data assimilation by statistical interpolation of forecast error fields. *J. Atmos. Sci., 29,* 809-815.

Rutherford, I. D., 1973: Experiments in the updating of P. E. forecasts with real wind and geopotential data. Preprint, *Third Conf. on Probability and Statistics in Atmos. Sci.,* Boulder, Colo., American Meteorological Society, 198-201.

Rutherford, I. D., 1976: An operational three-dimensional multi-variate statistical analysis scheme. *Proceedings of the JOC Study Group Conference on Four Dimensional Data Assimilation,* Paris 17-21 November, 1975. *Rept. No. 11, the GARP Program on Numerical Experimentation,* 98-121.

Rutherford, I. D., 1978: An operational three-dimensional multivariate statistical objective analysis scheme. *Notes Scientifiques et Techniques, 1,* Division de Recherche en Prevision Numerique, Montreal, Canada.

Sadourny, R., 1975: The dynamics of finite-difference models of the shallow-water equations. *J. Atmos. Sci., 32,* 680-689.

Saha, K., and R. Suryanarayana, 1971: Numerical solution of geopotential with different forms of balance relationship in the tropics. *J. Meteor. Japan, 49,* 510-515.

Sanders, F., 1973: Skill in forecasting daily temperature and precipitation, some experimental results. *Bull. Amer. Meteor. Soc., 54,* 1171-1179.

Sarkisyan, A. S., 1977: The diagnostic calculations of a large-scale oceanic circulation. *The Sea, Vol. 1,* Editors, E. D. Goldberg, N. McCane, J. J. O'Brien, and J. H. Steele, John Wiley and Sons, 363-458.

Sasaki, Y., 1958: An objective analysis based on the variational method. *Soc. Japan, 36,* 77-78.

Sasaki, Y., 1969: Proposed inclusion of time variation terms, observational in numerical variational objective analysis. *J. Meteor. Soc.,* 115-124.

Sasaki, Y., 1975: An experiment of noise suppression in data assimilation, ''noise freezing technique''. *Proceedings of the JOC Study Group Conference on Four-Dimensional Data Assimilation.* Paris, 17-21 November 1975. *GARP Rept. No. 11.*

Schemm, C. E., and F. B. Lipps, 1976: Some results from a simplified three-dimensional model of atmospheric turbulence. *J. Atmos. Sci., 33,* 1021-1041.

Schlatter, T. W., 1975: Some experiments with a multivariate statistical objective analysis scheme. *Mon. Wea. Rev., 103,* 246-257.

Schlatter, T. W., 1978: Statistical objective analysis of meteorological data, an overview. Task Group on Space and Time Dependent Data Committee on Data for Science and Technology, International Council of Scientific Unions.

Schoenstadt, A. L., and R. T. Williams, 1976: The computational properties of the Shuman pressure gradient averaging technique. *J. Comp. Phys., 21,* 166-177.

Schoenstadt, A. L., 1977: The effect of spatial discretization on the steady state and transient behavior of a dispersive wave equation. *J. Comp. Phys., 23,* 364-379.

Schoenstadt, A. L., 1978: A transfer function analysis of numerical schemes used to simulate geostrophic adjustment. *NPS Rept. NPS-53-79-001,* 44 pp.

Schubert, W. H., and A. Arakawa, 1974: Interaction of a cumulus cloud ensemble with the large-scale environment, Part II., *J. Atmos. Sci., 31.*

Schubert, W. H., 1974: Cumulus parameterization in terms of feedback and control. Colorado State University. *Atmos. Science Paper No. 226.*

Semtner, A. J., Jr., and Y. Mintz, 1977: Numerical simulation of the Gulf Stream and ocean eddies. *J. Phys. Oceanogr., 7,* 208-230.

Shapiro, R., 1970: Smoothing, filtering, and boundary effects. *Rev. Geophys. and Space Phys., 8,* 359-387.

Shapiro, R., 1975: Linear filtering, *Math. Comp., 29,* 1094-1097.

Shapiro, R., 1977: The treatment of lateral boundary conditions in limited-area model: A pragmatic approach. *APGL-TR-0092, Env. Res. Paper No. 594.*

Shapiro, M. A., 1975: Simulation of upper-level frontogenesis with a 20-level isentropic coordinate primitive equation model. *Mon. Wea. Rev., 103,* 591-604.

Shuman, F. G., 1955: A method for solving the balance equation. *Joint Numerical Weather Prediction Unit Tech. Memo. No. 6,* 12 pp.

Shuman, F. G., 1955: A method of designing finite-different smoothing operators to meet specification. *Joint Numerical Weather Prediction Unit Tech. Memo No. 7,* 44 pp.

Shuman, F. G., 1957: Predictive consequences of certain physical inconsistencies in the geostrophic barotropic model. *Mon. Wea. Rev., 85,* no. 7, 229-234.

Shuman, F. G., 1960: Numerical experiments with the primitive equations. *Proc. Intern. Symp. Numerical Weather Prediction,* Tokyo.

Shuman, F. G., and J. B. Hovermale, 1968: An operational six-layer primitive equation model. *J. Appl. Meteor., 7,* 525-547.

Shuman, F. G., 1971: Resuscitation of an integration procedure. *NWC Office Note 54.*

Shuman, F. G., 1974: Analysis and experiment in nonlinear computational stability. Difference and spectral methods for atmosphere and ocean dynamics problems. *Proc. Symp., Novosibirsk, Part I,* 51-81.

Shuman, F. G., 1978: Numerical weather prediction, *Bull. Amer. Meteor. Soc. 59,* 5-17.

Shuman, F. G., 1978: Limitations on NOAA's ability to forecast the weather: A brief statement. *NMC Office Note 170, NOAA.*

Shuman, F. G., 1978: Long range weather forecasting: A brief statement. *NMC Office Note 168, NOAA.*

Silberman, I. S., 1954: Planetary waves in the atmosphere. *J. Meteor., 11,* 27-34.

Simmons, A. J., and B. J. Hoskins, 1977: A note on the wavelength of maximum growth rate for baroclinic instability. *J. Atmos. Sci., 34,* 1477-1478.

Smagorinsky, J., 1953: The dynamical influence of large-scale heat sources and sinks on the quasi-stationary mean motions of the atmosphere. *Quart. J. Roy. Meteor. Soc., 79,* 342-366.

Smagorinsky, J., and G. O. Collins, 1955: On the numerical prediction of precipitation. *Mon. Wea. Rev., 83,* 53-68.

Smagorinsky, J., 1956: On the inclusion of moist adiabatic processes in numerical prediction models. *Berichte Deutsch. Wetterdientes, 5,* no. 38, 82-90.

Smagorinsky, J., 1958: On the numerical integration of the primitive equations of motion for baroclinic flow in a closed region. *Mon. Wea. Rev., 86,* 457-466.

Smagorinsky, J., 1960a: On the application of numerical methods to the solution of systems of partial difference equations arising in meteorology. *Frontiers of Numerical Mathematics,* University of Wisconsin Press.

Smagorinsky, J., 1960b: On the dynamical prediction of large-scale condensation by numerical methods. Physics of Precipitation, *Geophysical Mon.,* no. 5, American Geophysical Union, 71-78.

Smagorinsky, J., 1962: A primitive equation model including condensation processes. *Proc. Intern. Symp. Numerical Weather Prediction, Tokyo. Meteor. Soc. Japan.*

Smagorinsky, J., 1963: General circulation experiments with the primitive equations: I. The basic experiment. *Mon. Wea. Rev., 91,* 99-164.

Smagorinsky, J., S. Manabe, and J. L. Holloway, 1965: Numerical results from a nine-level general circulation model of the atmosphere. *Mon. Wea. Rev., 93,* 727-768.

Smagorinsky, J., and Staff Members, 1965: Prediction experiments with a general circulation model. *Proc. Intern. Symp. Dynamics of Large Scale Processes in the Atmosphere (IAMAP/WMO), Moscow.*

Smagorinsky, J., 1969: Problems and promises of deterministic extended range forecasting. *Bull. Amer. Meteor. Soc., 50,* 286-313.

Smeda, M. S., 1977: Incorporation of planetary boundary layer processes into numerical forecasting models. *Dept. Met. Univ. of Stockholm Rept. UDC 551.513.*

Smith, S. D., and E. G. Banke, 1975: Variation of the sea surface drag coefficient with wind speed. *Quart J. Roy. Meteor. Soc., 101,* 665-673.

Sobel, J. P., 1976: Nested grids in numerical weather prediction and an application to a mesoscale jet streak. Ph.D. thesis, Pennsylvania State University, 135 pp.

Somerville, R. C. J., P. H. Stone, M. Halem, J. E. Hansen, J. S. Hogan, L. M. Druyan, G. Russell, A. A. Lacis, W. J. Quirk, and J. Tenenbaum, 1974: The GISS model of the global atmosphere. *J. Atmos. Sci., 31,* 84-117.

Somerville, R. C. J., 1979: Predictability and prediction of ultra-long planetary waves. *Preprints, Amer. Meteor. Soc. Fourth Conference on Numerical Prediction, Silver Spring, MD,* 182-185.

Sommeria, G., 1976: Three-dimensional simulation of turbulent processes in an undisturbed trade wind boundary layer. *J. Atmos. Sci., 33,* 216-241.

Staley, D. O., and R. L. Gall, 1977: On the wavelength of maximum baroclinic instability. *J. Atmos. Sci., 34,* 1679-1688.

Staniforth, A. N., and H. L. Mitchell, 1977: A semi-implicit finite-element barotropic model. *Mon. Wea. Rev., 105,* 154-169.

Stephens, J. J., 1970: Variational initialization with the balance equation. *J. Appl. Meteor., 9,* 732-739.

Stern, M. E., 1975: *Ocean Circulation Physics*. Academic Press, 246 pp.

Stommel, H., 1948: The westward intensification of wind-driven ocean currents. *Trans. Am. Geophys. Union, 29,* 202-206.

Stommel, H., 1965: *The Gulf Stream*. (2nd Ed.) University of California Press, 240 pp.

Strang, G. W., and G. J. Fix, 1973: *An Analysis of the Finite Element Method*. Prentice-Hall, 306 pp.

Stull, R. B., 1973: Inversion rise model based on penetrative convection. *J. Atmos. Sci., 30,* 1092-1099.

Sundquist, H., 1975: On initialization for models using sigma as vertical coordinate. *J. Appl. Meteor., 14,* 153-158.

Sundquist, H., 1978: A parameterization scheme for non-convective condensation including prediction of cloud water content. *Quart. J. Roy. Meteor. Soc., 104,* 677-690.

Sundström, A., 1973: Theoretical and practical problems in formulating boundary conditions for a limited-area model. *Rept. DM9,* Institute of Meteorology, University of Stockholm.

Swartztrauber, P. N., and Sweet, R. A., 1975: Efficient Fortran subprograms for the solution of elliptic partial differential equations. *NCAR Technical Note IN/IA-109,* 139 pp.

Sweet, R. A., 1973: Direct methods for the solution of Poisson's equation on a staggered grid. *J. Comp. Phys., 12,* 422-428.

Sweet, R. A. 1973: A generalized cyclic reduction algorithm. SIAM, *J. of Numerical Analysis, 10,* 506-520.

Syono, S., and M. Yamasaki, 1966: Stability of symmetrical motions driven by latent heat release by cumulus convection under the existence of surface friction. *J. Meteor. Soc. Japan,* Sec. II, *44,* No. 6.

Talagrand, O., 1972: On the damping of high-frequency motions in four-dimensional assimilation of meteorological data. *J. Atmos. Sci., 29,* 1571-1574.

Temperton, C., 1973: Some experiments in dynamic initialization for a simple primitive equation model. *Quart. J. Roy. Meteor., Soc., 99,* 303-319.

Temperton, C., 1976: Dynamic initialization for barotropic and multilevel models. *Quart. J. Roy. Met. Soc., 102,* 297-311.

Temperton, C., 1977: Normal modes of a barotropic version of the ECMWF grid point model. *ECMWF Internal Rept. No. 12,* 38 pp.

Temperton, C., and D. L. Williamson, 1979: Normal mode initialization for a multilevel gridpoint model. *ECMWF Tech. Rept. No. 11,* 91 pp.

Teweles, S., and H. Wobus, 1954: Vertification of prognostic charts. *Bull. Amer. Meteor. Soc., 35,* 455-463.

Teweles, S., 1963: Spectral aspects of the stratosphere circulation during the IGY. MIT Rept. No. 8.

Thompson, P. D., 1953: On the theory of large-scale disturbance in a two-dimensional baroclinic equivalent of the atmosphere. *Quart. J. Roy. Meteor. Soc., 79,* 51-69.

Thompson, P. D., 1956: A theory of large-scale disturbances in nongeostrophic flow. *J. Meteor., 13,* 251-261.

Thompson, P. D., 1957: Uncertainty of initial stage as a factor in the predictability of large-scale atmospheric flow patterns. *Tellus, 9,* 275-295.

Thompson, P. D., 1961: *Numerical Weather Analysis* and *Prediction*. New York, Macmillan, 170 pp.

Tokioka, T., 1978: Some considerations on vertical differencing. *J. Meteor. Soc. Japan, 44,* 25-43.

U.S. Committee for GARP, 1975: Understanding climatic change, A program for action, NAS, Wash., D.C., 20418, 239 pp.

U.S. POLYMODE Organizing Committee, 1976: *U.S. POLYMODE Program and Plan*. Massachusetts Institute of Technology, 98 pp.

Veronis, G., 1965: On parametric values and types of representation in wind-driven ocean circulation studies. *Tellus, 17,* 77-84.

Veronis, G., 1966a: Wind-driven ocean circulation: Part I. Linear theory and perturbation analysis. *Deep-Sea Res., 13,* 17-29.

Veronis, G., 1966b: Wind-driven ocean circulation: Part II. Numerical solutions of the non-linear problem. *Deep-Sea Res., 13,* 31-55.

Veronis, G., 1975: The role of models in tracer studies. *Proc. Symp. Numerical Models of Ocean Circulation.*

von Neumann, J., and R. D. Richtmyer, 1950: A method for the numerical calculation of hydrodynamical shocks. *J. Appl. Phys., 21,* 232.

Wallace, J., and V. Kousky, 1968: Observational evidence of Kelvin waves in the tropical stratosphere. *J. Atmos. Sci., 25,* 900-907.

Warren, B. A., 1963: Topographical influences on the path of the Gulf Stream. *Tellus, 15,* 167-183.

Webster, P. J., 1972: Response of the tropical atmosphere to local steady forcing. *Mon. Wea. Rev., 100,* 518-541.

Wiin-Nielsen, A., 1959: On certain integral constraints for the time integration of baroclinic models. *Tellus, 11,* 45-60.

Wiin-Nielsen, A., J. A. Brown, and M. Drake, 1964: On atmospheric energy conversion between the zonal flow and the eddies. *Tellus, 15,* 261-279.

Wiin-Nielsen, A., 1967: On the annual variation and spectral distribution of atmospheric energy. *Tellus, 19,* 540-559.

Williams, R. T., T. K. Schminke, and R. L. Newman, 1971: Effect of surface friction on the structure of barotropically unstable tropical disturbances. *Mon. Wea. Rev., 99,* 778-785.

Williamson, D. L., and A. Kasahara, 1972: Adaptation of meteorological variables forced by updating. *J. Atmos. Sci., 28,* 1313-1324.

Williamson, D. L., and G. L. Browning, 1973: Comparison of grids and difference approximations for numerical weather prediction over a sphere. *J. Appl. Meteor., 12,* 264-274.

Williamson, D. L., 1976a: Linear stability of finite-difference approximations on a uniform latitude-longitude grid with Fourier filtering. *Mon. Wea. Rev., 104,* 31-41.

Williamson, D. L., 1976b: Normal mode initialization procedure applied to forecasts with the global shallow water equations. *Mon. Wea. Rev., 104,* 195-206.

Williamson, D. L., and R. E. Dickinson, 1976: Free oscillations of the NCAR global circulation model. *Mon. Wea. Rev., 104,* 1372-1391.

Winninghoff, F. J., 1968: On the adjustment toward a geostrophic balance in a simple primitive equation model with application to the problems of initialization and objective analysis. Ph.D. thesis, Dept. Met., University of California, Los Angeles.

Wolff, P. M., 1958: The error in numerical forecasts due to retrogression of ultra-long waves. *Mon. Wea. Rev., 86,* 245-250.

Wurtele, M. G., 1961: On the problem of truncation error. *Tellus, 13,* 379-391.

Wyngaard, J. C., O. R. Cote, and K. S. Rao, 1974: Modeling the atmospheric boundary layer. *Advances in Geophysics, Vol. 18A,* Academic Press, 193-211.

Wyngaard, J. C., and R. Cotè, 1974: The evolution of a convective boundary layer, a higher order closure model study. *Bound. Layer Meteor., 7,* 289-308.

Wyngaard, J. C., 1975: Modeling the planetary boundary layer-extension to the stable case. *Bound. Layer Meteor., 9,* 441-460.

Yamada, T., 1976: On the similarity functions A, B and C of the planetary boundary layer. *J. Atmos. Sci., 33,* 781-793.

Yamamoto, G., 1952: On a radiation chart. Sci. Rept. Tohoku Univ., S.5, *Geophysics,* 4, 9-23.

Yamasaki, M., 1968: Detailed analysis of a tropical cyclone simulated with a 13-layer model. *Pap. Meteor. Geophys., 19,* 559-585.

Yamasaki, M., 1968: Numerical simulation of tropical cyclone development with the use of primitive equations. *J. Meteor. Soc. Japan, 46,* No. 3.

Yamasaki, M., 1968: A tropical cyclone model with parameterized partition of released latent heat. *J. Meteor. Soc. Japan, 46,* No. 3, 202-214.

Yamasaki, M., 1970: Large-scale disturbances in a conditionally unstable atmosphere in low latitudes. *Papers in Meteor. Geophys., 20.*

Yamasaki, M., 1975: A numerical experiment of the interaction between cumulus convection and larger-scale motion. *Pap. Meteor. Geophys., 26,* 63-91.

Yamasaki, M., 1977a: A preliminary experiment of the tropical cyclone without parameterizing the effects of cumulus convection. *J. Meteor. Soc. Japan, 55,* 11-31.

Yamasaki, M., 1977b: The role of surface friction in tropical cyclones. *J. Meteor. Soc. Japan, 55,* 559-571.

Yanai, M., and T. Maruyama, 1966: Stratospheric wave disturbance propagating over the equatorial Pacific. *J. Meteor. Soc. Japan, 44,* 291-294.

Young, J. A., 1968: Comparative properties of some time differencing schemes for linear and non-linear oscillations. *Mon. Wea. Rev., 96,* 357-364.

Yu, T. W., and R. Madala, 1977: Comments on certain boundary-layer parameterization schemes used in atmospheric circulation models. *Naval Research Laboratory Memo 3548*.

Zienkiewicz, O. C., 1971: *The Finite Element Model in Engineering Science*. McGraw-Hill, 521 pp.

Zilitinkevich, S. S., and D. L. Laikhtman, 1965: Turbulent regime in the surface layer of the atmosphere. *Izv. Akad. Nauk SSSR,* Ser. fiz. atm. i okean., *1,* 150-156.

Zilitinkevich, S. S., and A. S. Monin, 1974: Similarity theory for the atmospheric boundary layer. *Izvestiya. Atmos. and Ocean Physics, 10,* 587-599.

Zilitinkevich, S. S., and J. W. Deardorff, 1974: Similarity theory for the planetary boundary layer of time-dependent height. *J. Atmos. Sci., 31,* 1449-1452.

Zilitinkevich, S. S., 1975: Resistance laws and prediction equations for the depth of the planetary boundary layer. *J. Atmos. Sci., 32,* 741-752.

INDEX

Abel, J., 206
Abyssal circulation, 408
Adams, J., 166
Adams-Bashforth scheme, 151
Advection equation, 110
  finite element, 201
  two dimensional, 139
Alexander, R., 412
Aliasing, 173
Amplification matrix, 123
Anderson, J., 383
Angular momentum, 41, 91
Anthes, R. A., 321, 323, 389
Arakawa, A, 170, 174, 216, 219, 226, 230, 235, 237, 238, 242, 243, 244, 259, 265, 266, 306, 323, 328, 347
Arakawa Jacobian, 176, 190, 239
Arnason, G., 368
Asselin, R., 147

Baer, F., 190, 378, 381, 383
Balance equation, 67, 69, 256, 368
  system, 68, 213-214
Barker, E. H., 373, 376, 377
Baroclinic equations, 59
  baroclinic numerical models, 211, 215, 257, 409
Baroclinic instability, 81, 415
Barotropic instability, 72, 405, 415
  necessary condition, 73, 75
  unstable profiles, 75
Barotropic vorticity equations, 58, 70
  finite element form, 203
  spectral form, 187
Basis functions, 181, 187, 191, 201
Bengtsson, L., 388
Beta plane, 63, 70
  equatorial, 99
Bickley jet, 75
Bjerknes, J., 2
Bjerknes, V., 1, 108
Blackadar, A., 273, 296, 297, 298, 299
Blakeslee, R., 96
Blandford, R., 405
Bleck, R., 262, 264
Boundary conditions, 249, 250, 267
  upper, 264
Boundary effects, 398
Boundary layer, 267
Bourke, W., 193, 196, 197, 200, 257
Boussinesq approximation, 83, 301, 407
Brekhovskikh, L., 415
Brown, J., 144
Browning, G., 251
Brunt-Vaisala frequency, 34
Bryan, K., 404, 408, 412, 413, 421
Buneman, O., 159, 165
Burger, A., 53, 85
Burridge, D., 243
Businger, J., 279, 280, 282, 286, 296

Cahn, A., 48
Camerlengo, A., 253
Campana, K., 143
Case, K. M., 80
Chan, S., 421
Chang, C.-P., 106, 107
Characteristics, 110, 120, 441
Charney, J. G., 2, 53, 66, 68, 81, 83, 85, 97, 98, 108, 209, 266, 385, 404
Charnock, H., 282
Cho, H., 337
CISK, 338
Clarke, R., 288
Clausius-Clapeyron equation, 309, 318
Closure, 269, 272, 298, 300
Cloud process, 308, 315
  radiation, 348

work function, 329
Compatibility, 120
Computational instability, 119
energy method, 129
matrix method, 123
von Neumann method, 127
Computational mode, 114, 118
Consistency, 120
Continuity equation, 5, 13, 16, 17, 18, 19, 29, 40, 54, 59, 400
Convective adjustment, 312
Convergence, 122
Cooley, J., 196
Coordinate systems, 8, 12
isentropic, 262
lnp, (Z), 82
orthogonal, 441
sigma, 17, 216
vertical, 14, 59
Corby, G., 265
Coriolis force, 5
parameter, 8
Coté, R., 305
Courant-Friedrichs-Levy, 119
Cox, M., 412, 413, 421
Cressman, G. P., 210, 357, 423
Cullen, M., 203, 206, 207
Cumulus parameterization, 319

Daley, R., 201, 257, 377, 383
Data assimilation, 366, 387
Deardorff, J., 285, 289, 293, 294
Derome, J., 265
Desai, C., 206
DeSzoeke, R., 421
Dickinson, R., 265, 369, 377
Differencing schemes, 150
Adams-Bashforth, 151
compatibility, 120
consistency, 120
convergence, 122
Dufort-Frankel, 155
Euler backward, 134, 367
forward-backward, 143
fourth-order, 134
Lax-Wendroff, 149
leapfrog, 111
semi-implicit, 148, 197, 207, 412
trapexoidal implicit, 132
Diffusion, 155
Dispersion, 47
computational, 115
Divergence, 15, 44
damping, 367
equation, 27, 44, 56, 61, 64
removal, 375
Doron, E., 201
Drag coefficient, 270, 274, 282, 283
Drazin, P., 97
Dufort-Frankel scheme, 155
Dyer, A., 297

Eady, E. T., 2, 81, 83
Eddy stress, 268-307
Eddy viscosity coefficient, 272, 274, 278, 284, 285, 295, 296, 297, 307
Eigenvalues, 76, 123, 127
Ekman layer, 66, 272, 274, 283, 401
Eliasen, E., 193, 197
Eliassen, A., 2, 66, 97, 229, 262, 359
Elliptic equations, 157-159
Elsasser, W., 342
Elsberry, R., 415
Energy, 20, 25
available, 23-25
barotropic model, 210
conservation, 189, 205, 235, 238
cycle, 95
equations, 20, 21, 22, 74, 90
internal, 21
kinetic, 20
potential, 20, 23
total, 22, 218
transformation function, 21
turbulent, 419
vertical energy flux, 97
vertical propagation, 96
Enstrophy, 171, 189, 205
potential conserving schemes, 237
Enthalpy, 21
Entrainment, 419
Epstein, E., 434
Equivalent barotropic level, 209
Equivalent barotropic model, 208
Equivalent depth, 104
Error growth, 125, 429
Ertel, H., 41
Euler formula, 111

backward scheme, 134, 367
forward scheme, 130
Euler-Lagrange equation, 371
Exner function, 262

Faulkner, F. D., 159, 161, 167, 168
Filtered models, 208
Filtering, 392-397
time, 145
Fine mesh models, 248
Finite differences, 108
Finite element method, 182
Fix, G., 204, 206
Fjøtoft, R., 2, 108, 173, 209
Flattery, T., 377, 379
Fleming, R., 435
Fofonoff, N., 405
Forecasting skill, 423
Fourier series, integral, 442
Frequency equation, 32, 37, 42
Friction, 154, 267
Friction velocity, 273
Froude number, rotational, 55, 62, 65

Gadd, A., 144
Galerkin methods, 181
time dependence, 186
Gall, R., 96, 264
Gallagher, R., 421
Gambo, K., 85
Gandin, L., 359
Garrett, J., 282
Garwood, R. W., 421
Gas law, 5
Gates, W. L., 412
Gauss divergence theorem, 44
Gaussian elimination, 164
Gaussian quadrature, 194
Geostrophic, 17, 44, 49, 373
adjustment, 35, 47, 365, 374
divergence, 47, 58
omega, 66, 211
potential vorticity, 58, 64, 66
quasi-geostrophic, 58, 64, 66, 81, 97
vertical motion, 65
Gerald, C., 195
Gilchrist, A., 265
Girard, C., 201
Glahn, H. R., 433

Gordon, T., 257
Gravitation, 4
Gravity, 4
Gravity waves, 367, 375, 378
numerical solution, 140
see also Waves
Gray, W. G., 206
Green, J. S. A., 85
Greenspan, H., 403
Grotjahn, R., 117
Group velocity, 50, 116, 137, 203, 228
Gustafson, T., 43

Haltiner, G. J., 8, 39, 116, 268, 272, 310, 313, 373, 377, 387
Haney, R., 413, 421
Harrison, E., 254
Haseler, J., 243
Hayaski, Y., 106
Heating, 6, 68, 269, 310, 340
latent, 105
Helmholtz equation, 167, 200
Henderson, J., 201
Hinkelmann, K., 47, 369
Hinsman, D., 206
Hirschman, A., 413
Hoke, J., 389
Holl, M., 358
Holland, W., 413, 414, 415
Holton, J. R., 83, 98, 103, 105, 106, 107
Hoskins, B. J., 96, 257
Hough, S. S., 72
Hovermale, J., 226, 386
Hunt, K., 413
Hydrostatic equation, 7, 10, 15, 17, 19
approximation, 35, 37, 216, 225, 371

Image scale, 12-14
Inertial oscillations, 42, 410
Initialization, 45, 255, 365
dynamic, 385
normal mode, 377
static, 368
variational, 369, 377
Isentropic coordinate, 19, 262

Joint Organizing Committee, 237

Jones, R., 255
Julian, P., 107

Katayama, A., 340, 349, 354
Kessler, E., 315-317, 321
Kirkwood, E., 265
Kistler, R., 389
Klein, W., 433
Kluge, J., 359
Kolmogorov, A., 303
Koshlyakov, M., 415
Kousky, V., 106
Kraichman, R., 431, 433
Kraus, E., 416, 419
Kreitzberg, C., 251
Kullenberg, B., 43
Kuo, H. L., 73, 76, 85, 321, 323, 325, 336
Kurihara, Y., 150, 265
Kutta scheme, 153
Kwizak, M., 148

Laikhtman, D., 297
Lamb, V., 216, 219, 226, 235, 237, 238, 242, 244, 259, 265, 266
Lambert conformal map, 13
Lamb wave, 143, 266
  geostrophic adjustment, 143
Lax equivalence theorem, 122
Lax-Wendroff scheme, 149, 386
Leapfrog scheme, 111, 127, 202
Leith, C. E., 385, 432, 433, 435
Leslie, L., 159
Lilly, D., 151, 335
Lin, C. C., 70
Lin, L., 415
Lindzen, R., 102, 106, 107, 264
Lipps, F., 305
Lord, S., 337, 338
Lorenz, E. N., 23, 187, 191, 216, 221, 429, 430, 431
Lubeck, O., 257

McAlvaney, B., 159, 193
McCullough, J., 387
Machenhauer, B., 193, 196, 257, 378, 383
Madala, R., 292, 412
Madden, R., 107

Manabe, S., 312, 336, 350
Map factor, 12-14
Map projections, 10
Martin, F. L., 39, 116, 268, 272, 310, 313
Maruyama, T., 106
Matsuno, T., 98, 99, 104, 116, 367
Mellor, G., 301, 303, 304
Mercator projection, 13
Mesinger, F., 226, 230
Metric coefficients, 8
Millard, R., 418
Mintz, Y., 415
Mitchell, H., 207
Mixed layer, 287
  models, 285, 415
Mixing length, 273, 296
Miyakoda, K., 251, 304, 306, 336, 386
Moisture equation, 308
Möller, F., 350
Momentum flux, 74, 81
Monaco, A., 235
Monin, A., 415
Monin-Obukhov length, 271, 277, 286, 300
Montgomery stream function, 19, 262
Morgan, G., 404
Morton, K., 122, 129, 149
Motion equations, 2, 12, 13, 15, 17, 18, 19, 29, 40, 54, 59, 301
Mountain effects, 68, 265
Moyer, R., 386
Multivariate analysis, 359
Munk, W., 403

Namias, J., 399
NCAR, 168
NEPRF, 168
Neumann, J. von, 2, 108, 127, 130, 209
Newson, R., 265
Niiler, P., 416
Nitta, T., 383, 386
Nodal point, 183, 203
Nonlinear interaction, 172
  instability, 170-172
Normal mode solutions, 71, 79
  continuous spectrum, 80, 85
  initialization, 377
Nudging, Newtonian, 389

Numerical methods, 108

Objective analysis, 356-365
  statistical method, 359
O'Brien, J., 117, 253, 284, 415
Obukhov, A. M., 2, 271, 277, 286, 300
Ogura, Y., 315, 316, 337
Okamura, 383
Okland, H., 51
Omega equation, 17, 66, 211, 214, 215
Oort, A., 95
Ooyama, K., 323, 338
Optimum interpolation, 359
Orlanski, I., 250
Orszag, S., 193, 196
Oscillation equation, 138

Palm, E., 97
Panofsky, H., 296, 356
Parabolic differential equation, 153
Partial differential equations, 443
Paulson, C., 285
Pearce, R., 323
Pedlosky, J., 83, 85, 98
Perkey, D., 251
Perturbation method, 31
Petterssen, S., 2
Phase speed, 34, 71, 84, 89
  complex, 72
  numerical, 114, 115, 202
Phase tilt, 74
Phillips, N. A., 9, 17, 47, 53, 63, 66, 90, 170, 174, 225, 213, 230, 255, 265, 369
Piacsek, S., 412
Pinder, G., 206
Platzman, G., 190, 191, 193
Polar stereographic map, 11
Pollard, R., 418
Potential temperature, ϕ, 7, 16
  equivalent, 310
  wet-bulb, 311
Potential vorticity, 41, 414
  gradient, 83, 85
Prandtl number, 291
Prandtl (surface) layer, 272, 277
Precipitation, 310, 319
Pressure averaging, 144
Pressure coordinate, 17
Pressure tendency, 17, 18
Primitive equations, 69, 215
Puri, K., 193

Radiation, 340-355
  terrestrial (longwave), 340
  solar, 349
Randall, D., 294, 306
Rasmussen, E., 193, 196
Raustein, E., 262
Rayleigh, Lord, 73
Recker, E., 337
Reed, R. J., 1, 337
Refractive index, 98
Reid, R., 415
Relaxation method, 157
  Newtonian, 389
Response function, 146, 394
Reynold's equations, 268
Reynold's stress, 268-307, 400, 416, 418
Rhines, P., 421
Richardson, L. F., 1, 56, 62, 108
Richardson number, 281, 288, 299
Richtmyer, R., 122, 129, 149
Riehl, H., 323
Robert, A., 147, 148, 387, 423
Robinson, A., 408, 415
Robinson, G., 431
Rogers, D., 354
Rosati, A., 251
Rosenthal, L., 338
Rosmond, T., 159, 161, 257
Rossby, C. G., 2, 48, 72, 108, 383
  number, 47, 54, 65, 369, 400
  radius of deformation, 50, 55, 84, 228, 407, 414
  surface, 271, 311
  waves, *see* Waves
Rotta, J., 303
Roughness length, 273, 274
Rutherford, I., 359

Sadourney, R., 238, 243
Saha, K., 257
Sarkisyan, A., 413
Sasaki, Y., 369, 373, 377, 388
Scale analysis, 53, 401, 407
  advection time scale, 54

boundary current, 402, 403, 404
geostrophic scaling, 55, 60
mid-latitude, 62
planetary scale, 67
tropics, 67
Scale height, 33, 59
Schemm, C., 305
Schlatter, T., 359, 362, 363
Schoenstadt, A. L., 48, 145, 207, 226
Schrödinger equation, 100
Schubert, W., 306, 328, 331
Schwarzschild, 340
Semtner, B., 415
Sensible heat flux, 271
Shallow-water equations, 40, 48, 54, 99, 238
spectral form, 197
Shapiro, M., 263
Shapiro, R., 250, 252, 392
Shiver, W., 413
Shukla, J., 255
Shuman, F. G., 144, 226
Silberman, I., 191
Similarity theory, 273, 285, 291, 293
Simmonds, I., 201
Simmons, A., 96, 257
Sirutis, J., 304, 306, 336
Smagorinsky, J., 412, 421, 430
Smeda, M., 293
Smoothing, 392
Sobel, J., 255
Solar radiation, 349
clear sky, 350
cloudy sky, 351
Somerville, R., 96, 430
Sommeria, G., 305
Spectral method, 182
baroclinic, 257
transform method, 193, 198
Spherical coordinates, 8
grids, 243
Stability, computational, 122
Stability analysis, 122
matrix method, 123
Staggered grid, 141, 226, 230
Staley, D., 96
Staniforth, A., 207
State equation, 5
Static energy, 310
Static stability, 34, 61, 66, 82, 88, 211
Stern, M. E., 83, 407, 408
Stern, W., 257
Stokes theorem, 441
Stommel, H., 401, 408
Strang, G., 206
Stream function, 56
Sundquist, H., 315, 317, 369
Sundström, A., 250
Surface layer, 272, 286
neutral, 273
non-neutral, 277
Surface temperature, 298
Suryanarayana, R., 257
Sverdrup balance, 402
Sweet, R., 164
Synoptic-scale eddies, ocean, 414

Takahashi, T., 315, 316
Talagrand, O., 367
Temperton, C., 383, 384, 385, 386, 387
Tennekes, H., 273
Terrain, 271
Terrestrial radiation, 340
clear sky, 345
cloudy sky, 348
Teweles, S., 424
Thermocline, 406
Thermodynamic equation, 6, 7, 16, 29, 59, 61, 310
Thermohaline ocean models, 406
forcing, 412
Thompson, P., 430
Thunderstorm, 321
Thurling, R., 193
Tokioka, T., 225, 265
Topography, 208, 413
Transfer coefficients, 288, 291
Trapezoidal implicit scheme, 132, 152
Truncation error, 109, 120
Tukey, J., 196
Turbulent fluxes, 268-307
bulk formulas, 269, 271
Two-level model, 86
Two-way interaction, 254

U. S. POLYMODE, 415

Variational method, 369, 377
Velocity:
  divergent part, 56, 60
  rotational part, 56, 60
  vertical, 17, 18, 60, 211, 214, 215, 270
Velocity potential, 56
Veronis, G., 403, 404, 405, 421
Vertical coordinates, 14, 59
Vertical velocity, 17, 18, 60, 211, 214, 215, 270
Von Karman constant, 274
von Neumann, J., 2, 108, 127, 130, 209
Vorticity, 26, 40, 44, 56, 61, 406

Wallace, J. M., 106
Warren, B., 414
Water vapor flux, 271
Waves, 29-52
  equatorial, 99, 102
  gravity:
    deep-water, 38, 39
    external, 35, 39, 410
    inertial, 40, 42, 47, 48, 105
    internal, 33, 35, 39, 410
    shallow-water, 38, 42
    surface, 36
  Kevin (equatorial), 67, 69, 102, 106
  Kelvin-Helmholtz, 40
  Lamb, 35, 105, 143
  mixed Rossby-gravity, 67, 101, 106
  Rossby, 40, 43, 47, 56, 57, 68, 70, 92, 105, 189, 253, 265, 383, 405, 410
    internal, 92
  sound, 31, 33
  ultra long, 430
Wave structure, 91
Webster, P., 107
Wiin Nielsen, A., 431
Williams, R. T., 77, 145, 235, 257
Williamson, D., 235, 251, 369, 377, 383, 384, 385
Wind stress, 400, 412
Winninghoff, F., 226
Wobus, H., 424
Wolff, P., 210
Wurtele, M., 117
Wyngaard, J., 285, 305

Yamada, T., 291, 301, 303, 304
Yamamoto, G., 344
Yamasaki, M., 338
Yanai, M., 106
Young, J., 153
Yu, T., 292

Zienkiewicz, O. C., 206
Zilitinkevich, S., 297